D0617183

TOWN AND LAKE OF TIBERIAS.

FROM THE NORTH WEST.

NOTES
ON THE
NEW TESTAMENT
EXPLANATORY AND PRACTICAL

BY

ALBERT BARNES

ENLARGED TYPE EDITION

EDITED BY

ROBERT FREW, D.D.

WITH NUMEROUS ADDITIONAL NOTES AND A SERIES OF ENGRAVINGS

MATTHEW AND MARK

BAKER BOOK HOUSE
GRAND RAPIDS 6, MICHIGAN
1949

V-1

PREFACE

TO THE REVISED EDITION OF THE NOTES ON THE NEW TESTAMENT.

THE first volumes of these Notes on the New Testament—those on the Gospels—were published in 1832. The other volumes were published at intervals between that year and 1851, when the Notes on the Book of Revelation were published.

In 1840 the stereotype plates of the Gospels had become greatly worn, and it was found necessary to recast them, and a careful revision of the Notes was made. In that edition many errors were corrected; in some places the notes were enlarged, and at the close of the second volume a chronological table and an index, which it was supposed would be of value to the teachers in Sabbath-schools, were appended.

Since that time more than a quarter of a century has elapsed, and the Notes on the Gospels, as well as on other parts of the New Testament, have passed through numerous editions. During that time, also, great advances have been made in all the departments of knowledge necessary to a proper illustration of the Scriptures. Palestine has been explored more accurately than before; a better knowledge of Oriental manners and customs has been obtained; more accurate maps and illustrations have been published; and the best minds in Europe and in this country have been employed in illustrating the language employed and the manners and customs referred to in the New Testament. The means of explaining the Bible have fully kept up with the progress of the world in other things, and it is every way desirable that a commentary on the Scriptures should be such as to meet the wants of society as it advances in other respects.

In the revision the essential character of the work has not been changed. It would have been easy to have enlarged it very greatly, and by one competent to the task it might have been made much more learned; but it was supposed that the fact that since the first edition of the Gospels was issued more than five hundred and fifty thousand volumes have been sold in this country, and probably a larger number in Great Britain, and that it has been translated, in whole or in part, into the Welsh, French, and Tamil languages, and that numerous imitations of the general form and style of the work have been made in different religious denominations in this country, has shown that the plan of the work met a *want* in the public mind, and was adapted in some measure to supply that want, and that no essential change in its plan and character should be attempted. As the usefulness of the work, it is believed, has been much promoted by the fact that it was at first issued in small and convenient volumes, especially adapted to the use of Sabbath-schools and Bible-classes, that form of publication has not been changed.

While, however, no material change has been made in the character and plan of the work, I have endeavoured to improve it in every way in my power. In some places it has been abridged, but new matter has been added that will possibly somewhat enlarge the size of the volume. I have availed myself freely of such works as have been published bearing on the subject since the first edition was issued.

In now finishing my labours on the New Testament, after so many years, I cannot better express my emotions than in the words which I used when, in 1840, I sent forth the revised edition of the Gospels to the world, and which I supposed then would be the last time that I should address the public on the subject:

"I dismiss the work, therefore, finally, with deep feeling; feeling more deep by far than when I first submitted it to the press. I cannot be insensible to the fact that I have been, by my expositions of the New Testament, doing something—and it may be much—to mould the hearts and intellects of thousands of the rising generation in regard to the great doctrines and duties of religion—thousands who are to act their parts, and to develop these principles, when I am dead. Nor can I be insensible to the fact that in the form in which these volumes now go forth to the public, I may continue, though dead, to speak to the living; and that the work may be exerting an influence on immortal minds when I am in the eternal world. I need not say that, while I am sensitive to this consideration, I earnestly desire it. There are no sentiments in these volumes which I wish to alter; none that I do not believe to be truth that will abide the investigations of the great day; none of which I am ashamed. That I *may* be in error I know; that a better work than this might be prepared by a more gifted mind and a better heart, I know; but the truths here set forth are, I am persuaded, those which are destined to abide, and to be the means of saving millions of souls, and of ultimately converting this whole world to God. That these volumes may have a part in this great work is my earnest prayer; and with many thanks to the public for its favours, and to God, the Great Source of all blessings, I send them forth again, commending them to *his* care, and asking in a special manner the continued favour of Sabbath-school teachers and of the young."

ALBERT BARNES.

Washington Square, Philadelphia, Dec., 1868.

ORIGINAL PREFACE

TO THE NOTES ON THE GOSPELS.

In the preparation of the following Notes, free use has been made of all the helps within the reach of the author. . . . The object has been to express, in as few words as possible, the *real meaning* of the Gospels; the *results* of their critical study, rather than the *process* by which these results were reached.

This work is designed to occupy a place which is supposed to be unappropriated in attempts to explain the New Testament. It was my wish to present to Sunday-school teachers a plain and simple *explanation* of the more common difficulties of the book which it is their province to teach. This wish has given character to the work. If it should occur to anyone that more minute explanations of *words*, *phrases*, and *customs* have been attempted than might seem to them desirable, it will be recollected that many Sunday-school teachers have little access to means of information, and that no small part of their success is dependent on the *minuteness* and *correctness* of the explanation which is given to children.

This work is designed also to be a *Harmony of the Gospels*. Particular attention has been bestowed, especially in the Notes on Matthew, to bring the different narratives of the Evangelists together, and to show that, in their narration of the same events, there is no real contradiction. It will be recollected that *the sacred narrative of an event is what it is reported to be by all the Evangelists*. It will also be recollected that the most plausible objections to the New Testament have been drawn from the apparent contradictions in the Gospels. The importance of meeting these difficulties in the education of the young, and of showing that these objections are not well founded, will be apparent to all.

Particular attention has been paid to the *references* to parallel passages of Scripture. *In all instances in these Notes they are an essential part of the explanation of the text.* The authority of the Bible has been deemed the only authority that was necessary in such cases; and it is hoped that no one will condemn any explanation offered without a candid examination of the *real* meaning of the passages referred to.

The main design of these notes will be accomplished if they furnish a just *explanation* of the text. Practical remarks could not have been more full without materially increasing the size of the book, and, as was supposed, without essentially limiting its circulation and its usefulness. All that has been attempted, therefore, in this part of the work, has been to furnish *leading thoughts*, or heads of practical remark, to be enlarged on at the discretion of the teacher.

These Notes have been prepared amid the pressing and anxious cares of a responsible pastoral charge. Of their imperfection no one can be more sensible than the author. Of the time and patience indispensable in preparing even such brief Notes on the Bible, under the conviction that the opinions expressed *may* form the sentiments of the young on the subject of the Book of God, and determine their eternal destiny, no one can be sensible who has not made the experiment. The great truth is becoming more and more impressed on the minds of this generation that the Bible is the only authoritative source of religious belief; and if there is any institution pre-eminently calculated to deepen this impression, and fix it permanently in the minds of the coming age, it is the Sunday-school. Every minister of the gospel, every parent, every Christian, must therefore feel it important that *just views of interpretation* should be imbibed in these schools. I have felt more deeply than I have any other sentiment the importance of inculcating on the young proper modes of explaining the sacred Scriptures. If I can be one of the instruments, however humble, in extending such views through the community, my wish in this work will be accomplished. I commit it, therefore, to the blessing of the God of the Bible, with the prayer that it may be one among many instruments of forming correct religious views, and promoting the practical love of God and man, among the youth of this country.

ALBERT BARNES.

Philadelphia, August 25th, 1832.

INTRODUCTION.

The writings which are regarded by Christians as the sole standard of faith and practice have been designated at various periods by different names. They are frequently called *The Scriptures,* to denote that they are the most important of all *writings; The Holy Scriptures,* because composed by persons divinely inspired, and containing sacred truth; and *The Canonical Scriptures.* The word *canon* means a *rule,* and it was applied by the Christian fathers to the books of the Bible because they were regarded as *an authoritative rule* of faith and practice; and also to distinguish them from certain *spurious* or *apocryphal* books, which, although some of them might be true as matter of history, or correct in doctrine, were not regarded as a *rule* of faith, and were therefore considered as not *canonical.*

But the most common appellation given now to these writings is The Bible. This is a Greek word signifying *book.* It is given to the Scriptures by way of eminence, to denote that this is the Book of books, as being infinitely superior to every unassisted production of the human mind. In the same way, the name *Koran* or *reading* is given to the writings of Mohammed, denoting that they are the chief writings to be *read,* or eminently the *reading.*

The most common and general division of the Bible is into the Old and New Testaments. The word *testament* with us means a *will;* an instrument in writing, by which a person declares his *will* in relation to his property after his death. This is not, however, its meaning when applied to the Scriptures. It is taken from the Greek translation of the Hebrew word meaning *covenant, compact,* or *agreement.* The word is applied to the *covenant* or *compact* which God made with the Jews to be their God, and thus primarily denotes the agreement, the compact, the promises, the institutions of the old dispensation, and then the *record* of that compact in the writings of Moses and the Prophets. The name "Old Testament," or "Old Covenant," therefore, denotes the books containing the records of God's covenant with his people, or his dispensations under the Mosaic or Jewish state. The phrase New Covenant, or Testament, denotes the books which contain the record of his *new* covenant or compact with his people under the Messiah, or since Christ came. We find mention made of *the Book of the Covenant* in Ex. xxiv. 7, and in the New Testament the word is once used (2 Co. iii. 14) with an undoubted reference to the sacred books of the Jews. By whom, or at what time, these terms were first used to designate the two divisions of the sacred Scriptures, is not certainly known. There can be no doubt, however, of the great antiquity of the application.

The Jews divided the Old Testament into three parts, called The Law, The Prophets, and The Hagiographa, or the holy writings.

This division is noticed by our Saviour in Lu. xxiv. 44,[1] "All things must be fulfilled which were written in the law of Moses and in the Prophets, and in the Psalms, concerning me." Josephus, the Jewish historian, also makes mention of the same division.[2] "We have," says he, "only twenty-two books which are to be believed to be of divine authority; of which five are the books of Moses. From the death of Moses to the reign of Artaxerxes, son of Xerxes, king of Persia, the prophets who were the successors of Moses have written in thirteen books. The remaining four books contain hymns to God and documents of life for the use of men." It is probable that precisely the same books were not always included in the same division; but there can be no doubt that the *division* itself was always retained. The division into twenty-two books was made partly, no doubt, for the convenience of the memory. This was the number of letters in the Hebrew alphabet. The English Bible contains thirty-nine instead of twenty-two books in the Old Testament. The number which Josephus reckons may be accurately made out as follows: The first division, comprehending the five books of Moses, or THE LAW. The second, including 1st, Joshua; 2d, Judges, with Ruth; 3d, Samuel; 4th, Kings; 5th, Isaiah; 6th, Jeremiah, with Lamenations; 7th, Ezekiel; 8th, Daniel; 9th, the twelve minor prophets; 10th, Job; 11th, Ezra, including Nehemiah; 12th, Esther; 13th, Chronicles: these thirteen books were called THE PROPHETS. The four remaining will be Psalms, Proverbs, Ecclesiastes, and the Song of Solomon. In regard to the second division, it is a fact well known that the twelve smaller prophets, from Hosea to Malachi, were for convenience uniformly united in one volume; that the small books of Ruth and Lamentations were attached to the larger works mentioned, and that Ezra and Nehemiah were long reckoned as one book.

The arrangement of the books of the Bible has not always been the same. The order followed in the English Bible is taken from the Greek translation called the Septuagint. Probably the best way to read the Bible is to read the books as nearly as possible in the order in which they were written. Thus Isaiah informs us (Is. i. 1) that his prophecies were delivered in the reigns of Uzziah, Jotham, Ahaz, and Hezekiah; and, to be correctly understood, they should be read in connection with the record of those reigns in Kings and Chronicles.

The names of most of the books in the Bible are taken from the Greek translation above mentioned.

The books of the Bible were anciently written without any breaks, or divisions into chapters and verses. For convenience the Jews early divided the Old Testament into greater and smaller sections. These sections in the law and prophets were read in the worship of the synagogues. The New Testament was also early divided in a similar manner.

The division into chapters and verses is of recent origin. It was first adopted in the 13th century by Cardinal Hugo, who wrote a celebrated commentary on the Scriptures. He divided the Latin Vulgate, the version used in the Church of Rome, into chapters nearly the same as those which now exist in our English translation. These chapters

[1] See Note on that place. [2] *Against Apion.*

he divided into smaller sections by placing the letters A, B, C, &c., at equal distances from each other in the margin.

The division into verses was not made until a still later period. The division of Cardinal Hugo into chapters became known to Rabbi Nathan, a distinguished Jew, who adopted it for the Hebrew Bible, and placed the Hebrew letters, used also as numerals, in the margin. This was used by Rabbi Nathan in publishing a concordance, and adopted by Athias in a printed edition of the Hebrew Bible in 1661.

The verses into which the New Testament is divided are still more modern, and are an imitation of those used by Rabbi Nathan in the fifteenth century. This division was invented and first used by Stephens in an edition of the New Testament printed in 1551. The division was made as an amusement while he was on a journey from Lyons to Paris, during the intervals in which he rested in travelling. It has been adopted in all the subsequent editions of the Bible.

In regard to this division into chapters and verses, it is clear that they are of no authority whatever. It has been doubted whether the sacred writers used *any* points or divisions of any kind. It is certain that they were wholly unacquainted with those now in use. It is farther evident that these divisions have not been judiciously made in all cases. The sense is often interrupted by the close of a chapter, and still oftener by the break in the verses. In *reading* the Scriptures little regard should be had to this division. It is of use now only for reference; and, inaccurate as it is, it must evidently be substantially retained. All the books that have been printed for three hundred years, which refer to the Bible, have made their references to these chapters and verses; and to attempt any change now would be to render almost useless a great part of the religious books in our language, and to introduce inextricable confusion in all attempts to quote the Bible.

The first translation of the Old Testament was made about the year 270 before the Christian era. It was made at Alexandria in Egypt into the Greek language, and probably for the use of the Jews who were scattered among Pagan nations. Ancient writers inform us, indeed, that it was made at the command of Ptolemy Philadelphus, to be deposited in the Library at Alexandria. It bears internal marks of having been made by different individuals, and no doubt at different times. It came to be extensively used in Judea, and no small part of the quotations in the New Testament were taken from it. There is no doubt that the apostles were familiar with it; and as it had obtained general currency, they chose to quote it rather than translate the Hebrew for themselves. It is called the Septuagint, or the version by the seventy, from a tradition that seventy elders of Israel, deputed for that purpose, were employed in making the translation.[1]

The language spoken by our Saviour and his apostles was a corruption of the Hebrew, a mixture of that and the language spoken in Chaldee, called Syro-Chaldaic, or more commonly the Syriac. The reason why the New Testament was not written in this language was, that the Greek had become the common language used throughout

[1] For an account of this translation, see Introduction to my Notes on Isaiah, vol. i. pages 46, 47.

the Eastern nations subject to the Romans. This general use of the Greek language was produced by the invasion and conquest of those nations by Alexander the Great, about 330 years before Christ. The New Testament was, however, early translated into the Syriac language. A translation is now extant in that language, held in great veneration by Syrian Christians, said to have been made in the first century, or in the age of the apostles, and acknowledged by all to have been made before the close of the second century, and is one of the most valuable translations of the New Testament ever made. It has been translated into English by the late Dr. Murdock.

About the beginning of the fourth century the Bible was translated into Latin by Jerome. This translation was made in consequence, as he says, of the incorrectness of a version then in use, called the *Italic*. The translation made by Jerome, now called the Latin Vulgate, is the authorized version of the Church of Rome.[1]

The Bible was translated by Luther in the beginning of the Reformation. This translation has done much to fix the German language, and is now the received version among the Lutheran churches.

There have been many other translations of the Bible, and there are many more still in progress. More than one hundred and fifty translations of the whole Bible, or parts of it, have been made during the last half century. Those which have been mentioned, together with the English, have been, however, the principal, and are most relied on as faithful exhibitions of the meaning of the sacred Scriptures.

The English translation of the Bible now in use was made in the reign of James I. This translation was intended only as an improvement of those previously in existence. A short account of the translation of the Bible into our own language cannot fail to be interesting.

It is not easy to ascertain the precise time when the gospel was introduced into Britain, or when the inhabitants were first in possession of the Bible. The earliest version of which we have any account is a translation of the Psalms into the Saxon language about the year 706; but the principal translation at that early period was made by the "venerable Bede," about the year 730. He translated the whole Bible into the Saxon language.

The first English translation of the Bible was executed about the year 1290, by some unknown individual. About the year 1380, John Wickliffe, the morning star of the Reformation, translated the entire Bible into English from the Latin. The great labour and expense of transcribing books before the invention of printing probably prevented a very extensive circulation of the Scriptures among the people.[2] Yet the translation of Wickliffe is known to have produced a vast effect on the minds of the people. Knowledge was sought for with avidity. The minds of the people were beginning to be opened to the abominations of the Church of Rome, and the national mind was preparing for the great change which followed in the days of Luther. So deep was the impression made by Wickliffe's translation, and so dan-

[1] For an account of this version, see also my Notes on Isaiah, vol. i. pages 47, 48.

[2] So great was the expense of transcribing the Bible at that time, that the price of one of Wickliffe's New Testaments was not less than forty pounds sterling, or one hundred and seventy-seven dollars seventy-eight cents of our money. And it should be matter of devout gratitude to God that, by the art of printing, the New Testament can now be obtained for the trifling sum of ten cents, and the entire Bible for twenty-five.

gerous was it thought to be to the interest of the Romish religion, that a bill was brought into the House of Lords for the purpose of suppressing it. The bill was rejected through the influence of the Duke of Lancaster, and this gave encouragement to the friends of Wickliffe to publish a more correct translation of the Bible. At a convocation, however, held at Oxford in 1408, it was decreed that no one should translate any text of the Holy Scripture into English by way of a book, or little book, or tract, and that no book of this kind should be read that was composed in the time of John Wickliffe, or since his death. This decree led the way to a great persecution, and many persons were punished severely, and some even with death, for reading the Bible in English. The *Bible* translated by Wickliffe was never printed. Some years since the New Testament was printed in England.[1]

For the first printed English translation of the Scriptures we are indebted to William Tindal. He printed this translation at Antwerp in Flanders, and the copies were brought thence into England. So great was the opposition to this by the Roman Catholic clergy, that the Bishop of London endeavoured to buy up whole editions as fast as they were printed, to burn them. This, however, produced little effect. Copies of the New Testament were multiplied. It is said that on one occasion Sir Thomas More, then Chancellor of England, asked how Tindal contrived to maintain himself abroad: to which it was replied that the Bishop of London supported him by purchasing the Scriptures as fast as they could be printed.

In 1535 the whole Bible, translated into English, was printed in folio, and dedicated to the king, by Miles Coverdale. This was the first English translation of the Bible allowed by royal authority.

Various editions and translations of the Scriptures, with various degrees of correctness, were printed in successive years, till, in 1568, the edition appeared which was called "the Bishop's Bible," or "the great English Bible." This was prepared by royal authority. It was the work of much care. Different learned men undertook to translate different parts of the Bible, and after those portions had been carefully

[1] The following is a specimen of this translation:—
Matthew, chap. v.—And Jhesus seynge the people, went up into an hil; and whanne he was sett, his disciplis camen to him. And he openyde his mouthe, and taughte them; and seide, Blessid be pore men in spirit; for the kyngdom of hevenes is hereun.* Blessid ben mylde men: for thei schulen weelde the erthe. Blessid ben thei that mournen: for thei schal be comfortid. Blessid be thei that hungren and thirsten rigtwisnesse:† for thei schal be fulfilled. Blessid ben merciful men: for thei schul gete mercy. Blessid ben thei that ben of clene herte: for thei schulen se god. Blessid ben pesible men: for thei schulen be clepid goddis children. Blessid ben thei that suffren persecucioun for rightwisnesse: for the kyngdom of hevenes is hern. Ye schul be blessid whanne men schul curse you, and schul pursue you: and schul seye al yvel agens you liynge for me. Joie ye and be ye glade: for your meede is plenteous in hevenes: for so thei han pursued also prophets that weren bifore you. Ye ben salt of the erthe, that if the salt vanishe awey wherynne schal it be salted? to nothing it is worth over, no but it be cast out, and be defoulid of men. Ye ben light of the world, a citee sett on an hill may not be hid. Ne me teendith not a lanterne and puttith it under a bushel; but on a candlestik that it give light to alle that ben in the hous. So, schyne your light bifore men, that thei see youre gode workis, and glorifie your fadir that is in hevenes. Nyle ghe deme that I cam to undo the Lawe or the prophetis, I cam not to undo the lawe but to fulfille. Forsothe I sey to you till hevene and erthe passe, oon lettre, or oon title, schal not passe fro the Lawe till alle thingis be don. Therefore he that brekith oon of these leeste maundementis, and techith thus men, schal be clepid the Leest in the rewme of hevenes; but he that doth and techith, schal be clepid greet in the kyngdom of hevenes.—*Baber's Edit.*

* Theirs. † Rightfulnesse, MS. *plures.*

compared, the whole was printed, and directed to be used as an authorized English translation of the Scriptures. This, after being reprinted many times, and after being in use for half a century, was succeeded by the translation at present in use.

As this is, in many respects, the most important of all English translations of the sacred Scriptures, it is proper to dwell more fully on the circumstances under which it was made.

It was undertaken by the authority of King James I. of England. He came to the throne in 1603. Several objections having been made to the "Bishop's Bible," then in general use, he ordered a new translation to be made. This work he committed to fifty-four men; but, before the translation was commenced, seven of them had either died or had declined the task, so that it was actually accomplished by forty-seven. All of them were eminently distinguished for their piety, and for their profound acquaintance with the original languages. This company of men was divided into six classes, and to each class was allotted a distinct part of the Bible to be translated. "Ten were to meet at Westminster, and to translate from Genesis to the end of the second book of Kings. Eight assembled at Cambridge, and were to translate the remaining historical books, the Psalms, Job, Canticles, and Ecclesiastes. At Oxford seven were to translate the four greater Prophets, the Lamentations of Jeremiah, and the twelve minor Prophets. The four Gospels, the Acts of the Apostles, and the Revelation, were assigned to another company of eight at Oxford, and the Epistles were allotted to a company of seven at Westminster. Lastly, another company at Cambridge were to translate the Apocrypha."

To these companies the king gave instructions to guide them in their work, of which the following is the substance:

The Bishop's Bible, then used, to be followed, and to be altered as little as the original would permit.

The names of the sacred writers to be retained as they were commonly used.

When a word had different significations, that to be kept which had been most commonly used by the fathers and most eminent writers.

No alteration to be made in the chapters and verses. No marginal notes to be affixed, except to explain the Greek and Hebrew words that could not be briefly and fitly explained in the text. Reference to parallel places to be set down in the margin.

Each man of a company to take the same chapters and translate them according to the best of his abilities; and when this was done all were to meet together and compare their translations, and agree which should be regarded as correct.

Each book, when thus translated and approved, to be sent to every other company for their approbation.

Besides this, the translators were authorized, in cases of great difficulty, to send letters to any learned men in the kingdom to obtain their opinion.

In this manner the Bible was translated into English. First, each individual translated each book allotted to his company. Second, the readings to be adopted were agreed upon by that company assembled together. Third, the book thus finished was sent to each of the other companies to be examined. At these meetings one read the English, and the rest held in their hands some Bible of Hebrew, Greek, Latin, French, Spanish, &c. If they found any fault, says Selden, they spoke; if not, he read on.

The translation was commenced in 1607, and completed in about three years. At the end of that time three copies of it were sent to London. Here a committee of six revised the work, which was afterward revised by Dr. Smith, who wrote the preface, and by Dr. Bilson. It was first printed in 1611 at London by Robert Barker.

From this account it is clear that no ordinary care was taken to furnish to English readers a correct translation of the sacred Scriptures. No version of the Bible was ever made under more happy auspices, and it would now be impossible to furnish another translation in our language under circumstances so propitious. Whether we contemplate the number, the learning, or the piety of the men employed in it; the cool deliberation with which it was executed; the care taken that it should secure the approbation of the most learned men in a country that embosomed a vast amount of literature; the harmony with which they conducted their work, or the comparative perfection of the translation, we see equal cause of gratitude to the great Author of the Bible that we have so pure a translation of his word.

From this time the English language became fixed. More than two hundred years have elapsed, and yet the simple and majestic purity and power of the English tongue is expressed in the English translation of the Bible as clearly as when it was given to the world. It has become the standard of our language, and nowhere can the purity and expressive dignity of this language be so fully found as in the sacred Scriptures.

The friends of this translation have never claimed for it inspiration or infallibility. Yet it is the concurrent testimony of all who are competent to express an opinion, that no translation of the Bible into any language has preserved so faithfully the sense of the original as the English. Phrases there may be, and it is confessed there are, which modern criticism has shown not to express the exact meaning of the original; but, as a whole, it indubitably stands unrivalled. Nor is it probable that any translation can now supply its place, or improve upon its substantial correctness. The fact that it has for two hundred years poured light into the minds of millions, and guided the steps of generation after generation in the way to heaven, has given to it somewhat of the venerableness which appropriately belongs to a book of God. Successive ages may correct some of its few unimportant errors, may throw light on some of its obscure passages; but to the consummation of all things it must stand, wherever the English language is spoken, as the purest specimen of its power to give utterance to the meaning of ancient tongues, and of the simple and pure majesty of the language which we speak.

These remarks are made, because it is easy for men who dislike the plain doctrines of the Bible, and for those ignorant of the true history of its translation, to throw out insinuations of its unfaithfulness. From various quarters are often heard demands for a new translation. I by no means assert the entire infallibility, much less the inspiration, of the English translation of the Bible; yet of its general faithfulness to the original there can be no doubt. It would be easy to multiply testimonies of the highest authority to this fact. But the general testimony of the world; the profound regard paid to it by men of the purest character and most extensive learning; the fact that it has warmed the hearts of the pious, ministered to the comforts of the wretched and the dying, and guided the steps of millions to glory for two hundred years, and that it now commands the high regard of Christians of so many different denominations, evinces that it is to no ordinary extent faithful to the original, and has a claim on the continued regard of coming generations.

It is perfectly clear, also, that it would be impossible *now* to translate the Scriptures into the English language under so favourable circumstances as those which attended the translation in the time of James I. No set of men could so command the confidence of the Christian world; no convention who claim the Christian name could be formed competent to the task, or if formed, could prosecute the work with harmony; no single denomination could make a translation that would secure the undisputed respect of others. The probability is, therefore, that while the English language is spoken, and as far as it is used, the English Bible will continue to form the faith and direct the lives of those who use that language, and that the words which now pour light into *our* minds will continue to illuminate the understandings and mould the feelings of unnumbered millions in their path to immortal life.

PREFACE

TO THE GOSPEL ACCORDING TO MATTHEW.

THE word Gospel means *good news*, or *a joyful message*. It commonly signifies the message itself; but it is here used to denote *the book* containing the record of the message. The title "saint," given to the sacred writers of the New Testament, is of Roman Catholic origin, and is of no authority.

It has been pretty generally believed that Matthew wrote his Gospel in his native tongue; that is, the language of Palestine. That language was not pure Hebrew, but a mixture of the Hebrew, Chaldaic, and Syriac, commonly called *Syro-Chaldaic* or *Aramæan*. This language our Saviour undoubtedly used in his conversation;[1] and his disciples would naturally use this language also, unless there were good reasons why they should write in a foreign tongue. It is agreed that the remainder of the New Testament was written in Greek. The reason for this, in preference to the native language of the writers, was that Greek was the language then generally spoken and understood throughout the eastern countries conquered by Alexander the Great, and particularly in Judea, and in the regions where the apostles first laboured.

The Christian fathers, without any exception, assert that Matthew wrote his Gospel for the use of the Christians in Palestine, and say that it was written in the Hebrew dialect. It should be remarked, however, that many modern critics of much eminence do not suppose the evidence that Matthew wrote in Hebrew to be decisive, and believe that there is sufficient proof that, like the other writers of the New Testament, Matthew wrote in Greek. See Lardner's Works, vol. v. p. 308–318, London edition, 1829.

The Gospel of Matthew exists now, however, only in Greek. The original Hebrew, or Syro-Chaldaic, if it was written in that language, has been designedly laid aside or undesignedly lost. The question, then, naturally arises, Who is the author of the *Greek* translation which we possess? and is it to be regarded as of divine authority?

It has been conjectured by some that Matthew himself furnished a Greek translation of the Hebrew. This conjecture, in itself probable enough, is destitute, however, of testimony to support it. Athanasius, one of the early fathers, says that it was translated by "James, the brother of our Lord according to the flesh." Papias, another of the early fathers, says that "each one translated it as he was able." If James translated it, there can be no question about its inspiration and canonical authority. Nor does it affect the question of its inspiration, even if we are ignorant of the name of the translator. The proper

[1] See instances in Mar. vii. 34, and Mat. xxvii. 46.

inquiry is whether it had such evidence of inspiration as to be satisfactory to the Church in the times when they were under the direction of the apostles. That it *had* such evidence, none acquainted with ancient history will doubt.

Epiphanius says that the Gospel by Matthew was written while Peter and Paul were preaching at Rome. This was about the year of our Lord 63, about the time of the destruction of Jerusalem. It is now generally supposed that this Gospel was written about this time. There is very clear evidence *in* the Gospel that it was written before the destruction of Jerusalem. The destruction of the Holy City is clearly and minutely foretold, but there is not the slightest intimation in it that these predictions had been accomplished—a thing which we should naturally expect if the Gospel was not written until after these calamities came upon the Jews. Comp. Ac. xi. 28. It has been till lately uniformly regarded as having been written before either of the other evangelists. Some of late have, however, endeavoured to show that the Gospel by Luke was written first. All testimony, and all ancient arrangements of the books, are against the opinion; and when such is the fact, it is of little consequence to attend to other arguments.

In all copies of the New Testament, and in all translations, this Gospel has been placed first. This, it is probable, would not have been done had not Matthew published his Gospel before any other was written.

Matthew, the writer of this Gospel, called also Levi, son of Alphæus, was a publican, or tax-gatherer, under the Romans. See Notes on Mat. ix. 9; Lu. v. 27. Of his life and death little is certainly known. Socrates, a writer of the fifth century, says that he went to Ethiopia after the apostles were scattered abroad from Judea, and died a martyr in a city called Nadebbar, but by what kind of death is altogether uncertain. However, others speak of his preaching and dying in Parthia or Persia, and the diversity of their accounts seems to show that they are all without good foundation. See Lardner's Works, vol. v. p. 296, 297.

BETHLEHEM,

FROM THE NORTH-WEST

THE PLAIN OF JERICHO AND THE DEAD SEA.

Court of Eastern House—Damascus.

[Matthew, page 96.]

Court of Inn, or Caravanserai, at Aleppo.

[Luke, page 18.]

THE RIVER JORDAN.—Ford between Scythopolis and Pella.

[Matthew, page 26.]

MAGDALA (*el Mejdel*), LAKE OF TIBERIAS.

[Matthew, page 165.]

THE
GOSPEL ACCORDING TO MATTHEW.

CHAPTER I.

THE book of the [a]generation of Jesus Christ, the [b]son of David, [c]the son of Abraham.

2 Abraham[d] begat Isaac; and [e]Isaac begat Jacob; and [f]Jacob begat Judas and his brethren;

3 And [g]Judas begat Phares and

a Lu.3.23, &c. *b* Ps.132.11; ch.22.45; Ac.2.30. *c* Ge.22.18; Ga.3.16.

d Ge.21.2-5. *e* Ge.25.26. *f* Ge.29.35, &c. *g* Ge. 38.29,30, &c.

1. *The book of the generation.* This is the proper title of the chapter. It is the same as to say, "the account of the ancestry or family, or the genealogical table of Jesus Christ." The phrase is common in Jewish writings. Compare Ge. v. 1. "This is the book of the generations of Adam," *i.e.* the genealogical table of the family or descendants of Adam. See also Ge. vi. 9. The Jews, moreover, as we do, kept such tables of their own families, and it is probable that this was copied from the record of the family of Joseph. ¶ *Jesus.* See Notes on ver. 21. ¶ *Christ.* The word *Christ* is a Greek word, signifying *anointed.* The Hebrew word signifying the same is *Messiah.* Hence, Jesus is called either the *Messiah*, or the *Christ*, meaning the same thing. The Jews speak of *the Messiah;* Christians speak of him as *the Christ.* Anciently, when kings and priests were set apart to their office, they were *anointed with oil*, Le. iv. 3; vi. 20; Ex. xxviii. 41; xxix. 7; 1 Sa. ix. 16; xv. 1; 2 Sa. xxiii. 1. To *anoint*, therefore, means often the same as to *consecrate*, or to set apart to an office. Hence those thus set apart are said to be *anointed*, or to be the anointed of God. It is for this reason that the name is given to the Lord Jesus. Comp. Notes on Da. ix. 24. He was set apart by God to be the King, and High-priest, and Prophet of his people. Anointing with oil was, moreover, supposed to be emblematic of the influences of the Holy Spirit; and as God gave him the Spirit *without measure* (Jn. iii. 34), so he is called peculiarly the Anointed of God. ¶ *The Son of David.* The word *son* among the Jews had a great variety of significations. It means literally a son; then a grandson; a descendant; an adopted son; a disciple, or one who is an object of tender affection—one who is to us *as a son.* In this place it means a *descendant* of David; or one who was of the *family* of David. It was important to trace the genealogy of Jesus up to David, because the promise had been made that the Messiah should be of his family, and all the Jews expected that it would be so. It would be impossible, therefore, to convince a *Jew* that Jesus was the Messiah, unless it could be shown that he was descended from *David.* See Je. xxiii. 5; Ps. cxxxii. 10, 11, compared with Ac. xiii. 23, and Jn. vii. 42. ¶ *The son of Abraham.* The descendant of Abraham. The promise was made to Abraham also. See Ge. xii. 3; xxi. 12; compare He. xi. 13; Ga. iii. 16. The Jews expected that the Messiah would be descended from him; and it was important, therefore, to trace the genealogy up to him also. Though Jesus was of humble birth, yet he was descended from most illustrious ancestors. Abraham, the father of the faithful—"the beauteous model of an Eastern prince," and David, the sweet psalmist of Israel, the conqueror, the magnificent and victorious leader of the people of God, were both among his ancestors. From these two persons, the most eminent for piety, and the most renowned for their excellencies of all the men of antiquity, sacred or profane, the Lord Jesus was descended; and though his birth and life were humble, yet they who regard an illustrious descent as of value, may find here all that is to be admired in piety, purity, patriotism, splendour, dignity, and renown.

2-16. These verses contain the genealogy of Jesus. Luke also (ch. iii.) gives a genealogy of the Messiah. No two passages of Scripture have caused more difficulty than these, and various attempts have been made to explain them. There are two sources of difficulty in these catalogues. 1st. Many

Zara of Thamar; and [h]Phares begat Esrom; and [i]Esrom begat Aram;

4 And Aram begat Aminadab; and [k]Aminadab begat Naasson; and [l]Naasson begat Salmon;

5 And [m]Salmon begat Booz of Rachab; and [n]Booz begat Obed of Ruth; and Obed begat Jesse;

6 And [o]Jesse begat David the king; and [p]David the king begat Solomon of her *that had been the wife* of Urias;

7 And [q]Solomon begat Roboam; and Roboam begat Abia; and Abia begat Asa;

8 And Asa begat Josaphat; and Josaphat begat Joram; and Joram begat Ozias;

9 And Ozias begat Joatham; and Joatham begat Achaz; and Achaz begat Ezekias;

10 And [r]Ezekias begat Manasses; and Manasses begat Amon; and Amon begat Josias;

h Ge.46.12. *i* Ru.4.19. *k* 1 Ch.2.10; Nu.1.7. *l* Ru.4.20. *m* Jos.6.25; Ru.4.21. *n* Ru.4.13.

o 1 Sa.17.12. *p* 2 Sa.12.24. *q* 1 Ch.3.10, &c. *r* 2 Ki.20.21; 1 Ch.3.13.

names that are found in the Old Testament are here omitted; and, 2d, the tables of Matthew and Luke appear in many points to be different. From Adam to Abraham Matthew has mentioned no names, and Luke only has given the record. From Abraham to David the two tables are alike. Of course there is no difficulty in reconciling these two parts of the tables. The difficulty lies in that part of the genealogy from David to Christ. There they are entirely different. They are manifestly different lines. Not only are the *names* different, but Luke has mentioned, in this part of the genealogy, no less than forty-two names, while Matthew has recorded but twenty-seven.

Various ways have been proposed to explain this difficulty, but it must be admitted that none of them is perfectly satisfactory. It does not comport with the design of these Notes to enter minutely into an explanation of the perplexities of these passages. All that can be done is to suggest the various ways in which attempts have been made to explain them. 1. It is remarked that in nothing are mistakes more likely to occur than in such tables. From the similarity of names, and the different names by which the same person is often called, and from many other causes, errors would be more likely to creep into genealogical tables than in other writings. Some of the difficulties may have possibly occurred from this cause. 2. Most interpreters have supposed that Matthew gives the genealogy of *Joseph*, and Luke that of *Mary*. They were both descended from David, but in different lines. This solution derives some plausibility from the fact that the promise was made to *David*, and as Jesus was not the son of Joseph, it was important to show that *Mary* was also descended from him. But though this solution is plausible, and *may be* true, yet it wants evidence. It cannot, however, be proved that this was *not* the design of Luke. 3. It has been said also that Joseph was the *legal* son and heir of *Heli*, though the *real* son of Jacob, and that thus the two lines terminated in him. This was the explanation suggested by most of the Christian fathers, and on the whole is the most satisfactory. It was a law of the Jews that if a man died without children, his brother should marry his widow. Thus the two lines might have been intermingled. According to this solution, which was first proposed by Africanus, Matthan, descended from Solomon, married Estha, of whom was born Jacob. After Matthan's death, Matthat being of the same tribe, but of another family, married his widow, and of this marriage Heli was born. Jacob and Heli were therefore children of the same mother. Heli dying without children, his brother Jacob married his widow, and begat *Joseph*, who was thus the *legal* son of Heli. This is agreeable to the account in the two evangelists. Matthew says that *Jacob begat Joseph;* Luke says that Joseph was *the son of Heli*, i. e. was his *legal* heir, or was reckoned in law to be his son. This can be seen by the plan on the next page, showing the nature of the connection.

Though these solutions may not seem to be entirely satisfactory, yet there are two additional considerations which should set the matter at rest, and lead to the conclusion that the narratives are not really inconsistent. 1. No difficulty was ever found, or alleged, in regard to them, by any of the early enemies of

11 And [1]Josias begat Jechonias and his brethren, about the time they were carried away to Babylon;

1 Some read *Josias begat Jakim, and Jakim begat Jechonias.*

12 And after they were brought to Babylon, [s]Jechonias begat Salathiel; and [t]Salathiel begat Zorobabel;

s 1 Ch.3.17, &c. t Ne.12.1.

Christianity. There is no evidence that they ever adduced them as containing a contradiction. Many of those enemies were acute, learned, and able; and they show by their writings that they were not *indisposed* to detect all the errors that could possibly be found in the sacred narrative. Now it is to be remembered that the *Jews* were fully competent to show that these tables were incorrect, if they were really so; and it is clear that they were fully disposed, if possible, to do it. The fact, therefore, that it is not done, is clear evidence that *they* thought it to be correct. The same may be said of the acute pagans who wrote against Christianity. None of them have called in question the correctness of these tables. This is full proof that, in a time when it was easy to understand these tables, they were believed to be correct. 2. The evangelists are not responsible for the *correctness* of these tables. They are responsible only for what was their real and professed object to do. What was

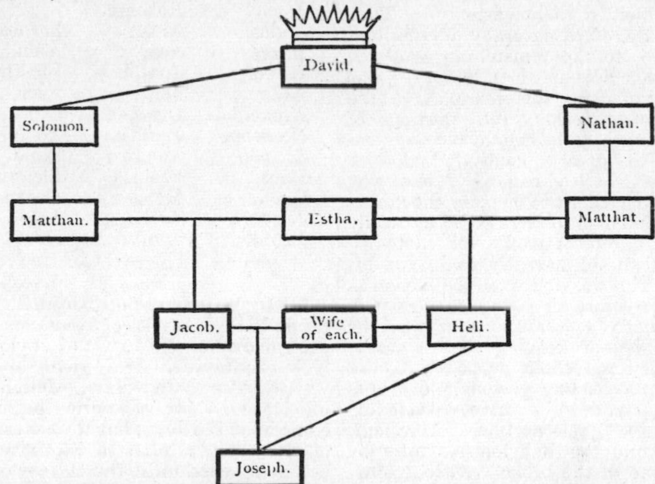

that object? It was to prove to the satisfaction of *the Jews* that Jesus was descended from *David*, and therefore that there was no argument from his ancestry that he was not the promised Messiah. Now to make this out, it was not necessary, nor would it have conduced to their argument, to have formed a *new* table of genealogy. All that could be done was to go to the *family records* —to the *public tables*, and copy them as they were *actually* kept, and show that, *according to the records of the nation*, Jesus was descended from David. This, among the Jews, would be full and decided testimony in the case. And this was doubtless done. In the same way, the records of a family among us, as they are kept by the family, are proof in courts of justice now of the birth, names, &c., of individuals. Nor is it necessary or proper for a court to call them in question or to attempt to correct them. So the tables here are good evidence to the only point that the writers wished to establish: that is, *to show to the Jews that Jesus of Nazareth was descended from David.* The only inquiry which can *now* be fairly made is whether they copied those tables *correctly*. It is clear that no man can prove that they did *not* so copy them, and therefore that no one can adduce them as an argument against the correctness of the New Testament.

17. *So all the generations*, &c. This

13 And Zorobabel begat Abiud; and Abiud begat Eliakim; and Eliakim begat Azor;

14 And Azor begat Sadoc; and Sadoc begat Achim; and Achim begat Eliud;

15 And Eliud begat Eleazar; and Eleazar begat Matthan; and Matthan begat Jacob;

16 And Jacob begat Joseph the husband of Mary, of whom was born Jesus, who is called Christ.

17 So all the generations from Abraham to David *are* fourteen generations; and from David until the carrying away into Babylon *are* fourteen generations; and from the carrying away into Babylon

---

division of the names in the genealogical tables was doubtless adopted for the purpose of aiding the memory. It was common among the Jews; and other similar instances are preserved. The Jews were destitute of books besides the Old Testament, and they had but few copies of that among them, and those chiefly in their synagogues. They would therefore naturally devise plans to keep up the remembrance of the principal facts in their history. One method of doing this was to *divide* the tables of genealogy into portions of equal length, to be committed to memory. This greatly facilitated the remembrance of the names. A man who wished to commit to memory the names of a regiment of soldiers would naturally divide it into companies and platoons, and this would greatly facilitate his work. This was doubtless the reason in the case before us. And, though it is not strictly accurate, yet it was the *Jewish* way of keeping their records, and answered their purpose. There were three leading persons and events that nearly, or quite, divided their history into equal portions: Abraham, David, and the Babylonish captivity. From one to the other was *about* fourteen generations, and by omitting a few names it was sufficiently accurate to be made a general guide or directory in recalling the principal events in their history.

In counting these divisions, however, it will be seen that there is some difficulty in making out the number *fourteen* in each division. This may be explained in the following manner: In the first division, Abraham is the first and David the last, making together fourteen. In the second series, David would naturally be placed first, and the fourteen was completed in *Josiah*, about the time of the captivity, as sufficiently near for the purpose of convenient computation, 2 Ch. xxxv. In the third division Josiah would naturally be placed first, and the number was completed in Joseph; so that David and Josiah would be reckoned twice. This may be shown by the following table of the names:—

First division.	*Second division.*	*Third division.*
Abraham,	David,	Josias,
Isaac,	Solomon,	Jechonias,
Jacob,	Roboam,	Salathiel,
Judas,	Abia,	Zorobabel,
Phares,	Asa,	Abiud,
Esrom,	Josaphat,	Eliakim,
Aram,	Joram,	Azor,
Aminadab,	Ozias,	Sadoc,
Naasson,	Joatham,	Achim,
Salmon,	Achaz,	Eliud,
Booz,	Ezekias,	Eleazar,
Obed,	Manasses,	Matthan,
Jessè,	Amon,	Jacob,
David.	Josias.	Joseph.
——14	——14	——14

¶ *Carrying away into Babylon.* This refers to the captivity of Jerusalem, and the removal of the Jews to Babylon by Nebuchadnezzar, 588 years before Christ. See 2 Ch. xxxvi. Josiah was king when these calamities began to come upon the Jews, but the exact time of the seventy years of captivity did not commence until the eleventh year of Zedekiah's reign, or 32 years after the death of Josiah. Babylon was situated on the Euphrates, and was encompassed with walls which were about 60 miles in circuit, 87 feet broad, and 350 feet high, and the city was entered by a hundred brazen gates, 25 on each side. It was the capital of a vast empire, and the Jews remained there for seventy years. See my Notes on Isaiah xiii.

18. *Now the birth of Jesus Christ.* The circumstances attending his birth. ¶ *Was on this wise.* In this manner. ¶ *Espoused.* Betrothed, or engaged to be married. There was commonly an interval of ten or twevle months, among the Jews, between the contract of marriage and the celebration of the nuptials

unto Christ *are* fourteen generations.

18 Now the [u]birth of Jesus Christ was on this wise: When as his mother Mary was espoused to Joseph, *before they came together, she was found with child of the Holy Ghost.

19 Then Joseph her husband, being a just *man*, and not willing to make her a public example, was minded [v]to put her away privily.

20 But while he thought on these things, behold, the angel of the Lord appeared unto him in a dream, saying, [w]Joseph, thou son

u Lu.1.27, &c.
* 5th year before the account called *A.D.*

v De.24.1.
w ver.16.

(see Ge. xxiv. 55; Ju. xiv. 8; De. xx. 7), yet such was the nature of this engagement, that unfaithfulness to each other was deemed adultery. See De. xxii. 25, 28. ¶ *With child by the Holy Ghost.* See Note, Lu. i. 35.

19. *Her husband.* The word in the original does not imply that they were married. It means here the man to whom she was espoused. ¶ *A just* man. *Justice* consists in rendering to every man his own. Yet this is evidently not the character intended to be given here of Joseph. The meaning is that he was kind, tender, merciful; that he was so attached to Mary that he was not willing that she should be exposed to public shame. He sought, therefore, secretly to dissolve the connection, and to restore her to her friends without the punishment commonly inflicted on adultery. The word *just* has not unfrequently this meaning of mildness, or mercy. See 1 Jn. i. 9.; comp. Cicero, *De Fin.* 5, 23. ¶ *A public example.* To expose her to public shame or infamy. Adultery has always been considered a crime of a very heinous nature. In Egypt it was punished by cutting off the nose of the adulteress; in Persia the nose and ears were cut off; in Judea the punishment was death by stoning, Le. xx. 10; Eze. xvi. 38, 40; Jn. viii. 5. This punishment was also inflicted where the person was not married, but betrothed, De. xxi. 23, 24. In this case, therefore, the regular punishment would have been death in this painful and ignominious manner. Yet Joseph was a religious man—mild and tender; and he was not willing to *complain* of her to the magistrate, and expose her to death, but sought to avoid the shame, and to put her away privately. ¶ *Put her away privily.* The law of Moses gave the husband the power of divorce, De. xxiv. 1. It was customary in a bill of divorce to specify the causes for which the divorce was made, and witnesses were also present to testify to the divorce. But in this case, it seems, Joseph resolved to put her away *without specifying the cause;* for he was not willing to make her a public example. This is the meaning here of *privily.* Both to Joseph and Mary this must have been a great trial. Joseph was ardently attached to her, but her character was likely to be ruined, and he deemed it proper to separate her from him. Mary was innocent, but Joseph was not yet satisfied of her innocence. We may learn from this to put our trust in God. He will defend the innocent. Mary was in danger of being exposed to shame. Had she been connected with a cruel, passionate, and violent man, she would have died in disgrace. But God had so ordered it that she was betrothed to a man mild, amiable, and tender; and in due time Joseph was apprised of the truth in the case, and took his faithful and beloved wife to his bosom. Thus our only aim should be to preserve a conscience void of offence, and God will guard our reputation. We may be assailed by slander; circumstances may be against us; but in due time God will take care to vindicate our character and save us from ruin. See Ps. xxxvii. 5, 6.

20. *He thought on these things.* He did not act hastily. He did not take the course which the law would have *permitted* him to do, if he had been hasty, violent, or unjust. It was a case deeply affecting his happiness, his character, and the reputation and character of his chosen companion. God will guide the thoughtful and the anxious. And when *we* have looked patiently at a perplexed subject, and know not what to do, then God, as in the case of Joseph, will interpose to lead us and direct our way. Ps. xxv. 9. ¶ *The angel of the Lord.* The word *angel* literally means a *messenger.* It is applied chiefly in the Scriptures to those invisible holy beings who have not fallen into sin; who live in heaven (1 Ti. v. 21; compare Jude 6);

of David, fear not to take unto thee Mary thy wife; for that which is [2]conceived in her is of the Holy Ghost.

21 And she shall bring forth a son, and thou shalt call his name [3]JESUS: for [x]he shall save his people from their sins.

22 Now all this was done, that it might be fulfilled which was

[2] *begotten.*

[3] i.e. *Saviour.* *x* Ac.5.31; 13.23,38.

and who are sent forth to minister to those who shall be heirs of salvation. See Notes on He. i. 13, 14, and on Da. ix. 21. The word is sometimes applied to *men*, as messengers (Lu. vii. 24; ix. 52; Ja. ii. 25); to the winds (Ps. civ. 4); to the pestilence (Ps. lxxviii. 49); or to whatever is appointed to *make known* or *to execute* the will of God. It is commonly applied, however, to the unfallen, happy spirits that are in heaven, whose dignity and pleasure it is to do the will of God. Various ways were employed by them in making known the will of God, by dreams, visions, assuming a human appearance, &c. ¶ *In a dream.* This was a common way of making known the will of God to the ancient prophets and people of God, Ge. xx. 3; xxx. 1, 11, 24; xxxvii. 5; xli. 1; 1 Ki. iii. 5; Dan. vii. 1; Job iv. 13-15; compare my Notes on Isaiah, vol. i. p. xi, xii, xiii. In what way it was ascertained that these dreams were from God cannot now be ascertained. It is sufficient for us to know that in this way many of the prophecies were communicated, and to remark that there is no evidence that we are to put reliance on *our* dreams. Dreams are wild, irregular movements of the mind when it is unshackled by reason, and it is mere superstition to suppose that God *now* makes known his will in this way. ¶ *Son of David.* Descendant of David. See ver. 1. The angel put him in mind of his relation to *David* perhaps to prepare him for the intelligence that Mary was to be the mother of the Messiah—the promised heir of David. ¶ *Fear not.* Do not hesitate, or have any apprehensions about her virtue and purity. Do not fear that she will be unworthy of you, or will disgrace you. ¶ *To take unto thee Mary thy wife.* To take her *as* thy wife; to recognize her as such, and to treat her as such. ¶ *For that which is conceived in her is of the Holy Ghost.* Is the direct creation of divine power. A body was thus prepared pure and holy, and free from the corruption of sin, in order that he might be qualified for his great work—the offering of a pure sacrifice to God. As this was necessary in order to the great work which he came to perform, Joseph is directed by an angel to receive her as pure and virtuous, and as every way worthy of his love. Comp. Notes on He. x. 5.

21. *His name JESUS.* The name *Jesus* is the same as *Saviour.* It is derived from the verb signifying *to save.* In Hebrew it is the same as *Joshua.* In two places in the New Testament it is used where it means Joshua, the leader of the Jews into Canaan, and in our translation the name *Joshua* should have been retained, Ac. vii. 45; He. iv. 8. It was a very common name among the Jews. ¶ *He shall save.* This expresses the same as the name, and on this account the name was given to him. He saves men by dying to redeem them; by giving the Holy Spirit to renew them (Jn. xvi. 7, 8); by his power in enabling them to overcome their spiritual enemies, in defending them from danger, in guiding them in the path of duty, in sustaining them in trials and in death; and he will raise them up at the last day, and exalt them to a world of purity and love. ¶ *His people.* Those whom the Father has given to him. The Jews were called the people of God because he had chosen them to himself, and regarded them as his peculiar and beloved people, separate from all the nations of the earth. Christians are called the people of Christ because it was the purpose of the Father to give them to him (Is. liii. 11; Jn. vi. 37); and because in due time he came to redeem them to himself, Tit. ii. 14; 1 Pe. i. 2. ¶ *From their sins.* This was the great business of Jesus in coming and dying. It was not to save men IN their sins, but FROM their sins. Sinners could not be happy in heaven. It would be a place of wretchedness to the guilty. The design of Jesus was, therefore, to save them *from* sin; and from this we may learn, 1st, That Jesus had a *design* in coming into the world. He came to save *his people;* and that design will surely be accomplished. It is impossible that in any part of it he should

spoken[y] of the Lord by the prophet, saying,

23 Behold, a virgin shall be with child, and shall bring forth a son, and [4]they shall call his name Emmanuel; which being interpreted, is, [z]God with us.

24 Then Joseph, being raised

y Is.7.14.

4 or, *his name shall be called.* z Jn. 1.14.

fail. 2d. We have no evidence that we are his people unless we are saved from the power and dominion of sin. A mere *profession* of being his people will not answer. Unless we give up our sins; unless we renounce the pride, pomp, and pleasure of the world, we have no evidence that we are the children of God. It is impossible that we should be Christians if we indulge in sin and live in the practice of any known iniquity. See 1 Jn. iii. 7, 8. 3d. That all professing Christians should feel that there is no salvation unless it is *from sin*, and that they can never be admitted to a holy heaven hereafter unless they are made pure, by the blood of Jesus, here.

22. *Now all this was done.* The prophecy here quoted is recorded in Is. vii. 14. See Notes on that passage. The prophecy was delivered about 740 years before Christ, in the reign of Ahaz, king of Judah. The land of Judea was threatened with an invasion by the united armies of Syria and Israel, under the command of Rezin and Pekah. Ahaz was alarmed, and seems to have contemplated calling in aid from Assyria to defend him. Isaiah was directed, in his consternation, to go to Ahaz, and tell him to ask a sign from God (Is. vii. 10, 11); that is, to look to *God* rather than to Assyria for aid. This he refused to do. He had not confidence in God, but feared that the land would be overrun by the armies of Syria (ver. 12), and relied only on the aid which he hoped to receive from Assyria. Isaiah answered that, in these circumstances, the Lord would himself give a sign, or a pledge, that the land should be delivered. The sign was, that a virgin should have a son, and that before that son would arrive to years of discretion, the land would be forsaken by these hostile kings. The prophecy was therefore designed *originally* to signify to Ahaz that the land would *certainly* be delivered from its calamities and dangers, and that the deliverance would not be long delayed. The land of *Syria* and *Israel*, *united* now in confederation, would be deprived of both their kings, and thus the land of Judah would be freed from the threatening danger. This appears to be the *literal* fulfilment of the passage in Isaiah. ¶ *Might be fulfilled.* It is more difficult to know in what sense this could be said to be *fulfilled* in the birth of Christ. To understand this, it may be remarked that the word *fulfilled* is used in the Scriptures and in other writings in many senses, of which the following are some: 1st. When a thing is *clearly predicted*, and comes to pass, as the destruction of Babylon, foretold in Is. xiii. 19-22; and of Jerusalem, in Mat. xxiv. 2d. When one thing is *typified* or shadowed forth by another, and when the event occurs, the type is said to be fulfilled. This was the case in regard to the types and sacrifices in the Old Testament, which were *fulfilled* by the coming of Christ. See He. ix. 3d. When prophecies of future events are expressed in language more elevated and full than the particular thing, at first denoted, demands. Or, in other words, when the language, though it may express one event, is also so full and rich as *appropriately* to express other events *in similar circumstances* and of similar import, they may be said to be *fulfilled*. Thus, *e.g.*, the last chapters of Isaiah, from the fortieth chapter, foretell the return of the Jews into Babylon, and every circumstance mentioned occurred in their return. But the language is more expanded and sublime than was necessary to express their return. It will also *express appropriately* a much more important and magnificent deliverance—that of the redeemed under the Messiah; and the return of the people of God to him, and the universal spread of the gospel; and therefore it may be said *to be fulfilled* in the coming of Jesus and the spread of the gospel. So, if there were any other magnificent and glorious events, still, *in similar circumstances*, and of like character, it might be said also that these prophecies were fulfilled in all of them. The language is so full and rich, and the promises are so grand, that they may appropriately express *all* these deliverances. This may be the sense in which

from sleep, did as the angel of the Lord had bidden him, and took unto him his wife:

25 And knew her not till she had brought [a]forth her first-born son: and he called his name [b]JESUS.

a Ex.13.2. *b* Lu.2.21.

the prophecy now under consideration may be said to have been fulfilled. 4th. Language is said to be fulfilled when, though it was used to express one event, it may be used also to express another. Thus a *fable* may be said to be fulfilled when an event occurs similar to the one concerning which it was first spoken. A parable has its fulfilment in all the cases to which it is applicable; and the same remark applies to a proverb, or to a declaration respecting human nature. The statement that "there is none that doeth good" (Ps. xiv. 3) was at first spoken of a particular race of wicked men. Yet it is applicable to others, and in this sense may be said to have been fulfilled. See Ro. iii. 10. In this use of the word *fulfilled*, it means, not that the passage was at first *intended* to apply *to this particular thing*, but that the words aptly or appropriately express the thing spoken of, and *may* be applied to it. We may say the same of this which was said of another thing, and thus the words express *both*, or *are fulfilled*. The writers of the New Testament seem occasionally to have used the word in this sense.

23. *Behold, a virgin shall be with child.* Matthew clearly understands this as applying literally *to a virgin*. Compare Lu. i. 34. It thus implies that the conception of Christ was *miraculous*, or that the body of the Messiah was *created* directly by the power of God, agreeably to the declaration in He. x. 5: "Wherefore, when he cometh into the world, he saith, Sacrifice and offering thou wouldest not, *but a body hast thou prepared me.*" ¶ *And they shall call his name Emmanuel.* That is, his name shall be so called. See Notes on Is. vii. 14. The word *Immanuel* is a Hebrew word, and means literally *God with us*. Matthew doubtless understands it as denoting that the Messiah was really "God with us," or that the divine nature was united with the human. He does not affirm that this was its meaning when used in reference to the child to whom it was first applied, but this is its signification as applicable to the Messiah. *It was fitly expressive of his character;* and in this sense it was fulfilled. When *first* used by Isaiah, it denoted simply that the birth of the child was a sign that God was with the Jews to deliver them. The Hebrews often incorporated the name of Jehovah, or God, into their proper names. Thus, Isaiah means "the salvation of Jehovah;" Eleazer, "help of God;" Eli, "my God," &c. But Matthew evidently intends more than was denoted by the simple use of such names. He had just given an account of the miraculous conception of Jesus; of his being begotten by the Holy Ghost. God was therefore his Father. He was divine as well as human. His appropriate name, therefore, was "God with us." And though the mere use of such a name would not prove that he had a divine nature, yet as *Matthew uses it*, and meant evidently to apply it, it *does* prove that Jesus was more than a man; that he was God as well as man. And it is this which gives glory to the plan of redemption. It is this which is the wonder of angels. It is this which makes the plan so vast, so grand, so full of instruction and comfort to Christians. See Phi. ii. 6–8. It is this which sheds such peace and joy into the sinner's heart; which gives him such security of salvation, and which renders the condescension of God in the work of redemption so great and his character so lovely.

"Till God in human flesh I see,
My thoughts no comfort find,
The holy, just, and sacred Three
Are terror to my mind.

"But if IMMANUEL's face appears,
My hope, my joy, begins.
His grace removes my slavish fears,
His blood removes my sins.'

For a full examination of the passage, see my Notes on Is. vii. 14.

24. *Being raised from sleep.* Having fully awoke. ¶ *Did as the angel of the Lord had bidden him.* That is, he took Mary to wife. Probably this was done immediately, as he was now convinced of her innocence, and he would not by delay leave any ground of suspicion that he had not confidence in her.

25. *Knew her not.* The doctrine of the virginity of Mary *before* the birth of Jesus is a doctrine of the Scriptures, and is very important to be believed. But the Bible does not affirm that she had no children afterward. Indeed, all

CHAPTER II.

NOW when Jesus was born* in Bethlehem of Judea, in the days of Herod the king, behold, there came wise men from the east to Jerusalem,

* 4th year before the account called *A.D.*

the accounts in the New Testament lead us to suppose that she had. See Notes on Mat. xiii. 55, 56. The language here evidently implies that she lived as the wife of Joseph after the birth of Jesus. ¶ *Her first-born son.* Her eldest son, or he that by the law had the privilege of birthright. This does not *of necessity* imply that she had other children, though it seems probable. It was the name given to the son which was first born, whether there were others or not. ¶ *His name JESUS.* This was given by divine appointment, ver. 21. It was conferred on him on the eighth day, at the time of his circumcision, Lu. ii. 21.

CHAPTER II.

1. *When Jesus was born.* See the full account of his birth in Lu. ii. 1–20. ¶ *In Bethlehem of Judea.* Bethlehem, the birthplace of Christ, was a small town about six miles south of Jerusalem. The word *Bethlehem* denotes "house of bread"—perhaps given to the place on account of its great fertility. It was also called *Ephrata*, a word supposed likewise to signify fertility, Ge. xxxv. 19; Ru. iv. 11; Ps. cxxxii. 6. It was called the city of David (Lu. ii. 4), because it was the city of his nativity, 1 Sa. xvi. 1, 18. It was called Bethlehem *of Judea*, to distinguish it from a town of the same name in Galilee, Jos. xix. 15. The soil of Bethlehem was noted for its fertility. Ancient travellers frequently spoke of its productions. The town is situated on an eminence, in the midst of hills and vales. At present it contains about two hundred houses, inhabited chiefly by Christians and Mohammedans, who live together in peace. About two hundred paces east of Bethlehem the place is still shown where our Saviour is supposed to have been born. There is a church and a convent there; and beneath the church a subterranean chapel, which is lighted by thirty-two lamps, which is said to be the place where was the stable in which Jesus was born, though no certain reliance is to be placed on the tradition which makes this the birthplace of the Saviour. ¶ *Herod the king.* Judea, where our Saviour was born, was a province of the Roman Empire. It was taken about 63 years before his birth by Pompey, and placed under tribute. Herod received his appointment from the Romans, and had reigned at the time of the birth of Jesus thirty-four years. Though he was permitted to be called *king*, yet he was in all respects dependent on the Roman emperor. He was commonly called Herod the Great because he had distinguished himself in the wars with Antigonus and his other enemies, and because he had evinced great talents in governing and defending his country, in repairing the temple, and in building and ornamenting the cities of his kingdom. He was, however, as much distinguished for his cruelty and his crimes as he was for his greatness. At this time Augustus was Emperor of Rome. The world was at peace. A large part of the known nations of the earth was united under the Roman emperor. Intercourse between different nations was easy and safe. Similar laws prevailed. The use of the Greek language was general throughout the world. All these circumstances combined to render this a favourable time to introduce the gospel, and to spread it through the earth; and the providence of God was remarkable in preparing the nations in this manner for the easy and rapid spread of the Christian religion. ¶ *Wise men.* The original word here is *magoi*, from which comes our word *magician*, now used in a bad sense, but not so in the original. The persons here denoted were philosophers, priests, or astronomers. They dwelt chiefly in Persia and Arabia. They were the learned men of the Eastern nations, devoted to astronomy, to religion, and to medicine. They were held in high esteem by the Persian court, were admitted as counsellors, and followed the camps in war to give advice. ¶ *From the east.* It is not known whether they came from Persia or Arabia. Both countries might be denoted by the word East—that is, east from Judea. ¶ *Jerusalem.* The capital of Judea. As there is frequent reference in the New Testament to Jerusalem; as it was the place of the

public worship of God; as it was the place where many important transactions in the life of the Saviour occurred, and where he died; and as no Sabbath-school teacher can intelligently explain the New Testament without some knowledge of that city, it seems desirable to present a brief description of it. A more full description may be seen in Calmet's *Dictionary*, and in the common works on Jewish antiquities. Jerusalem was the capital of the kingdom of Judah, and was built on the line dividing that tribe from the tribe of Benjamin. It was once called *Salem* (Ge. xiv. 18; Ps. lxxvi. 2), and in the days of Abraham was the abode of Melchizedek. When the Israelites took possession of the promised land, they found this stronghold in the possession of the *Jebusites*, by whom it was called *Jebus* or *Jebusi*, Jos. xviii. 28. The name *Jerusalem* was probably compounded of the two by changing a single letter, and calling it, for the sake of the sound, *Jerusalem* instead of *Jebusalem*. The ancient Salem was probably built on Mount Moriah or Acra—the eastern and western mountains on which Jerusalem was subsequently built. When the Jebusites became masters of the place, they erected a fortress in the southern quarter of the city, which was subsequently called Mount Zion, but which they called *Jebus;* and although the Israelites took possession of the adjacent territory (Jos. xviii. 28), the Jebusites still held this fortress or upper town until the time of David, who wrested it from them (2 Sa. v. 7–9), and then removed his court from Hebron to Jerusalem, which was thenceforward known as the city of David, 2 Sa. vi. 10, 12; 1 Ki. viii. 1. Jerusalem was built on several hills—Mount Zion on the south, Mount Moriah on the east, on which the temple was subsequently built (see Notes on ch. xxi. 12), Mount Acra on the west, and Mount Bezetha on the north. Mount Moriah and Mount Zion were separated by a valley, called by Josephus the *Valley of Cheesemongers*, over which there was a bridge or raised way leading from the one to the other. On the south-east of Mount Moriah, and between that and Mount Zion, there was a bluff or high rock capable of strong fortification, called *Ophel*. The city was encompassed by hills. On the west there were hills which overlooked the city; on the south was the valley of Jehoshaphat, or the valley of Hinnom (see Notes on Mat. v. 22), separating it from what is called the *Mount of Corruption;* on the east was the valley or the brook Kedron, dividing the city from the Mount of Olives. On the north the country was more level, though it was a broken or *rolling* country. On the south-east the valleys of the Kedron and Jehoshaphat united, and the waters flowed through the broken mountains in a south-easterly direction to the Dead Sea, some fifteen miles distant. The city of Jerusalem stands in 31° 50′ north latitude, and 35° 20′ east longitude from Greenwich. It is thirty-four miles south-easterly from Jaffa—the ancient Joppa—which is its seaport, and one hundred and twenty miles south-westerly from Damascus. The best view of the city of Jerusalem is from Mount Olivet on the east (comp. Notes on Mat. xxi. 1), the mountains in the east being somewhat higher than those on the west. The city was anciently inclosed within walls, a part of which are still standing. The position of the walls has been at various times changed, as the city has been larger or smaller, or as it has extended in different directions. The wall on the south formerly included the whole of Mount Zion, though the modern wall runs over the summit, including about half of the mountain. In the time of the Saviour the northern wall inclosed only Mounts Acra and Moriah north, though after his death Agrippa extended the wall so as to include Mount Bezetha on the north. About half of that is included in the present wall. The limits of the city on the east and the west, being more determined by the nature of the place, have been more fixed and permanent. The city was watered in part by the fountain of Siloam on the east (for a description of which, see Notes on Lu. xiii. 4, and on Is. vii. 3), and in part by the fountain of Gihon on the west of the city, which flowed into the vale of Jehoshaphat; and in the time of Solomon by an aqueduct, part of which is still remaining, by which water was brought from the vicinity of Bethlehem. The "pools of Solomon," three in number, one rising above another, and adapted to hold a large quantity of water, are still remaining in the vicinity of Bethlehem. The fountain of Siloam still flows freely (see Note on Is. vii. 3), though the fountain of Gihon is commonly dry. A reservoir or tank, how-

2 Saying, Where is he that is born [a]King of the Jews? for we have seen [b]his star in the east, and are come to [c]worship him.

a Zec.9.9. b Nu.24.17; Is.60.3. c Jn.5.23.

ever, remains at Gihon. Jerusalem had, probably, its highest degree of splendour in the time of Solomon. About four hundred years after, it was wholly destroyed by Nebuchadnezzar. It lay utterly desolate during the seventy years of the Jewish captivity. Then it was rebuilt, and restored to some degree of its former magnificence, and remained about six hundred years, when it was utterly destroyed by Titus, A.D. 70. In the reign of Adrian the city was partly rebuilt under the name of Ælia. The monuments of Pagan idolatry were erected in it, and it remained under Pagan jurisdiction until Helena, the mother of Constantine, overthrew the memorials of idolatry, and erected a magnificent church over the spot which was supposed to be the place of the Redeemer's sufferings and burial. Julian, the apostate, with the design to destroy the credit of the prophecy of the Saviour that the temple should remain in ruins (Mat. xxiv.), endeavoured to rebuild the temple. His own historian, Ammianus Marcellinus (see Warburton's *Divine Legation of Moses*), says that the workmen were impeded by balls of fire coming from the earth, and that he was compelled to abandon the undertaking. Jerusalem continued in the power of the Eastern emperors till the reign of the Caliph *Omar*, the third in succession from Mohammod, who reduced it under his control about the year 640. The Saracens continued masters of Jerusalem until the year 1099, when it was taken by the Crusaders under Godfrey of Bouillon. They founded a new kingdom, of which Jerusalem was the capital, which continued eighty-eight years under nine kings. At last this kingdom was utterly ruined by Saladin; and though the Christians once more obtained possession of the city, yet they were obliged again to relinquish it. In 1217 the Saracens were expelled by the Turks, who have ever since continued in possession of it. Jerusalem has been taken and pillaged seventeen times, and millions of men have been slaughtered within its walls. At present there is a splendid mosque—the mosque of Omar—on the site of the temple. The present population of Jerusalem is variously estimated at from 15,000 to 30,000. Turner estimates it at 26,000; Richardson, 20,000; Jowett, 15,000; Dr. Robinson at 11,000, viz., Mohammedans 4500, Jews 3000, Christians 3500.—*Biblical Researches*, vol. ii. p. 83, 84. The Jews have a number of synagogues. The Roman Catholics have a convent, and have the control of the church of the Holy Sepulchre. The Greeks have twelve convents; the Armenians have three convents on Mount Zion and one in the city; the Copts, Syrians, and Abyssinians have each of them one convent. The streets are narrow, and the houses are of stone, most of them low and irregular, with flat roofs or terraces, and with small windows only toward the street, usually protected by iron grates. The above description has been obtained from a great variety of sources, and it would be useless to refer to the works where the facts have been obtained.

2. *Where is he*, &c. There was at that time a prevalent expectation that some remarkable personage was about to appear in Judea. The Jews were anxiously looking for the coming of the Messiah. By computing the time mentioned by Daniel (ch. ix. 25-27), they knew that the period was approaching when he would appear. This personage, *they* supposed, would be a temporal prince, and they were expecting that he would deliver them from Roman bondage. It was natural that this expectation should spread into other countries. Many Jews at that time dwelt in Egypt, in Rome, and in Greece; many, also, had gone to Eastern countries, and in every place they carried their sacred writings, and diffused the expectation that some remarkable person was about to appear. Suetonius, a Roman historian, speaking of this rumour, says: "An ancient and settled persuasion prevailed throughout the East that the Fates had decreed some one to proceed from Judea who should attain universal empire."* Tacitus, another Roman historian, says: "Many were persuaded that it was contained in the ancient books of their priests, that at that very time the East should

* Vespasian, ch. 4.

3 When Herod the king had heard *these things*, he was troubled, and all Jerusalem with him.

4 And when he had [d]gathered all the chief priests and scribes of the people together, he demanded of them where Christ should be born.

d Ps.2.2.

prevail, and that some one should proceed from Judea and possess the dominion."* Josephus also, and Philo, two Jewish historians, make mention of the same expectation.† The *fact* that such a person was expected is clearly attested. Under this expectation these wise men came to do him homage, and inquired anxiously *where he was born?* ¶ *His star.* Among the ancients the appearance of a new star or comet was regarded as an omen of some remarkable event. Many such appearances are recorded by the Roman historians at the birth or death of distinguished men. Thus they say that at the death of Julius Cæsar a comet appeared in the heavens and shone seven days. These wise men also considered this as an evidence that the long-expected Prince was born. It is possible that they had been led to this belief by the prophecy of Balaam, Nu. xxiv. 17: "There shall come a *star* out of Jacob," &c. What this star was is not known. There have been many conjectures respecting it, but nothing is revealed concerning it. We are not to suppose that it was what *we* commonly mean by a *star*. The stars are vast bodies fixed in the heavens, and it is absurd to suppose that one of them was sent to guide the wise men. It is most probable that it was a luminous appearance, or meteor, such as we now see sometimes shoot from the sky, which the wise men saw, and which directed them to Jerusalem. It is possible that the same thing is meant which is mentioned by Lu. ii. 9: "*The glory of the Lord shone round about them;*" i.e. (see Note on this place), a great *light* appeared shining around them. That *light* might have been visible from afar, and *might* have been seen by the wise men in the East. ¶ *In the East.* This does not mean that they had seen the star to the east of themselves, but that, when *they* were in the East, they had seen this star. As this star was in the direction of Jerusalem, it must have been *west* of them. It might be translated, "We, being in the East,' have seen his star." It is called *his* star, because they supposed it to be intended to indicate the time and place of his birth. ¶ *To worship him.* This does not mean that they had come to pay him *religious* homage, or to *adore* him. They regarded him as the King of the Jews, but there is no evidence that they supposed that he was divine. They came to honour him as *a Prince*, or a king, not as God. The original word implies no more than this. It means to prostrate one's self before another; to fall down and pay homage to another. This was the mode in which homage was paid to earthly kings, and this they wished to pay to the new-born King of the Jews. See the same meaning of the word in Mat. xx. 20; xviii. 26; Ac. x. 25; Lu. xiv. 10. The English word *worship* also meant formerly "to respect, to honour, to treat with civil reverence" (Webster).

3. *Had heard* these things. Had heard of their coming, and of the star, and of the design of their coming. ¶ *He was troubled.* Herod had obtained the kingdom by great crimes, and by shedding much blood. He was therefore easily alarmed by any remarkable appearances; and the fact that this star appeared, and that it was regarded as proof that a King of the Jews was born, alarmed him. Besides, it was a common expectation that the Messiah was about to appear, and he feared that his reign was about to come to an end. He therefore began to inquire in what way he might secure his own safety and the permanency of his government. ¶ *All Jerusalem.* The people of Jerusalem, and particularly the friends of Herod. There were many in Jerusalem to whom the coming of the Messiah would be a matter of joy; but all of Herod's friends would doubtless be alarmed at his coming.

4. *The chief priests.* By the *chief priests* here are meant not only the high-priest and his deputy, but also the heads or chiefs of the twenty-four classes into which David had divided the sacerdotal families, 1 Ch. xxiii. 6; xxiv.; 2 Ch. viii. 14; Ezr. viii. 24. ¶ *Scribes.* By the *scribes*, in the New Testament, are meant learned men; men skilled in the law, or the lawyers

* Annals, 5. 13. † Josephus, b. 1. 5. 5. 7. 31.

5 And they said unto him, In Bethlehem of Judea: for thus it is written by the prophet;

6 And[e] thou Bethlehem, *in* the land of Juda, art not the least among the princes of Juda: for out of thee shall come a Governor, [f]that shall [1]rule my people Israel.

7 Then Herod, when he had privily called the wise men, inquired of them diligently what time the star appeared.

8 And he sent them to Bethle-

e Mi.5.2; Jn.7.42. f Re.2.27. 1 or, *feed*, Is.40.11.

of the nation. They kept the records of the courts of justice, the registers of the synagogues, wrote articles of contract and sale, bills of divorce, &c. They were also called *lawyers*, Mat. xxii. 35, and *doctors of the law*, Lu. v. 17. They were called *scribes*, from the fact of their *writing* the public records. They were not, however, a *religious* sect, but might be either Pharisees or Sadducees. By *the chief priests and scribes* here mentioned is denoted the *Sanhedrim* or great council of the nation. This was composed of seventy-two men, who had the charge of the civil and religious affairs of the Jews. On this occasion Herod, in alarm, called them together, professedly to make inquiry respecting the birth of the Messiah. ¶ *Demanded of them.* Inquired, or asked of them. As they were the learned men of the nation, and as it was their business to study and explain the Old Testament, they were presumed to know what the prophecies had declared on that point. His object was to ascertain from prophecy *where* he was born, that he might put him to death, and thus calm the anxieties of his own mind. He seems not to have had any doubt about the *time when* he would be born. He was satisfied that the time had come.

5, 6. *By the prophet.* The Sanhedrim answered without hesitation. The question where he would be born had been settled by prophecy. This prophecy is found in Mi. v. 2. In that prophecy both the place of his birth and the character of the Messiah are so clearly set forth that there was no room to doubt. It will be observed that there is a considerable difference between the passage as quoted by the Sanhedrim and as it stands in Micah. The *main point*, however, is retained—the place of his birth. We are not concerned, therefore, in showing how these passages can be reconciled. Matthew, moreover, is not responsible for the correctness of the quotation. He affirms only that *the chief priests and scribes gave this answer to Herod*, and that Herod was satisfied. Admitting that *they* did not quote the passage correctly, it does not prove that Matthew has not reported *their answer* as they gave it, and this is all that he pretends to give. ¶ *Art not the least.* In Micah, "though thou be little." Though a small place so far as population is concerned, yet it shall *not* be small, or be the least in honour; for the Messiah shall be born there. His birth gave the place an honour which could not be conferred on the larger cities by all their numbers, their splendour, and their wealth. The birth of a distinguished personage was always supposed to give honour and importance to a city or country. Thus seven cities contended for the honour of giving birth to Homer; Stratford-upon-Avon is distinguished as the birthplace of Shakspeare; and Corsica as the birthplace of Napoleon. ¶ *A Governor.* A ruler. This is one of the characters of the Messiah, who is the king of his people, Jn. xviii. 37. The word *rule* here means to rule as a shepherd does his flock, in faithfulness and tenderness. Comp. Jn. x. 11; Is. xl. 10, 11; ix. 7.

7. *Privily.* Secretly, privately. He did this to ascertain the *time* when Jesus was born. ¶ *Diligently.* Accurately, exactly. He took pains to learn the precise time when the star appeared. He did this because he naturally concluded that the star appeared just at the time of his birth, and he wished to know precisely how old the child was.

8. *Go, and search diligently*, &c. Herod took all possible means to obtain accurate information respecting the child, that he might be sure of destroying him. He not only ascertained the probable time of his birth, and the *place* where he would be born, but he sent the wise men that they might actually see him, and bring him word. All this might have looked suspicious if he had not clothed it with the appearance of religion. He said to them, therefore, that he did it that he might go and worship him also. From this we may

hem; and said, Go and search diligently for the young child; and when ye have found *him*, bring me word again, that I may come and[g] worship him also.

9 When they had heard the king, they departed: and, lo, the star, which they saw [h] in the east, went before them, till it came and stood over where the young child was.

10 When they saw the star, they [i] rejoiced with exceeding great joy.

11 And when they were come into the house, they saw the young child with Mary his mother, and fell down, and worshipped him:

g Pr.26.24. h ver.2. i Ps.67.4.

---

learn, 1. That wicked men often cloak their evil designs under the appearance of religion. They attempt to deceive those who are really good, and to make them suppose that they have the same design. 2. Wicked men often attempt to make use of the pious to advance their evil purposes. Men like Herod will stop at nothing if they can carry their ends. They endeavour to deceive the simple, to allure the unsuspecting, and to beguile the weak, in order to accomplish their own purposes of wickedness. 3. The plans of wicked men are often well laid. Those plans occupy a long time. Such men make diligent inquiry, and all of it has the appearance of religion. But God sees the design; and though *men* are deceived, yet *God* cannot be, Pr. xv. 3.

9, 10. *The star—went before them.* From this it appears that the *star* was a luminous meteor, perhaps at no great distance from the ground. It is not unlikely that they lost sight of it after they had commenced their journey from the East. It is probable that it appeared to them first in the direction of Jerusalem. They concluded that the expected King had been born, and immediately commenced their journey to Jerusalem. When they arrived there, it was important that they should be directed to the very place where he was, and the star again appeared. It was for this reason that they rejoiced. They felt assured that they were under a heavenly guidance, and would be conducted to the new-born King of the Jews. And this shows, 1. That the birth of Jesus was an event of great moment, worthy of the divine interposition in directing these men to find the place of his nativity. 2. God will guide those who are disposed to find the Saviour. Even if for a time the light should be withdrawn, yet it will again appear, and direct us in the way to the Redeemer. 3. Our being led to Christ should fill us with joy. He is the way, the truth, and the life; the Saviour, the friend, the all in all; there is no other way of life, and there is no peace to the soul till he is found. When we are guided to *him*, therefore, our hearts should overflow with joy and praise; and we should humbly and thankfully follow every direction that leads to the Son of God, Jn. xii. 35, 36.

11. *The house.* The place where he was born, or the place where they lived at that time. ¶ *Fell down.* This was the usual way of showing respect or homage among the Jews, Es. viii. 3; Job i. 20; Da. iii. 7; Ps. lxxii. 11; Is. xlvi. 6. ¶ *Worshipped him.* Did him homage as King of the Jews. See Notes on ver. 2. ¶ *Had opened their treasures.* The treasures which they had brought, or the boxes, &c., in which they had brought their gold, &c. ¶ *They presented unto him gifts.* These were presented to him as King of the Jews, because they supposed he was to be a distinguished prince and conqueror. It was customary in the East to show respect for persons of distinction by making presents or offerings of this kind. See Ge. xxxii. 14; xliii. 11; 1 Sa. x. 27; 1 Ki. x. 2; Ps. lxxii. 10-15. This custom is still common in the East, and it is everywhere there unusual to approach a person of distinguished rank without a valuable present. ¶ *Frankincense.* Frankincense is a white resin or gum. It is obtained from a tree by making incisions in the bark, and suffering the gum to flow out. It is highly odoriferous or fragrant when burned, and was therefore used in worship, where it was burned as a pleasant offering to God. See Ex. xxx. 8; Le. xvi. 12. It is found in the East Indies, but chiefly in Arabia; and hence it has been supposed probable that the wise men came from Arabia. ¶ *Myrrh.* This was also a production of Arabia, and was obtained from a tree in the same

and when they had opened their treasures, [k]they [2]presented unto him gifts; gold, and frankincense, and myrrh.

12 And [l]being warned of God in a dream that they should not return to Herod, they departed into their own country another way.

13 And when they were departed, behold, the angel of the Lord appeareth to Joseph in a dream, saying, Arise, and take the young child and his mother, and flee into Egypt, and be thou there until I bring thee word: for Herod [m]will seek the young child, to destroy him.

14 When he arose, he took the young child and his mother by night, and departed into Egypt:

15 And was there until the death

k Ps.72.10; Is.60.6. 2 or, *offered.* l ch.1.20. m Job 33.15,17.

manner as frankincense. The name denotes *bitterness,* and was given to it on account of its great bitterness. It was used chiefly in embalming the dead, because it had the property of preserving dead bodies from putrefaction. Compare Jn. xix. 39. It was much used in Egypt and in Judea. It was obtained from a thorny tree, which grows 8 or 9 foot high. It was at an early period an article of commerce (Ge. xxxvii. 25), and was an ingredient of the holy ointment, Ex. xxx. 23. It was also used as an agreeable perfume, Es. ii. 12; Ps. xlv. 8; Pr. vii. 17. It was also sometimes mingled with wine to form an article of drink. Such a drink was given to our Saviour, when about to be crucified, as a stupefying potion, Mar. xv. 23; compare Mat. xxvii. 34. The offerings here referred to were made because they were the most valuable which the country of the Magi or wise men produced. They were tokens of respect and homage which they paid to the new-born King of the Jews. They evinced their high regard for him, and their belief that he was to be an illustrious prince; and the fact that their deed is recorded with approbation shows us that we should offer *our* most valuable possessions, our all, to the Lord Jesus Christ. Wise men came from far to do him homage, and bowed down, and presented their best gifts and offerings. It is right that *we* give to him also our hearts, our property, our all.

12. *Warned of God.* This was done, doubtless, because, if they had given Herod precise information where he was, it would have been easy for him to send forth and slay him. And from this we learn that God will watch over those whom he loves; that he knows how to foil the purposes of the wicked, and to deliver his own out of the hands of those who would destroy them. ¶ *In a dream.* See Note on ch. i. 20.

13. *The angel appeareth to Joseph in a dream.* See ch. i. 20. ¶ *Flee into Egypt.* Egypt is situated to the south-west of Judea, and is distant from Bethlehem perhaps about 60 miles. It was at this time a Roman province. There were many Jews there, who had a temple and synagogues (see Notes on Is. xix. 18), and Joseph, therefore, would be among his own countrymen, and yet beyond the reach of Herod. The jurisdiction of Herod extended only to the River Sihon, or "river of Egypt," and, of course, beyond that Joseph was safe from his designs. For a description of Egypt, see Notes on Is. xix. It is remarkable that this is the only time in which our Saviour was out of Palestine, and that this was in the land where the children of Israel had suffered so much and so long under the oppression of the Egyptian kings. The very land which was the land of bondage and groaning for the Jews, became now the land of refuge and safety for the new-born King of Judea. God can overturn nations and kingdoms, so that those whom he loves shall be safe anywhere.

14. *When he arose.* Having arisen; that is, he arose immediately after awaking from his dream, and prepared at once to obey the command. ¶ *By night.* Thus he showed his prompt obedience to the command, and at the same time so concealed his departure as to render himself and Mary and the child safe from pursuit.

15. *The death of Herod.* Herod died in the thirty-seventh year of his reign. It is not certainly known in what year he began his reign, and hence it is impossible to determine the time that Joseph remained in Egypt. The best chronologers have supposed that he

of Herod, that it might be fulfilled which was spoken of the Lord by the prophet, saying, [n]Out of Egypt have I called my son.

16 Then Herod, when he saw that he was mocked of the wise men, was exceeding wroth, and sent forth, and slew all the chil-

n Ho.11.1.

died somewhere between two and four years after the birth of Christ, but at what particular time cannot now be determined. Nor can it be ascertained at what age Jesus was taken into Egypt. It seems probable that he was supposed to be a year old (see ver. 16), and of course the time that he remained in Egypt was not long. Herod died of a most painful and loathsome disease in Jericho. See Notes on ver. 16; also Josephus, *Ant.* xvii. 6. 5. ¶ *That it might be fulfilled,* &c. This language is recorded in Ho. xi. 1. It there evidently speaks of God's calling his people out of Egypt, under Moses. See Ex. iv. 22, 23. It might be said to be *fulfilled* in his calling Jesus from Egypt, because the words in Hosea aptly expressed this also. The same love which led him to deliver his people Israel from the land of Egypt, now led him also to deliver his Son from that place. The words used by Hosea would express both events. See Notes on ch. i. 22. Perhaps, also, the place in Hosea became *a proverb,* to express any great deliverance from danger; and thus it could be said to be *fulfilled* in Christ, as other proverbs are in cases to which they are applicable. It cannot be supposed that the passage in Hosea was a *prophecy* of the Messiah. It is evidently used by Matthew only because the *language* is appropriate to *express* the event.

16. *Then Herod, when he saw that he was mocked of the wise men.* When he saw that he had been deceived by them; that is, that they did not return as he had expected. It does not mean that they did it *for the purpose* of mocking or deriding him, but that he was *disappointed* in their not returning, or that he had been trifled with. ¶ *Exceeding wroth.* Very angry. He had been disappointed and deceived. He expected to send an executioner and kill Jesus alone. But, since he was disappointed in this, he thought he would accomplish the same thing, and be sure to destroy him, if he sent forth and put *all the children in the place* to death.—This is an illustration of the power of anger. It stops at nothing. If it cannot accomplish *just what* it wishes, it does not hesitate to go much farther, and accomplish much more evil than it at first designed. He that has a wicked heart, and indulges in anger, knows not where it will end, and will commonly commit far more evil than he at first intended. ¶ *Slew all the children.* That is, all the *male* children. This is implied in the original. The design of Herod was to cut off him that had been born *king* of the Jews. His purpose, therefore, did not require that he should slay the female children; and though he was cruel, yet we have no right to think that he attempted anything except what he thought to be for his own safety, and to secure himself from a rival. ¶ *In all the coasts thereof.* The word *coast* is commonly applied now to the regions around the sea, as the *sea-coast.* Here it means the adjacent places, the settlements or hamlets around Bethlehem—all that were in that neighbourhood. We do not know how large a place Bethlehem was, nor, of course, how many were slain; but it was never a large town, and the number could not be very great. It is not probable that it contained more than one or two thousand inhabitants, and in this case the number of children slain was not over twenty or thirty. ¶ *From two years old and under.* Some writers have said that this does not mean, in the original, that they had *completed* two years; but that they had *entered* on the second year, or had completed about one year, and entered on the second. But the meaning of the word is doubtful. It is quite probable that they would not be particular about the *exact* age, but slew all that were about that age. ¶ *According to the time,* &c. He had endeavoured to ascertain of the wise men the exact time of his birth. He supposed he knew the age of Jesus. He slew, therefore, all that were of his age; that is, all that were born *about* the time when the star appeared—perhaps from six months old to two years. There is no reason to think that he would command those to be slain who had been born *after* the star appeared.

This destruction of the infants of

dren that were in Bethlehem, and in all the coasts thereof, from two years old and under, according to the time which he had °diligently inquired of the wise men.

17 Then was fulfilled that which

o ver. 7.

Bethlehem is not mentioned by Josephus, but for this omission three reasons may be given. 1. Josephus, a Jewish historian and a *Jew*, would not be likely to record anything that would appear to confirm the truth of Christianity. 2. This act of Herod was really so small, compared with his other crimes, that the historian might not think it worthy of record. Bethlehem was a small and obscure village, and the other crimes of Herod were so great and so public, that it is not to be wondered at that the Jewish historian has passed over this. 3. The order was probably given in secret, and might not have been known to Josephus. It pertained to the Christian history; and if the evangelists had not recorded it, it might have been unknown or forgotten. Besides, no argument can be drawn from the silence of the Jewish historian. No reason can be given why Matthew should not be considered to be as fully entitled to credit as Josephus. Yet there is no improbability in the account given by Matthew. Herod was an odious and bloody tyrant, and the facts of his reign prove that he was abundantly capable of this wickedness. The following bloody deeds will show that the slaying of the infants was in perfect accordance with his character. The account is taken from Josephus, as arranged by Dr. Lardner. Aristobulus, brother of his wife Mariamne, was murdered by his direction at eighteen years of age, because the people of Jerusalem had shown some affection for his person. —In the seventh year of his reign, he put to death Hyrcanus, grandfather of Mariamne, then eighty years of age, and who had formerly saved Herod's life; a man who had, in every revolution of fortune, shown a mild and peaceable disposition. — His beloved and beautiful wife, Mariamne, had a public execution, and her mother Alexandra followed soon after.—Alexander and Aristobulus, his two sons by Mariamne, were strangled in prison by his orders upon groundless suspicions, as it seems, when they were at man's estate, were married, and had children. —In his last sickness, a little before he died, he sent orders throughout Judea requiring the presence of all the chief men of the nation at Jericho. His orders were obeyed, for they were enforced with no less penalty than that of death. When they were come to Jericho he had them all shut up in the circus, and calling for his sister Salome and her husband Alexis, he said to them, "My life is now short. I know the Jewish people, and nothing will please them better than my death. You have them now in your custody. As soon as the breath is out of my body, and before my death can be known, do you let in the soldiers upon them and kill them. All Judea, then, and every family, will, though unwillingly, mourn at my death." Nay, Josephus says that with tears in his eyes he conjured them, by their love to him and their fidelity to God, not to fail of doing him this honour. — What objection, after this account, can there be to the account of his murdering the infants at Bethlehem? Surely there could be no cruelty, barbarity, or horrid crime which such a man was not capable of perpetrating.

17. *Then was fulfilled.* The word "fulfilled," here, is used evidently in the sense that the words in Jeremiah *aptly express* the event which Matthew was recording. Compare Notes on ch. i. 22. ¶ *That which was spoken by Jeremy the prophet.* Jeremiah. This quotation is taken from Je. xxxi. 15. The original design of the prophecy was to describe the sorrowful departure of the people of Israel into captivity after the conquest of Jerusalem by Nebuzaradan. The captives were assembled at Rama, Jeremiah himself being in chains, and there the fate of those who had escaped in the destruction of the city was decided at the will of the conqueror, Je. xl. 1. The nobles had been slain; the sons of the king had been murdered in his presence; the eyes of the king had been put out, and the people were then gathered at Rama in chains, whence they were to start on their mournful journey, slaves to a cruel monarch, leaving behind them all that was dear in life. The sadness of such a scene is well expressed in the language of the prophet, and it no less beautifully and fitly applies to the melancholy event which the evangelist records, and there

was spoken by [p]Jeremy the prophet, saying,

18 In Rama was there a voice heard, lamentation, and weeping, and great mourning, Rachel weeping *for* her children, and would not be comforted because they are not.

p Je.31.15.

could be no impropriety in his using it as a quotation.

18. *In Rama was there a voice heard.* Rama was a small town in the tribe of Benjamin. Rachel was the mother of Benjamin, and was buried near to Bethlehem, Ge. xxxv. 16–19. Rama was about 6 miles north-west of Jerusalem, near Bethel, and was some 10 or 12 miles from Bethlehem. The name *Rama* signifies *an eminence*, and was given to the town because it was situated on a hill. Rama is commonly supposed to be the same as the Arimathea of the New Testament—the place where Joseph lived who begged the body of Jesus. See Mat. xxvii. 57. This is also the same place in which Samuel was born, where he resided, died, and was buried, and where he anointed Saul as king, 1 Sa. i. 1, 19; ii. 11; viii. 4; xix. 18; xxv. 1. Mr. King, an American missionary, was at Rama—now called *Romba*—in 1824; and Mr. Whiting, another American missionary, was there in 1835. Mr. Whiting says: "The situation is exceedingly beautiful. It is about two hours distant from Jerusalem to the north-west, on an eminence commanding a view of a wide extent of beautiful diversified country. Hills, plains, and valleys, highly cultivated fields of wheat and barley, vineyards and oliveyards, are spread out before you as on a map, and numerous villages are scattered here and there over the whole view. To the west and north-west, beyond the hill-country, appears the vast plain of Sharon, and farther still you look out upon the *great and wide sea.* It occurred to me as not improbable that in the days of David and Solomon this place may have been a favourite retreat during the heat of summer, and that here the former may have often struck his sacred lyre. Some of the Psalms, or at least one of them (see Ps. civ. 25), seem to have been composed in some place which commanded a view of the Mediterranean; and this is the only place, I believe, in the vicinity of Jerusalem that affords such a view."

Rama was once a strongly fortified city, but there is no city here at present. A half-ruined Mohammedan mosque, which was originally a Christian church, stands over the tomb of the prophet; besides which, a few miserable dwellings are the only buildings that remain on this once-celebrated spot. Comp. Notes on Is. x. 29. The tomb of Rachel, which is supposed to mark the precise spot where Rachel was buried (comp. Ge. xxxv. 18–20; xlviii. 7), is near to Bethlehem, and she is represented as rising and weeping again over her children. "The tomb is a plain Saracenic mausoleum, having no claims to antiquity in its present form, but deeply interesting in sacred associations; for, by the singular consent of all authorities in such questions, it marks the actual site of her grave."—*The Land and the Book*, vol. ii. 501.

By a beautiful figure of speech, the prophet introduces the mother weeping over the tribe, her children, and with them weeping over the fallen destiny of Israel, and over the calamities about to come upon the land. Few images could be more striking than thus to introduce a mother, long dead, whose sepulchre was near, weeping bitterly over the terrible calamities that befell her descendants. The language and the image also aptly and beautifully expressed the sorrows of the mothers in Bethlehem when Herod slew their infant children. Under the cruelty of the tyrant almost every family was a family of tears, and well might there be lamentation, and weeping, and great mourning.

We may remark here that the sacred writers were cautious of speaking of the characters of wicked men. Here was one of the worst men in the world, committing one of the most awful crimes, and yet there is not a single mark of exclamation; there is not a single reference to any other part of his conduct; there is nothing that could lead to the knowledge that his character in other respects was not upright. There is no wanton and malignant *dragging him* into the narrative that they might gratify malice in making free with a very bad character. What was to their purpose, they recorded; what was not, they left to others. This is the nature

19 But when Herod was dead, behold, an angel of the Lord appeareth in a dream to Joseph in Egypt,

20 Saying, Arise, and take the young child and his mother, and go into the land of Israel: [q]for they are dead which sought the young child's life.

21 And he arose, and took the young child and his mother, and came into the land of Israel.

22 But when he heard that Archelaus did reign in Judea in the room of his father Herod, he was afraid to go thither: notwithstanding, being warned of God in

q Ex.4.19.

of religion. It does not speak evil of others except when necessary, nor then does it take pleasure in it.

19. *Herod was dead.* See Notes on ver. 15. Herod left three sons, and the kingdom was at his death divided between them. To Archelaus was given Judea, Idumea, and Samaria; to Philip, Batanea and Trachonitis; to Antipas, Galilee and Perea. Each of these was

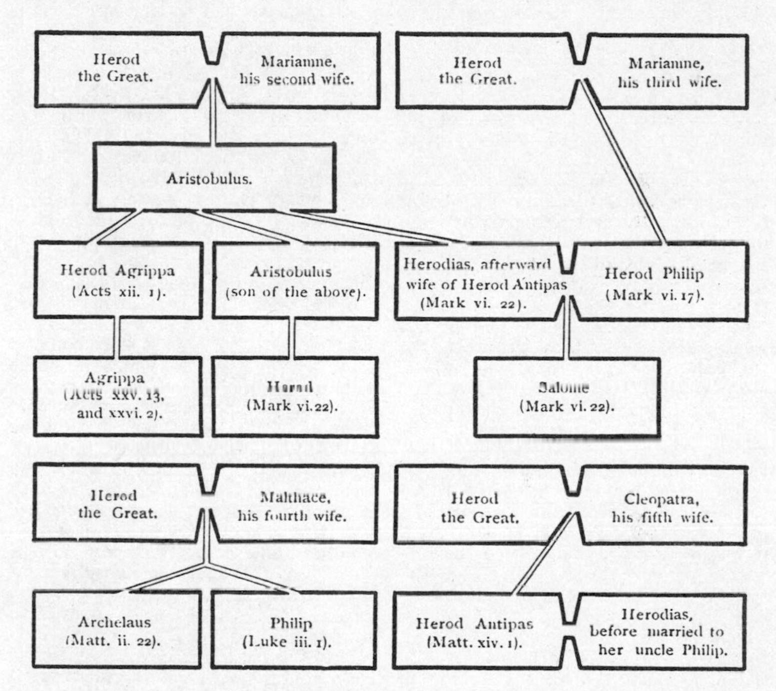

also called *Herod*, and these are the individuals who are so frequently referred to in the New Testament during the ministry of the Saviour and the labours of the apostles. The above table will show at a glance the chief connections of this family, as far as they are mentioned in the sacred history.

20. *They are dead who sought*, &c. This either refers to Herod alone, as is not uncommon, using the plural number for the singular; or it may refer to Herod and his son *Antipater*. He was of the same cruel disposition as his father, and was put to death by his father about five days before his own death.

22. *He heard that Archelaus did reign.* Archelaus possessed a cruel and tyrannical disposition similar to his father. At one of the Passovers he caused 3000 of the people to be put to death in the temple and city. For his crimes, after he had reigned nine years, he was banished by Augustus, the Ro-

a dream, he turned aside [r]into the parts of Galilee:

23 And he came and dwelt in a city called [s]Nazareth: that it might

r ch.3.13; Lu.2.39.

s Jn.1.45.

man emperor, to Gaul, where he died. Knowing his character, and fearing that he would not be safe, Joseph hesitated about going there, and was directed by God to go to Galilee, a place of safety. ¶ *The parts of Galilee.* The country of Galilee. At this time the land of Palestine was divided into three parts: GALILEE, on the north; SAMARIA, in the middle; and JUDEA, on the south. Galilee was under the government of Herod Antipas, who was comparatively a mild prince, and in his dominions Joseph might find safety.

23. *And he came and dwelt.* That is, he made it his permanent residence. The Lord Jesus, in fact, resided there until he entered on the work of his ministry—until he was about thirty years of age. ¶ *In a city called Nazareth.* This was a small town, situated in Galilee, west of Capernaum, and not far from Cana. It was built partly in a valley and partly on the declivity of a hill, Lu. iv. 29. A hill is yet pointed out, to the south of Nazareth, as the one from which the people of the place attempted to precipitate the Saviour. It was a place, at that time, proverbial for wickedness, Jn. iv. 46. It is now a large village, with a convent and two churches. One of the churches, called *the Church of the Annunciation*, is the finest in the Holy Land, except that of the Holy Sepulchre in Jerusalem.

A modern traveller describes Nazareth as situated upon the declivity of a hill, the vale which spreads out before it resembling a circular basin encompassed by mountains. Fifteen mountains appear to meet to form an inclosure for this beautiful spot, around which they rise like the edge of a shell, to guard it against intrusion. It is a rich and beautiful field, in the midst of barren mountains.

Another traveller speaks of the streets as narrow and steep. The houses, which are flat-roofed, are about two hundred and fifty in number, and the inhabitants he estimates at 2000. The population of the place is variously stated, though the average estimate is 3000, of whom about 500 are Turks, and the residue nominal Christians.

As all testimony to the truth and fidelity of the sacred narrative is important, I will here introduce a passage from the journal of Mr. Jowett, an intelligent modern traveller, especially as it is so full an illustration of the passage of Luke already cited.

"Nazareth is situated on the side, and extends nearly to the foot, of a hill, which, though not very high, is rather steep and overhanging. The eye naturally wanders over its summit in quest of some point from which it might probably be that the men of this place endeavoured to cast our Saviour down (Lu. iv. 29), but in vain; no rock adapted to such an object appears here. At the foot of the hill is a modest, simple plain, surrounded by low hills, reaching in length nearly a mile; in breadth, near the city, 150 yards; but farther south, about 400 yards. On this plain there are a few olive and fig trees, sufficient, or rather scarcely sufficient, to make the spot picturesque. Then follows a ravine, which gradually grows deeper and narrower toward the south; till, after walking about another mile, you find yourself in an immense chasm, with steep rocks on either side, from whence you behold, as it were beneath your feet and before you, the noble plain of Esdraelon. Nothing can be finer than the apparently immeasurable prospect of this plain, bounded on the south by the mountains of Samaria. The elevation of the hills on which the spectator stands in this ravine is very great; and the whole scene, when we saw it, was clothed in the most rich mountain-blue colour that can be conceived. At this spot, on the right hand of the ravine, is shown the rock to which the men of Nazareth are supposed to have conducted our Lord for the purpose of throwing him down. With the Testament in our hands we endeavoured to examine the probabilities of the spot; and I confess there is nothing in it which excites a scruple of incredulity in my mind. The rock here is perpendicular for about fifty feet, down which space it would be easy to hurl a person who should be unawares brought to the summit, and his perishing would be a very certain consequence. That the spot might be at a considerable distance from the city is an idea not inconsistent with St. Luke's account; for the expres-

be fulfilled which was spoken by the prophets, He shall be called a Nazarene.[t]

t Nu.6.13; Ju.13.5; 1 Sa.1.11; Am.2.10-12; Ac.24.5.

CHAPTER III.

IN those days came [a]John the Baptist, preaching in the wilderness of Judea,

a Lu.3.2; Jn. 1.28.

sion, *thrusting Jesus out of the city, and leading him to the brow of the hill on which their city was built*, gives fair scope for imagining that in their rage and debate the Nazarenes might, without originally intending his murder, press upon him for a considerable distance after they had quitted the synagogue. The distance, as already noticed, from modern Nazareth to the spot is scarcely two miles; a space which, in the fury of persecution, might soon be passed over. Or, should this appear too considerable, it is by no means certain but that Nazareth may at that time have extended through the principal part of the plain, which I have described as lying before the modern town. In this case, the distance passed over might not exceed a mile. I can see, therefore, no reason for thinking otherwise than that this may be the real scene where our divine prophet Jesus received so great a dishonour from the men of his own country and of his own kindred."

Mr. Fisk, an American missionary, was at Nazareth in the autumn of 1823. His description corresponds generally with that of Mr. Jowett. He estimates the population to be from 3000 to 5000, viz. Greeks, three hundred or four hundred families; Turks, two hundred; Catholics, one hundred; Greek Catholics, forty or fifty; Maronites, twenty or thirty; say in all seven hundred families. ¶ *That it might be fulfilled which was spoken*, &c. The words here are not found in any of the books of the Old Testament, and there has been much difficulty in ascertaining the meaning of this passage. Some have supposed that Matthew meant to refer to Ju. xiii. 5, to Samson as a type of Christ; others that he refers to Is. xi. 1, where the descendant of Jesse is called "a Branch;" in the Hebrew *Netzer*. Some have supposed that he refers to some prophecy which was not recorded, but handed down by tradition. But these suppositions are not satisfactory. It is much more probable that Matthew refers not to any particular place, but to the *leading characteristics* of the prophecies respecting him. The following remarks may make this clear: 1st. He does not say "by the *prophet*," as in ch. i. 22; ii. 5, 15, but "by the *prophets*," meaning no one particularly, but the general character of the prophecies. 2d. The leading and most prominent prophecies respecting him were, that he was to be of humble life; to be despised and rejected. See Is. liii. 2, 3, 7, 8, 9, 12; Ps. xxii. 3d. The phrase "he shall be called" means the same as *he shall be*. 4th. The character of the people of Nazareth was such that they were proverbially despised and contemned, Jn. i. 46; vii. 52. To come from Nazareth, therefore, or *to be a Nazarene*, was the same as to be despised, or to be esteemed of low birth; *to be a root out of dry ground, having no form or comeliness*. This was what had been predicted by all the prophets. When Matthew says, therefore, that the prophecies were "*fulfilled*," his meaning is, *that the predictions of the prophets that he would be of a low and despised condition, and would be rejected, were fully accomplished in his being an inhabitant of Nazareth, and despised as such.*

CHAPTER III.

1. *In those days.* The days here referred to cannot be those mentioned in the preceding chapter, for John was but six months older than Christ. Perhaps Matthew intended to embrace in his narrative the *whole time* that Jesus dwelt at Nazareth; and the meaning is, "*in those days while Jesus still dwelt at Nazareth,*" John began to preach. It is not probable that John began to baptize or preach long before the Saviour entered on his ministry; and, consequently, from the time that is mentioned in the close of the second chapter to that mentioned in the beginning of the third, an interval of twenty-five or more years elapsed. ¶ *John the Baptist.* Or John *the baptizer*—so called from his principal office, that of baptizing. Baptism, or the application of water, was a rite well known to the Jews, and practised when they admitted proselytes to their religion from heathenism.—*Lightfoot.* ¶ *Preaching.* The word rendered *preach* means to proclaim in the manner of a public crier; to make proclamation. The discourses recorded in the New

2 And saying, Repent ye: for the kingdom of heaven is at hand.

Testament are mostly brief, sometimes consisting only of a single sentence. They were public proclamations of some great truth. Such appear to have been the discourses of John, calling men to repentance. ¶ *In the wilderness of Judea.* This country was situated along the Jordan and the Dead Sea, to the east of Jerusalem. The word translated *wilderness* does not denote, as with us, a place of boundless forests, entirely destitute of inhabitants; but a mountainous, rough, and thinly settled country, covered to some considerable extent with forests and rocks, and better fitted for pasture than for tilling. There were inhabitants in those places, and even villages, but they were the comparatively *unsettled* portions of the country, 1 Sa. xxv. 1, 2. In the time of Joshua there were six cities in what was then called *a wilderness*, Jos. xv. 61, 62.

2. *Repent ye.* Repentance implies sorrow for past offences (2 Co. vii. 10); a deep sense of the evil of sin as committed against God (Ps. li. 4); and a full purpose to turn from transgression and to lead a holy life. A true penitent has sorrow for sin, not only because it is ruinous to his soul, but chiefly because it is an offence against God, and is that abominable thing which he hates, Je. xliv. 4. It is produced by seeing the great danger and misery to which it exposes us; by seeing the justice and holiness of God (Job xlii. 6); and by seeing that our sins have been committed against *Christ*, and were the cause of his death, Ze. xii. 10; Lu. xxii. 61, 62. There are two words in the New Testament translated *repentance*, one of which denotes a *change of mind*, or a *reformation* of life; and the other, *sorrow* or *regret* that sin has been committed. The word used here is the former, calling the Jews to a change of life, or a *reformation* of conduct. In the time of John the nation had become extremely wicked and corrupt, perhaps more so than at any preceding period. Hence both he and Christ began their ministry by calling the nation to repentance. ¶ *The kingdom of heaven is at hand.* The phrases kingdom of heaven, kingdom of Christ, kingdom of God, are of frequent occurrence in the Bible. They all refer to the same thing. The expectation of such a kingdom was taken from the Old Testament, and especially from Daniel, ch. vii. 13, 14. The prophets had told of a successor to David that should sit on his throne, 1 Ki. ii. 4; viii. 25; Je. xxxiii. 17. The Jews expected a great national deliverer. They supposed that when the Messiah should appear, all the dead would be raised; that the judgment would take place; and that the enemies of the Jews would be destroyed, and that they themselves would be advanced to great national dignity and honour.

The *language* in which they were accustomed to describe this event was retained by our Saviour and his apostles. Yet they early attempted to correct the common notions respecting his reign. This was one design, doubtless, of John in preaching repentance. Instead of summoning them to *military exercises*, and collecting an army, which would have been in accordance with the expectations of the nation, he called them *to a change of life;* to the doctrine of repentance—a state of things far more accordant with the approach of a kingdom of purity.

The phrases "kingdom of God" and "kingdom of heaven" have been supposed to have a considerable variety of meaning. Some have supposed that they refer to the state of things in heaven; others, to the personal reign of Christ on earth; others, that they mean the church, or the reign of Christ in the hearts of his people. There can be no doubt that there is reference in the words to the condition of things in heaven after this life. But the church of God is a preparatory state to that beyond the grave—a state in which Christ pre-eminently rules and reigns—and there is no doubt that the phrases sometimes refer to the state of things in the church; and that they may refer, therefore, to the state of things which the Messiah was to set up—*his spiritual reign begun in the church on earth, and completed in heaven.*

The expression "the kingdom of heaven is at hand" would be best translated, "the *reign* of God draws near." We do not say commonly of a *kingdom* that it is *movable*, or that it *approaches.* A *reign* may be said to be at hand; and it may be said with propriety that the time when Christ would

3 For this is he that was spoken of by the prophet Esaias, saying, The[b] voice of one crying in the wilderness, Prepare ye the way of the Lord, make his paths straight.

4 And the same John [c]had his

b Is.40.3.

c 2 Ki.1.8; ch.11.8.

reign was at hand. In this sense it is meant that the time when Christ should *reign*, or set up his kingdom, or *begin* his dominion on earth, under the Christian economy, was about to commence. The phrase, then, should not be confined to any period of that reign, but includes his whole dominion over his people on earth and in heaven.

In the passage here it clearly means that the coming of the Messiah was near, or that the time of the reign of God which the Jews had expected was coming.

The word *heaven*, or *heavens*, as it is in the original, means sometimes the *place* so called; and sometimes it is, by a figure of speech, put for the Great Being whose residence is there, as in Da. iv. 26: "the *Heavens* do rule." See also Mar. xi. 30; Lu. xv. 18. As that kingdom was one of purity, it was proper that the people should prepare themselves for it by turning from their sins, and by bringing their hearts into a state suitable to his reign.

3. *The prophet Esaias.* The prophet *Isaiah.* Esaias is the Greek mode of writing the name. This passage is taken from Is. xl. 3. It is here said to have been spoken in reference to John, the forerunner of Christ. The language is such as was familiar to the Jews, and such as they would understand. It was spoken at first with reference to the return from the captivity at Babylon. Anciently it was customary in the march of armies to send messengers, or pioneers, before them to proclaim their approach; to provide for them; to remove obstructions; to make roads, level hills, fill up valleys, &c. Isaiah, describing the return from Babylon, uses language taken from that custom. A crier, or herald, is introduced. In the vast deserts that lay between Babylon and Judea he is represented as lifting up his voice, and, with authority, commanding a public road to be made for the return of the captive Jews, with the Lord as their deliverer. "Prepare his ways, make them straight," says he. The meaning in Isaiah is, "Let the valleys be exalted, or filled up, and the hills be levelled, and a straight, level highway be prepared, that they may march with ease and safety." See Notes on Is. xl. 3, 4. The custom here referred to is continued in the East at the present time. "When Ibrahim Pasha proposed to visit certain places on Lebanon, the emeers and sheiks sent forth a general proclamation, somewhat in the style of Isaiah's exhortation, to all the inhabitants, to assemble along the proposed route and prepare the way before him. The same was done in 1845, on a grand scale, when the present sultan visited Brousa. The stones were gathered out, the crooked places straightened, and the rough ones made level and smooth."—*The Land and the Book*, vol. i. p. 105, 106.

As applied to John, the passage means that he was sent to remove obstructions, and to prepare the people for the coming of the Messiah, like a herald going before an army on the march, to make preparations for its coming.

4. *His raiment of camel's hair.* His clothing. This is not the fine hair of the camel from which our elegant cloth is made called *camlet*, nor the more elegant stuff brought from the East Indies under the name of camel's hair, but the long shaggy hair of the camel, from which a coarse cheap cloth is made, still worn by the poorer classes in the East, and by monks. This dress of the camel's hair, and a leathern girdle, it seems, was the common dress of the prophets, 2 Ki. i. 8; Zec. xiii. 4. ¶ *His meat was locusts.* His food. These constituted the food of the common people. Among the Greeks the vilest of the people used to eat them; and the fact that John made his food of them is significant of his great poverty and humble life. The Jews were allowed to eat them, Le. xi. 22. Locusts are flying insects, and are of various kinds. The green locusts are about 2 inches in length and about the thickness of a man's finger. The common brown locust is about 3 inches long. The general form and appearance of the locust is not unlike the grasshopper. They were one of the plagues of Egypt (Ex. x.). In Eastern countries they are very numerous. They appear in such quantities as to darken the sky, and devour in a short time every green thing.

raiment of camel's hair, and a leathern girdle about his loins: and his meat was [d]locusts and wild honey.

d Le.11.22.

The whole earth is sometimes covered with them for many leagues, Joel i. 4; Is. xxxiii. 4, 5. "Some species of the locust are eaten at this day in Eastern countries, and are even esteemed a delicacy when properly cooked. After tearing off the legs and wings, and taking out the entrails, they stick them in long rows upon wooden spits, roast them at the fire, and then proceed to devour them with great zest. There are also other ways of preparing them. For example: they cook them and dress them in oil; or, having dried them, they pulverize them, and, when other food is scarce, make bread of the meal. The Bedouins pack them with salt in close masses, which they carry in their leathern sacks. From these they cut slices as they may need them. It is singular that even learned men have suffered themselves to hesitate about understanding these passages of the literal locust, when the fact that these are eaten by the Orientals is so abundantly proved by the concurrent testimony of travellers. One of them says they are brought to market on strings in all the cities of Arabia, and that he saw an Arab on Mount Sumara who had collected a sackful of them. They are prepared in different ways. An Arab in Egypt, of whom he requested that he would immediately eat locusts in his presence, threw them upon the glowing coals; and after he supposed they were roasted enough, he took them by the legs and head, and devoured the remainder at one mouthful. When the Arabs have them in quantities they roast or dry them in an oven, or boil them and eat them with salt. The Arabs in the kingdom of Morocco boil the locusts; and the Bedouins eat locusts, which are collected in great quantities in the beginning of April, when they are easily caught. After having been roasted a little upon the iron plate on which bread is baked, they are dried in the sun, and then put into large sacks, with the mixture of a little salt. They are never served up as a dish, but every one takes a handful of them when hungry" (*Un. Bib. Dic.*). Burckhardt, one of the most trustworthy of travellers, says: "*All* the Bedawins of Arabia and the inhabitants of towns in Nejd and Hedjaz are accustomed to eat locusts." "I have seen at Medina and Tayf *locust-shops*, where these animals were sold by *measure*. In Egypt and Nubia they are only eaten by the poorest beggars" (*The Land and the Book*, ii. 107). "Locusts," says Dr. Thomson (*The Land and the Book*, ii. 108), "are not eaten in Syria by any but the Bedawin on the extreme frontiers, and it is always spoken of as an inferior article of food, and regarded by most with disgust and loathing—tolerated only by the very poorest people. John the Baptist, however, was of this class either from necessity or election." It is remarkable that not only in respect to his food, but also in other respects, the peculiarities in John's mode of life have their counterparts in the present habits of the same class of persons. "The coat or mantle of camel's hair is seen still on the shoulders of the Arab who escorts the traveller through the desert, or of the shepherd who tends his flocks on the hills of Judea or in the valley of the Jordan. It is made of the thin, coarse hair of the camel, and not of the fine hair, which is manufactured into a species of rich cloth. I was told that both kinds of raiment are made on a large scale at Nablus, the ancient Shechem. The 'leathern girdle' may be seen around the body of the common labourer, when fully dressed, almost anywhere; whereas men of wealth take special pride in displaying a rich sash of silk or some other costly fabric" (Hackett's *Illustrations of Scripture*, p. 104). ¶ *Wild honey.* This was probably the honey that he found in the rocks of the wilderness. Palestine was often called the land flowing with milk and honey, Ex. iii. 8, 17; xiii. 5. Bees were kept with great care, and great numbers of them abounded in the fissures of trees and the clefts of rocks. "Bees abound there still, not only wild, but hived, as with us. I saw a great number of hives in the old castle near the Pools of Solomon; several, also, at Deburieh, at the foot of Tabor; and again at Mejdel, the Magdala of the New Testament, on the Lake of Tiberias. Maundrell says that he saw 'bees very industrious about the blossoms' between Jericho and the Dead Sea, which must have been within the limits of the very 'desert' in which John 'did eat locusts and

5 Then went out to him Jerusalem, and all Judea, and all the region round about Jordan,

6 And were baptized of him in Jordan, [e]confessing their sins.

e Ac.1.5; 2.38; 19.4,15,18.

wild honey'" (Hackett's *Illustrations of Scripture*, p. 104). There is also a species of honey called wild honey, or *wood honey* (1 Sa. xiv. 27, margin), or honey-dew, produced by certain little insects, and deposited on the leaves of trees, and flowing from them in great quantities to the ground. See 1 Sa. xiv. 24–27. This is said to be produced still in Arabia, and perhaps it was this which John lived upon.

5. *Jerusalem.* The people of Jerusalem. ¶ *All Judea.* Many people from Judea. It does not mean that literally *all* the people went, but that great multitudes went. It was general. Jerusalem was in the part of the country called Judea. Judea was situated on the *west* side of the Jordan. See Notes on Mat. ii. 22. ¶ *Region about Jordan.* On the east and west side of the river. Near to Jordan.

6. *Were baptized.* The word *baptize* signifies originally to *tinge*, to *dye*, to *stain*, as those who *dye* clothes. It here means to cleanse or wash anything by the application of water. See Notes on Mar. vii. 4. Washing, or ablution, was much in use among the Jews, as one of the rites of their religion, Nu. xix. 7; He. ix. 10. It was not customary, however, among them to *baptize* those who were converted to the Jewish religion until after the Babylonish captivity. At the time of John, and for some time previous, they had been accustomed to administer a rite of *baptism*, or *washing*, to those who became proselytes to their religion; that is, to those who were converted from being Gentiles. This was done to signify that they renounced the errors and worship of the Pagans, and as significant of their becoming *pure* by embracing a new religion. It was a solemn rite of *washing*, significant of *cleansing* from their former sins, and purifying them for the peculiar service of Jehovah. John found this custom in use; and as he was calling the Jews to a *new dispensation*—to a change in their form of religion—he administered this rite of *baptism*, or washing, to signify the cleansing from sin, the adopting of the new dispensation, or the fitness for the pure reign of the Messiah. He applied an old ordinance to a new purpose. As it was used by him it was a significant rite, or ceremony, intended to denote the putting away of impurity, and a purpose to be pure in heart and life. The Hebrew word (*Tabal*) which is rendered by the word baptize, occurs in the Old Testament in the following places, viz.: Le. iv. 6; xiv. 6, 51; Nu. xix. 18; Ru. ii. 14; Ex. xii. 22; De. xxxiii. 24; Ezr. xxiii. 15; Job ix. 31; Le. ix. 9; 1 Sa. xiv. 27 (*twice*); 2 Ki. v. 14; viii. 15; Ge. xxxvii. 31; Jos. iii. 15. It occurs in no other places; and from a careful examination of these passages its meaning among the Jews is to be derived. From these passages it will be seen that its radical meaning is neither to sprinkle nor to immerse. It is to *dip*, commonly for the purpose of sprinkling, or for some other purpose. Thus, to dip the *finger*, *i.e.* a part of the finger, in blood—enough to sprinkle with, Le. iv. 6. To dip a living bird, *and* cedar wood, and scarlet, and hyssop, in the blood of the bird that was killed, for the purpose of sprinkling; where it could *not* be that *all these* would be *immersed* in the blood of a single bird, Le. xiv. 6. To dip hyssop in the water, to sprinkle with, Nu. xix. 18. To dip a portion of bread in vinegar, Ru. ii. 14. To dip the feet in oil—an emblem of plenty, De. xxxiii. 24. To *dye*, or stain, Eze. xxiii. 15. To plunge into a ditch, so as to defile the clothes, Job ix. 31. To dip the *end* of a staff in honey, 1 Sa. xiv. 27. To dip in Jordan—a declaration respecting Naaman the Syrian, 2 Ki. v. 14. The direction of the prophet was to wash himself (ver. 10), and this shows that he understood *washing* and *baptizing* to mean the same thing. To dip a *towel*, or *quilt*, so as to spread it on the face of a man to smother him, 2 Ki. viii. 15. In none of these cases can it be shown that the meaning of the word is to *immerse* entirely. But in nearly all the cases the notion of applying the water to a part only of the person or object, though it was by dipping, is necessarily to be supposed.

In the New Testament the word, in various forms, occurs eighty times; fifty-seven with reference to *persons*. Of these fifty-seven times, it is followed by "in" (ἐν) eighteen times, as *in* water, *in* the desert, *in* Jordan; nine times by

7 But when he saw many of the Pharisees and Sadducees come to his baptism, he said unto them, [f]O generation of vipers, who hath warned you to [g]flee from the wrath to come?

f Is.59.5; ch.12.34; 23.33; Lu.3.7.

g Je.51.6; Ro.1.18.

"into" (εἰς), as *into* the name, &c., *into* Christ; once it is followed by ἐπι (Ac. ii. 38), and twice by "for" (ὑπερ), 1 Cor. xv. 29.

The following remarks may be made in view of the investigation of the meaning of this word: 1st. That in baptism it is possible, perhaps probable, that the notion of dipping would be the one that would occur to a Jew. 2d. It would *not* occur to him that the word meant of necessity to dip entirely, or completely to immerse. 3d. The notion of *washing* would be the one which would most readily occur, as connected with a religious rite. See the cases of Naaman, and Mar. vii. 4 (Greek). 4th. It cannot be proved from an examination of the passages in the Old and New Testaments that the idea of a complete immersion *ever* was connected with the word, or that it *ever* in any case occurred. If those who were baptized went into the water, still it is not proved by that that the *only* mode of baptism was by immersion, as it might have been by *pouring*, though they were in the water. 5th. It is not positively enjoined anywhere in the New Testament that the only mode of baptism shall be by an entire submersion of the body under water. Without such a precept it cannot be made obligatory on people of all ages, nations, and climes, even if it were probable that in the mild climate of Judea it was the usual mode. ¶ *In Jordan.* The River Jordan is the eastern boundary of Palestine or Judea. It rises in Mount Lebanon, on the north of Palestine, and runs in a southerly direction, *underground*, for 13 miles, and then bursts forth with a great noise at Cesarea Philippi. It then unites with two small streams, and runs some miles farther, and empties into the Lake *Merom.* From this small lake it flows 13 miles, and then falls into the Lake Gennesareth, otherwise called the Sea of Tiberias or the Sea of Galilee. Through the middle of this lake, which is 15 miles long and from 6 to 9 broad, it flows undisturbed, and preserves a southerly direction for about 70 miles, and then falls into the Dead Sea. The Jordan, at its entrance into the Dead Sea, is about 90 feet wide. It flows in many places with great rapidity, and when swollen by rains pours like an impetuous torrent. It formerly regularly overflowed its banks in time of harvest, that is, in March, in some places 600 paces, Jos. iii. 15; 1 Ch. xii. 15. These banks are covered with small trees and shrubs, and afford a convenient dwelling for wild beasts. Allusion is often made to these thickets in the sacred Scriptures, Je. xlix. 19; l. 44. On the reason why a river, or a place abounding in water, was selected for administering baptism, see Notes on Jn. iii. 23.

7. *Pharisees and Sadducees.* The Jews were divided into three great sects—the Pharisees, the Sadducees, and the Essenes. In addition to these, some smaller sects are mentioned in the New Testament and by Josephus: the Herodians, probably political friends of Herod; the Galileans, a branch of the Pharisees; and the Therapeutæ, a branch of the Essenes, but converts from the Greeks. The three principal sects are supposed to have originated about 150 years before Christ, as they are mentioned by Josephus at that time in his history. Of course nothing is said of them in the Old Testament, as that was finished about 400 years before the Christian era.

I. THE PHARISEES were the most numerous and wealthy sect of the Jews. They derived their name from the Hebrew word *Pharash,* which signifies to set apart, or to separate, because they *separated* themselves from the rest of their countrymen, and professedly devoted themselves to peculiar strictness in religion. Their leading tenets were the following: that the world was governed by fate, or by a fixed decree of God; that the souls of men were immortal, and were either eternally happy or miserable beyond the grave; that the dead would be raised; that there were angels, good and bad; that God was under obligation to bestow peculiar favour on the Jews; and that they were justified by their own conformity to the law. They were proud, haughty, self-righteous, and held the common people in great disrespect, Jn.

vii. 49. They sought the offices of the state, and affected great dignity. They were ostentatious in their religious worship, praying in the corners of the streets, and seeking publicity in the bestowment of alms. They sought principally external cleanliness, and dealt much in ceremonial ablutions and washing.

Some of the laws of Moses they maintained very strictly. In addition to the written laws, they held to a multitude which they maintained had come down from Moses by tradition. These they felt themselves as much bound to observe as the written law. Under the influence of these laws they washed themselves before meals with great scrupulousness; they fasted twice a week—on Thursday, when they supposed Moses ascended Mount Sinai, and on Monday, when he descended; they wore broad phylacteries, and enlarged the fringe or borders of their garments; they loved the chief rooms at feasts, and the chief seats in the synagogues. They were in general a corrupt, hypocritical, office-seeking, haughty class of men. There are, however, some honourable exceptions recorded, Ac. v. 34; perhaps, also, Mar. xv. 43; Lu. ii. 25; xxiii. 51; Jn. xix. 38, 39–42; iii. 1; vii. 50.

II. THE SADDUCEES are supposed to have taken their name from Sadok, who flourished about 260 years before the Christian era. He was a pupil of Antigonus Sochæus, president of the sanhedrim, or great council of the nation. He had taught the duty of serving God *disinterestedly*, without the hope of reward or the fear of punishment. Sadok, not properly understanding the doctrine of his master, drew the inference that there was no future state of rewards or punishments, and on this belief he founded the sect. The other notions which they held, all to be traced to this leading doctrine, were: 1st. That there is no resurrection, neither angel nor spirit (Mat. xxii. 23; Ac. xxiii. 8); and that the soul of man perishes with the body. 2d. They rejected the doctrine of fate or decrees. 3d. They rejected all traditions, and professed to receive only the books of the Old Testament. They were far less numerous than the Pharisees, but their want of numbers was compensated, in some degree, by their wealth and standing in society. Though they did not generally *seek* office, yet several of them were advanced to the high-priesthood.

III. THE ESSENES, a third sect of the Jews, are not mentioned in the New Testament. They differed from both the Pharisees and the Sadducees. They were Jewish monks or hermits, passing their time little in society, but mostly in places of obscurity and retirement. It is not probable, therefore, that our Saviour often, if ever, encountered them; and this, it is supposed, is the reason why they are not mentioned in the New Testament. They were a contemplative sect, having little to do with the common business of life. The property which they possessed they held *in common.* They denied themselves, in a great measure, the usual comforts of life, and were exceedingly strict in the observance of the duties of religion. They were generally more pure than the rest of the Jews, and appear to have been an unambitious, a modest, and retiring sort of people. The two sexes were not in company except on the Sabbath, when they partook of their coarse fare, bread and salt only, together. They practised dancing in their worship. Few of them were married; they were opposed to oaths, and they asserted that *slavery* was repugnant to nature. In regard to doctrine, they did not differ materially from the Pharisees, except that they objected to the sacrifices of slain animals, and of course did not visit the temple, and were not, therefore, likely to come into public contact with the Saviour. They perpetuated their sect by proselytes, and by taking orphan children to train up.

The other sects of the Jews were too insignificant to demand any particular notice here. It may be said of the Jews generally that they possessed little of the spirit of religion; that they had corrupted some of the most important doctrines of the Bible; and that they were an ignorant, proud, ambitious, and sensual people. There was great propriety, therefore, in John's proclaiming to them the necessity of *repentance*.

Generation of vipers. Vipers are a species of serpents, from 2 to 5 feet in length and about an inch thick, with a flat head. They are of an ash or yellowish colour, speckled with long brown spots. There is no serpent that is more poisonous. The person bitten by them swells up almost immediately, and falls down dead. See Ac. xxviii. 6. The word *serpent*, or *viper*, is used to denote

8 Bring forth therefore fruits meet for repentance[1]:

9 And think not to say within yourselves, We have Abraham to *our* father: for I say unto you, that God is able of these stones to raise up children unto Abraham.

10 And now also the axe is laid unto the root of the trees: therefore every tree which bringeth not forth good fruit, [h]is hewn down, and cast into the fire.

11 I[i] indeed baptize you with water unto repentance: but he

1 or, *answerable to amendment of life.*

h Jn.15.6. *i* Lu.3.16; Ac.19.4.

both cunning and malignancy. In the phrase "be ye wise as serpents" (Mat. x. 16), it means be prudent, or wise, referring to the account in Ge. iii. 1–6. Among the Jews the serpent was regarded as the symbol of cunning, circumspection, and prudence. It was so regarded in the Egyptian hieroglyphics. In the phrase "generation of vipers" (Mat. xii. 34), the viper is the symbol of wickedness, of envenomed malice—a symbol drawn from the *venom* of the serpent. It is not quite certain in which of these senses the phrase is used in this place. Probably it is used to denote their malignancy and wickedness. ¶ *Wrath to come.* John expresses his astonishment that sinners so hardened and so hypocritical as they were should have been induced to flee from coming wrath. The wrath to come means the divine indignation, or the punishment that will come on the guilty. See 1 Th. i. 10; 2 Th. i. 8, 9.

8. *Bring forth therefore fruits,* &c. That is, the proper fruits of reformation; the proper evidence that you are sincere. Do not bring your cunning and dissimulation to this work; carry not your hypocrisy into your professed repentance, but evince your sincerity by forsaking sin, and thus give evidence that this coming to Jordan to be baptized is not an act of dissimulation. No discourse could have been more appropriate or more *cutting.* ¶ *Fruits.* Conduct. See Mat. vii. 16–19. ¶ *Meet for repentance.* Fit for repentance; appropriate to it—the proper expression of repentance.

9. *And think not to say,* &c. They regarded it as sufficient righteousness that they were descended from so holy a man as Abraham. Comp. Jn. viii. 33–37, 53. John assured them that this was a matter of small consequence in the sight of God. Of the very stones of the Jordan he could raise up children to Abraham. The meaning seems to be this: God, from these stones, could more easily raise up those who should be *worthy* children of Abraham, or be *like him,* than simply, because you are descendants of Abraham, make you, who are proud and hypocritical, subjects of the Messiah's kingdom. Or, in other words, mere *nativity,* or the privileges of birth, avail nothing where there is not righteousness of life. Some have supposed, however, that by *these stones* he meant the Roman soldiers, or the heathen, who might also have attended on his ministry; and that God could *of them* raise up children to Abraham.

10. *The axe is laid at the root of the tree.* Laying the axe at the root of a tree is intended to denote that the tree is to be cut down. It was not merely to be *trimmed,* or to be cut *about the limbs,* but the very *tree* itself was to be struck. That is, a searching, trying kind of preaching has been commenced. A kingdom of justice is to be set up. Principles and conduct are to be investigated. No art, no dissimulation, will be successful. Men are to be tried by their lives, not by birth or profession. They who are not found to bear this test are to be rejected. The very *root* shall feel the *blow,* and the fruitless tree shall fall. This is a beautiful and very striking figure of speech, and a very direct threatening of future wrath. John regarded them as making a fair and promising profession, as trees do in *blossom.* But he told them, also, that they should bear *fruit* as well as *flowers.* Their *professions* of repentance were not enough. They should show, by a holy life, that their profession was genuine.

11. *Whose shoes I am not worthy to bear.* The word here translated *shoes* has a signification different from what it has in our language. At first, in order to keep the feet from the sharp stones or the burning sand, small pieces of wood were fastened to the soles of the feet, called *sandals.* Leather, or skins of beasts dressed, afterward were used. The foot was not covered at all, but the sandal, or piece of leather or wood, was bound by thongs. The people put off these when they enter

that cometh after me is mightier than I, whose shoes I am not worthy to bear: [k]he shall baptize you with the Holy Ghost, and *with* fire:

k Ac.1.5.

12 Whose[l] fan *is* in his hand, and he will thoroughly purge his floor, and gather his wheat into the garner; but he will [m]burn up the chaff with unquenchable fire.

l Mal.3.2,3. m Ps.1.4; Mal.4.1; Mar.9.44.

---

a house, and put them on when they leave it. To unloose and bind on sandals, on such occasions, was formerly

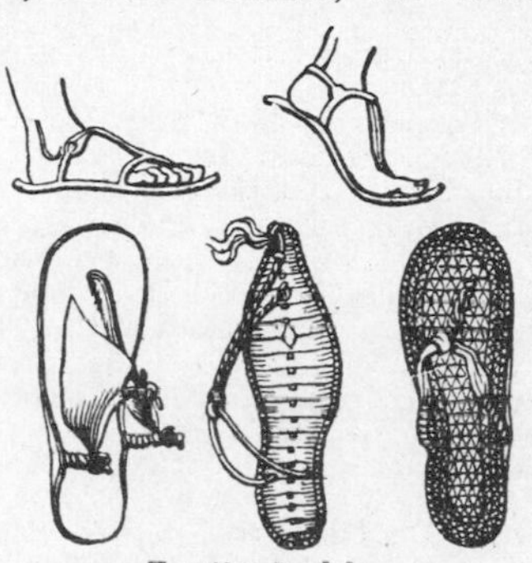

Egyptian Sandals.

the business of the lowest servants. The expression in this place, therefore, denotes great humility, and John says that he was not worthy to be the servant of him who should come after him. ¶ *Shall baptize you.* Shall send upon you the Holy Spirit. The Spirit of God is frequently represented as being poured out upon his people, Pr. i. 23; Is. xliv. 3; Joel ii. 28, 29; Ac. ii. 17, 18. The baptism of the Holy Spirit is the same, therefore, as the sending of his influences to convert, purify, and guide the soul. ¶ *The Holy Ghost.* The third person of the adorable Trinity, whose office it is to enlighten, renew, sanctify, and comfort the soul. He was promised by the Saviour *to convince* of sin, Jn. xvi. 8; to enlighten or teach the disciples, Jn. xiv. 26; xvi. 13; to comfort them in the absence of the Saviour, Jn. xiv. 18; xvi. 7; to change the heart, Tit. iii. 5. To be baptized with the Holy Ghost means that the Messiah would send upon the world a far more powerful and mighty influence than had attended the preaching of John. Many more would be converted. A mighty change would take place. His ministry would not affect the external life only, but *the heart, the motives, the soul;* and would produce rapid and permanent changes in the lives of men. See Ac. ii. 17, 18. ¶ With *fire.* This expression has been variously understood. Some have supposed that John refers to the afflictions and persecutions with which men would be tried under the Gospel; others, that the word *fire* means *judgment* or wrath. According to this latter interpretation, the meaning is that he would baptize a portion of mankind—those who were willing to be his followers—with the Holy Ghost, but the rest of mankind—the wicked—with fire; that is, with judgment and wrath. Fire is a symbol of vengeance. See Is. v. 24; lxi. 2; lxvi. 24. If this be the meaning, as seems to be probable, then John says that the ministry of the Messiah would be far more powerful than his was. It would be more searching and trying; and they who were not fitted to abide the test would be cast into eternal fire. Others have supposed, however, that by *fire*, here, John intends to express the idea that the preaching of the Messiah would be refining, powerful, purifying, as fire is sometimes an emblem of purity, Mal. iii. 2. It is difficult to ascertain the precise meaning farther than that his ministry would be very trying, purifying, searching. Multitudes would be converted; and those who were not true penitents would not be able to abide the trial, and would be driven away.

12. *His fan.* The word here used and rendered *fan* rather means a *winnowing shovel,* used for throwing the grain, after it was threshed, into the air, that the chaff might be driven away by the wind. This mode of separating the grain from the chaff is still practised in the East. It is not probable that the *fan*, as the term is now used, was known to the Orientals as an instrument for cleaning grain. See Notes on Is. xxx. 24. ¶ *His floor.* The threshing-floor was an open space, or area, in the field, usually on an elevated part of the land, Ge. l. 10. It had no covering or walls. It was a space of ground thirty or forty paces in diameter, and made smooth by rolling it or treading it hard. A high place

13 Then[n] cometh Jesus from Galilee to Jordan, unto John to be baptized of him.

14 But John forbade him, saying, I have need to be baptized of thee, and comest thou to me?

15 And Jesus answering said unto him, Suffer *it to be so* now: for thus it becometh us to fulfil all righteousness. Then he suffered him.

16 And Jesus, when he was baptized, went up straightway out of the water: and, lo, the heavens

n Mar.1.9; Lu.3.21.

was selected for the purpose of keeping it dry, and for the convenience of winnowing the grain by the wind. The grain was usually trodden out by oxen. Sometimes it was beaten with flails, as with us; and sometimes with a sharp threshing instrument, made to roll over the grain and to cut the straw at the same time. See Notes on Is. xli. 15. ¶ *Shall purge.* Shall cleanse or purify. Shall remove the chaff, &c. ¶ *The garner.* The granary, or place to deposit the wheat. ¶ *Unquenchable fire.* Fire that shall not be extinguished, that will utterly consume it. By the *floor*, here, is represented the Jewish people. By the *wheat*, the righteous, or the people of God. By the *chaff*, the wicked. They are often represented as being driven away like chaff before the wind, Job xxi. 18; Ps. i. 4; Is. xvii. 13; Ho. xiii. 13. They are also represented as chaff which the fire consumes, Is. v. 24. This image is often used to express judgments, Is. xli. 15: "Thou shall thresh the mountains and beat them small, and shalt make the hills as chaff." By the unquenchable fire is meant the eternal suffering of the wicked in hell, 2 Th. i. 8, 9; Mar. ix. 48; Mat. xxv. 41.

13. *Then cometh Jesus.* The Saviour is now introduced as about to enter on his work, or as about to be solemnly set apart to his great office of Messiah and Redeemer. The expression "cometh" implies that the act was voluntary on his part; that he went for that purpose and for no other. He left the part of Galilee—Nazareth—where he had lived for nearly thirty years, and went to the vicinity of the Jordan, where John was baptizing the people in great numbers, that he might be set apart to his work. The occasion was doubtless chosen in order that it might be as public and solemn as possible. It is to be remembered, also, that it was the *main* purpose of John's appointment to *introduce* the Messiah to the world, ver. 3. ¶ *To be baptized of him.* *By* him. Baptism was not in his case a symbol of personal reformation and repentance, for he was sinless; but it was a solemn rite by which he was set apart to his great office. It is true, also, that although he was personally holy, and that the baptism in his case had a different signification, in this respect, from that which is implied when it is administered now, yet that even in *his* case the great idea always implied in the ordinance of baptism had a place; for it was a symbol of *holiness* or *purity* in that great system of religion which he was about to set up in the world.

14. *John forbade him.* Refused him. ¶ *I have need.* It is more fit that *I* should be baptized with *thy* baptism, the Holy Ghost, than that thou shouldest be baptized in water by me. I am a sinner, and unworthy to administer this to the Messiah.

15. *Thus it becometh us.* It is fit and proper. And though you may feel yourself unworthy, yet it is proper it should be done. ¶ *All righteousness.* There was no particular precept in the Old Testament requiring this, but he chose to give the sanction of his example to the baptism of John, as to a divine ordinance. The phrase "all righteousness," here, is the same as *a righteous institution or appointment.* Jesus had no sin. But he was about to enter on his great work. It was proper that he should be set apart by his forerunner, and show his connection with him, and give his approbation to what John had done. He submitted to the ordinance of baptism, also, in order that occasion might be taken, at the commencement of his work, for God publicly to declare his approbation of him, and his solemn appointment to the office of the Messiah.

16. *Out of the water.* This shows that he had descended *to* the river. It literally means, "he went up directly FROM *the water.*" The original does not imply that they had descended *into* the river, and it cannot be *proved*, therefore, from this passage, that *his* baptism was by *immersion;* nor can it be proved that even *if* his baptism was by immersion,

were opened unto him, and he saw the[o] Spirit of God descending like a dove, and lighting upon him:

o Is.11.2; 42.1; 61.1; Jn.3.34.

17 And, lo, a voice from heaven, saying, [p]This is my beloved Son, in whom I am well pleased.

p Ps.2.7; Lu.9.35; Ep.1.6; 2 Pe.1.17.

that *therefore* the same mode is binding on men now. In order to demonstrate from this passage that immersion is *essential*, it is necessary to demonstrate, (*a*) that he went *into* the river; (*b*) that, being there, he was wholly immersed; (*c*) that the fact that *he* was immersed, if he was, proves that all others *must be*, in order that there could be a valid baptism. Neither of these three things has ever been demonstrated from this passage, nor can they be. ¶ *The heavens were opened unto him.* This was done while he was praying, Lu. iii. 21. The ordinances of religion will be commonly ineffectual without prayer. If in those ordinances we look to God, we may expect that he will bless us; the heavens will be opened, light will shine upon our path, and we shall meet with the approbation of God. The expression, "the heavens were opened," is one that commonly denotes the appearance of the clouds when it lightens. The heavens appear to open or give way. Something of this kind probably appeared to John at this time. The same appearance took place at Stephen's death, Ac. vii. 56. The expression means, he was permitted to see far into the heavens beyond what the natural vision would allow. ¶ *To him.* Some have referred this to Jesus, others to John. It probably refers to John. See Jn. i. 33. It was a testimony given to *John* that this was the Messiah. ¶ *He saw.* John saw. ¶ *The Spirit of God.* See ver. 11. This was the third person of the Trinity, descending upon him in the form of a dove, Lu. iii. 22. The *dove*, among the Jews, was the symbol of purity of heart, harmlessness, and gentleness, Mat. x. 16; comp. Ps. lv. 6, 7. The form chosen here was doubtless an emblem of the innocence, meekness, and tenderness of the Saviour. The gift of the Holy Spirit, in this manner, was the public approbation of Jesus (Jn. i. 33), and a sign of his being set apart to the office of the Messiah. We are not to suppose that there was any change wrought in the moral character of Jesus, but only that he was publicly set apart to his work, and solemnly approved by God in the office to which he was appointed.

17. *A voice from heaven.* A voice from God. Probably this was heard by all who were present. This voice, or sound, was repeated on the mount of transfiguration, Mat. xvii. 5; Lu. ix. 35, 36; 2 Pe. i. 17. It was also heard just before his death, and was then supposed by many to be thunder, Jn. xii. 28–30. It was a public declaration that Jesus was the Messiah. ¶ *My beloved Son.* This is the title which God himself gave to Jesus. It denotes the nearness of his relation to God, and the love of God for him, He. i. 2. It implies that he was equal with God, He. i. 5–8; Jn. x. 29–33; xix. 7. The term *Son* is expressive of love—of the nearness of his relation to God, and of his dignity and equality with God. ¶ *Am well pleased.* Am ever delighted. The language implies that he was constantly or uniformly well pleased with him; and in this solemn and public manner he expressed his approbation of him as the Redeemer of the world.

The baptism of Jesus has usually been regarded as a striking manifestation of the doctrine of the Trinity, or the doctrine that there are three persons in the divine nature. (1.) There is the person of *Jesus Christ*, the Son of God, baptized in Jordan, elsewhere declared to be equal with God, Jn. x. 30. (2.) *The Holy Spirit* descending in a bodily form upon the Saviour. The Holy Spirit is also equal with the Father, or is also God, Ac. v. 3, 4. (3.) The *Father*, addressing the Son, and declaring that he was well pleased with him. It is impossible to explain this transaction consistently in any other way than by supposing that there are three equal persons in the divine nature or essence, and that each of these sustains an important part in the work of redeeming men.

In the preaching of John the Baptist we are presented with an example of a faithful minister of God. Neither the wealth, the dignity, nor the power of his auditors deterred him from fearlessly declaring the truth respecting their character. He called things by their right names. He did not apologize for their sins. He set their transgressions fairly before them, and

CHAPTER IV.

THEN was Jesus [a]led up of the Spirit into the wilderness, [b]to be tempted of the devil.

2 And when he had fasted forty days and forty nights, he was afterward an hungered.

3 And when the tempter came

a 1 Ki.18.12; Eze.11.1,24; Ac.8.39. *b* Mar.1.12; Lu.4.1.

---

showed them faithfully and fearlessly what must be the consequence of a life of sin. So should all ministers of the Gospel preach. Rank, riches, and power should have nothing to do in shaping and gauging their ministry. In respectful terms, but without shrinking, all the truth of the Gospel must be spoken, or woe will follow the ambassador of Christ, 1 Cor. ix. 16.

In John we have also an example of humility. Blessed with great success, attended by the great and noble, and with nothing but *principle* to keep him from turning it to his advantage, he still kept himself out of view, and pointed to a far greater personage at hand. So should every minister of Jesus, however successful, keep the Lamb of God in his eye, and be willing—nay, rejoice—to lay all his success and honours at his feet.

Everything about the work of Jesus was wonderful. No person had before come into the world under such circumstances. God would not have attended the commencement of his life with such wonderful events if it had not been of the greatest moment to our race, and if he had not possessed a dignity above all prophets, kings, and priests. His "name" was to be called "Wonderful, Councillor, The mighty God, The everlasting Father, The Prince of Peace;" "of the increase of his government and peace" there was to be "no end;" "upon the throne of David and of his kingdom, to order it, and to establish it with judgment and with justice forever" (Is. ix. 6, 7); and it was proper that a voice from heaven should declare that he was the long-promised prince and Saviour; that the angels should attend him, and the Holy Spirit signalize his baptism by his personal presence. And it is proper that *we*, for whom he came, should give to him our undivided affections, our time, our influence, our hearts, and our lives.

CHAPTER IV.

1. *Then was Jesus led up of the Spirit.* Led up *by* the Spirit. Luke says (iv. 1) that Jesus was "full of the Holy Ghost;" and it was by his influence, therefore, that he went into the desert to be tempted. It was not done by presumption on the part of Jesus, nor was it for a mere display of his power in resisting temptation; but it was evidently that it might be seen that his holiness was such that he *could not* be seduced from allegiance to God. When the first Adam was created he was subjected to the temptation of the devil, and he fell and involved the race in ruin: it was not improper that the second Adam—the Redeemer of the race—should be subjected to temptation, in order that it might be seen that there was no power that could alienate him from God; that there *was* a kind and a degree of holiness which no art or power could estrange from allegiance. Mark (i. 12) says that this occurred "immediately" after his baptism; that is, in his case, as not unfrequently happens, the great temptation followed *immediately* the remarkable manifestation of the divine approbation and favour. In the clearest manifestations of the divine favour to us we may not be far from most powerful temptations, and then may be the time when it is necessary to be most carefully on our guard. ¶ *Into the wilderness.* See Notes on ch. iii. 1. ¶ *To be tempted.* The word *tempt*, in the original, means to try, to endeavour, to attempt to do a thing; then, to try the nature of a thing, as metals by fire; then, to test moral qualities by *trying* them, to see how they will endure; then, to endeavour to draw men away from virtue by suggesting motives to evil. This is the meaning here, and this is now the established sense of the word in the English language. ¶ *The devil.* This word originally means an adversary, or an accuser; then, any one opposed to us; then, an enemy of any kind. It is given in the Scriptures, by way of eminence, to the leader of evil angels—a being characterized as full of subtlety, envy, art, and hatred of mankind. He is known, also, by the name *Satan*, Job i. 6–12; Mat. xii. 26; *Beelzebub*, Mat. xii. 24; *the old Serpent*, Re. xii. 9; and *the Prince of the power of the air*, Ep. ii. 2. The name is once given

to him, he said, If thou be the Son of God, command that these stones be made bread.

4 But he answered and said, It is written, [c]Man shall not live by bread alone, but by every word that proceedeth out of the mouth of God.

c De.8.3.

to women (1 Ti. iii. 11): "Even so must their wives be grave, not *slanderers;*" in the original, *devils.*

2. *Had fasted.* Abstained from food. ¶ *Forty days and forty nights.* It has been questioned by some whether Christ abstained wholly from food, or only from the food to which he was accustomed. Luke says (ch. iv. 2) that he *ate nothing.* This settles the question. Mark says (ch. i. 13) that angels came and ministered unto him. At first view this would seem to imply that he did eat during that time. But Mark does not mention the *time* when the angels performed this office of kindness, and we are at liberty to suppose that he means to say that it was done at the close of the forty days; and the rather as Matthew, after giving an account of the temptation, says the same thing (ch. iv. 2). There are other instances of persons fasting forty days recorded in the Scriptures. Thus Moses fasted forty days, Ex. xxxiv. 28. Elijah also fasted the same length of time, 1 Ki. xix. 8. In these cases they were no doubt miraculously supported.

3. *The tempter.* The devil, or Satan. See ver. 1. ¶ *If thou be the Son of God.* If thou art God's own Son, then thou hast power to work a miracle, and here is a fit opportunity to try thy power, and show that thou art sent from God. ¶ *Command that these stones,* &c. The stones that were lying around him in the wilderness. No temptation could have been more plausible, or more likely to succeed, than this. He had just been *declared* to be the Son of God (ch. iii. 17), and here was an opportunity to show that he was *really* so. The circumstances were such as to make it appear plausible and proper to work this miracle. "Here you are," was the language of Satan, "hungry, cast out, alone, needy, poor, and yet the Son of God! If you have this power, how easy could you satisfy your wants! How foolish is it, then, for the Son of God, having all power, to be starving in this manner, when by a *word* he could *show* his power and relieve his wants, and when *in the thing itself* there could be nothing wrong!"

4. *But he answered and said,* &c. In reply to this artful temptation Christ answered by a quotation from the Old Testament. The passage is found in De. viii. 3. In that place the discourse is respecting *manna.* Moses says that the Lord humbled the people, and fed them with manna, an unusual kind of food, that they might learn that man did not live by *bread* only, but that there were other things to support life, and that everything which God had commanded was proper for this. The term "word," used in this place, means very often, in Hebrew, *thing,* and clearly in this place has that meaning. Neither Moses nor our Saviour had any reference to *spiritual food,* or to the *doctrines* necessary to support the faith of believers; but they simply meant that God could support life by other things than *bread;* that man was to live, not by *that* only, but by every other thing which proceeded out of his mouth; that is, which he chose to command men to eat. The substance of his answer, then, is: "It is not so imperiously necessary that I should have *bread* as to make a miracle proper to procure it. Life depends on the will of God. He can support it in other ways as well as by *bread.* He has created other things to be eaten, and man may live by everything that his Maker has commanded." And from this temptation we may learn: 1. That Satan oftens takes advantage of our circumstances and wants to tempt us. The poor, the hungry, and the naked he often tempts to repine and complain, and to be dishonest in order to supply their necessities. 2. Satan's temptations are often the strongest immediately after we have been remarkably favoured. Jesus had just been called the Son of God, and Satan took this opportunity to try him. He often attempts to fill us with pride and vain self-conceit when we have been favoured with any peace of mind, or any new view of God, and endeavours to urge us to do something which may bring us low and lead us to sin. 3. His temptations are plausible. They often seem to be only urging us to do what is good and proper. They seem even to urge us to promote

5 Then the devil taketh him up into [d]the holy city, and setteth him on a pinnacle of the temple,

6 And saith unto him, If thou be the Son of God, cast thyself down: for it is written, [e]He shall give his angels charge concerning thee: and in *their* hands they shall bear

d Ne.11.1; ch.27.53.

e Ps.91.11,12.

the glory of God, and to honour him. We are not to think, therefore, that because a thing *may seem to be good in itself*, that therefore it is to be done. Some of the most powerful temptations of Satan occur when he seems to be urging us to do what shall be for the glory of God. 4. We are to meet the temptations of Satan, as the Saviour did, with the plain and positive declarations of Scripture. We are to inquire whether the thing is *commanded*, and whether, therefore, it is right to do it, and not trust to our own feelings, or even our *wishes*, in the matter.

5. *Then the devil taketh him up.* This does not mean that he bore him through the air, or that he *compelled* him to go against his will, or that he wrought a miracle in any way to place him there. There is no evidence that Satan had *power* to do any of these things, and the word translated *taketh him up* does not imply any such thing. It means to conduct one; to lead one; to attend or accompany one; or to induce one to go. It is used in the following places in the same sense: Nu. xxiii. 14: "And he (Balak) *brought him* (Balaam) into the field of Zophim," &c. That is, he *led him*, or induced him to go there. Mat. xvii. 1: "And after six days Jesus *taketh* Peter, James," &c.; that is, led or conducted them—not by any means implying that he bore them by force. Mat. xx. 17: "Jesus, going to Jerusalem, *took* the twelve disciples apart," &c. See also Mat. xxvi. 37; xxvii. 27; Mar. v. 40. From these passages, and many more, it appears that all that is meant here is, that Satan *conducted* Jesus, or *accompanied* him; but not that this was done against the *will of Jesus.* ¶ *The holy city.* Jerusalem, called *holy* because the temple was there, and because it was the place of religious solemnities. ¶ *Setteth him on a pinnacle of the temple.* It is not perfectly certain to what part of the temple the sacred writer here refers. It has been supposed by some that he means the roof. But Josephus says that the roof was covered by spikes of gold, to prevent its being polluted by birds; and such a place would have been very inconvenient to stand upon. Others suppose that it was the top of the porch or entrance to the temple. But it is more than probable that the porch leading to the temple was not as high as the main building. It is more probable that he refers to that part of the sacred edifice which was called Solomon's Porch. The temple was built on the top of Mount Moriah. The temple itself, together with the courts and porches, occupied a large space of ground. See Notes on Mat. xxi. 12. To secure a level spot sufficiently large, it was necessary to put up a high wall on the east. The temple was surrounded with porches or piazzas 50 feet broad and 75 feet high. The porch on the south side was, however, 67 feet broad and 150 high. From the top of this to the bottom of the valley below was more than 700 feet, and Josephus says that one could scarcely look down without dizziness. The word *pinnacle* does not quite express the force of the original. It is a word given usually to *birds*, and denotes *wings*, or anything in the form of wings, and was given to the roof of this porch because it resembled a bird *dropping its wings.* It was on this place, doubtless, that Christ was placed.

6. *And saith unto him, If thou be the Son of God, cast thyself down.* The temptation here was, that he should at once avail himself of the protection of a promise of safety made to him, and thus demonstrate that he was the Messiah. If he was the true Messiah he had a certain assurance of protection, a promise that no harm could befall him; and thus, by so surprising a miracle, and such a clear proof of the divine interposition, he could at once establish his claim to the Messiahship. How much more easy would this be than to engage in a slow work of years to establish that claim; to encounter fatigue, and want, and poverty, and persecution, before that claim would be admitted! And where could be a more fit place for thus at once demonstrating that he was the Son of God, than on this pinnacle of the temple, in the very midst of Jerusalem, and perhaps in the presence of thousands who would see the wonderful performance? The *temp-*

thee up, lest at any time thou dash thy foot against a stone.

7 Jesus said unto him, It is written again, [f]Thou shalt not tempt the Lord thy God.

f De.6.16.

8 Again, the devil taketh him up into an exceeding high mountain, and showeth him all the kingdoms of the world, and the glory of them;

9 And saith unto him, All these

---

tation, therefore, in this case was, that by thus establishing his claim he would avoid all the obloquy, persecution, and suffering which he must otherwise endure if he attempted to prove that he was the Son of God by a life of toil and privation. ¶ *It is written.* That is, there is a passage of Scripture which promises special protection in such a case, and on which you may rely. The argument was not, perhaps, that this applied *exclusively* to the Messiah, but that, if applicable in any case, it would be in this; if *any* one could plead this promise, assuredly he could who claimed to be the Son of God. ¶ *He shall give his angels charge concerning thee*, &c. That is, they shall protect thee. ¶ *And in* their *hands they shall bear thee up.* They shall sustain thee, or hold thee up, so that thou shalt not be endangered by the fall. ¶ *Lest at any time thou dash thy foot against a stone.* This would be peculiarly appropriate in such a case. The promise, as Satan applied it, was that he should not be injured by the stones lying at the bottom of the wall or in the valley below. The case, therefore, seemed to be one that was especially contemplated by the promise.

7. *Jesus said unto him, It is written again.* Again the Saviour replied to Satan by a text of Scripture—a passage which expressly forbade an act like this. ¶ *Thou shalt not tempt the Lord thy God.* This is quoted literally from De. vi. 16. The meaning is, thou shalt not *try* him; or, thou shalt not, by throwing thyself into voluntary and uncommanded dangers, appeal to God for protection, or trifle with the promises made to those who are thrown into danger *by his providence.* It is true, indeed, that God aids those of his people who are placed *by him* in trial or danger; but it is *not* true that the promise was meant to extend to those who wantonly provoke him and trifle with the promised help. Thus Satan, artfully using and perverting Scripture, was met and repelled by Scripture rightly applied.

8. *An exceeding high mountain.* It is not known what mountain this was. It was probably some elevated place in the vicinity of Jerusalem, from the top of which could be seen no small part of the land of Palestine. The Abbé Mariti speaks of a mountain on which he was, which answers to the description here. "This part of the mountain," says he, "overlooks the mountains of Arabia, the country of Gilead, the country of the Amorites, the plains of Moab, the plains of Jericho, the River Jordan, and the whole extent of the Dead Sea." So Moses, before he died, went up into Mount Nebo, and from it God showed him "all the land of Gilead unto Dan, and all Naphtali, and the land of Ephraim and Manasseh, and all the land of Judah, unto the utmost sea, and the south, and the plain of the valley of Jericho, and the city of palm-trees, unto Zoar," De. xxxiv. 1-3. This shows that there were mountains from which no small part of the land of Canaan could be seen; and we need not suppose that there was any miracle when they were shown to the Saviour. ¶ *All the kingdoms of the world.* It is not probable that anything more is intended here than the kingdoms of Palestine, or of the land of Canaan, and those in the immediate vicinity. Judea was divided into three parts, and those parts were called *kingdoms;* and the sons of Herod, who presided over them, were called *kings.* The term *world* is often used in this limited sense to denote a part or a large part of the world, particularly the land of Canaan. See Ro. iv. 13, where it means *the land of Judah;* also Lu. ii. 1, and the Note on the place. ¶ *The glory of them.* The riches, splendour, towns, cities, mountains, &c., of this beautiful land.

9. *All these things*, &c. All these kingdoms. All these dominions Satan claimed a right to bestow on whom he pleased, and with considerable justice. They were excessively wicked; and with no small degree of propriety, therefore, he asserted his claim to give them away. This temptation had much plausibility. Satan regarded Jesus as the king of the Jews. As the Messiah he supposed he had come to take possession of all that country. He was poor, and unarmed,

things will I give thee, if thou wilt fall down and worship me.

10 Then saith Jesus unto him, Get thee hence, Satan: for it is written, [g]Thou shalt worship the Lord thy God, and him only shalt thou serve.

11 Then the devil leaveth him, and, behold, [h]angels came and ministered unto him.

12 Now when Jesus had heard

g De.6.13; 1 Sa.7.3.

h He.1.6,14.

and without followers or armies. Satan proposed to put him in possession of it *at once,* without any difficulty, if he would acknowledge *him* as the proper *lord* and disposer of that country; if he would trust to *him* rather than *to God.* ¶ *Worship me.* See Notes on Mat. ii. 2. The word here seems to mean, to acknowledge Satan as having a right to give these kingdoms to him; to acknowledge his dependence on him rather than God; that is, really to render *religious* homage. We may be surprised at his boldness. But he had been twice foiled. He supposed it was an object dear to the heart of the Messiah to obtain these kingdoms. He claimed a *right* over them; and he *seemed* not to be asking too much, if he *gave* them to Jesus, that Jesus should be willing to *acknowledge* the gift and express *gratitude* for it. So plausible are Satan's temptations, even when they are blasphemous; and so artfully does he present his allurements to the mind.

10. *Get thee hence.* These temptations, and this one especially, the Saviour met with a decided rebuke. This was a bolder attack than any which had been made before. The other temptations had been founded on an appeal to his necessities, and an offer of the protection of God in great danger; in both cases plausible, and in neither a direct violation of the law of God. Here was a higher attempt, a more decided and deadly thrust at the piety of the Saviour. It was a proposition that the Son of God should *worship* the devil, instead of honouring and adoring Him who made heaven and earth; that he should bow down before the Prince of wickedness and give him homage. ¶ *It is written.* In De. vi. 13. Satan asked him to worship him. This was expressly forbidden, and Jesus therefore drove him from his presence.

11. *Then the devil leaveth him.* He left him for a time, Lu. iv. 13. He intended to return again to the temptation, and, if possible, to seduce him yet from God. Comp. Jn. xiv. 30; Lu. xxii. 53. See Notes on He. xii. 4. ¶ *The angels came and ministered.* See Notes on ch. i. 20. They came and supplied his wants and comforted him. From this narrative we may learn:

(*a.*) That no one is so *holy* as to be free from temptation, for even the Son of God was sorely tempted.

(*b.*) That when God permits a temptation or trial to come upon us, he will, if we look to him, give us grace to resist and overcome it, 1 Co. x. 13.

(*c.*) We see the *art* of the tempter. His temptations are adapted to times and circumstances. They are plausible. What could have been more plausible than his suggestions to Christ? They were applicable to his circumstances. They had the appearance of much piety. They were backed by passages of Scripture—misapplied, but still most artfully presented. Satan never comes boldly and tempts men to sin, telling them that they are committing sin. Such a mode would defeat his design. It would put people on their guard. He commences, therefore, artfully and plausibly, and the real purpose does not appear till he has prepared the mind for it. This is the way with all temptation. No wicked man would *at once* tempt another to be profane, to be drunk, to be an infidel, or to commit adultery. The *principles* are first corrupted. The confidence is secured. The affections are won. And then the allurement is by little and little presented, till the victim falls. How should every one be on his guard at the very *first appearance* of evil, at the first suggestion that may possibly lead to sin!

(*d.*) One of the best ways of meeting temptation is by applying Scripture. So our Saviour did, and they will always best succeed who best wield the sword of the Spirit, which is the word of God, Ep. vi. 17.

12. *John was cast into prison.* For an account of the imprisonment of John see Mat. xiv. 1-13. ¶ *He departed into Galilee.* See Mat. ii. 22. The reasons why Jesus then went into Galilee were probably: 1st. Because the attention of the people had been much excited by John's preaching, and things seemed to

that John was [1]cast into prison, he departed into Galilee:

13 And leaving Nazareth, he came and dwelt in Capernaum, which is upon the sea coast, in the borders of Zabulon and Nephthalim:

14 That it might be fulfilled which was spoken by Esaias the prophet, saying,

15 The[i] land of Zabulon, and the land of Nephthalim, *by* the way of the sea, beyond Jordan, Galilee of the Gentiles:

16 The[k] people which sat in darkness saw great light: and to them

[1] or, *delivered up*.

i Is.9.1,2. *k* Is.42.6,7; Lu.2.32.

be favourable for success in his own ministry. 2d. It appeared desirable to have some one to second John in the work of reformation. 3d. It was less dangerous for him to commence his labours *there* than near Jerusalem. Judea was under the dominion of the scribes, and Pharisees, and priests. They would naturally look with envy on any one who set himself up for a public teacher, and who should attract much attention there. It was important, therefore, that the work of Jesus should begin in Galilee, and become somewhat established and known before he went to Jerusalem.

13. *Leaving Nazareth.* Because his townsmen cast him out, and rejected him. See Lu. iv. 14-30. ¶ *Came and dwelt in Capernaum.* This was a city on the north-west corner of the Sea of Tiberias. It is not mentioned in the Old Testament, but is repeatedly referred to in the Gospels. Though it was once a city of renown, and the metropolis of all Galilee, the site it occupied is now uncertain. When Mr. Fisk, an American missionary, travelled in Syria in 1823, he found twenty or thirty uninhabited Arab huts occupying what are supposed to be the ruins of the once-celebrated city of Capernaum.

The exact site of this ancient city has been a question of much interest, and is not supposed to be as yet fully settled; perhaps it is not possible that it should be. Dr. Robinson (*Biblical Researches*, iii. p. 283, 284, 288-295) supposes that the site of the ancient city is a place now called Khan Minyeh. Dr. Thomson (*The Land and the Book*, vol. ii. p. 542-547) supposes that it was at a place now called Tell Hum. This place is a short distance *north* of Khan Minyeh, or the site supposed by Dr. Robinson to be Capernaum. It is at the north-west corner of the Sea of Tiberias.

In this place and its neighbourhood Jesus spent no small part of the three years of his public ministry. It is hence called *his own city*, Mat. ix. 1. Here he healed the nobleman's son (Jn. iv. 47); Peter's wife's mother (Mat. viii. 14); the centurion's servant (Mat. viii. 5-13); and the ruler's daughter (Mat. ix. 23-25). ¶ *Upon the sea coast.* The Sea of Tiberias. ¶ *In the borders of Zabulon and Nephthalim.* These were two tribes of the children of Israel which were located in this part of the land of Canaan, and constituted in the time of Christ a part of Galilee. Comp. Ge. xlix. 13; Jos. xix. 10, 32. The word *borders* here means *boundaries.* Jesus came and dwelt in the *boundaries* or *regions* of Zabulon and Naphthali.

14-16. *That it might be fulfilled*, &c. This place is recorded in Is. ix. 1, 2. Matthew has given the *sense*, but not the very words of the prophet. For the meaning of the passage as employed by Isaiah, see Notes on Is. ix. 1, 2. ¶ *By the way of the sea.* Which is *near to the sea*, or in the vicinity of the sea. ¶ *Beyond Jordan.* This does not mean to the *east* of Jordan, as the phrase sometimes denotes, but rather in the vicinity of the Jordan, or perhaps in the vicinity of the sources of the Jordan. See De. i. 1; iv. 49. ¶ *Galilee of the Gentiles.* Galilee was divided into *upper* and *lower* Galilee. Upper Galilee was called *Galilee of the Gentiles*, because it was occupied chiefly by Gentiles. It was in the neighbourhood of Tyre, Sidon, &c. The word *Gentiles* includes in the Scriptures all who are not Jews. It means the same as *nations*, or, as we should say, the *heathen nations.*

16. *The people which sat in darkness.* This is an expression denoting great ignorance. As in darkness or night we can see nothing, and know not where to go, so those who are ignorant of God and their duty are said to be in darkness. The instruction which removes this ignorance is called *light.* See Jn. iii. 19; 1 Pe. ii. 9; 1 Jn. i. 5; ii. 8. As ignorance is often connected with crime and vice, so *darkness* is sometimes used

which sat in the region and shadow of death, light is sprung up.

17 From that time Jesus began to preach, and to say, [l]Repent: for the kingdom of heaven is at hand.

l ch.3.2; 10.7.

18 And Jesus, walking by the sea of Galilee, saw two brethren, Simon [m]called Peter, and Andrew his brother, casting a net into the sea: for they were fishers.

m Jn.1.42.

---

to denote sin, 1 Th. v. 5; Ep. v. 11; Lu. xxii. 53. ¶ *Saw great light.* That is, as the passage is employed by Matthew, the light under the Messiah would spring up among them. In that region he grew up, and in that region he preached a great part of his discourses and performed a great part of his miracles. ¶ *The region and shadow of death.* This is a forcible and beautiful image, designed also to denote ignorance and sin. It is often used in the Bible, and is very expressive. A *shadow* is caused by an object coming between us and the sun. So the Hebrews imaged death as standing between us and the sun, and casting a long, dark, and baleful shadow abroad on the face of the nations, denoting their great ignorance, sin, and woe. It denotes a dismal, gloomy, and dreadful shade, where death and sin reign, like the chills, damps, and horrors of the dwelling-place of the dead. See Job x. 21; xvi. 16; xxxiv. 22; Ps. xxiii. 4; Je. ii. 6. See also Notes on Is. ix. 2. These expressions denote that the country of Galilee was peculiarly dark. We know that the people were proverbially ignorant and stupid. They were distinguished for a coarse, outlandish manner of speech (Mar. xiv. 70), and are represented as having been also distinguished by a general profligacy of morals and manners. It shows the great compassion of the Saviour, that he went to preach to such poor and despised sinners. Instead of seeking the rich and the learned, he chose to minister to the needy, the ignorant, and the contemned. His office is to enlighten the ignorant; his delight to guide the wandering, and to raise up those that are in the shadow of death. In doing this, Jesus set an example for all his followers. It is their duty to seek out those who are sitting in the shadow of death, and to send the gospel to them. No small part of the world is still lying in wickedness—as wicked and wretched as was the land of Zabulon and Naphthali in the time of Jesus. The Lord Jesus is able to enlighten them also, and every Christian should regard it a privilege, as well as a duty, to imitate his Saviour in this, and to be permitted to send to them the light of life. See Mat. xxviii. 19.

17. See Notes on Mat. iii. 2.

18. *Sea of Galilee.* This was also called the Sea of Tiberias and the Lake of Gennesareth, and also the Sea of Chinnereth, Nu. xxxiv. 11; De. iii. 17; Jos. xii. 3. Its form is an irregular *oval*, with the large end to the north. It is about 14 miles in length, and from 6 to 9 in width. It is about 600 feet lower than the Mediterranean, and this great depression accounts for some of its peculiar phenomena. There is no part of Palestine, it is said, which can be compared in beauty with the environs of this lake. Many populous cities once stood on its shores, such as Tiberias, Bethsaida, Capernaum, Chorazin, Hippo, &c. The shores are described by Josephus as a perfect paradise, producing every luxury under heaven at all seasons of the year, and its remarkable beauty is still noticed by the traveller. "Seen from any point of the surrounding heights, it is a fine sheet of water—a burnished mirror set in a framework of surrounding hills and rugged mountains, which rise and roll backward and upward to where hoary Hermon hangs the picture on the blue vault of heaven." The lake is fed mainly by the Jordan; but besides this there are several great fountains and streams emptying into it during the rainy seasons, which pour an immense amount of water into it, raising its level several feet above the ordinary mark. See *The Land and the Book* (Thomson), vol. ii. p. 77. Lieutenant Lynch reports its greatest ascertained depth at 165 feet. The waters of the lake are sweet and pleasant to the taste, and clear. The lake still abounds with fish, and gives employment, as it did in the time of our Saviour, to those who live on its shores. It is, however, stormy, owing probably to the high hills by which it is surrounded. ¶ *Simon called Peter.* The name *Peter* means a rock, and is the same as *Cephas.* See Notes on Mat. xvi. 18; also Jn. i. 42; 1 Co. xv. 5.

19 And he saith unto them, Follow me, and I will make you [n]fishers of men.

20 And they straightway [o]left *their* nets, and followed him.

21 And going on from thence, he saw other two brethren, [p]James *the son* of Zebedee, and John his brother, in a ship with Zebedee their father, mending their nets: and he called them.

22 And they immediately left the ship and their father, and followed him.

23 And Jesus went about all Galilee, [q]teaching in their synagogues, and preaching [r]the gospel of the kingdom, and [s]healing all

n Lu.5.10; 1 Co.9.20–22; 2 Co.12.16. *o* Mar.10. 28-31. *p* Mar.1.19,20.

q ch.9.35; Lu.4.15,44. *r* ch.24.14; Mar.1.14. *s* Ps. 103.3; ch.8.16,17.

---

19. *Fishers of men.* Ministers or preachers of the gospel, whose business it shall be to win souls to Christ.

20. *Straightway.* Immediately—as all should do when the Lord Jesus calls them. ¶ *Left* their *nets.* Their nets were the means of their living, perhaps all their property. By leaving them immediately, and following him, they gave every evidence of sincerity. They showed, what we should, that they were willing to forsake *all* for the sake of Jesus, and to follow him wherever he should lead them. They went forth to persecution and death for his sake; but also to the honour of saving souls from death, and establishing a church that shall continue to the end of time. Little did they know what awaited them when they left their unmended nets to rot on the beach, and followed the unknown and unhonoured Jesus of Nazareth. So we know not what awaits us when we become his followers; but we should cheerfully go when our Saviour calls, willing to commit all into his hands—come honour or dishonour, sickness or health, riches or poverty, life or death. Be it ours to do our duty at once, and to commit the result to the great Redeemer who has called us. Comp. Mat. vi. 33; viii. 21, 22; Jn. xxi. 21, 22. ¶ *Follow him.* This is an expression denoting that they became his disciples, 2 Ki. vi. 19.

21. *And going on from thence.* From the place where he had found Peter and Andrew, ver. 18. ¶ *Saw two other brothers.* They were men engaged in the same employment, as it is probable that there were many such in the neighbourhood of the lake. ¶ *In a ship.* A small vessel. In fact, it was little more, probably, than a sail-boat. ¶ *Mending their nets.* A very common employment when they were not actually engaged in fishing.

22. *Left their father.* This showed how willing they were to follow Jesus. They showed us what we ought to do. If necessary, we should leave father, and mother, and every friend, Lu. xiv. 26. If they will go with us, and be Christians, it is well; if not, yet they should not hinder us. We should be the followers of Jesus. And, while in doing it we should treat our friends kindly and tenderly, yet we ought at all hazards to obey God, and do our duty to him. We may add that many, very many children, since Sabbath-schools have commenced, have been the means of their parents' conversion. Many children have spoken to their parents, or read the Bible to them, or other books, and prayed for them, and God has blessed them and converted them. Every child in a Sunday-school ought to be a Christian; and then should strive and pray that God would convert his parents, and make them Christians too. We see here, too, what humble instruments God makes use of to convert men. He chose fishermen to convert the world. He chooses the foolish to confound the wise. And it shows that religion is true, and is the power of God, when he makes use of such instruments to change the hearts of men and save their souls. See Notes on 1 Co. i. 26–28.

23. *All Galilee.* See Notes on ch. ii. 22. ¶ *Synagogues.* Places of worship, or places where the people *assembled* together to worship God. The origin of synagogues is involved in much obscurity. The *sacrifices* of the Jews were appointed to be held in *one* place, at Jerusalem. But there was nothing to forbid the other services of religion to be performed at any other place. Accordingly the praises of God were sung in the schools of the prophets; and those who chose were assembled by the prophets and seers on the Sabbath, and the new moons, for religious worship,

manner of sickness, and all manner of disease among the people.

24 And his fame went throughout all Syria: and they brought unto him all sick people that were taken with divers diseases and tor-

---

2 Ki. iv. 23; 1 Sa. x. 5-11. The people would soon see the necessity of providing convenient places for their services, to shelter them from storms and from the heat, and this was probably the origin of synagogues. At what time they were commenced is unknown. They are mentioned by Josephus a considerable time before the coming of Christ; and in his time they were multiplied, not only in Judea, but wherever there were Jews. There were no less than 480 in Jerusalem alone before it was taken by the Romans.

Synagogues were built in any place where ten men were found who were willing to associate for the purpose, and were the regular customary places of worship. In them the *law, i.e.* the Old Testament, divided into suitable portions, was read, prayers were offered, and the Scriptures were expounded. The law was so divided that the five books of Moses, and portions of the prophets, could be read through each year. The Scriptures, after being read, were expounded. This was done, either by the officers of the synagogue, or by any person who might be invited by the officiating minister. Our Saviour and the apostles were in the habit of attending at those places continually, and of speaking to the people, Lu. iv. 15-27; Ac. xiii. 14, 15.

The synagogues were built in imitation of the temple, with a centre building, supported by pillars, and a *court* surrounding it. See Notes on Mat. xxi. 12. In the centre building, or chapel, was a place prepared for the reading of the law. The law was kept in a chest, or ark, near to the pulpit. The uppermost seats (Mat. xxiii. 6) were those nearest to the pulpit. The people sat round, facing the pulpit. When the law was read, the officiating person rose; when it was expounded, he was seated. Our Saviour imitated their example, and was commonly seated in addressing the people, Mat. v. 1; xiii. 1. ¶ *Teaching.* Instructing the people, or explaining the gospel. ¶ *The gospel of the kingdom.* The good news respecting the kingdom he was about to set up; or the good news respecting the coming of the Messiah and the nature of his kingdom. ¶ *Preaching.* See Notes on ch. iii. 1. ¶ *All manner of sickness.* All kinds of sickness.

24. *And his fame went throughout all Syria.* It is not easy to fix the exact bounds of Syria in the time of our Saviour. It was, perhaps, the general name for the country lying between the Euphrates on the east, and the Mediterranean on the west; and between Mount Taurus on the north, and Arabia on the south. Through all this region his celebrity was spread by his power of working miracles; and, as might be expected, the sick from every quarter were brought to him, in the hope that he would give relief. ¶ *Those possessed with devils.* Much difficulty exists, and much has been written respecting those in the New Testament said to be possessed with the devil. It has been maintained by many that the sacred writers only meant by this expression to denote those who were *melancholy* or *epileptic*, or afflicted with some other grievous disease. This opinion has been supported by arguments too long to be repeated here. On the other hand, it has been supposed that the persons so described were under the influence of evil spirits, who had complete possession of the faculties, and who produced many symptoms of disease not unlike melancholy, madness, and epilepsy. That such was the fact will appear from the following considerations: 1st. Christ and the apostles spoke *to* them and *of* them *as such;* they addressed them, and managed them, precisely *as if* they were so possessed, leaving their hearers to infer beyond a doubt that such was their real opinion. 2d. Those who were thus possessed spake, conversed, asked questions, gave answers, and expressed their knowledge of Christ, and their fear of him—things that certainly could not be said of *diseases*, Mat. viii. 28; Lu. viii. 27. 3d. The devils, or evil spirits, are represented as going out of the persons possessed, and entering the bodies of others, Mat. viii. 32. 4th. Jesus spake to them, and asked their name, and they answered him. He threatened them, commanded them to be silent, to depart, and not to return, Mar. i. 25; v. 8; ix. 25. 5th. Those possessed are said *to know Christ; to be acquainted with the Son of God*, Lu. iv. 34;

ments, and those which were possessed with devils, and those which were lunatic, and those that had the palsy; and he healed them.

Mar. i. 24. This could not be said of diseases. 6th. The early fathers of the Church interpreted these passages in the same way. They derived their opinions probably from the apostles themselves, and their opinions are a fair interpretation of the apostles' sentiments. 7th. If it is denied that Christ believed in such possessions, it does not appear why any other clearly-expressed sentiment of his may not in the same way be disputed. There is, perhaps, no subject on which he expressed himself more clearly, or acted more uniformly, or which he left more clearly impressed on the minds of his disciples.

Nor is there any absurdity in the opinion that those persons were really under the influence of devils. For, 1st, It is no more absurd to suppose that an angel, or many angels, should have *fallen* and become wicked than that so many *men* should. 2d. It is no more absurd that Satan should have possession of the human faculties, or inflict diseases, than that *men* should do it—a thing which is done every day. What is more common than for a wicked man to corrupt the morals of others, or, by inducing them to become intemperate, to produce a state of body and mind quite as bad as to be possessed with the devil? 3d. We still see a multitude of cases that no man can prove *not* to be produced by the presence of an evil spirit. Who would attempt to say that some evil being may not have much to do in the case of madmen? 4th. It afforded an opportunity for Christ to show his power over the enemies of himself and of man, and thus to evince himself qualified to meet every enemy of the race, and triumphantly to redeem his people. He came to destroy the power of Satan, Ac. xxvi. 18; Ro. xvi. 20, 21. ¶ *Those which were lunatic.* This name is given to the disease from the Latin name of the *moon* (Luna). It has the same origin in Greek. It was given because it was formerly imagined that the patient was affected by the increase or the decrease of the moon. The name is still retained, although it is certain that the moon has no effect on the disease. The disease is mentioned only in this place, and in Mat. xvii. 15. It was probably the *falling-sickness* or *epilepsy*, the same as the disease mentioned Mar. ix. 18–20; Lu. ix. 39, 40. ¶ *And those that had the palsy.* Many infirmities were included under the general name of *palsy* in the New Testament. 1st. The paralytic shock, affecting the whole body. 2d. The hemiplegy, affecting only one side of the body; the most frequent form of the disease. 3d. The paraplegy, affecting all the system below the neck. 4th. The catalepsy. This is caused by a contraction of the muscles in the whole or a part of the body, and is very dangerous. The effects are very violent and fatal. For instance, if, when a person is struck, he happens to have his hand extended, he is unable to draw it back; if not extended, he is unable to stretch it out. It gradually becomes diminished in size, and dried up in appearance. Hence it was called *the withered hand*, Mat. xii. 10–13. 5th. The cramp. This, in Eastern countries, is a fearful malady, and by no means unfrequent. It originates from chills in the night. The limbs, when seized by it, remain unmovable, and the person afflicted with it resembles one undergoing a torture. This was probably the disease of the servant of the centurion, Mat. viii. 6; Lu. vii. 2. Death follows from this disease in a few days. ¶ *And he healed them.* This was done evidently by miraculous power. A miracle is an effect produced by divine power above, or opposed to, what are regular effects of the laws of nature. It is not a *violation* of the laws of nature, but is a suspension of their *usual operation*, for some important purpose. For instance, the regular effect of death is that the body returns to corruption. The ordinary laws of chemistry had been suspended by the operation of *life*—a power superior to those laws, and producing new combinations of matter in the animal or vegetable organization. When life is extinct those laws act in their proper power, and the body is *decomposed;* that is, the materials of which it is composed, under chemical laws, return to their natural forms of gases and earths. When one who claims to be from God suspends that regular effect, and gives life to a dead body for some important purpose, it is a miracle. Such an effect is clearly the result of divine power. No other being

25 And there followed him [t]great multitudes of people from Galilee, and *from* Decapolis, and *from* Jerusalem, and *from* Judea, and *from* beyond Jordan.

t Lu.6.17,19.

CHAPTER V.

AND seeing the multitudes, he went up into a mountain: and when he was set, his disciples came unto him:

but God can do it. When, therefore, Christ and the apostles exercised this power, it was clear evidence that God *approved* of their doctrines; that he had commissioned them; and that they were authorized to declare his will. He would not give this attestation to a false doctrine. Most or all of these diseases were incurable. When Christ cured them *by a word*, it was the clearest of all proofs that he was sent from heaven. This is one of the strong arguments for Christianity.

25. From *Decapolis. Decapolis* was the name of a region of country in the bounds of the half-tribe of Manasseh, mainly on the east of Jordan. It was so called because it included *ten cities*—the meaning of the word Decapolis in Greek. Geographers generally agree that Scythopolis was the chief of these cities, and was the only one of them west of the Jordan; that Hippo (Hippos), Gadara, Dion (or Dios), Pelea (or Pella), Gerasa (or Gergesa), Philadelphia, and Raphana (or Raphanæ), were seven of the remaining nine, and the other two were either Kanatha and Capitolias, or Damascus and Otopos. These cities were inhabited chiefly by foreigners (Greeks) in the days of our Saviour, and not by Jews. Hence the keeping of swine by the Gergesenes (Mat. viii. 30-33), which was forbidden by the Jewish law.

CHAPTER V.

1. *And seeing the multitudes.* The great numbers that came to attend on his ministry. The substance of this discourse is recorded also in Lu. vi. It is commonly called the Sermon on the Mount. It is not improbable that it was repeated, in substance, on different occasions, and to different people. At those times parts of it may have been omitted, and Luke may have recorded it as it was pronounced on one of those occasions. See Notes on Lu. vi. 17-20. ¶ *Went up into a mountain.* This mountain, or hill, was somewhere in the vicinity of Capernaum, but where precisely is not mentioned. He ascended the hill, doubtless, because it was more convenient to address the multitude from an eminence than if he were on the same level with them. A hill or mountain is still shown a short distance to the north-west of the ancient site of Capernaum, which tradition reports to have been the place where this sermon was delivered, and which is called on the maps the *Mount of Beatitudes.* The hill commonly believed to be that on which the sermon was delivered is on the road from Nazareth to Tiberias, not far from the latter place. The hill is known by the name of Kuran Huttin, the Horns of Huttin. Of this hill Professor Hackett (*Illustrations of Scripture*, p. 323, 324) says: "Though a noontide heat was beating down upon us with scorching power, I could not resist the temptation to turn aside and examine a place for which such a claim has been set up, though I cannot say that I have any great confidence in it. The hill referred to is rocky, and rises steeply to a moderate height above the plain. It has two summits, with a slight depression between them, and it is from these projecting points, or horns, that it receives the name given to it. From the top the observer has a full view of the Sea of Tiberias. The most pleasing feature of the landscape is that presented by the diversified appearance of the fields. The different plots of ground exhibit various colours, according to the state of cultivation: some of them are red, where the land has been newly ploughed up, the natural appearance of the soil; others yellow or white, where the harvest is beginning to ripen, or is already ripe; and others green, being covered with grass or springing grain. As they are contiguous to each other, or intermixed, these particoloured plots present at some distance an appearance of gay chequered work, which is really beautiful.

"In rhetorical descriptions of the delivery of the Sermon on the Mount, we often hear the people represented as looking up to the speaker from the sides of the hill, or listening to him from the plain. This would not be possible with reference to the present locality; for it is too precipitous and

2 And he opened his mouth, and taught them, saying,

3 Blessed[a] *are* the [b]poor in spirit: [c]for theirs is the kingdom of heaven.

4 Blessed[d] *are* they that mourn: [e]for they shall be comforted.

a Lu.6.20,&c. b Is.57.15; 66.2. c Ja.2.5. d Is.61.3; Eze.7.16. e Jn.16.20; 2 Co.1.7.

too elevated to allow of such a position. The Saviour could have sat there, however, in the midst of his hearers, for it affords a platform amply large enough for the accommodation of the hundreds who may have been present on that occasion." ¶ *And when he was set.* This was the common mode of teaching among the Jews, Lu. iv. 20; v. 3; Jn. viii. 2; Ac. xiii. 14; xvi. 13. ¶ *His disciples came unto him.* The word *disciples* means *learners*, those who are taught. Here it is put for those who attended on the ministry of Jesus, and does not imply that they were all Christians. See Jn. vi. 66.

3. *Blessed* are *the poor in spirit.* The word *blessed* means *happy*, referring to that which produces felicity, from whatever quarter it may come. ¶ *Poor in spirit.* Luke says simply, *Blessed are* THE POOR. It has been disputed whether Christ meant the *poor* in reference to the things of this life, or to *the humble.* The gospel is said to be preached to the poor, Lu. iv. 18; Mat. xi. 5. It was predicted that the Messiah would preach to the poor, Is. lxi. 1. It is said that they have peculiar facilities for being saved, Mat. xix. 23; Lu. xviii. 24. The state of such persons is therefore comparatively blessed, or happy. Riches produce care, anxiety, and dangers, and not the least is the danger of losing heaven by them. To be poor *in spirit* is to have a humble opinion of ourselves; to be sensible that we are sinners, and have no righteousness of our own; to be willing to be saved only by the rich grace and mercy of God; to be willing to be where God places us, to bear what he lays on us, to go where he bids us, and to die when he commands; to be willing to be in his hands, and to feel that we deserve no favour from him. It is opposed to pride, and vanity, and ambition. Such are happy: 1st. Because there is more real enjoyment in thinking of ourselves *as we are*, than in being filled with pride and vanity. 2d. Because such Jesus chooses to bless, and on them he confers his favours here. 3d. Because theirs will be the kingdom of heaven hereafter. It is remarkable that Jesus began his ministry in this manner, so unlike all others. Other teachers had taught that happiness was to be found in honour, or riches, or splendour, or sensual pleasure. Jesus overlooked all those things, and fixed his eye on the poor and the humble, and said that happiness was to be found in the lowly vale of poverty more than in the pomp and splendours of life. ¶ *Theirs is the kingdom of heaven.* That is, either they have peculiar facilities for entering the kingdom of heaven, and of *becoming Christians* here, or they shall enter heaven hereafter. Both these ideas are probably included. A state of poverty—a state where we are despised or unhonoured by men—is a state where men are most ready to seek the comforts of religion here, and a home in the heavens hereafter. See Notes on ch. ii. 2.

4. *Blessed* are *they that mourn.* This is capable of two meanings: either, that those are blessed who are afflicted with the loss of friends or possessions, or that they who mourn over *sin* are blessed. As Christ came to preach repentance, to induce men to mourn over their sins and to forsake them, it is probable that he had the latter particularly in view. Comp. 2 Cor. vii. 10. At the same time, it is true that the gospel only can give true comfort to those in affliction, Is. lxi. 1-3; Lu. iv. 18. Other sources of consolation do not reach the deep sorrows of the soul. They may blunt the sensibilities of the mind; they may produce a sullen and reluctant submission to what we cannot help; but they do not point to the true source of comfort. In the God of mercy only; in the Saviour; in the peace that flows from the hope of a better world, and there only, is there consolation, 2 Co. iii. 17, 18; v. 1. Those that mourn thus shall be comforted. So those that grieve over sin; that sorrow that they have committed it, and are afflicted and wounded that they have offended God, shall find comfort in the gospel. Through the merciful Saviour those sins may be forgiven. In him the weary and heavy-laden soul shall find peace (Mat. xi. 28–30); and the presence of the *Comforter*, the Holy Ghost, shall sustain them

5 Blessed *are* the meek: [f]for they shall inherit the earth.

f Ps.37.11.

6 Blessed *are* they which do hunger and thirst after righteousness: [g]for they shall be filled.

g Ps.145.19; Is.65.13.

here (Jn. xiv. 26, 27), and in heaven all their tears shall be wiped away, Re. xxi. 4.

5. *The meek.* Meekness is patience in the reception of injuries. It is neither meanness nor a surrender of our rights, nor cowardice; but it is the opposite of sudden anger, of malice, of long-harboured vengeance. Christ insisted on his right when he said, "If I have done evil, bear witness of the evil; but if well, why smitest thou me?" Jn. xviii. 23. Paul asserted his right when he said, "They have beaten us openly uncondemned, being Romans, and have cast us into prison; and now do they thrust us out privily? nay, verily; but let them come themselves, and fetch us out," Ac. xvi. 37. And yet Christ was the very model of meekness. It was one of his characteristics, "I am meek," Mat. xi. 29. So of Paul. No man endured more wrong, or endured it more patiently than he. Yet the Saviour and the apostle were not passionate. They bore all patiently. They did not press their rights through thick and thin, or trample down the rights of others to secure their own.

Meekness is the reception of injuries with a belief that God will vindicate us. "Vengeance is his; he will repay," Ro. xii. 19. It little becomes us to take his place, and to do what he has promised to do.

Meekness produces peace. It is proof of true greatness of soul. It comes from a heart too great to be moved by little insults. It looks upon those who offer them with pity. He that is constantly ruffled; that suffers every little insult or injury to throw him off his guard and to raise a storm of passion within, is at the mercy of every mortal that chooses to disturb him. He is like "the troubled sea that cannot rest, whose waters cast up mire and dirt." ¶ *They shall inherit the earth.* This might have been translated *the land.* It is probable that here is a reference to the manner in which the Jews commonly expressed themselves to denote any great blessing. It was promised to them that they should inherit the *land* of Canaan. For a long time the patriarchs looked forward to this, Ge. xv. 7, 8; Ex. xxxii. 13. They regarded it as a great blessing. It was so spoken of in the journey in the wilderness, and their hopes were crowned when they took possession of the promised land, De. i. 38; xvi. 20. In the time of our Saviour they were in the constant habit of using the Old Testament, where this promise perpetually occurs, and they used it *as a proverbial expression to denote any great blessing, perhaps as the sum of all blessings,* Ps. xxxvii. 20; Is. lx. 21. Our Saviour used it in this sense, and meant to say, not that the meek would own *great property* or have many lands, but that they would possess peculiar blessings. The Jews also considered the land of Canaan as a type of heaven, and of the blessings under the Messiah. To *inherit the land* became, therefore, an expression denoting those blessings. When our Saviour uses this language here, he means that the meek shall be received into his kingdom, and partake of its blessings here, and of the glories of the heavenly Canaan hereafter.—The value of *meekness,* even in regard to worldly property and success in life, is often exhibited in the Scriptures, Pr. xxii. 24, 25; xv. 1; xxv. 8, 15. It is also seen in common life that a meek, patient, mild man is the most prospered. An impatient and quarrelsome man raises up enemies; often loses property in lawsuits; spends his time in disputes and broils rather than in sober, honest industry; and is harassed, vexed, and unsuccessful in all that he does. "Godliness is profitable unto all things, having promise of the life that now is, and of that which is to come," 1 Ti. iv. 8. Comp. 1 Ti. vi. 3-6.

6. *Blessed* are *they which do hunger,* &c. Hunger and thirst, here, are expressive of strong desire. Nothing would better express the strong desire which we *ought* to feel to obtain righteousness than hunger and thirst. No wants are so keen, none so imperiously demand supply, as these. They occur daily, and when long continued, as in case of those shipwrecked, and doomed to wander months or years over burning sands, with scarcely any drink or food, nothing is more distressing. An ardent *desire* for anything is often represented in the Scriptures by hunger and thirst,

7 Blessed *are* the merciful: [h]for they shall obtain mercy.

h Ps.41.1,2.

8 Blessed[i] *are* the pure in heart: for they shall see God.

9 Blessed[k] *are* the peacemakers:

i Ps.24.3.4; Heb.12.14; 1 Jn.3.2,3. k Ps.34.14.

Ps. xlii. 1, 2; lxiii. 1, 2. A desire for the blessings of pardon and peace; a deep sense of sin, and want, and wretchedness, is also represented by thirsting, Is. lv. 1, 2. ¶ *They shall be filled.* They shall be satisfied—as a hungry man is when supplied with food, or a thirsty man when supplied with drink. Those who are perishing for want of righteousness; those who feel that they are lost sinners and strongly desire to be holy, shall be thus satisfied. Never was there a desire to be *holy* which God was not willing to gratify, and the gospel of Christ has made provision to satisfy all who truly desire to be holy. See Is. lv. 1-3, and lxv. 13; Jn. iv. 14; vi. 35; vii. 37, 38; Ps. xvii. 15.

7. *Blessed* are *the merciful.* That is, those who are so affected by the *sufferings* of others as to be disposed to alleviate them. This is given as an evidence of piety, and it is said that they who show mercy to others shall obtain it. The same sentiment is found in Mat. x. 42: "Whosoever shall give to drink unto one of these little ones a cup of cold water only, *in the name of a disciple*, verily I say unto you he shall in no wise lose his reward." See also Mat. xxv. 34-40. This should be done with a wish to glorify God; that is, in obedience to his commandments, and with a desire that he should be honoured, and with a feeling that we are benefiting one of his creatures. Then he will regard it as done *to him*, and will reward us. See the sentiment of this verse, that the merciful shall obtain mercy, more fully expressed in 2 Sa. xxii. 26, 27; and in Ps. xviii. 25, 26.

Nowhere do we imitate God more than in showing mercy. In nothing does God more delight than in the exercise of mercy, Ex. xxxiv. 6; Eze. xxxiii. 11; 1 Ti. ii. 4; 2 Pe. iii. 9. To us, guilty sinners; to us, wretched, dying, and exposed to eternal woe, he has shown his mercy by giving his Son to die for us; by expressing his willingness to pardon and save us; and by sending his Spirit to renew and sanctify our hearts. Each day of our life, each hour, and each moment, we partake of his undeserved mercy. All the blessings we enjoy are proofs of his mercy. If *we*, then, show mercy to the poor, the wretched, the guilty, it shows that we are *like God.* We have his spirit, and shall not lose our reward. And we have abundant opportunity to do it. Our world is full of guilt and woe, which we may help to relieve; and every day of our lives we have opportunity, by helping the poor and wretched, and by forgiving those who injure us, to show that we are like God. See Notes on ch. vi. 14, 15.

8. *Blessed* are *the pure in heart.* That is, whose minds, motives, and principles are pure; who seek not only to have the *external actions* correct, but who desire to be holy *in heart*, and who *are so.* Man looks on the outward appearance, but God looks on the heart. ¶ *They shall see God.* There is a sense in which *all* will see God, Re. i. 7. That is, they will behold him as a *Judge*, not as a *Friend.* In this place it is spoken of as a peculiar favour. So also in Re. xxii. 4: "And they shall *see his face.*" To see the face of one, or to be in the presence of any one, were terms among the Jews expressive of great favour. It was regarded as a high honour to be in the presence of kings and princes, and to be permitted to see them, Pr. xxii. 29: "He shall stand *before kings.*" See also 2 Ki. xxv. 19: "Those that stood in the king's presence;" in the Hebrew, those that saw the *face* of the king; that is, who were his favourites and friends. So here, to see God, means to be his friends and favourites, and to dwell with him in his kingdom.

9. *Blessed* are *the peacemakers.* Those who strive to prevent contention, strife, and war; who use their influence to reconcile opposing parties, and to prevent lawsuits and hostilities in families and neighbourhoods. Every man may do *something* of this; and no man is more like God than he who does it. There ought not to be unlawful and officious interference in that which is none of our business; but without any danger of acquiring this character, every man has many opportunities of reconciling opposing parties. Friends, neighbours, men of influence, lawyers, physicians, ministers of the gospel, may do much to promote peace. And it should be taken in hand in the beginning. "The

for they shall be called the children of God.

10 Blessed[l] *are* they which are persecuted for righteousness' sake: for theirs is the kingdom of heaven.

11 Blessed are ye when *men* shall revile you, and persecute *you*, and shall say all manner of evil against you [1]falsely for my sake.

12 Rejoice, and be exceeding

l 1 Pe.3.13,14.

1 *lying*.

---

beginning of strife," says Solomon, "is like the letting out of water." "An ounce of prevention," says the English proverb, "is worth a pound of cure." Long and most deadly quarrels might often be prevented by a little kind interference in the beginning. ¶ *Children of God.* See Notes on Mat. i. 1. Those who *resemble* God, or who manifest a spirit like his. He is the Author of peace (1 Co. xiv. 33); and all those who endeavour to promote peace are *like* him, and are worthy to be called his children.

10. *Blessed* are *they which are persecuted.* To *persecute* means literally to pursue, follow after, as one does a flying enemy. Here it means to vex, or oppress one, on account of his religion. They persecute others who injure their names, reputation, property, or who endanger or take their life, on account of their religious opinions. ¶ *For righteousness' sake.* Because they are righteous, or are the friends of God. We are not to seek persecution. We are not to provoke it by strange sentiments or conduct; by violating the laws of civil society, or by modes of speech that are unnecessarily offensive to others. But if, in the honest effort to be Christians, and to live the life of Christians, others persecute and revile us, we are to consider this as a blessing. It is an evidence that we are the children of God, and that he will defend us. "All that live godly in Christ Jesus shall suffer persecution," 2 Ti. iii. 12. ¶ *Theirs is the kingdom of heaven.* They have evidence that they are Christians, and that they will be brought to heaven.

11. *Blessed are ye when* men *shall revile you.* Reproach you; call you by evil and contemptuous names; ridicule you because you are Christians. Thus they said of Jesus that he was a Samaritan and had a devil (Jn. viii. 48); that he was mad (Jn. x. 20); and thus they reviled and mocked him on the cross, Mat. xxvii. 39–44. But, being reviled, he reviled not again (1 Pe. ii. 23); and thus being reviled, we should bless (1 Co. iv. 12); and thus, though the contempt of the world is not in itself desirable, yet it is blessed to tread in the footsteps of Jesus, to imitate his example, and even to suffer for his sake, Phi. i. 29. ¶ *All manner of evil against you falsely.* An emphasis should be laid on the word *falsely* in this passage. It is not blessed to have evil spoken of us if we *deserve it;* but if we deserve it not, then we should not consider it as a calamity. We should take it patiently, and show how much the Christian, under the consciousness of innocence, can bear, 1 Pe. iii. 13–18. ¶ *For my sake.* Because you are attached to me; because you are Christians. We are not to *seek* such things. We are not to do things to offend others; to treat them harshly or unkindly, and to *court* revilings. We are not to say or do things, though they may be on the subject of religion, designed to disgust or offend. But if, in the faithful endeavour to be Christians, we are reviled, as our Master was, then we are to take it with patience, and to remember that thousands before us have been treated in like manner. When thus reviled or persecuted, we are to be meek, patient, humble; not angry; not reviling again; but endeavouring to do good to our persecutors and slanderers, 2 Ti. ii. 24, 25. In this way many have been convinced of the power and excellence of that religion which they were persecuting and reviling. They have seen that nothing else *but* Christianity could impart such patience and meekness to the persecuted; and have, by this means, been constrained to submit themselves to the gospel of Jesus. Long since it became a proverb, "that the blood of the martyrs is the seed of the church."

12. *Rejoice, and be exceeding glad.* Regard it as a great privilege thus to be persecuted and to suffer—a thing not to be mourned over, but as among the chief blessings of life. ¶ *For great is your reward in heaven.* That is, your reward *will be* great in the future world. To those who suffer most, God imparts the highest rewards. Hence the crown of martyrdom has been thought to be the brightest that any of the redeemed

glad: for [m]great *is* your reward in heaven: for so persecuted they the prophets which were before you.

m 2 Co.4.17.

13 Ye are the [n]salt of the earth: but if the salt have lost his savour, wherewith shall it be salted? it is

n Mar.9.50.

shall wear; and hence many of the early Christians *sought* to become martyrs, and threw themselves in the way of their persecutors, that they might be put to death. They literally rejoiced, and leaped for joy, at the prospect of death for the sake of Jesus. Though God does not require us to *seek* persecution, yet all this shows that there is something in religion to sustain the soul which the world does not possess. Nothing but the consciousness of innocence, and the presence of God, could bear up the sufferers in the midst of these trials; and the flame, therefore, kindled to consume the martyr, has also been a bright light, showing the truth and power of the gospel of Jesus. ¶ *The prophets*, &c. The holy men who came to predict future events, and who were the religious teachers of the Jews. For an account of their persecution, see He. xi.

13. *Ye are the salt of the earth.* Salt renders food pleasant and palatable, and preserves from putrefaction. So Christians, by their lives and instructions, are to keep the world from entire moral corruption. By bringing down the blessing of God in answer to their prayers, and by their influence and example, they save the world from universal vice and crime. ¶ *Salt have lost its savour.* That is, if it has become tasteless, or has lost its preserving properties. The salt used in this country is a chemical compound—chloride of sodium—and if the *saltness* were lost, or it were to lose its *savour*, there would be nothing remaining. It enters into the very *nature* of the substance. In eastern countries, however, the salt used was impure, or mingled with vegetable or earthy substances, so that it might lose the whole of its saltness, and a considerable quantity of earthy matter remain. This was good for nothing, except that it was used to place in paths, or walks, as we use gravel. This kind of salt is common still in that country. It is found in the earth in veins or layers, and when exposed to the sun and rain, loses its saltness entirely. Maundrell says, "I broke a piece of it, of which that part that was exposed to the rain, sun, and air, though it had the sparks and particles of salt, yet it had perfectly lost its savour. The inner part, which was connected to the rock, retained its savour, as I found by proof." So Dr. Thomson (*The Land and the Book*, vol. ii. p. 43, 44) says, "I have often seen just such salt, and the identical disposition of it that our Lord has mentioned. A merchant of Sidon having farmed of the government the revenue from the importation of salt, brought over an immense quantity from the marshes of Cyprus—enough, in fact, to supply the whole province for at least twenty years. This he had transferred to the mountains, to cheat the government out of some small percentage. Sixty-five houses in Jûne—Lady Stanhope's village—were rented and filled with salt. These houses have merely earthen floors, and the salt next the ground, in a few years, entirely spoiled. I saw large quantities of it literally thrown into the street, to be trodden under foot of men and beasts. It was 'good for nothing.'

"It should be stated in this connection that the salt used in this country is not manufactured by boiling clean salt water, nor quarried from mines, but is obtained from marshes along the sea-shore, as in Cyprus, or from salt lakes in the interior, which dry up in summer, as the one in the desert north of Palmyra, and the great lake of Jebbûl, south-east of Aleppo.

"Maundrell, who visited the lake at Jebbûl, tells us that he found salt there which had entirely 'lost its savour,' and the same abounds among the debris at Usdum, and in other localities of rock-salt at the south end of the Dead Sea Indeed, it is a well-known fact that the salt of *this country*, when in contact with the ground, or exposed to rain and sun, does become insipid and useless. From the manner in which it is gathered, much earth and other impurities are necessarily collected with it. Not a little of it is so impure that it cannot be used at all, and such salt soon effloresces and turns to dust—not to fruitful soil, however. It is not only good for nothing itself, but it actually destroys all fertility wherever it is thrown; and this is the reason why it is

thenceforth good for nothing, but to be cast out, and to be trodden under foot of men.

14 Ye are the [o]light of the world. A city that is set on an hill cannot be hid.

15 Neither do men light a candle, and put it under a [2]bushel, but on

o Phi.2.15.

2 The word in the original signifieth *a measure containing about a pint less than a peck.*

---

cast into the street. There is a sort of verbal verisimilitude in the manner in which our Lord alludes to the act: 'it is cast out' and 'trodden under foot;' so troublesome is this corrupted salt, that it is carefully swept up, carried forth, and thrown into the street. There is no place about the house, yard, or garden where it can be tolerated. No man will allow it to be thrown on to his field, and the only place for it is the street, and there it is cast to be trodden under foot of men."

14. *The light of the world.* The light of the world often denotes the *sun*, Jn. xi. 9. The sun renders objects visible, shows their form, their nature, their beauties, their deformities. The term *light* is often applied to religious teachers. See Mat. iv. 16; Lu. ii. 32; Jn. i. 4; viii. 12; Is. xlix. 6. It is pre-eminently applied to Jesus in these places, because he is, in the moral world, what the sun is in the natural world. The apostles, Christian ministers, and all Christians, are lights of the world, because they, by their instructions and example, show what God requires, what is the condition of man, what is the way of duty, peace, and happiness—the way that leads to heaven. ¶ *A city that is set on a hill*, &c. Many of the cities of Judea were placed on the summits or sides of mountains, and could be seen from afar. Perhaps Jesus *pointed* to such a city, and told his disciples that they were like it. Their actions could not be hid. The eyes of the world were upon them. They *must be seen;* and as this was the case, they ought to be holy, harmless, and undefiled.

Maundrell, Jowett, and others suppose that the Sermon on the Mount was delivered in the vicinity of the present city of *Safed*, or "the Horns of Huttin" (see Notes on ver. 1), and that this city may have been in his eye, and may have been directly referred to by the Saviour when he uttered this sentiment. It would give additional force and beauty to the passage to suppose that he pointed to the city. Of this Dr. Thomson (*The Land and the Book*, vol. i. p. 420, 421) says, "The shape of the hill is a well-described oval, and the wall corresponds to it. The bottom of the outer ditch is now a very flourishing vineyard, and the entire circuit is not far from half a mile. The wall is mostly modern, but built on one more ancient, portions of which can be seen on the east side. The interior summit rises about a hundred feet higher than this wall, and was a separate castle, strongly defended. Here are *bevelled* stones, as heavy, and as aged in appearance, as those of the most celebrated ruins in the country; and they prove that this has been a place of importance from a remote age. These ancient parts of the castle render it all but certain that there was then a city or citadel on this most conspicuous 'hill' top; and our Lord might well point to it to illustrate and confirm his precept. The present Hebrew name is Zephath, and may either refer to its elevation like a watch-tower, or to the beauty and grandeur of the surrounding prospects. Certainly they are quite sufficient to suggest the name. There lies Gennesaret, like a mirror set in framework of dark mountains and many-faced hills. Beyond is the vast plateau of the Hauran, faintly shading with its rocky ranges the utmost horizon eastward. Thence the eye sweeps over Gilead and Bashan, Samaria and Carmel, the plains of Galilee, the coasts of Phœnicia, the hills of Naphtali, the long line of Lebanon, and the lofty head of Hermon—a vast panorama, embracing a thousand points of historic and sacred interest."

15. *Neither do men light a candle*, &c. The word rendered *candle* means any portable light, as a lamp, candle, lantern. Comp. Mar. iv. 21; Lu. viii. 16; xii. 35. Jesus proceeded here to show them that the very reason why they were enlightened was that others might also see the light, and be benefited by it. When men light a candle, they do not *conceal* the light, but place it where it may be of use. So it is with religion. It is given that we may benefit others. It is not to be concealed, but suffered to show itself, and to shed light on a surrounding wicked world. ¶ *A bushel. Greek*, a measure containing nearly a

a candlestick; and it giveth light unto all that are in the house.

16 Let your light so shine before men, that they may see your good works, and [p]glorify your Father which is in heaven.

17 Think not that I am come to [q]destroy the law or the prophets: I am not come to destroy, [r]but to fulfil.

18 For verily I say unto you, [s]Till heaven and earth pass, one jot

p 1 Pe.2.12. q ch.3.15. r Is.42.21; Ps.40.6,8. s Lu.16.17.

peck. It denotes anything, here, that might *conceal the light.*

16. *Let your light so shine*, &c. Let your holy life, your pure conversation, and your faithful instructions, be everywhere seen and known. Always, in all societies, in all business, at home and abroad, in prosperity and adversity, let it be seen that you are real Christians. ¶ *That they may see your good works.* The proper *motive* to influence us is not simply that we *may be seen* (comp. ch. vi. 1), but it should be that our heavenly Father may be glorified. The Pharisees acted to be *seen of men;* true Christians act to glorify God, and care little what *men* may think of them, except as by their conduct others may be brought to honour God, yet they should so live that men *may* see from their conduct what is the proper nature of their religion. ¶ *Glorify your Father.* Praise, or honour God, or be led to worship him. Seeing in your lives the excellency of religion, and the power and purity of the gospel, they may be won to be Christians also, and give praise and glory to God for his mercy to a lost world.

We learn here, 1. That religion, if it exist, cannot be concealed. 2. That where it is not manifest in the life, it does not exist. 3. That professors of religion, who live like other men, give evidence that they have never been truly converted. 4. That to attempt to conceal or hide our Christian knowledge or experience is to betray our trust, injure the cause of piety, and to render our lives useless. And, 5. That good actions will be seen, and will lead men to honour God. If we have no other way of doing good—if we are poor, and unlearned, and unknown—yet we may do good by our lives. No sincere and humble Christian lives in vain. The feeblest light at midnight is of use.

"How far the little candle throws his beams!
So shines a good deed in a naughty world!"

17. *Think not that I am come*, &c. Our Saviour was just entering on his work. It was important for him to state what he came to do. By his setting up to be a teacher in opposition to the scribes and Pharisees, some might charge him with an intention to destroy their law, and to abolish the customs of the nation. He therefore told them that he did not come for that end, but really to *fulfil* or accomplish what was in the law and the prophets. ¶ *To destroy.* To abrogate; to deny their divine authority; to set men free from the obligation to obey them. ¶ *The law.* The five books of Moses called the law. See Notes on Lu. xxiv. 44. ¶ *The prophets.* The books which the prophets wrote. These two divisions here seem to comprehend the Old Testament, and Jesus says that he came not to do away or destroy the authority of the Old Testament. ¶ *But to fulfil.* To complete the design; to fill up what was predicted; to accomplish what was intended in them. The word fulfil also means sometimes to *teach* or inculcate, Col. i. 25. The law of Moses contained many sacrifices and rites which were designed to shadow forth the Messiah. See Notes on He. ix. These were *fulfilled* when he came and offered himself a sacrifice to God,

"A sacrifice of nobler name,
And richer blood than they."

The prophets contained many predictions respecting his coming and death. These were all to be fulfilled and fully accomplished by his life and his sufferings.

18. *Verily.* Truly, certainly. A word of strong affirmation. ¶ *Till heaven and earth pass.* This expression denotes that the law *never would be destroyed* till it should be *all* fulfilled. It is the same as saying everything else may change; the very earth and heaven may pass away, but the law of God shall not be destroyed till its whole design has been accomplished. ¶ *One jot.* The word *jot*, or *yod*—'—is the name of the Hebrew letter *I*, the smallest letter in the Hebrew alphabet. ¶ *One tittle.* The word here used, in the Greek, means literally *a little horn*, then *a point, an extremity.* Several of

or one tittle shall in no wise pass from the law, till all be fulfilled.

19 Whosoever therefore shall break one of these least commandments, and shall teach men so, he shall be called the least in the kingdom of heaven: but whosoever shall do and teach *them*, the

---

the Hebrew letters were written with small points or apices, as in the letter *schin*—שׁ—or *sin*—שׂ—which serve to distinguish one letter from another. To change a small point of one letter, therefore, might vary the meaning of a word, and destroy the sense. The name "little horn" was given to these points probably from the manner in which they were written, resembling *a little horn*. Professor Hackett says of a manuscript which he saw a Jew transcribing: "One peculiarity, that struck me at once as I cast my eye over the parchment, was the horn-like appearance attached to some of the letters. I had seen the same mark, before this, in Hebrew manuscripts, but never where it was so prominent as here. The sign in question, as connected with the Hebrew Letter Lamedh in particular, had almost the appearance of an intentional imitation of a ram's head. It was to that appendage of the Hebrew letters that the Saviour referred when he said, 'Not one jot or little horn' (as the Greek term signifies, which our version renders 'tittle,') 'shall pass from the law until all be fulfilled.'"—*Illustrations of Scripture*, p. 234. Hence the Jews were exceedingly cautious in writing those letters, and considered the smallest change or omission a reason for destroying the whole manuscript when they were transcribing the Old Testament. The expression, "one jot or tittle," became proverbial, and means that the *smallest part* of the law should not be destroyed.

The laws of the Jews are commonly divided into moral, ceremonial, and judicial. The moral laws are such as grow out of the *nature of things*, and which cannot, therefore, be changed—such as the duty of loving God and his creatures. These cannot be abolished, as it can never be made right to *hate* God, or to hate our fellow-men. Of this kind are the ten commandments, and these our Saviour has neither abolished nor superseded.—The ceremonial laws are such as are appointed to meet certain states of society, or to regulate the religious rites and ceremonies of a people. These can be changed when circumstances are changed, and yet the moral law be untouched. A general in an army may command his soldiers to appear sometimes in a red coat and sometimes in blue or in yellow. This would be a *ceremonial* law, and might be changed as he pleased. The duty of *obeying him*, and of being faithful to his country, could not be changed. This is a moral law. A parent might suffer his children to have fifty different dresses at different times, and love them equally in all. The dress is a mere matter of *ceremony*, and may be changed. The child, in all these garments, is bound to *love* and *obey* his father. This is a *moral* law, and cannot be changed. So the laws of the Jews. Those designed to regulate mere matters of ceremony and rites of worship might be changed. Those requiring *love and obedience to God* and love to men could not be changed, and Christ did not attempt it, Mat. xix. 19; xxii. 37-39; Lu. x. 27; Ro. xiii. 9.—A third species of law was the *judicial*, or those laws regulating courts of justice which are contained in the Old Testament. These were of the nature of the ceremonial law, and might also be changed at pleasure. The *judicial* law of the Hebrews was adapted to their own civil society. When the form of their polity was changed this was of course no longer binding. The *ceremonial* law was *fulfilled* by the coming of Christ: the shadow was lost in the substance, and ceased to be binding. The *moral* law was confirmed and unchanged.

19. *Whosoever therefore shall break.* Shall violate or disobey. ¶ *One of these least commandments.* The Pharisees, it is probable, divided the precepts of the law into *lesser* and *greater*, teaching that they who violated the former were guilty of a trivial offence only. See Mat. xxiii. 23. Christ teaches that in his kingdom they who make this distinction, or who taught that any laws of God might be violated with impunity, should be called *least;* while *they* should be held in high regard who observed *all* the laws of God without distinction. ¶ *Shall be called least.* That is, shall *be* least. See ver. 9. The meaning of this passage seems to be

same shall be [t]called great in the kingdom of heaven.

20 For I say unto you, That except your righteousness shall exceed [u]*the righteousness* of the scribes and Pharisees, ye shall in no case enter into the kingdom of heaven.

21 Ye have heard that it was said [3]by them of old time, [v]Thou shalt not kill; and whosoever shall

t 1 Sa.2.30. *u* ch.23.23-28; Phi.3.9.

[3] or, *to them.* *v* Ex.20.13; De.5.17.

this: in the kingdom of heaven, that is, in the kingdom of the Messiah, or in the church which he is about to establish (see Notes on Mat. iii. 2), he that breaks the least of these commandments shall be in no *esteem*, or shall not be regarded *as a proper religious teacher*. The Pharisees, by dividing the law into *greater* and *lesser* precepts, made no small part of it void by their traditions and divisions, Mat. xxiii. 23; xv. 3-6. Jesus says that in his kingdom all this vain division and tradition would cease. Such divisions and distinctions would be a small matter. He that attempted it should be the *least* of all. Men would be engaged in yielding obedience to *all* the law of God without any such vain distinctions. ¶ *Shall be called great.* He that teaches that *all* the law of God is binding, and that *the whole* of it should be obeyed, without attempting to specify what is most important, shall be a teacher worthy of his office, and shall be called great. We learn hence, 1. That *all* the law of God is binding on Christians. Comp. Ja. ii. 10. 2. That all the commands of God should be preached, in their proper place, by Christian ministers. 3. That they who pretend that there are any laws of God so small that they need not obey them, are unworthy of his kingdom. And, 4. That true piety has respect to *all* the commandments of God. Comp. Ps. cxix. 6.

20. *Your righteousness.* Your holiness; your *views* of the nature of righteousness, and your conduct and lives. Unless you are more holy than they are, you cannot be saved. ¶ *Shall exceed.* Shall excel, or *abound* more. The righteousness of true Christians is seated in the *heart*, and is therefore genuine. Jesus means that unless they had more *real* holiness of character than the scribes and Pharisees, they could not be saved. ¶ The righteousness *of the scribes and Pharisees.* See Notes on ch. iii. 7. Their righteousness consisted in *outward* observances of the ceremonial and traditional law. They offered sacrifices, fasted often, prayed much, were punctilious about ablutions, and tithes, and the ceremonies of religion, but neglected justice, truth, purity, and holiness of heart. See Mat. xxiii. 13-33. The righteousness that Jesus required in his kingdom was purity, chastity, honesty, temperance, the fear of God, and the love of man. It is pure, eternal, reaching the motives, and making the life holy. ¶ *The kingdom of heaven.* See Notes on ch. iii. 2. Shall not be a fit subject of his kingdom here, or saved in the world to come.

21. *Ye have heard.* Or, this is the common interpretation among the Jews. Jesus proceeds here to comment on some prevailing opinions among the Jews; to show that the righteousness of the scribes and Pharisees was defective; and that men needed a better righteousness, or they could not be saved. He illustrates what he meant by that better righteousness by showing that the common opinions of the scribes were erroneous. ¶ *By them of old time.* This *might* be translated *to the ancients*, referring to Moses and the prophets. But it is more probable that Jesus here refers to the *interpreters* of the law and the prophets. He did not set himself against the law of Moses, but against the false and pernicious interpretations of the law prevalent in his time. ¶ *Thou shalt not kill.* See Ex. xx. 13. This properly denotes taking the life of another with malice, or with an intention to murder him. The Jews understood it as meaning no more. The comment of our Saviour shows that it was spiritual, and was designed to extend to the *thoughts* and *feelings* as well as the external act. ¶ *Shall be in danger of.* Shall be held guilty, and be punished by. The law of Moses declared that the murderer should be put to death, Le. xxiv. 21; Nu. xxxv. 16. It did not say, however, by whom this should be done, and it was left to the Jews to organize courts to have cognizance of such crimes, De. xvi. 18. ¶ *The judgment.* This was the tribunal that had cognizance of cases of murder, &c. It was a *court* that sat in each city or town, and consisted

kill shall be in danger of the judgment:

22 But I say unto you, That [w] whosoever is angry with his brother without a cause, shall be in danger of the judgment: and whosoever shall say to his brother, [4] Raca, shall be in danger of the council:

w 1 Jn.3.15.

4 i.e. *vain fellow*, 2 Sa.6.20.

---

commonly of seven members. It was the lowest court among the Jews, and from it an appeal might be taken to the Sanhedrim.

22. *But I say unto you.* Jesus being God as well as man (Jn. i. 1, 14), and therefore, being the original giver of the law, had a right to expound it or change it as he pleased. Comp. Mat. xii. 6, 8. He therefore spoke here and elsewhere as *having authority*, and not as the scribes. It may be added here that no mere man ever spake as Jesus did, when explaining or enforcing the law. He did it as having a *right* to do it; and he that has a right to ordain and change laws in the government of God must be himself divine. ¶ *Is angry with his brother without a cause.* Anger, or that feeling which we have when we are injured, and which prompts us to defend ourselves when in danger, is a natural feeling, given to us—1st. As a proper expression of our disapprobation of a course of evil conduct; and 2d. That we may defend ourselves when suddenly attacked. When excited against sin, it is lawful. God is angry with the wicked, Ps. vii. 11. Jesus looked on the hypocritical Pharisees *with anger*, Mar. iii. 5. So it is said, "Be ye angry, and sin not," Ep. iv. 26. This anger, or indignation against *sin*, is not what our Saviour speaks of here. What he condemns here is anger *without a cause;* that is, unjustly, rashly, hastily, where no offence has been given or intended. In that case it is evil; and it is a violation of the sixth commandment, because *he that hateth his brother is a murderer*, 1 Jn. iii. 15. He has a feeling which would lead him to *commit* murder, if it were fully acted out. The word *brother* here refers not merely to one to whom we are nearly related, having the same parent or parents, as the word is commonly used, but includes also a neighbour, or perhaps anyone with whom we may be associated. As all men are descended from one Father and are all the creatures of the same God, so they are all brethren, and so every man should be regarded and treated as a brother, He. xi. 16. ¶ *Raca.* This is a Syriac word, expressive of great contempt. It comes from a verb signifying to be *empty, vain;* and hence, as a word of contempt, denotes *senseless, stupid, shallow-brains.* Jesus teaches here that to use such words is a violation of the *spirit* of the sixth commandment, and if indulged, may lead to a more open and dreadful infraction of that law. Children should learn that to use such words is highly offensive to God, for we must give an account for every *idle word* which we speak in the day of judgment, Mat. xii. 36. ¶ *In danger of the council.* The word translated *council* is in the original *Sanhedrim*, and there can be no doubt that the Saviour refers to the Jewish tribunal of that name. This was instituted in the time of the Maccabees, probably about 200 years before Christ. It was composed of seventy-two judges; the high-priest was the president of this tribunal. The seventy-two members were made up of the chief priests and elders of the people and the scribes. The chief priests were such as had discharged the office of the high-priest, and those who were the *heads* of the twenty-four classes of priests, who were called in an honorary way *high* or *chief* priests. See Mat. ii. 4. The *elders* were the princes of the tribes or heads of the family associations. It is not to be supposed that *all* the elders had a right to a seat here, but such only as were *elected* to the office. The *scribes* were learned men of the nation elected to this tribunal, being neither of the rank of priests or elders. This tribunal had cognizance of the great affairs of the nation. Till the time when Judea was subjected to the Romans, it had the power of life and death. It still retained the power of passing *sentence*, though the Roman magistrate held the right of execution. It usually sat in Jerusalem, in a room near the temple. It was before this tribunal that our Saviour was tried. It was then assembled in the palace of the high-priest, Mat. xxvi. 3-57; Jn. xviii. 24. ¶ *Thou fool.* This term expressed *more* than want of wisdom. It was expressive of the highest guilt. It had been commonly used to denote those who were idolaters (De. xxii. 21), and also one

but whosoever shall say, Thou fool, shall be in danger of hell fire.

23 Therefore, [x]if thou bring thy gift to the altar, and there remem- berest that thy brother hath aught against thee,

24 Leave there thy gift before the altar, and go thy way; first be

x De.16.16,17.

who is guilty of great crimes, Jos. vii. 15; Ps. xiv. 1. ¶ *Hell fire.* The original of this is "*the* GEHENNAH *of fire.*" The word GEHENNA, commonly translated *hell*, is made up of two Hebrew words, and signifies the *valley of Hinnom.* This was formerly a pleasant valley near to Jerusalem, on the south. A small brook or torrent usually ran through it and partly encompassed the city. This valley the idolatrous Israelites devoted formerly to the horrid worship of Moloch, 2 Ki. xvi. 3; 2 Ch. xxviii. 3. In that worship, the ancient Jewish writers inform us, the idol of Moloch was of brass, adorned with a royal crown, having the head of a calf, and his arms extended as if to embrace anyone. When they offered children to him they heated the statue within by a great fire, and when it was burning hot they put the miserable child into his arms, where it was soon consumed by the heat; and, in order that the cries of the child might not be heard, they made a great noise with drums and other instruments about the idol. These drums were called TOPH, and hence a common name of the place was TOPHET, Je. vii. 31, 32.

After the return of the Jews from captivity, this place was held in such abhorrence that, by the example of Josiah (2 Ki. xxiii. 10), it was made the place where to throw all the dead carcasses and filth of the city, and was not unfrequently the place of public executions. It became, therefore, extremely offensive; the sight was terrific; the air was polluted and pestilential; and to preserve it in any manner pure, it was necessary to keep fires continually burning there. The extreme loathsomeness of the place; the filth and putrefaction, the corruption of the atmosphere, and the lurid fires blazing by day and night, made it one of the most appalling and terrific objects with which a Jew was acquainted. It was called the GEHENNA *of fire*, and was the image which our Saviour often employed to denote the future punishment of the wicked.

In this verse it denotes a degree of suffering higher than the punishment inflicted by the *court of seventy*, or the *Sanhedrim*, and the whole verse may therefore mean, "He that hates his brother without a cause is guilty of a violation of the sixth commandment, and shall be punished with a severity similar to that inflicted by the *court of judgment.* He that shall suffer his passions to transport him still farther, so that he shall make his brother an object of derision and contempt, shall be exposed to severer punishment, corresponding to that which the *Sanhedrim*, or *council*, inflicts. But he who shall load his brother with odious appellations and abusive language shall incur the severest degree of punishment, represented by being burned alive in the horrid and awful valley of Hinnom."

The amount, then, of this difficult and important verse is this: The Jews considered but *one crime* a violation of the sixth commandment, viz. actual murder, or wilful, unlawful taking *life.* Jesus says that the commandment is much broader. It relates not only to the *external* act, but to the feelings and words. He specifies three forms of such violation. 1st. Unjust *anger.* 2d. Anger accompanied with an expression of *contempt.* 3d. Anger, with an expression not only of contempt, but *wickedness.* Among the Jews there were three degrees of condemnation: that by the "judgment," the "council," and the "fire of Hinnom." Jesus says likewise there shall be grades of condemnation for the different ways of violating the sixth commandment. Not only *murder* shall be punished by God, but *anger* and *contempt* shall be regarded by him as a violation of the law, and punished according to the offence. As these offences were not actually cognizable before the Jewish tribunals, he must mean that they will be punished *hereafter*, and *all* these expressions therefore relate to *degrees of punishment* proportionate to crime in the future world —the world of justice and of woe.

23, 24. *Therefore, if thou bring thy gift to the altar*, &c. The Pharisees were intent only on the *external* act in worship. They looked not at all to the internal state of the mind. If a man conformed to the *external* rites of religion, however much envy, and malice, and secret ha-

reconciled to thy brother, and then come and offer thy gift.

25 Agree[y] with thine adversary quickly, whiles thou art in the way with him; lest at any time the adversary deliver thee to the judge, and the judge deliver thee to the officer, and thou be cast into prison.

26 Verily I say unto thee, Thou shalt by no means come out thence,

y Pr.25.8; Lu.12.58,59.

tred he might have, they thought he was doing well. Our Saviour taught a different doctrine. It was of more consequence to have the *heart* right than to perform the outward act. If, therefore, says he, a man has gone so far as to bring his gift *to the very altar*, and should remember that anyone had anything against him, it was his duty there to leave his offering and go and be reconciled. While a difference of this nature existed, his offering could not be acceptable. He was not to *wait* till the offended brother should come to him; he was to *go* and seek him out, and be reconciled. So now the worship of God will not be acceptable, however well performed *externally*, until we are at peace with those that we have injured. "To obey is better than sacrifice," 1 Sa. xv. 22. He that comes to worship his Maker filled with malice, and hatred, and envy, and *at war with his brethren*, is a hypocritical worshipper, and must meet with God's displeasure. God is not deceived, and he will not be mocked. ¶ *Thy gift.* Thy sacrifice. What thou art about to devote to God as an offering. ¶ *To the altar.* The altar was situated in front of the temple, and was the place on which sacrifices were made. See the Notes on plan, Mat. xxi. 12. To bring a gift to the altar was expressive of worshipping God, for this was the way in which he was formerly worshipped. ¶ *Thy brother.* Any man, especially any fellow-worshipper. Anyone of the same religious society. ¶ *Hath aught.* Is offended, or thinks he has been injured by you in any manner. ¶ *First be reconciled.* This means to settle the difficulty; to make proper acknowledgment or satisfaction for the injury. If you have wronged him, make restitution. If you owe him a debt which ought to be paid, pay it. If you have injured his character, confess it and seek pardon. If he is under an erroneous impression, if your conduct has been such as to *lead* him to suspect that you have injured him, make an explanation. Do all *in your power*, and all you *ought to do*, to have the matter settled. From this we learn: 1st. That, in order to worship God acceptably, we must do justice to our fellowmen. 2d. Our worship will not be acceptable unless we do all we can to live *peaceably* with others. 3d. It is our duty to *seek* reconciliation with others when we have injured them. 4th. This should be done *before* we attempt to worship God. 5th. This is often the reason why God does not accept our offerings, and we go empty away from our devotions. We do not do what we ought to others; we cherish improper feelings or refuse to make proper acknowledgments, and God *will not* accept such attempts to worship him.

25, 26. *Agree with thine adversary quickly.* This is still an illustration of the sixth commandment. To be in hostility, to go to law, to be litigious, is a violation always, on one side or the other, of the law requiring us to love our neighbour, and our Saviour regards it as a violation of the sixth commandment. While you are in the *way* with him, says he, that is, while you are *going* to the court, *before the trial has taken place*, it is your duty, if possible, to come to an agreement. It is wrong to carry the contention to a court of law. See 1 Co. vi. 6, 7. The consequence of *not* being reconciled, he expresses in the language of courts. The adversary shall deliver to the judge, and he to the executioner, and he shall throw you into prison. He did not mean to say that this would be *literally* the way with God, but that *His* dealings with those that harboured these feelings, and would not be *reconciled* with their brethren, were *represented* by the punishment inflicted by human tribunals. That is, he would hold all such as *violators* of the sixth commandment, and would punish them accordingly.

There is no propriety in the use sometimes made of this verse, in representing *God* as the "adversary" of the sinner, and urging him to be reconciled to God while in the way to judgment. Nor does the phrase "thou shalt by no means come out thence till thou hast paid the uttermost farthing" refer to the *eternity* of future punishment. It is language taken from courts of justice,

till thou hast paid the uttermost farthing.

27 Ye have heard that it was said by them of old time, Thou shalt not commit adultery:

28 But I say unto you, That whosoever [z]looketh on a woman to lust after her hath committed adultery with her already in his heart.

29 And if thy right eye [5]offend thee, pluck it out, and cast *it* from thee: for it is profitable for thee

z Job 31.1; Pr.6.25. 5 or, *do cause thee to offend.*

to illustrate the truth that God will *punish* men according to *justice* for not being reconciled to him. The punishment in the future world will be eternal indeed (Mat. xxv. 46), but *this* passage does not prove it. ¶ *Thine adversary.* A man that is opposed to us in law. It here means a *creditor;* a man who has a just claim on us. ¶ *In the way with him.* While you are going before the court. Before the trial comes on. It is remarkable that this *very direction* is found in the Roman law of the Twelve Tables, which expressly directed the plaintiff and defendant to make up the matter while they were *in the way*, or going to the prætor—*in via, rem uti pacunt orato.—Blackstone's Comm.*, iii. p. 299. Whether the Saviour had any reference to this cannot be determined. As the Roman laws prevailed to some extent in Palestine, however, it is possible that there was such an allusion. ¶ *The officer.* The executioner; or, as we should say, the sheriff. ¶ *The uttermost farthing.* The last farthing. All that is due. The *farthing* was a small coin used in Judea, equal to two *mites.* It was not quite equal to half a farthing of English money.

27, 28. *Ye have heard that it was said by them of old time, Thou shalt not commit adultery.* See Notes on ver. 21. Our Saviour in these verses explains the seventh commandment. It is probable that the Pharisees had explained this commandment, as they had the *sixth,* as extending only to the external act; and that they regarded evil thoughts and a wanton imagination as of little consequence, or as not forbidden by the law. Our Saviour assures them that the commandment did not regard the external act merely, but the secrets of the heart, and the movements of the *eye.* He declares that they who indulge a wanton desire, that they who *look* on a woman to increase their lust, have already, in the sight of God, violated the commandment, and committed adultery in the heart. Such was the guilt of David, whose deep and awful crime fully shows the danger of indulging in evil desires, and in the rovings of a wanton eye. See 2 Sa. xi.; Ps. li. See also 2 Pe. ii. 14. So exceeding strict and broad is the law of God! And so heinous in *his* sight are thoughts and feelings which may be for ever concealed from the world!

29. *Thy right eye.* The Hebrews, like others, were accustomed to represent the affections of the mind by the members or parts of the body, Ro. vii. 23; vi. 13. Thus the *bowels* denoted compassion; the *heart*, affection or feeling; the *reins*, understanding, secret purpose. An *evil eye* denotes sometimes *envy* (Mat. xx. 15), and sometimes an evil passion, or sin in general. Mar. vii. 21, 22: "Out of the heart proceedeth an *evil eye.*" In this place, as in 2 Pe. ii. 14, the expression is used to denote strong adulterous passion, unlawful desire, or wicked inclination. The *right* eye and hand are mentioned, because they are of most *use* to us, and denote that, however *strong* the passion may be, or difficult to part with, yet that we should do it. ¶ *Offend thee.* The noun from which the verb "offend," in the original, is derived, commonly means a *stumbling-block*, or a *stone* placed in the way, over which one might fall. It also means a *net*, or a certain part of a net against which, if a *bird* strikes, it springs the net, and is taken. It comes to signify, therefore, anything by which we fall, or are ensnared; and applied to *morals*, means anything by which we *fall* into sin, or by which we are *ensnared.* The English word *offend* means now, commonly, to displease; to make angry; to affront. This is by no means the sense of the word in Scripture. It means to cause to fall *into sin.* The eye does this when it wantonly *looks* on a woman to lust after her. ¶ *Pluck it out,* &c. It cannot be supposed that Christ intended this to be taken literally. His design was to teach that the *dearest* objects, if they cause us to sin, are to be abandoned; that by all sacrifices and self-denials we must overcome the evil propensities of our nature, and resist our wanton imaginations. Some of

that one of thy members should perish, and not *that* thy whole body should be [a]cast into hell.

30 And if thy right hand offend thee, cut it off, and cast *it* from thee: for it is profitable for thee that one of thy members should perish, and not *that* thy whole body should be cast into hell.

31 It hath been said, [b]Whosoever shall put away his wife, let him give her a writing of divorcement:

32 But I say unto you, That [c]whosoever shall put away his wife, saving for the cause of fornication, causeth her to commit adultery: and whosoever shall marry her that is divorced committeth adultery.

33 Again, ye have heard that it hath been said by them of old

a Ro.8.13; 1 Co.9.27. *b* De.24.1; Je.3.1; Mar.10.2-9. *c* ch.19.9; 1 Co.7.10,11.

---

the fathers, however, took this commandment literally. Our Saviour several times repeated this sentiment. See Mat. xviii. 9; Mar. ix. 43-47. Comp. also Col. iii. 5. ¶ *It is profitable for thee.* It is *better* for thee. You will be a gainer by it. ¶ *One of thy members perish.* It is better to deny yourself the gratification of an evil passion here, however much it may cost you, than to go down to hell for ever. ¶ *Thy whole body should be cast into hell.* Thy body, with all its unsubdued and vicious propensities. This will constitute no small part of the misery of hell. The sinner will be sent there *as he is*, with every evil desire, every unsubdued propensity, every wicked and troublesome passion, and yet with no possibility of gratification. It constitutes our highest notions of misery when we think of a man filled with anger, pride, malice, avarice, envy and lust, and with no opportunity of gratifying them for ever. This is all that is necessary to make an eternal hell. On the word *hell*, see Notes on ver. 22.

30. *And if thy right hand offend thee.* The right hand is selected for the same reason as the right eye, because it is one of the most important members of the human body. The idea is, that the dearest earthly objects are to be sacrificed rather than that we should commit sin; that the most rigid self-denial should be practised, and that the most absolute self-government should be maintained at any sacrifice, rather than that we should suffer the mind to be polluted by unholy thoughts and impure desires.

31, 32. *It hath been said*, &c. That is, by Moses, De. xxiv. 1, 2. The husband was directed, if he put his wife away, to give her a bill of divorce, that is a certificate of the fact she had been his wife, and that he had dissolved the marriage. There was considerable difference of opinion among the Jews for what *causes* the husband was permitted to do this. One of their famous schools maintained that it might be done for any cause, however *trivial*. The other maintained that *adultery* only could justify it. The truth was, however, that the husband exercised this right at pleasure; that he was judge in the case, and dismissed his wife when and for what cause he chose. And this seems to be agreeable to the law in Deuteronomy. Our Saviour in Mar. x. 1-12, says that this was permitted on account of the hardness of their hearts, but that in the beginning it was not so. God made a single pair, and ordained marriage for life. But Moses found the people so much hardened; so long accustomed to the practice, and so rebellious, that, as a matter of *civil* appointment, he thought it best not to attempt any change. Our Saviour brought marriage back to its original intention, and declared that whosoever put away his wife henceforward, except for one offence, should be guilty of adultery. This is now the law of God. This was the original institution. This is the *only* law that is productive of peace and good morals, and that secures the respect due to a wife, and the good of children. Nor has any man or set of men—any legislature or any court, civil or ecclesiastical—a right to interfere, and declare that divorces may be granted for any other cause. They, therefore, whoever they may be, who are divorced for any cause except the single one of adultery, if they marry again, are, according to the Scriptures, living in adultery. No earthly laws can trample down the laws of God, or make that *right* which he has solemnly pronounced *wrong*.

33. *Thou shalt not forswear thyself.* Christ here proceeds to correct another false interpretation of the law. The

time, [d]Thou shalt not forswear thyself, but shalt perform unto the Lord thine oaths:

34 But I say unto you, [e]Swear not at all: neither by heaven; for it is God's throne:

35 Nor by the earth; for it is his footstool: neither by Jerusalem; for it is [f]the city of the great King.

d Le.19.12; Nu.30.2; De.23.23. e ch.23.16-22; Ja.5.12. f Re.21.2,10.

law respecting oaths is found in Le. xix. 12, and De. xxiii. 23. By those laws men were forbid to perjure themselves, or to *forswear*, that is, swear falsely. ¶ *Perform unto the Lord.* Perform literally, really, and religiously what is promised in an oath. ¶ *Thine oaths.* An oath is a solemn affirmation or declaration, made with an appeal to God for the truth of what is affirmed, and imprecating his vengeance, and renouncing his favour if what is affirmed is false. A false oath is called perjury, or, as in this place, *forswearing.*

It appears, however, from this passage, as well as from the ancient writings of the Jewish rabbins, that while the Jews professedly adhered to the law, they had introduced a number of oaths *in common conversation*, and oaths which they by no means considered to be binding. For example, they would swear by the temple, by the head, by heaven, by the earth. So long as they kept from swearing by the name *Jehovah*, and so long as they observed the oaths *publicly* taken, they seemed to consider all others as allowable, and allowedly broken. This is the abuse which Christ wished to correct. *It was the practice of swearing in common conversation, and especially swearing by created things.* To do this, he said that they were mistaken in their views of the *sacredness* of such oaths. They were very closely connected with God; and to *trifle* with them was a species of trifling with God. Heaven is *his* throne; the earth *his* footstool; Jerusalem *his* peculiar abode; the head was made *by him*, and was so much under his control that we could not make one hair white or black. To swear by these things, therefore, was to treat irreverently objects *created* by God, and could not be without guilt. It is remarkable that the sin here condemned by the Saviour prevails still in Palestine in the same form and manner referred to here. Dr. Thomson (*The Land and the Book*, vol. ii. p. 284) says, "The people now use the very same sort of oaths that are mentioned and condemned by our Lord. They swear by the head, by their life, by heaven, and by the temple, or what is in its place, the church. The forms of cursing and swearing, however, are almost infinite, and fall on the pained ear all day long."

Our Saviour here evidently had no reference to *judicial* oaths, or oaths taken in a court of justice. It was merely the foolish and wicked habit of swearing in private conversation; of swearing on every occasion and by everything that he condemned. This he *does* condemn in a most unqualified manner. He himself, however, did not refuse to take an oath in a court of law, Mat. xxvi. 63, 64. So Paul often *called God to witness* his sincerity, which is all that is meant by an oath. See Ro. i. 9; ix. 1; Ga. i. 20; He. vi. 16. Oaths were, moreover, prescribed in the law of Moses, and Christ did not come to repeal those laws. See Ex. xxii. 11; Le. v. 1; Nu. v. 19; De. xxix. 12, 14.

34, 35. *But I say unto you, Swear not at all.* That is, in the manner which he proceeds to specify. Swear not in any of the common and profane ways customary at that time. ¶ *By heaven; for it is God's throne.* To swear by that was, if it meant anything, *to swear by Him that sitteth thereon*, Mat. xxiii. 22. ¶ *Nor by the earth; for it is his footstool.* Swearing by that, therefore, is really swearing by God. Or perhaps it means, 1st. We have no right to *pledge*, or swear by, what belongs to God; and, 2d. That oaths by inanimate objects are unmeaning and wicked. If they are *real* oaths, they are by a living Being, who has power to take vengeance. A *footstool* is that on which the foot rest when sitting. The term is applied *to the earth* to denote how lowly and humble an object it is when compared with God. ¶ *Jerusalem.* See Notes on ch. ii. 1. ¶ *City of the Great King.* That is, of *God;* called the Great King because he was the King of the Israelites, and Jerusalem was the capital of the nation, and the place where he was peculiarly honoured *as king.* Comp. Ps. xlvi. 4; xlviii. 1, 2; lxxxvii. 3.

36. *Neither shalt thou swear by thy*

36 Neither shalt thou swear by thy head, because thou canst not make one hair white or black.

37 But [g]let your communication be, Yea, yea; Nay, nay: for whatsoever is more than these cometh of evil.

38 Ye have heard that it hath been said, [h]An eye for an eye, and a tooth for a tooth:

39 But I say unto you, [i]That ye resist not evil: [k]but whosoever shall smite thee on the right cheek, turn to him the other also.

g Ja.5.12. h Ex.21.24. i Pr.20.22; 24.29; Ro.12.17-19. k Is.50.6.

head. This was a common oath. The Gentiles also used this oath. To swear by the *head* was the same as to swear by the *life;* or to say, I will forfeit my *life* if what I say is not true. God is the author of the life, and to swear by *that*, therefore, is the same as to swear by *him.* ¶ *Because thou canst not make one hair white or black.* You have no control or right over your own life. You cannot even change one single *hair. God* has all that control; and it is therefore *improper* and profane to pledge what is God's gift and God's property; and it is the same as swearing by God himself.

37. *But let your communication. Your word;* what you say. ¶ *Be, Yea.* Yes. This does not mean that we should always use the word *yea*, for it might as well have been translated *yes;* but it means that we should simply *affirm* or *declare* that a thing is so. ¶ *More than these.* More than these *affirmations.* ¶ *Cometh of evil.* Is evil. Proceeds from some evil disposition or purpose. And from this we may learn: 1st. That profane swearing is always the evidence of a depraved heart. To trifle with the name of God, or with any of his works, is itself most decided proof of depravity. 2d. That no man is believed any sooner in common conversation because he *swears* to a thing. When we hear a man swear to a thing, it is pretty good evidence that he knows what he is saying to be false, and we should be on our guard. He that will break the third commandment will not hesitate to break the ninth also. And this explains the fact that profane swearers are seldom believed. The man who is *always* believed is he whose character is beyond suspicion in all things, who obeys *all* the laws of God, and whose simple declaration, therefore, is enough. A man that is truly a Christian, and leads a Christian life, does not need oaths and profaneness to make him believed. 3d. It is no mark of a gentleman to swear. The most worthless and vile, the refuse of mankind, the drunkard and the prostitute, swear as well as the best dressed and educated *gentleman.* No particular endowments are requisite to give a *finish* to the art of cursing. The basest and meanest of mankind swear with as much tact and skill as the most refined, and he that wishes to degrade himself to the very lowest level of pollution and shame should learn to be a common swearer. Any man has talents enough to learn to curse God and his fellow-men, and to *pray*—for every man who swears prays—that God would sink him and others into hell. No profane man knows but that God will *hear his prayer,* and send him to the regions of woe. 4th. Profaneness does no man any good. No man is the richer, or wiser, or happier for it. It helps no one's morals or manners. It commends no one to any society. The profane man *must be,* of course, shut out from female society, and no refined intercourse can consist with it. It is disgusting to the refined; abominable to the good; insulting to those with whom we associate; degrading to the mind; unprofitable, needless, and injurious in society; and awful in the sight of God. 5th. God will not hold the profane swearer guiltless. Wantonly to profane his name, to call his vengeance down, to curse him on his throne, to invoke damnation, is perhaps of all offences the most awful. And there is not in the universe more cause of amazement at his forbearance, than that God does not rise in vengeance, and smite the profane swearer at once to hell. Verily, in a world like this, where his name is profaned every day, and hour, and moment by thousands, God shows that he is slow to anger, and that his mercy is without bounds!

38–41. *An eye for an eye,* &c. This command is found in Ex. xxi. 24; Le. xxiv. 20, and De. xix. 21. In these places it was given as a rule *to regulate the decisions of judges.* They were to take eye for eye, and tooth for tooth, and to inflict burning for burning. As a *judicial rule* it is not unjust. Christ

40 And if any man will sue thee at the law, and take away thy coat, let him have *thy* cloak also.

41 And whosoever shall compel thee to go a mile, go with him twain.

---

finds no fault with the rule as applied to *magistrates*, and does not take upon himself to repeal it. But instead of confining it to magistrates, the Jews had extended it to *private* conduct, and made it the rule by which to take *revenge*. They considered themselves justified by this rule to inflict the same injury on others that they had received. Against this our Saviour remonstrates. He declares that the law had no reference to private revenge, that it was given only to regulate the magistrate, and that their private conduct was to be governed by different principles.

The general principle which he laid down was, that we are not *to resist evil;* that is, as it is in the Greek, not to set ourselves against an evil person who is injuring us. But even this general direction is not to be pressed too strictly. Christ did not intend to teach that we are to see our families murdered, or be murdered ourselves, rather than to make resistance. The law of nature, and all laws, human and divine, justify self-defence when *life* is in danger. It cannot surely be the intention to teach that a father should sit by coolly and see his family butchered by savages, and not be allowed to defend them. Neither natural nor revealed religion ever did, or ever can, inculcate this doctrine. Our Saviour immediately explains what *he* means by it. Had he intended to refer it to a case where *life* is in danger, he would most surely have mentioned it. Such a case was far more worthy of statement than those which he *did* mention. A doctrine so unusual, so unlike all that the world had believed, and that the best men had acted on, deserved to be formally stated. Instead of doing this, however, he confines himself to smaller matters, to things of comparatively trivial interest, and says that in these we had better take wrong than to enter into strife and lawsuits. The first case is where we are smitten on the cheek. Rather than contend and fight, we should take it patiently, and turn the other cheek. This does not, however, prevent our remonstrating firmly yet mildly on the injustice of the thing, and insisting that justice should be done us, as is evident from the example of the Saviour himself. See Jn. xviii. 23. The second evil mentioned is where a man is *litigious* and determined to take all the advantage the law can give him, following us with vexatious and expensive lawsuits. Our Saviour directs us, rather than to imitate him—rather than to contend with a revengeful spirit in courts of justice—to take a trifling injury, and yield to him. This is merely a question about property, and not about conscience and life.

"*Coat.*" The Jews wore two principal garments, an interior and an exterior. The *interior*, here called the "*coat,*" or the tunic, was made commonly of linen, and encircled the whole body, extending down to the knees. Sometimes beneath this garment, as in the case of the priests, there was another garment corresponding to pantaloons. The coat, or tunic, was extended to the neck, and had long or short sleeves. *Over* this was commonly worn an upper garment, here called "*cloak*," or mantle. It was made commonly nearly square, of different sizes, 5 or 6 cubits long and as many broad, and was wrapped around the body, and was thrown off when labour was performed. *If*, said Christ, an adversary wished to obtain, *at law*, *one* of these garments, rather than contend with him let him have the other also. A reference to various articles of apparel occurs frequently in the New Testament, and it is desirable to have a correct view of the ancient mode of dress, in order to a proper understanding of the Bible. The Asiatic modes of dress are nearly the same from age to age, and hence it is not difficult to illustrate the passages where such a reference occurs. The ordinary dress consisted of the inner garment, the outer garment, the girdle, and the sandals. In regard to the *sandals*, see Notes on ch. iii. 11.

In the girdle was the place of the purse (Mat. x. 9), and to it the sword and dirk were commonly attached. Comp. 2 Sa. xx. 8. In modern times the pistols are also fastened to the girdle. It is the usual place for the handkerchief, smoking materials, inkhorn, and, in general, the implements of one's profession. The girdle served to confine the loose flowing robe or

42 Give to him that asketh thee, and [l]from him that would borrow of thee turn not thou away.

43 Ye have heard that it hath been said, [m]Thou shalt love thy neighbour, and hate thine enemy:

44 But I say unto you, [n]Love your enemies, bless them that curse you, do good to them that hate you, and [o]pray for them which despitefully use you, and persecute you;

l De.15.7,11. m De.23.6. n Ro.12.14,20. o Lu.23.34; Ac.7.60.

outer garment to the body. It held the garment when it was tucked up, as it was usually in walking or in labour. Hence *to gird up the loins* became a significant figurative expression, denoting readiness for service, activity, labour, and watchfulness; and *to loose the loins* denoted the giving way to repose and indolence, 2 Ki. iv. 29; Job xxxviii. 3; Is. v. 27; Lu. xii. 35; Jn. xxi. 7.

Whosoever shall compel thee to go a mile. The word translated *shall compel* is of Persian origin. Post-offices were then unknown. In order that the royal commands might be delivered with safety and despatch in different parts of the empire, Cyrus stationed horsemen at proper intervals on all the great public highways. One of those delivered the message to another, and intelligence was thus rapidly and safely communicated. These heralds were permitted to *compel* any person, or to press any horse, boat, ship, or other vehicle that they might need for the quick transmission of the king's commandments. It was to this custom that our Saviour refers. Rather, says he, than *resist* a public authority requiring your attendance and aid for a certain distance, go peaceably twice the distance. ¶ *A mile.* A Roman *mile* was a thousand paces. ¶ *Twain.* Two.

42. *Give to him that asketh thee.* This is the general rule. It is better to give sometimes to an undeserving person than to turn away one really necessitous. It is good to be *in the habit* of giving. At the same time, the rule must be interpreted so as to be consistent with our duty to our families (1 Ti. v. 8) and with other objects of justice and charity. It is seldom, perhaps never, good to give to a man that is able to work, 2 Th. iii. 10. To give to such is to encourage laziness, and to support the idle at the expense of the industrious. If such a man is indeed hungry, feed him; if he wants anything farther, give him employment. If a widow, an orphan, a man of misfortune, or a man infirm, lame, or sick, is at your door, never send any of them away empty. See He. xiii. 2; Mat. xxv. 35-45. So of a poor and needy friend that wishes to borrow. We are not to turn away or deny him. This deserves, however, some limitation. It must be done in consistency with other duties. To lend to every worthless man would be to throw away our property, encourage laziness and crime, and ruin our families. It should be done consistently with every other obligation, and of this every man is to be the judge. Perhaps our Saviour meant to teach that where there was a *deserving* friend or brother in want, we should *lend* to him without usury, and without *standing much* about the security.

43. *Ye have heard that it hath been said, Thou shalt love thy neighbour, and hate thine enemy.* The command to love our neighbour was a law of God, Le. xix. 18. That we must therefore hate our enemy was an inference drawn from it by the Jews. They supposed that if we loved the one, we must of course hate the other. They were total strangers to that great, peculiar law of religion which requires us to love both. *A neighbour* is literally one that *lives* near to us; then, one that *is near* to us by acts of kindness and friendship. This is its meaning here. See also Lu. x. 36.

44. *Love your enemies.* There are two kinds of love, involving the same general feeling, or springing from the same fountain of good-will to all mankind, but differing so far as to admit of separation in idea. The one is that feeling by which we *approve of the conduct* of another, commonly called *the love of complacency;* the other, that by which we wish well to the *person* of another, though we cannot approve *his conduct.* This is *the love of benevolence*, and this love we are to bear toward our enemies. It is impossible to love the *conduct* of a man that curses and reviles us, that injures our person or property, or that violates all the laws of God; but, though

45 That ye may be the children of your Father which is in heaven: for [p]he maketh his sun to rise on the evil and on the good, and sendeth rain on the just and on the unjust.

46 For if ye love them which love you, what reward have ye? do not even the publicans the same?

47 And if ye salute your brethren only, what do ye more *than others?* do not even the publicans so?

48 Be ye therefore [q]perfect, even as your Father which is in heaven is perfect.

p Job 25.3.

q Ge.17.1; De.18.13; Lu.6.36,40; Col.1.28.

---

we may hate his conduct, and suffer keenly when *we* are affected by it, yet we may still wish well to the *person;* we may pity his madness and folly; we may speak kindly *of* him and *to* him; we may return good for evil; we may aid him in the time of trial; we may seek to do him good here and to promote his eternal welfare hereafter, Ro. xii. 17-20. This seems to be what is meant by loving our enemies; and this is a peculiar law of Christianity, and the highest possible test of piety, and probably the most difficult of all duties to be performed. ¶ *Bless them that curse you.* The word *bless* here means to *speak well of* or *to:*—not to curse again or to slander, but to speak of those things which we can *commend* in an enemy; or, if there is nothing that we can commend, to say nothing about him. The word *bless*, spoken of God, means to regard with favour or to confer benefits, as when God is said to bless his people. When we speak of our *blessing God*, it means to praise him or give thanks to him. When we speak of blessing *men*, it *unites* the two meanings, and signifies to confer favour, to thank, or to speak well of. ¶ *Despitefully use you.* The word thus translated means, first, to injure by prosecution in law; then, wantonly and unjustly to accuse, and to injure in any way. This seems to be its meaning here. ¶ *Persecute.* See Notes on ch. v. 10.

45. *That ye may be the children of your Father.* In Greek, the *sons* of your Father. The word son has a variety of significations. See Notes on Mat. i. 1. Christians are called the *sons* or *children* of God in several of these senses: as his offspring; as adopted; as his disciples; as imitators of him. In this passage the word is applied to them because, in doing good to enemies, they *resemble* God. *He* makes his sun to rise on the evil and good, and sends rain, without distinction, on the just and unjust. So his people should show that they *imitate* or resemble him, or that they possess his spirit, by doing good in a similar way.

46. *What reward have ye?* The word reward seems to be used in the sense of *deserving of praise.* If you only love those that love you, you are selfish; it is not genuine love for the *character*, but love for the *benefit*, and you deserve no commendation. The very *publicans* would do the same. ¶ *The publicans.* The publicans were tax-gatherers. Judea was a province of the Roman empire. The Jews bore this foreign yoke with great impatience, and paid their taxes with great reluctance. It happened, therefore, that those who were appointed to collect taxes were objects of great detestation. They were, besides, men who would be supposed to execute their office at all hazards; men who were willing to engage in an odious and hated employment; men often of abandoned character, oppressive in their exactions, and dissolute in their lives. By the Jews they were associated in character with thieves and adulterers; with the profane and the dissolute. Christ says that even these wretched men would love their benefactors.

47. *And if you salute your brethren,* &c. The word *salute* here means to show the customary tokens of civility, or to treat with the common marks of friendship. See Notes on Lu. x. 4. The Saviour says that the *worst* men, the very publicans, would do this. Christians should do more; they should show that they have a different spirit; they should treat their *enemies* as well as wicked men do their *friends.* This should be done: 1st. Because it is *right;* it is the only really amiable spirit; and, 2d. We should show that religion is not *selfish*, and is superior to all other principles of action.

48. *Be ye therefore perfect,* &c. The Saviour concludes this part of the discourse by commanding his disciples to be *perfect.* This word commonly means finished, complete, pure, holy. Origin-

ally it is applied to a piece of mechanism, as a machine that is complete in its parts. Applied to men, it refers to completeness of parts, or *perfection*, where no part is defective or wanting. Thus Job (i. 1) is said to be "perfect;" that is, not holy as God, or *sinless*—for fault is afterward found with him (Job ix. 20; xlii. 6); but his piety was *proportionate*—had a completeness of parts —was consistent and regular. He exhibited his religion as a prince, a father, an individual, a benefactor of the poor. He was not merely a pious man in one place, but uniformly. He was consistent everywhere. See Notes on that passage. This is the meaning in Matthew. Be not religious merely in loving your friends and neighbours, but let your piety be shown in loving your enemies; imitate God; let your piety be *complete, proportionate, regular*. This every Christian *may be;* this every Christian *must be.*

REMARKS ON CHAPTER V.

1st. The gospel pronounces blessings on things far different from what the world has thought to be a source of happiness. Men suppose that happiness is to be found in mirth, in wealth, in honour, in esteem, in freedom from persecution. Christ says that it is to be sought in the reverse. Often men are most happy in poverty, in sickness, in persecution, when supported by the presence and promises of a merciful God. And if God appoints our station there, we should submit to it, and learn therewith to be content.

2d. We may see the evil of anger. It is a species of murder. If secretly cherished, or exhibited by contempt and injury, it must bring down the displeasure of God. It is a source of misery. True enjoyment is found in meekness, peace, calmness, and benevolence. In such a firmness, and steadiness, and dependence on God as to keep the soul unruffled in the midst of provocation, is happiness. Such was Christ.

3d. We see the evil of indelicacy of feeling and sentiment, and the strictness and severity of the law respecting the intercourse of the sexes (ver. 28). And yet what law is more frequently violated? By obscene anecdotes and tales; by songs and gibes; by double meanings and innuendoes; by looks and gestures; by conversation, and obscene books and pictures, this law of our Saviour is perpetually violated. If there is any one sentiment of most value for the comfort, the character, the virtuous sociability of the young—one that will shed the greatest charm over society, and make it the most pure, it is that which inculcates *perfect delicacy* and *purity* in the intercourse of the sexes. Virtue of any kind never blooms where this is not cherished. Modesty and purity once gone, every flower that would diffuse its fragrance over life withers and dies with it. There is no one sin that so withers and blights *every* virtue, none that so enfeebles and prostrates every ennobling feeling of the soul, as the violation of the seventh commandment in spirit or in form, in thought or in act. How should purity dwell in the heart, breathe from the lips, kindle in the eye, live in the imagination, and dwell in the intercourse of all the young! An eternal, avenging God is near to every wanton thought, marks every eye that kindles with impure desire, rolls the thunder of justice over every polluted soul, and is preparing woe for every violator of the laws of purity and chastity, Pr. vii. 22, 23; v. 5; ii. 18.

4th. Revenge is equally forbidden. Persecution, slander, a spirit of litigation, anger, personal abuse, duelling, suicide, murder, are all violations of the law of God, and all must call down his vengeance.

5th. We are bound to love our enemies. This is a law of Christianity, original and peculiar. No system of religion but Christianity has required it, and no act of Christian piety is more difficult. None shows more the power of the grace of God; none is more ornamental to the character; none more like God; and none furnishes better evidence of piety. He that can meet a man kindly who is seeking his hurt; who can speak well of one that is perpetually slandering and cursing him; that can pray for a man that abuses, injures, and wounds him; and that can seek heaven for him that wishes *his* damnation, is in the way to life. This is religion, beautiful as its native skies; pure like its Source; kind like its Author; fresh like the dews of the morning; clear and diffusive like the beams of the rising sun; and holy like the feelings and words that come from the bosom of the Son of God. He that can do this need not doubt that he is a Christian. He has caught the very spirit of the Saviour, and he *must* inherit eternal life.

CHAPTER VI.

TAKE heed that ye do not your [1]alms before men, to be seen of them: otherwise ye have no reward [2]of your Father which is in heaven.

2 Therefore when thou doest *thine* alms, [3]do not sound a trumpet before thee, as the hypocrites do in the synagogues and in the streets, that they may have glory of men. Verily I say unto you, They have their reward.

3 But when thou doest alms, let not thy left hand know what thy right hand doeth:

4 That thine alms may be in secret; and thy Father, which seeth in secret, himself [a]shall reward thee openly.

1 or, *righteousness*, Ps.112.9.
2 or, *with*. 3 or, *cause not a trumpet to be sounded.*

a Lu.8.17; 14.14.

CHAPTER VI.

1. *Take heed that ye do not your alms.* The word *alms* here denotes liberality to the poor and needy. In the margin, as in the best editions of the Greek, it is *righteousness;* either referring to almsgiving as eminently a righteous act, or more probably including all that is specified in this and the following verses—almsgiving, prayer, fasting, ver. 2–18. Our Saviour here does not positively *command* his disciples to aid the poor, but supposes that they *would do* it of course, and gives them directions *how* to do it. It is the nature of religion to help those who are really needy; and a real Christian does not wait to be *commanded* to do it, but only asks for the opportunity. See Ga. ii. 10; Ja. i. 27; Lu. xix. 8. ¶ *Before men, &c.* Our Lord does not require us never to give alms before men, but only forbids our doing it *to be seen of them*, for the purposes of ostentation and to seek their praise. To a person who is disposed to do good from a right motive, it matters little whether it be in public or in private. The only thing that renders it even desirable that our good deeds should be seen is that God may be glorified. See ch. v. 16. ¶ *Otherwise.* If your only motive for doing it is to be seen of men, God will not reward you. Take heed, therefore, that you do not do it to be seen, *otherwise* God will not reward you

2. *Do not sound a trumpet before thee, as the hypocrites do.* The word *hypocrite* is taken from *stage-players*, who act the part of others, or speak not their own sentiments, but the sentiments of others. It means here, and in the New Testament generally, those who *dissemble* or hide their real sentiments, and assume or express other feelings than their own—those who, for purposes of ostentation, gain, or applause, put on the appearance of religion. It is probable that such persons, when they were about to bestow alms, caused a trumpet to be sounded, *professedly* to call the poor together to receive it, but *really* to call the people to see the proofs of their liberality and piety; or perhaps it may mean that they should not make a great noise about it, *like* sounding a trumpet. ¶ *In the synagogues.* The word *synagogue* commonly means the place of assembling for religious worship known by that name. See Notes on Mat. iv. 23. It might mean, however, any *collection of people* assembled for any purpose, and it is not improbable that it has that meaning here. It does not appear that they made a noise in bestowing charity in the *synagogues*, or that charity was commonly bestowed there; but it was probably done on occasion of any great *assemblage*, in any place of concourse, and at the *corners of the streets*, where it could be seen by many. ¶ *They have their reward.* That is, they obtain the applause they seek the reputation of being charitable; and as this applause was *all* they wished, there is, of course, no farther reward to be looked for or obtained.

3, 4. *Let not thy left hand know, &c.* This is a proverbial expression, signifying that the action should be done as secretly as possible. The Hebrews often attribute actions to *members* which properly belong to *persons.* The encouragement for performing our acts of charity in secret is that it will be pleasing to God; that he will see the act, however secret it may be, and will openly reward it. If the reward is not granted in *this* life, it will be in the life to come. In multitudes of cases, however, alms given to the poor are "lent to the Lord" (Pr. xix. 17), and will be repaid in this life. Rarely, perhaps never, has it been found that the man who is liberal to the poor has ever

5 And when thou prayest, thou shalt not be as the hypocrites *are:* for they love to pray standing in the synagogues and in the corners of the streets, that they may be seen of men. Verily I say unto you, [b]They have their reward.

6 But thou, when thou prayest,

b Pr.16.5; Ja.4.6.

suffered by it in his worldly circumstances.

5. *And when thou prayest*, &c. Hypocrites manifested the same spirit about prayer as almsgiving; it was done in public places. The word *synagogues*, here, clearly means, not the place of worship of that name, but places where many were accustomed to assemble—near the markets or courts, where they could be seen of many. Our Lord evidently could not mean to condemn prayers in the synagogues. It might be said that he condemned *ostentatious* prayer there, while they neglected *secret* prayer; but this does not appear to be his design. The Jews were much in the habit of praying in public places. At certain times of the day they always offered their prayers. Wherever they were, they suspended their employment and paid their devotions. This is also practised now everywhere by Mohammedans, and in many places by Roman Catholics. It seems, also, that they *sought* publicity, and regarded it as proof of great piety.

6. *Enter into thy closet.* Every Jewish house had a place for secret devotion. The roofs of their houses were *flat* places, well adapted for walking, conversation, and meditation. See Notes on Mat. ix. 2. Professor Hackett (*Illustrations of Scripture*, p. 82) says: "On the roof of the house in which I lodged at Damascus were chambers and rooms along the side and at the corners of the open space or terrace, which constitutes often a sort of upper story. I observed the same thing in connection with other houses." Over the *porch*, or entrance of the house, there was frequently a small room of the size of the porch, raised a story above the rest of the house, expressly appropriated for the place of retirement. Here, in secrecy and solitude, the pious Jew might offer his prayers, unseen by any but the Searcher of hearts. To this place, or to some similar place, our Saviour directed his disciples to repair when they wished to hold communion with God. This is the place commonly mentioned in the New Testament as the *upper room*, or the place for secret prayer. The meaning of the Saviour is, that there should be some place where we may be in secret—where we may be alone with God. There should be some *place* to which we may resort where no ear will hear us but *His* ear, and no eye can see us but *His* eye. Unless there is such a place, secret prayer will not be long or strictly maintained. It is often said that we have no such place, and can secure none. We are away from home; we are travelling; we are among strangers; we are in stages and steamboats, and how can we find such places of retirement? I answer, the *desire* to pray, and the love of prayer, will *create* such places in abundance. The Saviour had all the difficulties which we can have, but yet he lived in the practice of secret prayer. To be alone, he rose up "a great while before day," and went into a solitary place and prayed, Mar. i. 35. With him a grove, a mountain, a garden, furnished such a place, and, though a traveller, and among strangers, and without a house, he lived in the habit of secret prayer. What excuse can they have for not praying who have a home, and who spend the precious hours of the morning in sleep, and who will practise no self-denial that they may be alone with God? O Christian! thy Saviour would have broken in upon these hours, and would have trod his solitary way to the mountain or the grove that he might pray. He *did* do it. He did it to pray for thee, too indolent and too unconcerned about thy own salvation and that of the world to practise the least self-denial in order to commune with God! How can religion live thus? How can such a soul be saved?

The Saviour does not specify the *times* when we should pray in secret. He does not say how *often* it should be done. The reasons may have been: (1.) That he designed that his religion should be *voluntary*, and there is not a better *test* of true piety than a disposition to engage often in secret prayer. He intended to leave it to his people to show attachment to him by coming to God often, and as often as they chose. (2.) An attempt to specify the times when this should be done would tend to make religion formal and heartless.

enter into thy closet, and, when thou hast shut thy door, pray to thy Father which is in secret; and thy Father, which seeth in secret, [c]shall reward thee openly.

7 But when ye pray, [d]use not

c Ps.34.15; Is.65.24. d Ec.5.2.

Mohammed undertook to regulate this, and the consequence is a cold and formal prostration at the appointed hours of prayer all over the land where his religion has spread. (3.) The periods are so numerous, and the seasons for secret prayer vary so much, that it would not be easy to fix rules when this should be done. Yet without giving rules, where the Saviour has given none, we may suggest the following as times when secret prayer is proper: 1. In the morning. Nothing can be more appropriate when we have been preserved through the night, and when we are about to enter upon the duties and dangers of another day, than to render to our great Preserver thanks, and to commit ourselves to his fatherly care. 2. In the evening. When the day has closed, what more natural than to offer thanksgiving for the mercies of the day, and to implore forgiveness for what we have said or done amiss? and when about to lie down again to sleep, not knowing but it may be our *last* sleep and that we may awake in eternity, what more proper than to commend ourselves to the care of Him "who never slumbers nor sleeps?" 3. We should pray in times of embarrassment and perplexity. Such times occur in every man's life, and it is then a privilege and a duty to go to God and seek his direction. In the most difficult and embarrassed time of the American Revolution, Washington was seen to retire to a grove in the vicinity of the camp at Valley Forge. Curiosity led a man to observe him, and the father of his country was seen on his knees supplicating the God of hosts in prayer. Who can tell how much the liberty of this nation is owing to the answer to the secret prayer of Washington? 4. We should pray when we are beset with strong temptations. So the Saviour prayed in the garden of Gethsemane (comp. He. v. 7, 8), and so we should pray when we are tempted. 5. We should pray when the Spirit prompts us to pray; when we feel *just like praying;* when nothing can satisfy the soul but prayer. Such times occur in the life of every Christian, and they are "spring-times" of piety—favourable gales to waft us on to heaven. Prayer to the Christian, at such times, is just as congenial as conversation with a friend when the bosom is filled with love; as the society of father, mother, sister, child is, when the heart glows with attachment; as the strains of sweet music are to the ear best attuned to the love of harmony; as the most exquisite poetry is to the heart enamoured with the muses; and as the most delicious banquet is to the hungry. Prayer, then, is the element of being—the breath—the vital air; and, then, the Christian must and should pray. He is the most eminent Christian who is most favoured with such strong emotions urging him to prayer. The heart is then full; the soul is tender; the sun of glory shines with unusual splendour; no cloud intervenes; the Christian rises above the world, and pants for glory. *Then* we may go to be alone with God. We may enter the closet, and breathe forth our warm desires into his ever-open ear, and he who sees in secret will reward us openly. ¶ *In secret.* Who is unseen. ¶ *Who seeth in secret.* Who sees what the human eye cannot see; who sees the real designs and desires of the heart. Prayer should always be offered, remembering that God is acquainted with our *real desires;* and that it is those real desires, and not the *words* of prayer, that he will answer.

7. *Use not vain repetitions.* The original word here is supposed to be derived from the name of a Greek poet, who made long and weary verses, declaring by many forms and endless repetitions the same sentiment. Hence it means to repeat a thing often; to say the same thing in different words, or to repeat the same words, as though God did not *hear* at first. An example of this we have in 1 Ki. xviii. 26: "They called on Baal from morning until noon, saying, O Baal, hear us!"* It may serve to illustrate this passage, and to show how true is the description here of prevailing modes of prayer, to refer to the forms and modes of devotion still practised in Palestine by the Mohammedans. Dr. Thomson (*The Land and the Book*) gives

* The following is a *specimen* of the *vain repetitions* of the Romans: "Pious Antonine, the gods preserve thee. Gentle Antonine, the gods preserve thee. Gentle Antonine, the gods preserve thee."

vain repetitions, as the [h]heathen *do:* [e]for they think that they shall be heard for their much speaking.

8 Be not ye therefore like unto them: [f]for your Father knoweth what things ye have need of before ye ask him.

9 After this manner therefore

e 1 Ki.18.26,&c.

f Lu.12.30; Jn.16.23-27.

---

the following description of what actually occurs:—"See those men on that elevated terrace. One has spread his cloak, others their Persian rugs toward the south. They are Moslems, preparing to say prayers—*perform* them rather, in this most public place, and in the midst of all this noise and confusion.

"Let us stop and watch the ceremony as it goes on. That man next us raises his open hands till the thumbs touch the ears, exclaiming aloud, *Allah-hû-akbar*—'God is great.' After uttering mentally a few short petitions, the hands are brought down and folded together near the girdle, while he recites the first chapter of the Koran, and two or three other brief passages from the same book. And now he bends forward, rests his hands upon his knees, and repeats three times a formula of praise to 'God most great.' Then, standing erect, he cries *Allah-hû-akbar*, as at the beginning. Then see him drop upon his knees, and bend forward until his nose and forehead touch the ground directly between his expanded hands. This he repeats three times, muttering all the while the same short formulas of prayer and praise. The next move will bring him to his knees, and then, settling back upon his heels, he will mumble over various small petitions, with sundry grunts and exclamations, according to taste and habit. He has now gone through one regular Rek'āh; and, standing up as at the first, and on exactly the same spot, he will perform a second, and even a third, if specially devout, with precisely the same genuflections.

"They are obliged to repeat some expressions thirty times, others many hundred times. Would that these remarks did not apply to nominal Christians in this land as well as to Moslems!" ¶ *The heathen* do. The original word is that which is commonly translated *Gentile.* The world was divided into two parts, the Jews and the Gentiles; that is, in the original, the "*nations*," the nations destitute of the true religion. Christ does not fix the *length* of our prayers. He says that we should not repeat the same thing, as though God did not hear; and it is not improbable that he intended to condemn the practice of long prayers. His own supplications were remarkably short.

9–13. This passage contains the Lord's prayer, a composition unequalled for comprehensiveness and for beauty. It is supposed that some of these petitions were taken from those in common use among the Jews. Indeed some of them are still to be found in Jewish writings, but they did not exist in this beautiful combination. This prayer is given as a *model.* It is designed to express the *manner* in which we are to pray, evidently not the precise words or petitions which we are to use. The substance of the prayer is recorded by Luke, ch. xi. 2, 3, 4. In Luke, however, it varies from the form given in Matthew, showing that he intended not to prescribe this as a *form* of prayer to be used always, but to express the *substance* of our petitions, or to show what petitions it would be proper to present to God. That he did not intend to prescribe this as a *form* to be invariably used is farther evident from the fact that there is no proof that either he or his disciples ever used exactly this form of prayer, but clear evidence that they prayed often in other language. See Mat. xxvi. 39–42, 44; Lu. xxii. 42; Jn. xvii.; Ac. i. 24.

9. *Our Father.* God is called a Father, 1st, as he is the Creator and the Great Parent of all; 2d, the Preserver of the human family and the Provider for their wants, ch. v. 45; vi. 32; 3d, in a peculiar sense he is the Father of those who are adopted into his family; who put confidence in him; who are the true followers of Christ, and made heirs of life, Ro. viii. 14–17. ¶ *Hallowed be thy name.* The word hallowed means to render or pronounce holy. God's name is essentially holy; and the meaning of this petition is, "Let thy name be celebrated, venerated, and *esteemed as holy* everywhere, and receive from all men proper honour." It is thus the expression of a *wish* or desire, on the part of the worshipper, that the name of God, or that God himself, should be held everywhere in proper veneration.

pray ye: [g]Our [h]Father which art in[i] heaven, [k]Hallowed be thy name:

10 Thy [l]kingdom come. [m]Thy will be done, in earth as *it is* in heaven:

11 Give us this day our [n]daily bread:

12 And [o]forgive us our debts, as we forgive our debtors:

g Lu.11.2,&c. h Ro.8.15. i Ps.115.3. k Ps.111.9; 139.20. l ch.16.28; Re.11.15. m Ps.103.20,21. n Pr.30.8; Is.33.16. o ch.18.21-35; Lu.7.40-48.

10. *Thy kingdom come.* The word *kingdom* here means *reign.* Note, Mat. iii. 2. The petition is the expression of a wish that God may *reign* everywhere; that his laws may be obeyed; and especially that the gospel of Christ may be advanced everywhere, till the world shall be filled with his glory. ¶ *Thy will be done.* The will of God is, that men should obey his law, and be holy. The word *will*, here, has reference to his law, and to what would be *acceptable* to him. To pray, then, that his will may be done, on earth as in heaven, is to pray that his *law*, his *revealed will*, may be obeyed and loved. His law is perfectly obeyed in heaven, and his true children most ardently desire and pray that it may also be obeyed on the earth.

The object of these three *first* petitions, is, that God's name should be glorified and his kingdom established; and by being placed *first*, we learn that *his glory* and *kingdom* are of more consequence than *our* wants, and that these should be *first* in our hearts and petitions before a throne of grace.*

11. *Give us this day*, &c. The word bread, here, denotes doubtless everything necessary to sustain life. See Notes on Mat. iv. 4. Comp. De. viii. 3. This petition implies our dependence on God for the supply of our wants. As we are dependent on him one day as much as another, it was evidently the intention of the Saviour that prayer should be offered every day. The petition, moreover, is expressed in the plural number—give US—and it is evidently, therefore, intended to be used by more than one, or by some community of people. No community or congregation can meet every day for worship but families. It is therefore evident that this prayer contains a strong implied command for daily family prayer. It can nowhere else be used so as fully to come up to the meaning of the original intention; and nowhere else can it be breathed forth with so much propriety and beauty as from the lips of a father, the venerable priest of his household, and the pleader with God for those rich blessings which a parental bosom desires on his beloved offspring.

12. *And forgive us our debts*, &c. The word *debts* is here used figuratively. It does not mean *literally* that we are *debtors to God*, but that our sins have a resemblance to debts. Debtors are those who are bound to others for some claim in commercial transactions; for something which we have had, and for which we are bound to pay according to contract. *Literally* there can be no such transaction between God and us. It must be used figuratively. We have not met the claims of law. We have violated its obligations. We are exposed to its penalty. We are guilty, and God only can forgive, in the same way as none but a *creditor* can forgive a debtor. The word *debts* here, therefore, means *sins*, or offences against God—offences which none but God can forgive. In the parallel place in Lu. xi. 4, the word *sins* is used. The measure by which we may expect forgiveness is that which *we use* in reference to others. See Ps. xviii. 25, 26; Mat. xviii. 23; Mar. xi. 26; Lu. xi. 4. This is the invariable rule by which God dispenses pardon. He that comes before him unwilling to forgive, harbouring dark and revengeful thoughts, how can he expect that God will show him that mercy which he is unwilling to show to others? It is not, however, required that we should forgive *debts* in a pecuniary sense. To them we have a right, though they should not be pushed with an overbearing and oppressive spirit; not so as to

* Several of the petitions in this prayer are found in the writings of the Jews, and were doubtless familiar in the time of Christ. "That prayer," say the Rabbins, "in which there is no mention made of the kingdom of heaven, is *not* a prayer," "What," say they, "is a short prayer? *Answer.* Do thy will in heaven, and give rest to the spirits fearing thee below." "Give us this day," &c. The Jews had a prayer like this: "The necessities of thy people are many, and their knowledge small, so that they do not know how to make known their wants: let it be thy good pleasure to give to each one what is necessary for his sustenance," &c. "Deliver us from evil." The Jews prayed, "Be it thy good pleasure to free us from an evil man, and an evil event; from evil affections, from an evil companion and neighbour, from Satan," &c. The prayers of the Jews were generally closed with a doxology, or ascription of praise, not unlike this in the Lord's prayer. The people, at the close of the prayer, generally responded "Amen."

13 And [p]lead us not into temptation, but [q]deliver us from evil: for[r] thine is the kingdom, and the power, and the glory for ever. Amen.

14 For[s] if ye forgive men their

p ch.26.41; Lu.22.40,46. q Jn.17.15. r Re.5.12,13. s Ep.4.31.

sacrifice the feelings of mercy in order to secure the claims of justice. No man has a right to oppress; and when a debt cannot be paid, or when it would greatly distress a debtor's wife and children, or a widow and an orphan, or when calamity has put it out of the power of an honest man to pay the debt, the spirit of Christianity requires that it should be forgiven. To such cases this petition in the Lord's prayer doubtless extends. But it was probably intended to refer principally to injuries of character or person which we have received from others. If we cannot from the heart forgive *them*, we have the assurance that God will *never* forgive us.

13. *And lead us not into temptation.* A petition similar to this is offered by David, Ps. cxli. 4: "Incline not my heart to any evil thing, to practise wicked works with the workers of iniquity." God tempts no man. See Ja. i. 13. This phrase, then, must be used in the sense of *permitting*. Do not *suffer* us, or *permit* us, to be tempted to sin. In this it is implied that God has such control over the tempter as to save us from his power if we call upon him. The word *temptation*, however (see Note ch. iv. 1), means sometimes *trial*, *affliction*, anything that *tests* our virtue. If this be the meaning here, as it may be, then the import of the prayer is, "Do not afflict or try us." It is not wrong to pray that we may be saved from suffering if it be the will of God. See Lu. xxii. 42. ¶ *Deliver us from evil.* The original in this place has the article —deliver us from THE *evil*—that is, as has been supposed, the Evil One, or Satan. He is elsewhere called, by way of eminence, the *Evil One*, Mat. xiii. 19; 1 Jn. ii. 13, 14; iii. 12. The meaning here is, "deliver us from his power, his snares, his arts, his temptations." He is supposed to be the great parent of evil, and to be delivered from him is to be safe. Or it may mean, "deliver us from the various evils and trials which beset us, the heavy and oppressive calamities into which we are continually liable to fall." ¶ *Thine is the kingdom.* That is, thine is the *reign* or *dominion*. Thou hast control over all these things, and canst so order them as to answer these petitions. ¶ *Thine is the power.* Thou hast power to accomplish what we ask. *We* are weak, and cannot do it; but thou art Almighty, and all things are possible with thee. ¶ *Thine is the glory.* That is, thine is the honour or praise. Not for *our honour*, but that thy glory, thy goodness, may be displayed in providing for our wants; thy power exerted in defending us; thy praise be celebrated by causing thy kingdom to spread through the earth.

This *doxology*, or ascription of praise, is connected with the prayer by the word "*for*," to signify that all these things—the reign, power, and glory of God—will be manifested by granting these petitions. It is not because *we* are to be benefited, but that God's name and perfections may be manifested. *His* glory is, then, the first and principal thing which we are to seek when we approach him. We are to suffer *our* concerns to be lost sight of in the superior glory and honour of his name and dominion. We are to seek temporal and eternal life chiefly because the honour of our Maker will be promoted, and his name be more illustriously displayed to his creatures. He is to be "first, last, supremest, best," in our view; and all selfish and worldly views are to be absorbed in that one great desire of the soul that God may be "all in all." Approaching him with these feelings, our prayers will be answered; our devotions will ascend like incense, and the lifting up our hands will be like the evening sacrifice.

Amen. This is a word of Hebrew origin, from a verb signifying *to be firm*, *secure*, *to be true* and *faithful*. It is a word expressing consent or strong approbation; a word of strong asseveration. It means *verily*, *certainly*, *so be it*. It is probable that this word was used by the people in the synagogue to signify their assent to the prayer that was uttered by the minister, and, to some extent, it was probably so used in the Christian Church. See 1 Co. xiv. 16.

It may be proper to remark that this doxology, "for thine is the kingdom," &c., is wanting in many manuscripts, and that its authenticity is doubtful.

trespasses, your heavenly Father will also forgive you.

15 But[t] if ye forgive not men their trespasses, neither will your Father forgive your trespasses.

16 Moreover, [u]when ye fast, be not, as the hypocrites, of a sad countenance: for they disfigure their faces, that they may appear unto men to fast. Verily I say unto you, They have their reward.

17 But thou, when thou fastest,

t Ja.2.13. u Is.58.3,5.

14, 15. *For if ye forgive men their trespasses.* If ye forgive others when they offend or injure you. ¶ *Your heavenly Father will also forgive you.* This is constantly required in the Bible. See Notes on ver. 12. Our Saviour says we should forgive even if the offence be committed seventy times seven times, Mat. xviii. 22. By this is meant, that when a man *asks* forgiveness, we are cordially and for ever to pardon the offence; we are to *declare* our willingness to forgive him. If he does not *ask* forgiveness, yet we are still to treat him kindly; not to harbour malice, not to speak ill of him, to be ready to do him good, and be always *prepared* to *declare* him forgiven when he asks it, and if we are not ready and willing to forgive him, we are assured that God will not forgive us.

16. *Moreover, when ye fast.* The word *fast* literally signifies to abstain from food and drink, whether from necessity or as a religious observance. It is, however, commonly applied in the Bible to the latter. It is, then, an expression of grief or sorrow. Such is the constitution of the body, that in a time of grief or sorrow we are not *disposed* to eat; or, we have no appetite. The grief of the *soul* is so absorbing as to destroy the natural appetites of the *body*. Men in deep affliction eat little, and often pine away and fall into sickness, because the *body* refuses, on account of the deep sorrow of the *mind*, to discharge the functions of health. *Fasting, then, is the natural expression of grief.* It is not arbitrary; it is what every person in sorrow naturally does. This is the foundation of its being applied to religion as a sacred rite. It is because the soul, when oppressed and burdened by a sense of sin, is so filled with grief that the body refuses food. It is, therefore, appropriate to scenes of penitence, of godly sorrow, of suffering, and to those facts connected with religion which are fitted to produce grief, as the prevalence of iniquity, or some dark impending calamity, or storm, or tempest, pestilence, plague, or famine. It is also useful to humble us, to bring us to reflection, to direct the thoughts away from the allurements of this world to the bliss of a better. It is not acceptable except it be the *real expression* of sorrow; the natural effect of the feeling that we are burdened with crime.

The Jews fasted often. They had four *annual fasts*—in commemoration of the capture of Jerusalem (Je. lii. 7), of the burning of the temple (Zec. vii. 3), of the death of Gedaliah (Je. xli. 4), and of the commencement of the attack on Jerusalem (Zec. viii. 19). In addition to these, they had a multitude of occasional fasts. It was customary, also, for the Pharisees to fast twice a week, Lu. xviii. 12. ¶ *Of a sad countenance.* That is, sour, morose; with assumed expressions of unfelt sorrow. ¶ *They disfigure their faces.* That is, they do not anoint and wash themselves as usual; they are uncombed, filthy, squalid, and haggard. It is said that they were often in the habit of throwing *ashes* on their heads and faces; and this, mixing with their tears, served still farther to disfigure their faces. So much pains will men take, and so much suffering will they undergo, and so much that is ridiculous will they assume, to impose on God and men. But they deceive neither. God sees through the flimsy veil. Human eyes can pierce a disguise so thin. Hypocrites overact their part. Not having the genuine principles of piety at heart, they know not what is its proper expression, and hence they appear supremely contemptible and abominable. Never should men exhibit outwardly more than they *feel;* and never should they attempt to *exhibit* anything for the mere sake of ostentation. ¶ *They have their reward.* They have all that they desired—the praise of men and *the pleasure of ostentation.* See Notes on ver. 2.

17, 18. *But thou when thou fastest, anoint,* &c. That is, appear as you do daily. Do not assume any new appearance, or change your visage or dress. The Jews and all neighbouring nations

anoint thine head, and wash thy face:

18 That thou appear not unto men to fast, but unto thy Father which is in secret: and thy Father, which seeth in secret, shall reward thee openly.

19 Lay[v] not up for yourselves treasures upon earth, where moth and rust doth corrupt, and where thieves break through and steal;

20 But[w] lay up for yourselves treasures in heaven, where neither moth nor rust doth corrupt, and where thieves do not break through nor steal:

21 For where your treasure is, there will your heart be also.

22 The[x] light of the body is the eye: If, therefore, thine eye be single, thy whole body shall be full of light:

23 But if thine eye be evil, thy whole body shall be full of dark-

v Pr.23.4; Lu.18.24,35; He.13.5.
w Is.33.6; Lu.12.33,34; 1 Ti.6.19.

x Lu.11.34,36.

---

were much in the habit of washing and anointing their bodies. This washing was performed at every meal; and where it could be effected, the head, or other parts of the body, was daily anointed with sweet or olive oil. In a warm climate, exposed to the great heat of the sun, this practice conduced much to health, preserved the skin smooth and tender, and afforded a most grateful sensation and odour. See Mar. vii. 2, 3; Ja. v. 14; Mar. xi. 13; Jn. xii. 3.

The meaning of this whole commandment is, when you regard it to be your duty to fast, do it as a thing expressing deep feeling or sorrow for sin, not by assuming unfelt gravity and moroseness, but in your ordinary dress and appearance; not to attract attention, but as an expression of feeling towards God, and he will approve and reward it.

19. *Lay not up for yourselves treasures upon earth.* Treasures, or wealth, among the ancients, consisted in clothes or changes of raiment, as well as in gold, silver, gems, wine, lands, and oil. It meant an abundance of *anything* that was held to be conducive to the ornament or comfort of life. As the Orientals delighted much in display, in splendid equipage, and costly garments, their treasures, in fact, consisted much in beautiful and richly-ornamented articles of apparel. See Ge. xlv. 22, where Joseph gave to his brethren *changes of raiment;* Jos. vii. 21, where Achan coveted and secreted *a goodly Babylonish garment.* Compare also Ju. xiv. 12. This fact will account for the use of the word *moth.* When *we* speak of *wealth*, we think at once of gold, and silver, and lands, and houses. When a Hebrew or an Orientalist spoke of wealth, he thought first of what would make a *display;* and included, as an essential part, splendid articles of dress. The *moth* is a small insect that finds its way to clothes and garments, and destroys them. The *moth* would destroy their apparel, the *rust* their silver and gold; thus all their treasure would waste away. The word rendered *rust* signifies anything which *eats into*, and hence anything which would consume one's property, and may have a wider signification than mere *rust.* ¶ *And where thieves break through and steal.* The houses in the East were not unfrequently made of clay hardened in the sun, or of loose stones, and hence it was comparatively easy, as it was not uncommon, for thieves to *dig through* the wall, and effect an entrance in that way. See Notes on Job xxiv. 16.

20, 21. *Lay up for yourselves treasures in heaven.* That is, have provision made for your eternal felicity. Do not exhaust your strength and spend your days in providing for the life here, but let your *chief* anxiety be to be prepared for eternity. Comp. Notes on Is. lv. 2. In heaven nothing corrupts; nothing terminates; no enemies plunder or destroy. To have treasure in heaven is to possess evidence that its purity and joys will be ours. It is to be heirs of God, and joint-heirs with Christ, to an inheritance incorruptible, undefiled, and that fadeth not away, 1 Pe. i. 4. The *heart*, or affections, will of course be fixed on the treasure. To *regulate* the heart, it is therefore important that the treasure, or object of attachment, should be right.

22, 23. *The light of the body*, &c. The sentiment stated in the preceding verses —the duty of fixing the affections on heavenly things — Jesus proceeds to illustrate by a reference to the *eye.*

ness. If, therefore, the light that is in thee be darkness, how great *is* that darkness!

24 No[y] man can serve two masters: for either he will hate the one, and love the other; or else he will hold to the one, and despise the other. Ye[z] cannot serve God and Mammon.

25 Therefore I say unto you,

y Lu.16.13.

z Ga.1.10; 2 Ti.4.10; Ja.4.4.

When the eye is directed steadily toward an object, and is in health, *or is single*, everything is clear and plain. If it *vibrates*, flies to different objects, is fixed on no one singly, or is diseased, nothing is seen clearly. Everything is dim and confused. The man, therefore, is unsteady. The *eye* regulates the motion of the body. To have an object distinctly in view is necessary in order to correct and regulate action. Rope-dancers, that they may steady themselves, fix the eye on some object on the wall, and look steadily at that. If they should look *down* on the rope or the people, they might become dizzy, and fall. A man crossing a stream on a log, if he will look *across* at some object steadily, will be in little danger. If he looks down on the dashing and rolling waters, he will become dizzy, and fall. So Jesus says, in order that the *conduct* may be right, it is important to fix the affections on heaven. Having the affections there—having the eye of faith *single*, steady, unwavering—all the conduct will be correspondent. ¶ *Single.* Steady, directed to one object. Not confused, as persons' eyes are when they see *double.* ¶ *Thy body shall be full of light.* Your *conduct* will be regular and steady. All that is needful to direct the *body* is that the *eye* be fixed right. No other *light* is required. So all that is needful to direct the *soul* and the *conduct* is, that the eye of *faith* be fixed on heaven; that the affections be there. ¶ *If, therefore, the light that is in thee*, &c. The word *light*, here, signifies *the mind*, or principles of the soul. If this be dark, how great is that darkness! The meaning of this passage may be thus expressed: The light of the body, the guide and director, is the eye. All know how calamitous it is when that light is irregular or extinguished, as when the eye is diseased or lost. So the light that is in us is the soul. If that soul is debased by attending exclusively to earthly objects—if it is diseased, and not fixed on heaven—how much darker and more dreadful will it be than any darkness of the eye! Avarice darkens the mind, obscures the view, and brings in a dreadful and gloomy night over all the faculties.

24. *No man can serve two masters*, &c. Christ proceeds to illustrate the necessity of laying up treasures in heaven from a well-known fact, that a servant cannot serve two masters at the same time. His affections and obedience would be divided, and he would fail altogether in his duty to one or the other. One he would love, the other he would hate. To the interests of the one he would adhere, the interests of the other he would neglect. This is a law of human nature. The supreme affections can be fixed on only one object. So, says Jesus, the servant of God cannot at the same time obey *him* and be avaricious, or seek treasures supremely on earth. One interferes with the other, and one or the other *will* be, and *must* be, surrendered. ¶ *Mammon.* Mammon is a Syriac word, a name given to an idol worshipped as the god of riches. It has the same meaning as Plutus among the Greeks. It is not known that the Jews ever formally worshipped this idol, but they used the word to denote wealth. The meaning is, ye cannot serve the true God, and at the same time be supremely engaged in obtaining the riches of this world. One *must* interfere with the other. See Lu. xvi. 9–11.

25–34. *Therefore I say unto you, Take no thought*, &c. The general design of this paragraph, which closes the chapter, is to warn his disciples against avarice, and, at the same time, against anxiety about the supply of their wants. This he does by *four* arguments or considerations, expressing by unequalled beauty and force the duty of depending for the things which we need on the providence of God. The *first* is stated in the 25th verse: "Is not the life more than meat, and the body than raiment?" In the beginning of the verse he charged his disciples to take *no thought*—that is, not to be *anxious*—about the supply of their wants. In illustration of this he says

Take[a] no thought for your life, what ye shall eat, or what ye shall drink; nor yet for your body, what ye shall put on. Is not the life more than meat, and the body than raiment?

26 Behold the fowls of the air: for they sow not, neither do they reap, nor gather into barns; [b]yet your heavenly Father feedeth them. Are ye not much better than they?

27 Which of you, by taking

a 1 Co.7.32; Phi.4.6.

b Job 38.41; Lu.12.24,&c.

---

that God has given *life*, a far greater blessing than *meat;* that he has created the *body*, of far more consequence than raiment. Shall not he who has conferred the *greater* blessing be willing to confer the *less?* Shall not he who has formed the body so curiously, and made in its formation such a display of power and goodness, see that it is properly protected and clothed? He who has displayed *so great* goodness as to form the body, and breathe into it the breath of life, will surely *follow up* the blessing, and confer the *smaller* favour of providing that that body shall be clothed, and that life preserved. ¶ *No thought.* The word *thought*, when the Bible was translated, meant *anxiety*, and is so used frequently in old English authors. Thus Bacon says, "Haweis died with *thought* and anguish before his business came to an end." As such it is here used by our translators, and it answers exactly to the meaning of the original. Like many other words, it has since somewhat changed its signification, and would convey to most readers an improper idea. The word *anxiety* would now exactly express the sense, and is precisely the thing against which the Saviour would guard us. See Lu. viii. 14; xxi. 34; Phi. iv. 6. *Thought* about the future is right; *anxiety*, *solicitude*, *trouble* is wrong. There is a degree of *thinking* about the things of this life which is proper. See 1 Ti. v. 8; 2 Th. iii. 10; Ro. xii. 11. But it should not be our *supreme* concern; it should not lead to anxiety; it should not take time that ought to be devoted to religion. ¶ *For your life.* For what will *support* your life. ¶ *Meat.* This word here means *food* in general, as it does commonly in the Bible. *We* confine it now to animal food. When the Bible was translated, it denoted all kinds of food, and is so used in the old English writers. It is one of the words which has changed its meaning since the translation of the Bible was made. ¶ *Raiment.* Clothing.

26. *Behold the fowls of the air.* The second argument for confidence in the providence of God is derived from a beautiful reference to the fowls or feathered tribes. See, said the Saviour, see the fowls of the air: they have no anxiety about the supply of their wants; they do not sow or reap; they fill the grove with music, and meet the coming light of the morning with their songs, and pour their notes on the zephyrs of the evening, unanxious about the supply of their wants; yet how few die with hunger! how regularly are they fed from the hand of God! how he ministers to their unnumbered wants! how cheerfully and regularly are their necessities supplied! You, said the Saviour to his disciples, you are of more consequence than they are; and shall God feed *them* in such numbers, and suffer you to want? It cannot be. Put confidence, then, in that Universal Parent that feeds all the fowls of the air, and do not fear but that he will also supply *your* wants. ¶ *Better than they.* Of more consequence. Your lives are of more importance than theirs, and God will therefore provide for them.

27. *Which of you, by taking thought.* The third argument is taken from their extreme weakness and helplessness. With all your care you cannot increase your stature a single cubit. God has ordered your height. Beyond his appointment your powers are of no avail, and you can do nothing. So of raiment. He, by his providence, orders and arranges the circumstances of your life. *Beyond* that appointment of his providence, beyond *his* care for you, your efforts avail nothing. Seeing, then, that he alike orders your *growth* and the supply of your wants, how obvious is the duty of *depending* on him, and of beginning all your efforts, feeling that he only can grant you the means of preserving life. ¶ *One cubit.* The cubit was originally the length from the elbow to the end of the middle finger. The cubit of the Scriptures is not far from 22 inches. Terms of *length* are often applied to life, and it is

thought, can add one cubit unto his stature?

28 And why take ye thought for raiment? Consider the lilies of the field, how they grow; they toil not, neither do they spin:

29 And yet I say unto you, that even Solomon in all his glory was not arrayed like one of these.

30 Wherefore, if God so clothe the grass of the field, which to-day is, and to-morrow is cast into the oven, *shall he* not much more *clothe* you, O ye of little faith?

31 Therefore[c] take no thought, saying, What shall we eat? or, What shall we drink? or, Wherewithal shall we be clothed?

32 (For after all these things do the Gentiles seek:) for your heavenly Father knoweth that ye have need of all these things.

33 But [d]seek ye first the king-

c Ps.37.3; 55.22; 1 Pe.5.7. d 1 Ti.4.8.

---

thought by many to be so here. Thus it is said, "Thou hast made my days as a handbreadth" (Ps. xxxix. 5); "Teach me the MEASURE of my days" (Ps. xxxix. 4). In this place it is used to denote a *small length.* You cannot increase your stature even a cubit, or in the smallest degree. Comp. Lu. xii. 26. ¶ *Stature.* This word means *height.* The original word, however, means oftener *age,* Jn. ix. 21: "He is of *age;*" so also ver. 23. If this be its meaning here, as is probable (comp. Robinson, *Lex.*), it denotes that a man cannot increase the length of his life at all. The utmost anxiety will not prolong it one hour beyond the time appointed for death.

28, 29. ¶ *Consider the lilies of the field.* The fourth consideration is taken from the care which God bestows on lilies. Watch the growing of the lily. It toils not, and it spins not; yet night and day it grows. With a beauty with which the most splendid monarch of the East was never adorned, it expands its blossom and fills the air with fragrance. Yet this beauty is of short continuance. Soon it will fade, and the beautiful flower will be cut down and burned. God *so little* regards the bestowment of beauty and ornament as to give the highest adorning to this which is soon to perish. When he thus clothes a lily—a fair flower, soon to perish—will he be unmindful of his children? Shall *they*—dear to his heart and imbued with immortality—lack that which is proper for them, and shall *they* in vain trust the God that decks the lily of the valley? ¶ *Even Solomon in all his glory,* &c. The common dress of Eastern kings was purple, but they sometimes wore white robes. See Es. viii. 15; Da. vii. 9. It is to this that Christ refers. Solomon, says he, the richest and most magnificent king of Israel, was not clothed in a robe *of so pure a white* as the lily that grows wild in the field.

30. *Wherefore, if God so clothe the grass of the field.* What grows up in the field, or grows wild and without culture. The word *grass,* applied here to the lily, denotes merely that it is a vegetable production, or that it is among the things which grow wild, and which are used for fuel. ¶ *Which to-day is.* It lives to-day, or it lives for a day. It is short-lived, and seems to be a thing of no value, and is so treated. ¶ *Is cast into the oven.* The Jews had different modes of baking. In early times they frequently baked in the sand, warmed with the heat of the sun. They constructed, also, movable ovens made of clay, brick, or plates of iron. But the most common kind, and the one here probably referred to, was made by excavating the earth 2½ feet in diameter, and from 5 to 6 feet deep. This kind of oven still exists in Persia. The bottom was paved with stones. It was heated by putting wood or dry grass *into* the oven, and, when heated, the ashes were removed and the bread was placed on the heated stones. Frequently, however, the oven was an earthen vessel without a bottom, about 3 feet high, smeared outside and inside with clay, and placed upon a frame or support. Fire was made within or below it. When the sides were sufficiently heated, thin patches of dough were spread on the inside, and the top was covered, without removing the fire as in the other cases, and the bread was quickly baked.

32, 33. *For after all these things do the Gentiles seek.* That is, those destitute of the true doctrines of religion, and unacquainted with proper dependence on Divine Providence, make it their *chief anxiety* thus to seek food and rai-

dom of God, and his righteousness, and[e] all these things shall be added unto you.

34 Take, therefore, no thought for the morrow; for the morrow shall take [f]thought for the things of itself. Sufficient unto the day *is* the evil thereof.

e Le.25.20,21; 1 Ki.3.13; Ps.37.25; Mar.10.30.

f De.33.25; He.13.5,6.

ment. But *you*, who have a knowledge of your Father in heaven; who know that he will provide for your wants, should not be anxious. Seek first his kingdom; seek first to be righteous, and to become interested in his favour, and all necessary things will be added to you. He has control over all things, and he can give you that which you need. He *will* give you that which *he* deems best for you.

34. *Take therefore no thought*, &c. That is, no anxiety. Commit your way to God. The evil, the trouble, the anxiety of each day as it comes, is sufficient without perplexing the mind with restless cares about another day. It is wholly uncertain whether you live to see another day. If you do, it will bring its own trouble, and it will also bring the proper supply of your wants. God will be the same Father then as to-day, and will make then, as he does now, proper provision for your wants. ¶ *The morrow shall take thought*. The morrow will have anxieties and cares of its own, but it will also bring the proper provision for those cares. Though you will have *wants*, yet God will provide for them as they occur. Do not, therefore, increase the cares of *this day* by borrowing trouble from the future. Do your duty faithfully *now*, and depend on the mercy of God and his divine help for the troubles which are yet to come.

REMARKS ON CHAPTER VI.

1st. Christ has here forcibly taught the necessity of charity, of prayer, and of all religious duties.

2d. We see the necessity of sincerity and honesty in our religious duties. They are not to be done to be seen of men. If they are, they cannot be performed acceptably. God looks on the heart, nor is it possible to deceive him. And of what avail is it to deceive men? How poor and pitiable is the reward of a hypocrite! How contemptible the praise of men when God is displeased! How awful the condition of such a one beyond the grave!

3d. Christ has here, in a particular manner, urged the duty of prayer. He has given a model for prayer. Nothing can equal this composition in simplicity, beauty, and comprehensiveness. At the same time that it is so simple that it can be understood by a child, it contains the expression of all the wants of man at any age and in every rank of life.

The duty of prayer is urged by every consideration. None but God can provide for us; none but he can forgive, and guide, and support us; none but he can bring us into heaven. He is ever ready to hear us. The humble he sends not empty away. Those who ask receive, and they who seek find. How natural and proper, then, is prayer! How strange that any man can live, and not pour out his desires to God! How strange that anyone is willing to go to eternity with this sad reflection: "I have gone through this world, spent my probation, wasted my strength, and am dying, and have never prayed!" How awful will be the reflection of the soul through all eternity: "I was *offered* eternal life, but I never *asked* for it. I lived from day to day and from year to year in God's world, breathed his air, rioted on his beneficence, forgot his goodness, and never once asked him to save my soul!" Who will be to blame if the prayerless soul is lost?

Secret and family prayer should be daily. We daily have the same necessities, are exposed to the same dangers, tread on the borders of the same heaven or hell. How should the voice of praise and prayer go up as incense in the morning, and rise as a rich perfume in the shades of each evening! What more lovely object on earth is there than that of one in the bloom of health and the dew of youth, bending with reverence before the King of heaven, seeking forgiveness, peace, guidance, and salvation! And what a strange, misguided, and piteous object is a soul that never prays!

4th. Forgiveness is essential in prayer. If we come to God harbouring malice and unwilling to forgive, we have his solemn assurance that we shall not be ourselves forgiven.

5th. *Avarice* is alike foolish and an insult to God, ver. 19-24. It is the parent of many foolish and hurtful lusts. It alienates the affections from God; produces envy of another's prosperity; leads to fraud, deception, and crime to obtain wealth, and degrades the soul. Man is formed for nobler pursuits than the mere desire to be rich. He lives for eternity, where silver will not be needed and where gold will be of no value. That eternity is near; and though we have wealth like Solomon, and though we be adorned as the lily, yet like Solomon we must soon die, and like the lily our beauty will soon fade. Death will lay us alike low; the rich and the poor will sleep together; and the worm will feed no more sweetly on the unfed and unclothed son of poverty, than on the man clothed in fine linen, and the daughter of beauty and pride. As avarice is moreover the parent of discontent, he only that is contented with the allotments of Providence, and is not restless for a change, is happy. After all, this is the true source of enjoyment. Anxiety and care, perplexity and disappointment, find their way more readily to the mansions of the rich than to the cottages of the poor. It is the *mind*, not mansions, and gold, and adorning, that gives ease; and he that is content with his situation will "smile upon his stool, while Alexander weeps upon the throne of the world."

6th. We see how comparatively valueless is *beauty*. How little it is regarded by God! He gives it to the lily, and in a day it fades and is gone. He gives it to the wings of the butterfly, and soon it dies and its beauty is forgotten. He gives it to the flowers of the spring, soon to fall; to the leaves of the forest, soon to grow yellow and decay in the autumn. How many lilies and roses does he cause to blossom in solitude where no man is, where they "waste their sweetness on the desert air!" How many streams ripple in the wilderness, and how many cataracts, age after age, have poured their thunders on the air, unheard and unseen by mortals! So little does God think of beauty. So the human form and "face divine." How soon is all that beauty marred; and, as in the lily, how soon is its last trace obliterated! In the cold grave, among the undistinguished multitudes of the dead, who can tell which of all the mouldering host was blessed with a "lovely set of features or complexion?" Alas! all has faded like the morning flower. How vain, then, to set the affections on so frail a treasure!

7th. We see the duty and privilege of depending for our daily wants on the bounties of Providence. Satisfied with the troubles of to-day, let us not add to those troubles by anxieties about to-morrow. The heathen, and they who know not God, will be anxious about the future; but they who know him, and have caught the spirit of Jesus, may surely trust him for the supply of their wants. The young lions do roar, and seek their meat at the hand of God, Ps. civ. 21. The fowls of heaven are daily supplied. Shall man only, of all the creatures on earth, vex himself and be filled with anxious cares about the future? Rather, like the rest of the creation, let us depend on the aid of the universal Parent, and feel that HE who hears the young ravens which cry will also supply our necessities.

8th. Especially is the remark just made of value in reference to those in early life. Life is a stormy ocean. Over that ocean no being presides but God. He holds the winds in his hands, and can still their howlings, and calm the heaving billows. On that ocean the young have just launched their frail bark. Daily they will need protection; daily will they need supplies; daily will they be in danger, and exposed to the rolling of the billows that may ingulf them for ever. Ignorant, inexperienced, and in danger, how should they look to God to guide and aid them! Instead of vexing themselves with anxious cares about the future, how should they place humble reliance on God! Safe in his hand, we shall outride the storm and come to a haven of peace. *He* will supply our wants if we *trust* him, as he does those of the songsters of the grove. He will be the guide of our youth and the strength of our manhood. If we seek him, he will be found of us; if we forsake him, he will cast us off for ever, 1 Ch. xxviii. 9.

9th. From all this, how manifest is the propriety of seeking *first* the kingdom of God! First in our affections, first in the objects of pursuit, first in the feelings and associations of each morning, be the desire and the aim for heaven. Having this, we have assurance of all that we need. GOD, *our Father*, will then befriend us, and in life and death all will be well.

CHAPTER VII.

JUDGE[a] not, that ye be not judged.

2 For with what judgment ye judge, ye shall be judged; and with[b] what measure ye mete, it shall be measured to you again.

3 And why beholdest thou the mote that is in thy brother's eye, but considerest not the beam that is in thine own eye?

4 Or how wilt thou say to thy brother, Let me pull out the mote out of thine eye: and, behold, a beam *is* in thine own eye?

5 Thou hypocrite, [c]first cast out the beam out of thine own eye; and then shalt thou see clearly to cast out the mote out of thy brother's eye.

6 Give not that which is holy unto the dogs, neither [d]cast ye

a Lu.6.37; Ro.2.1; 1 Co.4.5. *b* Ju.1.7. *c* Ga.6.1. *d* Pr.9.7,8; 23.9.

CHAPTER VII.

1. *Judge not*, &c. This command refers to rash, censorious, and unjust judgment. See Ro. ii. 1. Luke (vi. 37) explains it in the sense of *condemning*. Christ does not condemn judging as a magistrate, for that, when according to justice, is lawful and necessary. Nor does he condemn our *forming an opinion* of the conduct of others, for it is impossible *not* to form an opinion of conduct that we know to be evil. But what he refers to is a habit of forming a judgment hastily, harshly, and without an allowance for every palliating circumstance, and a habit of *expressing* such an opinion harshly and unnecessarily when formed. It rather refers to *private* judgment than *judicial*, and perhaps primarily to the customs of the scribes and Pharisees.

2. *With what judgment*, &c. This was a *proverb* among the Jews. It expressed a truth; and Christ did not hesitate to adopt it as conveying his own sentiments. It refers no less to the way in which *men* will judge of us, than to the rule by which God will judge us. See 2 Sa. xxii. 27; Mar. iv. 24; Ja. ii. 13. ¶ *Mete.* Measure. You shall be judged by the same rule which you apply to others.

3. *And why beholdest thou the mote*, &c. A mote signifies any *light substance*, as dry chaff, or fine spires of grass or grain. It probably most usually signified the small *spiculæ* or *beards* on a head of barley or wheat. It is thus placed in opposition to the word *beam.* ¶ *Beam.* The word here used signifies a large piece of squared timber. The one is an exceedingly small object, the other a large one. The meaning is, that *we are much more quick and acute to judge of small offences in others, than of much larger offences in ourselves.* Even a very *small* object in the eye of another we discern much more quickly than a much larger one in our own; a small fault in our neighbour we see much more readily than a large one in ourselves. This was also a proverb in frequent use among the Jews, and the same sentiment was common among the Greeks, and deserves to be expressed in every language.

5. *Thou hypocrite, first cast out*, &c. Christ directs us to the proper way of forming an opinion of others, and of reproving and correcting them. By first amending our own faults, or casting the beam out of our eye, we can *consistently* advance to correct the faults of others. There will then be no hypocrisy in our conduct. We shall also *see clearly* to do it. The beam, the thing that obscured our sight, will be removed, and we shall more clearly discern the *small* object that obscures the sight of our brother. The sentiment is, that the readiest way to judge of the imperfections of others is to be free from greater ones ourselves. This qualifies us for judging, makes us candid and consistent, and enables us to see things as they are, and to make proper allowances for frailty and imperfection.

6. *Give not that which is holy*, &c. By some the word *holy* has been supposed to mean *flesh offered in sacrifice*, made holy, or separated to a sacred use; but it probably means here *anything connected with religion*—admonition, precept, or doctrine. Pearls are precious stones found in shell-fish, chiefly in India, in the waters that surround Ceylon. They are used to denote anything peculiarly precious, Re. xvii. 4; xviii. 12–16; Mat. xiii. 45. In this place they are used to denote the doctrines of the gospel. *Dogs* signify men who spurn, oppose, and abuse that doctrine; men

your pearls before swine, lest they trample them under their feet, and turn again and rend you.

7 Ask,[e] and it shall be given you; seek, and ye shall find; knock, and it shall be opened unto you:

8 For [f]every one that asketh receiveth; [g]and he that seeketh findeth; and to him that knocketh it shall be opened.

9 Or what man is there of you, whom if his son ask bread, will he give him a stone?

10 Or if he ask a fish, will he give him a serpent?

11 If[h] ye then, being evil, know

e Is.55.6; Lu.18.1. f Ps.81.10,16; Jn.14.13,14; 16.23,24; 1 Jn.3.22; 5.14,15. g Pr.8.17; Je.29.12,13.

h Lu.11.11,&c.

of peculiar sourness and malignity of temper, who meet it like growling and quarrelsome curs, Phi. iii. 2; 2 Pe. ii. 22; Re. xxii. 15. *Swine* denote those who would trample the precepts under feet; men of impurity of life; those who are corrupt, polluted, profane, obscene, and sensual; those who would not know the value of the gospel, and who would tread it down as swine would pearls, 2 Pe. ii. 22; Pr. xi. 22. The meaning of this proverb, then, is, do not offer your doctrine to those violent and abusive men who would growl and curse you; nor to those peculiarly debased and profligate who would not perceive its value, would trample it down, and would abuse you. This verse furnishes a beautiful instance of what has been called the *introverted parallelism.* The usual mode of poetry among the Hebrews, and a common mode of expression in proverbs and apothegms, was by the parallelism, where one member of a sentence answered to another, or expressed substantially the same sense with some addition or modification. See the Introduction to the Book of Job, vol. i. p. xxviii.-xxxix. Sometimes this was alternate, and sometimes it was introverted—where the first and fourth lines would correspond, and the second and third. This is the case here. The dogs would rend, and not the swine; the swine would trample the pearls under their feet, and not the dogs. It may be thus expressed:

Give not that which is holy unto the dogs,
Neither cast ye your pearls before swine,
Lest they [that is, the swine] trample them under their feet,
And turn again [that is, the dogs] and rend you.

7-11. *Ask, and it shall be given you,* &c. There are here three different forms presented of seeking the things which we need from God—*asking, seeking,* and *knocking.* The latter is taken from the act of knocking at a door for admittance. See Lu. xiii. 45; Re. iii. 20. The phrases signify to seek with earnestness, diligence, and perseverance.

The promise is, that what we seek shall be given us. It is of course implied that we seek with a proper spirit, with humility, sincerity, and perseverance. It is implied, also, that we ask the things which it may be consistent for God to give—that is, things which he has promised to give, and which would be best for us, and most for his own honour, 1 Jn. v. 14. Of that God is to be the judge. And here there is the utmost latitude which a creature can ask. God is willing to provide for us, to forgive our sins, to save our souls, to befriend us in trial, to comfort us in death, to extend the gospel through the world. Man *can* ask no higher things of God; and these he *may* ask, assured that he is willing to grant them.

Christ encourages us to do this by the conduct of parents. No parent turns away his child with that which would be injurious. He would not give him a stone instead of bread, or a serpent instead of a fish. God is better and kinder than the most tender earthly parents; and with what confidence, therefore, may we come as his children, and ask what we need! Parents, he says, are evil; that is, are imperfect, often partial, and not unfrequently passionate; but God is free from all this, and therefore is ready and willing to aid us. ¶ *Every one that asketh receiveth.* That is, every one that asks aright; that prays in faith, and in submission to the will of God. He does not always give the very thing which we ask, but he gives what would be better. A parent will not always confer the *very thing* which a child asks, but he will seek the welfare of the child, and give what *he* thinks will be most for its good. Paul asked that the thorn from his flesh might be removed. God did not *literally* grant the request, but told him that his *grace* should be *sufficient* for him. See Notes on 2 Co. xii. 7, 8, 9. ¶ *A fish.* A

how to give good gifts unto your children, how much more shall your Father which is in heaven give good things to them that ask him?

12 Therefore all things whatsoever ye would that men should do to you, do ye even so to them: [i]for this is the law and the prophets.

13 Enter[k] ye in at the strait gate: for wide *is* the gate, and broad *is* the way, that leadeth to destruction, and many there be which go in thereat:

14 Because[1] strait *is* the gate, and narrow *is* the way, which leadeth unto life; and [l]few there be that find it.

15 Beware[m] of false prophets, which come to you in sheep's clothing, but inwardly they are [n]ravening wolves:

i Le.19.18; Ro.13.8-10; Ga.5.14. *k* Lu.3.24.

1 or, *how.* *l* ch.20.16; 25.1-12; Ro.9.27,29. *m* De. 13.1-3; Je.23.13-16; 1 Jn.4.1. *n* Ac.20.29-31.

fish has some resemblance to a serpent; yet no parent would attempt to deceive his child in this. So God will not give to us that which might appear to be of use, but which would be injurious.

12. *All things whatsoever*, &c. This command has been usually called the *Saviour's golden rule*, a name given to it on account of its great value. All that you *expect* or *desire* of others in similar circumstances, do to them. Act not from selfishness or injustice, but put yourself in the place of the other, and ask what you would expect of him. This would make you impartial, candid, and just. It would destroy avarice, envy, treachery, unkindness, slander, theft, adultery, and murder. It has been well said that this law is what the balance-wheel is to machinery. It would prevent all irregularity of movement in the moral world, as that does in a steam-engine. It is easily applied, its justice is seen by all men, and all must acknowledge its force and value. ¶ *This is the law and the prophets.* That is, this is the sum or substance of the Old Testament. It is nowhere found in so many words, but it is a summary expression of all that the law required. The sentiment was in use among the Jews. Hillel, an ancient Rabbi, said to a man who wished to become a proselyte, and who asked him to teach him the whole law, "Whatever is hateful to you, do not do to another." Something of the same sentiment was found among the ancient Greeks and Romans, and is found in the writings of Confucius.

13, 14. *Enter ye in at the strait gate.* Christ here compares the way to life to an entrance through a gate. The words *straight* and *strait* have very different meanings. The former means *not crooked;* the latter, *pent up, narrow, difficult to be entered.* This is the word used here, and it means that the way to heaven is *pent up, narrow, close*, and not obviously entered. The way to death is open, broad, and thronged. The Saviour here referred probably to ancient cities. They were surrounded with walls and entered through gates. Some of those, connected with the great avenues to the city, were broad and admitted a throng; others, for more private purposes, were narrow, and few would be seen entering them. So, says Christ, is the path to heaven. It is narrow. It is not *the great highway* that men tread. Few go there. Here and there one may be seen—travelling in solitude and singularity. The way to death, on the other hand, is broad. Multitudes are in it. It is the great highway in which men go. They fall into it easily and without effort, and go without thought. If they wish to *leave that* and go by a narrow gate to the city, it would require effort and thought. So, says Christ, *diligence* is needed to enter life. See Lu. xiii. 24. None go of course. All must strive, to obtain it; and so narrow, unfrequented, and solitary is it, that few find it. This sentiment has been beautifully versified by Watts:

"Broad is the road that leads to death,
And thousands walk together there;
But wisdom shows a narrower path,
With here and there a traveller."

15. *False prophets.* The word prophet originally means one who foretells future events. As prophets, however, were commonly regarded as public instructors on the subject of religion, the word came to denote all who were religious teachers. See Notes on Ro. xii. 6. In this sense it is probably used here. A false prophet is a teacher of incorrect doctrine, or one falsely and unjustly laying claims to divine inspira-

16 Ye[o] shall know them by their fruits. Do men gather grapes of thorns, or figs of thistles?

17 Even so [p]every good tree bringeth forth good fruit; but a corrupt tree bringeth forth evil fruit.

18 A good tree cannot bring forth evil fruit, neither *can* a corrupt tree bring forth good fruit.

19 Every[q] tree that bringeth not forth good fruit, is hewn down, and cast into the fire.

20 Wherefore by their fruits ye shall know them.

21 Not every one that saith unto me, [r]Lord, Lord, shall enter into the kingdom of heaven; but he that doeth the will of my Father which is in heaven.

22 Many will say to me in that day, Lord, Lord, have we not [s]prophesied in thy name? and in thy name have cast out devils? and in thy name done many wonderful works?

o ch.12.33. p Lu.6.43,45. q ch.3.10; Jn.15.2,6.

r Is.48.1,2; ch.25.11,12; Lu.6.46; 13.25; Ro.2.13. s Nu.24.4; 1 Ki.22.11,&c.; Je.23.13,&c.; Ac.19.13-15; 1 Co.13.2.

tion. It probably had reference to the false teachers then among the Jews. ¶ *Who come in sheep's clothing.* The sheep is an emblem of innocence, sincerity, and harmlessness. To come in sheep's clothing is to assume the appearance of sanctity and innocence, when the heart is evil. ¶ *Ravening wolves.* Rapacious; voraciously devouring; hungry even to rage. Applied to the false teachers, it means that they assumed the appearance of holiness in order that they might the more readily get the *property* of the people. They were full of extortion and excess. See Mat. xxiii. 25.

16. *Ye shall know them by their fruits.* The Saviour gives the proper test of their character. Men do not judge of a tree by its leaves, or bark, or flowers, but by the fruit which it bears. The flowers may be beautiful and fragrant, the foliage thick and green; but these are merely ornamental. It is the *fruit* that is of chief service to man; and he forms his opinion of the nature and value of the tree by that fruit. So of pretensions to religion. The profession may be fair; but the *conduct*—the fruit—is to determine the nature of the principles.

17. *A corrupt tree.* The word corrupt here does not signify, as our translation would seem to indicate, that the tree *had been* good, but had become *vitiated;* but that it was a tree of a useless character, of a nature that produced nothing beneficial.

21. *Not every one that saith,* &c. The Saviour goes on to say that many, on the ground of a mere profession such as he had just referred to, would claim admittance into his kingdom. Many would plead that they had done miracles, and preached or prophesied much, and on the ground of that would demand an entrance into heaven. The power of working miracles had no necessary connection with piety. God may as well, if he chooses, give the power of raising the dead to a wicked man, as the skill of healing to a wicked physician. A miracle is a display *of his own power* through the medium of another. An act of healing the sick is also a display of *his power* through the agency of another. In neither of these cases is there any necessary connection with moral character. So of preaching or prophesying. God may use the agency of a man of talents, though not pious, to carry forward his purposes. Saving power on the mind is the work of God, and he may convey it by any agency which he chooses. Accordingly, many may be found in the day of judgment who may have been endowed with powers of prophecy or miracle, as Balaam or the magicians of Egypt; in the same way as many men of distinguished talents may be found, yet destitute of piety, and who will be shut out of his kingdom. See Mat. vii. 21; 1 Co. i. 26; xiii. 1-3. In this last place Paul says that, though he spoke with the tongue of angels, and had the gift of prophecy, and could remove mountains, and had not charity or love, all would be of no avail. See Notes on 1 Co. xiii. 1-3.

22. *In that day.* That is, in the last day, the day of judgment; the time when the principles of all pretenders to prophecy and piety shall be tried.

23. *Profess unto them.* Say unto them; plainly declare. ¶ *I never knew*

23 And then will I profess unto them, I never knew you: [t]depart from me, ye that work iniquity.

24 Therefore [u]whosoever heareth these sayings of mine, and doeth them, I will liken him unto a [v]wise man, which built his house upon a rock:

25 And the rain descended, and the floods came, and the winds blew, and beat upon that house; and it fell not: for it was [w]founded upon a rock.

26 And every one that heareth these sayings of mine, and doeth them not, shall be likened unto a [x]foolish man, which built his house upon the sand:

27 And the rain descended, and the floods came, and the winds

t Ps.5.5; ch.25.41; Re.22.15. *u* Lu.6.47,&c. *v* Ps.111.10; 119.99,130. *w* Ps.92.13-15. *x* 1 Sa.2.30; Je.8.9.

you. That is, I never approved your conduct; never loved you; never regarded you as my friends. See Ps. i. 6; 2 Ti. ii. 19; 1 Co. viii. 3. This proves that, with all their pretensions, they had never been true followers of Christ. Jesus will not then say to false prophets and false professors of religion that he had once known them and then rejected them; that they had been once Christians and then had fallen away; that they had been pardoned and then had apostatized—but that he had *never known them*—THEY HAD NEVER BEEN TRUE CHRISTIANS. Whatever might have been their pretended joys, their raptures, their hopes, their self-confidence, their visions, their zeal, they had never been regarded by the Saviour as his true friends. I know not a more decided proof that Christians do not fall from grace than this text. It settles the question; and proves that whatever else such men had, they never had any true religion. See 1 Jn. ii. 19.

24-27. Jesus closes the sermon on the mount by a beautiful comparison, illustrating the benefit of attending to his words. It was not sufficient to *hear* them; they must be *obeyed.* He compares the man who should hear and obey him to a man who built his house on a rock. Palestine was to a considerable extent a land of hills and mountains. Like other countries of that description, it was subject to sudden and violent rains. The Jordan, the principal stream, was annually swollen to a great extent, and became rapid and furious in its course. The streams which ran among the hills, whose channels might have been dry during some months of the year, became suddenly swollen with the rain, and would pour down impetuously into the plains below. Everything in the way of these torrents would be swept off. Even houses, erected within the reach of these sudden inundations, and especially if founded on sand or on any unsolid basis, would not stand before them. The rising, bursting stream would shake it to its foundation; the rapid torrent would gradually wash away its base; it would totter and fall. Rocks in that country were common, and it was easy to secure for their houses a solid foundation. No comparison could, to a Jew, have been more striking.—So tempests, and storms of affliction and persecution, beat around the soul. Suddenly, when we think we are in safety, the heavens may be overcast, the storm may lower, and calamity may beat upon us. In a moment, health, friends, comforts may be gone. How desirable, then, to be possessed of something that the tempest cannot reach! Such is an interest in Christ, reliance on his promises, confidence in his protection, and a hope of heaven through his blood. Earthly calamities do not reach these; and, possessed of *religion*, all the storms and tempests of life may beat harmlessly around us.

There is another point in this comparison. The house built on the sand is beat upon by the floods and rains; its foundation gradually is worn away; it falls, and is borne down the stream and is destroyed. So falls the sinner. The floods are wearing away his sandy foundation; and soon one tremendous storm shall beat upon him, and he and his hopes shall fall, for ever fall. Out of Christ; perhaps having *heard* his words from very childhood; perhaps having taught them to others in the Sabbath-school; perhaps having been the means of laying the foundation on which others shall build for heaven, he has laid for himself no foundation, and soon an eternal tempest shall beat around his naked soul. How great will

blew, and [y]beat upon that house; and it fell: and [z]great was the fall of it.

28 And it came to pass, when Jesus had ended these sayings, the people were [a]astonished at his doctrine:

29 For he taught them as *one* having authority, and not as the scribes.

y 1 Co.3.13. z He.10.26,27. a Je.23.29; Mar.6.2.

be that fall! What will be his emotions when sinking for ever in the flood, and when he realizes that he is destined for ever to live and writhe in the peltings of that ceaseless storm that shall beat when "God shall rain snares, fire, and a horrible tempest" upon the wicked!

28, 29. *His doctrine.* His teaching. ¶ *As* one *having authority, and not as the scribes.* The scribes were the learned men and teachers of the Jewish nation, and were principally Pharisees. They taught chiefly the sentiments of their Rabbins, and the traditions which had been delivered; they consumed much of their time in useless disputes and "vain jangling." Jesus was open, plain, grave, useful, delivering truth as *became* the oracles of God; not spending his time in trifling disputes and debating questions of no importance, but confirming his doctrine by miracles and argument; teaching *as having power,* as it is in the original, and not in the vain and foolish manner of the Jewish doctors. He showed that he had authority to explain, to enforce, and to *change* the ceremonial laws of the Jews. He came with authority such as no *man* could have, and it is not remarkable that his explanations astonished them. From this chapter we may learn,

1st. The evil of censorious judging, ver. 1-5. We cannot see the heart. We have ourselves possibly greater faults than the persons that we condemn. They may possibly be of a different kind; but it is nevertheless not uncommon for persons to be very censorious toward faults in others, which they have to much greater extent themselves.

2d. We see how we are to treat men who are opposers of the gospel, ver. 6. We are *not* to present it to them when we know they will despise it and abuse us. We should, however, be cautious in forming that opinion of them. Many men may be far more ready to hear the gospel than we imagine, and a word seasonably and kindly spoken may be the means of saving them, Pr. xxv. 11; Ec. xi. 6. We should not meet violent and wicked opposers of the gospel with a harsh, overbearing, and lordly spirit—a spirit of dogmatizing and anger; nor should we violate the laws of social intercourse under the idea of *faithfulness.* Religion gains nothing by outraging the established laws of social life, 1 Pe. iii. 8. If men will not hear us when we speak to them kindly and respectfully, we may be sure they will not when we abuse them and become angry. We harden them against the truth, and confirm them in the opinion that religion is of no value. Our Saviour was always mild and kind, *and in not a single instance did he do violence to the laws of social intercourse, or fail in the respect due from one man to another.* When with harshness men speak to their superiors; when they abuse them with unkind words, coarse epithets, and unfeeling denunciations; when children and youth forget their station, and speak in harsh, authoritative tones to the aged, they are violating the very first principles of the gospel—meekness, respect, and love. Give honour to whom honour is due, and be *kind,* be *courteous.*

3d. Christ gives peculiar encouragement to prayer, ver. 7-11. Especially his remarks apply to the young. What child is there that would not go to his parent and ask him for things which were necessary? What child doubts the willingness of a kind parent to give what he thinks will be best for him? But God is more willing to give than the *best* parent. We need of *him* gifts of far more importance than we ever can of an earthly father. None but God can forgive, enlighten, sanctify, and save us. How strange that many ask favours of an *earthly* parent daily and hourly, and never ask of the Great Universal Father a single blessing for time or eternity!

4th. There is danger of losing the soul, ver. 13, 14. The way to ruin is broad, the path to heaven is narrow. Men naturally and readily go in the former; they never go in the latter without design. When we enter on the journey of life, we naturally fall into the broad and thronged way to ruin.

Our original propensity, our native depravity, our disinclination to God and religion, lead us to that, and we never leave it without effort. How much more natural to tread in a way in which multitudes go, than in one where there are few travellers, and which requires an effort to find it! And how much danger is there that we shall continue to walk in that way until it terminates in our ruin! No one is saved without effort. No one enters on the narrow way without design; no one by following his natural inclination and propensities. And yet how indisposed we are to effort! how unwilling to listen to the exhortations which would call us from the broad path to a narrower and less frequented course! How prone are men to feel that they are safe if they are with the many, and that the multitude that attend them constitute a safeguard from danger!

> "Encompassed by a throng,
> On *numbers* they depend;
> They say so many can't be wrong,
> And miss a happy end."

Yet did God ever spare a guilty city because it was large? Did he save the army of Sennacherib from the destroying angel because it was mighty? Does he hesitate to cut men down by the plague, the pestilence, and by famine, because they are numerous? Is he deterred from consigning men to the grave because they swarm upon the earth, and because a mighty throng is going to death? So in the way to hell. Not numbers, nor power, nor might, nor talent will make that way safe; nor will the path to heaven be a dangerous road because few are seen travelling there. The Saviour knew and *felt* that men are in danger; and hence, with much solemnity, he warned them when he lived, and now warns *us*, to strive to enter in at the strait gate.

5th. Sincerity is necessary in religion, ver. 15–23. Profession is of no value without it. God sees the heart, and the day is near when he will cut down and destroy all those who do not bring forth the fruits of righteousness in their lives. If in anything we should be honest and sincere, surely it should be in the things of religion. God is never deceived (Ga. vi. 7), and the things of eternity are of too much consequence to be lost by deluding ourselves or others. We may deceive our fellow-men, but we do not deceive our Maker; and soon he will strip off our thin covering, and show us as we are to the universe. If anything is of prominent value in religion, it is *honesty*—honesty to ourselves, to our fellow-men, and to God. Be willing to know the worst of your case. Be willing to be thought of, by God and men, *as you are*. Assume nothing which you do not possess, and pretend to nothing which you have not. Judge of yourselves as you do of others—not by words and promises, but by the *life*. Judge of yourselves as you do of trees; not by leaves and flowers, but by the *fruit*.

6th. We may learn the importance of building our hopes of heaven on a firm foundation, ver. 24–27. No other foundation can any man lay than that which is laid, which is Jesus Christ, 1 Co. iii. 11. He is the tried Corner Stone, 1 Pe. ii. 6; Ep. ii. 20. On an edifice raised on that foundation the storms of persecution and calamity will beat in vain. Hopes thus reared will sustain us in every adversity, will remain unshaken by the terrors of death, and will secure us from the tempests of wrath that shall beat upon the guilty. How awful, in the day of judgment, will it be to have been deceived! How dreadful the shock to find then that the house has been built on the sand! How dreadful the emotions, to see our hopes totter on the brink of ruin; to see sand after sand washed away, and the dwelling reel over the heaving deep, and fall into the abyss to rise no more! Ruin, awful and eternal ruin, awaits those who thus deceive themselves, and who trust to a name to live, while they are dead.

7th. Under what obligations are we for this *Sermon on the Mount!* In all languages there is not a discourse to be found that can be compared with it for purity, and truth, and beauty, and dignity. Were there no other evidence of the divine mission of Christ, this alone would be sufficient to prove that he was sent from God. Were these doctrines obeyed and loved, how pure and peaceful would be the world! How would hypocrisy be abashed and confounded! How would impurity hang its head! How would peace reign in every family and nation! How would anger and wrath flee! And how would the race—the lost and benighted tribes of men, the poor, and needy, and sorrowful—bend themselves before their common Father, and seek peace and eternal life at the hands of a merciful and faithful God!

CHAPTER VIII.

WHEN he was come down from the mountain, great multitudes followed him.

2 And, behold, [a]there came a leper and worshipped him, saying, Lord, if thou wilt, thou canst make me clean.

a Mar.1.40,&c.; Lu.5.12,&c.

CHAPTER VIII.

1. *When he was come down from the mountain.* That is, immediately on his descending from the mountain. His discourse had attracted great attention, and the fame of it drew together great multitudes, who were convinced that he had come from God. Then follows, in this chapter and the chapter succeeding, a succession of *miracles* not less remarkable than his teaching was; miracles that tended to confirm beyond a doubt the impression made by his sermon that he was sent from God. ¶ *Great multitudes followed him.* Great numbers of those who had been with him in the mountain, and great numbers of others who were attracted by the fame of that discourse.

2. *There came a leper.* No disease with which the human family has been afflicted has been more dreadful than that which is often mentioned in the Bible *as the leprosy.* It first exhibits itself on the surface of the skin. The appearance is not always the same, but it commonly resembles the spot made by the puncture of a pin or the pustules of a ringworm. The spots generally make their appearance very suddenly. Perhaps its appearance might be hastened by any sudden passion, as fear or anger. See Nu. xii. 10; 2 Ch. xxvi. 19. The spots commonly exhibit themselves at first on the face, about the nose and eyes, and increase in size a number of years, till they become as large as a pea or a bean.

There are three kinds of leprosy, distinguished by the appearance of the spots—the white, the black, and the red leprosy. These spots, though few at first, gradually spread till they cover the whole body.

But, though the *appearance* of the disease is at first in the skin, yet it is deeply seated in the bones, and marrow, and joints of the body. We have reason to suppose that in children it is concealed in the system for a number of years till they arrive at the age of puberty; and in adults for three or four years, till at last it gives fearful indications on the *skin* of its having gained a well-rooted and permanent existence. A leprous person may live twenty, or thirty, or even fifty years, if he received the disease at his birth, but they will be years of indescribable misery. The bones and marrow are pervaded with the disease. The malady advances from one stage to another with slow and certain ruin. "Life still lingers amid the desolation;" the joints, and hands, and feet lose their power; and the body *collapses*, or falls together in a form hideous and awful. There is a form of the disease in which it commences at the extremities: the joints separate; the fingers, toes, and other members one by one fall off; and the malady thus gradually approaches the seat of life. The wretched victim is thus doomed to see himself dying *piecemeal*, assured that no human power can arrest for a moment the silent and steady march of this foe to the seat of life.

This disease is contagious and hereditary. It is easily communicated from one to another, and is transmitted to the third and fourth generation. The last generation that is afflicted with it commonly exhibits the symptoms by decayed teeth, by a fetid breath, and by a diseased complexion.

Moses gave particular directions by which the real leprosy was to be distinguished from other diseases. See Le. xiii. The leprous person was, in order to avoid contagion, very properly separated from the congregation. The inspection of the disease was committed to the priest; and a declaration on his part that the person was healed, was sufficient evidence to restore the afflicted man to the congregation. It was required, also, that the leprous person should bring an offering to the priest of two birds, probably *sparrows* (see Le. xiv. 4, *margin*), one of which was slain and the other dismissed, Le. xiv. 5–7. In compliance with the laws of the land, Jesus directed the man that he had healed to make the customary offering, and to obtain the testimony of the priest that he was healed. The leprosy has once, and but once, appeared in America. This loathsome and most painful disease has in all other instances been confined to the

3 And Jesus put forth *his* hand, and touched him, saying, I will; be thou clean: and immediately his leprosy was cleansed.

4 And Jesus saith unto him,[b] See thou tell no man; but go thy way, shew thyself to the priest, and offer the gift that[c] Moses commanded, for a testimony unto them.

5 And when Jesus was entered into Capernaum, there came unto him a [d] centurion, beseeching him,

b ch.9.30; Mar.5.43. c Le.14.3,&c. d Lu.7.2,&c.

Old World, and chiefly to the Eastern nations. It is matter of profound gratitude to a benignant God that this scourge has been permitted *but* once to visit the New World. That awful calamity was in the island of Guadaloupe, in the West Indies, about the year 1730, and is thus described by an eye-witness:* "Its commencement is imperceptible. There appear only some few white spots on the skin. At first they are attended with no pain or inconvenience, but no means whatever will remove them. The disease imperceptibly increases for many years. The spots become larger, and spread over the whole body. When the disease advances, the upper part of the nose swells, the nostrils become enlarged, and the nose itself soft. Tumours appear on the jaws; the eye-brows swell; the ears become thick; the points of the fingers, as also the feet and the toes, swell; the nails become scaly; *the joints of the hands and feet separate and drop off.* In the last stage of the disease the patient becomes a hideous spectacle, *and falls to pieces.*" ¶ *Worshipped him.* Bowed down before him, to show him respect. See Notes on Mat. ii. 2. ¶ *If thou wilt.* This was an exhibition of great faith, and also an acknowledgment of his dependence on the *will* of Jesus, in order to be healed. So every sinner must come. He must feel that Jesus *can* save him. He must also feel that he has no claim on him; that it depends on his sovereign will; and must cast himself at his feet with the feelings of the leper:

> "I can but perish if I go;
> I am resolved to try;
> For if I stay away, I know
> I shall for ever die."

Happily, no one ever came to Jesus with this feeling who was not received and pardoned. ¶ *Make me clean.* Heal me. The leprosy was regarded as an unclean and disgusting disease. To be *healed*, therefore, was expressed by being *cleansed* from it.

* M. Peyssanel.

3. *And Jesus—touched him.* It was an offence to the Jews to *touch* a leprous person, and was regarded as making him who did it ceremonially impure, Le. xiii. 3. The act of putting forth his hand and *touching* him, therefore, expressed the intention of Jesus to cure him, and was a pledge that he *was*, in fact, already cured.

4. *See thou tell no man.* This command is to be understood as extending only to the time until he had made the proper representation to the priest. It was his duty to *hasten* to him immediately (Le. xiv. 2); not to delay by talking about it, but, as the *first* thing, to obey the laws of God, and make proper acknowledgments to him by an offering. The place where this cure was wrought was in Galilee, a distance of forty or fifty miles from Jerusalem; and it was his duty to make haste to the residence of the priest, and obtain his sanction to the reality of the cure. Perhaps, also, Christ was apprehensive that the report would go *before* the man if he delayed, and the priest, through opposition to Jesus, might pronounce it an imposition. ¶ *And offer the gift that Moses commanded:* That Moses directed to be offered by a leper when he was cured. That gift consisted of "two birds alive and clean, cedar-wood, scarlet, and hyssop," Le. xiv. 4. ¶ *For a testimony unto them.* Not to the *priest*, but to the people. Show thyself to the *priest*, and get his *testimony* to the reality of the cure, as a proof to the *people* that the healing is genuine. It was necessary that he should have that testimony before he could be received to the congregation or allowed to mingle with the people. Having this, he would be, of course, restored to the privileges of social and religious life, and the proof of the *miracle*, to the people, would be put beyond a doubt.

5. *Capernaum.* See Notes on chap. iv. 13. ¶ *There came unto him a centurion.* A centurion was the commander of a *hundred men* in the Roman armies. Judea was a Roman province, and gar-

6 And saying, Lord, my servant lieth at home sick of the palsy, grievously tormented.

7 And Jesus saith unto him, I will come and heal him.

8 The centurion answered and said, Lord, [e]I am not worthy that thou shouldst come under my roof: but [f]speak the word only, and my servant shall be healed.

9 For I am a man under authority, having soldiers under me: and I say to this *man*, Go, and he goeth; and to another, Come, and he cometh; and to my servant, Do this, and he doeth *it*.

10 When Jesus heard *it*, he marvelled, and said to them that followed, Verily I say unto you, I have not found so [g]great faith, no, not in Israel.

11 And I say unto you, That

e Ps.10.17; Lu.15.19,21. f Ps.33.9; 107.20. g ch.15.28.

---

risons were kept there to preserve the people in subjection. This man was probably by birth a Pagan. See verse 10.

6. *Sick of the palsy.* See Notes on ch. iv. 24. The particular form which the palsy assumed in this case is not mentioned. It seems it was a violent attack. Perhaps it was the painful form which produced violent *cramps*, and which immediately endangered his life.

8. *I am not worthy*, &c. This was an expression of great humility. It refers, doubtless, to his view of his *personal* unworthiness, and not merely to the fact that he was a *Gentile*. It was the expression of a conviction of the great dignity and power of the Saviour, and of a feeling that he was so unlike him that he was not fit that the Son of God should come into his dwelling. So every truly penitent sinner feels—a feeling which is appropriate when he comes to Christ.

9. *I am a man*, &c. He had full confidence in the ability of Jesus to heal his servant, and requested him simply to give the command. This request he presented in a manner appropriate to a soldier. I am a man, says he, under authority. That is, I am subject to the commands of others, and know how to obey. I have also under me soldiers who are accustomed to obedience. I say to one, Go, and he goes; and to another, Come, and he comes. I am *prepared*, therefore, to believe that your commands will be obeyed. As these obey me, so do diseases, storms, and seas obey you. If men obey me, who am an *inferior* officer, subject to another, how much more shall diseases obey you—the original source of power—having control over all things! He asked, therefore, simply that Christ would give commandment, and he felt assured he would be obeyed.

10. *When Jesus heard* it, *he marvelled.* He *wondered* at it, or *he deemed it remarkable.* ¶ *I have not found so great faith.* The word *faith*, here, means *confidence* or belief that Christ had power to heal his servant. It does not *of necessity* imply that he had saving faith; though, from the connection and the spirit manifested, it seems probable that he had. If this was so, then he was the first Gentile convert to Christianity, and was a very early illustration of what was more clearly revealed afterward—that the heathen were to be brought to the knowledge of the truth. ¶ *Not in Israel.* Israel was a name given to *Jacob* (Ge. xxxii. 28, 29), because, as a prince, he had power with God; because he persevered in wrestling with the angel that met him, and obtained the blessing. The name is derived from two Hebrew words signifying *Prince* and *God.* He was one of the patriarchs, a progenitor of the Jewish nation; and the names *Israel and Israelites* were given to them, as the name Romans to the Roman people was in honour of Romulus, and the name *American* to this continent from *Americus Vespuccius.* The name Israel was given to the whole nation till the time of Jeroboam, when only the ten tribes that revolted received the name, probably because they were a majority of the nation. After the captivity of Babylon it was given to *all* the Jews indiscriminately. See Mat. x. 6; Ac. vii. 42; He. viii. 8; Mar. xv. 32. It here means, "I have not found such an instance of *confidence* among the Jews."

11. *Many shall come from the east*, &c. Jesus takes occasion from the faith of a Roman centurion to state that this

many[h] shall come from the east and west, and shall sit down with Abraham, and Isaac, and Jacob, in the kingdom of heaven:

12 But the [i]children of the kingdom shall be cast out into outer darkness: [k]there shall be weeping and gnashing of teeth.

13 And Jesus said unto the centurion, Go thy way; and as thou

h Is.2.2,3; Lu.13.29; Ac.11.18; Ep.3.6; Re.7.9.
i ch.7.22,23.
k ch.13.42,50.

---

conversion would not be solitary; that *many* Pagans—many from the east and west—would be converted to the gospel, and be saved, as Abraham, Isaac, and Jacob were. The phrase "from the east and from the west," in the Scripture, is used to denote the *whole world*, Is. xlv. 6; lix. 19. The phrase, *shall sit down*, in the original, refers to the manner of sitting at meals (see Notes on Mat. xxiii. 6); and the enjoyments of heaven are described under the similitude of a feast or banquet—a very common manner of speaking of it, Mat. xxvi. 29; Lu. xiv. 15; xxii. 30. It is used here to denote *felicity*, *enjoyment*, or *honour*. To sit with those distinguished men was an honour, and would be expressive of great felicity.

12. *The children of the kingdom.* That is, the children, or the people, who *expected the kingdom*, or to whom it properly belonged; or, in other words, the Jews. *They* supposed themselves peculiarly the favourites of heaven. They thought that the Messiah would enlarge their nation and spread the triumphs of *their* kingdom. They called *themselves*, therefore, the children or the members of the kingdom of God, to the exclusion of the Gentiles. Our Saviour used the manner of speech to which they were accustomed, and said that *many of the Pagans would be saved, and many Jews lost.* ¶ *Shall be cast out into outer darkness*, &c. This is an image of future punishment. It is not improbable that the image was taken from Roman dungeons or prisons. They were commonly constructed under ground. They were shut out from the light of the sun. They were, of course, damp, dark, and unhealthy, and probably most filthy. Masters were in the habit of constructing such prisons for their slaves, where the unhappy prisoner, without light, or company, or comfort, spent his days and nights in weeping from grief, and in vainly gnashing his teeth from indignation. The image expresses the fact that the wicked who are lost will be shut out from the light of heaven, and from peace, and joy, and hope; will weep in hopeless grief, and will gnash their teeth in indignation against God, and murmur against his justice. What a striking image of future woe! Go to a damp, dark, solitary, and squalid dungeon; see a miserable and enraged victim; add to *his* sufferings the idea of eternity, and then remember that this, after all, is but an *image*, a faint image, of hell! Comp. Notes on Mat. xxii. 13.

13. *He was healed in that self-same hour.* This showed decisively the goodness and power of Jesus. No miracle could be more complete. There could be no imposition or deception.

This account, or one similar to this, is found in Lu. vii. 1–10. There has been a difference of opinion whether the account in Luke refers to the same case as that recorded in Matthew, or whether a *second* centurion, encouraged by the success of the first, applied to our Saviour in a similar case and manner, and obtained the same success. In support of the supposition that they are different narratives, it is said that they disagree so far that it is impossible to reconcile them, and that it is not *improbable* that a similar occurrence might take place, and be attended with similar results.

To a plain reader, however, the narratives appear to be the same. They agree in the character of the person, the place, and apparently the time; in the same substantial *structure* of the account; in the expression of similar feelings, the same answers, and the same result. It is very difficult to believe that all these circumstances would coincide in two different stories.

They differ, however. Matthew says that the centurion *came himself*. Luke says that he at first sent elders of the Jews, and then his particular friends. He also adds that he was friendly to the Jews, and had built them a synagogue. An infidel will ask whether there is not here a palpable contradiction. In explanation of this, let it be remarked: 1st. That the fact that the centurion came himself, supposing that to have

hast believed, *so* be it done unto thee. And his servant was healed in the self-same hour.

14 And when Jesus was come into Peter's house, he saw *l*his wife's mother laid, and sick of a fever.

15 And he touched her hand, and the fever left her: and she arose, and ministered unto them.

l Mar.1.30,31; Lu.4.38,39.

been the fact, is no evidence that others did not come also. It was *in* the city. The centurion was a great favourite, and had conferred on the Jews many favours, and they would be anxious that the favour which he desired of Jesus should be granted. At his suggestion, or of their own accord, his Jewish friends might apply to Jesus, and press the subject upon him, and be anxious to represent the case as favourably as possible. All this was probably done, as it would be in any other city, in considerable haste and apparent confusion; and one observer might fix his attention strongly on one circumstance, and another on another. It is not at all improbable that the *same* representation and request might have been made both by the centurion and his friends. Matthew might have fixed his eye very strongly on the fact that the centurion came *himself*, and been particularly *struck* with his deportment; and Luke on the remarkable zeal shown by the friends of a heathen, the interest they took in his welfare, and the circumstance that he had done much for them. Full of these interesting circumstances, he might comparatively have overlooked the centurion himself. But, 2d. It was a maxim among the Jews, as it is now in law, *that what a man does by another, he does himself*. So, in Mar. x. 35, James and John are represented as coming to the Saviour with a request: in Mat. xx. 20, it appears that they presented their request through their mother. In Jn. iv. 1, Jesus is said to baptize, when, in fact, he did not do it himself, but by his disciples. In Jn. xix. 1, Pilate is said to have scourged Jesus; but he certainly did not do it with his own hands. In the case of the centurion, Matthew narrates what occurred very briefly; Luke goes more into detail, and states more of the circumstances. Matthew was intent on the great leading facts of the cure. He was studious of brevity. He did not choose to explain the particular circumstances. He says that the centurion *made the application* and received the answer. He does not say whether by himself or by *an agent*. Luke explains particularly *how* it was done. There is no more contradiction, therefore, than there would be if it should be said of a man in a court of law that he came and made application for a new trial, when the application was really made by his lawyer. Two men, narrating the fact, might exhibit the same variety that Matthew and Luke have done, and both be true. It should never be forgotten that *the sacred narrative of an event is what it is stated to be by all the sacred writers; as the testimony in a court in which a case is decided is what is stated by all the credible witnesses, though one may have stated one circumstance and another another.*

One thing is most clearly shown by this narrative: that this account was not *invented* by the evangelists for the sake of imposition. If it had been, they would have *agreed in all the circumstances.*

14, 15. This account is contained also in Mar. i. 29-31, and Lu. iv. 38-41. Mark says that Simon and Andrew lived together, and that James and John went with them to the house. He adds, also, that *before* the miracle they spake to him about the sick person. The miracle was direct and complete. She that had been sick was so completely restored as to attend to them and minister to them. The mention of "*Peter's wife's mother*" proves that Peter either then was or had been married. The fair and obvious interpretation is, that his wife was then living. Comp. 1 Co. ix. 5, and see the Note on that place. Peter is claimed by the Roman Catholics to be the head of the church and the vicegerent of Christ. The Pope, according to their view, is the successor of this apostle. On what pretence do they maintain that it is wrong for *priests* to marry? Why did not Christ at once reject Peter from being an apostle for having a wife? How remarkable that *he* should be set up as the head of the church, and an example and a model to all who were to succeed him! But all this is human law, and is contrary to the New Testament.

16 When the even was come, they brought unto him [m]many that were possessed with devils: and he cast out the spirits with *his* word, and healed all that were sick:

17 That it might be fulfilled which was spoken by Esaias the prophet, saying, [n]Himself took our infirmities, and bare *our* sicknesses.

18 Now when Jesus saw great multitudes about him, he gave commandment to depart unto the other side.

19 And a certain scribe came, and said unto him, Master, [o]I will follow thee whithersoever thou goest.

20 And Jesus saith unto him, The foxes have holes, and the birds of the air *have* nests; but the Son of man hath not where to lay *his* head.

m Mar.1.32,&c. *n* Is.53.4; 1 Pe.2.24. *o* Lu.9.57,58.

Comp. 1 Ti. iii. 2, 4, 5. That Peter had a wife was no objection to his being an apostle, and marriage has been expressly declared to be "honourable in ALL," He. xiii. 4.

16. *When the even was come*, &c. The fame of the miracles of Jesus would probably draw together a crowd, and those who had friends that were afflicted would bring them. All that were brought to him he healed. This was proof of two things: first, of his great benevolence; and, secondly, of his divine mission. He might have established the latter by miracles that would do no good. None of his miracles were performed, however, merely to make a display of power, unless the cursing of the barren fig-tree be an exception. Comp. Mar. xi. 11–14. What is here recorded occurred on the evening of the Sabbath, Mar. i. 21–32. The Jews kept the Sabbath from evening to evening, Le. xxiii. 32. On the Sabbath they would not even bring their sick to be healed (Lu. xiii. 14); but as soon as it was closed, on the evening of the same day, they came in multitudes to be cured. ¶ *Possessed with devils.* See Notes on Mat. iv. 24. ¶ *With* his *word.* By his *command;* by a word.

17. *That it might be fulfilled*, &c. This passage is found in Is. liii. 4. Our English translation of that important passage is, "Surely he hath borne our griefs and carried our sorrows." The Greek in Matthew is an exact translation of the Hebrew, and the same translation should have been made in both places. In the fifty-third chapter, Isaiah fully states the doctrine of the atonement, or that the Messiah was to suffer for sin. In the verse quoted here, however, he states the very truth which Matthew declares. The word translated *griefs* in Isaiah, and *infirmities* in Matthew, means properly, in the Hebrew and Greek, *diseases of the body.* In neither does it refer to the disease of the mind, or to sin. To bear those griefs is clearly to bear them *away*, or to remove them. This was done by his miraculous power in healing the sick. The word rendered "sorrows" in Isaiah, and "sicknesses" in Matthew, means *pain, grief*, or *anguish of mind.* To *carry* these is to sympathize with the sufferers; to make provision for alleviating those sorrows, and to take them away. This he did by his precepts and by his example; and the *cause* of all sorrows—*sin*—he removed by the atonement. The passage in Isaiah and Matthew, therefore, mean precisely the same thing. See *Magee on Atonement*, and Notes on Isaiah, ch. liii.

18. *Unto the other side.* Jesus was now in Capernaum, a city at the north-west corner of the Sea of Tiberias, or Sea of Galilee. See Notes on Mat. iv. 18. The country to which he purposed to go was the region on the east of the Sea of Tiberias.

19, 20. *And a certain scribe came*, &c. It is not improbable that this man had seen the miracles of Jesus, and had formed an expectation that by following him he would obtain some considerable worldly advantage. Christ, in reply to his professed purpose to follow him, proclaimed his own poverty, and dashed the hopes of the avaricious scribe. The very foxes and birds, says he, have places of repose and shelter, but the Son of man has no home and no pillow. He is a stranger in his own world—a wanderer and an outcast from the abodes of men. Comp. Jn. i. 11. ¶ *Son of man.* This means, evidently, Jesus himself. No title is more frequently given to the Saviour than this, and yet there is much difficulty in ex-

21 And another of his disciples said unto him, [p]Lord, suffer me first to go and bury my father.

p 1 Ki.19.20.

22 But Jesus said unto him, Follow me; and let the dead bury their dead.

plaining it. The word *son* is used in a great variety of significations. See Notes on Mat. i. 1. The name *Son of man* is given to Jesus only three times in the New Testament (Ac. vii. 56; Re. i. 13; xiv. 14), except by himself. When he speaks of himself, this is the most common appellation by which he is known. The phrase *Son of God*, given to Christ, denotes a *peculiar* connection with God, Jn. x. 36. The name *Son of man* probably denotes a corresponding *peculiar* connection with man. Perhaps the Saviour used it to signify the interest he felt in man; his peculiar love and friendship for him; and his willingness to devote himself to the best interests of the race. It is sometimes, however, used as synonymous with *Messiah*, Mat. xvi. 28; Jn. i. 34; Ac. viii. 37; Jn. xii. 34.

21. *And another of his disciples*, &c. The word disciple properly signifies *learner*, and was given to the followers of Jesus because they received him as their teacher. See Notes on Mat. v. 1. It does not of necessity mean that a *disciple* was a pious man, but only one of the multitude, who, for various causes, might attend on his instructions. See Jn. vi. 66; ix. 28. ¶ *Suffer me first to go and bury my father.* This seemed to be a reasonable request, as respect for parents, living or dead, is one of the first duties of religion. But the Saviour saw that in his circumstances there might be danger, if he was thus permitted to go, that he would not return to him; and he commanded him, therefore, to perform the more important duty—the duty of attending to the salvation of his soul—even at the risk of the apparent neglect of another duty. The first duty of man is religion, and everything else should be made subordinate to that.

22. *Let the dead bury their dead.* The word dead is used in this passage in two different senses. It is apparently a paradox, but is fitted to convey the idea very distinctly to the mind. The Jews used the word *dead* often to express indifference toward a thing; or, rather, to show that that thing has no *influence* over us. Thus, to be dead to the world; to be dead to the law (Ro. vii. 4); to be dead to sin (Ro. vi. 11), means that the world, law, and sin have not influence or control over us; that we are free from them, and act *as though they were not.* A body in the grave is unaffected by the pomp and vanity, by the gaiety and revelry, by the ambition and splendour that may be near the tomb. So men of the world are dead to religion. They see not its beauty, hear not its voice, are not won by its loveliness. This is the class of men to which the Saviour refers here. Let men, says he, who are uninterested in my work, and who are *dead in sin* (Ep. ii. 1), take care of the dead. Your duty is now to follow me.

There may have been several reasons for this apparently harsh direction. One may have been to *test* the character and attachment of the man. If he had proper love for Christ, he would be willing to leave his friends, even in the most tender and trying circumstances. This is required, Mat. x. 27; Lu. xiv. 26. A second reason may have been, that if he returned *at that time*, his friends might ridicule or oppose him, or present plausible arguments, *in the afflictions of the family*, why he should not return to Christ. The thing to which he was called was moreover of more importance than any earthly consideration; and, for that time, Christ chose to require of the man a very extraordinary sacrifice, to show his sincere attachment to him. Or it may have been that the Saviour saw that the effect of visiting his home at that time might have been to drive away all his serious impressions, and that he would return to him no more. His impressions may not have been deep enough, and his purpose to follow the Saviour may not have been strong enough to bear the trial to which he would be subjected. Strange as it may seem, there are few scenes better fitted to drive away serious impressions than those connected with a funeral. We should have supposed it would be otherwise; but facts show it to be so, and demonstrate that if this was one of the reasons which influenced the Saviour, he had a thorough knowledge of human nature. The arrangements for the funeral, the preparation of mourning

23 And when he was entered into a ship, his disciples followed him.

24 And behold, [q]there arose a great tempest in the sea, insomuch that the ship was covered with the waves: but he was asleep.

25 And his disciples came to him, and awoke him, saying, Lord, save us: we perish.

26 And he saith unto them, Why are ye fearful, O ye of little faith? Then he arose, and [r]rebuked the winds and the sea; and there was a great calm.

27 But the men marvelled, say-

q Mar.4.37,&c.; Lu.8.23,&c.

r Job 38.11; Ps.89.9; 107.29.

---

apparel, and the depth of sorrow in such cases, divert the mind from its sins and its personal need of a Saviour; and hence few persons are awakened or converted as the result of death in a family. The case here was a *strong* one—it was as strong as can well be conceived; and the Saviour meant to teach by this that nothing is to be allowed to divert the mind from religion—nothing to be an excuse for not following him. Not even the death of a father, and the sorrows of an afflicted family, are to be suffered to lead a man to defer religion, or to put off the purpose to be a Christian. That is a fixed duty—a duty not to be deferred or neglected, whether in sickness or health, at home or abroad—whether surrounded by living and happy kindred, or whether a father, a mother, a child, or a sister lies in our house dead.

It is the *regular* duty of children to obey their parents, and to show them kindness in affliction, and to evince proper care and respect for them when dead. Nor did our Saviour show himself insensible to these duties. He taught here, however, as he always taught, that a regard to friends, and ease, and comfort, should be *subordinate to the gospel;* and that we should always be ready to sacrifice these when duty to God requires it.

23. *Into a ship.* This was on the Sea of Tiberias. The *ship* in which they sailed was probably a small open boat with sails, such as was commonly used for fishing on the lake. ¶ *His disciples.* Not merely the apostles, but probably many others. There were many other ships in company with him, Mar. iv. 36. This circumstance would render the miracle much more striking and impressive.

24. *A great tempest.* A violent storm; or a *wind* so strong as to endanger their lives. This lake was subject to sudden squalls. Dr. Thomson (*The Land and the Book*, vol. ii. p. 59) says: "Small as the lake is, and placid, in general, as a molten mirror, I have repeatedly seen it quiver, and leap, and boil like a caldron, when driven by fierce winds from the eastern mountains." ¶ *The ship was covered with the waves.* The billows dashed against the ship (Mar. iv. 37), so that it was fast filling and in danger of sinking. ¶ *He was asleep.* On the hinder part of the vessel, on a pillow, Mar. iv. 38. It was in the night, and Jesus had retired to rest. He was probably weary, and slept calmly and serenely. He apprehended no danger, and showed to his disciples how calmly one can sleep with a pure conscience, and who feels safe in the hands of God.

25. *Save us.* Save our lives. ¶ *We perish.* We are in danger of perishing. This showed great confidence in the Saviour. It shows, also, where sinners and Christians should always go who feel that they are in danger of perishing. There is none that can save from the storms of divine wrath but the Son of God.

26. *Why are ye fearful?* You should have remembered that the Son of God, the Messiah, was on board. You should not have forgotten that he had power to save, and that with him you are safe. So Christians should never fear danger, disease, or death. With Jesus they are safe. No enemy can reach *him;* and as *he* is safe, so they shall be also, Jn. xiv. 19. ¶ *Rebuked the winds.* Reproved them, or commanded them to be still. What a power was this! What irresistible proof that he was divine! His word awed the tempest and allayed the storm! There is not anywhere a sublimer description of a display of power. Nor could there be clearer proof that he was truly the Son of God. ¶ *A great calm.* The winds were still, and the sea ceased to dash against the vessel and to endanger their lives.

27. *The men marvelled.* Wondered,

ing, What manner of man is this, that even the winds and the sea obey him?

28 And[s] when he was come to the other side, into the country of the Gergesenes, there met him two

s Mar.5.1; Lu.8.26,&c.

or were amazed. ¶ *What manner of man.* What kind of a personage. How unlike other men! What a vast display of power! and how far exalted above mortals must he be!

Jesus spake to the winds; rebuked their raging, and the sea was suddenly calm. The storm subsided; the ship glided smoothly; danger fled; and in amazement they stood in the presence of him who controlled the tempests that God had raised; and they felt that *he* must be God himself, for none but God could calm the heaving billows and scatter the tempest. No scene could have been more grand than this display of the power of Jesus. The darkness; the dashing waves; the howling winds; the heaving and tossing ship; the fears and cries of the seamen, all by a single word hushed into calm repose, present an image of power and divinity irresistibly grand and awful. So the tempest rolls and thickens over the head of the awakened sinner. So he trembles over immediate and awful destruction. So, while the storm of wrath howls, and hell threatens to ingulf him, he comes trembling to the Saviour. He hears; he rebukes the storm, and the sinner is safe. An indescribable peace takes possession of the soul, and he glides on a tranquil sea to the haven of eternal rest. See Is. lvii. 20, 21; Ro. v. 1; Phi. iv. 7.

28-34. The same account of the demoniacs substantially is found in Mar. v. 1-20, and Lu. viii. 26-38.

28. *The other side.* The other side of the Sea of Tiberias. ¶ *Country of the Gergesenes.* Mark (v. 1) says that he came into the country of the *Gadarenes.* This difference is only apparent. *Gadara* was a city not far from the Lake Gennesareth, one of the ten cities that were called *Decapolis.* See Notes on Mat. iv. 25. *Gergesa* was a city about 12 miles to the south-east of Gadara, and about 20 miles to the east of the Jordan. There is no contradiction, therefore, in the evangelists. He came into the region in which the two cities were situated, and one evangelist mentioned one, and the other another. It shows that the writers had not *agreed* to impose on the world; for if they had, they would have mentioned the *same* city; and it shows, also, they were familiar with the country. No men would have written in this manner but those who were acquainted with the facts. Impostors do not mention *places* or *names* if they can avoid it. ¶ *There met him two.* Mark and Luke speak of only *one* that met him. "There met him out of the tombs *a man,*" Mar. v. 2. "There met him out of the tombs *a certain man,*" Lu. viii. 27. This difference of statement has given rise to considerable difficulty. It is to be observed, however, that neither Mark nor Luke say that there was *no more* than one. For particular reasons, they might have been led to fix their attention on the one that was more notorious, and furious, and difficult to be managed. Had they denied plainly that there was more than *one*, and had Matthew affirmed that there were *two*, there would have been an irreconcilable contradiction. As it is, they relate the affair as other men would. It shows that they were honest witnesses. Had they been impostors; had Matthew and Luke *agreed* to write books to deceive the world, they would have agreed exactly in a case so easy as this. They would have told the story with the same circumstances. Witnesses in courts of law often differ in unimportant matters; and, provided the *main* narrative coincides, their testimony is thought to be more valuable.

Luke has given us a hint why he recorded only the cure of *one* of them. He says there met him "*out of the city,*" a man, &c.; or, as it should be rendered, "*a man of the city,*" a *citizen.* Yet the man did not dwell in the city, for he adds in the same verse, "neither abode he in any house, but in the tombs." The truth of the case was, that he was born and educated in the city. He had probably been a man of wealth and eminence; he was well known, and the people felt a deep interest in the case. Luke was therefore particularly struck with his case; and as *his* cure fully established the power of Jesus, he recorded it. The other person that Matthew mentions was probably a stranger, or one less notorious as a maniac, and he felt less

possessed with devils, coming out of the tombs, exceeding fierce, so that no man might pass by that way.

29 And, behold, they cried out, saying, What have we to do with thee, Jesus, thou Son of God? art

interest in the cure. Let two persons go into a lunatic asylum and meet two insane persons, one of whom should be exceedingly fierce and ungovernable, and well known as having been a man of worth and standing; let them converse with them, and let the more violent one attract the principal attention, and they would very likely give the same account that Matthew and Luke do, and no one would doubt the statement was correct. ¶ *Possessed with devils.* See Notes on Mat. iv. 24. ¶ *Coming out of the tombs.* Mark and Luke say that they dwelt in the tombs. The sepulchres of the Jews were frequently *caves* beyond the walls of the cities in which they dwelt, or excavations made in the sides of hills, or sometimes in solid rocks. These caves or excavations were sometimes of great extent. They descended to them by flights of steps. These graves were not in the midst of cities, but in groves, and mountains, and solitudes. They afforded, therefore, to insane persons and demoniacs a place of retreat and shelter. They delighted in these gloomy and melancholy recesses, as being congenial to the wretched state of their minds. Josephus also states that these sepulchres were the haunts and lurking-places of those desperate bands of robbers that infested Judea. For further illustration of this subject see my Notes on Is. xiv. 9; xxii. 16; and lxv. 4. The ancient Gadara is commonly supposed to be the present Umkeis. "Near there Burckhardt reports that he found many sepulchres in the rocks, showing how naturally the conditions of the narrative respecting the demoniacs could have been fulfilled in that region. Reliable writers state that they have seen lunatics occupying such abodes of corruption and death."—Hackett's *Illustrations of Scripture*, p. 109. Dr. Thomson, however (*The Land and the Book*, vol. ii. p. 34-37), maintains that Gadara could not have been the place of the miracle, since that place is about "three hours" (some 10 or 12 miles) to the south of the extreme shore of the lake in that direction. He supposes that the miracle occurred at a place now called *Kerza* or *Gersa*, which he supposes was the ancient *Gergesa*. Of this place he says: "In this Gersa or Chersa we have a position which fulfils every requirement of the narratives, and with a name so near that in Matthew as to be in itself a strong corroboration of the truth of this identification. It is within a few rods of the shore, and an immense mountain rises directly above it, in which are ancient tombs, out of some of which the two men possessed of the devils may have issued to meet Jesus. The lake is so near the base of the mountain that the swine, rushing madly down it, could not stop, but would be hurried on into the water and drowned. The place is one which our Lord would be likely to visit, having Capernaum in full view to the north, and Galilee 'over against it,' as Luke says it was. The *name*, however, pronounced by Bedawin Arabs is so similar to Gergesa, that, to all my inquiries for this place, they invariably said it was at Chersa, and they insisted that they were identical, and I agree with them in this opinion."

29. *What have we to do with thee?* This might have been translated with great propriety, What hast thou to do with us? The meaning is "Why dost thou trouble or disturb us?" See 2 Sa. xvi. 10; 2 Ki. ix. 18; Ezr. iv. 3. ¶ *Son of God.* The title, *Son of God*, is often given to Christ. Men are sometimes called sons, or children of God, to denote their adoption into his family, 1 Jn. iii. 1. But the title given to Christ denotes his superiority to the prophets (He. i. 1); to Moses, the founder of the Jewish economy (He. iii. 6); it denotes his *peculiar* and near relation to the Father, as evinced by his resurrection (Ps. ii. 7; Ac. xiii. 33); it denotes his peculiar relation to God from his miraculous conception (Lu. i. 35); and is equivalent to a declaration that he is divine, or equal to the Father. See Notes on Jn. x. 36. ¶ *Art thou come hither to torment us?* &c. By *the time* here mentioned is meant the day of judgment. The Bible reveals the doctrine that evil spirits are not *now* bound as they will be after that day; that they are permitted to tempt and afflict men, but that in the day of judgment *they* also will be condemned to everlasting punishment with all the

thou come hither to torment us before the time?

30 And there was a good way off from them a herd of many swine, feeding.

31 So the devils besought him, saying, If thou cast us out, [t]suffer us to go away into the herd of swine.[u]

32 And he said unto them, Go. And when they were come out, they went into the herd of swine: and, behold, the whole herd of swine ran violently down a steep place into the sea, and perished in the waters.

33 And they that kept them fled, and went their ways into the city,

t Job 1.10-12; 2.3-6. u De.14.8; Is.65.3,4.

wicked, 2 Pe. ii. 4; Jude 6. These spirits seemed to be apprised of that, and were alarmed lest the day that they feared had come. They besought him, therefore, not to send them out of that country, not to consign them then to hell, but to put off the day of their final punishment.

Mark and Luke say that Jesus inquired the name of the principal demoniac, and that he called his name *Legion, for they were many*. The name legion was given to a division in the Roman army. It did not always denote the same number, but in the time of Christ it consisted of 6000—3000 foot and 3000 horsemen. It came, therefore, to signify *a large number*, without specifying the exact amount.

30. *A herd of many swine.* The word *herd*, here applied to swine, is now commonly given to *cattle*. Formerly it signified any collection of beasts, or even of men. The number that composed this *herd* was 2000, Mar. v. 13.

33. *They that kept them fled.* These swine were doubtless owned by the inhabitants of the country. Whether they were Jews or Gentiles is not certainly known. It was not properly in the territory of Judea; but, as it was on its borders, it is probable that the inhabitants were a mixture of Jews and Gentiles. Swine were to Jews unclean animals, and it was unlawful for them to eat them, Le. xi. 7. They were forbidden by their own laws to keep them, even for the purpose of traffic. Either, therefore, they had expressly violated the law, or these swine were owned by the Gentiles.

The keepers fled in consternation. They were amazed at the power of Jesus. Perhaps they feared a farther destruction of property; or, more likely, they were acquainted with the laws of the Jews, and regarded this as a judgment of heaven for keeping forbidden animals, and for tempting the Jews to violate the commands of God.

This is the only one of our Saviour's miracles, except the case of the fig-tree that he cursed (Mat. xxi. 18–20), in which he caused any destruction of property. It is a striking proof of his benevolence, that his miracles tended directly to the comfort of mankind. It was a proof of goodness *added* to the direct purpose for which his miracles were wrought. That purpose was to confirm his divine mission; and it might have been as fully done by splitting rocks, or removing mountains, or causing water to run up steep hills, as by any other display of power. He chose to exhibit the proof of his divine power, however, in such a way as to benefit mankind.

Infidels have objected to this whole narrative. They have said that this was a wanton and unauthorized violation of private rights in the destruction of property. They have said, also, that the account of devils going into swine, and destroying them, was ridiculous. In regard to these objections the narrative is easily vindicated. 1st. If Christ, as the Bible declares, is divine as well as human—God as well as man—then he had an original right to that and all other property, and might dispose of it as he pleased, Ps. l. 10–12. If God had destroyed the herd of swine by pestilence or by lightning, by an inundation or by an earthquake, neither the owners or anyone else would have had reason to complain. No one now feels that he has a right to murmur if God destroys a thousand times the amount of this property by overturning a city by an earthquake. Why, then, should complaints be brought against him if he should do the same thing in another way? 2d. If this property was held *by the Jews*, it was a violation of their law, and it was right that they should suffer the loss; if *by the Gentiles*, it was known also to be a violation of the law of the

and told every thing, and what was befallen to the possessed of the devils.

34 And, behold, the whole city came out to meet Jesus: and when they saw him, they besought *him* that he would [v]depart out of their coasts.

v Job 21.14; Lu.5.8; Ac.16.39.

people among whom they lived; a temptation and a snare to them; an abomination in their sight; and it was proper that the nuisance should be removed. 3d. The cure of two men, one of whom was probably a man of distinction and property, was of far more consequence than the amount of property destroyed. To restore a *deranged* man now would be an act for which *property* could not compensate, and which could not be measured in value by any pecuniary consideration. But, 4th. Jesus was not at all answerable for this destruction of property. He did not *command*, he only *suffered* or *permitted* the devils to go into the swine. He commanded them merely to *come out of the man. They* originated the purpose of destroying the property, doubtless for the sake of doing as much mischief as possible, and of destroying the effect of the miracle of Christ. In this they seem to have had most disastrous success, and they only are responsible. 5th. If it should be said that Christ *permitted* this, when he might have prevented it, it may be replied that the difficulty does not stop there. He *permits* all the evil that exists, when he might prevent it. He permits *men* to do much evil, when he might prevent it. He permits one bad man to injure the person and property of another bad man. He permits the bad to injure the good. He often permits a wicked man to fire a city, or to plunder a dwelling, or to rob a traveller, destroying property of many times the amount that was lost on this occasion. Why is it any more absurd to suffer a wicked spirit to do injury than a wicked man? or to suffer a *legion of devils* to destroy a herd of swine, than for *legions of men* to desolate nations, and cover fields and towns with ruin and slaughter?

34. *The whole city came out.* The people of the city probably came with a view of arresting him for the injury done to the property; but, seeing him, and being awed by his presence, they only besought him to leave them. ¶ *Out of their coasts.* Out of their country. This shows, 1st. That the design of Satan is to prejudice men against the Saviour, and even to make what Christ does an occasion why they should desire him to leave them. 2d. The power of avarice. These men preferred their property to the Saviour. They loved it so much that they were blind to the evidence of the miracle, and to the good he had done to the miserable men whom he had healed. It is no uncommon thing for men to love the world so much; to love property—even like that owned by the people of Gadara—so much as to see no beauty in religion and no excellence in the Saviour; and, rather than part with it, to beseech Jesus to withdraw from them. The most grovelling employment, the most abandoned sins, the most loathsome vices, are often loved more than the presence of Jesus, and more than all the blessings of his salvation.

REMARKS.

1st. The leprosy, the disease mentioned in this chapter, is a fit representation of the nature of sin. Like that, sin is loathsome; it is deep fixed in the frame; penetrating every part of the system; working its way to the surface imperceptibly, but surely; loosing the joints, and consuming the sinews of moral action; and adhering to the system till it terminates in eternal death. It goes down from age to age. It shuts out men from the society of the pure in heaven; nor can man be admitted there till God has cleansed the soul by his Spirit, and man is made pure and whole.

2d. The case of the centurion is a strong instance of the nature and value of humility, ver. 5–10. He sustained a fair character, and had done much for the Jews. Yet he had no exalted conception of himself. Compared with the Saviour, he felt that he was unworthy that he should come to his dwelling. So feels every humble soul. *Humility is an estimate of ourselves as we are.* It is a willingness to be known, and talked of, and treated just according to truth. It is a view of ourselves as lost, poor, and wandering creatures. Compared with other men—with angels, with Jesus, and with God—it is a feeling by which we regard ourselves as unworthy of notice. It is a readiness to occupy our appropriate station in the universe, and to put on humbleness of mind as our proper array, 1 Pe. v. 5.

3d. We have in the case of the centurion an equally beautiful exhibition of *faith*. He had unwavering confidence in the power of Jesus. He did not doubt at all that he was able to do for him just what he *needed, and what he wished him to do*. This is faith; and every man who has this *trust* or confidence in Christ for salvation, has *saving faith*.

4th. Humility and faith are always connected. The one prepares the mind for the other. Having a deep sense of our weakness and unworthiness, we are prepared to look to Him who *has* strength. Faith also produces humility. Jesus was humble; and believing on him, we catch his spirit and learn of him, Mat. xi. 28–30. Compared with him, we see our unworthiness. Seeing HIS *strength*, we see OUR *feebleness;* seeing *his* strength exerted to save creatures impure and ungrateful as we are, we sink away into an increased sense of our unfitness for his favour.

5th. We see the compassion and kindness of Jesus, ver. 16, 17. He has borne *our* heavy griefs. He provides comfort for us in sickness and sustains us in dying. But for his merciful arm, we should sink; and dying, we should die without hope. But

"Jesus can make a dying bed
Feel soft as downy pillows are;
While on his breast we lean our head,
And breathe our life out sweetly there."

6th. We are forcibly struck with his condescension, ver. 19, 20. Men of wickedness and crime dwell in splendid mansions, and stretch themselves on couches of ease; when afflicted, they recline on beds of down; but Jesus had no home and no pillow. The birds that fill the air with music and warble in the groves, nay, the very foxes, have homes and a shelter from the storms and elements; but He that made them, clothed in human flesh, was a wanderer, and had not where to lay his head. His sorrows he bore alone; his dwelling was in the mountains. In the palaces of the men for whom he toiled, and for whom he was about to bleed on a cross, he found no home and no sympathy. Surely this was compassion worthy of a God.

7th. It is no disgrace to be poor. The Son of God was poor, and it is no dishonour to be like him. If our Maker, then, has cast our lot in poverty; if he takes away by sickness or calamity the fruits of our toils; if he clothes us in homely and coarse apparel; if he bids the winds of heaven to howl around our open and lonely dwellings, let us remember that the Redeemer of mankind trod the same humble path, and that it can be no dishonour to be likened to him who was the beloved Son of God.

8th. We should be willing to embrace the gospel without hope of earthly reward, ver. 19–23. Religion promises no earthly honours or wealth. It bids its disciples to look beyond the grave for its highest rewards. It requires men to love religion *for its own sake;* to love the Saviour, even when poor, and cast out, and suffering, *because he is worthy of love;* and to be willing to forsake all the allurements which the world holds out to us for the sake of the purity and peace of the gospel.

9th. We learn the necessity of forsaking all for the sake of the gospel. Our *first* duty is to God, our Creator and Saviour; our second, to friends, to our relations, and to our country, ver. 22. When *God* commands we must follow him, nor should any consideration of ease, or safety, or imaginary duty deter us. To us it is of no consequence what men say or think of us. Let the will of God be prayerfully ascertained, and then let it be done though it carry us through ridicule and flames.

10th. Jesus can preserve us in the time of danger, ver. 23–27. He hushed the storm and his disciples were safe. *His* life was also in danger with *theirs*. Had the ship sunk, without a miracle he would have perished with them. So in every storm of trial or persecution, in every heaving sea of calamity, he is united to his followers. *His* interest and *theirs* is the same. He feels for them, he is touched with their infirmities, and he will sustain them. Because *I* live, says he, ye shall live also. Never, never, then, shall man or devil pluck one of his faithful followers from his hand, Jn. x. 27, 28.

11th. All that can disturb or injure us is under the control of the Christian's Friend, ver. 28–32. The very inhabitants of hell are bound, and beyond his permission they can never injure us. In spite, then, of all the malice of malignant beings, the friends of Jesus are safe.

12th. It is no uncommon thing for men to desire Jesus to depart from

CHAPTER IX.

AND he entered into a ship, and passed over, and came into his own city.

2 And,[a] behold, they brought to him a man sick of the palsy, lying on a bed: and Jesus, seeing

a Mar.2.3,&c.; Lu.5.18,&c.

---

them, ver. 34. Though he is ready to confer on them important favours, yet they hold *his* favours to be of far less consequence than some unimportant earthly possession. Sinners never love him, and always wish him away from their dwellings.

13th. It is no uncommon thing for Jesus to take men at their word, and leave them. He gives them over to worldly thoughts and pursuits; he suffers them to sink into crime, and they perish for ever. Alas! how many are there, like the dwellers in the country of the Gergesenes, that ask him to depart; that see him go without a sigh; and that never, never again behold him coming to bless them with salvation!

CHAPTER IX.

1. *And he entered into a ship*, &c. Jesus acceded to the request of the people of Gadara (ch. viii. 34), recrossed the Lake of Gennesareth, and returned to his own city. By *his own city* is meant Capernaum (Mar. ii. 1), the city which was at that time his home, or where he had his dwelling. See Notes on ch. iv. 13. This same account, with some additional circumstances, is contained in Mar. ii. 3–12, and Lu. v. 18–26.

2. *A man sick of the palsy*. See Notes on Mat. iv. 24. ¶ *Lying on a bed*. This was probably a mattress, or perhaps a mere blanket spread to lie on, so as to be easily borne. Being light, Jesus might with propriety command him to take it up and walk, ver. 6.

Mark says "*they uncovered the roof*," ch. ii. 4. Luke says "*they went upon the housetop, and let him down through the tiling*," ch. v. 19. To us it would appear that much injury must have been done to the house where Jesus was, and that they must be much incommoded by the removal of tiles and rafters, &c. An acquaintance, however, with the mode of building in the East removes every difficulty of this nature. Houses in Eastern countries are commonly square in their form, and of a single story. On approaching them from the street a single door is seen in the centre, and usually, directly above it, a single latticed window. This destitution of doors and lights from the streets, though it gives their dwellings a sombre appearance, is yet adapted to the habits of retirement and secrecy among the people of the East, where they are desirous of keeping their *females* from observation. See Notes on Mat. vi. 6. On entering the only door in front, the first room is a small square room, surrounded with benches, called the *porch*. In this room the master of the family commonly transacts business, and on private occasions receives visits. Passing through the porch, you enter a large square room directly in the centre of the building, called the *court*. Luke says that the *paralytic* was let down "*into the midst;*" not in the midst of the *people*, but of the *building*—the *middle place* of the house. This *court* is paved commonly with marble; and, if possible, a fountain of water is formed in the centre, to give it beauty, and to diffuse a grateful coolness. This room is surrounded by a gallery or covered walk on every side. From *that* covered walk doors open into the other apartments of the house.

This centre room, or court, is commonly uncovered or open above. In wet weather, however, and in times of great heat of the sun, it is covered with an awning or canvas, stretched on cords, and capable of being easily removed or rolled up. This is what Mark means when he says *they uncovered the roof*. They *rolled up* or removed this awning.

From the court to the roof the ascent is by flights of stairs, either in the covered walk or gallery or in the porch. The roof is nearly flat. It is made of earth; or, in houses of the rich, is a firmly constructed flooring, made of coals, chalk, gypsum, and ashes, made hard by repeated blows. On those roofs spears of grass, wheat, or barley sometimes spring up; but these are soon withered by the sun, Ps. cxxix. 6–8. The roof is a favourite place for walking, for repose in the cool of the day, for conversation, and for devotion. See Notes on Mat. vi. 6. On such a roof Rahab concealed the spies (Jos. ii. 6), Samuel talked with Saul (1 Sa. ix. 25), David walked at eventide (2 Sa. xi. 2),

their faith, said unto the sick of the palsy, [b]Son, be of good cheer; thy sins be forgiven thee.

b Mar.5.34.

3 And, behold, certain of the scribes said within themselves, This *man* blasphemeth.

and Peter went up to pray (Ac. x. 9). This roof was surrounded with a *balustrade*, or railing, breast-high, on the sides; but where a house was contiguous to another, and of the same height, the railing was lower, so as to walk from one roof to another. In cities where the houses were constructed in this manner, it was possible to walk through a considerable part of the city on the roofs. A breastwork or railing was of course built in the same manner around the *open space* in the centre, to prevent persons from falling *into* the court below. This railing, or breastwork, is what Luke (v. 19) says they let him down through. They removed it, probably, so that the couch could be conveniently let down with cords; and, standing on the roof *over* the Saviour, they let the man down directly before him. The perseverance they had manifested was the *evidence* of their faith or confidence in his power to heal the sick man.

The following cut exhibits the ground-plan of an Eastern dwelling, and illus-

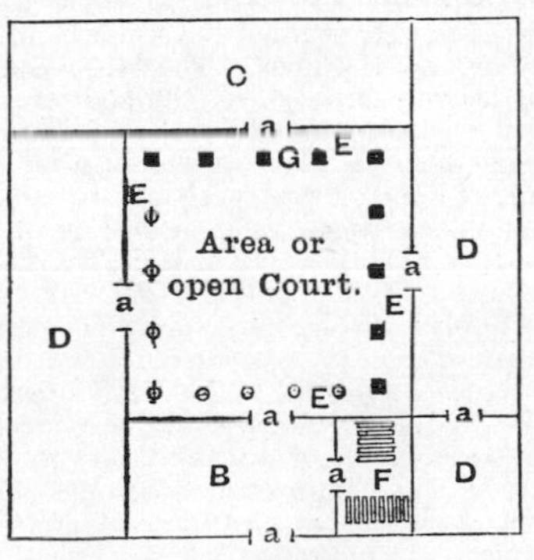

a Doors. B Porch.
C Harem, or room for women.
D Other rooms, for the family.
E Galleries, or walks between the court and rooms.
F Stairs to the second story, or to the roof.

trates the account of the cure of the sick man.

By looking at this it may be easily seen how the paralytic was presented to Jesus. Suppose the Saviour to be seated in the open court, say at G. The room was thronged. There was but one way of access, through *a*. It would be easy to ascend the stairs at F, and go round on the gallery till they came over Jesus, and remove a part of the balustrade or breastwork, and let him down directly before him. ¶ *Be of good cheer: thy sins be forgiven thee.* It may seem remarkable, since the man came only to be *healed*, that Jesus should have first declared his sins forgiven. For this the following reasons may be suggested: 1st. The man might have brought on this disease of the palsy by a long course of vicious indulgence. Conscious of guilt, he may have feared that he was so great a sinner that Christ would not regard him. He therefore assured him that his offences were pardoned, and that he might lay aside his fears. 2d. Jesus might be willing to show his power to forgive sins. Had he stated it without any miracle, the Jews would not have believed it, and even his disciples might have been staggered. In proof of it, he worked a miracle; and no one, therefore, could doubt that he had the power. The miracle was wrought in *express attestation* of the assertion that he had power to forgive sins. As God would not work a miracle to confirm a falsehood or to deceive men, the miracle was a solemn confirmation, on the part of God, that Jesus had the power to forgive sins. 3d. The Jews regarded disease as the effect of sin, Jn. ix. 2; Ja. v. 14, 15. There is a *real* connection between sin and suffering, as in the case of gluttony, intemperate drinking, lewdness, debauchery. Jesus might be willing to direct the minds of the spectators *to this fact;* and, by pointing them to a manifest instance of the effect of sin, to lead them to hate and forsake it. Diseases are sometimes the direct judgment of God for sin, 1 Co. v. 3–5; xi. 30; 2 Sa. xxiv. 10–14. This truth, also, Christ might have been desirous of impressing on the people.

3. *This* man *blasphemeth.* The word *blaspheme* originally means to speak evil of anyone; to injure by words; to blame unjustly. When applied to God, it means to speak of him unjustly; to ascribe to him acts and attributes which he does not possess; or to speak

4 And Jesus, [c]knowing their thoughts, said, Wherefore think ye evil in your hearts?

5 For whether is easier to say, *Thy* sins be forgiven thee; or to say, Arise, and walk?

6 But that ye may know that the Son of man hath power on earth to [d]forgive sins (then saith he to the sick of the palsy), Arise, take up thy bed, and go unto thine house.

7 And he arose, and departed to his house.

8 But when the multitude saw *it*, they marvelled, and [e]glorified God, which had given such power unto men.

9 And[f] as Jesus passed forth from thence, he saw a man, named

c Ps.139.2; Jn.2.24,25; He.4.12,13; Re.2.23. d Mi.7.18.

e Ac.4.21; Ga.1.24. f Mar.2.14; Lu.5.27,&c.

impiously or profanely. It also means to say or do anything by which his name or honour is insulted, or which conveys an *impression* unfavourable to God. It means, also, to attempt to do, or say a thing, which belongs to him alone, or which he only can do. This is its meaning here. Christ was charged *with saying a thing in his own name, or attempting to do a thing, which properly belonged to God;* thus assuming the *place* of God, and doing him injury, as the scribes supposed, by an invasion of his prerogatives. "None," said they (see Mark and Luke), "can forgive sins but God only." In this they reasoned correctly. See Is. xliii. 25; xliv. 22. None of the prophets had this power; and by saying that *he forgave sins*, Jesus was understood to affirm that he was divine; and as he proved this by working a miracle *expressly* to confirm the claim, it follows that he is divine, or equal with the Father.

4. *Jesus, knowing their thoughts.* Mark says, "Jesus perceived *in his spirit* that they so reasoned." The power of searching the heart, and of knowing the thoughts of men, belongs only to God, 1 Ch. xxviii. 9; Ro. viii. 27; Re. ii. 23; Je. xvii. 10. In claiming this, as Jesus did here, and often elsewhere, he gave clear proofs of his omniscience, Jn. ii. 24, 25.

5. *For whether is easier to say,* Thy *sins be forgiven thee; or to say, Arise and walk?* The one involves divine *power*, the other divine *authority*, and neither can be done but by God. One is as easy as the other; and to be able to do the one, involves the right and the power to do the other.

6. *But that ye may know,* &c. That you may have full proof on that point; that you may see that I have power to forgive sin, I will perform an act which all must perceive and admit to require the power of God. ¶ *Arise, take up thy bed, and go unto thine own house.* The fact that the paralytic man could do this would *prove* that a miracle was wrought. He was healed by a word; it was done instantaneously; it was done in the most public manner. The fact that a man, just before perfectly helpless, could now take up and carry his own bed or couch, proved that a divine *power* had been exerted; and that fact proved that he who had performed the miracle *must* also have the *power* and the *authority* to forgive sin. It is proper to add, in illustrating this, that in the East a "*bed*" is often nothing more than a bolster and a blanket spread on the floor. "The bed provided for me," says Professor Hackett (*Illustrations of Scripture*, p. 112) "consisted merely of a bolster and a blanket spread on the floor. The latter could be drawn partially over the body if any one wished, though the expectation seemed to be that we should sleep in our ordinary dress, without any additional covering. Such a bed is obviously a portable one; it is easy to take it up, fold it together, and carry it from place to place, as convenience may require."

8. *They glorified God.* See Notes on Mat. v. 16. To *glorify* God, here, means to *praise him*, or to acknowledge his power. The expression, *which had given such power to men*, was a part of *their* praise. It expresses no sentiment of the evangelist about the nature of Christ, but is a record of *their* feelings and *their* praise.

9. *He saw a man, named Matthew, sitting at the receipt of custom.* That is, at the place where *custom*, or *tribute*, was received; or, in other words, he was a *publican* or tax-gatherer. See Notes on Mat. v. 47. This man was the writer of this gospel. The same

Matthew, sitting at the receipt of custom: and he saith unto him, Follow me. And he arose, and followed him.

10 And it came to pass, as Jesus sat at meat in the house, behold, many publicans and sinners came and sat down with him and his disciples.

11 And when the Pharisees saw *it*, they said unto his disciples, Why eateth your Master with [g]publicans and sinners?

12 But when Jesus heard *that*, he said unto them, They that be whole need not a physician, but they that are sick.

13 But go ye and learn what

g ch.11.19; Lu.15.2; He.5.2.

account is found in Mar. ii. 14, and Lu. v. 27, 28. Both those evangelists call him *Levi*. That it was the same man is known by the circumstances in which he was called being the same in all the evangelists, and by their all concurring in the statement that the Saviour was present at a feast soon after he called him, and by the fact that *Levi* is not mentioned in the catalogue of the apostles. The Jews were in the habit of giving several names to the same person. Thus Peter was also called Simon and Cephas. It is worthy of remark that Luke has mentioned a circumstance favourable to Matthew, which Matthew himself has omitted. Luke says "*he left all.*" Had Matthew said this, it would have been a commendation of himself utterly unlike the evangelists. No men were ever farther from *praising themselves* than they were.

10. *And it came to pass, as Jesus sat at meat in the house.* This was at a feast given to him by *Levi* or *Matthew*, Lu. v. 29. This is another circumstance favourable to Matthew, but omitted by him, and recorded by Luke; showing also that the apostles were averse to praising themselves. To receive Christ hospitably and kindly was a commendable act, and it strongly evinces Matthew's freedom from ostentation that he has not himself mentioned the fact. It thus illustrates the command of the Saviour, as recorded by himself, Mat. vi. 1-4. ¶ *At meat.* At the table; at supper. ¶ *Many publicans and sinners came.* Probably the old friends of Matthew who had been invited by him. The character of a *publican*, or tax-gatherer, among the Jews was commonly not very respectable (see Notes on ch. v. 47; xviii. 17), and there is no improbability in supposing that Matthew, before his conversion, had sustained the general character of such men, and that his associations and friendships had been among those who were not remarkable for their morality.

11. *Why eateth and drinketh*, &c. To eat and drink with others denotes intimacy and familiarity. The Pharisees, by asking this question, accused him of seeking the society of such men, and of being the companion of the wicked. The inference which *they* would draw was, that he could not be himself righteous, since he delighted in the company of abandoned men.

12. *They that be whole*, &c. Jesus, in reply, said that the whole needed not a physician. Sick persons only needed his aid. A physician would not commonly be found with those that were in health. His proper place was among the sick. So, says he, "If you Pharisees are such as you think yourselves—already pure and holy—you do not need *my* aid. It would be of no use to you, and you would not thank me for it. With those persons who feel that they are sinners I may be useful, and there is my proper place." Or the expression may mean, "I came on purpose to save sinners: my business is with them. There are none righteous; and as a physician is in his proper place with the *sick*, so am I with guilty and miserable sinners."

13. *But go ye and learn*, &c. To reprove them, and to vindicate his own conduct, he appealed to a passage of Scripture with which they ought to have been acquainted: "I will have mercy, and not sacrifice," Ho. vi. 6. This is not a declaration on the part of God that he was opposed to *sacrifices* or *offerings for sin;* for he had appointed and commanded many, and had therefore expressed his approbation of them. It is a Hebrew mode of speaking, and means, *I prefer mercy to sacrifice;* or, *I am more pleased with acts of benevolence and kindness than with a mere external compliance with the duties of religion. Mercy* here means benevolence or kind-

that meaneth, [h]I will have mercy, and not sacrifice: for I am not come to call the righteous, [i]but sinners to repentance.

14 Then came to him the disciples of John, saying, Why do we and the Pharisees fast oft, but thy disciples fast not?

15 And Jesus said unto them, Can the children of the bride-chamber mourn as long as [k]the bridegroom is with them? but the days will come when the bridegroom shall be taken from them, and [l]then shall they fast.

16 No man putteth a piece of [1]new cloth unto an old garment; for that which is put in to fill it

h Pr.21.3; Ho.6.6; Mi.6.8; ch.12.7.
i Lu.24.47; Ac.5.31; 2 Pe.3.9.
k ch.25.1,10; Jn.3.29; Re.21.2.
l Is.22.12. [1] or, *raw*, or, *unwrought cloth.*

ness towards others. *Sacrifices* were offerings made to God on account of sin, or as an expression of thanksgiving. They were commonly bloody offerings, or animals slain; signifying that the sinner offering them deserved to die himself, and pointing to the great sacrifice or offering which Christ was to make for the sins of the world. *Sacrifices* were the principal part of the worship of the Jews, and hence came to signify *external worship in general.* This is the meaning of the word here. The sense in which our Saviour applies it is this: "You Pharisees are exceedingly tenacious of the *external* duties of religion; but God has declared that he prefers benevolence or mercy to those external duties. It is proper, therefore, that I should associate with sinners for the purpose of doing them good." ¶ *I came not to call the righteous,* &c. No human beings are by nature righteous, Ps. xiv. 3; Ro. i. 18–32; iii. 10–18. The Pharisees, however, *pretended* to be righteous. Christ might have meant by this answer that it was not the design of his coming to call such persons to repentance, knowing that they would spurn his efforts, and that to a great extent they would be vain; or, more probably, he meant to affirm that his proper and only business was to call to repentance such men as he was now with. He came to seek and save such, and it was his *proper business,* therefore, to associate with them. ¶ *Repentance.* See Notes on Mat. iii. 2.

14–17. *Then came the disciples of John,* &c. This narrative is found also in Mar. ii. 18–22; Lu. v. 33–39. The reference here is to John the Baptist. It is probable that they had understood that John was the forerunner of the Messiah; and if such was the case, they could not account for the fact that there was such a difference between them and the disciples of Jesus. The Pharisees fasted often—regularly twice a week, besides the great national days of fasting, Lu. xviii. 12. See Notes on Mat. vi. 16–18. This was the established custom of the land, and John did not feel himself authorized to make so great a change as to dispense with it. They were desirous of knowing, therefore, why Jesus had done it.

Besides, it is probable that this question was put to Jesus when John was in prison, and his disciples, involved in deep grief on account of it, observed days of fasting. Fasting was the natural expression of sorrow, and they wondered that the followers of Jesus did not join with them in lamenting the captivity of him who was the forerunner and baptizer of their Lord.

Christ, in reply to them, used three illustrations, all of them going to establish the same thing—that *we should observe a fitness and propriety in things.* The first is taken from a marriage. The children of the bride-chamber—that is, the bridemen, or *men who had the special care of the bridal chamber, and who were therefore his special friends*—do not think of fasting while he is with them. With them it is a time of festivity and rejoicing, and mourning would not be appropriate. When he is removed or taken away, then their festivity will be ended, and *then* will be the proper time for sorrow. So, says he, John, your friend and teacher, is in captivity. With you it is a time of deep grief, and it is fit that *you* should fast. I am *with* my disciples. It is with them a time of joy. It is not fit that they should use the tokens of grief, and fast now. When *I* am taken away, it will then be proper that they should fast. For an account of the ceremonies of an Eastern marriage, see Notes on Mat. xxv. 1–13.

16. *No man putteth a piece of new cloth,* &c. A second illustration was drawn

up taketh from the garment, and the rent is made worse.

17 Neither do men put new wine into old bottles; else [m] the bottles break, and the wine runneth out, and the bottles perish: but they put new wine into new bottles, and both are preserved.

18 While[n] he spake these things unto them, behold, there came a certain ruler and worshipped him, saying, My daughter is even now dead; but come and lay thy hand upon her, and [o] she shall live.

19 And Jesus arose and followed him, and *so did* his disciples.

m Job 32.19.

n Mar.5.22; Lu.8.41,&c. o Jn.11.22,25.

---

from a well-known fact, showing also that there was *a propriety or fitness of things.* None of you, says he, in mending an old garment, would take a piece of entire new cloth. There would be a waste in it. An old piece, or a piece *like* the garment, would be better. The word here translated *new*, in the original means *rude, undressed, not fulled* by the cloth-dresser. In this state, if applied to an old garment, and if wet, it would *contract* and draw off a part of the garment to which it was attached, and thus make the rent worse than it was. So, says he, my *new* doctrines do not *match* with the old rites of the Pharisees. There is a fitness of things. Their doctrines require much fasting. In my system it would be incongruous; and if my *new* doctrines were to be attached to their old ones, it would only make the matter worse.

17. *Neither do men put new wine, &c.* The third illustration was taken from wine put into bottles. Bottles, in Eastern nations, were made, and are still made, of skins of beasts. Generally the skin was taken entire from a sheep or a goat, and, properly prepared, was filled with wine or water. Such bottles are still used, because, in crossing deserts of sand, they have no other conveyances but camels, or other beasts of burden. It would be difficult for them to carry glass bottles or kegs on them. They therefore fill two skins, and fasten them together and lay them across the back of a camel, and thus carry wine or water to a great distance. These bottles were, of course, of different sizes, as the skins of kids, goats, or oxen might be used. Bruce describes particularly a bottle which he saw in Arabia, made in this manner of an ox-skin, which would hold 60 gallons, and two of which were a load for a camel. By long usage, however, bottles of skins became tender and would be easily ruptured. New wine put into them would ferment, and swell and burst them open. New skins or bottles would *yield* to the fermenting wine, and be strong enough to hold it from bursting. So, says Christ, there is a *fitness* or propriety of things. It is not *fit* that my doctrine should be attached to or connected with the old and corrupt doctrines of the Pharisees. New things should be put together, and made to *match.*

This account of Eastern bottles may illustrate the following passages in the Bible: The Gibeonites took "wine-bottles, old, and rent, and bound up," Jos. ix. 4. "My belly is ready to burst, like new bottles," Job xxxii. 19. "I am become like a bottle in the smoke," Ps. cxix. 83; *i.e.* like a bottle of skin hung up in a tent filled with smoke.

18-26. The account contained in these verses is also recorded, with some additional circumstances, in Mar. v. 22-43, and Lu. viii. 41-56.

18. *There came a certain ruler.* Mark and Luke say that his name was Jairus, and that he was a *ruler of the synagogue;* that is, one of the elders to whom was committed the care of the synagogue. See Notes on Mat. iv. 23. ¶ *And worshipped him.* That is, fell down before him, or expressed his respect for him by a token of profound regard. See Notes on Mat. ii. 2. ¶ *My daughter is even now dead.* Luke says that this was his only daughter, and that she was twelve years of age. Mark and Luke say that she was *at the point of death*, and that information of her actual death was brought to him by one who was sent by the ruler of the synagogue, while Jesus was going. Matthew combined the two facts, and stated the representation which was made to Jesus, without stopping particularly to exhibit the *manner* in which it was done. In a summary way he says that the *ruler* communicated the information. Luke and Mark, dwelling more particularly on the circumstances, state at length the way in which it was done; that is, by himself stating, in a hurry, that she

20 And,[p] behold, a woman, which was diseased with an issue of blood twelve years, came behind *him*, and touched the hem of his garment:

21 For she said within herself, If I may but touch [q]his garment, I shall be whole.

22 But Jesus turned him about; and when he saw her, he said, Daughter, be of good comfort; [r]thy faith hath made thee whole. And the woman was made whole [s]from that hour.

23 And[t] when Jesus came into the ruler's house, and saw [u]the

p Mar.5.25; Lu.8.43. q Ac.19.12.

r Lu.7.50; 17.19; 18.42; Ac.14.9. s Jn.4.53. t Mar.5.38; Lu.8.51. u 2 Ch.35.25.

was *about to die*, or *was dying*, and then in a few moments sending word that *she was dead*. The Greek word, rendered *is even now dead*, does not of necessity mean, as our translation would express, that she had actually expired, but only that she was *dying* or about to die. Comp. Ge. xlviii. 21. It is likely that a father, in these circumstances, would use a word as nearly expressing actual death as would be consistent with the fact that she was alive. The passage may be expressed thus: "My daughter was so sick that she must be by this time dead." ¶ *Come and lay thy hand upon her.* It was customary for the Jewish prophets, in conferring favours, to lay their hand on the person benefited. Jesus had probably done so also, and the ruler had probably witnessed the fact.

20. *And, behold, a woman*, &c. This disease was by the Jews reckoned unclean (Le. xv. 25), and the woman was therefore unwilling to make personal application to Jesus, or even to touch his person. The disease was regarded as incurable. She had expended all her property, and grew worse, Mar. v. 26. ¶ *Touched the hem of his garment.* This garment was probably the square garment which was thrown over the shoulders. See Notes on Mat. v. 40. This was surrounded by a border or *fringe;* and this *fringe*, or the loose threads hanging down, is what is meant by the *hem*. The Jews were commanded to wear this, in order to distinguish them from other nations. See Nu. xv. 38, 39; De. xxii. 12.

Mark says that *the woman, fearing and trembling*, came and told him all the truth. Perhaps she feared that, from the impure nature of her disease, he would be offended that she touched him.

22. *But Jesus turned him about, and when he saw her, he said, Daughter, be of good comfort.* Jesus silenced her fears, commended her faith, and sent her away in peace. He used an endearing appellation, calling her *daughter*, a word of tenderness and affection, and dismissed her who had been twelve long and tedious years labouring under a weakening and offensive disease, now in an instant made whole. Her faith, her strong confidence in Jesus, had been the means of her restoration. It was the *power* of Jesus that cured her; but that power would not have been exerted but in connection with faith. So in the salvation of a sinner. No one is saved who does not believe; but faith is the *instrument*, and not the *power*, that saves.

23. *And when Jesus came into the ruler's house*, &c. Jesus permitted only three of his disciples, Peter, James, and John the brother of James, and the father and mother of the damsel, to go in with him where the corpse lay, Mar. v. 37–40. It was important that there should be *witnesses* of the miracle, and he chose a sufficient number. *Five* witnesses were enough to establish the fact. The witnesses were impartial. The fact that she was dead was established beyond a doubt. Of this the mourners, the parents, the messengers, the people, were satisfied. If she was presented to the people *alive*, the proof of the miracle was complete. The presence of more than the *five* witnesses would have made the scene tumultuous, and have been less satisfactory evidence of the fact of the restoration of the child. Five sober witnesses are always better than the confused voices of a rabble. These were the same disciples that were with him in the mount of transfiguration and in the garden of Gethsemane, Mar. ix. 2, and xiv. 33; 2 Pe. i. 17, 18. ¶ *And saw the minstrels and the people making a noise. Minstrels* are persons who play on instruments of music. The people of the East used to bewail the dead by cutting the flesh, tearing the hair, and crying bitterly.

minstrels and the people making a noise,

24 He said unto them, Give place; [v]for the maid is not dead, but sleepeth. And they laughed him to scorn.

v Ac.20.10.

See Je. ix. 17; xvi. 6, 7; Eze. xxiv. 17. The expressions of grief at the death of a friend, in Eastern countries, are extreme. As soon as a person dies, all the females in the family set up a loud and doleful cry. They continue it as long as they can without taking breath, and the shriek of wailing dies away in a low sob. Nor do the relatives satisfy themselves with these expressions of violent grief. They hire persons of both sexes, whose employment it is to mourn for the dead in the like frantic manner. See Am. v. 16; Je. ix. 20. They sing the virtues of the deceased, recount his acts, dwell on his beauty, strength, or learning; on the comforts of his family and home, and in doleful strains ask him why he left his family and friends. To all this they add soft and melancholy music. They employ *minstrels* to aid their grief, and to increase the expressions of their sorrow. This violent grief continues, commonly, eight days. In the case of a king, or other very distinguished personage, it is prolonged through an entire month. This grief does not cease at the house; it is exhibited in the procession to the grave, and the air is rent with the wailings of real and of hired mourners. Professor Hackett (*Illustrations of Scripture*, p. 121, 122) says: "During my stay at Jerusalem I frequently heard a singular cry issuing from the houses in the neighbourhood of the place where I lodged, or from those on the streets through which I passed. It was to be heard at all hours—in the morning, at noonday, at evening, or in the deep silence of night. For some time I was at a loss to understand the cause of this strange interruption of the stillness which, for the most part, hangs so oppressively over the lonely city. Had it not been so irregular in its occurrence, I might have supposed it to indicate some festive occasion; for the tones of voice (yet hardly tones so much as shrieks) used for the expression of different feelings sound so much alike to the unpractised ear, that it is not easy always to distinguish the mournful and the joyous from each other. I ascertained, at length, that this peculiar cry was, no doubt, in most instances, the signal of the death of some person in the house from which it was heard. It is customary, when a member of the family is about to die, for the friends to assemble around him and watch the ebbing away of life, so as to remark the precise moment when he breathes his last, upon which they set up instantly a united outcry, attended with weeping, and often with beating upon the breast, and tearing out the hair of the head. This lamentation they repeat at other times, especially at the funeral, both during the procession to the grave and after the arrival there, as they commit the remains to their last resting-place."

The Jews were forbidden to tear their hair and cut their flesh. See Le. xix. 28; De. xiv. 1. They showed *their* grief by howling, by music, by concealing the chin with their garment, by rending the outer garment, by refusing to wash or anoint themselves, or to converse with people, by scattering ashes or dust in the air, or by lying down in them, Job i. 20; ii. 12; 2 Sa. i. 2–4; xiv. 2; xv. 30; Mar. xiv. 63. The expressions of grief, therefore, mentioned on this occasion, though excessive and foolish, were yet strictly in accordance with Eastern customs.

24. *The maid is not dead, but sleepeth.* It cannot be supposed that our Lord means *literally* to say that the child was not dead. Every possible evidence of her death had been given, and he acted on that himself, and conveyed to the people the idea that he raised her *from the dead*. He meant to speak in opposition to their opinions. It is not unlikely that Jairus and the people favoured the opinions of the Sadducees, and that *they* understood by her being dead that she had *ceased to be*, and that she would never be raised up again. In opposition to this, the Saviour used the expression *she sleepeth;* affirming mildly both that the *body* was dead, and *implying* that *her spirit* still lived, and that she would be raised up again. A similar mode of speaking occurs in Jn. xi. 11: "Our friend Lazarus *sleepeth.*" The sacred writers often spoke of the pious dead as *sleeping*, 2 Pe. iii. 4; Ac. vii. 60; 1 Co. xv. 6, 18; 1 Th. iv. 13–15. The meaning of this passage, then, is, the maid has not ceased to *exist;* but,

25 But[w] when the people were put forth, he went in, and took her by the hand, and the maid arose.

26 And [2]the fame hereof went abroad into all that land.

27 And when Jesus departed thence, two blind men followed him, crying, and saying, [x]*Thou* Son of David, have mercy on us.

28 And when he was come into the house, the blind men came to him: and Jesus saith unto them, Believe ye that I am able to do this? They said unto him, Yea, Lord.

29 Then touched he their eyes, saying, According to your faith be it unto you.

30 And their eyes were opened: and Jesus straitly charged them, saying, [y]See *that* no man know *it*.

w 2 Ki.4.33,&c. x ch.15.22; 20.30,31. 2 or, *this fame.*

y Is.42.2; 52.13; ch.12.16.

though her body is dead, yet her spirit lives, and she sleeps in the hope of the resurrection. ¶ *Laughed him to scorn.* Derided him; ridiculed him.

25. *He went in.* With the father, and mother, and three disciples, Mar. v. 37–40. ¶ *The maid arose.* She returned to life. There could be no deception here. *Parents* could not be imposed on in such a case, nor could such a multitude be deceived. The power of Jesus was undoubtedly shown to be sufficient to raise the dead.

27. *And when Jesus departed thence.* The scene of this miracle was near Capernaum. The blind men probably followed him with their cry for aid immediately on his leaving the house of Jairus. ¶ Thou *Son of David.* By the Son of David the Jews meant the Messiah. He was *the* descendant or Son of David by way of eminence, Is. ix. 7; Lu. i. 32; Re. xxii. 16. See Notes on Mat. i. 1. This was therefore a profession of belief, on the part of these blind men, of the Messiahship of Jesus, and, at the same time, the expression of a belief that, *being* the Messiah, he could heal them. ¶ *Have mercy on us.* That is, show compassion towards us in our affliction, and restore to us the blessing of sight.

28. *And when he was come into the house.* That is, either into the house which he usually occupied in Capernaum, or the house of some friend. They had followed him, but thus far he had not seemed to heed their cries, and he entered the house *as if* he did not intend to regard them—probably for the trial of their faith. ¶ *The blind men came to him.* That is, they followed him into the house. They showed a determination to persevere until they obtained what they asked. ¶ *Believe ye that I am able to do this?* To work such a miracle. Though they had followed him and cried after him, yet he required of them an open profession of their faith in regard to his power. ¶ *They said unto him, Yea, Lord.* We have no doubt of this. We came with that assurance; we have followed thee with that belief. It was on this simple profession of their faith that the miracle was wrought, as it is on the simple profession of *our* faith that our souls will be saved.

29. *Then touched he their eyes.* Simply to indicate that the power proceeded from him. Comp. ch. viii. 3. ¶ *According to your faith,* &c. That is, you have *believed* that you could be healed, be healed accordingly. Your faith covered the whole extent of the work respecting my power and the absolute restoration to sight, and that power is exerted accordingly, and your sight is restored. So with the sinner. If he has faith on the Son of God; if he believes that he is able and willing to save him; and if he earnestly desires to be saved, the power of Jesus will be put forth to the full extent of his faith.

30. *And their eyes were opened.* Immediately. That is, their sight was restored. ¶ *And Jesus straitly charged them.* He enjoined it on them in the most earnest and solemn manner. ¶ *See* that *no man know* it. That is, do not make proclamation of this; do not make it your business to tell every man of it; do not go forth as if *I* wished that you should proclaim this abroad. The injunction could not mean that they should screen the fact that no one *should* know it, for there were witnesses of it, and it would be made known; but they were not to make it a point to proclaim to the world what was done

31 But they, when they were departed, spread abroad his fame in all that country.

32 As they went out, behold, they brought to him [z]a dumb man possessed with a devil.

33 And when the devil was cast out, [a]the dumb spake: and the multitudes marvelled, saying, It was never so seen in Israel.

34 But the Pharisees said, [b]He casteth out devils through the prince of the devils.

35 And[c] Jesus went about all the cities and villages, teaching in their synagogues, and preaching the gospel of the kingdom, and healing every sickness and every disease among the people.

36 But when he saw the multi-

z ch.12.22; Lu.11.14. a Is.35.6. b ch.12.24; Mar.3.22; Lu.11.15. c ch.4.23.

to them. This was in accordance with the usual habit of the Saviour (ch. viii. 4; xii. 16), and also with his own precepts to others (ch. vi. 1-4).

31. *But they, when they were departed, spread abroad his fame.* The report of what he had done. This was not unnatural for them. They were so filled with joy that they could not repress their feelings. In this, however, they violated the express command of the Saviour; but he was not responsible for that.

32. *And as they went out, behold, they brought unto him.* That is, the friends of the dumb man brought him. This seems to have occurred as soon as the blind men which had been healed left him. Possibly it was from what they had observed of his power in healing them. ¶ *A dumb man possessed with a devil.* That is, the effect of the "possession," in his case, was to deprive him of speech. Those "possessed with devils" were affected in different ways (see Notes on ch. iv. 24), and there is no improbability in supposing that if other forms of disease occurred under demoniacal possessions, this form might occur also.

33. *And when the devil was cast out, the dumb spake.* The miracle is narrated in the briefest terms; but the effect was immediate and the restoration was complete. ¶ *It was never so seen in Israel.* Never was there in our land among the Jews—such a succession of wonders, so striking, so marvellous, so full of the power of God. This was literally true.

34. *But the Pharisees said, He casteth out devils through the prince of the devils.* That is, Beelzebub. See Notes on Mat. xii. 24. They did not deny the reality of the miracle or the facts in the case, but they ascribed what was done to the power of the great leader of the fallen host, as if Jesus was in league with him. For the manner in which the Saviour met that reasoning, see Notes on Mat. xii. 25-28.

35. *And Jesus went about all the cities and villages, &c.* That is, in all parts of Galilee, for his labours were, as yet, confined to that part of Palestine. Comp. Notes on ch. iv. 24, 25.

36. *But when he saw the multitudes.* That followed him from place to place. When he saw their anxiety to be instructed and saved. ¶ *He was moved with compassion on them.* He pitied them. ¶ *Because they fainted.* The word used here refers to the weariness and fatigue which results from labour and being burdened. He saw the people *burdened* with the rites of religion and the doctrines of the Pharisees; sinking down under their ignorance and the weight of their traditions; neglected by those who *ought* to have been enlightened teachers; and *scattered* and driven out without care and attention. With great beauty he compares them to sheep wandering without a shepherd. Judea was a land of flocks and herds. The faithful shepherd, by day and night, was with his flock. He defended it, made it to lie down in green pastures, and led it beside the still waters, Ps. xxiii. 2. Without his care the sheep would stray away. They were in danger of wild beasts. They panted in the summer sun, and knew not where was the cooling shade and stream. So, said the Saviour, is it with this people. No wonder that the compassionate Redeemer was moved with pity.

37. *The harvest truly is plenteous, &c.* Another beautiful image. A waving field of golden grain invites many reapers and demands haste. By the reference to the harvest here, he meant that the multitude of people that flocked

tudes, he was moved with compassion on them, because they [3]fainted, and were scattered abroad, [d]as sheep having no shepherd.

37 Then saith he unto his disciples, [e]The harvest truly *is* plenteous, but the labourers *are* few:

38 Pray ye therefore the Lord of the harvest, that he will [f]send forth labourers into his harvest.

[3] or, *were tired and lay down.*
d Nu.27.17; 1 Ki.22.17; Eze.34.5; Zec.10.2.
e Lu.10.2; Jn.4.35.
f Ps.68.11.

to his ministry was great. The people expected the Messiah. They were prepared to receive the gospel; but the labourers were few. He directed them, therefore, to pray to the Lord of the harvest to send forth reapers. *God* is the proprietor of the great harvest of the world, and he only can send men to gather it in.

REMARKS.

1st. We are presented with an instance of proper perseverance in coming to Christ, ver. 1, 2. Nothing was suffered to prevent the purpose of presenting the helpless paralytic to the Saviour. So the poor helpless sinner should come. No obstacle should prevent him. He should lay himself at his feet, and feel that Jesus holds over him the power of life and death, and that no other being can save.

2d. Jesus has the power to forgive sins, ver. 6. He claimed it, and worked a miracle to prove it. If he had it then, he has it still. To him, then, the lost sinner may come with the assurance that as he freely *then* exerted that power, so he is ever the same, and will do it *now.*

3d. Jesus Christ is divine. Nothing could prove it more clearly than the power to pardon sinners. God only can pronounce what shall be done with transgressors of his law, Is. xliii. 25. He that claims this right must be either an impostor or God. But no impostor ever yet worked a real miracle. Jesus was therefore divine. He can save to the uttermost all that come to God through him.

4th. We see here the proper rule to be observed in mingling with the wicked, ver. 10-13. It should not be of choice or for pleasure. We should not enter into their follies or vices. We should not seek enjoyment in their society. We should mingle with them simply to transact necessary business and to do them good, *and no farther,* Ps. i. 1.

5th. In the case of the ruler and the woman that was diseased, we have a strong instance of the nature of faith. They came not doubting the power of Jesus—fully assured that he was able to heal. So all genuine believers come to him. They doubt not his power or willingness to save them. Poor, and lost, and ruined by sin, and in danger of eternal death, they come. His heart is open. He puts forth his power, and the soul is healed, and the sin and danger gone.

6th. The young must die, and may die in early life, ver. 18. Very short graves are in every burying-ground. Thousands and millions, not more than twelve years of age, have died. Thousands and millions, not more than twelve years of age, are yet to die. Many of these may be taken from Sunday-schools. Their class, their teacher—their parents, sisters, brothers—must be left, and the child be carried to the grave. Many children of that age that have been in Sunday-schools have died happy. They loved the Saviour, and they were ready to go to him. Jesus was near to them when they died, and they are now in heaven. Of every child we may ask, Are you ready also to go when God shall call you? Do you love the Lord Jesus, so as to be willing to leave all your friends here and go to him?

7th. Jesus can raise up the dead, and he will raise up all that love him, ver. 25. Many little children will be raised up to meet him in the last great day. He shall come in the clouds. The angel shall sound a trumpet, and all the dead shall hear. All shall be raised up and go to meet him. All that loved him here will go to heaven. All that were wicked, and did not love him here, will go to everlasting suffering.

8th. We see the duty of praying for the conversion of the world, ver. 37, 38. The harvest is as plenteous as it was in the time of Christ. More than six hundred millions are still without the gospel, and there are not yet many labourers to go into the harvest. The world is full of wickedness, and God only can qualify those who shall go and preach the gospel to the dark nations of the earth. Without ceasing we ought to

CHAPTER X.

AND when he had called unto *him* his twelve disciples, [a]he gave them power [1]*against* unclean spirits, to cast them out, and to heal all manner of sickness and all manner of disease.

2 Now the [b]names of the twelve apostles are these: The first, Simon, who is called Peter, and An-

a Mar.3.13,14; 6.7,&c.; Lu.9.1,&c. 1 or, *over*.

b Lu.6.13.

entreat of God to pity the nations, and to send to them faithful men who shall tell them of a dying Saviour.

CHAPTER X.

1. *And when he had called unto* him *his twelve disciples*, &c. This account of sending the apostles forth is recorded also in Mar. vi. 7–11, and Lu. ix. 1–6. Mark says that he sent them out two and two. This was a kind arrangement, that each one might have a companion, and that thus they might visit more places and accomplish more labour than if they were all together. These twelve were the original number of apostles. The word *apostle* means one that is *sent*, and was given to them because they were *sent forth* to preach the gospel. They were ambassadors of Christ. To this number Matthias was afterward added, to supply the place of Judas (Ac. i. 26), and Paul was specially called to be an apostle to the Gentiles, Ro. i. 1; 1 Co. xv. 8, 9; Ga. i. 1. In all, therefore, there were fourteen apostles.

In selecting *twelve* at first, it is probable that the Saviour was somewhat guided by the number of the tribes of Israel. Twelve was, with them, a well-known number, and it was natural that he should select one for every tribe. Their office was clearly made known. They were to heal the sick, cast out devils, raise the dead, preach the gospel. They were to be with him to receive his instructions, to learn the nature of his religion, be witnesses to his resurrection, and then to bear his gospel around the globe. The number twelve was the best number for these purposes that could be selected. It was sufficiently *large* to answer the purpose of testimony, and it was *so small* as not to tend to disorder, or that they could easily be divided into parties or factions. They were not *learned* men, and could not be supposed to spread their religion by art or talents. They were not men of wealth, and could not *bribe* men to follow them. They were not men of rank and office, and could not *compel* men to believe. They were just such men as are always found the best witnesses in courts of justice—plain men, of good sense, of fair character, of great honesty, and with favourable opportunities of ascertaining the facts to which they bore witness. Such men everybody believes, and especially when they are willing to lay down their lives to prove their sincerity.

It was important that the Saviour should choose them *early* in his ministry, in order that they might be fully acquainted with him; might treasure up his instructions, and observe his manner of life and his person, so that, by having been long acquainted with him, they might be able to testify to his identity and be competent witnesses of his resurrection. No witnesses were ever so well qualified to give testimony as they, and none ever gave so much evidence of their sincerity as they did. See Ac. i. 21, 22.

2. *Now the names of the twelve apostles.* The account of their being called is more fully given in Mar. iii. 13–18, and Lu. vi. 12–19. Each of those evangelists has recorded the circumstances of their appointment. They agree in saying it was done on a mountain; and, according to Luke, it was done *before* the sermon on the mount was delivered, perhaps on the same mountain, near Capernaum. Luke adds that the night previous had been spent *in prayer to God*. See Notes on Lu. vi. 12. ¶ *Simon, who is called Peter.* The word Peter means a rock. He was also called Cephas, Jn. i. 42; 1 Co. i. 12; iii. 22; xv. 5; Ga. ii. 9. This was a Syro-Chaldaic word signifying the same as Peter. This name was given probably in reference to the *resoluteness and firmness* which he *was* to exhibit in preaching the gospel. *Before* the Saviour's death he was rash, impetuous, and unstable. Afterward, as all history affirms, he was firm, zealous, steadfast, and immovable. The tradition is that he was at last crucified at Rome with his head downward, thinking it too great an honour to die as his Master did. See Notes on Jn. xxi. 18. There is no cer-

drew his brother; James *the son* of Zebedee, and John his brother;

3 Philip, and Bartholomew; Thomas, and Matthew the publican; James *the son* of Alpheus; and Lebbeus, whose surname was Thaddeus;

4 Simon the Canaanite; and Judas Iscariot, who also betrayed him.

5 These twelve Jesus sent forth, and commanded them, saying, Go not into the way of the Gentiles, and into *any* city of [c] the Samaritans enter ye not:

c 2 Ki.17.24; Jn.4.5,9,20.

---

tain proof, however, that this occurred at Rome, and no absolute knowledge as to the place where he died. ¶ *James* the son *of Zebedee, and John his brother.* This James was slain by Herod in a persecution, Ac. xii. 2. The other James, the son of Alpheus, was stationed at Jerusalem, and was the author of the epistle that bears his name. See Ga. i. 19; ii. 9; Ac. xv. 13. A James is mentioned (Ga. i. 19) as *the Lord's brother.* It has not been easy to ascertain why he was thus called. He is here called the son of *Alpheus*, that is, of Cleophas, Jn. xix. 25. Alpheus and Cleophas were but different ways of writing and pronouncing the same name. This Mary, called the mother of James and Joses, is called the wife of Cleophas, Jn. xix. 25.

3. *Philip and Bartholomew.* These two were probably sent out together. Philip was a native of Bethsaida, the city of Andrew and Peter. He is not the same as Philip the evangelist, mentioned in Ac. vi. 5; xxi. 8. Bartholomew (literally *the son of Tolmai*). ¶ *Thomas.* Literally *a twin*, in reference to which he is also called *Didymus*, Jn. xi. 16. For his character, see Notes on Jn. xx. 25. ¶ *And Matthew the publican.* See Notes on ch. ix. 9. ¶ *James* the son *of Alpheus.* See Note above. ¶ *And Lebbeus, called Thaddeus.* These two words have the same signification in Hebrew. Luke calls him *Judas*, by a slight change from the name *Thaddeus.* Such changes are common in all writings.

4. *Simon the Canaanite.* Luke calls him Simon *Zelotes*, the zealous. It is probable that he was one of a small sect of the Jews called *Zealots*, on account of peculiar zeal in religion. His native place was probably *Cana.* Afterward he might with propriety be called by either title. ¶ *Judas Iscariot.* It is probable this name was given to him to designate his native place. *Carioth* was a small town in the tribe of Judah.

5. *Into the way of the Gentiles.* That is, *among* the Gentiles, or nowhere but among the Jews. The full time for preaching the gospel to the Gentiles was not come. It was proper that it should be *first* preached to the Jews, the ancient covenant people of God, and the people among whom the Messiah was born. He afterward gave them a charge to go into all the world, Mat. xxviii. 19. ¶ *And into* any *city of the Samaritans enter ye not.* The Samaritans occupied the country formerly belonging to the tribe of Ephraim and the half-tribe of Manasseh. This region was situated between Jerusalem and Galilee; so that in passing from the one to the other, it was a direct course to pass through Samaria. The capital of the country was Samaria, formerly a large and splendid city. It was situated about 15 miles to the north-west of the city of Shechem or Sychar (see Notes on Jn. iv. 5), and about 40 miles to the north of Jerusalem. For a description of this city, see Notes on Is. xxviii. 1. Sychar or Shechem was also a city within the limits of Samaria.

This people was formerly composed of a few of the ten tribes and a mixture of foreigners. When the ten tribes were carried away into captivity to Babylon, the King of Assyria sent people from Cutha, Ava, Hamath, and Sepharvaim to inhabit their country, 2 Ki. xvii. 24; Ezr. iv. 2–11. These people at first worshipped the idols of their own nations; but, being troubled with lions, which had increased greatly while the country remained uninhabited, they supposed it was because they had not honoured the *God of the country.* A Jewish priest was therefore sent to them from Babylon to instruct them in the Jewish religion. They were instructed partially from the books of Moses, but still retained many of their old rites and idolatrous customs, and embraced a religion made up of Judaism and idolatry, 2 Ki. xvii. 26–28.

The grounds of difference between the two nations were the following:—

6 But[d] go rather to the [e]lost sheep of the house of Israel.

7 And as ye go, preach, saying, The[f] kingdom of heaven is at hand.

8 Heal the sick, cleanse the lepers, raise the dead, cast out devils: [g]freely ye have received, freely give.

9 [2]Provide[h] neither gold, nor silver, nor brass, in your purses:

10 Nor scrip for *your* journey,

d Ac.13.46. e Ps.119.176; Is.53.6; Je.50.6,17; Eze.34.5,6,8; 1 Pe.2.25. f ch.3.2; 4.17; Lu.9.2; 10.9. g Ac.8.18,20. 2 or, *Get.* h Lu.22.35; 1 Co.9.7,&c.

1st. The Jews, after their return from Babylon, set about rebuilding their temple. The Samaritans offered to aid them. The Jews, however, perceiving that it was not from a love of true religion, but that they might obtain a part of the favours granted to the Jews by Cyrus, rejected their offer. The consequence was, that a state of long and bitter animosity arose between them and the Jews.

2d. While Nehemiah was engaged in building the walls of Jerusalem, the Samaritans used every art to thwart him in his undertaking, Ne. vi. 1–14.

3d. The Samaritans at length obtained leave of the Persian monarch to build a temple for themselves. This was erected on *Mount Gerizim*, and they strenuously contended that that was the place designated by Moses as the place where the nation should worship. Sanballat, the leader of the Samaritans, constituted his son-in-law, Manasses, high-priest. The religion of the Samaritans thus became perpetuated, and an irreconcilable hatred arose between them and the Jews. See Notes on Jn. iv. 20.

4th. Afterward Samaria became a place of resort for all the outlaws of Judea. They received willingly all the Jewish criminals and refugees from justice. The violators of the Jewish laws, and those who had been excommunicated, betook themselves for safety to Samaria, and greatly increased their numbers and the hatred which subsisted between the two nations.

5th. The Samaritans received only the five books of Moses, and rejected the writings of the prophets and all the Jewish traditions. From these causes arose an irreconcilable difference between them, so that the Jews regarded them as the worst of the human race (Jn. viii. 48), and had no dealings with them, Jn. iv. 9.

Our Saviour, however, preached the gospel to them afterward (Jn. iv. 6–26), and the apostles imitated his example, Ac. viii. 25. The gospel was, however, *first* preached to the Jews.

6. *But go rather to the lost sheep*, &c. That is, to the Jews. He regarded them as wandering and lost, like sheep straying without a shepherd. They had been the chosen people of God; they had long looked for the Messiah; and it was proper that the gospel should be first offered to them.

7. *The kingdom of heaven is at hand.* Or, more literally, the *reign* of heaven, or of God, draws near. See Notes on Mat. iii. 2.

8. *Freely ye have received, freely give.* That is, they were not to *sell* their favours of healing, preaching, &c. They were not to make a *money-making* business of it, to bargain specifically to heal for so much, and to cast out devils for so much. This, however, neither then nor afterward precluded them from receiving a competent support. See Lu. x. 7; 1 Co. ix. 8 14; 1 Ti. v. 18.

9–15. See also Mar. vi. 8–11, and Lu. ix. 3–5. In both these places the *substance* of this account is given, though not so particularly as in Matthew. The general subject is the instructions given to the apostles.

9. *Provide neither gold nor silver, nor brass.* This prohibition of gold, silver, and brass is designed to prevent their providing *money* for their journey. Pieces of money of *small value* were made of brass. ¶ *In your purses.* Literally in your *girdles*. See Notes on Mat. v. 38 41. A *girdle* or *sash* was an indispensable part of the dress. This girdle was made *hollow*, and answered the purpose of a purse. It was convenient, easily borne, and safe.

10. *Nor scrip.* That is, *knapsack*. This was made of skin or coarse cloth, to carry provisions in. It was commonly hung around the neck. ¶ *Neither two coats.* See Notes on Mat. v. 40. ¶ *Neither shoes.* The original is the word commonly rendered *sandals*. See Notes on Mat. iii. 11.

Mark says, in recording this discourse,

neither two coats, neither shoes, nor yet [3]staves: [i]for the workman is worthy of his meat.

11 And into whatsoever city or town ye shall enter, inquire who in it is worthy; and there abide till ye go thence.

12 And when ye come into an house, salute it.

13 And if the house be worthy,

[3] *a staff.* [i] Lu.10.7,&c.

"*but be shod with sandals.*" Between him and Matthew there is an apparent contradiction, but there is really no difference. According to Matthew, Jesus does not forbid their *wearing* the sandals which they probably had on, but only forbids their *supplying themselves with more*, or with *superfluous* ones. Instead of making provision for their feet when their *present* shoes were worn out, they were to trust to Providence to be supplied, and *go as they were.* The meaning of the two evangelists may be thus expressed: "Do not procure anything more for your journey than you have on. Go as you are, shod with sandals, without making any more preparation." ¶ *Nor yet staves.* In the margin, in all the ancient versions, and in the common Greek text, this is in the singular number—*nor yet* A STAFF. But Mark says that they might have a *staff:* "Jesus commanded them that they should take nothing for their journey, *save a staff only.*" To many this would appear to be a contradiction. Yet the *spirit* of the instruction, the main thing that the writers aim at, is the same. That was, that they were *to go just as they were*, to trust to Providence, and not to spend any time in making preparation for their journey. Some of them, probably, when he addressed them, *had staves*, and some had not. To those who *had*, he did not say that they should throw them away, as the instructions he was giving them might seem to require, but he suffered them to take them (Mark). To those who had not, he said they should not spend time in procuring them (Matthew), but *they were all to go just as they were.* ¶ *The workman is worthy of his meat.* This implies that they were to expect a proper supply for their wants from those who were benefited. They were not to make *bargain and sale* of the power of working miracles, but they were to expect competent support from preaching the gospel, and that not merely as a gift, but because they were *worthy* of it, and had a right to it.

11. *Who in it is worthy.* That is, who in it sustains such a character that he will be disposed to show you hospitality and to treat you kindly. This shows that they were not needlessly to throw themselves in the way of *insult.* ¶ *And there abide.* There remain; as Luke adds, "Go not from house to house." They were to content themselves with one house; not to wander about in the manner of vagrants and mendicants; not to appear to be men of idleness and fond of change; not to seem dissatisfied with the hospitality of the people; but to show that they had regular, important business; that they valued their time; that they were disposed to give themselves to labour, and were intent *only* on the business for which he had sent them. If ministers of the gospel are useful, it will be by not spending their time in idle chit-chat, and wandering about as if they had nothing to do, but in an honest and laborious improvement of their time in study, in prayer, in preaching, and in visiting their people.

12. *And when ye come into a house, salute it.* The word *house* here evidently means *family*, as it does in the following verse. See also Mat. xii. 25, and Jn. iv. 53: "And himself believed and *his whole house.*" The apostles were directed to *salute* the family—to show them the customary tokens of respect, and to treat them with civility. Religion never requires or permits its friends to outrage the common rules of social intercourse. It demands of them to exhibit to all the customary and proper tokens of respect, according to their age and station, 1 Pe. ii. 12–25; iii. 8–11; Phi. iv. 8. For the mode of salutation, see Notes on Lu. x. 4, 5.

13. *If the house be worthy.* That is, if the *family* be worthy, or be willing to receive you as my disciples. ¶ *Let your peace come upon it.* That is, let the *peace* or happiness which you seek or for which you pray in saluting it (see Lu. x. 5), come upon it; or seek *their* peace and happiness by prayer, instruction, by remaining with them, and imparting to them the blessings of the gospel. ¶ *But if it be not worthy,* &c. If the family be unwilling to receive

let your peace come upon it: but if it be not worthy, [k]let your peace return to you.

14 And whosoever shall not receive you, nor hear your words, when ye depart out of that house or city, [l]shake off the dust of your feet.

15 Verily I say unto you, [m]It shall be more tolerable for the land of Sodom and Gomorrah in the day of judgment than for that city.

16 Behold, I send you forth as sheep in the midst of wolves: [n]be ye therefore wise as serpents, and [4]harmless [o]as doves.

17 But[p] beware of men: [q]for they will deliver you up to the

k Ps.35.13. l Ne.5.13; Ac.13.51; 18.6. m ch.11.22,24.

n Ro.16.19; Ep.5.15. 4 or, *simple.* o Phi.2.15. p Phi.3.2. q ch.24.9; Mar.13.9.

---

you; if they show themselves unfriendly to you and your message. ¶ *Let your peace return to you.* This is a Hebrew mode of saying that your peace shall *not* come upon it, Ps. xxxv. 13. It is a mode of speaking derived from bestowing a gift. If people were willing to receive it, they derived the benefit from it; if not, then of course the present came back or remained in the hand of the giver. So Christ *figuratively* speaks of the peace which their labour would confer. If received kindly and hospitably by the people, they would confer on them most valuable blessings. If rejected and persecuted, the blessings which they sought for others would come upon themselves. *They* would reap the benefit of being cast out and persecuted for their Master's sake, Mat. v. 10.

14. *Shake off the dust of your feet.* The Jews taught uniformly that the dust of the Gentiles was impure, and was to be shaken off. To shake off the dust from the feet, therefore, was a significant act, denoting that they regarded them as impure, profane, and heathenish, and that they declined all farther connection with them. It is recorded that this was actually done by some of the apostles. See Ac. xiii. 51; xviii. 6.

15. *It shall be more tolerable for the land of Sodom,* &c. The cities here mentioned, together with Admah and Zeboim, were destroyed by fire and brimstone on account of their great wickedness. They occupied the place afterward covered by the Dead Sea, bounding Palestine on the south-east, Ge. xix. 24, 25. Christ said that *their* punishment will be more *tolerable*—that is, more easily borne—than that of the people who reject his gospel. The reason is, that they were not favoured with so much light and instruction. See Mat. xi. 23, 24; Lu. xii. 47, 48. Sodom and Gomorrah are often referred to as signal instances of divine vengeance, and as sure proofs that the wicked shall not go unpunished. See 2 Pe. ii. 6; Jude 7.

16. *As sheep in the midst of wolves.* That is, I send you, inoffensive and harmless, into a cold, unfriendly, and cruel world. Your innocence will not be a protection. ¶ *Be wise as serpents,* &c. Serpents have always been an emblem of wisdom and cunning, Ge. iii. 1. The Egyptians used the serpent in their hieroglyphics as a symbol of wisdom. Probably the thing in which Christ directed his followers to imitate the serpent was in its caution in avoiding danger. No animal equals them in the rapidity and skill which they evince in escaping danger. So said Christ to his disciples, You need caution and wisdom in the midst of a world that will seek your lives. He directs them, also, to be harmless, not to provoke danger, not to do injury, and thus make their fellow-men justly enraged against them. Doves are, and always have been, a striking emblem of innocence. Most men would foolishly destroy a serpent, be it ever so harmless, yet few are so hard-hearted as to kill a dove.

17. *But beware of men.* That is, be on your guard against men who are like wolves, ver. 16. Do not run unnecessarily into danger. Use suitable prudence and caution, and do not needlessly endanger your lives. ¶ *Councils.* The word here used commonly signifies the great council of the nation, *the Sanhedrim.* See Notes on Mat. v. 22. Here it seems to refer to any judicial tribunal, of which there were some in every village. ¶ *They will scourge you in their synagogues.* Scourging, or *whipping*, is often mentioned in the New Testament as a mode of punishment. The law of Moses directed that the number of stripes should not exceed forty, but might be any number less, at the dis-

councils, and [r] they will scourge you in their synagogues;

18 And[s] ye shall be brought before governors and kings for my sake, for a testimony against them and the Gentiles.

19 But[t] when they deliver you up, take no thought how or what ye shall speak; for it shall be given you in that same hour what ye shall speak.

20 For it is not ye that speak, but the Spirit of your Father which speaketh in you.

21 And the brother shall deliver up the brother to death, and the father the child: and the children

r Ac.5.40; 2 Co.11.24. s Ac.24. and 25. t Mar.13.11; Lu.12.11; 21.14,15.

---

cretion of the judge, De. xxv. 2, 3. The person who was sentenced to scourging was formerly laid upon the ground, and the blows inflicted on his back in the presence of the judge. In later times the criminal was tied to a low post. Scourging is still practised in the East, but the blows are commonly inflicted on the soles of the feet. It is called the *bastinado.*

The instrument formerly used was a *rod.* Afterward they employed thongs or lashes attached to the rod. To make the blows severe and more painful, they sometimes fastened sharp points of iron or pieces of lead in the thongs. These were called *scorpions*, 1 Ki. xii. 11. The law was express that the number of stripes should not exceed forty. The Jews, to secure greater accuracy in counting, used a scourge with three lashes, which inflicted three stripes at once. With this the criminal was struck thirteen times, making the number of blows thirty-nine. Paul was five times scourged in this way. See 2 Co. xi. 24.

The Romans did not feel themselves bound by the law of the Jews in regard to the *number* of stripes, but inflicted them at pleasure. Thus our Saviour was scourged till he was so weak as not to be able to bear his cross. This was often done in the *synagogue.* See Mat. xxiii. 34; Ac. xxii. 19; xxvi. 11.

18. *And ye shall be brought*, &c. This prediction was completely and abundantly fulfilled, Ac. v. 26; xii. 1-4; xxiii. 33; xxvi. 1, 28, 30. Peter is said to have been brought before Nero, and John before Domitian, Roman emperors; and others before Parthian, Scythian, and Indian kings. They were to stand there to bear a testimony *against* them; or, as it might be rendered, *to them.* That is, they were to be *witnesses to them* of the great facts and doctrines of the Christian religion; and if they rejected Christianity, they would be witnesses *against* them in the day of judgment. The fulfilment of this prophecy is a signal evidence that Christ possessed a knowledge of the future. Few things were more improbable when this was uttered than that the fishermen of Galilee would stand before the illustrious and mighty monarchs of the East and the West.

19, 20. *Take no thought.* That is, be not anxious or unduly solicitous. See Notes on Mat. vi. 25. This was a full promise that they should be inspired, and was a most seasonable consolation. Poor, and ignorant, and obscure fishermen would naturally be solicitous what they should *say* before the great men of the earth. Eastern people regarded kings as raised far above common mortals—as approaching to divinity. How consoling, then, the assurance that God would aid them and speak within them!

21. *And the brother shall deliver up the brother*, &c. Were there no evidence that this *had* been done, it would scarcely be *credible.* The ties which bind brothers and sisters, and parents and children together, are so strong that it could scarcely be believed that division of sentiment on religious subjects would cause them to forget these tender relations. Yet history assures us that this has been often done. If this be so, then how inexpressibly awful must be the malignity of the human heart by nature against religion! Nothing else but this dreadful opposition to God and his gospel ever *has* induced or ever *can* induce men to violate the most tender relations, and consign the best friends to torture, racks, and flames. It adds to the horrors of this, that those who were put to death in persecution were tormented in the most awful modes that human ingenuity could devise. They were crucified; were thrown into boiling oil; were burned at the stake; were roasted slowly over coals; were compelled to drink melted lead; were torn in pieces by beasts of prey; were covered with pitch and set

shall rise up against *their* parents, and cause them to be put to death.

22 And ye shall be hated of all *men* for my name's sake; but [u]he that endureth to the end shall be saved.

23 But when they persecute you in this city, [v]flee ye into another: for verily I say unto you, Ye shall not [5]have gone over the cities of Israel till the Son of Man be come.

24 The [w]disciple is not above *his* master, nor the servant above his lord.

25 It is enough for the disciple that he be as his master, and the servant as his lord. If [x]they have called the master of the house [6]Beelzebub, how much more *shall they call* them of his household?

26 Fear them not therefore: [y]for there is nothing covered that

u De.12.12,13; Re.2.10. v Ac.8.8. 5 or, *end*, or, *finish*.

w Lu.6.40; Jn.13.16;15.20. x Jn.8.48. 6 *Beelzebul*. y Mar.4.22; Lu.12.2,3; 1 Co.4.5.

on fire. Yet, dreadful as this prediction was, it was fulfilled; and, incredible as it seems, parents and children, husbands and wives, were found wicked enough to deliver up each other to these cruel modes of death on account of attachment to the gospel. Such is the opposition of the heart of man to the gospel! That hostility which will overcome the strong ties of natural affection, and which will be satisfied with nothing else to show its power, can be no slight opposition to the gospel of God.

22. *Ye shall be hated of all* men. That is, of *all kinds* of men. The human heart would be opposed to them, because it is opposed to Christ. ¶ *But he that endureth to the end*, &c. That is, to the end of life, be it longer or shorter. He that bears all these unspeakable sufferings, and who does not shrink and apostatize, will give decisive evidence of attachment to me, and shall enter into heaven. See Re. iii. 21, 22.

23. *When they persecute*, &c. The apostles were not permitted to *throw away* their lives. Where they could preserve them without denying their Lord, they were to do it. Yet all the commands of Christ, as well as their conduct, show that they were rather to lay down their lives than deny their Saviour. We are to preserve our lives by all proper means, but we are rather to *die* than save ourselves by doing anything wrong. ¶ *Ye shall not have gone over the cities of Israel*, &c. That is, in fleeing from persecutors from one city to another, you shall not have gone to every city in Judea till the end of the Jewish economy shall occur. See Notes on Mat. xxiv. 28-30. By *the coming of the Son of Man*, that is, of *Christ*, is probably meant the destruction of Jerusalem, which happened about thirty years after this was spoken. The words are often used in this sense. See Mat. xxiv. 30; Mar. xiii. 26; Lu. xxi. 27, 32.

24, 25. *The disciple is not above* his *master*, &c. That is, you must expect the same treatment which *I* have received. They have called me, your Master and Teacher, Beelzebub, the prince of the devils (see Mat. xii. 24; Lu. xi. 15; Jn. viii. 48), and you must expect that they will call all of the family by the same name. *Beelzebub* was a god of the Ekronites. See 2 Ki. i. 2. The word literally means *the god of flies*, so called because this idol was supposed to protect them from the numerous swarms of flies with which that country abounded. The correct reading here, as in Lu. xi. 15, 18, 19; Mar. iii. 22, is supposed to be, not *Beelzebub*, but *Beelzebul* (Griesbach, Hahn, Rob., *Lex.*) an Aramean form of the word meaning the *god of dung* or *filth*. The name, thus altered by the Jews by changing a single letter, was given to Satan to express supreme contempt and aversion. The Jews seem to have first given to Satan the name of a heathen god, and then, to express their sense of the character of Satan, to have changed that name by altering a single letter so as to express their aversion in the most emphatic manner. By giving the name to Christ, they poured upon him the greatest possible abuse and contempt.

26. *Fear them not*, &c. He encouraged them by the assurance that God would protect them, and that their truth and innocence should yet be vindicated. It is probable that the declaration, There is nothing covered, &c., was a proverb among the Jews. By it our Saviour meant that their *innocence*, their *principles*, and their *integrity*, though then

shall not be revealed; and hid, that shall not be known.

27 What I tell you in darkness, *that* speak ye in light: and what ye hear in the ear, *that* preach ye upon the house-tops.

28 And[z] fear not them which kill the body, but are not able to kill the soul: but rather fear him which is able to destroy both soul and body in hell.

z Is.8.12,13; 51.7,12; 1 Pe.3.14.

29 Are not two sparrows sold for a [7]farthing? and one of them shall not fall on the ground without your Father.

30 But[a] the very hairs of your head are all numbered.

31 Fear ye not therefore; ye are of more value than many sparrows.

32 Whosoever therefore shall confess me before men, [b]him will

7 In value, *halfpenny farthing*, a 10th part of the Roman penny, ch.18.28. *a* Ac.27.34. *b* Re.3.5.

---

the world might not acknowledge them, in due time would be revealed, or God would vindicate them and the world would do them justice. They were, then, to be willing to be unknown, despised, persecuted for a time, with the assurance that their true characters would yet be understood and their sufferings appreciated.

27. *What I say to you in darkness*, &c. That is, *in secret*, in *private*, in *confidence*. The private instructions which I give you while with me do you proclaim publicly, on the *house-top*. The *house-top*, the flat roof, was a public, conspicuous place. See 2 Sa. xvi. 22. See also Notes on Mat. ix. 1-8.

28. *Them which kill the body*. That is, *men*, who have no power to injure the soul, the immortal part. The *body* is a small matter in comparison with the *soul*. Temporal death is a slight thing compared with eternal death. He directs them, therefore, not to be alarmed at the prospect of temporal death, but to fear *God*, who can destroy both soul and body for ever. This passage proves that the *bodies* of the wicked will be raised up to be punished for ever. ¶ *In hell*. See Notes on Mat. v. 22.

29-31. *Are not two sparrows*, &c. He encourages them not to fear by two striking considerations: first, that God takes care of sparrows, the smallest and least valuable of birds; and, secondly, by the fact that God numbers even the hairs of the head. The argument is, that if he takes care of *birds* of the least value, if he regards so small a thing as the hair of the head, and numbers it, he will certainly protect and provide for you. You need not, therefore, fear what man can do to you. ¶ *Sparrows*. The sparrows are well-known birds in Syria. They are small; they are found in great numbers; they are tame, intrusive, and nestle everywhere. "They are extremely pertinacious in asserting their right of possession, and have not the least reverence for any place or thing. David alludes to these characteristics of the sparrow in Ps. lxxxiv., when he complains that they had appropriated even the altars of God for their nests. Concerning himself, he says, I watch, and am as a sparrow upon the house-top, Ps. cii. 7. When one of them has lost its mate—a matter of everyday occurrence—he will sit on the house-top alone, and lament by the hour his sad bereavement. These birds are snared and caught in great numbers, but, as they are small, and not much relished for food, five sparrows may still be sold for two farthings; and when we see their countless numbers, and the eagerness with which they are destroyed as a worthless nuisance, we can better appreciate the assurance that our heavenly Father, who takes care of them, so that not one can fall to the ground without his notice, will surely take care of us, who are of more value than many sparrows."—*The Land and the Book* (Thomson), vol. i. p. 52, 53. ¶ *Farthing*. See Notes on Mat. v. 26. ¶ *Without your Father*. That is, God, your Father, guides and directs its fall. It falls only with *his* permission, and where *he* chooses.

30. *The very hairs of your head are all numbered*. That is, each one has exercised the care and attention of God. He has fixed the number; and, though of small importance, yet he does not think it beneath him to determine how few or how many they shall be. He will therefore take care of you.

32, 33. *Whosoever therefore shall confess me*, &c. The same word in the original is translated *confess* and *profess*, 1 Ti. vi.

I confess also before my Father which is in heaven.

33 But[c] whosoever shall deny me before men, him will I also deny before my Father which is in heaven.

34 Think not that I am come to send peace on earth: [d]I came not to send peace, but a sword.

35 For I am come to set a man at variance [e]against his father, and the daughter against her mother, and the daughter-in-law against her mother-in-law.

36 And[f] a man's foes *shall be* they of his own household.

37 He[g] that loveth father or mother more than me, is not worthy of me: and he that loveth son or daughter more than me, is not worthy of me.

38 And he that taketh not his cross, and followeth after me, is not worthy of me.

c 2 Ti.2.12. d Lu.12.49,53. e Mi.7.5,6. f Ps.41.9. g Lu.14.26.

12, 13; 2 Jn. 7; Ro. x. 10. It means to acknowledge the Lord Jesus Christ, and our dependence on him for salvation, and our attachment to him, *in every proper manner*. This profession may be made in uniting with a church, at the communion, in conversation, and in conduct. The Scriptures mean, by a profession of religion, an exhibition of it in every circumstance of the life and before all men. It is not merely in *one* act that we must do it, but in every act. We must be ashamed neither of the person, the character, the doctrines, nor the requirements of Christ. If we are; if we deny him in these things before men; if we are unwilling to express our attachment to him in every way possible, then it is *right* that he should *disown all connection with us*, or deny us before God, and he *will* do it.

34–36. *Think not that I am come*, &c. This is taken from Mi. vii. 6. Christ did not here mean to say that the *object* of his coming was to produce discord and contention, for he was the Prince of Peace, Is. ix. 6; xi. 6; Lu. ii. 14; but he means to say that such would be one of the *effects* of his coming. One part of a family that was opposed to *him* would set themselves against those who believed in him. The wickedness of men, and not the religion of the gospel, is the cause of this hostility. It is unnecessary to say that no prophecy has been more strikingly fulfilled; and it will *continue* to be fulfilled till all *unite* in obeying his commandments. Then his religion will produce universal peace. Comp. Notes on ver. 21. ¶ *But a sword*. The sword is an instrument of death, and *to send* a sword is the same as to produce hostility and war.

37. *He that loveth father or mother*, &c. The meaning of this is clear. Christ must be loved *supremely*, or he is not loved at all. If we are not willing to give up all earthly possessions, and forsake all earthly friends, and if we do not *obey* him rather than all others, we have no true attachment to him. ¶ *Is not worthy of me*. Is not fit to be regarded as a follower of me, or is not a Christian.

38. *And he that taketh not his cross*, &c. When persons were condemned to be crucified, a part of the sentence was that they should carry the *cross* on which they were to die to the place of execution. Thus Christ carried his, till he fainted from fatigue and exhaustion. See Notes on Mat. xxvii. 31. The cross was usually composed of two rough beams of wood, united in the form of this figure, ✝. It was an instrument of death. See Notes on ch. xxvii. 31, 32. To carry it was burdensome, was disgraceful, was trying to the feelings, was an addition to the punishment. So *to carry the cross* is a figurative expression, denoting that we must endure whatever is burdensome, or is trying, or is considered disgraceful, in following Christ. It consists simply in doing our duty, let the people of the world think of it or speak of it as they may. It does not consist in *making* trouble for ourselves, or doing things merely *to be opposed;* it is doing just what is *required* of us in the Scriptures, let it produce whatever shame, disgrace, or pain it may. This every follower of Jesus is required to do.

39. *He that findeth his life*, &c. The word *life* in this passage is used evidently in two senses. The meaning may be expressed thus: He that is anxious to save his *temporal* life, or his comfort and security here, shall lose *eternal* life, or shall fail of heaven. He that is

39 He[h] that findeth his life, shall lose it: and he that loseth his life for my sake, shall find it.

40 He[i] that receiveth you, receiveth me; and he that receiveth me, receiveth him that sent me.

41 He[k] that receiveth a prophet in the name of a prophet, shall receive a prophet's reward; and he that receiveth a righteous man in the name of a righteous man, shall receive a righteous man's reward.

42 And whosoever shall give to drink unto one of these little ones a cup of cold *water* only in the name of a disciple, verily I say unto you, he shall in no wise lose his reward.

h ch.16.25. i ch.18.5; 25.40,45; Jn.12.44. k 1 Ki.17.10; He.6.10.

---

willing to risk or lose his comfort and *life* here for my sake, shall find *life* everlasting, or shall be saved. The manner of speaking is similar to that where he said, "Let the dead bury their dead." See Notes on Mat. viii. 22.

40-42. *He that receiveth you,* &c. In all these three illustrations Christ meant to teach substantially the same thing—that he that would entertain kindly or treat with hospitality himself, his disciples, a prophet, or a righteous man, would show that he approved their character, and should not fail of proper reward. To receive in the *name of* a prophet is to receive *as* a prophet; to do proper honour to his character, and to evince attachment to the cause in which he was engaged.

42. *These little ones.* By *these little ones* are clearly meant his disciples. They are called *little ones* to denote their want of wealth, rank, learning, and whatever the world calls *great.* They were *little* in the estimation of the world and in their own estimation. They were *learners,* not yet *teachers;* and they made no pretensions to what attracts the admiration of mankind. ¶ *A cup of cold* water *only.* Few would refuse a cup of cold water to any man, if thirsty and weary, and yet not all men would give it to such a one *because he was a Christian,* or to express attachment to the Lord Jesus. In bestowing it on a man *because he was a Christian,* he would show love to the Saviour himself; in the other case he would give it from mere sympathy or kindness, evincing no regard for the Christian, the Christian's Master, or his cause. In one case he would show that he loved the cause of religion; in the other, not.

REMARKS.

1st. From the narrative in this chapter, in connection with that in Luke, we are permitted to see the Saviour's habits in regard to prayer. An important event was before him; an event on which, humanly speaking, depended the whole success of his religion—the choice of those who should be his messengers to mankind. He felt its importance; and even the Son of God sought the place of prayer, and during the night-watches asked the direction of his Father. His example shows that we, in great and trying circumstances, should seek particularly the direction of God.

2d. We see the *benevolence* of the gospel, ver. 7, 8. The apostles were to confer the highest favours on mankind without reward. Like air, and sunbeams, and water—gifts of God—they are without price. The poor are welcome; the rich, unaided by their wealth, are welcome also; the wide world may freely come and partake the rich blessings of the gospel of peace.

3d. Ministers of the gospel, and all the followers of Jesus, should depend on the providence of God for support and the supply of their wants, ver. 9, 10. He sent his apostles into a cold, unfriendly world, and he took care of them. So none that trust him shall want. The righteous shall not be forsaken. The God who has in his hand all the pearls of the ocean, the gold in the heart of the earth, and the cattle on a thousand hills, and that feeds the raven when it cries, will hear the cries of his children and supply their wants.

4th. We see the duty of treating kindly the messengers of salvation, ver. 11-13. Christ expected that in every city and town they would find some who would welcome them. He promised the reward of a prophet to those who should receive a prophet, and assured those of his favour who had nothing better to bestow than even a cup of cold water. The ministers of religion are sent to benefit the world.

CHAPTER XI.

AND it came to pass, when Jesus had made an end of commanding his twelve disciples, he departed thence, to teach and to preach in their cities.

2 Now[a] when John had heard in the prison the works of Christ, he sent two of his disciples,

3 And said unto him, Art thou he that should come, or do we look for another?

[a] Lu.7.18,&c.

It is but right that *in* that world they should be kindly received, and that their wants should be supplied.

5th. The guilt of rejecting the gospel, ver. 14, 15. It is not a small matter to reject an offer of heaven. A palace, a throne, a rich earthly inheritance, might be rejected, and, compared with rejecting the gospel, it would be a trifle. But life eternal is not like thrones, and gold, and palaces. This lost, all is lost. The gospel rejected, all is gone. Nor hope nor happiness awaits him that hath spurned this offer. God requires every one to believe the gospel; and woe, woe, a greater woe than befell guilty Sodom and Gomorrah, to him who rejects it.

6th. Judgment will certainly overtake the guilty, ver. 15. It fell on Sodom, and it will fall on all transgressors. None shall escape. Damnation may slumber long over the wicked, and they may long mock the God of truth, but in due time their feet will slide, and the whole creation shall not be able to save them from woe. How dangerous, how awful is the condition of an impenitent sinner!

7th. We are to take proper care of our lives, ver. 23. The apostles were to flee from danger, when they could do it without denying their Lord. So are we. He that throws away his life when it might have been, and ought to have been preserved, is a self-murderer. He that exposes himself when *duty* does not require it, and whose life pays the forfeit, goes before God "rushing unbidden into his Maker's presence," nor can he be held guiltless.

8th. We are to persevere *in our duty* through all trials, ver. 23. Neither the world, nor pain, nor poverty, nor persecution, nor death is to appal us. He that endures to the end shall be saved. We have but one thing to do—to do the will of God, to *be Christians everywhere*, and to leave the event with him.

9th. God exercises a particular providence, ver. 29, 30. He watches the falling sparrow, numbers the hairs of the head, and for the same reason he presides over all other things. The Lord reigneth, says the Psalmist, let the earth rejoice, Ps. xcvii. 1.

10th. The duty of making a profession of religion, ver. 32, 33. It must be done in a proper way, or Christ will disown us in the day of judgment. It is impossible to neglect it, and have evidence of piety. If ashamed of him, he will be ashamed of us.

11th. Religion is easy, and easily tested, ver. 40-42. What more easy than to give a cup of water to a stranger, and what more easy than to know from what motive we do it! Yet how many are there who, while they would do the thing, would yet *lose eternal life* rather than do it with a view of honouring Christ or showing attachment to him! How dreadful is the opposition of the human heart to religion! How amazing that man will not do the slightest act to secure an interest in the kingdom of God!

CHAPTER XI.

1. *And it came to pass*, &c. The directions to the apostles were given in the vicinity of Capernaum. The Saviour went from thence to preach in *their* cities; that is, in the cities in the vicinity of Capernaum, or in Galilee. He did not yet go into Judea.

2. The account contained in this chapter of Matthew, to the 19th verse, is found, with no material variation, in Lu. vii. 18-35. John was in prison. Herod had thrown him into confinement on account of his faithfulness in reproving him for marrying his brother Philip's wife. See Mat. xiv. 3, 4.

It is not certainly known why John sent to Jesus. It might have been to satisfy his disciples that he was the Messiah; or he might have been desirous of ascertaining for himself whether this person, of whom he heard so much, was the same one whom he had baptized, and whom he knew to be the Messiah. See Jn. i. 29.

3. *Art thou he that should come?* That is, Art thou the Messiah, or the Christ?

4 Jesus answered and said unto them, Go and show John again those things which ye do hear and see:

5 The blind receive their sight, and the lame walk, the lepers are cleansed, and the deaf hear, the dead are raised up, and the poor have the gospel preached to them.

6 And blessed is *he*, whosoever shall not [b]be offended in me.

7 And as they departed, Jesus began to say unto the multitudes concerning John, [c]What went ye

b Is.8.14,15; 1 Co.1.22,23; 1 Pe.2.8. c Lu.7.24-30.

The Jews expected a Saviour. His coming had been long foretold, Ge. xlix. 10; Is. ix. 1-6; xi. 1-5; xxxv. 4-6; liii.; Da. ix. 24-27. See also Jn. vi. 14. Comp. De. xviii. 18, 19. In common language, therefore, he was familiarly described as *he that was to come*. Luke adds here (ch. vii. 21), that at the time when the messengers came to him, Jesus "cured many of their infirmities, and plagues, and of evil spirits." An answer was therefore ready to the inquiries of John.

4, 5. *Go and show John again*, &c. Jesus referred them for an answer to these miracles. They were proof that he was the Messiah. Prophets had indeed wrought miracles, but no prophet had wrought so many, or any so important. Jesus, moreover, wrought them *in his own name* and by his own power. Prophets had done it by the power of God. Jesus, therefore, performed the works which none but the Messiah could do, and John might easily *infer* that he was the Christ. ¶ *The poor have the gospel preached to them.* It was predicted of the Messiah that he would preach good tidings to the meek (Is. lxi. 1); or, as it is rendered in the New Testament, "He hath anointed me to preach the gospel to the poor," Lu. iv. 18. By this, therefore, also, John might infer that he was truly the Messiah. It adds to the force of this testimony that the *poor* have always been overlooked by Pharisees and philosophers. No sect of philosophers had condescended to notice them before Christ, and no system of religion had attempted to instruct them before the Christian religion. In all other schemes the poor have been passed by as unworthy of notice.

6. *And blessed is* he, &c. The word *offence* means a *stumbling-block*. See Notes on Mat. v. 29. This verse might be rendered, "Happy is he to whom I shall not prove a stumbling-block." That is, happy is he who shall not take offence at my poverty and lowliness of life, so as to reject me and my doctrine. Happy is he who can, notwithstanding that poverty and obscurity, see the evidence that I am the Messiah, and follow me. It is not improbable that John wished Jesus publicly to proclaim himself as the Christ, instead of seeking retirement. Jesus replied that he gave sufficient evidence of that by his works; that a man might discover it if he chose; and that he was blessed or happy who should appreciate that evidence and embrace him as the Christ, in spite of his humble manner of life.

7. *And as they departed*, &c. Jesus took occasion, from the inquiries made by John's disciples, to instruct the people respecting the true character of John. Multitudes had gone out to hear him when he preached in the desert (Mat. iii.), and it is probable that many had been attracted by the novelty of his appearance or doctrines, or had gone simply to see and hear a man of singular habits and opinions. Probably many who followed Christ had been of that number. He took occasion, therefore, by some striking questions, to examine the motives by which they had been drawn to his ministry. ¶ *A reed shaken with the wind?* The region of country in which John preached, being overflowed annually by the Jordan, produced great quantities of *reeds* or *canes*, of a light fragile nature, easily shaken by the wind. They were therefore an image of a light, changing, inconstant man. John's sending to Christ to inquire his character might have led some to suppose that he was changing and inconstant, like a reed. He had once acknowledged him to be the Messiah, and now, being in prison and sending to him to inquire into the fact, they might have supposed he had no firmness or fixed principles. Jesus, by asking this question, declared that, notwithstanding this appearance, this was not the character of John.

8. *Clothed in soft raiment.* The kind of raiment here denoted was the light, thin clothing worn by effeminate per-

out into the wilderness to see? [d]a reed shaken with the wind?

8 But what went ye out for to see? a man clothed in soft raiment? Behold, they that wear soft *clothing* are in kings' houses.

9 But what went ye out for to see? a prophet? yea, I say unto you, and more than a prophet.

10 For this is *he* of whom it is written, [e]Behold, I send my messenger before thy face, which shall prepare thy way before thee.

11 Verily I say unto you, [f]Among them that are born of women there hath not risen a greater than John the Baptist: notwithstanding, [g]he that is least in the kingdom of heaven is greater than he.

12 And from the days of John the Baptist until now the kingdom

d Ep.4.14; Ja.1.6. *e* Is.40.3; Mal.3.1; Lu.1.76. *f* Jn.5.35. *g* Jn.1.15,27; 3.30.

sons. It was made commonly of fine linen, and was worn chiefly for ornament. Christ asks them whether they were attracted by anything like that. He says that the desert was not the place to expect it. In the palaces of kings, in the court of Herod, it might be expected, but not in the place where John was. This kind of clothing was an emblem of riches, splendour, effeminacy, feebleness of character. He meant to say that John was a man of a different stamp—coarse in his exterior, hardy in his character, firm in his virtue, fitted to endure trials and privations, and thus qualified to be the forerunner of the toiling and suffering Messiah.

9. *A prophet?* He next asks whether they went to see a prophet. They *had* regarded him as such, and Jesus tells them that in this their apprehensions of him were correct. ¶ *More than a prophet.* Sustaining a character more elevated and sacred than the most distinguished of the ancient prophets. Those had been regarded as the most eminent of the prophets who had most clearly predicted the Messiah. Isaiah had been distinguished above all others for the sublimity of his writings, and the clearness with which he had foretold the coming of Christ. Yet John surpassed even him. He lived in the time of the Messiah himself. He predicted his coming with still more clearness. He was the instrument of introducing him to the nation. He was, therefore, first among the prophets.

10. *For this is* he, &c. The passage of Scripture here quoted is found in Mal. iii. 1. The substance of it is contained also in Is. xl. 3. ¶ *Prepare thy way.* That is, to prepare *the people;* to make them ready, by proper instructions, to receive the Messiah.

11. *Among them that are born of women.* This is an emphatic way of saying that there *had never* been a greater *man* than John. See Job xiv. 1. ¶ *He that is least in the kingdom of heaven is greater than he.* The phrase "kingdom of heaven" is used in many senses. See Notes on Mat. iii. 2. It here probably means, *in preaching the kingdom of God*, or the gospel. It could hardly be affirmed of the obscurest and most ignorant Christian that he had clearer views than Isaiah or John; but of the apostles of the Saviour, of the first preachers who were with him and who heard his instructions, it might be said that they had more correct apprehensions than any of the ancient prophets, or than John.

12. *And from the days of John,* &c. That is, from the days when John began to preach. It is not known how long this was, but it was not probably more than a year. Our Saviour here simply states a fact. He says there was a great *rush* or a *crowd* pressing to hear John. Multitudes went out to hear him, as if they were about to take the kingdom of heaven by force. See Mat. iii. 5. So, says he, it has continued. Since *the kingdom of heaven*, or *the gospel*, has been preached, there has been a *rush* to it. Men have been *earnest* about it; they have come *pressing* to obtain the blessing, as if they would take it by violence. There is allusion here to the manner in which cities were taken. Besiegers *pressed* upon them with violence and demolished the walls. With such *earnestness* and *violence*, he says, men had pressed around him and John since they began to preach. There is no allusion here to the manner in which individual sinners seek salvation, but it is a simple record of the fact that multitudes had thronged around him and John to hear the gospel.

of heaven [1]suffereth violence, and the violent [h]take it by force.

13 For all the prophets and the law prophesied until John.

14 And if ye will receive *it*, this is [i]Elias which was for to come.

15 He[k] that hath ears to hear, let him hear.

16 But[l] whereunto shall I liken this generation? It is like unto children sitting in the markets, and calling unto their fellows,

17 And saying, We have piped unto you, and ye have not danced; we have mourned unto you, and ye have not lamented.

18 For John came neither eating nor drinking; and they say, [m]He hath a devil.

19 The Son of man came [n]eat-

1 or, *is gotten by force, and they that thrust men, take it*, &c. h Lu.16.16; Ep.6.11-13. i Mal.4.5; ch.17.12. k Re.2.7,&c. l Lu.7.31. m ch.10.25; Jn.7.20. n ch.9.10; Jn.2.2.

13. *All the prophets*, &c. It is meant by this verse that John introduced a new dispensation; and that the *old* one, under which the prophets and the law of Moses were the guide, was closed when he preached that the kingdom of heaven was at hand. By the *law* is meant here the five books of Moses; by the prophets, the remainder of the books of the Old Testament.

14. *If ye will receive* it. This is a mode of speaking implying that the doctrine which he was about to state was different from their common views; that he was about to state something which varied from the common expectation, and which therefore they might be disposed to reject. ¶ *This is Elias*, &c. That is, *Elijah*. Elias is the *Greek* mode of writing the Hebrew word *Elijah*. An account of him is found in the first and second books of Kings. He was a distinguished prophet, and was taken up to heaven in a chariot of fire, 2 Ki. ii. 11. The prophet Malachi (ch. iv. 5, 6) predicted that *Elijah* would be sent before the coming of the Messiah to prepare the way for him. By this was evidently meant, not that he should appear *in person*, but that one should appear with a striking resemblance to him; or, as Luke (ch. i. 17) expresses it, "in the spirit and power of Elijah." But the Jews understood it differently. They supposed that Elijah would appear in person. They also supposed that Jeremiah and some other of the prophets would appear also to usher in the promised Messiah and to grace his advent. See Mat. xvi. 14; xvii. 10; Jn. i. 21. This prevalent belief was the reason why he used the words *if ye will receive it*, implying that the affirmation that *John* was the promised Elijah was a doctrine contrary to their expectation.

15. *He that hath ears*, &c. This expression is frequently used by Christ. It is a proverbial expression, implying that the highest attention should be given to what was spoken. The doctrine about John he regarded as of the greatest importance. He among you, says he, that has the faculty of understanding this, or that will believe that this is the Elijah spoken of, let him attend to it and remember it.

16–19. *But whereunto shall I liken*, &c. Christ proceeds to reprove the inconsistency and fickleness of that age of men. He says they were like children—nothing pleased them. He refers here to the *plays* or *sports* of children. Instrumental music, or piping and dancing, were used in marriages and festivals as a sign of joy. See Notes on Is. v. 11, 12. Comp. Job xxi. 11; 2 Sa. vi. 14; Ju. xi. 34; Lu. xv. 25. Children imitate their parents and others, and *act over* in play what they see done by others. Among their childish sports, therefore, was probably an imitation of a wedding or festal occasion. We have seen also (Notes on Mat. ix. 23) that funerals were attended with mournful music, and lamentation, and howling. It is not improbable that children also, in play, imitated a mournful funeral procession. One part are represented as sullen and dissatisfied. They would not enter into the play: nothing pleased them. The others complained of it. We have, said they, taken all pains to please you. We have piped to you, have played lively tunes, and have engaged in cheerful sports, but you would not join with us; and then we have played different games, and imitated the mourning at funerals, and you are equally sullen; *you have not lamented;* you have not joined with us. Nothing pleases you. So, said Christ, is this generation of men. *John* came one

ing and drinking; and they say, Behold a man gluttonous, and a wine-bibber, a friend of [o]publicans and sinners. But [p]wisdom is justified of her children.

20 Then[q] began he to upbraid the cities wherein most of his mighty works were done, because they repented not:

21 Woe unto thee, Chorazin! woe unto thee, [r]Bethsaida! for if the mighty works which were

o Lu.15.2; 19.7. p Ps.92.5,6; Pr.17.24. q Lu.10.13,&c. r Jn.12.21.

way, *neither eating nor drinking*, abstaining as a Nazarite, and you were not pleased with him. I, the Son of man, have come in a different manner, *eating and drinking;* not practising any austerity, but living like other men, and you are equally dissatisfied—nay, you are less pleased. You calumniate him, and abuse me for not doing the very thing which displeased you in John. Nothing pleases you. You are fickle, changeable, inconstant, and abusive. ¶ *Markets.* Places to sell provisions; places of concourse, where also children flocked together for play. ¶ *We have piped.* We have played on musical instruments. A *pipe* was a wind instrument of music often used by shepherds. ¶ *Neither eating nor drinking.* That is, abstaining from some kinds of food and wine, as a Nazarite. It does not mean that he did not eat at all, but that he was remarkable for abstinence. ¶ *He hath a devil.* He is actuated by a bad spirit. He is irregular, strange, and cannot be a good man. ¶ *The Son of man came eating and drinking.* That is, living as others do; not practising austerity; and they accuse him of being *fond* of excess, and seeking the society of the wicked. ¶ *Gluttonous.* One given to excessive *eating.* ¶ *Wine-bibber.* One who drinks much wine. Jesus undoubtedly lived according to the general customs of the people of his time. He did not affect singularity; he did not separate himself as a Nazarite; he did not practise severe austerities. He ate that which was common and drank that which was common. As wine was a common article of beverage among the people, he drank it. It was the pure juice of the grape, and for anything that can be proved, it was without fermentation. In regard to the kind of wine which was used, see Notes on Jn. ii. 10. No one should plead the example, at anyrate, in favour of making use of the wines that are commonly used in this country—wines, many of which are manufactured here, and without a particle of the pure juice of the grape, and most of which are mixed with noxious drugs to give them colour and flavour. ¶ *Wisdom is justified of her children.* The children of wisdom are *the wise*—those who understand. The Saviour means that though that generation of Pharisees and fault-finders did not appreciate the conduct of John and himself, yet the *wise*, the candid—those who understood the reasons of their conduct—would approve of and do justice to it.

20. *Then began he to upbraid*, &c. That is, to reprove, to rebuke, to denounce heavy judgment.

21. *Chorazin and Bethsaida.* These were towns not far from Capernaum, but the precise situation is unknown. See *The Land and the Book* (Thomson), vol. ii. p. 8, 9. Bethsaida means literally a *house of hunting* or *of game*, and it was probably situated on the banks of the Sea of Galilee, and supported itself by hunting or fishing. It was the residence of Philip, Andrew, and Peter, Jn. i. 44. It was enlarged by Philip the Tetrarch, and called *Julia*, after the emperor's daughter. ¶ *Tyre and Sidon.* These were cities of Phœnicia, formerly very opulent, and distinguished for merchandise. They were situated on the shore of the Mediterranean Sea, and were in the western part of Judea. They were therefore well known to the Jews. Tyre is frequently mentioned in the Old Testament as being the place through which Solomon derived many of the materials for building the temple, 2 Ch. ii. 11–16. It was also a place against which one of the most important and pointed prophecies of Isaiah was directed. See Notes on Is. xxiii. Comp. Eze. xxvi. 4–14. Both these cities were very ancient. Sidon was situated within the bounds of the tribe of Asher (Jos. xix. 28), but this tribe could never get possession of it, Ju. i. 31. It was famous for its great trade and navigation. Its inhabitants were the first remarkable merchants in the world, and were much celebrated for

done in you had been done in Tyre and Sidon, they would have repented long ago in sackcloth and ashes.

22 But I say unto you, [s]It shall be more tolerable for Tyre and Sidon at the day of judgment than for you.

23 And thou, Capernaum, [t]which art exalted unto heaven, shalt be

s ch.10.15.

t Is.14.13-15; La.2.1.

their luxury. In the time of our Saviour it was probably a city of much splendour and extensive commerce. It is now called Seide, or Saide, and is far less populous and splendid than it was in the time of Christ. It was subdued successively by the Babylonians, Egyptians, and Romans, the latter of whom deprived it of its freedom.

Messrs. Fisk and King, American missionaries, passed through Sidon in the summer of 1823, and estimated the population, as others have estimated it, at 8000 or 10,000; but Mr. Goodell, another American missionary, took up his residence there in June, 1824, for the purpose of studying the Armenian language with a bishop of the Armenian Church who lives there, and of course had far better opportunities to know the statistics of the place. He tells us there are six Mohammedan mosques, a Jewish synagogue, a Maronite, Latin, and Greek church. Dr. Thomson (*The Land and the Book*, vol. i. p. 164) supposes that the population may now be about 10,000 — about 6800 Moslems, 850 Greek Catholics, 750 Maronites, 150 Greeks, and 300 Jews. It exports tobacco, oil, fruit, and silk, but the amount of exports is small.

Tyre was situated about twenty miles south of Sidon. It was built partly on a small island about seventy paces from the shore, and partly on the mainland. It was a city of great extent and splendour, and extensive commerce. It abounded in luxury and wickedness. It was often besieged. It held out against Shalmaneser five years, and was taken by Nebuchadnezzar after a siege of *thirteen* years. It was afterward rebuilt, and was at length taken by Alexander the Great, after a most obstinate siege of five months. There are no signs now of the ancient city. It is the residence only of a few miserable fishermen, and contains, amid the ruins of its former magnificence, only a few huts. Thus was fulfilled the prophecy of Ezekiel: *Thou shalt be built no more; though thou be sought for, yet shalt thou never be found again* (xxvi. 21). For a description of Tyre as it was formerly and as it is now, see Notes on Is. xxiii. ¶ *In sackcloth and ashes.* Sackcloth was a coarse cloth, like canvas, used for the dress of the poor, and for the more common articles of domestic economy. It was worn also as a sign of mourning. The Jews also frequently threw ashes on their heads as expressive of grief, Job i. 21; ii. 12; Jer. vi. 26. The meaning is, that they would have repented *with expressions of deep sorrow.* Like Nineveh, they would have seen their guilt and danger, and would have turned from their iniquities. *Heathen* cities would have received him better than the cities of the Jews, his native land.

23. *And thou, Capernaum.* See Notes on Mat. iv. 13. ¶ *Which art exalted to heaven.* This is an expression used to denote great privileges. He meant that they were peculiarly favoured with instruction. The city was prosperous. It was signally favoured by its wealth. Most of all, it was signally favoured by the presence, the preaching, and the miracles of the Lord Jesus Christ. Here he spent a large portion of his time in the early part of his ministry, and in Capernaum and its neighbourhood he performed his chief miracles. ¶ *Shalt be brought down to hell.* This does not mean that all the *people* would go to hell, but that the city which had flourished so prosperously would lose its prosperity, and occupy the *lowest place* among cities. The word *hell* is used here, not to denote a place of punishment in the future world, but a state of *desolation and destruction.* It stands in contrast with the word *heaven.* As their being exalted *to heaven* did not mean that the *people* would all be saved or dwell in heaven, so their being brought down to *hell* refers to the desolation of the *city.* Their privileges, honours, wealth, &c., would be taken away, and they would sink *as low* among cities as they had been before exalted. This has been strictly fulfilled. In the wars between the Jews and the Romans, Chorazin, Bethsaida, Capernaum, &c.,

brought down to hell: for if the mighty works which have been done in thee had been done in Sodom, it would have remained until this day.

24 But I say unto you, [u]That it shall be more tolerable for the land of Sodom in the day of judgment than for thee.

25 At[v] that time Jesus answered and said, I thank thee, O Father, Lord of heaven and earth, because [w]thou hast hid these things from the wise and prudent, and hast revealed them unto babes.

26 Even so, Father: for so it seemed good in thy sight.

27 All[x] things are delivered unto me of my Father: and no man knoweth the Son but the Father; [y]neither knoweth any man the Father save the Son, and *he* to whomsoever the Son will reveal *him*.

u ver.22. *v* Lu.10.21,&c.

w Ps.8.2; Je.1.7,8; 1 Co.1.27. *x* ch.28.18; Lu.10.22; Jn.3.35; 17.2; 1 Co.15.27. *y* Jn.1.18; 1 Jn.5.20.

---

were so completely desolated that it is difficult to determine their former situation. See Notes on ch. iv. 13. It is not to be denied, also, that he threatened future punishment on those who rejected him. The truth inculcated is, that those who are peculiarly favoured will be punished accordingly if they abuse their privileges. ¶ *If the mighty works—had been done in Sodom.* See Notes on Mat. x. 15. Sodom was destroyed on account of its great wickedness. Christ says if his miracles had been performed *there*, they would have repented, and consequently the city would not have been destroyed. As it was, it would be better for Sodom in the day of judgment than for Capernaum, for its inhabitants would not be called to answer for the abuse of so great privileges.

25, 26. *From the wise and prudent.* That is, from those who *thought* themselves wise—*wise* according to the world's estimation of wisdom, 1 Co. i. 26, 27. ¶ *Hast revealed them unto babes.* To the poor, the ignorant, and the obscure; the teachable, the simple, the humble. By the wise and prudent here he had reference probably to the proud and haughty scribes and Pharisees in Capernaum. They rejected his gospel, but it was the pleasure of God to reveal it to obscure and more humble men. The reason given, the only satisfactory reason, is, that it so seemed good in the sight of God. In this the Saviour acquiesced, saying, *Even so, Father;* and in the dealings of God it is fit that all should acquiesce. *Such is the will of God* is often the only explanation which can be offered in regard to the various events which happen to us on earth. *Such is the will of God* is the only account which can be given of the reason of the dispensations of his grace. Our understanding is often confounded. We are unsuccessful in all our efforts at explanation. Our philosophy fails, and all that we can say is, "Even so, Father; for so it seems good to thee." And this is enough. That GOD does a thing, is, after all, the best reason which we *can* have that it is right. It is a *security* that nothing wrong is done; and though now mysterious, yet light will hereafter shine upon it like the light of noonday. I have more certainty that a thing is right if I can say that I know such is the will of God, than I could have by depending on my own reason. In the one case I confide in the infallible and most perfect God; in the other I rely on the reason of a frail and erring man. God never errs; but nothing is more common than for men to err.

27. *All things are delivered,* &c. The same doctrine is clearly taught often in the New Testament. See Jn. iii. 35; vi. 46; x. 15; Col. i. 16, 17. It means that Christ has control over all things for the good of his church; that the government of the universe is committed to him *as Mediator*, that he may redeem his people and guide them to glory, Ep. i. 20–22. ¶ *No man knoweth the Son.* That is, such is the nature of the Son of God, such the mystery of the union between the divine and human nature, such his exalted character as *divine*, that no mortal can fully comprehend him. None but God *fully* knows him. Had he been a mere man, this language surely would not have been used of him. ¶ *Neither knoweth any man the Father*, &c. In the original this is, neither knoweth *any one* the Father except the Son. That is, no man or angel clearly and fully com-

28 Come unto me, [z]all *ye* that labour and are heavy laden, and I will give you rest.

29 Take my yoke upon you, and [a]learn of me; for I am meek and [b]lowly in heart: and [c]ye shall find rest unto your souls.

30 For[d] my yoke *is* easy, and my burden is light.

z Is.53.2,3. *a* Phi.2.5-8; 1 Pe.2.21. *b* Zec.9.9. *c* Je.6.16. *d* 1 Jn.5.3.

prehends the character of the infinite God; none but the Son—the Lord Jesus—and he to whom he makes him known, have any just apprehensions of his being and perfections.

28. *All* ye *that labour and are heavy laden.* The Saviour here, perhaps, refers primarily to the Jews, who groaned under the weight of their ceremonial laws and the traditions of the elders, Ac. xv. 10. He tells them that by coming to him, and embracing the new system of religion, they would be freed from these burdensome rites and ceremonies. There can be no doubt, however, that he meant here chiefly to address the poor, lost, ruined sinner: the man *burdened* with a consciousness of his transgressions, trembling at his danger, and seeking deliverance. For such there *is* relief. Christ tells them to come to him, to believe in him, and to *trust* him, and him only, for salvation. Doing this, he will give them rest—rest from their sins, from the alarms of conscience, from the terrors of the law, and from the fears of eternal death.

29. *Take my yoke.* This is a figure taken from the use of oxen, and hence signifying to labour for one, or in the service of anyone. The *yoke* is used in the Bible as an emblem (1.) of bondage or slavery, Le. xxvi. 13; De. xxviii. 38. (2.) Of afflictions or crosses, La. iii. 27. (3.) Of the punishment of sin, La. i. 14. (4.) Of the commandments of God. (5.) Of legal ceremonies, Ac. xv. 10; Ga. v. 1. It refers here to the religion of the Redeemer; and the idea is, that they should embrace his system of religion and obey him. All virtue and all religion imply *restraint*—the restraint of our bad passions and inclinations—and subjection to laws; and the Saviour here means to say that the restraints and laws of his religion are mild, and gentle, and easy. Let anyone compare them with the burdensome and expensive ceremonies of the Jews (see Ac. xv. 10), or with the religious rites of the heathen everywhere, or with the requirements of the Popish system, and he will see how true it is that *his* yoke is easy. And let his laws and requirements be compared with the laws which *sin* imposes on its votaries—the laws of fashion, and honour, and sensuality—and he will feel that religion is "freedom," Jn. viii. 36. "He is a freeman whom the truth makes free, and all are slaves besides." It is *easier* to be a Christian than a sinner; and of all the *yokes* ever imposed on men, that of the Redeemer is the lightest. ¶ *For I am meek*, &c. See Notes on Mat. v. 5. This was eminently Christ's personal character. But this is not its meaning here. He is giving a reason why they should embrace his religion. That was, that he was not harsh, overbearing, and oppressive, like the Pharisees, but meek, mild, and gentle in his government. His laws were reasonable and tender, and it would be easy to obey him.

30. *My yoke* is *easy*, &c. That is, the services that I shall require are easily rendered. They are not burdensome, like all other systems of religion. So the Christian always finds them. In coming to him there is *a peace which passeth all understanding*; in believing in him, *joy;* in following him *through evil and good report*, a comfort *which the world giveth not;* in bearing trials and in persecution, *the hope of glory;* and in keeping his commandments, *great reward.*

REMARKS.

1st. A spirit of inquiry about the person and works of Christ is peculiarly proper, ver. 2, 3. John was solicitous to ascertain his true character, and nothing is of more importance for all than to understand his true character. On him depends all the hope that man has of happiness beyond the grave. He saves, or man must perish. *He* will save, or we must die for ever. With what earnestness, therefore, should the old and the young inquire into his character. Our eternal all demands it; and while *this* is delayed, we are endangering our everlasting felicity.

2d. Clear proof has been furnished that Jesus is the Christ and can save us, ver. 4, 5. If his miracles did not prove that he came from God, nothing can prove it. If he could open the eyes of the blind, then he can enlighten the sinner; if he could unstop the ears of the deaf, then he can cause us to hear and live; if he could heal the sick, and make the lame walk, then he can heal *our* spiritual maladies, and make us walk in the way of life; if he could raise the dead, then he can raise those dead in sin, and breathe into us the breath of eternal life. If he was willing to do all this for the *body* which is soon to perish, then he will be much more willing to do it for the *soul*, that never dies. Then the poor, lost sinner may come and live.

3d. We see in this chapter Christ's manner of praising or complimenting men, ver. 7-15. He gave, in no measured terms, his exalted opinion of John—gave him praise which had been bestowed on no other mortal—ranked him far above the purest and sublimest of the prophets. But this was not done in the presence of John, *nor was it done in the presence of those who would inform John of it.* It was when the disciples of John had "*departed*," and his commendation of John was spoken to "the multitude," ver. 7. He waited till his disciples were gone, apprehending, doubtless, that *they* would be likely to report what he said in praise of their master, and *then* expressed his high opinion of his character. The practice of the *world* is to praise others to their faces, or in the presence of those who will be sure to inform them of it, and to speak evil of them when absent. Jesus delivered his unfavourable opinions of others to the men themselves; their excellences he took pains to commend where they would not be likely to hear of them. He did good to both, and in both prevented the existence of pride.

4th. The wicked take much pains, and are often fickle and inconsistent, for the sake of abusing and calumniating religious men, ver. 18, 19. They found much fault with the Saviour for doing the very same thing which they blamed John for *not* doing. So it is commonly with men who slander professors of religion. They risk their own characters, to prove that others are hypocrites or sinners. The object is not truth, but calumny and opposition to religion; and hitherto no means have been too base or too wicked to pour contempt on the followers of Christ.

5th. The purest characters may expect the shaft of calumny and malice, and often in proportion to their purity, ver. 19. Even the Saviour of the world was accused of being intemperate and a glutton. If the only perfectly pure being that ever trod the earth was thus accused, let not his followers think that any strange thing has happened to them if *they* are falsely accused.

6th. Judgments will overtake guilty men, and cities, and nations, ver. 21, 22. They fell on Sodom, Tyre, Sidon, and Capernaum. They may long linger; but in due time the hand of God will fall on the wicked, and they will die—for ever die.

7th. The wicked will suffer in proportion to their privileges, ver. 23, 24. So it was with Capernaum. And if they of ancient days suffered thus; if more tremendous judgments fell on them than even on guilty Sodom, what shall be the doom of those who go down to hell from this day of light? The Saviour was indeed there a few days; he worked a few miracles; but they had not, as *we* have, all his instructions; they had not Sabbath-schools, and Bible-classes, and the stated preaching of the gospel, nor was the world blessed then, as now, with extensive and powerful revivals of religion. How awful must be the doom of those who are educated in the ways of religion—who are instructed from Sabbath to Sabbath—who grow up amid the means of grace—and then are lost!

8th. The poor and needy; the weary and heavy-laden; the soul sick of sin and of the world; the sinner conscious of guilt and afraid to die, may come to Jesus Christ and live, ver. 28-30. The invitation is wide as the world. The child and the old man may seek and find salvation at the feet of the same Saviour. No child is too young; no man is too old; no one is too great a sinner. Christ is *full* of mercy, and all who come shall find peace. O how should we, in this sinful and miserable world, borne down with sin, and exposed each moment to death—how should we come and find the peace which he has promised to all, and take the yoke which all have found to be light!

CHAPTER XII.

1-8. The account contained in these verses is also recorded in Mar. ii. 23-28, and Lu. vi. 1-5.

1. *At that time.* Luke (chap. vi. 1) fixes the time more particularly. He says that it was *the second Sabbath after*

CHAPTER XII.

AT that time [a]Jesus went on the Sabbath day through the corn; and his disciples were an hungered, and began to [b]pluck the ears of corn, and to eat.

2 But when the Pharisees saw *it*, they said unto him, Behold, thy disciples do that which is [c]not lawful to do upon the Sabbath day.

3 But he said unto them, Have ye not read [d]what David did when he was an hungered, and they that were with him;

4 How he entered into the house of God, and did eat [e]the shew-bread, which was not lawful for him to eat, neither for them which were with him, [f]but only for the priests?

a Mar.2.23,&c.; Lu.6.1,&c. *b* De.23.25. *c* Ex.31.15. *d* 1 Sa.21.6. *e* Ex.25.30. *f* Ex.29.32,33.

---

the first. To understand this, it is proper to remark that the *Passover* was observed during the month *Abib*, or Nisan, answering to the latter part of March and the first of April. The feast was held seven days, commencing on the fourteenth day of the month (Ex. xii. 1–28; xxiii. 15), on the *second* day of the paschal week. The law required that a sheaf of *barley* should be offered up as the first-fruits of the harvest, Le. xxiii. 10, 11. From this day was reckoned seven weeks to the feast of *Pentecost* (Le. xxiii. 15, 16), called also the feast of *weeks* (De. xvi. 10), and the feast of the harvest, Ex. xxiii. 16. This second day in the feast of the Passover, or of unleavened bread, was the *beginning*, therefore, from which they reckoned *toward* the Pentecost. The Sabbath in the week following would be the *second Sabbath* after this first one in the reckoning, and this was doubtless the time mentioned when Christ went through the fields. It should be farther mentioned, that in Judea the barley harvest commences about the beginning of May, and both that and the wheat harvest are over by the twentieth. Barley is in full ear in the beginning of April. There is no improbability, therefore, in this narrative on account of the season of the year. This feast was always held at Jerusalem. ¶ *Through the corn.* Through the *barley*, or *wheat*. The word *corn*, as used in our translation of the Bible, has no reference to *maize*, or *Indian corn*, as it has with us. Indian corn was unknown till the discovery of America, and it is scarcely probable that the translators knew anything of it. The word was applied, as it is still in England, to wheat, rye, oats, and barley. This explains the circumstance that they *rubbed it in their hands* (Lu. vi. 1) to separate the grain from the chaff.

2. *Upon the Sabbath day.* The Pharisees, doubtless desirous of finding fault with Christ, said that in plucking the grain on the *Sabbath day* they had violated the commandment. Moses had commanded the Hebrews to abstain from all servile work on the Sabbath, Ex. xx. 10; xxxv. 2, 3; Nu. xv. 32–36. On any other day this would have been clearly lawful, for it was permitted, De. xxiii. 25.

3. *But he said unto them*, &c. To vindicate his disciples, he referred them to a similar case, recorded in the Old Testament, and therefore one with which they *ought* to have been acquainted. This was the case of David. The law commanded that twelve loaves of bread should be laid on the table in the holy place in the tabernacle, to remain a week, and then to be eaten by the *priests only*. Their place was then supplied by *fresh bread*. This was called the *shew-bread*, Le. xxiv. 5–9. David, fleeing before Saul, weary and hungry, had come to Ahimelech the priest; had found only this bread; had asked it of him, and had eaten it contrary to the *letter* of the law, 1 Sa. xxi. 1–7. David, among the Jews, had high authority. This act had passed uncondemned. It proved that in *cases of necessity the laws did not bind a man*—a principle which all laws admit. So the *necessity* of the disciples justified them in doing on the Sabbath what would have been otherwise unlawful.

4, 5. *How he entered into the house of God.* That is, the *tabernacle*, the temple not being then built. ¶ *Have ye not read in the law?* In the law, or in the books of Moses. ¶ *Profane the Sabbath.* He referred them to the conduct of the priests also. On the Sabbath days they were engaged, as well as on other days, in killing beasts for sacrifice, Nu. xxviii. 9, 10. Two lambs were killed on the

5 Or have ye not read in [g]the law how that on the Sabbath days the[h] priests in the temple profane the Sabbath, and are blameless?

6 But I say unto you, That in this place is [i]*one* greater than the temple.

7 But if ye had known what *this* meaneth, [k]I will have mercy, and not sacrifice, ye would not have condemned the guiltless.

8 For the Son of man is Lord even of the Sabbath day.

g Nu.28.9. h Jn.7.22,23.
i 2 Ch.6.18; Mal.3.1; ch.23.17-21. k Ho.6.6.

9 And[l] when he was departed thence, he went into their synagogue:

10 And, behold, there was a man which had his hand withered. And they asked him, saying, [m]Is it lawful to heal on the Sabbath days? that they might accuse him.

11 And he said unto them, What man shall there be among you that shall have one sheep, and [n]if it fall into a pit on the Sabbath day, will he not lay hold on it, and lift *it* out?

l Mar.3.1,&c.; Lu.6.6,&c. m Lu.14.3. n De.22.4.

Sabbath, in addition to the *daily* sacrifice. The priests must be engaged in slaying them, and making fires to burn them in sacrifice, whereas to kindle a fire was expressly forbidden the Jews on the Sabbath, Ex. xxxv. 3. They did that which, for other persons to do, would have been *profaning* the Sabbath. Yet they were blameless. They did what was necessary and commanded. This was done in the *very temple*, too, the place of holiness, where the law should be most strictly observed.

6, 7. One *greater than the temple.* Here the Saviour refers to himself, and to his own dignity and power. "I have power over the laws; I can grant to my disciples a dispensation from those laws. An act which *I* command or permit them to do is therefore right." This proves that he was divine. None but God can authorize men to do a thing contrary to the divine laws. He refers them again (ver. 7) to a passage he had before quoted (See Notes on Mat. ix. 13), showing that God preferred acts of righteousness, rather than a precise observance of a ceremonial law.

Mark adds (ii. 27) "the Sabbath was made for man, and not man for the Sabbath." That is, the Sabbath was intended for the welfare of man; it was designed to promote his happiness, and not to produce misery by harsh, unfeeling requirements. It is not to be so interpreted as to produce suffering by making the necessary supply of wants unlawful. Man was not made for the Sabbath. Man was created first, and then the Sabbath was appointed for his happiness, Ge. ii. 1-3. His *necessities*, his *real* comforts and wants, are not to be made to bend to that which was made *for him*. The laws are to be interpreted favourably to his *real* wants and comforts. This authorizes works only of *real* necessity, not of imaginary wants, or amusements, or common business and worldly employments.

8. *For the Son of man is Lord even of the Sabbath day.* To crown all, Christ says that he was Lord of the Sabbath. He had a right to direct the manner of its observance—undoubted proof that he is divine.

9-13. The account contained in these verses is recorded also in Mar. iii. 1-5, and Lu. vi. 6-10.

10. *A man which had his hand withered.* This was probably one form of the palsy. See Notes on Mat. iv. 24.

Mark and Luke have mentioned some circumstances omitted by Matthew. They say that Jesus first addressed the man, and told him to stand forth in the midst. He then addressed the people. He asked them if it was lawful to do *good* on the Sabbath day. This was admitted by all their teachers, and it could not be denied. They were therefore silent. He then appealed to *them*, and drew an argument from their own conduct. A man that had a sheep that should fall into a pit on the Sabbath day would exercise the common offices of humanity and draw it out. If it was lawful to save the life of a *sheep*, was it not proper to save the life of a man? By a reference to their own conduct he silenced them.

Mark adds that he looked on them *with anger*—that is, with strong disapprobation of their conduct. Their envy and malignity excited feelings of holy indignation. See Notes on Mar. iii. 5.

12. *How much, then, is a man better*

12 How much, then, is a man better than a sheep? Wherefore it is lawful to do well on the Sabbath days.

13 Then saith he to the man, Stretch forth thine hand. And he stretched *it* forth; and it was restored whole, like as the other.

14 Then the Pharisees went out, and [1]held a council against him, how they might destroy him.

15 But when Jesus knew *it*, he

[1] or, *took counsel*.

---

than a sheep? Of more consequence or value. If you would show an act of kindness to a brute beast on the Sabbath, how much more important is it to evince similar kindness to one made in the image of God! ¶ *It is lawful to do well on the Sabbath days.* This was universally allowed by the Jews in the abstract; and Jesus only showed them that the *principle* on which they acted in other things applied with *more force* to the case before him, and that the act which he was about to perform was, by their own confession, lawful.

13. *Then saith he to the man, Stretch forth thine hand.* This was a remarkable commandment. The man *might* have said that he had no strength—that it was a thing which he could not do. Yet, *being commanded*, it was his duty to obey. He did so, and was healed. So the sinner. It is his duty to obey whatever God commands. He will *give* strength to those who endeavour to do his will. It is not right to plead, when God commands us to do a thing, that we have no strength. He will give us strength, if there is a disposition to obey. At the same time, however, this passage should not be applied to the sinner as if it proved that he has no more strength or ability than the man who had the withered hand. It proves no such thing: it has no reference to any such case. It may be used to prove that man should *instantly obey* the commands of God, without pausing to examine the question about his ability, and especially without saying *that he can do nothing.* What would the Saviour have said to this man if he had objected that he *could not* stretch out his hand? ¶ *It was restored whole.* Christ had before *claimed* divine authority and power (ver. 6–9), he now showed that he *possessed* it. By his *own power* he healed him, thus evincing by a miracle that his claim of being Lord of the Sabbath was well founded.

These two cases determine what may be done on the Sabbath. The one was a case of *necessity*, the other of *mercy.* The example of the Saviour, and his explanations, show that these are a part of the proper duties of that holy day. Beyond an *honest* and *conscientious* discharge of these two duties, men may not devote the Sabbath to any secular purpose. If they do, they do it at their peril. They go beyond what *his* authority authorizes them to do. They do what *he* claimed the special right of doing, as being Lord of the Sabbath. They usurp *his* place, and act and legislate where God only has a right to act and legislate. Men may as well trample down any other law of the Bible as that respecting the Sabbath.

14–21. This account is found also in Mar. iii. 6–12.

14. *The Pharisees—held a council*, &c. Mark adds that the *Herodians* also took a part in this plot. They were probably a *political* party attached firmly to Herod Antipas, son of Herod the Great, tetrarch of Galilee. He was the same man who had imprisoned and beheaded John the Baptist, and to whom the Saviour, when arraigned, was sent by Pilate. See Notes on Lu. iii. 1. He was under Roman authority, and was a strong advocate of Roman power. All the friends of the family of Herod were opposed to Christ, and ever ready to join any plot against his life. They remembered, doubtless, the attempts of Herod the Great against him when he was the babe of Bethelem, and they were stung with the memory of the escape of Jesus from his bloody hands. The attempt against him now, on the part of the Pharisees, was the effect of *envy.* They hated his popularity, they were losing their influence, and they therefore resolved to take him out of the way.

15. *But when Jesus knew* it, *he withdrew himself*, &c. He knew of the plot which they had formed against his life; but his hour was not yet come, and he therefore sought security. By remaining, his presence would only have provoked them farther and endangered his own life. He acted, therefore, the part of prudence and withdrew. Comp. Notes on Mat. x. 23.

withdrew himself from thence: and great multitudes followed him, and he healed them all;

16 And charged them that they should not make him known:

17 That it might be fulfilled which was spoken by Esaias the prophet, saying,

18 Behold[o] my servant, whom I have chosen; my beloved, in whom my soul is well pleased: I will put my spirit upon him, and he shall show judgment to the Gentiles.

19 He shall not strive, nor cry; neither shall any man hear his voice in the streets.

20 A bruised reed shall he not break, and smoking flax shall he

o Is.42.1.

Mark adds that he withdrew *to the sea;* that is, to the Sea of Galilee, or Tiberias. He states also (ch. iii. 7, 8) that "*a great multitude* from Galilee followed him, and from Judea, and from Jerusalem, and from Idumea, and from beyond Jordan; and they about Tyre and Sidon, a great multitude, when they heard what great things he did, came unto him." As some of these places were without the limits of Judea or inhabited by *Gentiles*, this statement of Mark throws light on the passage quoted by Matthew (ver. 21), "In his name shall the *Gentiles* trust."

Pressed by the crowd (Mar. iii. 9), Jesus went aboard a *small vessel*, or *boat*, called by Mark a *ship*. This he did for the convenience of being separated from them and more easily addressing them. We are to suppose the lake still and calm; the multitudes, most of whom were sick and diseased, on the shore and pressing to the water's edge; and Jesus thus healing their diseases, and preaching to them the good news of salvation. No scene could be more sublime than this.

16. *And he charged them*, &c. He was *at this time* desirous of concealment. He wished to avoid their plots and to save his life.

17. *That it might be fulfilled*, &c. Matthew here quotes a passage from Is. xlii. 1-4, to show the *reason why he thus retired from his enemies and sought concealment*. The Jews, and the disciples also at first, expected that the Messiah would be a conqueror, and vindicate himself from all his enemies. When they saw him retiring before them, and, instead of subduing them by force, seeking a place of concealment, it was contrary to all their previous notions of the Messiah. Matthew by this quotation shows that *their* conceptions of him had been wrong. Instead of a warrior and an earthly conqueror, he was *predicted* under a totally different character. Instead of shouting for battle, lifting up his voice in the streets, oppressing the feeble—*breaking bruised reeds and quenching smoking flax, as a conqueror*—he would be peaceful, retiring; would strengthen the feeble, and would cherish the faintest desires of holiness. This appears to be the *general* meaning of this quotation here. Comp. Notes on Is. xlii. 1-4.

18. *My servant.* That is, the Messiah, the Lord Jesus; called a servant from his taking the *form* of a *servant*, or his being born in a humble condition (Phi. ii. 7), and from his obeying or *serving* God. See He. x. 9. ¶ *Shall show judgment to the Gentiles.* The word *judgment* means, in the Hebrew, *law, commands*, &c., Ps. xix. 9; cxix. 29, 30. It means the *whole system of truth;* the law of God in general; the purpose, plan, or *judgment* of God about human duty and conduct. Here it means, evidently, the system of *gospel truth*, the *Christian scheme*. ¶ *Gentiles.* All who were not Jews. This prophecy was fulfilled by the multitudes coming to him from Idumea and beyond Jordan, and from Tyre and Sidon, as recorded by Mar. iii. 7, 8.

19. *He shall not strive*, &c. He shall not shout as a warrior. He shall be meek, retiring, and peaceful. Streets were places of concourse. The meaning is, that he should not seek publicity and popularity.

20. *A bruised reed*, &c. The reed is an emblem of feebleness, as well as of fickleness or want of stability, Mat. xi. 7. A bruised, broken reed is an emblem of the poor and oppressed. It means that he would not oppress the feeble and poor, as victorious warriors and conquerors did. It is also an expressive emblem of the soul broken and contrite on account of sin; weeping and mourning for transgression. He will not break it; that is, he will not be severe, unforgiving, and cruel. He will heal it, pardon it, and give it

not quench, till he send forth judgment unto victory.

21 And in his name shall the Gentiles trust.

22 Then[p] was brought unto him one possessed with a devil, blind and dumb: and he healed him, insomuch that the blind and dumb both spake and saw.

23 And all the people were amazed; and said, Is not this the Son of David?

24 But when the Pharisees heard *it*, they said, This *fellow* doth not cast out devils, but by [2]Beelzebub the prince of the devils.

25 And Jesus [q]knew their thoughts, and said unto them,

p Mar.3.11; Lu.11.14.

2 *Beelzebul.* q Ps.139.2; Jn.2.24,25.

---

strength. ¶ *Smoking flax.* This refers to the *wick* of a lamp when the oil is exhausted—the dying, flickering flame and smoke that hang over it. It is an emblem, also, of feebleness and infirmity. He would not farther oppress those who had a little strength; he would not put out hope and life when it seemed to be almost extinct. He would not be like the Pharisees, proud and overbearing, and trampling down the poor. It is expressive, also, of the languishing graces of the people of God. He will not treat them harshly or unkindly, but will cherish the feeble flame, minister the *oil* of grace, and kindle it into a blaze. ¶ *Till he send forth judgment unto victory. Judgment* here means *truth*—the truth of God, the gospel. It shall be victorious—it shall not be vanquished. Though the Messiah is not *such* a conqueror as the Jews expected, yet he *shall* conquer. Though mild and retiring, yet he will be victorious.

21. *And in his name,* &c. The Hebrew in Isaiah is, "And the isles shall wait for his law." The idea is, however, the same. The *isles* denote the Gentiles, or a part of the Gentiles—those out of Judea. The meaning is, that the gospel should be preached to the Gentiles, and that they should receive it. See Notes on Is. xli. 1 for an explanation of the word *islands,* as it is used in the Bible.

22–30. *Then was brought unto him one possessed with a devil.* See Notes on Mat. iv. 24. The same account, substantially, is found in Mar. iii. 22–27, and Lu. xi. 14–26.

23. *Is not this the Son of David?* That is, Is not this the promised *descendant* of David, the Messiah? They were acquainted with the prophecy in Is. xxxv. 5, "Then the eyes of the blind shall be opened, and the ears of the deaf shall be unstopped," and they inferred that he must be the promised Messiah who was able to do this. This inference was drawn by the common people, and not by the proud and haughty Pharisees. It is not uncommon that men of plain common sense, though unlearned, see the true meaning of the Bible, while those who are filled with pride and science, falsely so called, are blinded.

24. *But when the Pharisees heard* it, &c. It was necessary for the Pharisees, who had determined to reject Jesus of Nazareth, to account in *some* way for the miracles he had wrought. Here was a manifest miracle, an exertion of power unquestionably superior to what *men* could put forth. The common people were fast drawing the proper inference from it, and coming into the belief that this was the Messiah. The authority and power of the Pharisees were declining. Unless, therefore, some way should be devised of accounting for these facts, their influence would be at an end. Whatever way of accounting for them was adopted, it was necessary that they should acknowledge that there was *superhuman power.* The people were fully persuaded of this, and no man could deny it. They therefore ascribed it to the prince of the devils—to Beelzebub. In this they had *two* objects: 1st. To concede to the people that here was a *miracle,* or a work above mere human power. 2d. To throw all possible contempt on Jesus. Beelzebub, or Beelzebul, as it is in the Greek, and correctly rendered in the margin, was an opprobrious name given to the leader of the devils as an expression of supreme contempt. See Notes on Mat. x. 25.

25, 26. *And Jesus knew their thoughts,* &c. To know the thoughts of the heart belongs only to God, Ps. cxxxix. 2; Je. xvii. 10. ¶ *Every kingdom,* &c. Their subtle and cunning device was completely foiled, and Jesus made their argument recoil on their own heads.

Every kingdom divided against itself is brought to desolation; and every city or house divided against itself shall not stand:

26 And if Satan cast out Satan, he is divided against himself; how shall then his kingdom stand?

27 And if I [r]by Beelzebub cast out devils, by whom do your children cast *them* out? Therefore they shall be your judges.

28 But if I cast out devils by the Spirit of God, then [s]the kingdom of God is come unto you.

29 Or else how can one enter into a strong man's house, [t]and spoil his goods, except he first bind the strong man? and then he will spoil his house.

30 He[u] that is not with me, is against me; and he that gathereth not with me, scattereth abroad.

31 Wherefore I say unto you, [v]All manner of sin and blasphemy shall be forgiven unto men; [w]but the blasphemy *against* the *Holy* Ghost shall not be forgiven unto men.

r ver.24.
s Da.2.44; ch.6.33; Lu.11.20; 17.21; Ro.14.17.
t Is.49.24; 53.12; Re.12.7-10; 20.2,3. *u* 1 Jn.2.19.
v Mar.3.28; Lu.12.10. *w* He.10.29; 1 Jn.5.16.

A kingdom or a family can prosper only by living in harmony. The different parts and members must unite in promoting the same objects. If divided—if one part *undoes* what the other *does*—it must fall. So with the kingdom of Satan. It is your doctrine that Satan has *possessed* these whom *I have cured*. It is also your doctrine that *he* has *helped me* to cure them. If so, then he has helped me to undo what he had done. He has aided me to cast himself out—that is, to oppose and discomfit himself. At this rate, how can there be any stability in his kingdom? It must fall, and Satan must have less than human prudence.

27. *By whom do your children cast* them *out?* Your disciples; your followers. See Notes on Mat. i. 1. Christ was not satisfied by showing them the intrinsic absurdity of their argument. He showed them that it might as well be applied to them as to him. *Your* disciples, taught by you and encouraged by you, pretend to cast out devils. If your argument be true that a man who casts out devils must be in league with the devil, then *your disciples* have made a covenant with him also. You must therefore either give up this argument, or admit that the working of miracles is proof of the assistance of God. ¶ *Therefore they shall be your judges.* They condemn you and your argument. They are conclusive witnesses against the force of your reasoning.

28. *But if I cast out devils by the Spirit of God,* &c. The Spirit of God, here, means the *power* of God—in Luke, by the *finger* of God. Comp. Ex. viii. 19; Ps. viii. 3. If this work is not by the aid of Satan, then it is by the aid of God. Then his kingdom, or *reign*, is come, Mat. iii. 2. The *reign* of Satan over men, and the *reign* of God are in opposition. If God *expels* Satan from his dominion over men, then *his* reign has come.

29. *Or else,* &c. The Saviour makes use of a new illustration to confute the Pharisees, drawn from breaking into a house. A man could not break into the house of a strong man and take his property unless he had rendered the man himself helpless. If he had taken his goods, it would therefore be sufficient proof that he had bound the man. So I, says he, have taken this *property—this possessed person*—from the dominion of Satan. It is clear proof that I have subdued *Satan himself*, the *strong* being that had him in possession. The words *or else* mean *or how:* "*How*, or *in what way*, can one," &c. ¶ *Spoil his goods.* The word *spoil* commonly means, now, to corrupt, injure, or destroy. Here it means *to plunder*, to take with violence, as it commonly does in the Bible. See Col. ii. 8, 15; Ex. iii. 22.

30. *He that is not with me,* &c. In addition to his other arguments, Jesus urges this general principle, that there can be but two parties in the universe. If anyone did not act *with* him, he was against him. If he gathered not with him, he scattered. This is taken from the practice of persons in harvest. He that did not gather with him, or *aid* him, scattered abroad, or opposed him. The application of this was, "As I have not united with Satan, but opposed him, there can be no league between us." The charge, therefore, is a false one.

32 And whosoever [x]speaketh a word against the Son of man, it shall be forgiven him: but whosoever speaketh against the Holy Ghost, it shall not be forgiven him, neither in this world, neither in the *world* to come.

33 Either make the tree good, and his fruit good; or else make the tree corrupt, and his fruit cor-

x Lu.7.34; Jn.7.12; 1 Ti.1.13.

31, 32. In this place, and in Mar. iii. 28–30, Jesus states the awful nature of the sin of which they had been guilty. That sin was the sin against the Holy Ghost. It consisted in charging him with being in league with the devil, or accusing him of working his miracles, not by the *spirit* or *power* of God, but by the aid of the prince of the devils. It was therefore a direct insult, abuse, or evil speaking against the Holy Ghost—the spirit by which Jesus worked his miracles. That this was what he intended by this sin, at that time, is clear from Mar. iii. 30, "BECAUSE they said he had an unclean spirit." All other sins—all speaking against the Saviour himself—might be remitted. But this sin was clearly against the Holy One; it was alleging that the highest displays of God's mercy and power were the work of the devil; and it argued, therefore, the deepest depravity of mind. The sin of which he speaks is therefore clearly stated. It was accusing him of working miracles by the aid of the devil, thus dishonouring the Holy Ghost. ¶ *All manner of sin and blasphemy shall be forgiven.* That is, only on condition that men repent and believe. If they *continue* in this sin they cannot be forgiven, Mar. xvi. 16; Ro. ii. 6–9. ¶ *Blasphemy.* Injurious or evil speaking of God. See Notes on Mat. ix. 3. ¶ *A word against the Son of man.* The Jews were offended at the humble life and appearance of the Saviour. They reproached him as being a Nazarene—sprung from Nazareth, a place from which no good was expected to proceed; with being a Galilean, from Galilee, a place from which no prophet came, Jn. vii. 52. Jesus says that reproaches of this kind could be pardoned. Reflections on his poverty, on his humble birth, and on the lowliness of his human nature might be forgiven; but for those which affected his divine nature, accusing him of being in league with the devil, denying his divinity, and attributing the power which manifestly *implied* divinity to the prince of fallen spirits, there could be no pardon. This sin was a very different thing from what is now often supposed to be the sin against the Holy Ghost. It was a wanton and blasphemous attack on the divine power and nature of Christ. Such a sin God would not forgive. ¶ *Speaketh against the Holy Ghost.* The word *ghost* means *spirit*, and probably refers here to the *divine nature* of Christ—the power by which he wrought his miracles. There is no evidence that it refers to the third person of the Trinity; and the meaning of the whole passage may be: "He that speaks against me as a man of Nazareth—that speaks contemptuously of my humble birth, &c., may be pardoned; but he that reproaches my divine nature, charging me with being in league with Satan, and blaspheming the power of God manifestly displayed *by me*, can never obtain forgiveness." ¶ *Neither in this world, nor in that which is to come.* That is, as Mark expresses it, *hath never forgiveness, but is in danger of eternal damnation.* This fixes the meaning of the phrase. It means, then, not the future age or dispensation, known among the Jews as the world to come, but it means that the guilt will be unpardoned for ever; that such is the purpose of God that he *will* not forgive a sin so direct, presumptuous, and awful. It cannot be inferred from this that any sins will be forgiven in hell. The Saviour meant simply to say that there were *no possible circumstances* in which the offender could obtain forgiveness. He certainly did *not* say that any sin unpardoned here would be pardoned hereafter.

33. *Either make*, &c. The fact asserted in this verse is, that a tree is known, not by its leaves, or bark, or form, but by its fruit. The application to the argument is this: "You are to judge of man's being in league with Satan by his works. If my doctrines and works be properly the works of Satan, then *I* am corrupt; if not, then your charge is blasphemy. So, on the other hand, if, notwithstanding *your* professions, your works are the works of the devil, and your doctrines are

rupt: [y]for the tree is known by *his* fruit.

34 O[z] generation of vipers! how can ye, being evil, speak good things? [a]for out of the abundance of the heart the mouth speaketh.

35 A good man out of the good treasure of the heart bringeth forth good things; and an evil man, out of the evil treasure, bringeth forth evil things.

36 But I say unto you, that every idle word that men shall speak, [b]they shall give account thereof in the day of judgment:

37 For[c] by thy words thou shalt be justified, and by thy words thou shalt be condemned.

38 Then certain of the scribes

y ch.7.16,17. z ch.3.7. a Lu.6.45. b Ec.12.14; Ep.5.4,6; Jude 15. c Pr.13.3.

such as *he* would teach, it would prove respecting you that which you charge on me." In this indirect but powerful manner he advances to the charge against them, which he urges in the following verses.

34, 35. *O generation of vipers!* Christ here applies the argument which he had suggested in the previous verse. They were a wicked race; like poisonous reptiles, with a corrupt and evil nature. They could not be *expected* to speak good things—that is, to speak favourably of *him* and his works. As the bad fruit of a tree was the proper effect of its *nature*, so were their *words* about him and his works the proper effect of *their* nature. The *abundance* or fulness of the *heart* produced the words of the lips. *Vipers* are a poisonous kind of serpents, not often a yard long, and about an inch thick, having a flat head. The males have two large teeth, through which a most deadly poison is thrown into the wound made by the bite. They are an emblem of malignity and mischief. These were strong expressions to be used by the *meek and lowly Jesus;* but they were not the effect of anger and malice; they were a declaration of the true character of the men with whom he was conversing—a declaration most justly deserved. See Notes on Mat. iii. 7.

36. *But I say unto you, &c.* Christ closes this address to his malignant and wicked hearers by a solemn declaration that for these things God would bring them into judgment. *They*, therefore, who had spoken so malignantly against him, could not escape. ¶ *Idle word.* This literally means a vain, thoughtless, useless word; a word that accomplishes no good. Here it means, evidently, *wicked, injurious, false, malicious,* for *such* were the words which they had spoken.

37. *By thy words thou shalt be justified,* &c. That is, *words* are the indication of the true principles of the heart; by *words* the heart shall be known, as the tree is by its fruit. If they are true, proper, chaste, instructive, pious, they will prove that the heart is right. If false, envious, malignant, and impious, they will prove that the heart is *wrong*, and will therefore be among the causes of condemnation. It is not meant that words will be the *only* thing that will condemn man, but that they will be an important *part* of the things for which he shall be condemned. See Ja. iii. 3–12.

38–42. *We would see a sign from thee.* See Lu. xi. 16, 29–32. A *sign* commonly signifies a miracle—that is, a *sign* that God was with the person or had sent him. Comp. Notes on Is. vii. 11. Luke adds that this was done *tempting him;* that is, trying him, doubting if he had the power to do it. If these persons had been present with him for any considerable time, they had already seen sufficient proofs that he was what he claimed to be. They might have been, however, those who had recently come, and then the emphasis must be laid on "*we*"—*we*, as well as the others, would see a proof that thou art the Christ. In either case it was a temptation. If they had not *seen* him work a miracle, yet they should have believed it by testimony. Comp. Jn. xx. 29. Perhaps, however, the emphasis is to be laid on the words *from heaven.* They might profess not to doubt that his miracles were real, but they were not quite satisfactory. They were desirous of seeing something, therefore, that should clear up their doubts—where there could be no opportunity for dispute. A comet, or lightning, or thunder, or sudden darkness, or the gift of food raining upon them,

and of the Pharisees answered, saying, [d]Master, we would see a sign from thee.

39 But he answered and said unto them, An evil and [e]adulterous generation seeketh after a sign; and there shall no sign be given to it but the sign of the prophet Jonas;

40 For[f] as Jonas was three days and three nights in the whale's belly, so shall the Son of man be three days and three nights in the heart of the earth.

41 The men of Nineveh shall rise in judgment with this generation, and [g]shall condemn it: [h]because they repented at the preaching

d ch.16.1; 1 Co.1.22. e Is.57.3. f Jonah 1.17. g Ro.2.27. h Jonah 3.5.

they supposed would be decisive. Possibly they referred in this to Moses. *He* had been with God amid thunders and lightnings, and *he* had given them manna — *bread from heaven* — to eat. They wished Jesus to show some miracle equally undoubted.

39. *An evil and adulterous generation.* The relation of the Jews to God was often represented as a marriage contract—God as the husband, and the Jewish people as the wife. See Is. lvii. 3; Ho. iii. 1; Eze. xvi. 15. Hence their apostasy and idolatry are often represented as adultery. This is the meaning, probably, here. They were *evil*, and unfaithful to the covenant or to the commandments of God — an apostate and corrupt people. There is, however, evidence that they were literally an adulterous people. ¶ *There shall no sign be given to it*, &c. They sought some direct miracle *from heaven*. Jesus replied that no *such* miracle should be given. He did not mean to say that he would work no more miracles, or give no more evidence that he was the Christ, but he would give *no such miracle* as they required. *He would give one that ought to be as satisfactory evidence to them that he was from God, as the miraculous preservation of Jonah was to the Ninevites that he was divinely commissioned.* As Jonah was preserved three days by miracle and then restored *alive*, so he would be raised from the dead after three days. As on the ground of this preservation the Ninevites believed Jonah and repented, so, on the ground of his resurrection, the men of an adulterous and wicked generation ought to repent, and believe that he was from God. "The sign of the prophet Jonas" means the *sign or evidence* which was given to the people of Nineveh that he was from God—to wit, that he had been miraculously preserved, and was therefore divinely commissioned. The word *Jonas* is the Greek way of writing the Hebrew word *Jonah*, as *Elias* is for *Elijah*.

40. *For as Jonas was three days*, &c. See Jonah i. 17. This event took place in the Mediterranean Sea, somewhere between Joppa and Tarshish, when he was fleeing *from* Nineveh. It is said that the *whale* seldom passes into that sea, and that its throat is too small to admit a man. It is probable, therefore, that a fish of the *shark kind* is intended. Sharks have been known often to swallow a man entire. The fish in the book of Jonah is described merely as a *great fish*, without specifying the kind. It is well known that the Greek word translated *whale*, in the New Testament, does not of necessity mean a whale, but may denote a large fish or sea-monster of any kind.—Robinson, *Lex*.

40. *Three days and three nights.* It will be seen in the account of the resurrection of Christ that he was in the grave but two nights and a part of three days. See Mat. xviii. 6. This computation is, however, strictly in accordance with the Jewish mode of reckoning. If it had *not* been, the Jews would have understood it, and would have charged our Saviour as being a false prophet, for it was well known to them that he had spoken this prophecy, Mat. xxvii. 63. Such a charge, however, was never made; and it is plain, therefore, that what was *meant* by the prediction was accomplished. It was a maxim, also, among the Jews, in computing time, that a part of a day was to be received as the whole. Many instances of this kind occur in both sacred and profane history. See 2 Ch. x. 5, 12; Ge. xlii. 17, 18. Comp. Es. iv. 16 with v. 1. ¶ *In the heart of the earth.* The Jews used the word *heart* to denote the *interior* of a thing, or to speak of being *in* a thing. It means, here, to be in the grave or sepulchre.

of Jonas; and, behold, a greater than Jonas *is* here.

42 The [i]queen of the south shall rise up in the judgment with this generation, and shall condemn it: for [k]she came from the uttermost parts of the earth to hear the wisdom of Solomon; and, behold, a greater than Solomon *is* here.

43 When[l] the unclean spirit is

i Lu.11.31,&c. *k* 2 Ch.9.1. *l* Lu.11.24.

---

41. *The men of Nineveh.* Nineveh was the capital of the Assyrian empire. It was founded by Asshur, Ge. x. 11. It was situated on the banks of the river Tigris, to the north-east of Babylon. It was a city of vast extent, and of corresponding wickedness. It was 48 miles in circuit; its walls were 100 feet high and 10 thick, and were defended by fifteen hundred towers, each 200 feet in height. It contained in the time of Jonah, it is supposed, six hundred thousand inhabitants. The destruction of Nineveh, threatened by Jonah in forty days, was suspended, by their repentance, two hundred years. It was then overthrown by the Babylonians about six hundred years before Christ. During the siege a mighty inundation of the river Tigris took place, which threw down a part of the walls, through which the enemy entered, and sacked and destroyed the city. This destruction had been foretold one hundred and fifteen years before by Nahum (ch. i. 8): "But with an overwhelming flood he will make an utter end of the place thereof;" and ii. 6: "The gates of the river shall be opened, and the palace shall be dissolved." Its ruins have been lately discovered by Layard, and have contributed much to the establishment of the truth of Scripture history. Those remains are on the east side of the river Tigris, nearly opposite to the city of Mosul. ¶ *Shall condemn it.* That is, their conduct, in repenting under the preaching of Jonah, shall condemn this generation. They, ignorant and wicked heathen, repented when threatened with *temporal* judgment by a mere man—Jonah; you, Jews, professing to be enlightened, though threatened for your great wickedness with eternal punishment *by the Son of God*—a far greater being than Jonah—repent not, and must therefore meet with a far heavier condemnation.

42. *The queen of the south.* That is, the Queen of Sheba, 1 Ki. x. 1. Sheba was probably a city of Arabia, situated to the south of Judea. Comp. Notes on Is. lx. 6. ¶ *From the uttermost parts of the earth.* This means simply from the most distant parts of the habitable world *then known.* See a similar expression in De. xxviii. 49. As the knowledge of geography was limited, the place was, *in fact*, by no means in the extreme parts of the earth. It means that she came from a remote country; and she would condemn that generation, for she came *a great distance* to hear the wisdom of Solomon, but the Jews of that age would not listen to the wisdom of one *much greater* than Solomon, *though present with them.*

43–45. *When the unclean spirit,* &c. The *general sentiment* which our Saviour here teaches is much more easily understood than the illustration which he uses. The Jews had asked a sign *from heaven* that should decisively prove that he was the Messiah, and satisfy their unbelief. He replies that, though he should give them such a sign—a proof conclusive and satisfactory, and though for a time they should profess to believe and apparently reform, yet such was the obstinacy of their unbelief and wickedness, that they would soon return to their former course, and become worse and worse. Infidelity and wickedness, like an evil spirit in a possessed man, were appropriately *at home* in them. If driven out, they would find no other place so comfortable and undisturbed as their bosoms. Everywhere they would be, comparatively, like an evil spirit going through deserts and lonely places, and finding no place of rest. They would return, therefore, and dwell with them. ¶ *He walketh through dry places.* That is, through *deserts*—regions of country unwatered, sandy, barren, desolate. That our Saviour here speaks according to the ancient belief of the Jews that evil spirits had their abodes in those desolate, uninhabited regions, there can be no doubt; nor can there be any doubt that the Bible gives countenance to the opinion. Thus Re. xviii. 2: "Babylon—is become the habitation *of devils* and the hold of *every foul spirit;* that is, has become *desolate*

gone out of a man, [m]he walketh through dry places, seeking rest, and findeth none.

44 Then he saith, I will return into my house, from whence I came out; and when he is come, he findeth *it* empty, swept, and garnished.

45 Then goeth he and taketh with himself seven other spirits more wicked than himself, and they enter in and dwell there: and the last *state* of that man is [n]worse than the first. Even so shall it be also unto this wicked generation.

46 While he yet talked to the people, behold, [o]*his* mother and [p]his brethren stood without, desiring to speak with him.

47 Then one said unto him, Behold, thy mother and thy brethren stand without, desiring to speak with thee.

m Job 1.7; 1 Pe.5.8.
n He.6.4; 10.26; 2 Pe.2.20,22.
o Mar.3.31,&c.; Lu.8.19,&c. *p* ch.13.55.

—a place where evil spirits appropriately dwell. So Is. xiii. 21: "And *satyrs* shall dance there;" *i.e.* according to the ancient Greek translation, "*devils* or *demons* shall dance there." See also Je. l. 39. Comp. Notes on Is. xxxiv. 14. De. xxxii. 17. ¶ *Seeking rest, and findeth none.* These desolate and dry regions are represented as uncomfortable habitations; so much so, that the dissatisfied spirit, better pleased with a dwelling in the bosoms of men, as affording an opportunity of doing evil, seeks a return there.

44. *Then he saith, I will return into my house*, &c. The *man* is called his *house*, because the spirit had dwelt in him. ¶ *He findeth* it *empty*, &c. There is here a continuance of the reference to the dwelling of the spirit in men. The man was called his *house*. By the absence of the evil spirit the house is represented as unoccupied, or *empty, swept*, and *garnished;* that is, while the evil spirit was away, the man was restored to his right mind, or was freed from the influence of the evil spirit. ¶ *Garnished.* Adorned, put in order, furnished. Applied to the *man*, it means that his mind was sane and regular when the evil spirit was gone, or he had a *lucid interval.*

45. *Then goeth he*, &c. Seeing the state of the man; dissatisfied with a lonely dwelling in the desert where he could do no evil; envious of the happiness of the individual, and supremely bent on wickedness, he resolved to increase his power of malignant influences and to return. He is therefore represented as taking seven other spirits still worse than himself, and returning to his former habitation. Seven denotes a large but indefinite number. It was a favourite number with the Jews, and was used to denote *completeness* or *perfection*, or any *finished* or *complete* number. See 1 Sa. ii. 5. Comp. Rev. i. 4. Here it means a sufficient number completely to occupy and harass his soul. ¶ *Even so shall it be with this generation.* This shows the scope and design of this illustration. The state of that man was a representation of that generation of men. Much might be done to cure their unbelief, much to reform them externally; but such was the firm hold which the principles of infidelity and wickedness had taken of their minds *as their proper habitation*, that they would return, after all the means used to reform them, and they would be worse and worse. And this was literally accomplished. After all the instructions and miracles of the Saviour and his apostles; after all that had been done for them by holy men and prophets, and by the judgments and mercies of God; and after all their external temporary reformations—like the temporary departure of an evil spirit from a man possessed—yet such was their love of wickedness that the nation became worse and worse. They increased in crime, like the seven-fold misery and wretchedness of the man into whose bosom the seven additional evil spirits came. They rejected God's messengers, abused his mercies, crucified his Son, and God gave their temple, and capital, and nation into the hands of the Romans, and thousands of the people to destruction.

It is not *proved* by this passage that evil spirits actually *dwell* in deserts. It is proved only that such was the opinion of the Jews; that that opinion was drawn from some expressions in the Bible; and that *such expressions were sufficiently clear to justify the Saviour in*

48 But he answered and said unto him that told him, Who is my mother? and who are my brethren?

49 And he stretched forth his hand toward his disciples, and said, Behold my mother, and my brethren!

50 For[q] whosoever shall do the will of my father which is in heaven, the same is my brother, and sister, and mother.

q ch.7.20; Jn.15.14; Ga.5.6; He.2.11; 1 Jn.2.17.

drawing an argument from them to confound those who firmly believed that such was the case. Nor is there any absurdity in the opinion; for, 1st. There are evil spirits. See Notes on ch. viii. 33. 2d. They must exist in *some place.* 3d. There is as much propriety that they should be located about our earth as anywhere. 4th. The clear doctrine of the Bible is, that many of them have much to do with our world. 5th. It is as reasonable that they should dwell commonly in desolate and uninhabited regions as anywhere else.

46-50. See also Mar. iii. 31-35; Lu. viii. 19-21. ¶ *His brethren.* There has been some difference of opinion about the persons who are referred to here, some supposing that they were children of Mary his mother, others that they were the children of Mary, the wife of Cleophas or Alpheus, his *cousins*, and called *brethren* according to the customs of the Jews. The natural and obvious meaning is, however, that they were the children of Mary his mother. See also Mar. vi. 3. To this opinion, moreover, there can be no valid objection.

48. *Who is my mother?* &c. There was no want of affection or respect in Jesus toward his mother, as is proved by his whole life. See especially Lu. ii. 51, and Jn. xix. 25-27. This question was asked merely *to fix the attention* of the hearers and to prepare them for the answer—that is, to show them who sustained toward him the nearest and most tender relation. To do this he pointed to his disciples. Dear and tender as were the ties which bound him to his mother and brethren, yet those which bound him to his disciples were more tender and sacred. How great was his love for his disciples, when it was more than even that for his mother! And what a bright illustration of his own doctrine, that we ought to forsake father, and mother and friends, and houses, and lands, to be his followers!

REMARKS.

1st. Our Saviour has taught us the right use of the Sabbath, ver. 1-13. His conduct was an explanation of the meaning of the fourth commandment. By his example we may learn what may be done. He himself performed only those works on the Sabbath which were strictly necessary for life, and those which tended to benefit the poor, the afflicted, and needy. Whatever work is done on the Sabbath that is not for these ends must be wrong. All labour that can as well be done on another day—all which is not for the support of life, or to aid the ignorant, poor, and sick, must be wrong. This example justifies teaching the ignorant, supplying the wants of the poor, instructing children in the precepts of religion, teaching those to read in Sabbath-schools who have no other opportunity for learning, and visiting the sick, when we go not for formality, or *to save time on some other day*, but to do them good.

2d. The Sabbath is of vast service to mankind. It was made for man—not for man to violate or profane, or to be a day of mere idleness, but to improve to his spiritual and eternal good. Where men are employed through *six* days in worldly occupations, it is kind toward *them* to give them *one* day particularly to prepare for eternity. Where there is no Sabbath there is no religion. This truth, from the history of the world, will bear to be recorded in letters of gold—*that true religion will exist among men only when they strictly observe the Sabbath.* They, therefore, who do most to promote the observance of the Sabbath, are doing most for religion and the welfare of man. In this respect Sunday-school teachers may do more, perhaps, than all the world besides for the best interests of the world.

3d. In the conduct of Christ (ver. 14, 15) we have an illustration of the nature of Christian prudence. He did not throw himself needlessly into danger. He did not remain to provoke opposition. He felt that his time was not come, and that his life, by a prudent course, should be preserved. He therefore withdrew. Religion requires us to sacrifice our lives rather than deny the Saviour. To throw our lives away when, with good conscience, they might be preserved, is self-murder.

4th. The rejection of the gospel in one place is often the occasion of its being received elsewhere, ver. 15. Men may reject it to their own destruction; but somewhere it *will* be preached, and will be the power of God unto salvation. The wicked cannot drive it out of the world. They only secure their own ruin, and, against their will, benefit and save others. To reject it is like turning a beautiful and fertilizing stream from a man's own land. He does not, he cannot dry it up. *It will flow somewhere else.* He injures himself and perhaps benefits multitudes. Men never commit so great foolishness and wickedness, and so completely fail in what they aim at, as in rejecting the gospel. A man, hating the light of the sun, might get into a cave or dungeon, and be in total darkness; but the sun will continue to shine, and millions, in spite of him, will be benefited by it. So it is with the gospel.

5th. Christ was mild, quiet, retiring—not clamorous or noisy, ver. 19. So is all religion. There is no piety in noise; if there was, then thunder and artillery would be piety. Confusion and discord are not religion. Loud words and shouting are not religion. Religion is love, reverence, fear, holiness, a deep and awful regard for the presence of God, profound apprehensions of the solemnities of eternity, imitation of the Saviour. It is still. It is full of awe — an awe too great to strive, or cry, or lift up the voice in the streets. If men ever should be overawed and filled with emotions *repressing* noise and clamour, it should be when they approach *the great God.*

6th. The feeble may trust to Jesus, ver. 20. A child of any age, an ignorant person, the poorest man, may come, and he shall in nowise be cast out. It is a sense of our weakness that Jesus seeks. Where that is *he* will strengthen us, and we shall not fail.

7th. Grace will not be extinguished, ver. 20. Jesus, where he finds it in the feeblest degree, will not destroy it. He will cherish it. He will kindle it to a flame. It will burn brighter and brighter, till it "glows like that of the pure spirits above."

8th. Men are greatly prone to ascribe all religion to the devil, ver. 24. Anything that is unusual, anything that confounds them, anything that troubles their consciences, they ascribe to fanaticism, overheated zeal, and Satan. It has always been so. It is sometimes an easy way to stifle their own convictions, and to bring religion into contempt. *Somehow or other*, like the Pharisees, infidels must account for revivals of religion, for striking instances of conversion, and for the great and undeniable effects which the gospel produces. How easy to *say* that it is *delusion*, and that it is the work of the devil! How easy to show at once the terrible opposition of their own hearts to God, and to boast themselves in their own wisdom, in having found a *cause* so simple for all the effects which religion produces in the world! How much pains, also, men will take to secure their own perdition, rather than to admit it to be *possible* that Christianity is true!

9th. We see the danger of blasphemy—the danger of trifling with the influences of the Holy Spirit, ver. 31, 32. Even if we do not commit the unpardonable sin, yet we see that *all* trifling with the Holy Ghost is a sin very near to God, and attended with infinite danger. He that *laughs away* the thoughts of death and eternity; he that seeks the society of the gay and trifling, or of the sensual and profane, for the *express* purpose of driving away these thoughts; and he that struggles directly against his convictions, and is resolved that he *will not* submit to God, may be, for aught he knows, making his damnation sure. Why should God *ever* return when a man has *once* rejected the gospel? Who would be to blame if the sinner is then lost? Assuredly not God. None but himself. Children sometimes do this. Then is the time, the very time, when they should begin to love God and Jesus Christ. Then the Spirit also strives. Many *have then* given their hearts to him and become Christians. Many more *might* have done so, if they had not grieved away the Spirit of God.

10th. We see the danger of rejecting Christ, ver. 38–42. All past ages, all the wicked and the good, the foolish and the wise, will rise up in the day of judgment, and condemn us, if we do not believe the gospel. No people, heretofore, have seen so much light as we do in this age. And no people can be so awfully condemned as those who,

CHAPTER XIII.

THE same day went Jesus out of the house, and sat by the sea-side.

2 And great multitudes were gathered together unto him, so that [a]he went into a ship, and sat; and the whole multitude stood on the shore.

a Lu.5.3.

---

in a land of light, of Sabbaths and Sabbath-schools, reject Christ and go to hell. Among the hundred and twenty thousand children of Nineveh (Jonah iv. 11) there was not one single Sunday-school. There was no one to tell them of God and the Saviour. They have died and gone to judgment. Children now living will die also, and go to meet them in the day of judgment. How will they condemn the children of this age, if they do not love the Lord Jesus Christ!

11th. Sinners, when awakened, if they grieve away the Spirit of God, become worse than before, ver. 43-45. They are never as they were before. Their hearts are harder, their consciences are more seared, they have a more bitter hatred of religious men, and they plunge deeper and deeper into sin. Seven devils often dwell where one did, and God gives the man over to blindness of mind and hardness of heart. This shows, also, the great guilt and danger of grieving the Holy Ghost.

12th. We see the love of Christ for his followers, ver. 46-50. Much as he loved his mother, yet he loved his disciples more. He still loves them. He will always love them. His heart is full of affection for them. And though poor, and despised, and unknown to the rich and mighty, yet to Jesus they are dearer than mother, and sisters, and brothers.

CHAPTER XIII.

1, 2. *The sea-side.* This was the Sea of Tiberias. The multitude stood on the shore near to him, so that he could be easily heard. He went into a ship—that is, a boat, and sat down to address them. Few spectacles could be more interesting than a vast crowd on the banks of a smooth and tranquil sea—an emblem of his instructions—and the Son of God addressing them on the great interests of eternity.

3-9. *In parables.* The word *parable* is derived from a Greek word signifying *to compare together*, and denotes a similitude taken from a natural object to illustrate a spiritual or moral subject. It is a narrative of some fictitious or real event, in order to illustrate more clearly some truth that the speaker wished to communicate. In early ages it was much used. Heathen writers, as Æsop, often employed it. In the time of Christ it was in common use. The prophets had used it, and Christ employed it often in teaching his disciples. It is not necessary to suppose that the narratives were strictly true. The main thing—*the inculcation of spiritual truth*—was gained equally, whether it was true or was only a supposed case. Nor was there any dishonesty in this. It was well understood—no person was deceived. The speaker was not *understood* to affirm the thing *literally narrated*, but only to fix the attention more firmly on the moral truth that he presented. The *design* of speaking in parables was the following: 1st. To convey truth in a more interesting manner to the mind, adding to the truth conveyed the beauty of a lovely image or narrative. 2d. To teach spiritual truth so as to arrest the attention of ignorant people, making an appeal to them through the *senses.* 3d. To convey some offensive truth, some pointed personal rebuke, in such a way as to bring it *home* to the conscience. Of this kind was the parable which Nathan delivered to David (2 Sa. xii. 1-7), and many of our Saviour's parables addressed to the Jews. 4th. To *conceal* from one part of his audience truths which he intended others should understand. Thus Christ often, by this means, delivered truths to his disciples in the presence of the Jews, which he well knew the Jews would not understand; truths pertaining to them particularly, and which he was under no obligations to explain to the Jews. See Mar. iv. 33; Mat. xiii. 13-16.

Our Saviour's parables are distinguished above all others for clearness, purity, chasteness, importance of instruction, and simplicity. They are taken mostly from the affairs of common life, and intelligible, therefore, to all men. They contain much of *himself*—his doctrine, life, design in coming, and claims, and are therefore of import-

3 And he spake many things unto them in parables, saying, Behold,[b] a sower went forth to sow:

4 And when he sowed, some *seeds* fell by the way-side, and the fowls came and devoured them up.

5 Some fell upon stony places, where they had not much earth; and forthwith they sprung up, because they had no deepness of earth:

6 And when the sun was up, they were scorched: and because they had no root, they withered away.

7 And some fell among thorns, and the thorns sprung up, and choked them.

8 But other fell into good ground, and brought forth fruit, some an hundred-fold, some sixty-fold, some thirty-fold.

9 Who[c] hath ears to hear, let him hear.

10 And the disciples came, and said unto him, Why speakest thou unto them in parables?

11 He answered and said unto

b Mar.4.2; Lu.8.5,&c.

c ch.11.15.

---

ance to all men; and they are told in a style of simplicity intelligible to the child, yet instructive to men of every rank and age. In his parables, as in all his instructions, he excelled all men in the purity, importance, and sublimity of his doctrine.

3. *A sower went forth to sow.* The image here is taken from an employment known to all men, and therefore intelligible to all. Nor can there be a more striking illustration of preaching the gospel than placing the seed in the ground, to spring up hereafter and bear fruit. ¶ *Sower.* One who sows or scatters seed—a farmer. It is not improbable that one was near the Saviour when he spoke this parable.

4. *Some* seeds *fell by the way-side.* That is, the hard *path* or headland, which the plough had not touched, and where there was no opportunity for it to sink into the earth.

5. *Stony places.* Where there was little earth, but where it was hard and rocky, so that the roots could not strike down into the earth for sufficient moisture to support the plant. When the sun became hot they of course withered away. They sprang up the sooner because there was little earth to cover them. ¶ *Forthwith.* Immediately. Not that they sprouted and grew any quicker or faster than the others, but they were not so long in reaching the surface. Having little root, they soon withered away.

7. *Among thorns.* That is, in a part of the field where the thorns and shrubs had been imperfectly cleared away and not destroyed. They grew with the grain, crowded it, shaded it, exhausted the earth, and thus choked it.

8. *Into good ground.* The fertile and rich soil. In sowing, by far the largest proportion of seed will fall into the good soil; but Christ did not intend to teach that these proportions would be exactly the same among those who heard the gospel. Parables are designed to teach some *general* truth, and the *circumstances* should not be pressed too much in explaining them. ¶ *An hundred-fold,* &c. That is, a hundred, sixty, or thirty *grains* for each one that was sowed—an increase by no means uncommon. Some grains of wheat will produce twelve or fifteen hundred grains. The usual proportion on a field sown, however, is not more than twenty, fifty, or sixty bushels for one.

9. *Who hath ears,* &c. This is a proverbial expression, implying that it was every man's duty to pay attention to what was spoken, Mat. xi. 15.

10–17. Christ, in these verses, gives a *reason* why he used this manner of instruction. See also Mar. iv. 10–12; Lu. viii. 9, 10.

11. *The mysteries of the kingdom.* The word *mystery,* in the Bible, properly means a thing that is *concealed,* or that *has been concealed.* It does not mean that the thing was *incomprehensible,* or even difficult to be understood. The thing might be *plain* enough if revealed, but it means simply that it *had* not been before made known. Thus the *mysteries of the kingdom* do not mean any doctrines incomprehensible in themselves considered, but simply doctrines about the preaching of the gospel and

them, Because it is given unto you [d]to know the mysteries of the kingdom of heaven, but to them it is not given.

12 For[e] whosoever hath, to him shall be given, and he shall have more abundance: but whosoever hath not, from him shall be taken away even that he hath.

13 Therefore speak I to them in parables: because they seeing, see not; and hearing, they hear not, neither do they understand.

14 And in them is fulfilled the prophecy of [f]Esaias, which saith, [g]By hearing ye shall hear, and shall not understand; and seeing ye shall see, and shall not perceive:

15 For this people's heart is waxed gross, and *their* ears are [h]dull of hearing, and their eyes they have closed; lest at any time

d ch.11.25; Mar.4.11; 1 Co.2.10,14; Ep.1.9,18; 3.9; Col.1.26,27; 1 Jn.2.27. e ch.25,29; Lu.19.26. f Is.6.9. g Eze.12.2; Jn.12.40; Ac.28.26,27; Ro.11.8; 2 Co.3.14,15. h He.5.11.

the establishment of the new kingdom of the Messiah, which *had not* been understood, and which were *as yet* concealed from the great body of the Jews. See Ro. xvi. 25; xi. 25; Ep. iii. 3, 4, 9. Of this nature was the truth that the gospel was to be preached to the Gentiles; that the Jewish polity was to cease; that the Messiah was to die, &c. To the disciples it was given to know these truths. This was important for them, as they were to carry the gospel around the globe. To the others it was not *then* given. They were too gross, too earthly; they had too grovelling conceptions of the Messiah's kingdom to understand these truths, even if communicated to them. They were not to preach the gospel, and hence our Saviour was at particular pains to instruct his apostles in the system which they were to preach. The Pharisees, and Jews generally, were not prepared to receive the system, and would not have believed it, and therefore he purposely employed a kind of teaching which was intended for his apostles only.

12. *Whosoever hath*, &c. This is a proverbial method of speaking. It means that a man who improves what light, grace, and opportunities he has, shall have them increased. From him that improves them not, it is proper that they should be taken away. The Jews had many opportunities of learning the truth, and some light still lingered among them; but they were gross and sensual, and misimproved them, and it was a just judgment that they should be deprived of them. Superior knowledge was given to the disciples of Christ: they improved it, however slowly, and the promise was that it should be greatly increased.

13. *Because they seeing, see not.* Mark (iv. 12) and Luke (viii. 10) say, "That seeing, they may not see," &c.; but there is no difference. Matthew simply states the *fact*, that though they saw the *natural* meaning of the story—though they literally understood the parable—yet they did not understand its *spiritual* signification. Mark and Luke do not state the *fact*, but affirm that he spoke with this *intention*—implying that such *was* the result. Nor was there any dishonesty in this, or any unfair disguise. He had truths to state which he wished his *disciples particularly* to understand. They were of great importance to their ministry. Had he clearly and fully stated them to the Jews, they would have taken his life long before they did. He therefore chose to state the doctrines so that if their *hearts* had been right, and if they had not been malignant and blind, *they might have understood them.* His doctrines he stated in the best possible way, and it was not *his* fault if they did not understand him. By little and little, in this way, he prepared many even of the Jews to receive the truth, by the only possible way of ever gaining access to their minds. It was, moreover, entirely proper and right to impart instruction to his disciples which he did not *intend* for others.

14. *And in them is fulfilled*, &c. This place is quoted substantially from Is. vi. 9, 10. It was literally fulfilled in the time of Isaiah. In the time of Christ the people had the same character. Like them, they closed their eyes upon the truth, and rejected the divine teaching. The words of Isaiah were therefore *as well fitted* to express the character of the people in the time of Christ as in that of the prophet. In this sense they were *fulfilled*, or *filled up;* that is, *a case occurred that corresponded to their*

they should see with *their* eyes, and hear with *their* ears, and should understand with *their* heart, and should be converted, and I should heal them.

16 But[i] blessed *are* your eyes, for they see; and your ears, for they hear.

17 For verily I say unto you, That[k] many prophets and righteous *men* have desired to see *those things* which ye see, and have not seen *them;* and to hear *those things* which ye hear, and have not heard *them.*

18 Hear[l] ye therefore the parable of the sower.

19 When any one heareth [m]the word of the kingdom, and understandeth *it* not, then cometh [n]the wicked *one,* and catcheth away that which was sown in his heart. This is he which received seed by the way-side.

20 But he that received the seed into stony places, the same

i ch.16 17; Lu.10.23,24; Jn.20.29; 2 Co.4.6. *k* Ep.3.5,6; He.11.13; 1 Pe.1.10,11.
l Mar.4.14,&c.; Lu.8.11,&c. *m* ch.4.23. *n* 1 Jn.2.13,14; 3.12.

meaning. See Notes on Mat. i. 22. It is not by any means intended that Isaiah, when he spoke these words, had any reference to the time of Christ. The meaning in both places is, that the people were so gross, sensual, and prejudiced, that they *would* not see the truth, or understand anything that was contrary to their grovelling opinions and sensual desires; a case by no means uncommon in the world. See the passage more fully explained in my Notes on Is. vi. ¶ *Waxed gross.* Literally, *has become fat.* This language is commonly applied to *the body*, but is also used to denote one who is stupid and foolish in mind. Here it means that the people were so sensual and corrupt that they did not see or understand the pure spiritual principles of the gospel. ¶ *Lest they should see,* &c. Lest they should see their lost condition as sinners, and turn and live. The reason given here why they did not hear and understand the gospel is, that their *heart* was *wrong.* They *would* not attend to the things that belonged to their peace. ¶ *I should heal them.* Should pardon, sanctify, and save them. Sin is often represented as a disease, and the pardon and recovery of the soul from sin as *healing.*

16. *Blessed* are *your eyes,* &c. That is, you are happy that you are permitted to see *truth* which they *will* not see. You are permitted to understand the spiritual meaning of the parables, and in some degree the plan of salvation.

17. *Many prophets and righteous* men, &c. They wished to see the times of the Messiah. They looked to it as a time when the hopes of the world would be fulfilled, and when the righteous would be happy, Jn. viii. 56. "Abraham rejoiced to see my day, and he saw it and was glad." Comp. also 1 Pe. i. 10–12; He. xi. 13. So Isaiah and the prophets looked forward to the coming of the Messiah as the consummation of their wishes and the end of the prophecies, Re. xix. 10. The object always dearest to the hearts of all righteous men is to witness the coming and advancement of the kingdom of Christ. Comp. Re. xxii. 20.

18–23. See also Mar. iv. 13–20; Lu. viii. 11–15. *Hear ye, therefore, the parable of the sower.* That is, hear the *explanation* or the *spiritual meaning* of the narrative given before. Mark adds (iv. 13), "Know ye not this parable? And how, then, shall ye know all parables?" By which it seems that the Saviour regarded this as one of the simplest and plainest of the parables, and gave an explanation of it that they might understand the general principles of interpreting others.

19. *When any one heareth,* &c. The seed represents the word of God communicated in any manner to the minds of men—by the Scriptures, by preaching, by acts of Providence, or by the direct influences of the Holy Spirit. ¶ *Then cometh the wicked* one. That is, Satan (Mar. iv. 15), or the devil (Lu. viii. 12)—the one eminently *wicked*, the accuser, the tempter. He is represented by the fowls that came and picked up the seed by the way-side. The gospel is preached to men hardened in sin. It makes no impression. It lies like seed on the *hard path;* it is easily taken away, and never suffered to take root.

20, 21. *But he that received the seed into stony places.* Jesus explains this as de-

is he that heareth the word, and anon [o]with joy receiveth it:

21 Yet hath he not root in himself, but dureth for a while; for when tribulation or persecution ariseth because of the word, by and by [p]he is offended.

22 He also that received seed among the thorns is he that heareth the word; and the [q]care of this world and the [r]deceitfulness of riches choke the word, and he becometh unfruitful.

23 But he that received seed into the good ground is he that heareth the word, and understandeth

o Is.58.2; Eze.33.31,32; Jn.5.35; Ga.4.15. p ch.24.10; 26.31; 2 Ti.4.16.

q Lu.14.16-24. r Mar.10.23; 1 Ti.6.9; 2 Ti.4.10.

---

noting those who hear the gospel; who are caught with it as something new or pleasing; who profess to be greatly delighted with it, and who are full of zeal for it. Yet they have no root in themselves. They are not true Christians. Their hearts are not changed. They have not seen their guilt and danger, and the true excellency of Christ. They are not *really* attached to the gospel; and when they are tried and persecution comes, they *fall*—as the rootless grain withers before the scorching rays of the noonday sun. ¶ *Anon.* *Quickly*, or *readily*. ¶ *With joy receiveth it.* They are under deep distress for sin; they are apprehensive of danger; they hear the offer of mercy, and they *seem* to themselves to embrace the gospel. It offers them peace, pardon, salvation, and religion assumes for a time a lovely aspect. They *imagine* that they are pardoned, and they have a temporary peace and joy. Their anxieties subside. Their fears are gone. They are for a time happy. *The mere subsiding of anxious feeling from any cause will make the mind for a time happy.* They have only to imagine, therefore, that their sins are forgiven, to produce a certain kind of peace and joy. But there is no ground of permanent joy, as there is in true pardon, and soon their joy subsides, and all evidence of piety disappears. There is no strength of *principle* to resist temptation; there is no real love of the Saviour; and in times of trial and persecution they show that they have no true religion, and fall away. ¶ *By and by.* Mark, *Immediately*. That is, it soon occurs, or this is an effect which may be expected *soon* to follow. ¶ *Is offended.* Stumbles or falls, for this is the meaning of the word *offend* in the New Testament. See Notes on ch. v. 29. Persecution and trial are placed in his path, and he falls as he would over a *stumbling-block*. He has no strength of principle--no real confidence in God—no true religion. Mere excited animal feeling is all that he ever had, and that is not sufficient to sustain him when the trial comes.

22. *He also that received seed among the thorns.* These represent the cares, the anxieties, and the deceitful lure of riches, or the way in which a *desire* to be rich deceives men. They take the time and attention. They do not leave opportunity to examine the state of the soul. Besides, riches allure, and promise what they do not yield. They promise to make us happy; but, when gained, they do not do it. The soul is not satisfied. There is the same desire to possess more wealth. And to this there is no end *but death*. In doing it there is every temptation to be dishonest, to cheat, to take advantage of others, to oppress others, and to wring their hard earnings from the poor. Every evil passion is therefore cherished by the love of gain; and it is no wonder that the word is choked, and every good feeling destroyed, by this "execrable love of gold." See Notes on 1 Ti. vi. 7-11. How many, O how many, thus foolishly drown themselves in destruction and perdition! How many more *might* reach heaven, if it were not for this deep-seated love of that which fills the mind with care, deceives the soul, and finally leaves it naked, and guilty, and lost!

23. *Into good ground.* Those whose hearts are prepared by grace to receive it honestly, and to give it full opportunity to grow. In a rich and mellow soil—in a heart that submits itself to the full influence of truth, unchecked by cares and anxieties; under the showers and summer suns of divine grace; with the heart spread open, like a broad, luxuriant field, to the rays of the morning and to evening dews, the gospel takes deep root and grows; it has full room, and then and there only shows *what it is*.

24-30. *The kingdom of heaven is*

it; which also [s]beareth fruit, and bringeth forth, some an hundred-fold, some sixty, some thirty.

24 Another[t] parable put he forth unto them, saying, The kingdom of heaven is likened unto a man which sowed [u]good seed in his field:

25 But while men slept, his enemy came and sowed tares among the wheat, and went his way.

s Jn.15.5. t Is.28.10,13. u 1 Pe.1.23.

---

likened, &c. That is, the *gospel resembles.* The kingdom of heaven (see Notes on Mat. iii. 2) means here the effect of the gospel by its being preached. The meaning of this parable is plain. The field represents the *world,* in which the gospel is preached. The *good seed,* the truths preached by Christ and his apostles.

25. *While men slept, his enemy came,* &c. That is, *in the night,* when it could be done without being seen, an enemy came and scattered bad seed on the new-ploughed field, perhaps before the good seed had been harrowed in. Satan thus sows false doctrine in darkness. In the very place where the truth is preached, and while the hearts of people are open to receive it, by false but plausible teachers he takes care to inculcate false sentiments. Often it is one of his arts, in a revival of religion, to spread secretly dangerous notions of piety. Multitudes are persuaded that they are Christians who are deceived. They are awakened, convicted, and alarmed. They take this for conversion. Or they find their burden gone; they fancy that they hear a voice; or a text of Scripture is *brought* to them, saying that their sins are forgiven; or they *see* Christ hanging on the cross in a vision; or they dream that their sins are pardoned, and they suppose they are Christians. But they are deceived. None of these things are any conclusive evidence of piety. All these *may* exist, and still there be no true love to God or Christ, and no real hatred of sin and change of heart. An enemy may do it to deceive them, and to bring dishonour on religion. ¶ *Sowed tares.* By *tares* is probably meant a degenerate kind of wheat, or the darnel-grass growing in Palestine. In its growth and form it has a strong resemblance to genuine wheat; but it either produces no grain, or that of a very inferior and hurtful kind. Probably it comes near to what we mean by *chess.* It was extremely difficult to separate it from the genuine wheat, on account of its similarity while growing. "The tare abounds all over the East, and is a great nuisance to the farmer. It resembles the American *cheat* [*chess*], but the *head* does not droop like cheat, nor does it branch out like oats. The grain, also, is smaller, and is arranged along the upper part of the stalk, which stands perfectly erect. The *taste* is bitter, and when eaten separately, or even when diffused in ordinary bread, it causes dizziness, and often acts as a violent emetic. Barn-door fowls also become dizzy from eating it. In short, it is a strong soporific poison, and must be carefully winnowed, and picked out of the wheat grain by grain, before grinding, or the flour is not healthy. Even the farmers, who in this country generally *weed* their fields, do not attempt to separate the one from the other. They would not only mistake good grain for them, but very commonly the roots of the two are so intertwined that it is impossible to separate them without plucking up both. Both, therefore, must be left to *grow together* until the time of harvest."—(Thomson) *The Land and the Book,* vol. ii. p. 111, 112. Thus *tares* aptly represented hypocrites in the church. Strongly resembling Christians in their experience, and, in some respects, their lives, it is impossible to distinguish them from genuine Christians, nor can they be separated until it is done by the Great Searcher of hearts at the day of judgment. An enemy—the devil—hath done it. And nowhere has he shown profounder cunning, or done more to adulterate the purity of the gospel. ¶ *And went his way.* There is something very expressive in this. He knew the soil; he knew how the seed would take root and grow. He had only to sow the seed and let it alone. So Satan knows the soil in which he sows his doctrine. He knows that in the human heart it will take deep and rapid root. It needs but little culture. Grace needs constant attendance and care. Error, and sin, and hypocrisy are the native products of the human heart, and, when left alone, start up with deadly luxuriancy.

26 But when the blade was sprung up, and brought forth fruit, then appeared the tares also.

27 So the servants of the householder came and said unto him, Sir, didst not thou sow good seed in thy field? from whence, then, hath it tares?

28 He said unto them, An enemy hath done this. The servants said unto him, Wilt thou, then, that we go and gather them up?

29 But he said, Nay; lest while ye gather up the tares, ye root up also the wheat with them.

30 Let both grow together until the harvest: and in [v]the time of harvest I will say to the reapers, Gather ye together first the tares, and bind them in bundles [w]to burn them; but [x]gather the wheat into my barn.

31 Another parable put he forth unto them, saying, The kingdom of heaven is like to [y]a grain of mustard-seed, which a man took and sowed in his field:

32 Which indeed is the least of all seeds; but when it is grown, it is the greatest among herbs,

v 1 Ti.5.24. w Mal.4.1. x Lu.3.17. y Mar.4.30.

26. *Then appeared the tares also.* That is, then the tares were *first discovered.* They had grown with the wheat, but were so much like it as not to be noticed till the wheat began to ripen. So true piety and false hopes are not known by professions, by "blades," and leaves, and flowers, but *by the fruit.*

29. *Ye root up also the wheat.* They so much resembled the true wheat that even then it would be difficult to separate them. By gathering them, they would tread down the wheat, loosen and disturb the earth, and greatly injure the crop. In the harvest it could be done without injury.

30. *Let both grow together.* They would not spoil the true wheat, and in time of harvest it would be easy to separate them. Our Saviour teaches us here—1st. That hypocrites and deceived persons must be expected in the church. 2d. That this is the work of the enemy of man. They are not the work of Christianity any more than traitors are of patriotism, or counterfeiters are of the proper effect of legislating about money. They belong to the world, and hypocrisy is only one form of sin. The Christian religion never *made* a hypocrite, nor is there a hypocrite on the earth whose principles and practice it does not condemn. 3d. That all hope of removing them entirely would be vain. 4th. That an *attempt* to remove them altogether would injure real Christianity, by causing excitements, discord, and hard feelings even among Christians. 5th. That Christ will himself separate them at the proper time. There is no doubt that it is the duty of the church to keep itself pure, and to cut off gross and manifest offenders, 1 Co. v. 4, 5; but the Saviour refers here to those who may be *suspected* of hypocrisy, but against whom it cannot be proved; to those who so successfully imitate Christians as to make it difficult or impossible for man to distinguish them.

31, 32. See also Mar. iv. 30–32. *The kingdom of heaven.* See Notes on Mat. iii. 2. It means here either piety in a renewed heart or the church. In either case the commencement is small. In the heart it is at first feeble, easily injured, and much exposed. In the church there were few at first, ignorant, unknown, and unhonoured; yet soon it was to spread through the world. ¶ *Grain of mustard-seed.* The plant here described was very different from that which is known among us. It was several years before it bore fruit and became properly a tree. Mustard, with us, is an annual plant: it is always small, and is properly an herb. The Hebrew writers speak of the mustard-tree as one on which they could *climb*, as on a fig-tree. Its size was much owing to the climate. All plants of that nature grow much larger in a warm climate, like that of Palestine, than in colder regions. The seeds of this tree were remarkably small, so that they, with the great size of the plant, were an apt illustration of the progress of the church and of the nature of faith, Mat. xvii. 20. "I have seen," says Dr. Thomson, "this plant on the rich plain of Akkar as tall as the horse and his rider. It has occurred to me on former visits that

and [z]becometh a tree, so that the birds of the air come and lodge in the branches thereof.

33 Another parable spake he unto them: The kingdom of heaven is like unto leaven, which a woman took, and hid in three measures[1] of meal, till the whole was leavened.

34 All these things spake Jesus unto the multitude [a]in parables; and without a parable spake he not unto them;

35 That it might be fulfilled which was spoken by the prophet, saying, [b]I will open my mouth in parables; I will utter things which have been [c]kept secret from the foundation of the world.

36 Then Jesus sent the multitude away, and went into the house; and his disciples came unto him, saying, Declare unto us the parable of the tares of the field.

37 He answered and said unto

z Eze.17.23.
1 The Greek word signifies *a measure about a peck and a half, wanting a little more than a pint.*
a Mar.4.33.

b Ps.78.2. c Lu.10.14; Ro.16.25,26; Col.1.26.

the mustard-tree of the parable probably grew at this spot, or possibly at Tabiga, near Capernaum, for the water in both is somewhat similar, and so are the vegetable productions. To furnish an adequate basis for the proverb, it is necessary to suppose that a variety of it was cultivated in the time of our Saviour, which grew to an enormous size, and shot forth large branches, so that the fowls of the air could lodge in the branches of it. It may have been perennial, and have grown to a considerable tree; and there are traditions in the country of such so large that a man could climb into them; and after having seen *red pepper* bushes grow on year after year, into tall shrubs, and the *castor-bean* line the brooks about Damascus like the willows and the poplars, I can readily credit the existence of mustard-trees large enough to meet all the demands of our Lord's parable." — *The Land and the Book*, vol. ii. p. 101.

Young converts often suppose they have much religion. It is not so. They are, indeed, in a new world. Their hearts glow with new affections. They have an elevation, an ecstasy of emotion, which they may not have afterward—like a blind man suddenly restored to sight. The sensation is new and peculiarly vivid, yet little is seen distinctly. His impressions are indeed more vivid and cheering than those of him who has long seen and to whom objects are familiar. In a little time, too, the young convert will see more distinctly, will judge more intelligently, will love more strongly, though not with so much *new emotion*, and will be prepared to make more sacrifices for the cause of Christ.

33. *The kingdom of heaven.* The meaning here is the same as in the last parable; perhaps, however, intending to denote more properly the secret and hidden nature of piety in the soul. The other parable declared the *fact* that the gospel would greatly spread, and that piety in the heart would greatly increase. This states the *way* or *mode* in which it would be done. It is secret, silent, steady; pervading all the faculties of the soul and all the kingdoms of the world, as leaven, or yeast, though hidden in the flour, and though deposited only in one place, works silently till *all* the mass is brought under its influence. ¶ *Three measures.* These were small measures (see the margin); but the particular amount is of no consequence to the story; nor is anything to be inferred from the fact that *three* are mentioned. That number is mentioned as a circumstance giving interest to the parable, but designed to convey no spiritual instruction. The *measure* mentioned here probably contained about a peck and a half.

34, 35. *That it might be fulfilled.* This is taken from Ps. lxxviii. 2, 3. The *sense*, and not the very words of the Psalm, are given. Christ taught, as did that prophet—Asaph—in parables. The words of Asaph described the manner in which Christ taught, and in this sense it could be said that they were fulfilled. See Notes on Mat. i. 22, 23.

36–43. *Declare unto us.* That is, explain the meaning of the parable. This was done in so plain a manner as to render comment unnecessary. The Son of man, the Lord Jesus, sows the good seed — that is, preaches the gospel.

them, He that soweth the good seed is the Son of man:

38 The field is [d]the world: the good seed are [e]the children of the kingdom; but the tares are [f]the children of the wicked *one*.

39 The enemy that sowed them is the devil: [g]the harvest is the end of the world; and [h]the reapers are the angels.

40 As, therefore, [i]the tares are gathered and burned in the fire, so shall it be in the end of this world.

41 The Son of man shall send forth his angels, and they shall gather out of his kingdom all [2]things that offend, [k]and them which do iniquity;

42 And[l] shall cast them into a furnace of fire: [m]there shall be wailing and gnashing of teeth.

43 Then shall the righteous [n]shine forth as the sun, in the kingdom of their Father. Who hath ears to hear, let him hear.

44 Again, the kingdom of heaven is like unto [o]treasure hid in a field; the which when a man hath found, he hideth,

d Ro.10.18; Col.1.6. *e* 1 Pe.1.23.
f Jn.8.44; Ac.13.10; 1 Jn.3.8.
g Joel 3.13; Re.14.15. *h* Re.14.15-19. *i* ver.30.

2 or, *scandals*. *k* Lu.13.27.
l ch.3.12; Re.19.20; 20.10. *m* ver.50; ch.8.12.
n Da.12.3; 1 Co.15.49. *o* Pr.2.4,5.

This he did personally, and does now by his ministers, his providence, and his Spirit, by all the means of conveying *truth* to the mind. This seed was, by various means, to be carried over all the world. It was to be confined to no particular nation or people. The good seed was the children of the kingdom; that is, of the kingdom of God, or Christians. For these the Saviour toiled and died. They are the fruit of his labours. Yet amid them were wicked men; and all hypocrites and unbelievers in the church are the work of Satan. Yet they must remain together till the end, when they shall be separated, and the righteous saved and the wicked lost. The one shall shine clear as the sun, the other be cast into a furnace of fire—a most expressive image of suffering. We have no idea of more acute suffering than to be thrown into the fire, and to have our bodies made capable of bearing the burning heat, and living on in this burning heat for ever and for ever. It is not certain that our Saviour meant to teach here that hell is made up of *material* fire; but it *is* certain that he meant to teach that this would be a proper *representation* of the sufferings of the lost. We may be farther assured that the Redeemer would not deceive us, or use words to torment and tantalize us. He would not talk of hell-fire which had no existence, nor would the Saviour of men hold out frightful images merely to terrify mankind. If *he* has spoken of hell, then there *is* a hell. If *he* meant to say that the wicked shall suffer, then they *will* suffer. If he did not mean to deceive mankind, then there *is* a hell, and then the wicked *will* be punished. The impenitent, therefore, should be alarmed. And the righteous, however much wickedness they may see, and however many hypocrites there may be in the church, should be cheered with the prospect that soon the just will be separated from the unjust, and that *they* shall shine as the sun in the kingdom of their Father.

44. *The kingdom of heaven.* The gospel. The new dispensation. The offer of eternal life. See Notes on Mat. iii. 2. The Saviour in this parable compares that kingdom to treasure hid in a field; that is, to money concealed; or more likely to a mine of silver or gold that was unknown to the owner of the field. ¶ *He hideth.* That is, he conceals the fact that he has found it; he does not tell of it. With a view of obtaining this, Jesus says that a man would go and sell his property and buy the field. The conduct of the man would be *dishonest*. It would be his duty to inform the owner of the field of the discovery. He would be really endeavouring to gain property belonging to another at far less than its real value, and the principle of real integrity would require him to inform the owner of the discovery. But Christ does not intend to vindicate his conduct. He merely states the way in which men do *actually* manage to obtain wealth. He states a case where a man *would* actually *sacrifice his property*, and practise diligence and watchfulness to obtain the wealth which

and for joy thereof goeth and selleth[p] all that he hath, and buyeth[q] that field.

45 Again, the kingdom of heaven is like unto a merchant-man seeking goodly pearls;

46 Who, when he had found one [r] pearl of great price, went and sold all that he had, and bought it.

47 Again, the kingdom of heaven is like unto a net, that was cast into the sea, and [s]gathered of every kind:

48 Which, when it was full, they drew to shore, and sat down, and gathered the good into vessels, but cast the bad away.

49 So shall it be at the end of the world: the angels shall come forth, and [t]sever the wicked from among the just;

50 And[u] shall cast them into the furnace of fire: there shall be wailing and gnashing of teeth.

51 Jesus saith unto them, Have ye understood all these things? They say unto him, Yea, Lord.

52 Then said he unto them, Therefore every scribe *which is*

p Phi.3.7,8. q Is.55.1; Re.3.18. r Pr.3.14,15; 8.11. s ch.22.10. t ch.25.32. u ver.42.

he had discovered. The *point* of the parable lies in his *earnestness*, his anxiety, his care, and his actually obtaining it. The gospel is more valuable than such a treasure, Ps. xix. 10; Pr. iii. 13–15. From most men it is hid. When a man sees it and hears it, it is his duty to sacrifice all that hinders his obtaining it, and to seek it with the earnestness with which other men seek for gold. The truth often lies buried; it is like rich veins of ore in the sacred Scriptures; it must be searched out with diligence, and its discovery will repay a man for all his sacrifices, Lu. xiv. 33; Phi. iii. 8.

45, 46. *The kingdom of heaven is like unto a merchantman.* The meaning is, that the proper seeking for salvation, or the proper conduct in reference to religion, is like the conduct of a *merchantman.* In his searches he found *one* pearl of great value, and sold all his possessions to obtain it. So, says the Saviour, men seeking for happiness and finding the gospel—the pearl of great price—should be willing to sacrifice all other things for this. Pearls are precious stones found in the shells of oysters, chiefly in the East Indies. See Notes on Mat. vii. 6. They are valuable on account of their beauty and because they are rare. The value of them is greatly increased by their size. The meaning of this parable is nearly the same as the other. It is designed to represent the gospel as of more value than all other things, and to impress on us the duty of sacrificing *all* that we possess in order to obtain it.

47–50. *The kingdom of heaven is like unto a net*, &c. This parable does not differ in meaning from that of the tares. The gospel is compared to a net dragging along on the bottom of a lake, and collecting all—good and bad. The gospel may be expected to do the same; but in the end of the world, when the net *is drawn in*, the bad will be separated from the good; the one will be cast away, and the other saved. Our Saviour never fails to keep before our minds the great truth that there is to be a day of judgment, and that there will be a separation of the good and the evil. He came to preach salvation; and it is a remarkable fact, also, that the most fearful accounts of hell and of the sufferings of the damned, in the Scriptures, are from his lips. How does this agree with the representations of those who say that all will be saved?

51–53. Jesus kindly asked them whether they had understood these things. If not, he was still willing to teach them. He enjoined on them their duty to make a proper use of this knowledge by speaking another parable. ¶ *Every scribe* which is *instructed unto the kingdom of heaven.* That is, every man that is acquainted with the gospel or with the truth. As the disciples had said that *they* had understood the truth, he says that it should not be unemployed. They should bring it forth in due time, like a householder bringing out of his treasury, or place of deposit, what had been laid up there at any time, as it was needed. ¶ *Bringeth forth.* As occasion demands; as sickness, or calamity, or the wants of his family, or the poor require. ¶ *Treasure.* The word *treasure* here means a place of

instructed unto the kingdom of heaven is like unto a man that *is* an householder, which [v]bringeth forth out of his treasure [w]*things* new and old.

53 And it came to pass, *that* when Jesus had finished these parables, he departed thence.

54 And[x] when he was come into his own country, he taught them in their synagogue, insomuch that they were astonished, and said, Whence hath this *man* this wisdom, and these mighty works?

55 Is not this the carpenter's son? is not his mother called Mary? and his brethren, James, and Joses, and Simon, and Judas?

56 And his sisters, are they not all with us? Whence, then, hath this *man* all these things?

v Pr.10.21; 15.7; 18.4. w Ca.7.13. x Mar.6.1,&c.; Lu.4.16,&c.

deposit, not for money merely, but for anything necessary for the comfort of a family. It is the same as *treasury* or a place of *deposit.* ¶ *New and old.* Things lately acquired, or things that had been laid up for a long time. *So,* said Christ, you, my disciples, are to be. The truth, new or old, which you have gained, keep it not laid up and hid, but bring it forth, in due season and on proper occasions, to benefit others. Every preacher should be properly instructed. Christ for three years gave instructions to the apostles; and they who preach should be able to understand the gospel, to defend it, and to communicate it to others. Human learning alone is indeed of no value to a minister; but all learning that will enable a man better to understand the Bible and communicate its truths *is* valuable, and should, if possible, be gained. A minister should be like the father of a family—distributing to the church as it needs; and out of his treasures bringing forth truth to confirm the feeble, to enlighten the ignorant, and to recover and guide those who are in danger of straying away.

54. *Into his own country.* That is, into Nazareth. Mark, who has also recorded this (ch. vi. 1-6), says that it took place on the Sabbath. It was common for our Saviour to speak in the synagogues. Any Jew had a right to address the people, if called on by the minister; and our Saviour often availed himself of the right to instruct the people and declare his doctrines. See Mat. iv. 23.

55, 56. *Is not this the carpenter's son?* Mark says, "Is not this the *carpenter,* the son of Mary?" Both these expressions would probably be used in the course of the conversation, and Matthew has recorded one and Mark the other. The expression recorded by Mark is a strong, perhaps decisive proof that he had himself worked at the business till he was thirty years of age. The people in the neighbourhood would understand well the nature of his early employments. It is therefore almost certain that this had been his manner of life. A useful employment is always honourable. Idleness is the parent of mischief. Our Saviour, therefore, spent the greatest part of his life in honest, useful industry. Till the age of thirty he did not choose to enter on his great work; and it was proper before that time that he should set an example to the world of honourable though humble industry. Life is not wasted in such employments. They are appointed as the lot of man; and in the faithful discharge of duties in the relations of life, though obscure; in honest industry, however humble; in patient labour, if connected with a life of religion, we may be sure that God will approve our conduct. It was, moreover, the custom of the Jews—even those of wealth and learning—to train all their children to some *trade* or manual occupation. Thus Paul was a tent-maker. Comp. Ac. xviii. 3.

This was, on the part of the Saviour, an example of great condescension and humility. It staggers the faith of many that the Son of God should labour in an occupation so obscure and lowly. The infidel sneers at the idea that *He that made the worlds* should live thirty years in humble life as a poor and unknown mechanic. Yet the same infidel will loudly praise Peter the Great of Russia because he laid aside his imperial dignity and entered the British service as a *ship-carpenter,* that he might learn the art of building a navy. Was the purpose of *Peter* of more importance

57 And they [y]were offended in him. But Jesus said unto them, A prophet is not without honour save in his own country and in his own house.

58 And he did not many mighty works there, because of their unbelief.

CHAPTER XIV.

AT that time [a]Herod the tetrarch heard of the fame of Jesus;

2 And said unto his servants,

y Is.49.7; 53.3; Jn.6.42.

a Mar.6.14; Lu.9.7,&c.

than that of the Son of God? If Peter, the heir to the throne of the Czars, might leave his elevated rank and descend to a humble employment, and secure by it the applause of the world, why might not the King of kings evince a similar character for an infinitely higher object? ¶ *His brethren, James,* &c. The fair interpretation of this passage is, that these were the sons and daughters of Joseph and Mary. The people in the neighbourhood thought so, and spoke of them as such.

57. *And they were offended in him.* That is, they took offence at his humble birth, and at the indigent circumstances of his family. They were too proud to be taught by one who, in family connections, they took to be their equal or inferior. Men always look with envy on those of their own rank who advance pretensions to uncommon wisdom or superior power. ¶ *A prophet is not without honour,* &c. This seems to be a proverbial expression. Jesus advances it as a *general* truth. There *might be* some exceptions to it, but *he* was not an exception. Everywhere else he had been more honoured than at home. There they knew his family. They had seen his humble life. They had been his companions. They were envious of his wisdom, and were too proud to be taught by him. A case remarkably similar to this occurs in the history of the discovery of America. Columbus, a native of Genoa, had by patient study conceived the idea that there was a vast continent which might be reached by sailing to the west. Of this his countrymen had no belief. Learned men had long studied the science of geography, and they had never imagined that such a continent could exist; and they were indignant that *he,* an obscure man, should suppose that he "possessed wisdom superior to all the rest of mankind united." It was accordingly a fact that he was obliged to seek for patrons of his undertaking out of his own country; that there he received his first honours; and that to other kingdoms the discoveries of the obscure Genoese gave their chief wealth and highest splendour.

58. *Did not many mighty works.* Miracles. This implies that he performed *some* miracles. Mark tells us what they were: "He laid his hands upon a few sick folk and healed them," Mar. vi. 5. ¶ *Because of their unbelief.* That is, it would have been useless to the great purposes of his mission to have worked miracles there. We are not to suppose that his *power* was limited by the belief or unbelief of men; but they were so *prejudiced,* so set against him, that they were not in a condition to *judge of evidence* and to be convinced. They would have charged it to derangement, or sorcery, or the agency of the devil. Comp. Jn. x. 20. It would have been of no use, therefore, in proving *to them* that he was from God, to have worked miracles. He did, therefore, only those things which were the proper work of benevolence, and which could not easily be charged on the devil. He gave *sufficient* proof of his mission, and left them in their chosen unbelief without excuse. It is also true, in spiritual things, that the unbelief of a people prevents the influences of the Holy Spirit from being sent down to bless them. God requires faith. He hears only the prayers of faith. And when there is little true belief, and prayer is cold and formal, there the people sleep in spiritual death and are unblessed.

CHAPTER XIV.

1. *Herod the tetrarch.* See also Mar. vi. 14-16; Lu. ix. 7-9. This was a son of Herod the Great. Herod the Great died probably in the first year after the birth of Christ, and left his kingdom to his three sons, of whom this *Herod Antipas* was one. He ruled over Galilee and Perea. See Notes on Mat. ii. 15. The title *tetrarch* literally denotes one who rules over a *fourth* part of any country. It came, however, to signify the governor or ruler of any province subject to the Roman emperor.—Robinson, *Lex.*

This is John the Baptist: he is risen from the dead; and therefore mighty works [1]do show forth themselves in him.

3 For Herod had laid hold on John, and bound him, and put *him* in prison for Herodias' sake, his brother Philip's wife.

4 For John said unto him, It[b] is not lawful for thee to have her.

5 And when he would have put him to death, he feared the multitude, because [c]they counted him as a prophet.

6 But when Herod's birthday was kept, the daughter of Herodias danced [2]before them, and pleased Herod.

7 Whereupon he promised with an oath to give her whatsoever she would ask.

1 or, *are wrought by him.* *b* Le.18.16; 20.21.

c ch.21.26; Lu.20.6. 2 *in the midst.*

¶ *Heard of the fame of Jesus.* Jesus had been a considerable time engaged in the work of the ministry, and it may seem remarkable that he had not before heard of him. Herod might, however, have been absent on some expedition to a remote part of the country. It is to be remembered, also, that he was a man of much dissoluteness of morals, and that he paid little attention to the affairs of the people. He might have *heard* of Jesus before, but it had not arrested his attention. He did not think it a matter worthy of much regard.

2. *This is John the Baptist.* Herod feared John. His conscience smote him for his crimes. He remembered that he had wickedly put him to death. He knew him to be a distinguished prophet; and he concluded that no other one was capable of working such miracles but he who had been so eminent a servant of God in his life, and who, he supposed, had again risen from the dead and entered the dominions of his murderer. The alarm in his court, it seems, was general. Herod's *conscience* told him that this was John. Others thought that it might be the expected Elijah or one of the old prophets, Mar. vi. 15.

3-5. *For Herod had laid hold on John,* &c. See Mar. vi. 17-20; Lu. iii. 19, 20. This Herodias was a granddaughter of Herod the Great. She was first married to Herod Philip, by whom she had a daughter, Salome, probably the one that danced and pleased Herod. Josephus says that this marriage of Herod Antipas with Herodias took place while he was on a journey to Rome. He stopped at his brother's; fell in love with his wife; agreed to put away his own wife, the daughter of Aretas, King of Petræa; and Herodias agreed to leave her own husband and live with him. They were living, therefore, in adultery; and John, in faithfulness, though at the risk of his life, had reproved them for their crimes. Herod was guilty of two crimes in this act: 1st. Of *adultery*, as she was the wife of another man. 2d. Of *incest*, as she was a near relation, and such marriages were expressly forbidden, Le. xviii. 16.

6-13. See also Mar. vi. 21-29. *But when Herod's birthday was come.* Kings were accustomed to observe the day of their birth with much pomp, and commonly, also, by giving a *feast* to their principal nobility. See Ge. xl. 20. Mark adds that this birthday was kept by making a supper to his "lords, high captains, and chief estates in Galilee;" that is, to the chief men in office. *High captains* means, in the original, commanders of *thousands*, or of a division of a thousand men. ¶ *The daughter of Herodias;* that is, *Salome*, her daughter by her former husband. This was a violation of all the rules of modesty and propriety. One great principle of all eastern nations is to keep their females from public view. For this purpose they are confined in a particular part of the house, called the *harem.* See Notes on Mat. ix. 1-8. If they appear in public, it is always with a veil, so closely drawn that their faces cannot be seen. No modest woman would have appeared in this manner before the court, and it is probable, therefore, that she partook of the dissolute principles of her mother. It is also probable that the *dance* was one well known in Greece—the lascivious and wanton dance of the *Ionics.*

7. *He promised with an oath.* This was a foolish and wicked oath. To please a wanton girl, the monarch called the eternal God to witness his willingness to give her half his kingdom,

8 And she, being before instructed of her mother, said, [d]Give me here John Baptist's head in a charger.

9 And[e] the king was sorry: nevertheless, [f]for the oath's sake, and them which sat with him at meat, he commanded *it* to be given *her*.

10 And he sent and beheaded John in the prison.

11 And his head was brought

d Pr.29.10. e Ju.11.31,35; Da.6.14-16. f Ju.21.1; 1 Sa.14.28; 25.22; Ec.5.2.

Mar. vi. 23. It seems, also, that he was willing to shed the holiest blood it contained. An oath like this it was not lawful to make, and it should have been broken. See ver. 9.

8. *Being before instructed of her mother.* Not before she danced, but afterward, and before she made the request of Herod. See Mar. vi. 24. The only *appearance* of what was right in the whole transaction was her *honouring* her mother by consulting her, but in this she only intended to accomplish the purposes of wickedness more effectually. ¶ *In a charger.* The original word means a large *platter* on which food is placed. We should have supposed that she would have been struck with abhorrence at such a direction from her mother; but she seems to have been gratified. John, by his faithfulness, had offended the whole family, and here was ample opportunity for an adulterous mother and her dissolute child to gratify their resentment. It was customary for princes to require the *heads* of persons ordered for execution to be brought to them. For this there were two reasons: 1st. To gratify their resentment—to feast their eyes on the proof that their enemy was dead; and, 2d. To ascertain the fact that the sentence had been executed. There is a similar instance in Roman history of a *woman* requiring the head of an enemy to be brought to her. Agrippina, the mother of Nero, who was afterward emperor, sent an officer to put to death Lollia Paulina, who had been her rival for the imperial dignity. When Lollia's head was brought to her, not knowing it at first, she examined it with her own hands till she perceived some particular feature by which the lady was distinguished.*

9. *And the king was sorry.* There might have been several reasons for this. 1st. Herod had a high respect for John, and feared him. He knew that he was a holy man, and had "*observed* him," Mar. vi. 20. In the margin (Mark) this is *kept him*, or *saved him*. In fact, he had interposed and saved John from being put to death by Herodias, who had had a quarrel with John, and would have killed him but for Herod, Mar. vi. 19. Herod, though a bad man, had a respect and veneration for John as a holy and just man, as wicked men often will have. 2d. John was in high repute among the people, and Herod might have been afraid that his murder might excite commotion. 3d. Herod, though a wicked man, does not appear to have been insensible to some of the common principles of human nature. Here was a great and most manifest crime proposed—no less than the *murder* of an acknowledged prophet of the Lord. It was deliberate. It was to gratify the malice of a wicked woman. It was the price of a few moments' entertainment. His *conscience*, though in feeble and dying accents, checked him. He would have preferred a request not so manifestly wicked, and that would not have involved him in so much difficulty. ¶ *For the oath's sake.* Herod felt that he was bound by this oath; but he was not. The oath should not have been taken; but, *being* taken, he could not be bound by it. No oath could justify a man in committing murder. The true principle is, that Herod was bound by a prior obligation—by the law of God—*not* to commit murder; and no act of his, be it an *oath* or anything else, could free him from that obligation. ¶ *And them which sat with him at meat.* This was the strongest reason why Herod murdered John. He had not firmness enough to obey the law of God and to follow the dictates of conscience against the opinions of wicked men. He was afraid of the charge of cowardice and want of spirit; afraid of ridicule and the contempt of the wicked. This is the principle of *the laws of honour;* this the foundation of *duelling*. It is not so much *for his own sake* that one man murders another in a duel, for the offence is often a mere trifle—it is a *word*, or *look*, that never would injure

* Lardner's *Credibility*, part i. book i. ch. i.

in a charger, and given to the damsel: and she brought *it* to her mother.

12 And his disciples came and took up the body, and [g]buried it, and went and told Jesus.

13 When Jesus heard *of it*, [h]he departed thence by ship into a desert place apart: and when the people had heard *thereof*, they followed him on foot out of the cities.

14 And Jesus went forth, [i]and saw a great multitude, and was

g Ac.8.2.

h ch.10.23; 12.15; Mar.6.32,&c.; Lu.9.10,&c.: Jn.6.1,2,&c. i ch.9.36; 15.32,&c.

---

him. It is because the *men of honour*, as they call themselves, his companions, would consider him a coward and would laugh at him. Those companions may be unprincipled contemners of the laws of God and man; and yet the duellist, against his own conscience, against the laws of God, against the good opinion of the virtuous part of the world, and against the laws of his country, seeks by deadly aim to *murder* another merely to gratify his dissolute companions. And this is the law of honour! This is the secret of duelling! This the source of that remorse that settles in awful blackness, and that thunders damnation around the duellist in his dying hours! It should be added, this is the course of all *youthful* guilt. Young men are led along by others. They have not firmness enough to follow the teachings of a father and of the law of God. They are afraid of being called *mean* and *cowardly* by the wicked, and they often sink low in vice and crime, never to rise again. ¶ *At meat;* that is, at supper. The word *meat*, at the time the Bible was translated, meant provisions of all kinds. It is now restricted to *flesh*, and does not convey a full idea of the original.

11. *And his head was brought in a charger*, &c. For the sake of these wicked men, the bloody offering—the head of the slaughtered prophet—was brought and given as the reward to the daughter and mother. What an offering to a woman! Josephus says of Herodias that "she was a woman full of ambition and envy, having a mighty influence on Herod, *and able to persuade him to things he was not at all inclined to.*" This is one of the many proofs that we have that the evangelists drew characters according to truth.

12. *And his disciples*, &c. The *head* was with Herodias. The body, with pious care, they buried. ¶ *And went and told Jesus.* This was done, probably, for the following reasons: 1st. It was an important event, and one particularly connected with the work of Jesus. John was his forerunner, and it was important that he should be made acquainted with his death. 2d. It is not unreasonable to suppose that in their affliction they came to him for consolation; nor is it improper in *our* affliction to follow their example, *and go and tell Jesus.* 3d. *Their* master had been slain by a cruel king. Jesus was engaged in the same cause, and they probably supposed that *he* was in danger. They therefore came to warn him of it, and he (ver. 13) sought a place of safety.

13-21. A full narrative of the feeding the five thousand is given in each of the other evangelists: in Mar. vi. 32-44; in Lu. ix. 10-17; in Jn. vi. 1-14.

13. *And when Jesus heard* of it, *he departed.* He went to a place of safety. He never threw himself unnecessarily into danger. It was proper that he should secure his life till the appointed time had come for him to die. ¶ *By a ship into a desert place.* That is, he crossed the Sea of Galilee. He went to the country *east* of the sea, into a place little inhabited. Luke says (ix. 10) he went to a place called Bethsaida. See Notes on Mat. xi. 21. *A desert place* means a place little cultivated, where there were few or no inhabitants. On the east of the Sea of Galilee there was a large tract of country of this description—rough, uncultivated, and chiefly used to pasture flocks.

14. *Was moved with compassion.* That is, pitied them. Mark (vi. 34) says he was moved with compassion because they were as sheep having no shepherd. A shepherd is one who takes care of a flock. It was his duty to feed it; to defend it from wolves and other wild beasts; to take care of the young and feeble; to lead it by green pastures and still waters, Ps. xxiii. In Eastern countries this was a principal employment of the inhabitants. When Christ says the people were as sheep without a shepherd, he means that they had no

moved with [k]compassion toward them, and he healed their sick.

15 And when it was evening his disciples came to him, saying, This is a desert place, and the time is now past; send the multitude away, that they may go into the villages and buy themselves victuals.

16 But Jesus said unto them, They need not depart; give ye them to eat.

17 And they say unto him, We have here but five loaves and two fishes.

18 He said, Bring them hither to me.

19 And he commanded the multitude to sit down on the grass; and took the five loaves and the

k He.4.15.

---

teachers and *guides* who cared for them and took pains to instruct them. The scribes and Pharisees were haughty and proud, and cared little for the common people; and when they *did* attempt to teach them, they led them astray. They therefore came in great multitudes to him who preached the gospel to the poor (Mat. xi. 5), and who was thus the good shepherd, Jn. x. 14.

15. *The time is now past.* That is, the day is passing away; it is near night, and it is proper to make some provision for the temporal wants of so many. Perhaps it may mean it was past the usual time for refreshment.

16. *Jesus said—They need not depart; give ye them to eat.* John adds (ch. vi. 5, 6) that previous to this Jesus had addressed Philip, and asked, Whence shall we buy bread that these may eat? and that he "said this to prove him; for he himself knew what he would do;" that is, he said this to try his *faith;* to *test* the confidence of Philip in himself. Philip, it seems, had not the *kind* of confidence which he ought to have had. He immediately began to think of their ability to *purchase* food for them. Two hundred pennyworth of bread, said he, would not be enough, Jn. vi. 7. In the original it is two hundred *denarii.* These were Roman coins amounting to about fourteen cents (7*d.*) each. The whole two hundred, therefore, would have been equal to about twenty-eight dollars. In the view of Philip this was a great sum—a sum which twelve poor fishermen were by no means able to provide. It was this fact, and not any unwillingness to provide for them, which led the disciples to request that they should be sent into the villages around in order to obtain food. Jesus knew how much they had, and he required of them, as he does of all, implicit faith, and told them to give them to eat. He requires us to do what he commands, and we need not doubt that he will give us strength to accomplish it.

17. *We have here but five loaves,* &c. These loaves were in the possession of a *lad,* or young man, who was with them, and were made of barley, Jn. vi. 9. It is possible that this lad was one in attendance on the apostles to carry their food, but it is most probable he was one who had provision to sell among the multitude. Barley was a cheap kind of food, scarcely one-third the value of wheat, and was much used by poor people. A considerable part of the food of the people in that region was probably fish, as they lived on the borders of a lake that abounded in fish.

19. *And he commanded the multitude to sit down.* In the original it is *to recline* on the grass, or to lie as they did at their meals. The Jews never *sat,* as we do, at meals, but *reclined* or lay at length. See Notes on Mat. xxiii. 6. Mark and Luke add that they reclined in companies, by hundreds and by fifties. ¶ *And looking up to heaven, he blessed.* Luke adds, he blessed *them;* that is, the loaves. The word *to bless* means, often, to give thanks; sometimes to pray for a blessing; that is, to pray for the divine favour and friendship; to pray that what we do may meet his approbation. In seeking a blessing on our food, it means that we pray that it may be made nourishing to our bodies; that we may have proper gratitude to God, the giver, for providing for our wants; and that we may remember the Creator while we partake the bounties of his providence. Our Saviour *always* sought a blessing on his food. In this he was an example for us. What he did we should do. It is right thus to seek the blessing of God. He provides for us; he daily opens his hand and satisfies our wants, and it is proper that we should render suitable acknowledgments for his goodness.

The custom among the Jews was

two fishes, and, looking up to heaven, he blessed, and brake; and gave the loaves to *his* disciples, and the disciples to the multitude.

20 And they did all eat and were filled: and they [l]took up of the fragments that remained twelve baskets full.

21 And they that had eaten were about five thousand men, beside women and children.

22 And straightway Jesus constrained his disciples to get into a ship, and to go before him unto the other side, while he sent the multitudes away.

23 And when he had sent the multitudes away, [m]he went up into a mountain apart to pray:

l 2 Ki.4.1-7.

m Mar.6.46.

---

universal. The form of prayer which they used in the time of Christ has been preserved by their writers, the Talmudists. It is this: "Blessed be thou, O Lord our God, the King of the world, who hast produced this food and this drink from the earth and the vine." ¶ *And brake.* The loaves of bread, among the Jews, were made *thin* and *brittle*, and were therefore broken and not cut.

20. *And they did all eat, and were filled.* This was an undoubted *miracle*. The quantity *must* have been greatly increased to have supplied so many. He that could *increase* that small quantity so much had the power of *creation;* and he that could do that could create the world out of nothing, and had no less than divine power. ¶ *Twelve baskets full.* The size of these *baskets* is unknown. They were probably such as travellers carried their provisions in. They were used commonly by the Jews in their journeys. In travelling among the Gentiles or Samaritans, a *Jew* could expect little hospitality. There were not, as now, public houses for the entertainment of strangers. At great distances there were *caravansaries*, but they were intended chiefly as lodging-places for the night, and not to provide *food* for travellers. Hence, in journeying among strangers or in deserts, they carried *baskets* of provisions, and this is the reason why they were furnished with them here. It is probable that each of the apostles had *one*, and they were all filled. John (vi. 12) says that Jesus *directed* them to gather up these fragments, that nothing might be lost—an example of economy. God *creates* all food; it has, therefore, a kind of sacredness; it is all *needed* by some person or other, and none should be lost.

21. *Five thousand men, besides,* &c. Probably the whole number might have been ten thousand. To feed so many was an act of great benevolence and a stupendous miracle.

22, 23. *And straightway Jesus constrained,* &c. See Mar. vi. 45-56; Jn. vi. 15-21. The word *straightway* means immediately; that is, as soon as the fragments were gathered up. To *constrain* usually means to *compel*. It here means to *command*. There was no need of *compulsion*. They were at this time on the east side of the Lake of Gennesareth. He directed them to get into a ship and cross over to the other side; that is, to Capernaum. Mark adds that he sent them to *Bethsaida* (vi. 45). Bethsaida was situated at the place where the Jordan empties into the lake on the east side of the river. Comp. Notes on ch. xi. 21. It is probable that he directed them to go in a ship or boat to *Bethsaida*, and remain there till he should dismiss the people, and that he would meet them there, and with them cross the lake. The effect of the miracle on the multitude was so great (Jn. vi. 14) that they believed him to be that prophet which should come into the world; that is, the *Messiah*, the *king* that they had expected, and they were about to take him *by force* and make him a king, Jn. vi. 15. To avoid this, Jesus got away from them as privately as possible. He went into a solitary mountain alone. In view of the temptation—when human honours were offered to him and almost *forced* upon him—he retired for private prayer; an example for all who are tempted with human honours and applause. Nothing is better to keep the mind humble and unambitious than to seek some lonely place; to shut out the world with all its honours; to realize that the great God, before whom all creatures and all honours sink to nothing, is round about us; and to ask

and when the evening was come, he was there alone.

24 But the ship was now in the midst of the sea, tossed with waves; for the wind was contrary.

25 And in the fourth watch of the night Jesus went unto them, walking on the sea.

26 And[n] when the disciples saw him walking on the sea, [o]they were troubled, saying, It is a spirit; and they cried out for fear.

27 But straightway Jesus spake unto them, saying, [p]Be of good cheer; it is I; be not afraid.

28 And Peter answered him and said, [q]Lord, if it be thou, bid me come unto thee on the water.

29 And he said, Come. And when Peter was come down out of the ship, he walked on the water to go to Jesus.

30 But when he saw the wind [3]boisterous, he was afraid; and beginning to sink, he cried, saying, [r]Lord, save me!

31 And immediately [s]Jesus stretched forth *his* hand, and caught him, and said unto him, O thou of little faith, [t]wherefore didst thou doubt?

n Job 9.8; Jn.6.19. *o* Lu.24.37. *p* Ac.23.11.

q Phi.4.13. [3] or, *strong*. *r* Ps.69.1,2; La.3.57. *s* Is.63.12. *t* Ja.1.6.

---

him to keep us from pride and vainglory.

24. *But the ship was now in the midst of the sea.* John says they had sailed about 25 or 30 furlongs. About $7\frac{1}{2}$ Jewish furlongs made a mile; so that the distance they had sailed was not more than about 4 miles. At no place is the Sea of Tiberias much more than 10 miles in breadth, so that they were literally in the midst of the sea.

25. *And in the fourth watch of the night.* The Jews anciently divided the night into three parts of four hours each, usually called *watches.* The *first* of these watches is mentioned in La. ii. 19, the *middle watch* in Ju. vii. 19, and the *morning watch* in Ex. xiv. 24. In the time of our Saviour they divided the night into four watches, the fourth having been introduced by the Romans. These watches consisted of three hours each. The first commenced at six and continued till nine; the second from nine to twelve; the third from twelve to three; and the fourth from three to six. The first was called evening; the second midnight; the third cock-crowing; the fourth morning, Mar. xiii. 35. It is probable that the term *watch* was given to each of these divisions from the practice of placing sentinels around the camp in time of war, or in cities, to *watch* or *guard* the camp or city; and that they were at first relieved *three* times in the night, but under the Romans *four* times. It was in the last of these watches, or between three and six in the morning, that Jesus appeared to the disciples, so that he had spent most of the night alone on the mountain in prayer. ¶ *Walking on the sea.* A manifest and wonderful miracle. It was a boisterous sea. It was in a dark night. The little boat was 4 or 5 miles from the shore, tossed by the billows.

26. *They were troubled.* They were afraid. The sight was remarkable. It was sufficient to awe them. In the dark night, amid the tumultuous billows appeared the form of a man. They thought it was a spirit—an apparition. It was a common belief among the ancients that the spirits of men after death frequently appeared to the living.

28–31. *And Peter answered,* &c. Here is an instance of the characteristic ardour and rashness of Peter. He had less *real* faith than he supposed, and more ardour than his faith would justify. He was rash, headlong, incautious, really attached to Jesus, but still easily daunted and prone to fall. He was afraid, therefore, when in danger, and, sinking, cried again for help. Thus he was suffered to learn his own character, and his dependence on Jesus; a lesson which all Christians are permitted sooner or later to learn by dear-bought experience.

32. *And when they were come into the ship the wind ceased.* Here was a new proof of the power of Jesus. He that has power over winds and waves has all power. John adds (vi. 21) that the ship was immediately at the land whither they went; another proof, amid this collection of wonders, that the Son of God was with them. They came, therefore, and worshipped him,

32 And when they were come into the ship [u]the wind ceased.

33 Then they that were in the ship came and worshipped him, saying, Of a truth thou art [v]the Son of God.

34 And[w] when they were gone over, they came into the land of Gennesaret.

35 And when the men of that place had knowledge of him, they sent out into all that country round about, and brought unto him all that were diseased;

36 And besought him that they might only touch [x]the hem of his garment: and [y]as many as touched were made perfectly whole.

u Ps.107.29. v Da.3.25; Lu.4.41; Jn.1.49; 6.69; 11.27; Ac.8.37; Ro.1.4. w Mar.6.53.

x Nu.15.38; ch.9.20; Mar.3.10; Lu.6.19; Ac.19.12. y Jn.6.37.

acknowledging him to be the Son of God. That is, they gave him homage, or honoured him as the Son of God.

34–36. *Land of Gennesaret.* This region was in Galilee, on the west side of the Sea of Tiberias; and *in* this land was situated Capernaum, to which he had directed his disciples to go. ¶ *The hem of his garment.* That is, the fringe or border on the outer garment. See Notes on Mat. ix. 20.

REMARKS.

1st. We learn from this chapter the power of conscience, ver. 1–4. Herod's guilt was the only reason why he thought John the Baptist had risen. At another time he would altogether have disbelieved it. Consciousness of guilt will at some period infallibly torment a man.

2d. The duty of faithfulness, ver. 4. John reproved Herod at the hazard of his life, and he died for it; but he had the approbation of conscience and of God. So will all who do their duty. Here was an example of fidelity to all ministers of religion. They are not to fear the face of man, however rich, or mighty, or wicked.

3d. The righteous will *command* the respect of the wicked. Herod was a wicked man, but he respected John and feared him, Mar. vi. 20. The wicked profess to despise religion, and many really do; but their consciences tell them that religion is a good thing. In times of trial they will sooner trust Christians than others. In sickness and death they are often glad to see them and hear them pray, and desire the comfort which *they* have; and, like Balaam, say, "Let me die the death of the righteous," Nu. xxiii. 10. No person, young or old, is ever the less really esteemed for being a Christian.

4th. Men are often restrained from great sins by mere selfish motives, as Herod was by the love of popularity, ver. 5. Herod would have put John to death long before had it not been that he feared the people. His constantly desiring to do it was a kind of *prolonged murder.* God will hold men guilty for *desiring* to do evil; and will not justify them if they are restrained, *not* by the fear of him, but by the fear of men.

5th. We see the effect of what is called the principle *of honour*, ver. 9. It was in obedience to this that Herod committed murder. This is the principle of duelling and war. No principle is so foolish and wicked. The great mass of men disapprove of it. The wise and good have always disapproved of it. This principle of honour is usually the mere love of revenge. It is often the fear of being laughed at. It produces evil. God cannot and will not love it. The way to prevent duels and murders is to restrain the passions and cultivate a spirit of meekness and forgiveness when young; that is, to come early under the full influence of the gospel.

6th. Men should be cautious about promises, and especially about oaths. Herod made a foolish promise, and confirmed it by a wicked oath, ver. 9. Promises should not be made without *knowing* what is promised, and without *knowing* that it will be *right* to perform them. Oaths are always wicked except when made before a magistrate, and on occasions of real magnitude. The practice of profane and common swearing, like that of Herod, is always foolish and wicked, and sooner or later will bring men into difficulty.

7th. Amusements are often attended with evil consequences, ver. 6–11. The dancing of a gay and profligate girl was the means of the death of one of the holiest of men. Dancing, balls, splendid parties, and theatres are by many thought innocent; but they are a profitless waste of time. They lead to forgetfulness of God. They nourish passion and sensual desires. They often lead to the seduction and ruin of the innocent. They are *unfit* for dying creatures. From the very midst of such scenes the gay may go to the bar of God. How poor a preparation to die! How dreadful the judgment-seat to such!

8th. Jesus will take care of the poor, ver. 14–21. He regarded the *temporal* as well as the spiritual wants of the people. Rather than see them suffer, he worked a miracle to feed them. So, rather than see *us* suffer, God is daily doing what man *cannot do*. He causes the grain to grow; he fills the land, and seas, and air with living creatures; nay, he provides in desert places for the support of man. How soon would all men and beasts die if he did not put forth continued power and goodness for the supply of our wants!

9th. It is the duty of Christians to be solicitous about the temporal wants of the poor, ver. 15. They are with us. By regarding them, and providing for them, we have an opportunity of showing our attachment to Christ, and our resemblance to God, who continually does good.

10th. A blessing should be sought on our enjoyments, ver. 19. It is always right to imitate Christ. It is right to acknowledge our dependence on God, and in the midst of mercies to pray that we may not forget the Giver.

11th. We see the duty of economy. The Saviour, who had power to create worlds by a word, yet commanded to take up the fragments, that nothing might be lost, Jn. vi. 12. Nothing that *God* has created and given to us should be *wasted*.

12th. It is proper to *make preparation* for private prayer. Jesus sent the people away that he might be alone, ver. 22, 23. So Christians should *take pains* that they may have times and places for retirement. A grove or a mountain was the place where our Saviour sought to pray, and there, too, may *we* find and worship God.

13th. In time of temptation, of prosperity, and honour, it is right to devote much time to secret prayer. Jesus, when the people were about to make him a king, retired to the mountain, and continued there till the early morning in prayer, Jn. vi. 15.

14th. When Christ commands us to do a thing we should do it, ver. 22. Even if it should expose us to danger, it should be done.

15th. In times of danger and distress, Jesus will see us and will come to our relief, ver. 25, 26. Even in the tempest that howls, or on the waves of affliction that beat around us, he will come, and we shall be safe.

16th. We should never be afraid of him. We should always have *good cheer* when we see him, ver. 27. When he says, "It is I," he also says, "be not afraid." He can still the waves, and conduct us safely to the port which we seek.

17th. Nothing is too difficult for us when we act under the command of Christ. Peter at his command leaves the ship and walks on the billows, ver. 29.

18th. Christ sometimes leaves his people to see their weakness and their need of strength. Without his continued aid they would sink. Peter had no strength of his own to walk on the deep, and Christ suffered him to see his dependence, ver. 30.

19th. The eye, in difficulty, should be fixed on Christ. As soon as Peter began to look at the waves and winds, rather than Christ, he began to sink, ver. 30. True courage in difficulties consists not in confidence in ourselves, but in confidence in Jesus, the Almighty Saviour and Friend.

20th. Prayer may be instantly answered. When we are in immediate danger, and offer a prayer of faith, we may expect immediate aid, ver. 31.

21st. Pride comes before a fall. Peter was self-confident and proud, and he fell. His confidence and rashness were the very means of showing the weakness of his faith, ver. 31.

22d. It is proper to render homage to Jesus, and to worship him as the Son of God, ver. 33.

23d. We should be desirous that all about us should partake of the benefits that Christ confers. When we *know* him and have tested his goodness, we should take pains that all around us may also be brought to him and be saved, ver. 35.

24th. Jesus only can make us perfectly whole. No other being can save us. He that could heal the *body* can save the soul. A word can save us. With what earnestness ought we to plead with him that we may obtain his saving grace! ver. 36.

CHAPTER XV.

THEN[a] came to Jesus scribes and Pharisees, which were of Jerusalem, saying,

2 Why do thy disciples transgress the tradition of the elders? for they wash not their hands when they eat bread.

3 But he answered and said unto them, [b]Why do ye also transgress the commandment of God by your tradition?

4 For God commanded, saying, [c]Honour thy father and mother: and, [d]He that curseth father or mother, let him die the death.

5 But ye say, Whosoever shall say to *his* father or *his* mother, *It is* a

a Mar.7.1,&c.

b Col.2.8,23; Tit.1.14. c Ex.20.12; De.5.16. d Ex.21.17; Le.20.9.

CHAPTER XV.

1-9. See also Mar. vii. 1-9. ¶ *Then came to Jesus*, &c. Mark says that they *saw* the disciples of Jesus eating with hands unwashed.

2. *Transgress the tradition of the elders.* The world *elders* means literally *old men.* It here means the *ancients*, or their *ancestors.* The *tradition of the elders* meant something handed down from one to another by memory; some precept or custom not commanded in the *written law*, but which scribes and Pharisees held themselves bound to observe. They supposed that when Moses was on Mount Sinai two sets of laws were delivered to him: one, they said, was recorded, and is that contained in the Old Testament; the other was handed down from father to son, and kept uncorrupted to their day. They believed that Moses, before he died, delivered this law to Joshua; he to the Judges; they to the prophets; so that it was kept pure till it was recorded in the Talmuds. In these books these pretended laws are now contained. They are exceedingly numerous and very trifling. They are, however, regarded by the Jews as more important than either Moses or the prophets. One point in which the Pharisees differed from the Sadducees was in holding to these traditions. It seems, however, that in the particular traditions here mentioned all the Jews were united; for Mark adds (ch. vii. 3) that "the Pharisees and *all the Jews*, except they wash their hands oft, eat not, *holding the tradition of the elders.*" Mark has also added that this custom of washing extended not merely to their hands before eating, but in coming from the market; and also to cups, and pots, and brazen vessels, and tables, Mar. vii. 3, 4. They did this professedly for the sake of *cleanliness.* So far it was well. But they made it also a matter of superstition. They regarded *external* purity as of much more importance than the purity of the heart. They had many foolish rules about it respecting the quantity of water that was to be used, the way in which it should be applied, the number of times it should be changed, the number of those that might wash at a time, &c. These rules our Saviour did not think it proper to regard, and this was the reason why they found fault with him.

3. *But he answered*, &c. They accused him of violating their traditions, as though they were obligatory. In his answer he *implied* that his disciples were not bound to obey their traditions—they were invented by men. He said, also, that those traditions *could not* be binding, as they violated the commandments of God. He proceeds to specify *a case* in which their tradition made void one of the plain laws of God; and if that was their character, then they could not blame him for not regarding them.

4. *For God commanded*, &c. That is, in the fifth commandment (Ex. xx. 12), and in Ex. xxi. 17. To *honour* is to obey, to reverence, to speak kindly *to*, to speak and think well *of*. To *curse* is to disobey, to treat with irreverence, *to swear at*, to speak ill of, to think evil of in the heart, to meditate or do *any* evil to a parent. All this is included in the original word. ¶ *Let him die the death.* This is a Hebrew phrase, the same as saying, *let him surely die.* The Jewish law punished this crime with death. This duty of honouring and obeying a parent was what Christ said they had violated by their traditions. He proceeds to state the way in which it was done.

5. It is *a gift.* In Mark it is *corban.* The word *corban* is a Hebrew word denoting *a gift.* It here means a thing *dedicated to the service of God, and therefore not to be appropriated to any other use.* The Jews were in the habit of

gift, by whatsoever thou mightest be profited by me;

6 And[e] honour not his father or his mother, *he shall be free.* Thus have ye made the commandment of God of none effect by your tradition.

7 *Ye* hypocrites! well did Esaias prophesy of you, saying,

8 This[f] people draweth nigh unto

e De.27.16.

f Is.29.13.

---

making such dedications. They devoted their property to him for sacred uses, as they pleased. In doing this they used the word *corban*, or some similar word, saying, this thing is *corban, i.e.* it is a gift to God, or is sacred to him. The law required that when a dedication of this kind was made it should be fulfilled. "Vow and pay unto the Lord your God," Ps. lxxvi. 11. See De. xxiii. 21. The law of God required that a son should *honour* his parent; *i.e.* among other things, that he should provide for his wants when he was old and in distress. Yet the Jewish teachers said that it was more important for a man *to dedicate his property to God* than to *provide for the wants of his parent.* If he had *once* devoted his property—once *said* it was *corban*, or a gift to God—it could not be appropriated even to the support of a parent. If a parent was needy and poor, and if he should apply to a son for assistance, and the son should reply, though in in anger, "It is devoted to God; this property which you need, *and by which you might be profited by me, is corban—I have given it to God;*" the Jews said the property could not be recalled, and the son was not under obligation to aid a parent with it. He had done a more important thing in giving it to God. The son was free. He could not be required to do anything for his father after that. Thus he might *in a moment* free himself from the obligation to obey his father or mother. In a sense somewhat similar to this, the chiefs and priests of the Sandwich Islands had the power of devoting anything to the service of the gods by saying that it was *taboo*, or *tabooed;* that is, it became consecrated to the service of religion; and, no matter who had been the owner, it could then be appropriated to no other use. In this way they had complete power over all the possessions of the people, and could appropriate them to their own use under the pretence of devoting them to religion. They thus deprived the *people* of their property under the plea that it was consecrated to the gods. The Jewish son deprived his *parents* of a support under the plea that the property was devoted to the service of religion. The principle was the same, and both systems were equally a violation of the rights of others.

Besides, the law said that a man should die that *cursed* his father, *i.e.* that refused to obey him, or to provide for him, or spoke in anger to him. Yet the *Jews* said that though in *anger*, and in real *spite* and *hatred*, a son said to his father, "All that I have which could profit *you* I have given to God," he should be free from blame. Thus the whole law was made void, or of no use, by what *appeared* to have the appearance of piety. *No man, according to their views, was bound to obey the fifth commandment and support an aged and needy parent, if, either from superstition or spite, he chose to give his property to God, that is, to devote it to some religious use.*

Our Saviour did not mean to condemn the practice of giving to God, or to religious and charitable objects. This the law and the gospel equally required. He commended even a poor widow that gave all her living, Mar. xii. 44. But he meant to condemn the practice of giving to God where it interfered with our duty to parents and relations; where it was done to *get rid* of the duty of aiding them; and where it was done out of a malignant and rebellious spirit, with the *semblance* of piety, to get clear of doing to earthly parents what God required.

7. Ye *hypocrites!* See Notes on Mat. vii. 5. Hypocrisy is the concealment of some base principle under the pretence of religion. Never was there a clearer instance of it than this—*an attempt to get rid of the duty of providing for needy parents under an appearance of piety towards God.* ¶ *Esaias.* That is, *Isaiah.* This prophecy is found in Is. xxix. 13. ¶ *Prophesy of you.* That is, he spoke of the people of his day—of the Jews, *as* Jews—in terms that apply to the whole people. He properly *characterized the nation* in calling

me with their mouth, and honoureth me with *their* lips; but their heart is far from me.

9 But in vain they do worship me, [g] teaching *for* doctrines the commandments of men.

10 And he called the multitude, and said unto them, Hear, and understand:

11 Not[h] that which goeth into the mouth defileth a man; but that which cometh out of the mouth, this defileth a man.

12 Then came his disciples, and said unto him, Knowest thou that the Pharisees were offended after they heard this saying?

13 But he answered and said, [i]Every plant which my heavenly Father hath not planted shall be rooted up.

14 Let them alone: [k]they be

g Col.2.22. h Ac.10.15; Ro.14.14,20; 1 Ti.4.4; Tit.1.15. i Jn.15.2,6. k ch.23.16; Lu.6.39.

---

them hypocrites. The words are applicable to the nation at all times, and they apply, therefore, to *you*. He did not mean particularly to speak of the nation in the time of Christ, but he spoke of them as having a national character of hypocrisy. Comp. Notes on ch. i. 22, 23.

8. *Draweth nigh unto me with their mouth*, &c. That is, they are regular in the *forms* of worship; they are strict in ceremonial observances, and keep the law outwardly; but God requires the heart, and *that* they have not rendered.

9. *In vain do they worship me.* That is, their attempts to worship are *vain*, or are not real worship — they are mere *forms*. ¶ *Teaching* for *doctrines*, &c. The word *doctrines*, here, means the requirements of religion—things to be believed and practised in religion. God only has a right to declare what shall be done in his service; but they held their traditions to be superior to the written word of God, and taught them as *doctrines* binding the conscience. See Notes on Is. xxix. 13.

10–14. See also Mar. vii. 15–17. *And he called the multitude.* In opposition to the doctrines of the Pharisees, the Saviour took occasion to show them that the great source of pollution was the *heart*. *They* supposed that external things chiefly defiled a man. On this all their doctrines about purification were founded. This opinion of the Jews it was of great importance to correct. The Saviour took occasion, therefore, to direct the people to the true source of defilement—their own hearts. He particularly directed them to it as of importance—*Hear and understand.*

11. *Not that which goeth into the mouth*, &c. The disciples were charged with being sinners for transgressing the tradition of the elders in eating with unwashed hands. Christ replies that what they should *eat* could not render them sinners. The *man*, the moral agent, the soul, could not be polluted by anything that was eaten. What proceeds from the man himself, from his *heart*, would defile him. ¶ *Defileth.* Pollutes, corrupts, or renders sinful.

12. *The Pharisees were offended.* They were so zealous of their traditions that they could not endure that their absurdities should be exposed.

13. *Every plant*, &c. Religious *doctrine* is not inaptly compared to a plant. See 1 Co. iii. 6–8. It is *planted* in the mind for the purpose of producing fruit in the life, or *right conduct*. Jesus here says that all those doctrines of which his Father was not the author must be *rooted up* or corrected. The false doctrines of the Pharisees, therefore, must be attacked, and it was no wonder if they were indignant. It could not be helped. It was his duty to attack them. He was not surprised that they were enraged; but, notwithstanding their opposition, their doctrine should be destroyed.

14. *Let them alone.* That is, do not be troubled at their rage. Be not anxious about it. This result is to be expected. They are greatly attached to their traditions, and you are not to wonder that they are indignant. They lead, also, the blind. They have a vast influence over the multitude, and it is to be expected that they will be enraged at any doctrines that go to lessen their authority or influence. By commanding them *to let them alone*, Christ does not mean that they were to be suffered to remain in error without any attempt to refute or correct them, for this *he* was doing then; but he meant to charge his disciples not *to mind them* or to regard their opposition—it was to

blind leaders of the blind. And if the blind lead the blind, both shall fall into the ditch.

15 Then answered Peter, and said unto him, Declare unto us this parable.

16 And Jesus said, Are ye also yet without understanding?

17 Do ye not yet understand that whatsoever entereth in at the mouth goeth into the belly, and is cast out into the draught?

18 But those things which [l]proceed out of the mouth come forth from the heart, and they defile the man.

19 For[m] out of the heart proceed evil thoughts, murders, adulteries,

l Lu.6.45; Ja.3.6. m Ge.6.5; 8.21; Pr.6.14; 24.9; Je.17.9; Ro.3.10-19; Ga.5.19-21; Ep.2.3; Tit.3.3.

---

be expected. ¶ *If the blind lead the blind*, &c. This was a plain proposition. A blind man, attempting to conduct blind men, would fall into every ditch that was in the way. So with religious teachers. If these Pharisees, themselves ignorant and blind, should be suffered to lead the ignorant multitude, both would be destroyed. This was another reason for confuting their errors, or for rooting up the plants which God had not planted. He wished, by doing it, to save the deluded multitude.

God often suffers one man to lead many to ruin. A rich and profligate man, an infidel, a man of learning, a politician, or a teacher, is allowed to sweep multitudes to ruin. This is not unjust, for those who are led are not *compelled* to follow such men. They are *free* in choosing such leaders, and they are answerable for *being led* to ruin.

15-20. See also Mar. vii. 17-23. *Then answered Peter, and said unto him, Declare unto us this parable.* See Notes on Mat. xiii. 3. The word *parable* sometimes means a *dark* or *obscure saying*, Ps. lxxviii. 2. Peter meant, "Explain to us more fully this obscure and novel doctrine." To us, now, it is plain; to the disciples, just coming out of Judaism, the doctrine of Jesus was obscure. Mark says that the *disciples* asked him. There is no contradiction. The question was put by Peter *in the name* of the disciples; or several of them put the question, though Matthew has mentioned only one. An omission is not a contradiction.

16. *Are ye also yet without understanding?* Jesus appeals, in explaining this, to their *common sense;* and he wonders that they had not yet learned to judge the foolish traditions of the Jews by the decisions of common sense and by his own instructions.

17. *Do ye not understand*, &c. The meaning of this may be thus expressed: The food which is eaten does not affect the *mind*, and therefore cannot pollute it. The doctrine of the Pharisees, that neglect of washing and of similar observances defiles a man, cannot be true. Those things pertain to the *body* as much as food does, and they cannot affect the soul. That must be purified by something else than external washing, and it is polluted by other things than a neglect of mere outward ceremonies. The seat of corruption is *within*—it is the heart itself; and if men would be made pure, this must be cleansed. If that is corrupt, the whole man is corrupt.

18-20. Christ proceeds to state what *does* defile the man, or render him a sinner: 1st. *Evil thoughts.* These are the first things—these are the fountains of all others. Thought precedes action. Thought, or purpose, or motive, gives its *character* to conduct. All evil thoughts are here intended. Though we labour to suppress them, yet they defile us. They leave pollution behind them. 2d. *Murders.* Taking the life of others *with malice.* The *malice* has its seat in the *heart*, and the murder therefore proceeds from the heart, 1 Jn. iii. 15. 3d. *Adulteries, fornication.* See Mat. v. 28. 4th. *Thefts.* Theft is the taking and carrying away the goods of others without their knowledge or consent. Thefts are caused by *coveting* the property of others. They proceed, therefore, from the heart, and violate at the same time two commandments—the *tenth* in thought and the *eighth* in act. 5th. *False witness.* Giving wrong testimony. *Concealing* the truth, or stating what we know to be false—a violation of the ninth commandment. It proceeds from a desire to injure others, to take away their character or property, or to do them injustice. It proceeds thus from the heart. 6th. *Blasphemies.* See Notes on Mat. ix. 3. Blasphemy proceeds from opposition to God, hatred of his character (Ro. viii. 7), and from

fornications, thefts, false witness, blasphemies:

20 These are *the things* which defile a man; but to eat with unwashen hands defileth not a man.

21 Then[n] Jesus went thence, and departed into the coasts of Tyre and Sidon.

22 And behold, a woman of Canaan came out of the same coasts, and cried unto him, saying, Have mercy on me, O Lord, [o]*thou* son of David! my daughter is grievously vexed with a devil.

23 But he [p]answered her not a word. And his disciples came and besought him, saying, Send her away; for she crieth after us.

24 But he answered and said, [q]I am not sent but unto the lost sheep of the house of Israel.

25 Then came she, and wor-

n Mar.7.24.

o Lu.18.38,39. p Ps.28.1; La.3.8. q ch.10.5,6; Ac.3.26.

---

a *desire* that there should be no God. It proceeds from the heart. See Ps. xiv. 1. Mark adds several things to those enumerated by Matthew: (*a*) *Covetousness.* This always proceeds from the heart the unlawful desire of what others possess. (*b*) *Wickedness.* The original here means *malice*, or a *desire of injuring others*, Ro. i. 29. (*c*) *Deceit*, *i.e.* fraud, concealment, cheating in trade. This proceeds from a desire to benefit ourselves by doing injustice to others, and thus proceeds from the heart. (*d*) *Lasciviousness.* Lust, obscenity, unbridled passion—a strong, evil desire of the heart. (*e*) *An evil eye.* That is, an eye sour, malignant, proud; or an eye of lust and passion. See Mat. v. 28; xx. 15; 2 Pe. ii. 14. "Having eyes full of adultery, that cannot cease from sin." (*f*) *Pride.* An improper estimate of our own importance; thinking that we are of much more consequence than we really are—always the work of an evil heart. (*g*) *Foolishness.* Not want of intellect—man is not to blame for that; but *moral folly*, consisting in choosing bad ends, and bad means of gaining them; or, in other words, sin and wickedness. All sin is folly. It is foolish for a man to disobey God, and foolish for anyone to go to hell.

20. *These are* the things *which defile a man.* These are the true sources of pollution in man. These are what corrupt and degrade. It is not the neglect of washing the *body* which defiles; it is the deep, inward corruption of the heart. And what a fountain of pollution is the human soul! What an array of crimes to proceed from the heart of man! What a proof of guilt! What strictness is there in the law of God! How universal is depravity!

21–28. This narrative is also found in Mar. vii. 24–30. ¶ *The coasts of Tyre and Sidon.* These cities were on the *sea-coast* or shore of the Mediterranean. See Notes on Mat. xi. 21. Jesus went there for the purpose of concealment (Mar. vii. 24), perhaps still to avoid Herod.

22. *A woman of Canaan.* This woman is called, also, a Greek, a Syro-Phœnician by birth, Mar. vii. 26. Anciently the whole land, including Tyre and Sidon, was in the possession of the Canaanites, and called Canaan. The Phœnicians were descended from the Canaanites. The country, including Tyre and Sidon, was called Phœnicia, or Syro-Phœnicia. That country was taken by the Greeks under Alexander the Great, and those cities, in the time of Christ, were Greek cities. This woman was therefore a Gentile, living under the Greek government, and probably speaking the Greek language. She was by birth a Syro-Phœnician, born in that country, and descended, therefore, from the ancient Canaanites. All these names might with propriety be given to her. ¶ *Coasts.* Regions or countries. ¶ Thou *son of David.* Descendant of David. See Notes on Mat. i. 1. The phrase here means the Messiah. ¶ *Is grievously vexed with a devil.* See Notes on Mat. iv. 24. The woman showed great earnestness. She *cried* unto him, and fell at his feet, Mar. vii. 25.

23. *But he answered her not a word.* This was done to test her faith, and that there might be exhibited to the apostles an example of the effect of persevering supplication. The result shows that it was not unwillingness to aid her, or neglect of her. It was proper that the strength of her faith should be fully tried.

24. *But he answered and said, I am not sent*, &c. This answer was made to

shipped him, saying, Lord, help me!

26 But he answered and said, It is not meet to take the children's bread, and to [r]cast *it* to dogs.

27 And she said, Truth, Lord: yet the dogs eat of the crumbs which fall from their masters' table.

28 Then[s] Jesus answered and said unto her, O woman, great *is* thy faith: [t]be it unto thee even as thou wilt. And her daughter was made whole [u]from that very hour.

29 And[v] Jesus departed from thence, and came nigh unto the sea of Galilee; and went up into a mountain, and sat down there.

30 And great multitudes came unto him, having with them *those that were* lame, blind, dumb, maimed, and many others, and cast them down at Jesus' feet; [w]and he healed them;

31 Insomuch that the multitude

r ch.7.6; Re.22.15.
s Job 13.15; 23.10; La.3.32. t Ps.145.19.
u Jn.4.50-53. v Mar.7.31.
w Ps.103.3; Is.35.5,6.

---

the *woman*, not to the disciples. *The lost sheep of the house of Israel* were the Jews. He came first to them. He came as their expected Messiah. He came to preach the gospel himself to the Jews only. Afterward it was preached to the Gentiles, but the ministry of Jesus was confined almost entirely to the Jews.

25. *She came and worshipped.* That is, bowed down to him or did him reverence. See Notes on Mat. viii. 2. ¶ *Lord, help me!* A proper cry for a poor sinner, who needs the help of the Lord Jesus.

26. *But he answered and said, It is not meet*, &c. That is, it is not *fit or proper*. ¶ *Children's bread.* The Jews considered themselves as the peculiar children of God. To all other nations they were accustomed to apply terms of contempt, of which *dogs* was the most common. The Mohammedans still apply the term *dogs* to Christians, and Christians and Jews to each other. The term is designed as an expression of the highest contempt. The Saviour means to say that he was sent to the Jews. The woman was a Gentile. He meant merely—using a term in common use, and designed to test her faith in the strongest manner—that it did not comport with the design of his personal ministry to apply benefits intended for the Jews to others. Evidently he cannot be understood as intending to justify or sanction the use of such terms, or *calling names.* He meant to try her faith. As if he had said, "You are a Gentile; I am a Jew. The Jews call themselves children of God. You they vilify and abuse, calling you *a dog.* Are you willing to receive of *a Jew*, then, a favour? Are you willing to submit to these appellations to receive a favour of one of that nation, and to acknowledge your dependence on a people that so despise you?" It was, therefore, a trial of her faith, and was not a lending of his sanction to the propriety of the abusive term. *He* regarded her with a different feeling.

27. *And she said, Truth, Lord*, &c. "What you say is true. Let it be that the *best* food should be given to the children—let the *Jews* have the chief benefit of thy ministry; but the dogs beneath the table eat the crumbs. So let me be regarded as a dog, a heathen, as unworthy of everything. Yet grant *one* exertion of that almighty power displayed so signally among the Jews, and heal the despised daughter of a despised heathen mother."

28. *Great* is *thy faith.* That is, thy trust, confidence. The word here seems to include, also, the humility and perseverance manifested in pressing her suit. The daughter was healed then. Going home, she found her well and composed, Mar. vii. 30.

29–31. *Sea of Galilee.* That is, the Lake of Gennesaret. For an account of the principal diseases mentioned here, see Notes on Mat. iv. 24. ¶ *Maimed.* Those to whom a hand or foot was wanting. See Mat. xviii. 8. To cure them—that is, to *restore* a hand or foot—was a direct act of *creative* power. It is no wonder, therefore, that the people wondered. ¶ *And they glorified the God of Israel.* To glorify here means to *praise;* to acknowledge his power and goodness. The God of Israel was the God that the Israelites or Jews worshipped.

32–39. The miracle recorded here—

wondered, when they saw the dumb to speak, the maimed to be whole, the lame to walk, and the blind to see: and they glorified the God of Israel.

32 Then[x] Jesus called his disciples *unto him*, and said, I have compassion on the multitude, because they continue with me now three days, and have nothing to eat: and I will not send them away fasting, lest they faint in the way.

33 And[y] his disciples say unto him, Whence should we have so much bread in the wilderness as to fill so great a multitude?

34 And Jesus saith unto them, How many loaves have ye? And they said, Seven, and a few little fishes.

35 And[z] he commanded the multitude to sit down on the ground.

36 And he took the seven loaves and the fishes, and [a]gave thanks, and brake *them*, and gave to his disciples, and the disciples to the multitude.

37 And they did all eat, and were filled: and they took up of the broken *meat* that was left seven baskets full.

38 And they that did eat were four thousand men, beside women and children.

39 And he sent away the multitude, and took ship, and [b]came into the coasts of Magdala.

x Mar.8.1,&c. y 2 Ki.4.43,44.

z ch.14.19,&c. a 1 Sa.9.13; Lu.22.19; 24.30. b Mar.8.10.

the feeding of the four thousand—took place on a mountain near the Sea of Galilee. The same account is recorded in Mar. viii. 1–10. The circumstances of the miracle are so similar to the one recorded in Mat. xiv. 14–21, as to need little additional explanation.

32. *Three days, and have nothing to eat.* This is not, perhaps, to be taken literally, but only that during that time they had been deprived of their ordinary or regular food. They had had only a very scanty supply, and on the third day even that began to fail.

39. *Coasts of Magdala.* Mark says, "*The parts of Dalmanutha.*" Magdala was probably the same place which was formerly called *Migdol*, Jos. xix. 38. It is now called Mejdel, and is situated a few miles north of the city of Tiberias, in the land of Gennesaret, on the western side of the Sea of Tiberias, and directly east of Cana of Galilee. "It is a wretched hamlet of a dozen low huts huddled into one, and the whole ready to tumble into a dismal heap of black basaltic rubbish."—*The Land and the Book* (Thomson), vol. ii. p. 108. This was the birthplace of Mary Magdalene, out of whom the Saviour cast seven devils, Mar. xvi. 9. Dalmanutha was probably a small village near to Magdala, of which no remains have been discovered. There is no contradiction in the statements of the two evangelists here, for they do not say that Jesus went to *either* of these towns, but only to the *coasts* or *parts* where they were situated.

REMARKS.

We learn from this chapter,

1st. That men are often far more attached to traditions and the commandments of men than to the law of God, ver. 1–6.

2d. That men are strongly disposed to *explain away* the law of God, if possible. It is too strict for them, and too spiritual. They dare not often attack it directly, but they will *explain* it and *dilute* it so as to make it mean nothing. Wicked men do not love God's law, ver. 4–6.

3d. Men are prone to introduce foolish *rites* into religion. They do not love what God has commanded, and they attempt to compensate for not loving *his* doctrines by being great sticklers for their own, ver. 2; Mar. vii. 3, 4.

4th. All addition to the law of God is evil, ver. 3. All ceremonies in religion which are not authorized by the New Testament are wrong. Man has no right to ordain rites to bind the conscience where God has commanded none, Col. ii. 23. Men come the nearest to that which is right when they live nearest to just what God has commanded in the Bible.

5th. Hypocrites should be unmasked and detected, ver. 7. He does a great service to men who detects their hypocrisy. That close and faithful preaching which lays open the heart, and shows men what they are, is that which comes nearest to the example of Christ. It may pain them, but the wounds of a friend are faithful (Pr. xxvii. 6); and we should honour and love the man that, by the grace of God, can show us our own hearts. We always honour most the physician of the body that is most skilled in detecting and curing disease, and so should we the physician of the soul.

6th. We should be exceedingly cautious in avoiding *formality* in worship, ver. 8, 9. It is hypocrisy. God requires the heart. To render to him only the service of the lips is to mock him. Nothing can be acceptable but true piety, genuine love, and hearty obedience; nothing more *hateful* than an appearance of worshipping God, while the *heart* is in sin and the world.

7th. The duty of honouring parents, ver. 4–6. Nothing can explain away this duty. It is binding on all. Parents should be obeyed, loved, respected. God requires it and we cannot be free from the duty. *Under age*, a child is bound always to obey a parent where the parent does not command anything contrary to the Bible; but when the parent commands anything contrary to the Bible, the child is not bound to obey, Ac. v. 29. *After* the child is of age, he is to respect, love, and honour the parent; and, if poor and needy, to provide for his wants till he dies. It is certainly proper that we should do all that we can to comfort those in old age who did so much for us in childhood. A child can never repay a parent for his kindness to him.

8th. We are not at liberty to give to anything else—not even to religious uses—what is *necessary* to render our parents comfortable, ver. 4–6. They have the first claim on us. And though it is our duty to do *much* in the cause of benevolence, yet our first duty should be to see that our parents do not suffer.

9th. Men easily take offence when they are faithfully reproved, and especially when their hypocrisy is exposed; and especially if this exposure is about some *small matter* on which they have greatly set their hearts—some ceremony in worship or some foolish rite, ver. 12.

10th. Every false doctrine is to be opposed and should be rooted up, ver. 13. It is to be opposed by arguments and candid investigation, and not by abuse and misrepresentation. Christ never *misrepresented* any man's doctrine. He always stated it just as it was—just as *they* held it; and then, by *argument* and the word of God, he showed it was wrong. This is the proper way to manage all controversies.

11th. It is of great importance to search the *heart*, ver. 19, 20. It is a fountain of evil. It is the source of all crime. External conduct is comparatively of little importance. In the sight of God the *heart* is of more importance; and if that were pure, all would be well.

12th. The doctrine of man's depravity is true, ver. 19. If the *heart* produces those things which are specified by the Saviour it cannot be pure. And yet who is there from whose heart, at some time, these things have not proceeded? Alas! the world is *full* of instances that prove that the human heart may produce *all* these things.

13th. In our distress, and the distress of our children and friends, we should go to Jesus. We should, indeed, use all proper means to restore our friends when they are sick; but we should feel that God only can grant returning health and life, ver. 22.

14th. We should not be discouraged that our prayers are not immediately answered. God knows the proper time to answer them, and it may be of great importance to *us* that the answer should be deferred, ver. 23.

15th. We should still persevere, ver. 24–27. We should not be discouraged. We should not be disheartened even by the appearance of neglect or unkind treatment.

16th. Our prayers will be answered if we persevere, ver. 28. They that seek shall find. In due time—in the *best* and most proper time—a gracious God will lend an ear to our request, and grant the thing we need.

17th. We should come with humility and faith, ver. 27. We can never think too little of ourselves, or too much of the mercy and faithfulness of Christ. Prayers of humility and faith only are answered.

18th. Christ will take care of his poor and needy followers. We may be assured that he has *power* to give us all we need, and that in times of necessity he will supply our wants, ver. 32–38.

19th. The great number of poor in the world is no reason why he should not supply them, ver. 38. He daily supplies the wants of nine hundred millions of

CHAPTER XVI.

THE Pharisees also, with the Sadducees, came, and, tempting, [a]desired him that he would show them a sign from heaven.

2 He answered and said unto them, When it is evening, ye say, *It will be* fair weather; for the sky is red:

3 And in the morning, *It will be* foul weather to-day; for the sky is red and lowering. O *ye* hypocrites! ye can discern the face of the sky, but can ye not *discern* the signs of the times?

4 A wicked and adulterous generation seeketh after a sign; and there shall no sign be given unto it but the sign of the prophet [b]Jonas. And he left them, and departed.

5 And when his disciples were come to the other side, they had forgotten to take bread.

6 Then Jesus said unto them, [c]Take heed, and beware of [d]the leaven of the Pharisees and of the Sadducees.

7 And they reasoned among themselves, saying, *It is* because we have taken no bread.

a ch.12.38,&c.; Mar.8.11,&c.; Lu.11.16; 12.54-56; 1 Co.1.22.
b Jonah 1.17. *c* Lu.12.1.
d 1 Co.5.6-8; Ga.5.9; 2 Ti.2.16,17.

---

human beings, besides countless numbers of the beasts of the field, of the fowls of heaven, and the fishes of the sea. It is a small thing to supply the wants of the few poor on the earth, and He who feeds the world will take care of *us* in the time of want.

20th. We should be grateful to God for our daily food. We should render to him proper thanksgiving, ver. 36.

CHAPTER XVI.

1-4. See also Mar. viii. 11, 12. *The Pharisees also, and the Sadducees.* See Notes on Mat. iii. 7. ¶ *Tempting.* That is, *trying him*—feigning a desire to see evidence that he was the Messiah, but with a real desire to see him make the attempt to work a miracle and fail, that they might betray and ruin him. ¶ *A sign from heaven.* Some miraculous appearance in the sky. Such appearances had been given by the prophets; and they supposed, if he was the Messiah, that his miracles would not all be confined *to the earth*, but that he was able to give some signal miracle from heaven. Samuel had caused it to thunder (1 Sa. xii. 16-18); Isaiah had caused the shadow to go back ten degrees on the dial of Ahaz (Is. xxxviii. 8); and Moses had sent manna from heaven, Ex. xvi. 4; Jn. vi. 31. It is proper to say, that though Christ did not choose *then* to show such wonders, yet far more stupendous *signs from heaven* than these were exhibited at his death.

2, 3. *He answered*, &c. The meaning of this answer is, There are certain indications by which you judge about the weather. In the evening you think you can predict the weather to-morrow. You have evidence in the redness of the sky by which you judge. So there are sufficient indications on which you should judge concerning *me* and these times. My miracles, and the state of affairs in Judea, are an indication by which you should judge. ¶ *Is red.* Almost all nations have observed this as an indication of fair weather. ¶ *In the morning—the sky is red and lowering.* That is, there are threatening clouds in the sky, which are made red by the rays of the rising sun. This, in Judea, was a sign of a tempest. In other places, however, the signs of a storm may be different. ¶ *The face of the sky.* The *appearance* of the sky.

4. *A wicked and adulterous generation*, &c. See Notes on Mat. xii. 38-40. Mark adds (viii. 12) *that he sighed deeply in spirit.* He did not say this without feeling; he was greatly affected with their perverseness and obstinacy.

5-12. The account in these verses is also recorded in Mar. viii. 13-21.

5. *And when his disciples were come to the other side.* That is, to the other side of the Sea of Galilee. Mark says that he entered into a ship again, and departed to the other side. The conversation with the Pharisees and Sadducees had been on the western side of the Sea of Galilee. See Notes on ch. xv. 39. They crossed from that side again to the east. ¶ *Had forgotten to take bread.* That is, had forgotten to *lay in* a sufficient supply. They had, it seems, not more than one loaf, Mar. viii. 14.

8 *Which* when Jesus perceived, he said unto them, [e]O ye of little faith, why reason ye among yourselves because ye have brought no bread?

9 Do ye not yet understand, neither remember the [f]five loaves of the five thousand, and how many baskets ye took up?

10 Neither the [g]seven loaves of the four thousand, and how many baskets ye took up?

11 How is it that ye do not understand that I spake *it* not to you concerning bread, that ye should beware of the leaven of the Pharisees and of the Sadducees?

12 Then understood they how that he bade *them* not beware of the leaven of bread, but of [h]the doctrine of the Pharisees and of the Sadducees.

13 When Jesus came into the coasts of Cesarea Philippi, he

e ch.6.30; 8.26; 14.31. *f* ch.14.19,&c. *g* ch.15.34,&c. *h* ch.15.1-9.

6-11. *Take heed*, &c. That is, be cautious, be on your guard. ¶ *The leaven of the Pharisees and Sadducees.* Leaven is used in making bread. It passes secretly, silently, but certainly through the mass of dough. See Notes on ch. xiii. 33. None can see its progress. So it was with the doctrines of the Pharisees. They were insinuating, artful, plausible. They *concealed* the real tendency of their doctrines; they instilled them secretly into the mind, until they pervaded all the faculties like leaven. ¶ *They reasoned*, &c. The disciples did not understand him as referring to the doctrine of the Pharisees and Sadducees, because the word *leaven* was not often used among the Jews to denote *doctrines*, no other instance of this use of the word occurring in the Scriptures. Besides, the Jews had many particular rules about the *leaven* which might be used in making bread. Many held that it was not lawful to eat bread made by the Gentiles; and the disciples, perhaps, supposed that he was cautioning them not to procure a supply from the Pharisees and Sadducees. ¶ *O ye of little faith!* Jesus, in reply, said that they should not be so anxious about the supply of their temporal wants. *They should not have supposed, after the miracles that he had wrought in feeding so many*, that HE would caution them to be *anxious* about procuring *bread* for their necessities. It was improper, then, for them to reason about a thing like that, but they should have supposed that he referred to something more important. The miracles had been full proof that he could supply all their wants without such anxiety.

12. *Then understood they*, &c. After this explanation they immediately saw that he referred to the *doctrines* of the Pharisees and Sadducees. Erroneous doctrines are like *leaven* in the following respects: 1st. They are at first slight and unimportant in appearance, as leaven is small in quantity as compared with the mass that is to be leavened. 2d. They are insinuated into the soul unawares and silently, and are difficult of detection. 3d. They act gradually. 4th. They act most certainly. 5th. They will pervade all the soul, and bring all the faculties under their control.

13-20. See also Mar. viii. 27-29, and Lu. ix. 18-20. ¶ *Cesarea Philippi.* There were two cities in Judea called Cesarea. One was situated on the borders of the Mediterranean (See Notes on Ac. viii. 40), and the other was the one mentioned here. This city was greatly enlarged and ornamented by Philip the tetrarch, son of Herod, and called Cesarea in honour of the Roman emperor, Tiberius Cæsar. To distinguish it from the other Cesarea the name of Philip was added to it, and it was called *Cesarea Philippi*, or *Cesarea of Philip.* It was situated in the boundaries of the tribe of Naphtali, at the foot of Mount Hermon. It is now called *Panias* or *Banias*, and contains about 200 houses, and is inhabited chiefly by Turks. The word *coasts* here—now usually applied to land in the vicinity of the sea—means *borders* or *regions.* He came into the part of the country which *appertained* to Cesarea Philippi. He was passing *northward* from the region of Bethsaida, on the coasts of Magdala (ch. xv. 39), where the transactions recorded in the previous verses had occurred. ¶ *When Jesus came.* The original is, *when Jesus was coming.* Mark says (viii. 27) that

asked his disciples, saying, [i]Whom do men say that I, the Son of man, am?

14 And they said, [k]Some *say that thou art* John the Baptist; some, Elias; and others, Jeremias, or one of the prophets.

15 He saith unto them, But whom say ye that I am?

16 And Simon Peter answered and said, [l]Thou art the Christ, the Son of the living God.

17 And Jesus answered and said unto him, Blessed art thou, Simon Bar-jona; [m]for flesh and blood hath not revealed *it* unto thee, [n]but my Father which is in heaven.

18 And I say also unto thee,

i Mar.8.27; Lu.9.18,&c. k ch.14.2; Lu.9.7-9.

l Ps.2.7; ch.14.33; Jn.1.49; Ac.9.20; He.1.2,5. m 1 Co.2.10; Ga.1.16; Ep.2.8. n 1 Jn.4.15; 5.20.

---

this conversation took place when they were *in the way*, and this idea should have been retained in translating Matthew. While in the way, Jesus took occasion to call their attention *to the truth that he was the Messiah.* This truth it was of much consequence that they should fully believe and understand; and it was important, therefore, that he should often learn their views, to establish them if right, and correct them if wrong. He began, therefore, by inquiring what was the common report respecting him. ¶ *Whom do men say*, &c. This passage has been variously rendered. Some have translated it, "Whom do men say that I am? the Son of man?" Others, "Whom do men say that I am—*I*, who am the Son of man—*i.e.* the Messiah?" The meaning is nearly the same. He wished to obtain the sentiments of the people respecting himself.

14. *And they said*, &c. See Notes on Mat. xi. 14. They supposed that he might be John the Baptist, as Herod did, risen from the dead. See Mat. xiv. 2. He performed many miracles, and strongly resembled John in his manner of life, and in the doctrines which he taught.

16. *And Simon Peter answered*, &c. Peter, expressing the views of the apostles, with characteristic forwardness answered the question proposed to them by Jesus: "Thou art the Christ, the Son of the living God." ¶ *The Christ.* The Messiah, the *Anointed* of God. See Notes on Mat. i. 1. ¶ *The Son.* That is, the Son by way of eminence—in a peculiar sense. See Notes on Mat. i. 17. This appellation was understood as implying divinity, Jn. x. 29-36. ¶ *Of the living God.* The term *living* was given to the true God to distinguish him from *idols*, that are dead, or lifeless—blocks and stones. He is also the Source of life, temporal, spiritual, and eternal. The term *living* is often given to him in the Old Testament, Jos. iii. 10; 1 Sa. xvii. 26, 36; Je. x. 9, 10, &c. In this noble confession Peter expressed the full belief of himself and of his brethren that he was the long-expected Messiah. Other men had very different opinions of him, but *they* were satisfied, and were not ashamed to confess it.

17. *And Jesus answered—Blessed art thou*, &c. Simon Bar-jona is the same as Simon *son of* Jona. *Bar* is a Syriac word signifying *son*. The father of Peter, therefore, was Jona, or Jonas, Jn. i. 42; xxi. 16, 17. ¶ *Blessed.* That is, happy, honoured, evincing a proper spirit, and entitled to the approbation of God. ¶ *For flesh and blood.* This phrase usually signifies *man* (see Ga. i. 16; Ep. vi. 12), and it has been commonly supposed that Jesus meant to say that *man* had not revealed it, but he seems rather to have referred to *himself.* "This truth you have not learned from my lowly appearance, from my human nature, from my apparent rank and standing in the world. You, Jews, were expecting to know the Messiah by his external splendour; his pomp and power *as a man;* but you have not learned me in this manner. I have shown no *such* indication of my Messiahship. Flesh and blood have not shown it. In spite of my appearance —my lowly state—my want of resemblance to what you have expected, you have learned it as of God." This they had been taught by his miracles, his instructions, and by the direct teachings of God on their minds. To *reveal* is to make known, or communicate something that was unknown or secret.

18. *And I say also unto thee, That thou art Peter.* The word *Peter*, in Greek, means a rock. It was given to Simon by Christ when he called him to be a disciple, Jn. i. 42. *Cephas* is a Syriac word, meaning the same as Peter—a

That thou art [o]Peter; and [p]upon this rock I will build my church; and [q]the gates of hell [r]shall not prevail against it.

o Jn.1.42. p Ep.2.20; Re.21.14. q Ps.9.13. r Is.54.17.

rock, or stone. The meaning of this phrase may be thus expressed: "Thou, in saying that I am the Son of God, hast called me by a name expressive of my true character. I, also, have given to *thee* a name expressive of your character. I have called you *Peter, a rock*, denoting firmness, solidity, stability, and your confession has shown that the name is appropriate. I see that you are worthy of the name, and will be a distinguished support of my religion." ¶ *And upon this rock*, &c. This passage has given rise to many different interpretations. Some have supposed that the word ROCK refers to Peter's *confession*, and that Jesus meant to say, upon this rock—this *truth* that thou hast confessed, that I am the Messiah—and upon confessions of this from all believers, I will build my church. Confessions like this shall be the test of piety, and in such confessions shall my church stand amid the flames of persecution, the fury *of the gates of hell*. Others have thought that Jesus referred to himself. Christ is called a *rock*, Is. xxviii. 16; 1 Pe. ii. 8. And it has been thought that he turned from Peter to himself, and said, "Upon this rock, this truth that I am the Messiah—*upon myself* as the Messiah, I will build my church." Both these interpretations, though plausible, seem forced upon the passage to avoid the main difficulty in it. Another interpretation is, that the word *rock* refers to *Peter himself*. This is the obvious meaning of the passage; and had it not been that the Church of Rome has abused it, and applied it to what was never intended, no other would have been sought for. "Thou art a rock. Thou hast shown thyself firm, and fit for the work of laying the foundation of the church. Upon thee will I build it. Thou shalt be highly honoured; thou shalt be *first* in making known the gospel to both Jews and Gentiles." This was accomplished. See Ac. ii. 14-36, where he *first* preached to the Jews, and Ac. x., where he preached the gospel to Cornelius and his neighbours, who were Gentiles. Peter had thus the honour of laying the foundation of the church among the Jews and Gentiles; and this is the plain meaning of this passage. See also Ga. ii. 9. But Christ did *not* mean, as the Roman Catholics say he did, to exalt Peter to supreme authority above all the other apostles, or to say that he was the *only one* on whom he would rear his church. See Ac. xv., where the advice of *James*, and not of *Peter*, was followed. See also Ga. ii. 11, where Paul withstood Peter to his face, because he was to be blamed—a thing which could not have happened if Christ, as the Roman Catholics say, meant that Peter should be absolute and infallible. More than all, it is not said here, or anywhere else in the Bible, that Peter should have infallible successors who would be the vicegerents of Christ and the head of the church. The whole meaning of the passage is this: "I will make you the honoured instrument of making known my gospel first to Jews and Gentiles, and will make you a firm and distinguished preacher in building my church." ¶ *Will build my church*. This refers to the custom of building in Judea on a *rock* or other very firm foundation. See Notes on Mat. vii. 24. The word *church* means literally those *called out*, and often means *an assembly* or *congregation*. See Ac. xix. 32, Gr.; Ac. vii. 38. It is applied to Christians as being *called out* from the world. It means sometimes the whole body of believers, Ep. i. 22; 1 Co. x. 32. This is its meaning in this place. It means, also, a particular society of believers worshipping in one place, Ac. viii. 1; ix. 31; 1 Co. i. 2, &c.; sometimes, also, a society in a single house, as Ro. xvi. 5. In common language it means the church *visible—i.e.* all who *profess* religion; or *invisible, i.e.* all who are real Christians, professors or not. ¶ *And the gates of hell*, &c. Ancient cities were surrounded by walls. In the *gates* by which they were entered were the principal places for holding courts, transacting business, and *deliberating* on public matters. See Notes on Mat. vii. 13. Comp. Notes on Job xxix. 7. See also De. xxii. 4; 1 Sa. iv. 18; Je. xxxvi. 10; Ge. xix. 1; Ps. lxix. 12; ix. 14; Pr. i. 21. The word *gates*, therefore, is used for *counsels, designs, machinations, evil purposes*. ¶ *Hell* means, here, the place of departed spirits, particularly *evil spirits;* and the meaning of the passage is, that all the

19 And I will give unto thee the keys of the kingdom of heaven: and [s]whatsoever thou shalt bind on earth shall be bound in heaven, and whatsoever thou shalt loose on earth shall be loosed in heaven.

20 Then [t]charged he his disciples that they should tell no man that he was Jesus the Christ.

21 From[u] that time forth began Jesus to show unto his disciples how that he must go unto Jeru-

s ch.18.18. *t* Mar.8.30. *u* Lu.9.22; 18.31; 24.6,7; 1 Co.15.3,4.

---

plots, stratagems, and *machinations* of the enemies of the church would not be able to overcome it—a promise that has been remarkably fulfilled.

19. *And I will give unto thee,* &c. A *key* is an instrument for opening a door. He that is in possession of it has the power of access, and has a general *care* of a house. Hence, in the Bible, a *key* is used as a symbol of superintendence—an emblem of power and authority. See Notes on Is. xxii. 22; Re. i. 18; iii. 7. The kingdom of heaven here means, doubtless, the church on earth. See Notes on Mat. iii. 2. When the Saviour says, therefore, he will give to Peter the keys of the kingdom of heaven, he means that he will make him *the instrument of opening the door of faith to the world*—the *first* to preach the gospel to both Jews and Gentiles. This was done, Ac. ii. 14–36, and x. The "power of the keys" was given, on this occasion, to Peter alone, *solely for this reason;* the power of "*binding* and loosing" on earth was given to the other apostles *with him.* See Mat. xviii. 18. The only pre-eminence, then, that Peter had was the honour of *first* opening the doors of the gospel to the world. ¶ *Whatsoever thou shalt bind,* &c. The phrase *to bind* and *to loose* was often used by the Jews. It meant *to prohibit* and *to permit.* To *bind* a thing was to forbid it; to *loose* it, to allow it to be done. Thus they said about gathering wood on the Sabbath day, "The school of Shammei *binds it*"—*i.e. forbids it;* "the school of Hillel *looses it*"—*i.e. allows it.* When Jesus gave this power to the apostles, he meant that whatsoever they *forbade* in the church should *have divine authority;* whatever they *permitted,* or commanded, should *also have divine authority*—that is, should be bound or loosed in heaven, or *meet the approbation of God.* They were to be guided infallibly in the organization of the church, 1st, by the teaching of Christ, and, 2d, by the teaching of the Holy Spirit.

This does not refer to *persons,* but to *things*—"*whatsoever,*" not *whosoever.* It refers to rites and ceremonies in the church. Such of the Jewish customs as they should forbid were to be forbidden, and such as they thought proper to permit were to be allowed. Such rites as *they* should appoint in the church were to have the force of divine authority. Accordingly, they commanded the Gentile converts to "abstain from pollutions of idols, and from fornication, and from things strangled, and from blood" (Ac. xv. 20); and, in general, they organized the church, and directed what was to be observed and what was to be avoided. The rules laid down by them in the Acts of the Apostles and in the Epistles, in connection with the teachings of the Saviour as recorded in the evangelists, constitute the *only* law binding on Christians in regard to the order of the church, and the rites and ceremonies to be observed in it.

20. *Then charged,* &c. That is, he *commanded* them. Mark (viii. 30) and Luke (ix. 21) say (Greek) that he *strictly* or *severely* charged them. He laid emphasis on it, as a matter of much importance. The reason of this seems to be that his time had not fully come; that he was not willing to rouse the Jewish malice, and to endanger his life, by having it proclaimed that he was the Messiah. The word *Jesus* is wanting in many manuscripts, and should probably be omitted: "Then he charged them strictly to tell no man that he was *the Christ* or *Messiah.*"

21–23. See also Mar. vii. 31–33; Lu. ix. 22. *From that time forth.* This was the first intimation that he gave that he was to die in this cruel manner. He had taken much pains to convince them that he was the Messiah; he saw by the confession of Peter that they *were* convinced, and he *then* began to prepare their minds for the awful event which was before him. Had he declared this when he first called them they would never have followed him. Their minds were not prepared for it. They expected a temporal, triumphant prince as the Messiah. He *first,* therefore, con-

salem, and suffer many things of the elders, and chief priests, and scribes, and be killed, and be raised again the third day.

22 Then Peter took him, and began to rebuke him, saying, [1]Be it far from thee, Lord: this shall not be unto thee.

23 But he turned and said unto Peter, Get thee behind me, [v]Satan; thou art [w]an offence unto me: for thou savourest not the things that be of God, but those that be of men.

24 Then said Jesus unto his disciples, [x]If any *man* will come after me, let him deny himself, and take up his cross, and follow me.

25 For[y] whosoever will save his life shall lose it, and whosoever will lose his life for my sake shall find it.

26 For what is a man profited if

1 *Pity thyself.*
v 2 Sa.19.22. *w* Ro.14.13.

x ch.10.38; Mar.8.34; Lu.9.23; 14.27; Ac.14.22; 1 Th.3.3. *y* Jn.12.25; Es.4.14.

vinced them that he was the Christ, and then, with great prudence, began to correct their apprehensions of the proper character of the Messiah. ¶ *Elders.* The men of the great council or Sanhedrim. See Notes on Mat. v. 7. ¶ *Chief priests and scribes.* See Notes on Mat. iii. 7.

22. *Then Peter took him.* This may mean either that he interrupted him, or that he took him aside, or that he *took him by the hand* as a friend. This latter is probably the true meaning. Peter was strongly attached to him. He could not bear to think of his death. He expected, moreover, that he would be the triumphant Messiah. In his ardour, and confidence, and strong attachment, he seized him by the hand as a friend, and said, "Be it *far* from thee." This phrase might have been translated, "God be merciful to thee; this shall not be unto thee." It expressed Peter's strong desire that it *might* not be. The word *rebuke* here means to *admonish* or *earnestly to entreat*, as in Lu. xvii. 3. It does not mean that Peter assumed *authority* over Christ, but that *he earnestly expressed his wish that it might not be so.* Even this was improper. He should have been submissive, and not have interfered.

23. *Get thee behind me, Satan.* The word Satan means literally an *adversary*, or one that opposes us in the accomplishment of our designs. It is applied to the devil commonly, as the *opposer* or *adversary* of man; but there is no evidence that the Lord Jesus meant to apply this term to Peter, as signifying that *he* was Satan or the devil, or that he used the term in anger. He may have used it in the *general* sense which the word bore as an *adversary* or *opposer;* and the meaning may be, that such sentiments as Peter expressed then were *opposed* to him and his plans. His interference was improper. His views and feelings stood in the way of the accomplishment of the Saviour's designs. There was, undoubtedly, a *rebuke* in this language, for the conduct of Peter was improper; but the idea which is commonly attached to it, and which, perhaps, our translation conveys, implies a more severe and harsh rebuke than the Saviour intended, and than the language which he used would express. ¶ *Thou art an offence.* That is, a stumbling-block. Your advice and wishes are *in my way.* If followed, they would *prevent* the very thing for which I came. ¶ *Thou savourest not.* Literally, *thou thinkest not upon;* or your language and spirit are not such as spring from a supreme regard to the will of God, or from proper views of him, but such as spring from the common views entertained by men. *You* think that those things should *not* be done which *God* wishes to be done. You judge of this matter as *men* do who are desirous of honour; and not as *God*, who sees it best that I should die, to promote the great interests of mankind.

24–28. This discourse is also recorded in Mar. viii. 34–38; ix. 1; and Lu. ix. 23–27. ¶ *Let him deny himself.* That is, let him surrender to God his will, his affections, his body, and his soul. Let him not seek his own happiness as the supreme object, but be willing to renounce all, and lay down his *life* also, if required. ¶ *Take up his cross.* See Notes on Mat. x. 38.

25. *Whosoever will save his life*, &c. See Notes on Mat. x. 39.

26. *For what is a man profited*, &c.

he shall gain the whole world and lose his own soul? or [z]what shall a man give in exchange for his soul?

27 For[a] the Son of man shall come in the glory of his Father, with his angels, and [b]then he shall reward every man according to his works.

28 Verily I say unto you, [c]There be some standing here which shall not [d]taste of death till they see the Son of man coming in his kingdom.

z Ps.49.7,8. a Da.7.9,10; Zec.14.5; Jude 14. b Re.22.12. c Mar.9.1. d He.2.9.

To gain the whole world means to possess it as our own—all its riches, its honours, and its pleasures. *To lose his own soul* means to be cast away, to be shut out from heaven, to be sent to hell. Two things are implied by Christ in these questions: 1st. That they who are striving to gain the world, and are unwilling to give it up for the sake of religion, will lose their souls; and, 2d. That if the soul *is* lost, nothing can be given in exchange for it, or that it can never afterward be saved. There is no redemption in hell.

27. *For the Son of man*, &c. That is, he will return to judge the world. He will come in glory—the glory of his Father—the majesty with which God is accustomed to appear, and which befits God. He will be attended by angels. He will judge all men. ¶ *Reward.* The word *reward* means recompense. He will deal with them according to their character. The righteous he will reward in heaven with glory and happiness. The wicked he will send to hell, as a reward or recompense for their evil works. This fact, *that he will come to judgment*, he gives as a reason why we should be willing to deny ourselves and follow him. Even though it should be *now* attended with contempt and suffering, yet *then* he will *reward* his followers for all their shame and sorrow, and receive them to his kingdom. He adds (Mar. viii. 38), that if we are ashamed of him here, he will be ashamed of us there. That is, if we reject and disown *him* here, he will reject and disown *us* there.

28. *Verily I say unto you*, &c. To encourage them, he assured them that, though his kingdom was now obscure and despised—though he was cast out and little known—yet the time was near when *he* would be regarded in a different manner, and his kingdom be established with great power. This cannot refer to the end of the world, and there is no need of referring it to the destruction of Jerusalem. ¶ *Taste of death.* That is, *die.* Before they die they shall see this. ¶ *Son of man coming in his kingdom.* Mark and Luke have explained this: Mar. ix. 1, "Until they have seen the kingdom of God come with power;" Lu. ix. 27, "Till they see the kingdom of God." The meaning evidently is, till they shall see my kingdom, *i.e.* my church, now small, feeble, and despised, greatly enlarged, established, and spreading with great rapidity and extent. All this was accomplished. All these apostles, except Judas, lived to see the wonders of the day of Pentecost; some of them, John particularly, saw the Jewish nation scattered, the temple destroyed, the gospel established in Asia, Rome, Greece, and in a large part of the known world.

REMARKS.

1st. Men will often judge far more correctly about natural than about spiritual things, ver. 1–3. In respect to natural objects they are watchful. In them they feel a deep interest, and they watch for every *sign* that may affect their interest. They are too much concerned to judge falsely. But they feel no such interest in religious things. Hence it happens that men who have good sense and much wisdom in regard to worldly concerns, are often exceedingly foolish in regard to religion. They believe reports respecting religion, revivals, and missions, which they would despise on any other subject. They read and believe newspapers and other publications, which they would hold in contempt on any other topic but religion. They give a degree of weight to arguments *against* the Bible, and *against* the doctrines of the gospel, to which they would attach little or no importance on any other subject. They sustain themselves in infidelity by arguments which they would regard as of no force if the same kind of reasoning was urged in defence of anything else.

2d. It is of importance to watch the

signs of the times, ver. 3. In the days of Christ it was the duty of the people to look at the evidence that he was the Messiah. The proofs were clear that he was the Messiah. It is also important to look at the signs of the times in which we live. They are clear also. Much is doing; and the diffusion of the Bible, the labours among the heathen, the distribution of tracts, and perhaps, above all, the institution of Sabbath-schools, betoken an eventful age, and are an indication that brighter days are about to dawn on the world. We should watch these signs that we may rejoice; that we may pray with more fervour, and that we may do *our* part to advance the kingdom of God. Little children should grow up believing that they live in an important age; that they enjoy many peculiar privileges, and that they *may* and *must* do much to spread the gospel through the earth. Even *when* children, they should pray, and they should give to benefit others; and, most of all, they should give *themselves* to Christ, that they may benefit others with a right spirit.

3d. Sinners should be addressed with deep feeling and faithfulness, Mar. viii. 12. Jesus *sighed deeply*. So should we. We should not be harsh, or sour, or cold and unfeeling when we address our fellow-men about eternity. We should weep over them, and pray for them, and speak to them, not as if we were better than they, but with an earnest desire for their salvation. Comp. Ac. xx. 31; Phi. iii. 18.

4th. Men easily mistake plain instruction, ver. 7. And especially is this the case where there is any chance of giving a worldly turn to the instruction. If men's thoughts—even those of Christians—were more off from the world, and they thought less of the supply of their temporal wants, they would understand the truths of religion much better than they do. No man can understand the doctrines of religion aright whose principal concern is what he shall eat, and drink, and wear. Hence even Christians are often strangely ignorant of the plainest truths of religion; and hence the importance of teaching those truths to children before their thoughts become engrossed by the world; and hence, too, the importance of Sabbath-schools.

5th. We should not have undue anxiety about the supply of our wants. Christ supplied many thousands by a word, and he can easily supply us, ver. 9–12.

6th. We should learn, from his past goodness, to trust him for the future, ver. 9–12.

7th. We should be on our guard against error, ver. 11. It is sly, artful, plausible, working secretly, but effectually. We should always be cautious of what we believe, and examine it by the word of God. False doctrines are often made as much *like* the truth as possible, for the very purpose of deceiving. "Satan himself is transformed into an angel of light," 2 Cor. xi. 14.

8th. It is important to ascertain our views of Christ, ver. 13–15. Our all depends on this. If we do not think and feel right respecting him we cannot be safe. We should often, then, ask ourselves—we should ask one another—what we think of Christ.

9th. It is our duty to profess attachment to Christ. It should be done boldly, and always, ver. 16. We should never be ashamed of him. And to do this, we should always, *in our own hearts*, believe that he *is* the Christ, the Son of the living God.

10th. We should esteem it a great happiness and honour to be enabled thus to show our attachment to him. The world may not honour us, but God will, and will pronounce us blessed, ver. 17.

11th. God only reveals to men right views of Christ, ver. 17. This he does by his word and Spirit. We should, then, search the Bible; and we should pray much that God would *reveal his Son in us*, and enable us boldly to confess him before men.

12th. The church is safe, ver. 18. It may be small—it may be feeble—it may weep much—it may be much opposed and ridiculed—it may have mighty enemies—the rich and the great may set themselves against it—but it is safe. It is founded on a rock. Its enemies shall never be able to overcome it. Jesus has promised it, and in all ages he has shown that he has remembered his promise. It has not been suffered to become extinct. It has been persecuted, opposed, ridiculed, and almost driven from the world; but *a few* have been found who have loved the Lord; and soon the flame has kindled, and the church has shone forth "fair as the sun, clear as the moon, and terrible as an army with banners." So it is still. Feeble churches may mourn

CHAPTER XVII.

AND[a] after six days Jesus taketh Peter, James, and John his brother, and bringeth them up into a high mountain apart,

2 And was transfigured before

a Mar.9.2,&c.; Lu.9.28,&c.

---

much—iniquity may abound—the few pious people may weep in secret places; but Jesus hears their groans and counts their tears, and they and the church *are safe*. *He* is their friend, and all the powers of hell shall not prevail against his church.

13th. The importance of prudence in delivering truth, ver. 21. It should be well-timed—it should be when people are prepared to receive it. Especially is this true of young converts. They have need of milk, and not of strong meat. They should not be surprised that many doctrines of the Bible are mysterious now; but they may fully comprehend them hereafter. Peter, a young convert, did not understand the plain doctrine that Jesus must die for sin; yet it was afterward clear to him, and most cordially he loved it.

14th. It is highly wicked and improper to attempt to counsel God, or to think that we understand things better than he does, ver. 22, 23. His plan is the best plan; and though it does not fall in with *our* views of wisdom, yet we should be still. It is all wise. What he does we know not now, yet we shall know hereafter.

15th. We see what religion requires, ver. 24. We must deny ourselves. We must submit to trials. We must do our duty. We must welcome persecution, Mat. v. 10. We must be, in all places, among all men, and in every employment, *Christians*, no matter what may happen. Come poverty, disease, persecution, death, it is ours to take up the cross and do our duty. So apostles, and martyrs, and the Saviour himself have gone before us, and *we* must follow in their steps.

> "Shall I be carried to the skies
> On flowery beds of ease,
> While others fought to win the prize,
> And sailed through bloody seas?
>
> "Sure I must fight if I would reign;
> Increase my courage, Lord,
> To bear the cross, endure the shame,
> Supported by thy word."

16th. How foolish are the men of this world! ver. 26. In a little time how worthless will be all their wealth! It is gained by anxiety, and toil, and tears. It never satisfies. It harasses them with constant care. It smooths no wrinkles on their brow, alleviates no pain when they are sick, saves no friend from death, gives no consolation in regard to the future, and may be left at any moment. Others will soon possess, and perhaps scatter in dissipation, what they have obtained by so much toil. See Ps. xxxix. 6. And while they scatter or enjoy it, where shall the soul of him be who spent all his probation to obtain it? Alas! lost, lost, lost—for ever lost! and no wealth, no man, no devil, no angel, can redeem him, or be given *for* his soul. The harvest will be past, the summer ended, and he not saved. In *gaining* the world he made two things certain—disappointment and trouble here, and an eternity of woe hereafter. How foolish and wicked is man!

17th. The righteous should rejoice that Jesus will come again to our world. He will reward them, ver. 27. He will come as their friend, and they shall ascend with him to heaven.

18th. The wicked should weep and wail that Jesus will come again to our world. He will punish them for their crimes, ver. 27. They cannot escape. See Re. i. 7.

19th. It will not be long before he will come, ver. 28. At anyrate, it will not be long before *we* shall meet him. Death is near; and then we must stand before him, and give an account of the deeds done in the body.

CHAPTER XVII.

1-9. See also Mar. ix. 2-10; Lu. ix. 28-36.

1. *And after six days*. That is, six days from the conversation recorded in the last chapter. Luke (ix. 28) says, about an eight days after. Matthew mentions the six days that intervened between the day of the conversation and the transfiguration. Luke *includes* both those days, and thus reckons eight. Besides, Luke does not pretend to fix the precise time. He says, "*about* an eight days after." ¶ *Taketh Peter, and James, and John*. These three disciples were with him, also, in the garden of Gethsemane, Mar. xiv. 33. He designed to fit them in an eminent degree for the work of the gospel ministry by the previous manifestations of his glory, and of his

them: and [b]his face did shine as the sun, and his raiment was white as the light.

3 And, behold, there appeared unto them Moses and Elias, talking with him.

4 Then answered Peter, and said unto Jesus, Lord, it is good

b Re.1.16.

patience in suffering. ¶ *Into a high mountain apart.* That is, *apart* from the other disciples. It is commonly supposed that this was Mount Tabor, a high mountain in Galilee. The name of the mountain is not, however, mentioned in the New Testament. Luke adds (ix. 28) that he went up there *to pray.* Our Saviour prayed much. When he did it he chose to be alone. For this purpose he often ascended mountains or went into the deserts. There is something in the solitude and deep and awful stillness of a lofty mountain favourable to devotion.

2. *And was transfigured before them.* The word *transfigure* means *to change the appearance or form.* It does not denote the change of the *substance* of a thing, but simply of its *appearance.* It puts on a new aspect. What this change was we are expressly told. 1st. His face shone as the sun; that is, with a peculiar brightness. A similar appearance is described respecting Moses when he came down from the mount, Ex. xxxiv. 29, 30. See also He. i. 3, where Christ is called the brightness of the glory of God; in the original, the *splendour* or *shining,* like the brightness of the sun. 2d. The second change was that of his garments. They were white as the light. Mark says, "exceeding white as snow; so as no fuller on earth could white them." The word "fuller" means, commonly, one who dresses cloth or *fulls* it, so as to make it more thick and strong. Here it means one who *bleaches* cloth or makes it white; one who cleanses garments when by wearing they become soiled. Among the Greeks that was a distinct trade. Luke says, "white *and* glistering;" that is, resplendent, shining, or a very bright white. There is no evidence here that what is commonly said of him is true, that his *body* was so changed as to show what his glorified body is. His body, so far as the sacred writers inform us, underwent no change. All this splendour and glory was a change *in appearance* only. The Scriptures should be taken *just as they are,* without any attempt to affix a meaning to them which the sacred writers did not intend. ¶ *Raiment.* Clothing. John may refer to this transfiguration in ch. i. 14, as Peter does in his second epistle, i. 16, 17.

3. *And behold there appeared unto them Moses and Elias.* Moses, a distinguished servant of God, by whom the *law* was given, and whose institutions typified the Messiah. It was particularly proper that *he* should appear, when his prophecies and types were about to be fulfilled, and the rites which he had instituted were about to be done away. Elias, or Elijah, a distinguished prophet, taken to heaven without seeing death. See 2 Ki. ii. 11. Elijah had been honoured eminently by being thus translated, and still more by being made the *model* of the forerunner of the Messiah, Mal. iv. 5; Lu. i. 17; Mat. xi. 14. They appeared "in glory" (Lu. ix. 31); *i.e.* as they are *in heaven*—with the glory which the redeemed have there. ¶ *Talking with him.* Luke (ix. 31) informs us that they conversed about "his decease which he should accomplish at Jerusalem." To redeemed spirits that death was an object of intense interest. By faith in that death they had been saved; and now that the Redeemer of mankind was about to die, it is no wonder that this was the burden of his and their thoughts.

Luke adds (ix. 32) that "Peter and they that were with him were heavy with sleep." It is not improbable that this was in the night; that Jesus was engaged in prayer; and that he had *permitted* his weary followers to compose themselves to rest. It was after they were awaked that they saw this vision. Probably the sudden splendour, the bright shining aroused them from sleep.

4. *Let us make here three tabernacles.* A tabernacle is a *tent.* It was made, commonly, by fixing posts into the ground, and stretching on them cloth fastened by cords. See Notes on Is. xxxiii. 20. In some instances they were made of branches of trees—a temporary shelter from the sun and rain, not a permanent dwelling. Peter was rejoiced at the vision and desirous of continuing it. He proposed, therefore, that they should prolong this interview and dwell

for us to be here: if thou wilt, let us make here three tabernacles; one for thee, and one for Moses, and one for Elias.

5 While he yet spake, behold, a bright cloud overshadowed them: and behold [c]a voice out of the cloud, which said, This is my beloved Son, [d]in whom I am well pleased; [e]hear ye him.

6 And when the disciples heard it, they fell on their face, and were sore afraid.

7 And Jesus came and [f]touched them, and said, Arise, and be not afraid.

8 And when they had lifted up their eyes, they saw no man, save Jesus only.

9 And as they came down from the mountain, Jesus charged them, saying, Tell the vision to no man

c ch.3.17; Mar.1.11; Lu.3.22; 2 Pe.1.17.
d Is.42.1,21. e De.18.15,19; Ac.3.22,23; He.1.1,2; 2.1-3.
f Da.10.10,18; Re.1.17.

---

there. Mark adds, "For he wist not [that is, knew not] what to say, for they were sore afraid." They were frightened, amazed, and rejoiced; and, in the ecstasy of the moment, Peter proposed to remain there.

5. *A bright cloud overshadowed them.* The word *overshadow* here means, rather, to *be diffused* or *spread* over them. It does not mean that it made *a shade.* A cloud was the symbol of the divine presence. Thus God went before the Israelites in a cloudy pillar—dark by day and bright by night (Ex. xiv. 19, 20); he appeared on Mount Sinai in a cloud bright by fire (Ex. xxiv. 15–17); and a *cloud,* the symbol of the divine presence—called the *Shechinah*—dwelt continually in the most holy place in the temple, 1 Ki. viii. 10, 11; Eze. i. 4; x. 4. When, therefore, the disciples saw this cloud, they were prepared to hear the word of the Lord. ¶ *This is my beloved Son.* This was the voice of God. This was the second time that, in a remarkable manner, God had declared this. See Mat. iii. 17. This was spoken to confirm the disciples; to make known to them that it was their duty to hear Christ rather than any other, and to honour *him* more than Moses and Elijah; and to strengthen their faith in him when they should go forth to preach the gospel after he was shamefully put to death. After this, it was impossible for them to doubt that he was truly the Son of God. See 2 Pe. i. 17, 18.

6. *They fell on their face.* They entered into the cloud, or the cloud enveloped them, Lu. ix. 34. They were therefore afraid. They were awed at the presence of God, and prostrated themselves in solemn adoration on the ground, and their fears were removed only by the voice of their beloved Master. No man can see God and live; and it is only the glory of God, as it shines in the face of Christ (see 2 Co. iv. 6), that mortals can bear.

9. *Tell the vision to no man.* This vision was designed particularly to confirm them in the truth that he was the Messiah. While he was with them it was unnecessary that they should relate what they had seen. When he was crucified they would need this evidence that he was the Christ. Then they were to use it. There were three witnesses of it—as many as the law required (De. xvii. 6; He. x. 28), and the proof that he was the Messiah was clear. Besides, if they had told it then, it would have provoked the Jews and endangered his life. His time was not yet come. ¶ *Vision.* Sight; appearance. What they had seen on the mount. ¶ *Charged them.* Gave them a commandment.

The *sole* design of this transfiguration was to convince them that he was the Christ; that he was greater than the greatest of the prophets; that he was the Son of God.

Mark adds (ix. 10), "they kept that saying with themselves, questioning one with another what the rising from the dead should mean." The Pharisees believed that the dead would rise, and there is no doubt that the disciples believed it; but their views were not clear, and, in particular, they did not understand what he meant by *his* rising from the dead. They do not appear to have understood, though he had told them (ch. xii. 40) that he would rise after three days.

10–13. See also Mar. ix. 11–13. *Why then say the scribes,* &c. The disciples appear to have been satisfied now that he was the Messiah. The *transfigura-*

until the Son of man be risen again from the dead.

10 And his disciples asked him, saying, [g]Why then say the scribes that Elias must first come?

11 And Jesus answered and said unto them, Elias truly shall first come, and restore all things.

12 But I say unto you, That Elias is come already, and they knew him not, but have done unto him whatsoever they listed. Likewise [h]shall also the Son of man suffer of them.

13 Then the disciples understood that he spake unto them of John the Baptist.

14 And[i] when they were come

g Mal.4.5,6; ch.11.14. h ch.16.21. i Mar.9.14,&c.; Lu.9.37,&c.

tion had taken away all their doubts, but they recollected that it was a common doctrine among the Jews that *Elijah* would appear before the Messiah came, and they did not then recollect that he had appeared. To this difficulty the word *then* refers. "We are satisfied that thou art the Christ, but Elijah has not yet come, as was expected; what, then, is the meaning of the common opinions of our learned men, the scribes? Were they right or wrong in their expectation of Elijah?" See Notes on Mat. xi. 14.

11. *Elias truly shall first come, and restore all things.* He did not mean by this that Elijah *was yet* to come, for he tells them immediately (ver. 12) that he *had* come; but he meant to affirm that it was *a true doctrine* which the scribes taught, that Elijah *would* appear before the coming of the Messiah. *To restore* means to put into the former situation. See Mat. xii. 13. Hence it means *to heal, to correct, to put in proper order.* Here it means that Elijah would put things in a proper state; he would be the instrument of *reforming* the people, or of *restoring* them, in some measure, to proper notions about the Messiah and preparing them for his coming. Before the coming of John their views were erroneous, their expectations worldly, and their conduct exceedingly depraved. He corrected many of their notions about the Messiah (see Mat. iii.), and was the instrument of an extensive reformation, and thus *restored* them, in some degree, to correct views of their own economy and of the Messiah, and to a preparation for his advent.

12. *Elias is come already.* That is, John the Baptist has come, in the spirit and power of Elias. See Lu. i. 17. ¶ *They have done unto him whatsoever they listed.* The word *list* is an old English word, signifying *to choose,* to desire, to be inclined. See Jn. iii. 8. It means, here, that they had done to John as they pleased; that is, they had put him to death, Mat. xiv. 10.

Mark adds (ix. 12) that Jesus told them that it was "written of the Son of man that he must suffer many things, and be set at naught." This was written of him particularly in Is. liii. To be set at naught is to be esteemed as worthless or as nothing; to be cast out and despised. No prophecy was ever more strikingly fulfilled. See Lu. xxiii. 11.

14–21. This narrative, with some additions, is found in Mar. ix. 14–29, and Lu. ix. 37–43.

14. *And when they were come to the multitude.* This took place on the day following the transfiguration, Lu. ix. 37. This multitude was probably composed of persons who had attended on his ministry, many of whom were his real disciples. *With them,* as Mark (ix. 15) informs us, were "scribes questioning with them." That is, they were probably *professedly* making inquiries about the Saviour, but *really* attempting to introduce their own sentiments, and to draw them off from him. They probably artfully asked them many questions about his birth, his family, his appearance, his manner of life, and his instructions, all which were contrary to the general expectation respecting the Messiah, and they intended, therefore, to insinuate that *such* a person could not be the Christ. The people were persuaded that he was the Messiah, and it would not have done to have attacked their opinions openly, but they attempted to gain the same point by sly insinuations. Error is always subtle, and often puts on the appearance of calm and honest inquiry. Well had he compared them to *leaven*, Mat. xvi. 11, 12. The multitude, seeing Jesus coming down, left the scribes, and ran to meet him (Mark). They were *amazed*, probably because they had not expected to see him there. In their joy at meeting him in this unexpected manner,

to the multitude, there came to him a *certain* man kneeling down to him, and saying,

15 Lord, have mercy on my son; for he is lunatic, and sore vexed; for ofttimes he falleth into the fire, and oft into the water.

16 And I brought him to thy disciples, and they could not cure him.

17 Then Jesus answered and said, O faithless and perverse generation! how long shall I be with

---

they *saluted* him (Mark); that is, probably they prostrated themselves before him after the manner of salutation in Eastern countries. See Notes on Lu. x. 4. Jesus, seeing the scribes and their artful design, reproved them by asking them *why* they questioned thus with his disciples, Mar. ix. 16. Conscious of their guilt and their base purpose, they returned no answer. ¶ *A certain man kneeling down to him.* That is, *saluting* him, or showing high regard for him. See Notes on Lu. x. 4. It did not imply religious homage, but merely high respect and earnest entreaty.

15. *Lord, have mercy.* The word Lord here means *Sir*, a title of civility, not implying divinity. ¶ *My son.* This was an only son (Luke). He was possessed with a devil. This calamity was attended with the following symptoms: he was *lunatic* (see Notes on Mat. iv. 24); he was sore vexed; that is, he suffered greatly, or was greatly afflicted; he fell often suddenly, in the manner of persons having epileptic fits; he was dumb—that is, he was dumb except when the fit was *coming on him*, for Luke says that when the spirit took him he cried suddenly out; he foamed and gnashed with his teeth, and wasted away, or became poor and emaciated. Luke (ix. 39) adds of the evil spirit, "it teareth him that he foameth again, and, bruising him, hardly departeth from him;" that is, scarcely departed from him, or he had only short intervals of reason, for so the passage in Luke, "bruising him, hardly departeth from him," should be translated.

16. *And I brought him to thy disciples*, &c. That is, not to the apostles, for they had power over unclean spirits (Mat. x. 8), but to others of his followers who attempted to work miracles. It is probable that many of his disciples attempted this who were not personal attendants on his ministry, Mar. ix. 38.

17. *Then Jesus answered and said, O faithless and perverse generation! Perverse* means that which is *twisted* or *turned* from the proper direction; and is often used of the *eyes*, when one or both are turned from their natural position. Applied to a *generation* or *race* of men, it means that they hold opinions *turned* or *perverted* from the truth, and that they were wicked in their conduct. Jesus applied this, probably, to the Jews, and not to his real disciples. ¶ *How long shall I suffer you?* That is, how long shall I bear with you? How long is it necessary to show such patience and forbearance with your unbelief and perversity? This was not so much an expression of impatience or complaint as a reproof for their being so slow to believe that he was the Messiah, notwithstanding his miracles.

Mark adds (ix. 20–22) that when he that was possessed was brought, the spirit, by a last desperate struggle, threw him down and tore him, and left him apparently dead. He adds farther, that the case had existed during the whole life of his son, from a child. This was a case of uncommon obstinacy. The affliction was fixed and lasting. The disciples, seeing the obstinacy of the case—seeing him dumb, wasted away, torn, and foaming—despaired of being able to cure him. They lacked the *faith* which was necessary; *doubted* whether they could cure him, and *therefore* could not.

The father of the child said (Mar. ix. 22), "*If thou canst do anything*, have compassion on us and help us;" an expression implying a weak faith, a lingering doubt whether he *could* restore him. Jesus replied to this, "*If thou canst* BELIEVE, all things are possible to him that believeth" (Mar. ix. 23); implying that the difficulty in the case was *not* that he could not heal him, but that he had not the proper kind and degree of faith with which to come to him. That is, this cure shall be effected if you have faith. Not that *his* faith would give Jesus the *power* to heal him, but it *would render it proper* that he should exert that power in his favour. In this way, and in this only, are all things possible to believers.

you? how long shall I suffer you? Bring him hither to me.

18 And Jesus rebuked the devil, and he departed out of him: and the child was cured from that very hour.

19 Then came the disciples to Jesus apart, and said, Why could not we cast him out?

20 And Jesus said unto them, Because[k] of your unbelief: for verily I say unto you, [l]If ye have faith as a grain of mustard-seed, ye shall say unto this mountain, Remove hence to yonder place, and it shall remove; and nothing shall be impossible unto you.

21 Howbeit, this kind goeth not out but by prayer and fasting.

22 And [m]while they abode in Galilee, Jesus said unto them, The Son of man shall be betrayed into the hands of men;

23 And they shall kill him, and

k He.3.19.
l ch.21.21; Mar.11.23; Lu.17.6; 1 Co.13.2.
m ch.16.21; 20.17; Mar.8.31; 9.30,31; 10.33; Lu.9.22,44; 18.31; 24.6,26,46.

The man had faith, Mar. ix. 24. The father came, as a father *should* do, weeping, and praying that his faith might be increased, so as to make it *proper* that Jesus should interpose in his behalf, and save his child.

Help my unbelief, Mar. ix. 24. This was an expression of humility. If my faith is defective, supply what is lacking. Help me to overcome my unbelief. Let not the defect of my faith be in the way of this blessing.

18. *And Jesus rebuked the devil.* The word *rebuke* has the combined force of *reproving* and *commanding*. He *reproved* him for having afflicted the child, and he *commanded* him to come out of him. Mark (ix. 25) has recorded the words which he used—words implying reproof and command: "Thou dumb and deaf spirit, I charge thee come out of him, and enter no more into him." And the spirit cried, and with a mighty convulsion came out, leaving the child apparently dead. Jesus lifted him up by the hand (Mark), and gave him to his father (Luke).

19. *Then came the disciples*, &c. This inquiry was made in some house to which they retired near the place where the miracle was performed (Mark). Jesus told them, in reply, that it was because of their unbelief that they had not been able to cast him out. They were appalled by the difficulty of the case and the obstinacy of the disease. Their *faith* would not have made it more easy for God to work this miracle, but such was his *will*—such the way in which he worked miracles, that he required faith in those who were the instruments.

20. *As a grain of mustard-seed.* See Notes on Mat. xiii. 31, 32. The mustard-seed was the smallest of all seeds. It has been supposed by some, therefore, that he meant to say, If you have the smallest or feeblest faith that is genuine, you can do all things. The mustard-seed produced the largest of all herbs. It has been supposed by others, therefore, to mean, If you have increasing, expanding, enlarged faith, growing and strengthening from small beginnings, you can perform the most difficult undertaking. There is a principle of vitality in the grain of seed stretching forward to great results, which illustrates the nature of faith. Your faith should be *like* that. This is probably the true meaning. ¶ *Ye shall say unto this mountain*, &c. Probably he pointed to a mountain near, to assure them that if they had such faith they might accomplish the most difficult undertakings—things that at first would appear impossible.

21. *Howbeit, this kind*, &c. This *kind* means this kind of devils—this species of possession. Where they have had long possession—where they produce such painful, fixed, and alarming effects, they can be expelled only in connection with prayer and fasting. ¶ *Goeth not out but by prayer and fasting.* That is, in order to work miracles of this kind—to cast out devils in cases so obstinate and dreadful as this, *faith of the highest kind is necessary.* That faith is produced and kept vigorous only by much prayer, and by such abstinence from food as fits the mind for the highest exercises of religion, and leaves it free to hold communion with God.

22, 23. See also Mar. ix. 30–33; Lu. ix. 43–45. *And while they abode in Galilee.* Galilee, the northern part of Palestine. See Notes on Mat. ii. 22. ¶ *The Son of man shall be betrayed*, &c.

the third day he shall be raised again. And they were exceeding sorry.

24 And when they were come to Capernaum, they that received tribute-*money*[1] came to Peter, and said, Doth not your master pay tribute?

25 He saith, Yes. And when he was come into the house, Jesus prevented him, saying, What thinkest thou, Simon? of whom do the kings of the earth take custom or tribute? of their own children, or of strangers?

26 Peter saith unto him, Of strangers. Jesus saith unto him, Then are the children free.

[1] *didrachma*, in value 15*d*., Ex.38.26.

To betray means to deliver up in a treacherous manner. This was done by Judas Iscariot, called for that act the traitor, Mat. xxvi. 14-16, 47-50. A traitor, or betrayer, is one who makes use of confidence reposed in him for the purpose of delivering him up who puts that confidence in him to the hands of enemies.

23. *And they shall kill him, and the third day he shall be raised again.* See Mat. xii. 40. Mark and Luke add that they understood not that saying, and it was hid from them, and they were afraid to ask him. The reasons of this may have been, 1st. They were strongly attached to him, and were *exceedingly sorry* (Matthew) at any intimation that he was soon to leave them. They learned with great slowness and reluctance, therefore, that he was to be treated in this manner. 2d. They were not *willing* to believe it. They knew that he was the Messiah, but they supposed that he was to be a distinguished prince, and was to restore the kingdom to Israel, Ac. i. 6. But to be betrayed into the hands of his enemies, and be put to death, appeared to them to be frustrating all these expectations. 3d. Though what he said was plain enough, yet they did not understand it; they *could not see* how he could be the Messiah, and yet be put to death in this manner; nor did they understand it fully till after the resurrection.

24-27. *And when they were come to Capernaum.* See Notes on Mat. iv. 13. ¶ *They that received tribute.* In the original this is, they who received *the didrachma*, or *double drachma*. The *drachma* was a Grecian coin worth about fifteen cents (7½*d*.) of our money. The didrachma, or double drachma, was a silver coin equal to the Attic drachma, and, in the time of Josephus, equal to the Jewish half shekel, that is, about thirty cents of our money. This *tribute*, consisting of the didrachma or double drachma, was not paid to the Roman government, but to the Jewish collectors for the use of the temple service. It was permitted in the law of Moses (see Ex. xxx. 11-16) that in numbering the people half a shekel should be received of each man for the services of religion. This was in addition to the *tithes* paid by the whole nation, and seems to have been considered as a voluntary offering. It was devoted to the purchase of animals for the daily sacrifice, wood, flour, salt, incense, &c., for the use of the temple. ¶ *Doth not your master pay tribute?* This tribute was voluntary, and they therefore asked him whether he was in the habit of paying taxes for the support of the temple. Peter replied that it was his custom to pay all the usual taxes of the nation.

25. *Jesus prevented him.* That is, Jesus *commenced speaking before Peter*, or spoke before Peter had told him what he had said. This implies that, though not present with Peter when he gave the answer, yet Jesus was acquainted with what he had said. ¶ *Prevent.* To go before, or precede. It did not mean, as it now does with us, *to hinder* or obstruct. See the same use of the word in Ps. lix. 10; lxxix. 8; lxxxviii. 13; 1 Th. iv. 15; Ps. cxix. 148. ¶ *Of whom do the kings of the earth*, &c. That is, earthly kings. ¶ *Their own children.* Their sons; the members of their own family. ¶ *Or of strangers?* The word strangers does not mean foreigners, but those that were not their own sons or members of their family. Peter replied that tribute was collected of those *out of* their own family. Jesus answered, Then are the children, or *sons* of the kings, *free;* that is, taxes are not required of them. The meaning of this may be thus expressed: "Kings do not tax their own sons. This tribute-money is taken up for the temple service; that is, the service of *my* Father. I, therefore, being *the Son of God*, for whom this is taken up, cannot be law-

27 Notwithstanding, lest we should [n]offend them, go thou to the sea, and cast a hook, and take up the fish that first cometh up; and when thou hast opened his mouth, thou shalt find [2]a piece of money: that take, and give unto them, for me and thee.

n Ro.14.21; 15.1-3; 2 Co.6.3.

2 *a stater*, which was half an ounce of silver.

fully *required* to pay this tribute." This argument is based on the supposition that this was a *religious*, and not a *civil* tax. If it had been the latter, the illustration would not have been pertinent.

27. *Notwithstanding, lest we should offend them.* That is, lest they should think that we despise the temple and its service, and thus provoke needless opposition; though we are not under *obligation* to pay it, yet it is best to pay it to them. ¶ *Go to the sea.* This was at Capernaum, on the shore of the Sea of Tiberias. ¶ *Thou shalt find a piece of money.* In the original, thou shalt find a *stater*, a Roman silver coin of the value of four drachmas, or *one* shekel, and of course sufficient to pay the tribute for two—himself and Peter. In whatever way this is regarded, it is proof that Jesus was possessed of divine attributes. If he *knew* that the first fish that came up would have such a coin in his mouth, it was proof of *omniscience.* If he *created* the coin for the occasion and placed it there, then it was proof of divine power. The former is the most probable supposition. It is by no means absurd that a *fish* should have swallowed a silver coin. Many of them *bite* eagerly at anything bright, and would not hesitate, therefore, at swallowing a piece of money.

REMARKS.

1st. It is proper to withdraw from those around us that we may engage in secret prayer; and it is desirable for every one to have a place where he may be alone with God, ver. 1. Christ often went into deserts and on mountains that he might be by himself. This should be done—1. To avoid the appearance of ostentation. 2. Pride is easily excited when we know that others hear us pray. Every one should have some place—some closet—to which he may retire at any time, with the assurance that none sees him but God. See Notes on ch. vi. 6.

2d. In such seasons we shall meet God, ver. 2. It was in such a season that the divine favour was peculiarly shown to Christ. Then the *transfiguration* took place—the brightest manifestation of his glory that ever occurred on earth. So the clearest and most precious manifestations of the love and glory of God will be made to *us* in prayer.

3d. We see the great glory of Christ, ver. 2. No such favour had been granted to any prophet before him. We see the regard in which he was held by Moses and Elias—among the greatest of the prophets. We see the honour which God put on him, exalting him far above them both, ver. 5. The glory of heaven encompasses the Lord Jesus, and all its redeemed pay him reverence. In him the divine nature shines illustriously; and of him and to him the divinity speaks in glory as the only begotten Son of God.

4th. It is right to have particular affection for some Christians more than others, at the same time that we should love them all. Christ loved *all* his disciples, but he admitted some to peculiar friendship and favours, ver. 1. Some Christians may be more *congenial* to us in feeling, age, and education than others; and it is proper, and may be greatly to our advantage, to admit them among our peculiar friends.

5th. The death of Jesus is an object of great interest to the redeemed. Moses and Elias talked of it, Lu. ix. 31. Angels also desire to look into this great subject, 1 Pe. i. 12. By that death all the redeemed are saved, and *in* that death the angels see the most signal display of the justice and love of God.

6th. Christians should delight to be where God has manifested his glory. The feeling of Peter was natural, ver. 4. His love of the glorious presence of Christ and the redeemed was right. He erred only in the *manner* of manifesting that love. *We* should always love the house of prayer—the sanctuary—the place where Christ has manifested himself as peculiarly glorious and precious to our souls, or as peculiarly our Friend and Deliverer.

7th. We need not be afraid of the most awful displays of deity if Christ be with us, ver. 7. Were we *alone* we *should* fear. None could see God and live, for he is a consuming fire, He. xii. 29. But with Jesus for our friend we may go confidently down to death; we may meet him at his awful bar; we may dwell in the full splendours of his presence to all eternity.

8th. Saints at death are taken to happiness and live now in glory, ver. 3. Moses and Elias were not *created anew*, but went to heaven as they were. They came from heaven and returned thither. The spirits of all men live, therefore, in happiness or woe after the body is dead.

9th. It is not unreasonable to suppose that saints may have *some* knowledge of what is done here on earth. Moses and Elias appear to have been acquainted with the fact that Jesus was about to die at Jerusalem.

10th. The Scriptures will be fulfilled. The fulfilment may take place when we little know it, or in events that we should not suppose were intended for a fulfilment, ver. 12.

11th. Erroneous teachers will endeavour to draw us away from the truth, Mar. ix. 14. They will do it by art, and caution, and the appearance of calm inquiry. We should always be on our guard against any teachers *appearing* to call in question what Christ has plainly taught us.

12th. Christ, in his word and by his Spirit, is a safe teacher, Mar. ix. 15. When men are suggesting plausible doubts about doctrine, or attempting to unsettle our minds by cavils and inquiry, we should leave them, and apply by prayer, and by searching the Bible, to Christ, the great Prophet, who is the way, the *truth*, and the life.

13th. Parents should be earnest for the welfare of their children, ver. 15. It is right for them to pray to God, in times of sickness, that he would heal them. Miracles are not to be expected, but God only can bless the means which parents use for their sick and afflicted children.

14th. Parents may do much by faith and prayer for their children. Here the faith of the parent was the means of saving the life of the child, ver. 14–18. So the faith of parents—a faith producing diligent instruction, a holy example, and much prayer, may be the means of saving their souls. God will not, indeed, save them *on account* of the faith of the parent, but the holy life of a father and mother may be the means of training up their children for heaven.

15th. It is proper to pray to Jesus to increase our faith, Mar. ix. 24. We may be sensible of our unbelief—may feel that we deserve condemnation, and that we deserve no favour that is usually bestowed on faith; but we may come to him and implore of him an increase of faith, and thus obtain the object of our desires.

16th. Our unbelief hinders our doing much that we *might* do, ver. 20. We shrink from great difficulties, we fail in great duties, because we do not put confidence in God, who is able to help us. The proper way to live a life of religion and peace is to do *just what God requires of us*, depending on his grace to aid us.

17th. We see the proper way of increasing our faith, ver. 21. It is by much prayer, self-denial, and fasting. Faith is a plant that never grows in an uncultivated soil, and is never luxuriant unless it is often exposed to the beams of the Sun of Righteousness.

18th. It is right to weep and mourn over the death of Jesus, ver. 23. It was a cruel death, and we should mourn that our *best Friend* passed through such sufferings. Yet we should rather mourn that *our sins* were the cause of such bitter sorrows; and that, but for our sins, and the sins of the rest of mankind, he might have been always happy.

> "'Twas you, my sins, my cruel sins,
> His chief tormentors were;
> Each of my crimes became a nail,
> And unbelief the spear.
>
> "'Twas you that pulled the vengeance down
> Upon his guiltless head.
> Break, break, my heart! O burst, mine eyes!
> And let my sorrows bleed."

19th. At the same time, we should rejoice that God made his death the source of the richest blessings that ever descended on mankind. He rose and brought life and immortality to light, ver. 23.

20th. We should comply with all the requirements of the laws of the land, if not contrary to the law of God. It is important that governments should be supported, ver. 25. See also Ro. xiii. 1–7.

21st. We should also be willing to contribute our just proportion to the support of the institutions of religion. The *tribute* which Jesus paid here by a miracle was for the support of religion in the temple, ver. 24–27. He under-

CHAPTER XVIII.

AT[a] the same time came the disciples unto Jesus, saying, Who is the greatest in the kingdom of heaven?

2 And Jesus called a little child unto him, and set him in the midst of them,

3 And said, Verily I say unto you, [b]Except ye be converted, and

a Mar.9.33,&c.; Lu.9.46,&c.; 22.24,&c.

b Ps.51.10-13; Jn.3.3.

---

stood of how much value are the institutions of religion to the welfare of man. He worked a miracle, therefore, to make a *voluntary offering* to support it. Religion promotes the purity, peace, intelligence, and order of the community, and every man is therefore under obligation to do his part toward its support. If any man doubts this, he has only to go to the places where there is no religion—among scoffers, and thieves, and adulterers, and prostitutes, and pickpockets, and drunkards. No money is ever lost that goes in any way to suppress these vices and to make men better.

CHAPTER XVIII.

1-6. See also Mar. ix. 33-41; Lu. ix. 46-50. *Who is the greatest in the kingdom of heaven?* By the kingdom of heaven they meant the kingdom which they supposed he was about to set up—his kingdom as the Messiah. They asked the question because they supposed, in accordance with the common expectation of the Jews, that he was about to set up a temporal kingdom of great splendour, and they wished to know who should have the principal offices, and posts of honour and profit. This was among them a frequent subject of inquiry and controversy. Mark (ix. 34) informs us that they had had a dispute on this subject in the way. Jesus, he says, inquired of them what they had been disputing about. Luke (ix. 47) says that Jesus perceived the thought of their heart—an act implying omniscience, for none can search the heart but God; Je. xvii. 10. The disciples, conscious that the subject of their dispute was known, requested Jesus to decide it, Mat. xviii. 1. *They* were at first *silent* through shame (Mark), but, perceiving that the subject of their dispute was known, they came, as Matthew states, and referred the matter to him for his opinion.

2, 3. *Except ye be converted.* The word "converted" means *changed* or turned. The verb means to change or turn from one habit of life or set of opinions to another, Ja. v. 19; Lu. xxii. 32. See also Mat. vii. 6; xvi. 23; Lu. vii. 9, &c., where the same word is used in the original. It sometimes refers to that great change called the new birth or regeneration (Ps. li. 13; Is. lx. 5; Ac. iii. 19), but not always. It is a *general* word, meaning *any* change. The word *regeneration* denotes a particular change—the beginning to live a spiritual life. The phrase, "Except ye be converted," does not imply, of necessity, that they were not Christians *before*, or had not been born again. It means that their opinions and feelings about the kingdom of the Messiah must be *changed.* They had supposed that he was to be a temporal prince. They expected he would reign as other kings did. They supposed he would have his great officers of state, as other monarchs had, and they were ambitiously inquiring who should hold the highest offices. Jesus told them that they were wrong in their views and expectations. No such things would take place. From these notions they must be *turned*, *changed*, or *converted*, or they could have no part in his kingdom. These ideas did not fit at all *the nature* of his kingdom. ¶ *And become as little children.* Children are, to a great extent, destitute of ambition, pride, and haughtiness. They are characteristically humble and teachable. By requiring his disciples to be *like them*, he did not intend to express any opinion about the native moral character of children, but simply that *in these respects* they must become like them. They must lay aside their ambitious views and their pride, and be willing to occupy their proper station—a very lowly one. Mark says (ix. 35) that Jesus, *before* he placed the little child in the midst of them, told them that "if any man desire to be first, the same shall be last of all and servant of all." That is, he shall be the most distinguished Christian who is the most humble, and who is willing to be esteemed *least* and last of all. To esteem ourselves as *God* esteems us is humility, and it cannot be degrading to think of ourselves *as*

become[c] as little children, ye shall not enter into the kingdom of heaven.

4 Whosoever therefore shall humble[d] himself as this little child, the same is greatest in the kingdom of heaven.

5 And whoso shall [e]receive one such little child in my name, receiveth me.

6 But whoso shall [f]offend one of these little ones which believe in me, it were better for him that a millstone were hanged about his neck, and *that* he were drowned in the depth of the sea.

7 Woe unto the world because of offences! [g]for it must needs be that offences come; but [h]woe to that man by whom the offence cometh!

8 Wherefore, [i]if thy hand or

c 1 Co.14.20; 1 Pe.2.2. d Lu.14.11; Ja.4.10. e ch.10.42. f Mar.9.42; Lu.17.1,2.

g 1 Co.11.19; Jude 4. h Jude 11. i ch.5.29,30; Mar.9.43,45.

---

we are; but pride, or an attempt to be thought of more importance than we are, is foolish, wicked, and degrading.

4. *The greatest*, &c. That is, shall be the most eminent Christian—shall have most of the *true spirit* of religion.

5. *And whoso shall receive one such little child.* That is, whoso shall receive and love one with a spirit like this child—one who is humble, meek, and unambitious—that is, a real Christian. ¶ *In my name.* As a follower of me, or because he is attached to me. Whoso receives one possessed of my spirit, or who loves him *because* he has that spirit, loves me also. The word "receive" means to approve, love, or treat with kindness; to aid in the time of need. See Mat. xxv. 35-40.

Mark (ix. 38) and Luke (ix. 49) add a conversation that took place on this occasion, which has been omitted by Matthew. John told him that they had seen one casting out devils in his name, and they forbade him, because he followed not with them. Jesus replied that he should not have been forbidden, for there was no one who could work a miracle in his name that could lightly speak evil of him. That is, though he did not attend them—though he had not joined himself to their society, yet he could not *really* be opposed to him. Indeed, they should have remembered that the power to work a miracle must always come from the same source, that is, God; and that he who had the ability given him to work a miracle, and who did it in the name of Christ, must be a real friend to him. It is probable, from this, that the power of working miracles in the name of Christ was given to many who did not attend on his ministry.

6. *Whoso shall offend.* That is, cause to fall, or to sin; or who should place anything in their way to hinder their piety or happiness. See Notes on Mat. v. 29. ¶ *These little ones.* That is, Christians manifesting the spirit of little children, 1 Jn. ii. 1, 12, 18, 28. ¶ *It were better for him that a millstone*, &c. Mills, anciently, were either turned by hand (see Notes on Mat. xxiv. 41), or by beasts, chiefly by *mules.* These last were of the larger kind, and the *original* words denote that it was this kind that was intended. This was one mode of capital punishment practised by the Greeks, Syrians, Romans, and by some other nations. The meaning is, it would be better for him to have died before he had committed the sin. To injure, or to cause to sin, the feeblest Christian, will be regarded by Christ as a most serious offence, and will be punished accordingly.

7. *Woe unto the world because of offences.* That is, offences will be the cause of woe or of suffering. *Offences*, here, mean things that will produce sin; that will cause *us* to sin, or temptations to induce others to sin. See Notes on Mat. v. 29. ¶ *It must needs be*, &c. That is, such is the depravity of man that there *will* be always some who are attempting to make others sin; some men of wickedness endeavouring to lead Christians astray, and rejoicing when they have succeeded in causing them to fall. Such, also, is the strength of our native corruption and the force of passion, that *our besetting sins* will lead us astray. ¶ *Woe to that man by whom the offence cometh.* He who leads others into sin is awfully guilty—no man can be more guilty. No wickedness can be more deeply seated in the heart than that which attempts to mar the peace, defile the purity, and destroy the souls of others; and yet in all ages there have been multitudes who, by

thy foot offend thee, cut them off, and cast *them* from thee: it is better for thee to enter into life halt or maimed, rather than, having two hands or two feet, to be cast into everlasting fire.

9 And if thine eye offend thee, pluck it out and cast *it* from thee: it is better for thee to [k]enter into life with one eye, rather than, [l]having two eyes, to be cast into hell fire.

10 Take heed that ye despise not one of these little ones; for I say unto you, that in heaven [m]their angels do always [n]behold the face of my Father which is in heaven.

11 For the Son of man is come to [o]save that which was lost.

12 How think ye? [p]if a man

k He.4.11.

l Lu.9.25. m Ac.12.15. n Ps.17.15. o ch.1.21; Lu.9.56; 19.10; Jn.3.17; 10.10; 12.47; 1 Ti.1.15. p Lu.15.4,&c.

persecution, threats, arts, allurements, and persuasion, have endeavoured to seduce Christians from the faith and to lead them into sin.

8, 9. *If thy hand*, &c. See Notes on Mat. v. 29, 30. The sense in all these instances is the same. Worldly attachments, friendships, and employments of any kind, that cannot be pursued without leading us into sin, be they ever so dear to us, must be abandoned, or the soul will be lost. ¶ *It is better for thee to enter into life halt or maimed*, &c. It is not meant, by this, that when the body shall be raised it will be maimed and disfigured in this manner. It will be perfect. See 1 Co. xv. 42–44. But these things are said for the purpose of carrying out or making complete *the figure* or the representation of cutting off the hands, &c. The meaning is, it is better to go to heaven *without enjoying* the things that caused us to sin, than to enjoy them *here* and then be lost. ¶ *Halt*. Lame. *Maimed*. With a loss of limbs. ¶ *Into hell fire*. It is implied, in all this, that if their sins, however dear to them, were not abandoned, the soul must go into everlasting fire. This is conclusive proof that the sufferings of the wicked will be eternal. See Notes on Mar. ix. 44, 46, 48.

10. *Take heed that ye despise not one of these little ones*, &c. That is, one who has become like a little child, or a Christian. ¶ *For I say unto you*, &c. Jesus then proceeds to state the reason why we should not despise his feeblest and obscurest follower. That reason is drawn from the *care* which God exercises over them. The first instance of that *care* is, that *in heaven their angels do always behold his face*. He does not mean, I suppose, to state that every good man has his guardian angel, as many of the Jews believed; but that the angels were, *in general*, the guards of his followers, and aided them and watched over them. See Notes on He. i. 14. ¶ *Do always behold the face of God*. This is taken from the practice of earthly courts. To be admitted to the presence of a king; to be allowed to see his face continually; to have free access to him at all times, was deemed a mark of peculiar favour (1 Ki. x. 8; Es. i. 14), and was esteemed a security for his protection. So, says our Saviour, we should not despise the obscurest Christian, for he is ministered to by the highest and noblest of beings—by beings who are always enjoying the favour and friendship of God.

11. *For the Son of man*, &c. This is a second reason why we should not despise Christians. That reason is, that the Son of man came to seek and save them. He came in search of them when lost; he found them; he redeemed them. It was the great object of his life; and, though they may be obscure and little in the eye of the world, yet that cannot be an object of contempt which the Son of God sought by his toils and his death. ¶ *Son of man*. See Notes on Mat. viii. 19, 20. ¶ *That which was lost*. Property is *lost* when it is consumed, mislaid, wasted, sunk in the ocean, &c.—when *we* have no longer the use of it. Friends are lost when they die—we enjoy their society no longer. A wicked and profligate man is said to be *lost* to virtue and happiness. He is useless to society. So all men are *lost*. They are wicked, miserable wanderers from God. They are lost to piety, to happiness, to heaven. These Jesus came to save by giving his own life a ransom, and shedding his own blood that they might be recovered and saved.

12–14. To show still further the reason why we should not despise Christians, he introduced a parable showing the

have a hundred sheep, and one of them be gone astray, doth he not leave the ninety and nine, and goeth into the mountains and seeketh that which is gone astray?

13 And if so be that he find it, verily I say unto you, he rejoiceth more of that *sheep*, than of the ninety and nine which went not astray.

14 Even so it is not the will of your Father which is in heaven [q]that one of these little ones should perish.

15 Moreover, [r]if thy brother shall trespass against thee, go and tell him his fault between thee and him alone: [s]if he shall hear thee, thou hast gained thy brother.

16 But if he will not hear *thee*, *then* take with thee one or two more, that in [t]the mouth of two or three witnesses every word may be established.

q 2 Pe.3.9. *r* Le.19.17; Lu.17.3. *s* Ja.5.20. *t* De.19.15.

joy felt when a thing lost is found. A shepherd rejoices over the recovery of one of his flock that had wandered more than over all that remained; so God rejoices that man is restored; so he seeks his salvation, and wills that not one thus found should perish. If *God* thus loves and preserves the redeemed, then surely *man* should not despise them. See this passage farther explained in Lu. xv. 4–10.

15. *Moreover, if thy brother.* The word *brother*, here, evidently means a fellow-professor of religion. Christians are called *brethren* because they belong to the same redeemed family, having a common Father—God; and because they are united in the same feelings, objects, and destiny. ¶ *Trespass against thee.* That is, *injure* thee in any way, by words or conduct. The original word means *sin* against thee. This may be done by injuring the character, person, or property. ¶ *Go and tell him his fault between thee and him alone.* This was required under the *law*, Le. xix. 17. In the original it is "go and *reprove* him." Seek an explanation of his conduct, and if he has done wrong, administer a friendly and brotherly reproof. This is required to be done *alone:* 1st. That he may have an opportunity of explaining his conduct. In nine cases out of ten, where one supposes that he has been injured, a little friendly conversation would set the matter right and prevent difficulty. 2d. That he may have an opportunity of acknowledging his offence or making reparation, if he has done wrong. Many would be *glad* of such an opportunity, and it is our duty to furnish it by calling on them. 3d. That we may admonish them of their error if they have done an injury to the cause of religion. This should not be blazoned abroad. It can do no good—it does injury; it is what the enemies of religion wish. Christ is often wounded in the house of his friends; and religion, as well as an injured brother, often suffers by spreading such faults before the world. ¶ *Thou hast gained thy brother.* To *gain* means, sometimes, to *preserve* or to save, 1 Co. ix. 19. Here it means thou hast *preserved* him, or *restored* him, to be a consistent Christian. Perhaps it may include the idea, also, thou hast reconciled him to thyself—thou hast gained him as a Christian brother.

16. *But if he will not hear* thee, &c. That is, if he spurns or abuses you, or will not be entreated by you, and will not reform. ¶ *Take with thee one or two more.* The design of taking them seems to be, 1st. That he might be induced to listen to *them*, ver. 17. They should be persons of influence or authority; his personal friends, or those in whom he could put confidence. 2d. That they might be witnesses of his conduct before the church, ver. 17. The law of Moses required two or three witnesses, De. xix. 15; 2 Co. xiii. 1; Jn. viii. 17.

17. *Tell it to the church.* See Notes on Mat. xvi. 18. The church may here mean the whole assembly of believers, or it may mean those who are authorized to try such cases—the representatives of the church, or those who act for the church. In the Jewish synagogue there was a bench of elders before whom trials of this kind were brought. It was to be brought to the church in order that he might be admonished, entreated, and, if possible, reformed. This was, and is always to be, the first business in disciplining an offending brother. ¶ *But if he neglect to hear the church, let him be,* &c. The Jews gave

17 And if he shall neglect to hear them, tell *it* unto the church: but if he neglect to hear the church, [u]let him be unto thee as an heathen man and a publican.

18 Verily I say unto you, [v]Whatsoever ye shall bind on earth shall be bound in heaven; and whatsoever ye shall loose on earth shall be loosed in heaven.

u Ro.16.17; 1 Co.5.3-5; 2 Th.3.6,14.
v ch.16.19; Jn.20.23; Ac.15.23-31; 2 Co.2.10.

19 Again I say unto you, That if two of you shall agree on earth as touching any thing that they shall ask, [w]it shall be done for them of my Father which is in heaven.

20 For where two or three are [x]gathered together in my name, there am I in the midst of them.

21 Then came Peter to him, and said, Lord, how oft shall my

w Mar.11.24; Jn.16.24; 1 Jn.5.14.
x Jn.20.19; 1 Co.5.4.

---

the name *heathen* or *Gentile* to all other nations but themselves. With them they had no *religious* intercourse or communion. ¶ *Publican.* See Notes on Mat. v. 47. Publicans were men of abandoned character, and the Jews would have no intercourse with them. The meaning of this is, cease to have *religious* intercourse with him, or to acknowledge him as a Christian brother. It does not mean that we should cease to show kindness to him and aid him in affliction or trial, for *that* is required toward all men; but it means that we should *disown* him as a *Christian brother*, and treat him as we do other men not connected with the church. This should not be done till *all* these steps are taken. This is the only way of kindness. This is the only way to preserve peace and purity in the church.

18. *Whatsoever ye shall bind*, &c. See Notes on Mat. xvi. 19. These words were spoken to the apostles. Jesus had before addressed the same words to Peter, ch. xvi. 19. He employs them here to signify that they *all had the same power;* that in ordering the affairs of the church he did not intend to give *Peter* any supremacy or any exclusive right to regulate it. The meaning of this verse is, whatever you shall do in the discipline of the church shall be approved by God or bound in heaven. This promise, therefore, cannot be understood as extending to all Christians or ministers, for all others but the apostles may err.

19. *Again I say unto you, That if two of you*, &c. This is connected with the previous verses. The connection is this: The obstinate man is to be excluded from the church, ver. 17. The care of the church—the power of admitting or excluding members—of organizing and establishing it—is committed to you, the apostles, ver. 18. Yet there is not need of *the whole* to give validity to the transaction. When two of you agree, or have the same mind, feelings, and opinion, about the arrangement of affairs in the church, or about things desired for its welfare, and shall ask of God, it shall be done for them. See Ac. i. 14-26; xv. 1-29. The promise *here* has respect to the apostles in organizing the church. It cannot with any propriety be applied to the ordinary prayers of believers. Other promises are made to them, and it is true that the prayer of faith will be answered, *but that is not the truth taught here.*

20. *For where two or three*, &c. This is a *general* assertion made to support the *particular* promise made (ver. 19) to his apostles. He affirms that *wherever* two or three are assembled together in his name, he is in the midst of them. ¶ *In my name.* That is, 1st. By *my authority*, acting *for me* in my church. See Jn. x. 25; xvi. 23. 2d. It may mean for my service; in the place of prayer and praise, assembled in obedience to my command, and with a desire to promote my glory. ¶ *There am I in the midst of them.* Nothing could more clearly prove that Jesus must be omnipresent, and, of course, be God. Every day, perhaps every hour, two or three, or many more, may be assembled in every city or village in the United States, in England, in Greenland, in Africa, in Ceylon, in the Sandwich Islands, in Russia, and in Judea—in almost every part of the world—and in the midst *of them all* is Jesus the Saviour. Millions thus at the same time, in every quarter of the globe, worship in his name, and experience the truth of the promise that he is present with them. It is impossible that he should be in all these places and not be God.

21. *Then came Peter*, &c. The men-

brother sin against me, and I [y]forgive him? till seven times?

22 Jesus saith unto him, I say not unto thee, Until seven times; but, Until seventy times seven.

23 Therefore is the kingdom of heaven likened unto a certain king which would [z]take account of his servants.

24 And when he had begun to reckon, one was brought unto him which owed him ten thousand [1]talents:

25 But forasmuch as he had not to pay, his lord commanded him [a]to be sold, and his wife and children, and all that he had, and payment to be made.

26 The servant therefore fell down, and [2]worshipped him, say-

y Mar.11.25; Lu.17.4; Col.3.13.
z Ro.14.12.

1 *A talent is 750 ounces of silver, which, at 5s. the ounce, is £187, 10s.*
a 2 Ki.4.1; Is.50.1. 2 or, *besought him.*

tion of the duty (ver. 15) of *seeing* a brother when he had offended us, *implying* that it was a duty to forgive him, led Peter to ask *how often* this was to be done. ¶ *Forgive him.* To forgive is to treat as though the offence was not committed—to *declare* that we will not harbour malice or treat unkindly, but that the matter shall be buried and forgotten. ¶ *Till seven times?* The Jews taught that a man was to forgive another *three* times, but not the *fourth.* Peter more than doubled this, and asked whether forgiveness was to be exercised to so great an extent. ¶ *I say not unto thee, Until seven times, but, Until seventy times seven.* The meaning is, that we are not to limit our forgiveness *to any fixed number of times.* See Ge. iv. 24. As often as a brother injures us and asks forgiveness, we are to forgive him. It is, indeed, his duty to *ask* forgiveness, Lu. xvii. 4. If he does this, it is our duty to *declare* that we forgive him, and to treat him accordingly. If he does not *ask* us to forgive him, yet we are not at liberty to follow him with revenge and malice, but are still to treat him kindly and to do him good, Lu. x. 30-37.

23. *Therefore is the kingdom of heaven likened,* &c. The phrase, "the kingdom of heaven," here has reference to the church, or to the way in which God will deal with his people. "It shall be in my church as it was with a certain king; or *God* will deal with the members of his church as a certain king did with his servants." See Notes on Mat. iii. 2. This *parable* (see Mat. xiii. 3) is related to show the duty of forgiving others. It is not necessary to suppose that it was a *true* narrative, but only that it *illustrated* the truth which he was teaching. At the same time it *may* be true that such an occurrence really took place. ¶ *Would take account of his servants.* To take account means to reckon, to settle up affairs. The word *servants* here means, probably, *petty princes,* or, more likely, *collectors of the revenue* or *taxes.* Among the ancients kings often *farmed out,* or sold for a certain sum, the taxes of a particular district or province. Thus, when Judea was subject to Egypt or Rome, the kings frequently *sold* to the high-priest the taxes to be raised from Judea on condition of a much smaller sum being paid to them. This *secured* to them a *certain sum,* but it gave occasion to much oppression in the collection of the taxes. It is probable that some such persons are intended by the word servants.

24. *Ten thousand talents.* A *talent* was a sum of money, or *weight* of silver or gold amounting to three thousand shekels. A silver *shekel* was worth, after the captivity, not far from half a dollar of our money. A talent of *silver* was worth $1519, 23 cts. = £312, 3s. 9*d.*; of gold, $243,098, 88 cts. = £5475. If these were *silver* talents, as is probable, then the sum owed by the servant was fifteen millions one hundred and eighty thousand dollars, or about £3,421,875 sterling, a sum which proves that he was not a domestic, but some tributary prince. The sum is used to show that the debt was immensely large, and that our *sins* are so great that they cannot be estimated or numbered. Comp. Job xxii. 5.

25. *His lord commanded him to be sold,* &c. By the laws of the Hebrews they were permitted to sell debtors, with their wives and children, into servitude for a time sufficient to pay a debt. See 2 Ki. iv. 1; Le. xxv. 39-46; Am. viii. 6.

26. *The servant therefore fell down, and worshipped him.* This does not

ing, Lord, have patience with me, and I will pay thee all.

27 Then the Lord of that servant was [b]moved with compassion, and loosed him, and forgave him the debt.

28 But the same servant went out, and found one of his fellow-servants which owed him an hundred [3]pence; and he laid hands on him, and took *him* by the throat, saying, Pay me that thou owest.

29 And his fellow-servant fell down at his feet, and besought him, saying, [c]Have patience with me, and I will pay thee all.

30 And he would not; but went and cast him into prison till he should pay the debt.

31 So when his fellow-servants saw what was done, they were very sorry, and came and told unto their lord all that was done.

32 Then his lord, after that he had called him, said unto him, O thou [d]wicked servant, I forgave

b Ps.78.38.
3 *The Roman penny is the 8th part of an ounce, which, at 5s. the ounce, is 7d. halfpenny,* ch.20.2.

c ver.26. d Lu.19.22.

---

mean that he paid him *religious* homage, but that in a humble, reverent, and earnest manner he entreated him to have patience with him. He prostrated himself before his lord, as is customary in all Eastern nations when *subjects* are in the presence of their king. See Notes on Mat. ii. 2.

27. *The lord of that servant was moved with compassion*, &c. He had pity on him. He saw his distressed condition. He pitied his family. He forgave him the whole debt. This represents the mercy of God to men. They have sinned. They owe to God more than can be paid. They are about to be cast off; but God has mercy on them, and, in connection with their prayers, forgives them. We are not to interpret the circumstances of a parable too strictly. The illustration taken from selling the wife and children (ver. 25) is not to be taken literally, as if *God* would punish a man for the sins of his father; but it is a circumstance thrown in *to keep up the story*—to make it consistent—to explain the reason *why* the servant was so anxious to obtain a *delay* of the time of payment.

28, 29. *But the same servant went out, and found one of his fellow-servants which owed him an hundred pence.* Greek, *denarion;* Latin, *denarius;* a Roman silver coin in common use. When Greece became subject to the Romans, and especially under the emperors, the denarius was regarded as of equal value with the Attic drachma—about $7\frac{1}{2}$*d.* sterling, or fifteen cents; consequently this debt was about fifteen dollars—a very small sum compared with what had been forgiven to the first servant. Perhaps our Saviour, by this, meant to teach that the offences which our fellow-men commit against us are very small and insignificant compared with our offences against God. Since God has forgiven us *so much*, we ought to forgive each other the *small* offences which are committed. ¶ *Took him by the throat.* Took him in a violent and rough manner—half choked or *throttled* him. This was the more criminal and base, as he had himself been so kindly treated and dealt so mildly with by his lord. ¶ *Besought.* Entreated, pled with him.

31. *So when his fellow-servants*, &c. This is a mere circumstance thrown into the story for the sake of *keeping*, or making a consistent narrative. It *cannot* be intended to teach that other Christians should go and tell God what a brother has done; for God well knows all the actions of his children, and does not need us surely to *inform* him of what is done. It is abusing the Bible, and departing from the *design* of parables, to press every circumstance, and to endeavour to extract from it some spiritual meaning. Our Saviour, in this parable, designed most clearly to exhibit only *one great truth*—the duty of forgiving our brethren, and the great evil of *not* forgiving a brother when he offends us. The circumstances of the parable are intended only to make the story *consistent* with itself, and thus to impress the general truth more fully on the mind.

34. *Delivered him to the tormentors.* The word *tormentors* here probably means *keepers of the prison.* Torments were inflicted on *criminals*, not on debtors. They were inflicted by stretching the limbs, or pinching the flesh, or putting out the eyes, or taking off the

thee all that debt, because thou desiredst me:

33 Shouldest not thou also have had compassion on thy fellow-servant, even as I had pity on thee?

34 And his lord was wroth, and delivered him to the tormentors till he should pay all that was due unto him.

35 So [e]likewise shall my heavenly Father do also unto you, if ye from your hearts forgive not every one his brother their trespasses.

e Pr.21.13; ch.6.12; Ja.2.13.

---

skin while alive, &c. It is not probable that anything of this kind is intended, but only that the servant was punished by imprisonment till the debt should be paid.

35. *So likewise*, &c. This verse contains the sum or *moral* of the parable. When Christ has explained one of his own parables, we are to receive it *just* as he has explained it, and not attempt to draw spiritual instruction from any parts or circumstances which he has not explained. The following seems to be the particulars of the general truth which he meant to teach: 1st. That our sins are great. 2d. That God freely forgives them. 3d. That the offences committed against us by our brethren are comparatively small. 4th. That we should therefore most freely forgive them. 5th. That if we do not, God will be justly angry with us, and punish us. ¶ *From your hearts.* That is, not merely in words, but really and truly to feel and act toward him as if he had not offended us. ¶ *Trespasses.* Offences, injuries. Words and actions designed to do us wrong.

REMARKS.

1st. We see that it is possible to make a profession of religion an occasion of ambition, ver. 1. The apostles at first sought honour, and expected office as a consequence of following Christ. So thousands have done since. Religion, notwithstanding all the opposition it has met with, *really* commands the confidence of mankind. To make a profession of it may be a way of access to that confidence. Thousands, it is to be feared, even yet enter the church merely to obtain some worldly benefit. Especially does this danger beset ministers of the gospel. There are few paths to the confidence of mankind so easily trod as to enter the ministry. Every minister, of course, if at all worthy of his office, has access to the confidence of multitudes, and is never despised but by the worst and lowest of mankind. No way is so easy to step at once to public confidence. Other men toil long to establish influence by personal character. The minister has it by virtue of his office. Those who now enter the ministry are tempted far more in this respect than were the apostles; and how should they search their own hearts, to see that no such abominable motive has induced them to seek that office!

2d. It is consummate wickedness thus to prostitute the most sacred of all offices to the worst of purposes. The apostles at this time were ignorant. They expected a kingdom in which it would be right to seek distinction. But we labour under no such ignorance. We *know* that the kingdom of Christ is not of this world, and woe to the man that acts *as though* it were. Deep and awful must be the doom of him who thus seeks the honours of the world while he is professedly following the meek and lowly Jesus!

3d. Humility is indispensable to religion, ver. 3. No man who is not humble can possibly be a Christian. He must be willing to esteem himself *as he is*, and to have others esteem him so also. This is humility, and humility is lovely. It is not meanness—it is not cowardice—it is not want of proper self-esteem; it is a view of ourselves *just as we are*, and a willingness that God and all creatures should so esteem us. What can be more lovely than such an estimation of ourselves! and how foolish and wicked is it to be proud—that is, to think more of ourselves, and wish others to think so, than we really deserve! To put on appearances, and to magnify our own importance, and to think that the affairs of the universe could not go on without us, and to be indignant when all the world does not bow down to do us homage—this is hypocrisy as well as wickedness; and there *may be*, therefore, hypocrites *out of the church* as well as *in it*.

4th. Humility is the best evidence of piety, ver. 4. The most humble man is the most eminent Christian. He is *greatest* in the kingdom of heaven. The effect of sin is to produce pride. Religion overcomes it by producing a just sense of ourselves, of other men, of angels, and of God. We may therefore measure the advance of piety in our own souls by the increase of humility.

5th. We see the danger of despising and doing injury to real Christians, and more especially the guilt of attempting to draw them into sin, ver. 6. God watches over them. He loves them. In the eye of the world they may be of little importance, but not so with God. The most obscure follower of Christ is dear, infinitely dear, to him, and he will take care of him. He that attempts to injure a Christian, attempts to injure God; for God has redeemed him, and loves him.

6th. Men will do much to lead others into sin, ver. 7. In all communities there are some who seem to *live* for this. They have often much wealth, or learning, or accomplishment, or address, or professional influence, and they employ it for the sake of seducing the unwary and leading them into ruin. Hence offences come, and many of the young and thoughtless are led astray. But He who has all power has pronounced *woe* upon them, and judgment will not always linger. No class of men have a more fearful account to render to God than they who thus lead others into vice and infidelity.

7th. We must forsake our dearest sins, ver. 8, 9. We must do this, or go to hell-fire. There is no way of avoiding it. We cannot love and cherish those sins and be saved.

8th. The wicked—they who will *not* forsake their sins—must certainly go to eternal punishment, ver. 8, 9. So said the compassionate Saviour. The fair and obvious meaning of his words is that the sufferings of hell are eternal, and Christ did not use words without meaning. He did not mean to frighten us by bugbears or to hold up imaginary fears. If *Christ* speaks of hell, then there is a hell. If he says it is eternal, then it is so. Of this we may be sure, that EVERY WORD *which the God of mercy has spoken about the punishment of the wicked is* FULL OF MEANING.

9th. Christians are protected, ver. 10. Angels are appointed as their friends and guardians. *Those friends* are very near to God. They enjoy his favour, and his children shall be safe.

10th. Christians are safe, ver. 11–14. Jesus came to save them. He left the heavens for this end. God rejoices in their salvation. He secures it at great sacrifices, and none can pluck them out of his hand. After the coming of Jesus to save them—after all that he has done for that, and that only—after the joy of God and of angels at their recovery, it is *impossible* that they should be wrested from him and destroyed. See Jn. x. 27, 28.

11th. It is our duty to admonish our brethren when they injure us, ver. 15. We have no right to speak of the offence to anyone else, not even to our best friends, until we have given them an opportunity to explain.

12th. The way to treat offending brethren is clearly pointed out, ver. 15–17. Nor have we a right to take any other course. Infinite Wisdom—the *Prince of Peace*—has declared that this is the way to treat our brethren. No other can be right; and no other, therefore, can be so well adapted to promote the peace of the church. And yet how different from this is the course commonly pursued! How few go honestly to an offending brother and tell him his fault! Instead of this, every breeze bears the report—it is magnified—mole-hills swell to mountains, and a quarrel of years often succeeds what *might* have been settled at once. No robber is so cruel as he who steals away the *character* of another. Nothing can compensate for the loss of this. Wealth, health, mansions, equipage, all are trifles compared with this. Especially is this true of a *Christian*. His reputation gone, he has lost his power of doing good; he has brought dishonour on the cause he most loved; he has lost his peace, and worlds cannot repay him.

> "Who steals my purse, steals trash: 'tis something, nothing:
> 'Twas mine, 'tis his, and has been slave to thousands.
> But he that filches from me my good name
> Robs me of that which not enriches him,
> And makes me poor indeed."

13th. We have every encouragement to pray, ver. 20. We are poor, and sinful, and dying, and none can comfort us but God. At his throne we may find all that we want. We know not which is most wonderful—that God deigns to hear our prayers, or that men are so unwilling to use so simple and easy a way of obtaining what they so much need.

14th. We should never be weary of forgiving our brethren, ver. 22. We

CHAPTER XIX.

AND it came to pass, *that* when Jesus had finished these sayings, [a]he departed from Galilee, and came into the coasts of Judea beyond Jordan:

2 And great multitudes followed him, and he healed them there.

a Mar.10.1; Jn.10.40.

should do it cheerfully. We should do it always. We are never better employed than when we are doing good to those who have injured us. Thus doing, we are most like God.

15th. There will be a day in which we must give up our account, ver. 23. It may tarry long; but God will *reckon* with us, and everything shall be brought into judgment.

16th. We are greatly indebted to God—far, far beyond what we are able to pay, ver. 24. We have sinned, and *in no way* can *we* make atonement for past sins; but Jesus the Saviour *has* made an atonement and paid our debt, and we may be free.

17th. It is right to pray to God when we feel that we have sinned, and are unable to pay the debt, ver. 26. We have no other way. Poor, and needy, and wretched, we *must* cast ourselves upon his mercy or *die*—die for ever.

18th. God will have compassion on those who do this, ver. 27. At *his* feet, in the attitude of prayer, the burdened sinner finds peace. We have nowhere else to go but to the very Being that we have offended. None but he can save us from death.

19th. From the kindness of God to us we should learn *not* to oppress others, ver. 28.

20th. It is our true *interest*, as well as duty, to forgive those that offend us, ver. 34. God will take vengeance, and in due time we *must* suffer if we do not forgive others.

21st. Christians are often great sufferers for harbouring malice. As a punishment, God withdraws the light of his countenance; they walk in darkness; they cannot enjoy religion; their conscience smites them, and they are wretched. No man ever did or ever can enjoy religion who did not from his heart forgive his brother his trespasses.

22d. One reason why Christians ever walk in darkness is, that there is some such duty neglected. They think they have been injured, and very possibly they may have been; they think they are in the right, and possibly they are so; but mingled with a consciousness of this is an unforgiving spirit, and they cannot enjoy religion till that is subdued.

23d. Forgiveness must not be in word merely, but from the heart, ver. 35. No other can be genuine. No other is like God.

CHAPTER XIX.

1-12. See also Mar. x. 1-12.

1. *Coasts of Judea beyond Jordan.* The narrative here refers to the last journey of the Saviour from Galilee to Jerusalem, to attend the last Passover which he celebrated. A considerable lapse of time occurred between his last discourse in the preceding chapter and what is recorded here, and several important events have been recorded by Luke and John which occurred in the interval, as the sending out of the seventy disciples (Lu. x. 1-16); the Saviour's going up to the feast of Tabernacles, and his final departure from Galilee, passing through Samaria (Lu. ix. 51-56; Jn. vii. 2-10); the healing of the ten lepers (Lu. xvii. 11-19); the public teaching of Jesus at the feast of Tabernacles (Jn. vii. 11-53); the account of the woman taken in adultery (Jn. viii. 1); the reproof of the unbelieving Jews, and the escape of the Saviour from their hands (Jn. viii. 12-59); the instruction of the lawyer, and the parable of the good Samaritan (Lu. x. 28-37); the incidents in the house of Martha and Mary (Lu. x. 38-42); the return of the seventy (Lu. x. 17-24); the healing of the blind man on the Sabbath (Jn. ix. 1-41); the festival of the Dedication (Jn. x. 22-42); the raising of Lazarus (Jn. xi. 1-46); and the counsel of Caiaphas against Jesus, and the retiring of Jesus from Jerusalem (Jn. xi. 47-54). See Robinson's *Harmony*. Matthew and Mark now resume the narrative by relating that after Jesus had left Galilee he approached Jerusalem by passing through the country beyond Jordan. The country was, in general, called *Perea*, and appertained to *Judea*, being the region formerly occupied by the tribes of Reuben, Gad, and Manasseh. The word *coasts* means *regions* or *parts*. See Notes on Mat. ii. 16.

3. *The Pharisees came.* See Notes on Mat. iii. 7. ¶ *Tempting him.* This

3 The Pharisees also came unto him, tempting him, and saying unto him, Is it lawful for a man to put away his wife for every cause?

4 And he answered and said unto them, Have ye not read, that [b]he which made *them* at the beginning made them male and female,

5 And said, [c]For this cause shall a man leave father and mother, and shall cleave to his wife; and they twain shall be one flesh?

6 Wherefore they are no more twain, but one flesh. What [d]therefore God hath joined together, let not man put asunder.

7 They say unto him, [e]Why did Moses then command to give a writing of divorcement, and to put her away?

b Ge.1.27; 5.2; Mal.2.15. c Ge.2.24; Ep.5.31. d 1 Co.7.10. e De.24.1; Is.50.1.

means, to get him, if possible, to express an opinion that should involve him in difficulty. ¶ *Is it lawful*, &c. There was the more art in the captious question which they proposed, as at that time the people were very much divided on the subject. A part, following the opinions of *Hillel*, said that a man might divorce his wife for any offence, or any dislike he might have of her. See Notes on Mat. v. 31. Others, of the school of *Shammai*, maintained that divorce was unlawful except in case of adultery. Whatever opinion, therefore, Christ expressed, they expected that he would involve himself in difficulty with one of their parties.

4–6. *And he answered and said*, &c. Instead of referring to the opinions of either party, Jesus called their attention to the original design of marriage, to the authority of *Moses*—an authority acknowledged by them both. ¶ *Have ye not read?* Ge. i. 27; ii. 21, 22. ¶ *And said, For this cause*, &c., Ge. ii. 24. That is, *God*, at the beginning, made but *one* man and *one* woman: their posterity should learn that the original intention of marriage was that a man should have but one wife. ¶ *Shall leave his father and mother.* This means, shall bind himself more strongly to his wife than he was to his father or mother. The marriage connection is the most tender and endearing of all human relations—more tender than even that bond which unites us to a parent. ¶ *And shall cleave unto his wife.* The word *cleave* denotes a union of the firmest kind. It is in the original taken from *gluing*, and means so firmly to *adhere* together that nothing can separate them. ¶ *They twain shall be one flesh.* That is, they *two*, or they that *were* two, shall be united as one—one in law, in feeling, in interest, in affection. They shall no longer have separate interests, but shall act in all things *as if* they were *one*—animated by one soul and one wish. The argument of Jesus here is, that since they are so intimately united as to be one, and since in the beginning God made but one woman for one man, it follows that they cannot be separated but by the authority of God. Man may *not* put away his wife for every cause. What *God* has joined together *man* may not put asunder. In this decision he *really* decided in favour of one of the parties; and it shows that when it was proper, Jesus answered questions without regard to consequences, from whatever cause they might have been proposed, and however much difficulty it might involve him in. Our Lord, in this, also showed consummate wisdom. He answered the question, not from Hillel or Shammai, their teachers, but from *Moses*, and thus defeated their malice.

7. *Why did Moses*, &c. To this they objected that *Moses* had allowed such divorces (De. xxiv. 1); and if *he* had allowed them, they inferred that they could not be unlawful. See Notes on Mat. v. 31.

8. *He saith unto them*, &c. Jesus *admits* that this was allowed, but still he contends that this was not the *original design* of marriage. It was only a *temporary* expedient growing out of a peculiar state of things, and not designed to be perpetual. It was on account *of the hardness of their hearts.* Moses found the custom in use. He found a hard-hearted and rebellious people. In this state of things he did not deem it prudent to forbid a practice so universal; but it might be regulated; and, instead of suffering the husband to divorce his wife *in a passion*, he required him, in order that he might take time to *consider* the matter, and thus make it probable that divorces

8 He saith unto them, Moses, because of the hardness of your hearts, suffered you to put away your wives; but from the beginning it was not so.

9 And I say unto you, [f]Whosoever shall put away his wife, except *it be* for fornication, and shall marry another, committeth adultery; and whoso marrieth her which is put away doth commit adultery.

10 His disciples say unto him, [g]If the case of the man be so with *his* wife, it is not good to marry.

11 But he said unto them, All *men* cannot receive this saying, save *they* to whom it is given.

12 For there are some eunuchs which were so born from *their* mothers' womb; and there are some eunuchs which were made eunuchs of men; and [h]there be eunuchs which have made them-

f ch.5.32; Lu.16.18.
g Pr.19.13; 21.9,19. h 1 Co.7.32.

---

would be less frequent, to give her a writing; to sit down deliberately to look at the matter, and probably, also, to bring the case before some *scribe* or learned man, to write a divorce in the legal form. Thus doing, there might be an opportunity for the matter to be reconciled, and the man to be persuaded *not* to divorce his wife. This, says our Saviour, was a permission growing out of a particular state of things, and designed to remedy a prevailing evil; but at first it was not so. God intended that marriage should be between one man and one woman, and that they were only to be separated, in the case specified, by him who had formed the union. ¶ *Hardness of your hearts.* He speaks here of his hearers as a part of the nation. The hardness of *you Jews;* as when we say, *we* fought with England and gained our independence; that is, we, the American people, though it was done by our fathers. He does not mean to say, therefore, that this was done on account of the people whom he addressed, but of the *national* hardness of heart—the stubbornness of the Jewish people as a people.

9. *And I say unto you.* Emphasis should be laid here on the word *I.* This was the opinion of Jesus—this he proclaimed to be the law of his kingdom—this the command of God ever afterward. Indulgence had been given by the laws of Moses; but that indulgence was to cease, and the marriage relation *to be brought back to its original intention.* Only *one* offence was to make divorce lawful. This is the law of God; and by the same law, all marriages which take place after divorce, where adultery is not the cause of divorce, are adulterous. Legislatures have no right to say that men may put away their wives for any other cause; and where they do, and where there is marriage afterward, by the law of God such marriages are adulterous.

10. *His disciples say,* &c. The disciples were full of Jewish notions. They thought that the privilege of divorcing a wife when there was a quarrelsome disposition, or anything else that rendered the marriage unhappy, was a great privilege; and that in such cases to be always *bound* to live with a wife was a great calamity. They said, therefore, that if such *was the case*—such the condition on which men married—it was better not to marry.

11. *All* men *cannot receive this saying.* The minds of men are not prepared for this. *This saying* evidently means what the disciples had just said—that it was *good for a man not to marry.* It might be good in certain circumstances—in times of persecution and trial, or for the sake of labouring in the cause of religion without the care and burden of a family. It might be good for many to live, as some of the apostles did, without marriage, but it was not *given* to all men, 1 Co. vii. 1, 7, 9. To be married, or unmarried, might be lawful, according to circumstances, 1 Co. vii. 26.

12. *For there are some eunuchs,* &c. Jesus proceeds to state that there *were* some who were able to receive that saying and to remain in an unmarried state. Some were so born; some were made such by the cruelty of men; and there were some who voluntarily abstained from marriage *for the kingdom of heaven's sake*—that is, that they might devote themselves entirely to the proper business of religion. Perhaps he refers here to the ESSENES, a sect of the Jews (see Notes on Mat. iii. 7), who held that

selves eunuchs for the kingdom of heaven's sake. He that is able to receive *it*, let him receive *it*.

13 Then were there brought unto him little children, that he should put *his* hands on them and pray: and the disciples rebuked them.

14 But Jesus said, [i]Suffer little children, and forbid them not, to come unto me; for of [k]such is the kingdom of heaven.

15 And he laid *his* hands on them, and departed thence.

16 And behold, one came and

i Mar.10.14; Lu.18.16,&c. *k* ch.18.3.

marriage was unsuitable to their condition; who had no children of their own, but perpetuated their sect by adopting the poor children of others. *Eunuchs* were employed chiefly in attending on the females or in the harem. They rose often to distinction, and held important offices in the state. Hence the *word* is sometimes used with reference to such an officer of state, Ac. viii. 27.

13. *Then were brought little children.* See also Mar. x. 13–16; Lu. xviii. 15–17. Probably these were brought by some of his followers, who desired not only to devote *themselves* to Jesus, but all that they had—their *children* as well as themselves. All the Jews were accustomed to devote their children to God by circumcision. It was natural, therefore, under the new dispensation, that it should be done. Luke says they were *infants*. They were undoubtedly those who were not old enough to come by choice, but their coming was *an act of the parents*. ¶ *Put* his *hands on them and pray.* It was customary among the Jews, when blessings were sought for others in prayer, to lay the hands on the head of the person prayed for, implying a kind of consecration to God. See Ge. xlviii. 14; Mat. ix. 18. They had also much confidence in the prayers of pious men, believing that those blessed by a saint or a prophet would be happy. See Nu. xxii. 6; Lu. ii. 28. ¶ *The disciples rebuked them.* That is, *reproved* them, or told them it was improper. This they did, probably, either, 1st, because they thought that they were too young; or, 2d, because they thought that they would be troublesome to their Master.

14. *Jesus said, Suffer little children,* &c. Mark adds, *he was much displeased* at what the disciples said. It was a thing highly gratifying to him, and which he earnestly sought, that children should be brought to him, and a case where it was very improper that they should interfere. ¶ *Of such is the kingdom of heaven.* The kingdom of heaven evidently means here *the church*. See Notes on Mat. iii. 2. In Mark and Luke it is said he immediately added, "Whosoever shall not receive the kingdom of God as a little child shall not enter therein." Whosoever shall not be humble, unambitious, and docile, shall not be a true follower of Christ or a member of his kingdom. *Of such as these*—that is, of persons with such tempers as these—is the church to be composed. He does not say *of those infants*, but of such persons as *resemble* them, or are *like* them in temper, is the kingdom of heaven made up. As emblematic, therefore, of what his own followers were to be, and as having traits of character so strongly resembling what he required in his followers, it was proper that they should be brought to him. At the same time, it was proper on their own account that they should be brought to him, and that his blessing should be sought on them. All are fallen; all have a tendency to sin, and none but Jesus can save them. Little children, too, are in a world of sickness and death, and in the beginning of life it is proper to invoke on them the blessing of the Saviour. They are to live for ever beyond the grave; and as they have just entered on a career of existence which *can never terminate*, it is an appropriate act to seek the blessing of that Saviour who only can make them happy for ever, as they enter on their career of existence. No act, therefore, can be more proper than that by which parents, in a solemn ordinance of religion, give them up to God in baptism, consecrating them to his service, and seeking for them the blessing of the Saviour. It is probable—it is greatly to be hoped—that all infants will be saved. No contrary doctrine is taught in the sacred Scriptures. But it does not appear to be the design of *this* passage to teach that all infants will be saved. It means simply that they should be suffered to be brought to Christ as amiable, lovely, and uncorrupted by

said unto him, [l]Good Master, what good thing shall I do, that I may have eternal life?

17 And he said unto him, Why callest thou me good? *there is* none good but one, *that is* God: but if thou wilt enter into life, keep the commandments.

l Mar.10.17; Lu.10.25; 18.18.

---

the world; as having traits of mind *resembling* those among real Christians; and as themselves needing his blessing.

15. *He laid* his *hands on them.* Mark says *he blessed them.* That is, he pronounced or sought a blessing on them.

16–30. This account is found also in Mar. x. 17–31; Lu. xviii. 18–30.

16. *One came.* This was a *young* man, ver. 20. He was a *ruler* (Luke); probably a ruler in a synagogue, or of the great council of the nation; a place to which he was chosen on account of his unblemished character and promising talents. He came *running* (Mark); evincing great earnestness and anxiety, He fell upon his knees (Mark); not to worship him, but to pay the customary respectful salutation; exhibiting the highest regard for Jesus as an extraordinary religious teacher. ¶ *Good Master.* The word *good* here means, doubtless, *most excellent;* referring not so much to the MORAL *character* of Jesus as to his *character as a religious teacher.* It was probably a title which the Jews were in the habit of applying to their religious teachers. The word *Master* here means *teacher.* ¶ *What good thing shall I do?* He had attempted to keep all the commandments. He had been taught by his Jewish teachers that men were to be saved by *doing* something—that is, by their works; and he supposed that this was to be the way under every system of religion. He had lived externally a blameless life, but yet he was not at peace; he was anxious, and he came to ascertain what, in the view of Jesus, was to be *done,* that his righteousness might be complete. To *have eternal life* means to be saved. The happiness of *heaven* is called *life,* in opposition to the pains of hell, called *death,* or an eternal *dying,* Re. ii. 2; xx. 14. The one is real *life,* answering the purposes of *living*—living to the honour of God and in eternal happiness; the other is a failure of the great ends of existence—prolonged, eternal suffering, of which temporal *death* is but the feeble image.

17. *Why callest thou me good?* Why do you give to me a title that belongs only to God? *You* suppose me to be only a man, yet you give me an appellation that belongs only to God. It is improper to use titles in this manner. As you Jews use them they are unmeaning; and though the title may apply to me, yet you did not *intend* to use it in the sense in which it is proper, as denoting infinite perfection or divinity; but you *intended* to use it as a complimentary or a flattering title, applied to me as if I were a mere man—a title which belongs only to God. The *intention,* the *habit* of using mere titles, and applying *as a compliment* terms belonging only to God, is wrong. Christ did not intend here to disclaim divinity, or to say anything about *his own character,* but simply to reprove the intention and habit of the young man—a most severe reproof of a foolish habit of compliment and flattery, and seeking pompous titles. ¶ *Keep the commandments.* That is, *do* what God has commanded. He in the next verses informs him what he meant by the commandments. Jesus said this, doubtless, to try him, and to *convince him* that he had by no means kept the commandments, and that in supposing he *had* he was altogether deceived. The young man *thought* he had kept them, and was relying on them for salvation. It was of great importance, therefore, to convince him that he was, after all, a sinner. Christ did not mean to say that any man *would* be saved by the works of the law, for the Bible teaches plainly that such *will not* be the case, Ro. iii. 20, 28; iv. 6; Ga. ii. 16; Ep. ii. 9; 2 Ti. i. 9. At the same time, however, it is true that if a man perfectly complied with the requirements of the law he would be saved, for there would be no reason why he should be condemned. Jesus, therefore, since he saw he was *depending* on his works, told him that if he would enter into life—that is, into heaven—he *must* keep the commandments; if he was *depending* on them he must keep them *perfectly,* and if this was done he would be saved. The reasons why Christ gave him this direction were, probably, 1st. Because it was his duty to keep them. 2d. Because the young man *depended* on them, and he ought to understand what was required if he did—that they should be

18 He saith unto him, Which? Jesus said, [m] Thou shalt do no murder, Thou shalt not commit adultery, Thou shalt not steal, Thou shalt not bear false witness;

19 Honour thy father and *thy* mother; and, [n] Thou shalt love thy neighbour as thyself.

20 The young man saith unto him, All these things have I kept from my youth up; what lack I yet?

21 Jesus said unto him, If thou

m Ex.20.13; De.5.17,&c.

n Le.19.18.

kept perfectly, or that they were not kept at all. 3d. Because he wanted to *test* him, to show him that he did *not* keep them, and thus to show him his need of a Saviour.

18, 19. *He saith unto him, Which?* In reply to the inquiry of the young man, Jesus directed him to the sixth, seventh, eighth, ninth, and fifth (Ex. xx. 12-16), as containing the *substance* of the whole—as containing *particularly* what he intended to show him that he had not kept. See Notes on Mat. v. 21, 27. ¶ *Jesus said, Thou shalt do no murder.* See Notes on Mat. v. 21-26. ¶ *Thou shalt not commit adultery.* See Notes on Mat. v. 27-32. ¶ *Thou shalt not steal.* To *steal* is to take the property of another without his knowledge or consent. ¶ *Thou shalt not bear false witness.* Give testimony contrary to *truth.* This may be done in a court of justice, or by private or public slander. It means to say things of another which are not true. ¶ *Honour thy father,* &c. That is, 1st. *Obey them,* keep their commands, Col. iii. 20; Ep. vi. 1-3. 2d. *Respect them,* show them reverence. 3d. Treat their *opinions* with respect—do not despise them or ridicule them. 4th. Treat their *habits* with respect. Those habits may be different from ours; they may be antiquated, and to us strange, odd, or whimsical; but they are the habits of a *parent,* and they are not to be ridiculed. 5th. Provide for them when sick, weary, old, and infirm. Bear with their weakness, comply with their wishes, speak to them kindly, and deny yourselves of rest, and sleep, and ease, to promote their welfare. To this he added another—the duty of loving our neighbour, Le. xix. 18. This Christ declared to be the *second* great commandment of the law, Mat. xxii. 39. *A neighbour* means, 1st. Any person who lives near to us. 2d. Any person with whom we have dealings. 3d. A friend or relative, Mat. v. 43. 4th. Any person—friend, relative, countryman, or foe, Mar. xii. 31. 5th. Any person who does us good or confers a favour on us, Lu. x. 27-37. This commandment means, evidently, 1st. That we should not *injure* our neighbour in his person, property, or character. 2d. That we should not be selfish, but should seek to do him good. 3d. That in a case of debt, difference, or debate, we should do what is *right,* regarding his interest *as much* as our own. 4th. That we should treat *his* character, property, &c., as we do our own, according to what is *right.* 5th. That, in order to benefit him, we should practise self-denial, or do as we would wish him to do to us, Mat. vii. 12. It does *not* mean, 1st. That the love of ourselves, *according to what we are,* or according to *truth,* is improper. The happiness of *myself* is of as much importance as that of any other man, and it is *as* proper that it should be sought. 2d. It does not mean that I am to neglect *my own business* to take care of my neighbour's. *My* happiness, salvation, health, and family are committed peculiarly to myself; and, provided I do not interfere with my neighbour's rights or violate my obligations to him, it is my duty to seek the welfare of my own as my first duty, 1 Ti. v. 8, 13; Tit. ii. 5. Mark adds to these commandments, "Defraud not;" by which he meant, doubtless, to express the substance of this—to love our neighbour as ourselves. It means, literally, to take away the property of another by violence or by deceiving him, thus showing that he is not loved as we love ourselves.

20. *All these things have I kept from my youth up.* I have made them the rule of my life. I have endeavoured to obey them. Is there anything that I lack—are there any new commandments to be kept? Do you, the Messiah, teach any command besides those which I have learned from the law and from the Jewish teachers, which it is necessary for me to obey in order to be saved?

21. *If thou wilt be perfect.* The word *perfect* means *complete* in all its parts, *finished,* having no part wanting. Thus

wilt be perfect, [o]go *and* sell that thou hast and give to the poor, and thou shalt have treasure in heaven; and come *and* [p]follow me.

22 But when the young man heard that saying, he went away sorrowful, for he had great possessions.

23 Then said Jesus unto his disciples, Verily I say unto you, [q]That a rich man shall hardly enter into the kingdom of heaven.

o Lu.12.33; 16.9; Ac.2.45; 4.34,35; 1 Ti.6.18,19. p Jn.12.26.

q 1 Ti.6.9,10.

---

a *watch* is perfect or complete when it has all its proper wheels, and hands, and casements in order. Job was said to be perfect (see Notes on Job i. 1), not that he was sinless, for he is afterward reproved by God himself (Job xxxviii., xxxix., xl. 4); but because his piety was properly proportioned, or had a completeness of parts. He was a pious father, a pious magistrate, a pious neighbour, a pious citizen. His religion was not confined to *one* thing, but it extended to all. *Perfect* means, sometimes, the *filling up*, or the *carrying out*, or the *expression* of a principle of action. Thus, 1 Jn. ii. 5: "Whoso keepeth his word, in him verily is the love of God *perfected.*" That is, the keeping of the commandments of God is the proper *expression, carrying out*, or *completion* of the love of God. This is its meaning here. If thou wilt be *perfect, complete, finished*—if thou wilt show the *proper expression* of this keeping of the commandments, go, &c. Make the obedience *complete.*

Mark says (x. 21), *Jesus, beholding him, loved him.* He was pleased with his amiableness, his correct character, his frankness, his ingenuousness. Jesus, as a man, was capable of all the emotions of most tender friendship. As a man, we may suppose that his disposition was tender and affectionate, mild and calm. Hence he loved with peculiar affection the disciple John, eminently endowed with these qualities; and hence he *was pleased* with the same traits in this young man. Still, with all this amiableness, there is reason to think he was not a Christian, and that the love of *mere amiable qualities* was all the affection that was ever bestowed on him by the Saviour.

One thing, adds Mark, *thou lackest.* There is one thing wanting. You are not *complete.* This done, you would show that your obedience lacked no essential part, but was *complete, finished, proportionate, perfect.* ¶ *Go and sell that thou hast*, &c. The young man declared that he had kept the law. That law required, among other things, that he should love his neighbour as himself. It required, also, that he should love the Lord his God supremely; that is, more than all other objects. If he *had* that true love to God and man—if he loved his Maker and fellow-creatures more than he did his property, he would be willing to give up his wealth to the service of God and of man. Jesus commanded him to do this, therefore, to *test* his character, and to show him that he had *not* kept the law as he pretended, and thus to show him that he needed a better righteousness than his own. ¶ *Treasure in heaven.* See Notes on Mat. vi. 20. ¶ *Follow me.* To follow Jesus *then* meant to be a personal attendant on his ministry; to go about with him from place to place, as well as to imitate and obey him. *Now* it means, 1st. To obey his commandments. 2d. To imitate his example, and to live like him.

22. *He had great possessions.* He was very rich. He made an *idol* of his wealth. He loved it more than God. *He had* NOT *kept the commandments from his youth up*, nor had he kept them at all; and rather than do good with his treasures, and seek his salvation by obeying God, he chose to turn away from the Saviour and give over his inquiry about eternal life. He probably returned no more. Alas! how many lovely and amiable young persons follow his example!

23. *A rich man shall hardly enter into the kingdom of heaven.* Shall *with difficulty* be saved. He has much to struggle with, and it will require the greatest of human efforts to break away from his temptations and idols, and to secure his salvation. Comp. Notes on 1 Ti. vi. 9, 10.

24. *It is easier for a camel*, &c. This was a *proverb* in common use among the Jews, and is still common among the Arabians. To denote that a thing was *impossible* or *exceedingly difficult*, they said that a *camel* or an *elephant* might as soon walk through a needle's

24 And again I say unto you, It is easier for a camel to go through the eye of a needle, than for a rich man to enter into the kingdom of God.

25 When his disciples heard *it*, they were exceedingly amazed, saying, Who then can be saved?

26 But Jesus beheld *them*, and said unto them, With men this is impossible; but [r]with God all things are possible.

27 Then[s] answered Peter and said unto him, Behold, [t]we have forsaken all and followed thee: what shall we have, therefore?

28 And Jesus said unto them, Verily I say unto you, that ye which have followed me, in the regeneration, when the Son of man shall sit

r Ps.3.8; 62.11; Zec.8.6.
s Mar.10.28; Lu.18.28. t Phi.3.8.

eye. In the use of such proverbs it is not necessary to understand them *literally.* They merely denote the extreme difficulty of the case. ¶ *A camel.* A beast of burden much used in Eastern countries. It is about the size of the largest ox, with one or two bunches on his back, with long neck and legs, no horns, and with feet adapted to the hot and dry sand. They are capable of carrying heavy burdens, will travel sometimes faster than the fleetest horse, and are provided with a stomach which they fill with water, by means of which they can live four or five days without drink. They are very mild and tame, and kneel down to receive and unload their burden. They are chiefly used in deserts and hot climates, where other beasts of burden are with difficulty kept alive. ¶ *A rich man.* This rather means one who *loves* his riches and makes an idol of them, or one who *supremely* desires to be rich. Mark says (x. 24) "How hard is it for them that trust in riches." While a man has this feeling—relying on his wealth alone—it is literally *impossible* that he should be a Christian; for religion is a love of God rather than the world—the love of Jesus and his cause more than gold. Still a man may have much *property*, and not have this feeling. He *may* have great wealth, and love God more; as a poor man may have little, and love that little more than God. The difficulties in the way of the salvation of a rich man are—1st. That riches engross the affections. 2d. That men consider wealth as the *chief good*, and when this is obtained they think they have gained all. 3d. That they are proud of their wealth, and unwilling to be numbered with the poor and despised followers of Jesus. 4th. That riches engross the *time*, and fill the mind with cares and anxieties, and leave little for God. 5th. That they often produce luxury, dissipation, and vice. 6th. That it is difficult to obtain wealth without sin, without avarice, without covetousness, fraud, and oppression, 1 Ti. vi. 9, 10, 17; Ja. v. 1-5; Lu. xii. 16-21; xvi. 19-31. Still, Jesus says (ver. 26), all these *may* be overcome. God can give grace to do it. Though to *men* it may appear impossible, yet it is easy for God.

27. *We have forsaken all.* Probably nothing but their fishing-nets, small boats, and cottages. But they were their *all*—their *living*, their *home;* and, forsaking *them*, they had as really shown their sincerity as though they had possessed the gold of Ophir and dwelt in the palaces of kings. ¶ *What shall we have, therefore?* We have *done* as thou didst command this young man to do. What reward may we expect for it?

28. *Verily I say unto you.* Jesus in this verse declares the reward which they would have. They were not to look for it *now*, but in a future period. ¶ *That ye which have followed me, in the regeneration.* This word occurs but once elsewhere in the New Testament, Tit. iii. 5. It literally means a new birth, or being born again. Applied to man, it denotes the great change when the heart is renewed, or when the sinner begins to be a Christian. This is its meaning, clearly, in the passage referred to in *Titus;* but this meaning cannot be applied here. Christ was not born again, and in no proper sense could it be said that they *had followed him in the new birth;* but the word also means any great change, or a restoration of things to a former state or *to a better state.* In this sense it is probably used here. It refers to that great revolution—that restoration of order in the universe—that universal *new birth* which will occur when the dead shall

in the throne of his glory, [u]ye also shall sit upon twelve thrones, judging the twelve tribes of Israel.

29 And[v] every one that hath forsaken houses, or brethren, or sisters, or father, or mother, or wife, or children, or lands, for my name's sake, shall receive an hundred-fold, and shall inherit everlasting life.

30 But[w] many *that are* first shall be last, and the last *shall be* first.

u ch.20.21; Lu.22.28-30; 1 Co.6.2,3; Re.2.26.
v Mar.10.29,30; Lu.18.29,30; 1 Co.2.9.
w ch.20.16; 21.31,32; Mar.10.31; Lu.13.30; Ga.5.7; He.4.1.

---

rise, and all human things shall be changed, and a new order of things shall start up out of the ruins of the old, when the Son of man shall come to judgment. The passage, then, should be read, "Ye which have followed me shall, as a reward in the great day of the resurrection of the dead, and of forming the new and eternal order of things—the day of judgment, the *regeneration*—be signally honoured and blessed." ¶ *When the Son of man shall sit in the throne of his glory.* That is, to judge the world. *Throne of glory* means *glorious throne* or a splendid throne. It is not to be taken literally, but is used to denote his character as a *king and judge*, and to signify the great dignity and majesty which will be displayed by him. See Mat. xxiv. 30; xxvi. 64; Ac. i. 11; xvii. 31. ¶ *Sit upon twelve thrones.* This is figurative. To sit on a throne denotes power and honour, and means here that they would be distinguished above others, and be more highly honoured and rewarded. ¶ *Judging the twelve tribes of Israel.* Jesus will be the Judge of quick and dead. He only is qualified for it, and the Father hath given all judgment to the Son, Jn. v. 22. To be a *judge* denotes rank, authority, power. The ancient *judges* of Israel were men of distinguished courage, patriotism, honour, and valour. Hence the word comes to denote *not so much an actual exercise of the power of passing judgment*, as the *honour* attached to the office; and as earthly kings have those around them dignified with honours and office—counsellors and judges, so Christ says that his apostles will occupy the same *relative* station in the great day. They will be honoured by him, and by all, *as* apostles, as having, in the face of persecution, left all; as having laid the foundations of his church, and endured all the persecutions of the world. ¶ *The twelve tribes of Israel.* This was the number of the ancient tribes. By *this name* the people of God were denoted. By this name Jesus here denotes *his redeemed people.* See also Ja. i. 1, where *Christians* are called the twelve tribes. Here it means also, not the *Jews*, not the *world*, not the *wicked*, not that the apostles are to pronounce sentence on the enemies of God, but *the people of God*, the redeemed. Among them Jesus says his apostles will be *honoured* in the day of judgment, as earthly kings place in posts of office and honour those who have signally served them. Comp. Notes on 1 Co. vi. 2.

29. *And every one that hath forsaken houses,* &c. In the days of Jesus, those who followed him were *obliged*, generally, to forsake houses and home, and to attend him. In our time it is not often required that we should *literally leave* them, except when the life is devoted to him among the heathen; but it is always required that we love them *less* than we do him, that we give up all that is inconsistent with religion, and that we be *ready* to give up all when he demands it. ¶ *For my name's sake.* From attachment to me. Mark adds, "and for the gospel's;" that is, from obedience to the requirements of the gospel, and love for the service of the gospel. ¶ *Shall receive a hundred-fold.* Mark says "a hundred-fold now in this time, houses, and brethren, and sisters," &c. *A hundred-fold* means a hundred times as much. This is not to be understood *literally*, but that he will give what will *be worth* a hundred times as much in the peace, and joy, and rewards of religion. It is also literally true that no man's *temporal interest* is injured by the love of God. Mark adds, "*with persecutions.*" These are not promised as a part of the *reward;* but *amid* their trials and persecutions they should find reward and peace.

30. This verse should have been connected with the following chapter. The parable there spoken is expressly to illustrate this sentiment. See it explained in the Notes on ch. xx. 16.

REMARKS.

1st. We should not throw ourselves *unnecessarily* in the way of the enemies of religion, ver. 1. Jesus, to avoid the dangers to which he was exposed, left Jerusalem, and passed over to the other side of the Jordan. If *duty* calls us to remain in the presence of our enemies and the enemies of religion, we should do it. If we can do them good, we should do it. If our presence will only provoke them to anger and bitterness, then we should turn aside. Comp. Notes on ch. x. 23.

2d. Men will seek every occasion to *ensnare* Christians, ver. 3. Questions will be proposed with great art, and with an appearance of sincerity, only for the purpose of leading them into difficulty. Cunning men know *well* how to propose such questions, and triumph much when they have perplexed believers. This is often the boast of men of some standing, who think they accomplish the great purposes of their existence if they can confound other men, and think it signal triumph if they can make others as miserable as themselves.

3d. We should not refuse to answer such persons with mildness, when the Bible has settled the question, ver. 4-6. Jesus answered a captious question, proposed on purpose to ensnare him. We may often do much to confound the enemies of religion, and to recommend it, when without passion we hear their inquiries, and deliberately inform them that the question has been settled by God. We had better, however, far better, say nothing in reply, than to answer in anger or to show that we are irritated. All the object of the enemy is gained if he can *make us angry*.

4th. Men will search and pervert the Bible for authority to indulge their sins and to perplex Christians, ver. 7. No device is more common than to produce a passage of Scripture *known* to be misquoted or perverted, yet plausible, for the purpose of perplexing Christians. In such cases, the best way, often, is to say nothing. If unanswered, men will be ashamed of it; if answered, they gain their point, and are ready for debate and abuse.

5th. We learn from this chapter that there is no union so intimate as the marriage connection, ver. 6. Nothing is so tender and endearing as this union appointed by God for the welfare of man.

6th. This union should not be entered into slightly or rashly. It involves *all* the happiness of this life and *much* of that to come. The union demands—1st, congeniality of feeling and disposition; 2d, of rank or standing in life; 3d, of temper; 4th, similarity of acquirements; 5th, of age; 6th, of talent; 7th, intimate acquaintance. It should also be a union on religious feelings and opinions: 1st, because religion is more important than anything else; 2d, because it will give more happiness in the married life than anything else; 3d, because where *one* only is pious, there is danger that the religion of the other will be obscured and blighted; 4th, because no prospect is so painful as that of eternal separation; 5th, because it is heathenish, brutal, and mad, to partake the gifts of God in a family and offer no thanksgiving; inexpressibly wicked to live from day to day as if there were no God, no heaven, no hell; 6th, because death is near, and nothing will soothe the pangs of parting but the hope of meeting in the resurrection of the just.

7th. No human legislature has a right to declare divorces except in one single case, ver. 9. If they do, they are accessories to the crime that may follow, and presume to legislate where *God* has legislated before them.

8th. Those *thus* divorced, or pretended to be divorced, and marrying again, are, by the declaration of Jesus Christ, living in adultery, ver. 9. It is no excuse to say that the law of the land divorced them. The law had no such right. If all the legislatures of the world were to say that it was lawful for a man to steal or to commit murder, it would not make it so, and, in spite of human permission, God would hold a man answerable for theft and murder. So, also, of adultery.

9th. The marriage union demands *kindness* and *love*, ver. 6. The husband and the wife are *one*. Love to each other is love to a second self. Hatred, and anger, and quarrels are against *ourselves*. The evils and quarrels in married life will descend on ourselves, and be gall and wormwood in our own cup.

10th. Infants may be brought to Jesus to receive his blessing, ver. 12-15. While on earth, he admitted them to his presence and blessed them with his prayers. If they might be brought *then*, they may be brought *now* Their souls are as precious; their dangers are as great; their salvation is as important. A parent should require the most indubitable evidence that Jesus will *not* receive his offspring, and will be *displeased* if the offering is made, to deter him from this inestimable privilege.

11th. If children *may* be brought, they *should* be brought. It is the solemn duty of a parent to seize upon all possible means of benefiting his children, and of presenting them to God to implore his blessing. In family prayer, in the sanctuary, and in the ordinance of baptism, the blessing of the Redeemer should be sought early and constantly on their precious and immortal souls.

12th. Earnestness and deep anxiety are proper in seeking salvation, ver. 16. The young man came running; he kneeled. It was not form and ceremony; it was life and reality. Religion is a great subject. Salvation is important beyond the power of language to express. Eternity is near, and damnation thunders along the path of the guilty. The sinner *must* be saved soon, or die for ever. He cannot be too earnest. He cannot press with too great haste to Jesus. He should come running, and kneeling, and humbled, and lifting the agonizing cry, "What must I do to be saved?"

13th. We should come young, ver. 20. No one can come *too young*. God has the *first* claim on our affections. He made us, he keeps us, he provides for us, and it is right that we should give our first affections to him. No one who has become a Christian ever yet felt that he had become one too young. No young person that has given his heart to the Redeemer ever yet regretted it. They may give up the gay world to do it; they may leave the circles of the dance and the song; they may be exposed to contempt and persecution, but no matter. He who becomes a true Christian, no matter of what age or rank, blesses God that he was inclined to do it, and the time never *can* come when for one moment he will regret it. Why, then, will not the young give their hearts to the Saviour, and do that which they know they never can for one moment regret?

14th. It is no dishonour for those who hold *offices*, and who are men of rank, to inquire on the subject of religion, Lu. xviii. 18. Men of rank often suppose that it is only the *weak*, the *credulous*, and the *ignorant* that ever feel any anxiety about religion. Never was a greater mistake. It has been only profligate, and weak, and ignorant men that have been thoughtless. Two-thirds of all the profound investigations of the world have been on this very subject. The wisest and best of the heathens have devoted their lives to inquire about God and their own destiny. So in Christian lands. Were Bacon, Newton, Locke, Milton, Hale, and Boerhaave men of weak minds? Yet their deepest thoughts and most anxious inquiries were on this very subject. So in our own land. Were Washington, Ames, Henry, Jay, and Rush men of weak minds? Yet they were professed believers in revelation. And yet young men of rank, and wealth, and learning often think that they show great independence in refusing to *think* of what occupied the profound attention of these men, and fancy they are great only by refusing to tread in their steps. Never was a greater or more foolish mistake. If anything demands attention, it is, surely, the inquiry whether we are to be happy for ever, or wretched; whether there is a God and Saviour; or whether we are "in a forsaken and fatherless world."

15th. It is as important for the *rich* to seek religion as the poor, ver. 22. They will as certainly die; they as much need religion. Without it they *cannot* be happy. Riches will drive away no pain on a death-bed—will not go with us when we die—will not save us.

16th. It is of *special* importance that wealthy young persons should be Christians. They are exposed to many dangers. The world—the gay and flattering world—will lead them astray. Fond of fashion, dress, and amusement, as many of them are, they are exposed to a thousand follies and dangers, from which nothing but religion can *secure* them. Besides, they may do much good, and God will hold them answerable for all the good they *might* have done with their wealth.

17th. The amiable, the lovely, the moral, need also an interest in Christ, Mar. x. 21. If amiable, we should suppose they would be ready to embrace the Saviour. None was ever so moral, so lovely, so pure as he. If we really *loved* amiableness, then we should come to him—we should love him. But, alas! how many amiable young persons turn

CHAPTER XX.

FOR the kingdom of heaven is like unto a man *that is* an householder, [a]which went out early in the morning to hire labourers into his vineyard.

a Ca.8.11,12.

away from him, and refuse to follow him! Can they be really lovers of that which is pure and lovely? If so, then why turn away from the Lamb of God?

18th. The amiable and the lovely need a better righteousness than their own. With all this, they may make an idol of the world; they may be proud, sensual, selfish, prayerless, and thoughtless about dying. Externally they appear lovely; but oh, how far is the heart from God!

19th. Inquirers about religion usually depend on their own works, ver. 16. They are not willing to trust to Jesus for salvation, and they ask what they shall *do;* and it is only when they find that they can do nothing—that they are poor, and helpless, and wretched—that they cast themselves on the mercy of God and find peace.

20th. Compliments and flattering titles are evil, ver. 17. They ascribe something to others which we know they do not possess. Often beauty is praised where we know there is no beauty—accomplishment where there is no accomplishment—talent where there is no talent. Such praises are *falsehood.* We know them to be such. We intend to to deceive by them, and we know that they will produce pride and vanity. Often they they are used for the purpose of destruction. If a man praises us too much, we should look to our purse or our virtue. We should feel that we are in danger, and the next thing will be a dreadful blow — the heavier for all this flattery. They that use compliments much, expect them from others; are galled and vexed when they are *not* obtained; and are in danger when they are.

21st. If we are to be saved, we must do just what God commands us, ver. 17, 18. This is *all* we have to do. We are not to *invent* anything of our own. God has marked out the course, and we must follow it.

22d. We are easily deceived about keeping the law, ver. 17. We often *think* we observe it, when it is only the *outward* form that we have kept. The law is spiritual, and God requires the heart.

23d. Riches are a blessing if used aright; if not, they are deceitful, dangerous, ruinous, ver. 23, 24. Thousands have lost their souls by the love of riches. None have ever been saved by it.

24th. It is our duty to forsake all for Christ, ver. 27–29. Be it little or much, it is all the same to him. It is the *heart* that he looks at; and we may as really show our love by giving up a fishing-boat and net, as by giving up a palace or a crown. If done in either case, it will be accepted.

25th. Religion has its own rewards, ver. 28, 29. It gives more than it takes. It more than compensates for all that we surrender. It gives peace, joy, comfort in trial and in death, and heaven beyond. This is the testimony of all Christians of all denominations—of all that *have* lived, and of all that *do* live—that they never knew true peace till they found it in the gospel. The testimony of so many must be true. They have tried the world in all its forms of gaiety, folly, and vice, and they come and say with one voice, Here only is true peace. On any other subject they would be believed. Their testimony here *must* be true.

26th. Those eminent for usefulness here will be received to distinguished honours and rewards in heaven, ver. 28. They that turn many to righteousness shall shine as stars in the firmament for ever. See Notes on Da. xii. 3.

CHAPTER XX.

1. *For the kingdom of heaven*, &c. The word "for" shows that this chapter should have been connected with the preceding. The parable was spoken expressly to illustrate the sentiment in the last verse of that chapter: "Many that are first shall be last, and the last shall be first." The kingdom of heaven means here the church, including, perhaps, its state here and hereafter. See Notes on Mat. iii. 2. It has reference to *rewards*, and the meaning may be thus expressed: "Rewards shall be bestowed in my kingdom, or on my followers, in the same manner as they were by a certain householder—in such a way that the last shall be equal to the first, and the first last." ¶ *A householder.* A master of a family. One at the head of family affairs. ¶ *His vineyard.* No

2 And when he had agreed with the labourers for a [b]penny a day, he sent them into his vineyard.

3 And he went out about the third hour, and saw others standing idle in the market-place,

4 And said unto them, Go ye also into the vineyard, and whatsoever is right, I will give you. And they went their way.

5 Again he went out about the sixth and ninth hour, and did likewise.

6 And about the eleventh hour he went out and found others standing idle, and saith unto them, [c]Why stand ye here all the day idle?

7 They say unto him, Because no man hath hired us. He saith unto them, [d]Go ye also into the vineyard; and whatsoever is right, *that* shall ye receive.

b ch.18.28.

c Pr.19.15; Eze.16.49; Ac.17.21; He.6.12.
d Ec.9.10; Jn.9.4.

inconsiderable part of Judea was employed in the culture of the grape. *Vineyards* are often used, therefore, to represent a fertile or well-cultivated place, and hence the church, denoting the care and culture that God has bestowed on it. See Notes on Is. v. 7. Comp. Je. xii. 10. For the manner of their construction, see Notes on Mat. xxi. 33.

2. *A penny a day.* The coin here referred to was a Roman coin, equal in value, at different periods, to fifteen or seventeen cents ($7\frac{1}{2}d.$ to $8\frac{1}{2}d.$) of our money. The original denotes the Roman denarius (δηναριον), a silver coin, which was originally equivalent to *ten ases* (a brass Roman coin), whence its name. The consular denarius bore on one side a head of Rome, and an X or a star, to denote the value in *ases*, and a chariot with either two or four horses. At a later period the casts of different deities were on the obverse, and these were finally superseded by the heads of the Cæsars. Many specimens of this coin have been preserved. The following cut shows their usual appearance.

Denarius of Tiberius.

It was probably at that time the price of a day's labour. See Tobit v. 14. This was the common wages of a Roman soldier. In England, before the discovery of the mines of gold and silver in South America, and consequently before money was plenty, the price of labour was about in proportion. In 1351 the price of labour was regulated by law, and was a *penny* a day; but provisions were of course proportionally cheap, and the avails of a man's labour in articles of food were nearly as much as they are now.

3. *About the third hour.* The Jews divided their days into *twelve* equal parts, or hours, beginning at sunrise and ending at sunset. This was, therefore, about nine o'clock in the morning. ¶ *Standing idle in the market-place.* A place where provisions are sold in towns. Of course, many resort to such places, and it would be the readiest place to meet persons and find employers. They were not, therefore, *disposed* to be idle, but were waiting in the proper place to find employers.

4. *Whatsoever is right.* Whatsoever it shall appear you can earn. The contract with the first was definite; with this one it depended on the judgment of the employer.

5. *The sixth and ninth hour.* That is, about twelve and three o'clock.

6. *The eleventh hour.* About five o'clock in the afternoon, or when there was but one working hour of the day left.

8. *When even was come.* That is, when the twelfth hour was come; the day was ended, and the time of payment was come. ¶ *The steward.* A *steward* is one who transacts business in the place of another. He was one who had the administration of affairs in the absence of the householder, who provided for the family, and who was intrusted with the payment of labourers and servants. He was commonly the most trusty and faithful of the servants, raised to that station as a reward for his fidelity. ¶ *Beginning from the last unto the first.* It was immaterial where he *began* to pay, provided he dealt justly by them. In the parable this order is mentioned

8 So when even was come, the lord of the vineyard saith unto his steward, Call the labourers, and give[e] them *their* hire, beginning from the last unto the first.

9 And when they came that *were hired* about the [f]eleventh hour, they received every man a penny.

10 But when the first came, they supposed that they should have received more; and they likewise received every man a penny.

11 And when they had received *it*, they [g]murmured against the goodman of the house,

12 Saying, These last [1]have wrought *but* one hour, and thou hast made them equal unto us, which have borne the burden and the heat of the day.

13 But he answered one of them, and said, [h]Friend, I do thee no wrong: didst not thou agree with me for a penny?

14 Take *that* thine *is*, and go thy way: [i]I will give unto this last even as unto thee.

15 Is[k] it not lawful for me to do what I will with mine own? Is[l] thine eye evil because I am good?

16 So[m] the last shall be first,

e Lu.10.7. f Lu.23.40-43. g Lu.15.29,30.
1 or, *have continued one hour only.*
h ch.22.12. i Jn.17.2. k Ro.9.15-24; Ja.1.18.
l De.15.9; ch.6.23. m ch.19.30.

to give opportunity for the remarks which follow. Had those first hired been first paid, they would have departed satisfied, and the *point* of the parable would have been lost.

9. *They received every man a penny.* There was no agreement how much they should receive, but merely that justice should be done, ver. 4, 5, 7. The householder supposed they had earned it, or chose to make a present to them to compensate for the loss of the first part of the day, when they were willing to work, but could not find employment.

10. *They supposed that they should have received more.* They had worked longer—they had been in the heat; they supposed that it was his intention to pay them, not according to *contract*, but according to the time of the labour.

11. *Murmured.* Complained; found fault with. ¶ *The goodman of the house.* The original here is the same word which in ver. 1 is translated *householder*, and should have been so translated here. It is the old English way of denoting the father of a family. It expresses no *moral* quality.

12. *The burden and heat of the day.* The *burden* means the heavy labour, the severe toil. We have *continued* at that toil in the heat of the day. The others had worked only a little while, and that in the cool of the evening, and when it was far more pleasant and much less fatiguing.

13. *Friend, I do thee no wrong.* I have fully complied with the contract. We had an agreement: I have paid all that I promised. If I choose to *give* a penny to another man if he labours little or not at all—if I should choose to give *all* my property away to others, it would not affect this contract with *you:* it is fully met; and with my own—with that on which *you* have no farther claim—I may do as I please. So, if Christians are *just*, and pay their lawful debts, and injure no one, the world has no right to complain if they give the rest of their property to the poor, or devote it to send the gospel to the heathen, or to release the prisoner or the captive. It is their *own*. They have a right to do with it as they please. They are answerable, not to men, but to God, and infidels, and worldly men, and cold professors in the church have no right to interfere.

14. *Take* that *thine* is. Take what is justly *due* to you—what is properly your own.

15. *Is thine eye evil because I am good?* The Hebrews used the word *evil*, when applied to the eye, to denote one *envious* and *malicious*, De. xv. 9; Pr. xxiii. 6. The eye is called *evil* in such cases, because envy and malice show themselves directly in the eye. No passions are so fully expressed by the eye as these. "Does *envy* show itself in the eye? is thine eye so soon turned to express envy and malice because I have chosen to do good?"

16. *So the last shall be first*, &c. This is the *moral* or *scope* of the parable. To teach this it was spoken. Many that, in the *order of time*, are brought last into the kingdom, shall be first in the re-

and the first last: for [n]many be called, but few chosen.

17 And[o] Jesus, going up to Jerusalem, took the twelve disciples apart in the way, and said unto them,

18 Behold, we go up to Jerusalem; and the Son of man shall be betrayed unto the chief priests and unto the scribes, and they shall condemn him to death,

19 And[p] shall deliver him to the

n ch.22.14; 2 Th.2.13; Ja.1.23-25.
o ch.16.21,&c.; Mar.10.32,&c.; Lu.18.31,&c.; Jn. 12.12,&c.
p ch.27.2,&c.; Mar.15.1,16,&c.; Lu.23.1,&c.; Jn 18. 28,&c.; Ac.3.13; 1 Co.15.3-7.

---

wards. Higher *proportionate* rewards shall be given to them than to others. To *all* justice shall be done. To all to whom the rewards of heaven are *promised* they shall be given. Nothing shall be withheld that was promised. If, among this number who are called into the kingdom, I choose to raise some to stations of distinguished usefulness, and to confer on them peculiar talents and higher rewards, I injure no other one. They shall enter heaven, as was promised. If, amid the multitude of Christians, I choose to signalize such men as Paul, and Martyn, and Brainerd, and Spencer, and Summerfield—to appoint some of them to short labour but to wide usefulness, and raise them to signal rewards, I injure not the great multitude of others who live long lives less useful and less rewarded. All shall reach heaven, and all shall receive what I promise to the faithful. ¶ *Many be called, but few chosen.* The meaning of this, in this connection, I take to be simply this: "Many are called into my kingdom; they come and labour as I command them; many of them are comparatively unknown and obscure; yet they are real Christians, and shall all receive the proper reward. A few I have chosen for higher stations in the church. I have endowed them with apostolic gifts or with superior talents, and fitted them for wider usefulness. They may not be as long in the vineyard as others; their race may be sooner run; but I have chosen to honour them in this manner, and I have a right to do it. I injure no one, and have a right to do what I will with my own." Thus explained, this parable has no reference to the call of the Gentiles, nor to the call of aged sinners, nor to the call of sinners out of the church at all. It is simply designed to teach that *in* the church, among the multitudes who will be saved, Christ makes a difference. He makes some more useful than others, without regard to the *time* which they serve, and he will reward them accordingly. The parable teaches *one* truth, and *but* one; and where Jesus has explained it, we have no right to add to it, and say that it teaches anything else. It adds to the reason for this interpretation, that Christ was conversing about the rewards that should be given to his followers, and not about the numbers that should be called, or about the doctrine of election. See ch. xix. 27–29.

17-19. See also Mar. x. 32–34; Lu. xviii. 31-34. *And Jesus, going up to Jerusalem.* That is, doubtless, to the Passover. This journey was from the east side of Jordan. See Notes on ch. xix. 1. At this time he was on this journey to Jerusalem, probably not far from Jericho. This was his last journey to Jerusalem. He was going up to die for the sins of the world. ¶ *Took the twelve disciples apart.* All the *males* of the Jews were required to be at this feast, Ex. xxiii. 17. The roads, therefore, on such occasions, would probably be thronged. It is probable, also, that they would travel in companies, or that whole neighbourhoods would go together. See Lu. ii. 44. By his *taking them apart* is meant his taking them aside from the company. He had something to communicate which he did not wish the others to hear. Mark adds: "And Jesus went before them, and they were amazed; and as they followed they were sore afraid." He led the way. He had told them before (ch. xvii. 22) that he should be betrayed into the hands of men and be put to death. They began now to be afraid that this would happen, and to be solicitous for his life and for their own safety, and they were "amazed" at his boldness and calmness, and at his fixed determination to go up to Jerusalem in these circumstances.

18, 19. *Behold, we go up to Jerusalem.* Jesus assured them that what they feared would come to pass, but he had, in some measure, prepared their minds for this state of suffering by the promises which he had made to them, ch.

Gentiles, to mock, and to [q]scourge, and to crucify *him:* and the third day he shall rise again.

20 Then[r] came to him the mother of Zebedee's children, with her sons, worshipping *him*, and desiring a certain thing of him.

21 And he said unto her, What wilt thou? She saith unto him, Grant that these my two sons may sit, the one on thy right hand, and the other on the left, in thy kingdom.

22 But Jesus answered and said, Ye know not what ye ask. Are ye able to drink of the cup that I shall drink of, and to be baptized with [s]the baptism that I am baptized

q Is.53.5. r Mar.10.35. s Lu.12.50.

xix. 27–30; xx. 1–16. In all their sufferings they might be assured that eternal rewards were before them. ¶ *Shall be betrayed.* See ch. xvii. 22. ¶ *Unto the chief priests and scribes.* The high-priest, and the learned men who composed the Sanhedrim or Great Council of the nation. He *was* thus betrayed by Judas, Mat. xxvi. 15. He *was* delivered to the chief priests and scribes, Mat. xxvi. 57. ¶ *And they shall condemn him to death.* They had not power to *inflict* death, as that power had been taken away by the Romans; but they had the power of *expressing an opinion*, and of delivering him to the Romans to be put to death. This they did, Mat. xxvi. 66; xxvii. 2. ¶ *Shall deliver him to the Gentiles.* That is, because they have not the right of inflicting capital punishment, they will deliver him to those who have—to the Roman authorities. *The Gentiles* here means Pontius Pilate and the Roman soldiers. See Mat. xxvii. 2, 27–30. ¶ *To mock.* See Notes on Mat. ii. 16. ¶ *To scourge.* That is, to *whip.* This was done with thongs, or a whip made for the purpose, and this punishment was commonly inflicted upon criminals before crucifixion. See Notes on ch. x. 17. ¶ *To crucify* him. That is, to put him to death on a cross—the common punishment of slaves. See Notes on Mat. xxvii. 31, 32. ¶ *The third day,* &c. For the evidence that this was fulfilled, see Notes on Mat. xxviii. 15. Mark and Luke say that he would be spit upon. *Spitting* on another has always been considered an expression of the deepest contempt. Luke says (xviii. 31), "All things that are written by the prophets concerning the Son of man shall be accomplished." Among other things, he says he shall be "spitefully entreated;" that is, treated with *spite* or malice; malice, implying contempt. These sufferings of our Saviour, and this treatment, and his death, had been predicted in many places. See Is. liii.; Da. ix. 26, 27.

20–28. See also Mar. x. 35–45.

20. *Then came to him the mother of Zebedee's children,* &c. This was probably Salome, Mar. xv. 40; xvi. 1. ¶ *With her sons.* The names of these sons were James and John, Mar. x. 35. Mark says *they* came and made the request. That is, they made it, as appears from Matthew, through the medium of their mother; they requested *her* to ask it for them. It is not improbable that she was an ambitious woman, and was desirous to see her sons honoured. ¶ *Worshipping* him. Showing him respect; respectfully saluting him. In the original, *kneeling.* See Notes on Mat. viii. 2.

21. *Grant that these my two sons may sit,* &c. They were still looking for a temporal kingdom. They expected that he would reign on the earth with great pomp and glory. They anticipated that he would conquer as a prince and a warrior. They wished to be distinguished in the day of his triumph. To sit on the right and left hand of a prince was a token of confidence, and the highest honour granted to his friends, 1 Ki. ii. 19; Ps. cx. 1; 1 Sa. xx. 25. The disciples, here, had no reference to the kingdom of heaven, but only to the kingdom which they supposed he was about to set up on the earth.

22. *Ye know not what ye ask.* You do not know the nature of your request, nor what would be involved in it. You suppose that it would be attended only with honour and happiness if the request was granted, whereas it would require much suffering and trial. ¶ *Are ye able to drink of the cup,* &c. To drink of a cup, in the Scriptures, often signifies *to be afflicted, or to be punished,* Mat. xxvi. 39; Is. li. 17, 22; Ps. lxxiii. 10; lxxv. 8; Jer. xxv. 15; Re. xvi. 9. The figure is taken from *a feast,* where the master of a feast ex-

with? They say unto him, We are able.

23 And he saith unto them, Ye[t] shall drink indeed of my cup, and be baptized with the baptism that I am baptized with; but to sit on my right hand, and on my left, is not mine to give, but *it shall be given to them* for whom it is prepared of my Father.

24 And when the ten heard *it*, they were moved with indignation against the two brethren.

25 But Jesus called them *unto him*, and said, [u]Ye know that the princes of the Gentiles exercise dominion over them, and they that are great exercise authority upon them.

26 But[v] it shall not be so among you: but [w]whosoever will be great among you, let him be your minister;

27 And whosoever will be chief among you, let him be your servant:

t Ac.12.2; Ro.8.17; 2 Co.1.7; Re.1.9.

u Lu.22.25,26. *v* 1 Pe.5.3. *w* ch.23.11; Mar.9.35; 10.43.

tends a cup to those present. Thus God is represented as extending to his Son a cup filled with a bitter mixture—one causing deep sufferings, Jn. xviii. 11. This was the cup to which he referred. ¶ *The baptism that I am baptized with.* This is evidently a phrase denoting the same thing. Are ye able *to suffer* with me—to endure the *trials* and *pains* which shall come upon you and me in endeavouring to build up my kingdom? Are you able to bear it when sorrows shall cover you like water, and you shall be sunk beneath calamities as floods, in the work of religion? Afflictions are often expressed by being sunk in the floods and plunged in deep waters, Ps. lxix. 2; Is. xliii. 2; Ps. cxxiv. 4, 5; La. iii. 54.

23. *Ye shall indeed drink of my cup, &c.* You will follow me, and you will partake of my afflictions, and will suffer as *I* shall. This was fulfilled. James was slain with the sword by Herod, Ac. xii. 2. John lived many years; but he attended the Saviour through his sufferings, and was himself banished to Patmos, a solitary island, for the testimony of Jesus Christ—a companion of others *in tribulation*, Re. i. 9. ¶ *Is not mine to give*, &c. The translation of this place evidently does not express the sense of the original. The translation expresses the idea that Jesus has nothing to do in bestowing rewards on his followers. This is at variance with the uniform testimony of the Scriptures, Mat. xxv. 31-40; Jn. v. 22-30. The correct translation of the passage would be, "To sit on my right hand and on my left is not mine to give, *except to those* for whom it is prepared by my Father." The passage thus declares that *Christ* would give rewards to his followers, but only to such as should be entitled to them according to the *purpose of his Father*. Much as he might be attached to these two disciples, yet he could not bestow any such signal favours on them out of the regular course of things. Rewards were prepared for his followers, and in due time they should be bestowed. *He* would bestow them according as they had been provided from eternity by God the Father, Mat. xxv. 34. The correct sense is seen by leaving out that part of the verse *in italics*, and this is one of the places in the Bible where the sense has been obscured by the introduction of words which have nothing to correspond with them in the original. See a similar instance in 1 Jn. ii. 23.

24. *The ten heard* it. That is, the ten other apostles. ¶ *They were moved with indignation.* They were offended at their ambition, and at their desire to be exalted above their brethren. The word "*it*" refers not to what Jesus said, but to their request. When the ten heard *the request* which they had made they were indignant.

25-27. *But Jesus called them* unto him. That is, he called *all* the apostles to him, and stated the principles on which they were to act. ¶ *The princes of the Gentiles exercise dominion over them.* That is, over *their subjects*. "You know that such honours are customary among nations. The kings of the earth raise their favourites to posts of trust and power—they give *authority* to some over others; but my kingdom is established in a different manner. All are to be on a level. The rich, the poor, the learned, the unlearned, the bond, the free, are to be equal. He will be the

28 Even as the Son of man came not to be ministered unto, but [x] to minister, and [y] to give his life a ransom for many.

x Lu.22.27; Jn.13.4,14; Phi.2.7.
y Is.53.5,8,11; Da.9.24,26; 1 Ti.2.6; Tit.2.14; He.9.28; 1 Pe.1.18,19; Re.1.5.

29 And as they departed from Jericho a great multitude followed him.

30 And,[z] behold, two blind men,

z ch.9.27; Mar.10.46; Lu.18.35.

---

most distinguished that shows most humility, the deepest sense of his unworthiness, and the most earnest desire to promote the welfare of his brethren." ¶ *Gentiles.* All who were not Jews—used here to denote the manner in which human governments are constituted. ¶ *Minister.* A servant. The original word is *deacon*—a word meaning a servant of any kind; one especially who served at the table, and, in the New Testament, one who *serves* the church, Ac. vi. 1-4; 1 Ti. iii. 8. Preachers of the gospel are called *ministers* because they are the servants of God and of the church (1 Co. iii. 5; iv. 1; 2 Co. iii. 6; vi. 4; Ep. iv. 12); an office, therefore, which forbids them to lord it over God's heritage, which is the very opposite of a station of superiority, and which demands the very lowest degree of humility.

28. *Even as the Son of man,* &c. See Notes on Mat. viii. 20. Jesus points them to his own example. He was in the form of God in heaven, Phi. ii. 6. He came to men in the form of a servant, Phi. ii. 7. He came not with pomp and glory, but as a man in humble life; and since he came he had not required them to minister to him. He laboured *for* them. He strove to do them good. He provided for their wants; fared as poorly as they did; went before them in dangers and sufferings; practised self-denial on their account, and for them was about to lay down his life. See Jn. xiii. 4, 5. ¶ *To give his life a ransom for many.* The word *ransom* means literally a price paid for the redemption of captives. In war, when prisoners are taken by an enemy, the money demanded for their release is called a ransom; that is, it is the *means* by which they are set at liberty. So anything that releases anyone from a state of punishment, or suffering, or sin, is called a ransom. Men are by nature captives to sin. They are sold under it. They are under condemnation, Ep. ii. 3; Ro. iii. 9-20, 23; 1 Jn. v. 19. They are under a curse, Ga. iii. 10. They are in love with sin. They are under its withering dominion, and are exposed to death eternal, Eze. xviii. 4; Ps. ix. 17; xi. 6; lxviii. 2; cxxxix. 19; Mat. xxv. 46; Ro. ii. 6-9. They must have perished unless there had been some way by which they could be rescued. This was done by *the death* of Jesus—by giving his life a ransom. The meaning is, that he died *in the place* of sinners, and that God was willing to *accept* the pains of *his death* in the place of the eternal suffering of the redeemed. The reasons why such a ransom was necessary are—1st. That God had declared that the sinner shall die; that is, that he would punish, or show his hatred to, all sin. 2d. That all men had sinned, and, if justice was to take its regular course, all must perish. 3d. That man could make no atonement for his own sins. All that he could do, were he holy, would be only to do his duty, and would make no amends for the past. Repentance and future obedience would not blot away one sin. 4th. No man was pure, and no angel could make atonement. God was pleased, therefore, to appoint his only-begotten Son to make such a ransom. See Jn. iii. 16; 1 Jn. iv. 10; 1 Pe. i. 18, 19; Re. xiii. 8; Jn. i. 29; Ep. v. 2; He. viii. 27; Is. liii. This is commonly called *the atonement.* See Notes on Ro. v. 2. ¶ *For many.* See also Mat. xxvi. 28; Jn. x. 15; 1 Ti. ii. 6; 1 Jn. ii. 2; 2 Co. v. 14, 15; He. ii. 9.

29-34. See Mar. x. 46-52, and Lu. xviii. 35-43; xix. 1, where this account of his restoring to sight two blind men is also recorded. *And as they departed from Jericho.* This was a large town about eight miles west of the Jordan, and about nineteen miles north-east from Jerusalem. Near to this city the Israelites crossed the Jordan when they entered into the land of Canaan, Jos. iii. 16. It was the first city taken by Joshua, who destroyed it to the foundation, and pronounced a curse on him who should rebuild it, Jos. vi. 20, 21, 26. This curse was literally fulfilled in the days of Ahab, nearly five hundred years after, 1 Ki. xvi. 34. It afterward became the place of the school of the prophets, 2 Ki. ii. 5. In this place Elisha

sitting by the way-side, when they heard that Jesus passed by, cried out, saying, Have mercy on us, O Lord, *thou* son of David!

worked a signal miracle, greatly to the advantage of the inhabitants, by rendering the waters near it, that were before bitter, sweet and wholesome, 2 Ki. ii. 21. In point of size it was second only to Jerusalem. It was sometimes called the city of palm-trees, from the fact that there were many palms in the vicinity. A few of them are still remaining, 2 Ch. xxviii. 15; Ju. i. 16; iii. 13. At this place died Herod the Great, of a most wretched and foul disease. See Notes on Mat. ii. 19. It is now a small village, wretched in its appearance, and inhabited by a very few persons, and called *Riha*, or *Rah*, situated on the ruins of the ancient city (or, as some think, three or four miles east of it), which a modern traveller describes as a poor, dirty village of the Arabs. There are perhaps fifty houses, of rough stone, with roofs of bushes and mud, and the population, two or three hundred in number, is entirely Mohammedan. Dr. Thomson (*The Land and the Book*, vol. ii. p. 443) says of this village, that there "are some forty or fifty of the most forlorn habitations that I have seen. And this is Jericho! These houses, or rather huts, are surrounded by a peculiar kind of fortification, made of nubk, a species of bush very abundant in this plain. Its thorns are so sharp and the branches are so plaited together that neither horse nor man will attack it." The road from Jerusalem to Jericho lies through what is called the *wilderness of Jericho*, and is described by modern travellers as the most dangerous and forbidding about Palestine. As lately as 1820, an English traveller, Sir Frederick Henniker, was attacked on this road by the Arabs with firearms, who left him naked and severely wounded. See Notes on Lu. x. 30. Jesus was going to Jerusalem from the east side of the Jordan (ch. xix. 1), his regular journey was therefore through Jericho. ¶ *As they departed from Jericho.* Luke says, "*As he was come nigh unto Jericho.*" The original word used in Luke, translated *was come nigh*, commonly expresses *approach to* a place, but it does not of necessity mean that always. It may denote *nearness* to a place, whether going to it or from it. It would be here rendered correctly, "*when they were near to Jericho*," or when they were in the *vicinity* of it, without saying whether they were going *to* it or *from* it. Matthew and Mark say they were going from it. The passage in Lu. xix. 1—*and Jesus entered and passed through Jericho*—which seems to be mentioned as having taken place *after* the cure of the blind man, does not necessarily suppose that. That passage might be intended to be connected with the account of Zaccheus, and not to denote *the order of time* in which these events took place; but simply that as he was passing through Jericho, Zaccheus sought to see him, and invited him to his house. Historians vary in the circumstances and order of events. The *main facts* of the narrative are observed; and such variations of circumstances and order, where there is no palpable contradiction, show the *honesty* of the writers—show that they did not *conspire together* to deceive, and are in courts of justice considered as confirmations of the truth of the testimony.

30. *Two blind men.* Mark and Luke mention but one. They do not say, however, that there was no more than one. They mention one because he was probably well known; perhaps the son of a distinguished citizen reduced to poverty. His name was Bartimeus. *Bar* is a Syraic word, meaning *son*: and the name means, therefore, "the son of Timeus." Probably *Timeus* was a man of distinction; and as the case of his son attracted most attention, Mark and Luke recorded it particularly. Had they said there was *only* one healed, there would have been a contradiction. As it is, there is no more contradiction or difficulty than there is in the fact that the evangelists, like all other historians, often omit many facts which they do not choose to record. ¶ *Heard that Jesus passed by.* They learned who he was by inquiring. They heard a noise, and asked who it was (Luke). They had doubtless heard much of his fame, but had never before been where he was, and probably would not be again. They were therefore more earnest in calling upon him. ¶ *Son of David.* That is, *Messiah*, or *Christ*. This was the name by which the Messiah was commonly known. He was the illustrious *descendant* of David in whom the pro-

31 And the multitude rebuked them, because they should hold their peace: but they cried the more, saying, Have mercy on us, O Lord, *thou* son of David!

32 And Jesus stood still, and called them, and said, What will ye that I shall do unto you?

33 They say unto him, Lord, that our eyes may be opened.

34 So Jesus had compassion *on them,* and touched their eyes: and immediately their eyes received sight, and they followed him.

---

mises especially centred, Ps. cxxxii. 11, 12; lxxxix. 3, 4. It was the universal opinion of the Jews that the Messiah was to be the descendant of David. See ch. xxii. 42. On the use of the word *son*, see Notes on Mat. i. 1.

31. *And the multitude rebuked them because*, &c. They chid or reproved them, and in a threatening manner told them to be silent. ¶ *They cried the more.* Jesus, standing still, ordered them to be brought to him (Mark). His friends *then* addressed the blind men and told them that Jesus called (Mark). Mark adds that Bartimeus cast away his garment, and rose and came to Jesus. *The garment* was not his only raiment, but was the *outer* garment, thrown loosely over him, and commonly laid aside when persons laboured or ran. See Notes on Mat. v. 40. His doing it denoted haste and earnestness in order to come to Jesus.

34. *And touched their eyes.* Mark and Luke say he added, *Thy faith hath saved thee.* Thy *confidence*, or *belief* that I could cure, has been the means of obtaining this blessing. Faith had no power to open the eyes, but it led the blind men to Jesus; it showed that they had just views of his power; it was connected with the cure. So *faith* has no power to save from sin, but it leads the poor, lost, blind sinner to him who *has* power, and in this sense it is said we are saved by faith. His *touching* their eyes was merely *a sign* that the power of healing proceeded from him.

Here was an undoubted miracle. 1st. These blind men were well known. One, at least, had been long blind. 2d. They were strangers to Jesus. They could not have, therefore, *feigned* themselves blind, or done this by any *collusion* or *agreement* between him and themselves in order to impose on the multitude. 3d. The miracle was in the presence of multitudes who took a deep interest in it, and who could easily have detected the imposition if there had been any. 4th. The men followed him. They praised or *glorified* God (Mark and Luke). The people gave praise to God also (Luke). They were all satisfied that a *real* miracle was performed.

REMARKS.

1st. From the parable at the beginning of this chapter (ver. 1–16) we learn that it is not so much the *time* that we serve Christ as the *manner*, that is to entitle us to high rewards in heaven. Some may be in the church many years, yet accomplish little. Others in a few years may be more distinguished in the success of their labours and in their rewards.

2d. God will do justice to all, ver. 13. He will give to every one of his followers all that he promised to give. To him entitled to the least he will give everything which he has promised, and to each one infinitely more than he has deserved.

3d. On some he will bestow higher rewards than on others, ver. 16. There is no reason to think that the condition of men in heaven will be *equal*, any more than it is on earth. Difference of rank may run through all God's government, and still no one be degraded or be deprived of his rights.

4th. God does as he pleases with his own, ver. 15. It is his right to do so—a right which *men* claim, and which God may claim. If he does injustice to *no one*, he has a right to bestow what favours on others he pleases. In doing good to another man he does no injury to me. He violated none of *my* rights by bestowing great talents on Newton or great wealth on Solomon. He did not injure *me* by making Paul a man of distinguished talents and piety, or John a man of much meekness and love. What he gives me I should be thankful for and improve; nor should I be envious or malignant that he has given to others more than he has to me. Nay, I should rejoice that he has bestowed such favours on undeserving men at all; that *the race* is in possession of such talents and rewards, to whomsoever given; and should believe that in the hands of God such favours will be well bestowed. God is a sovereign, and the Judge of all the earth will do that which is right.

5th. It is our duty to go into the vineyard and labour faithfully whenever the Lord Jesus calls us, and till he calls us to receive our reward, ver. 1–16. He has a right to call us, and there are none who are not invited to labour for him.

6th. Rewards are offered to all who will serve him, ver. 4. It is not that we *deserve* any favour, or that we shall not say at the end of life that we have been *unprofitable* servants, but he graciously promises that our rewards shall be measured by our faithfulness in his cause. *He* will have the glory of bringing us into his kingdom and saving us, while he will bestow rewards on us according as we have been faithful in his service.

7th. Men may be saved in old age, ver. 6. Old men are sometimes brought into the kingdom of Christ and made holy, but it is rare. Few aged men are converted—they drop into the grave as they lived; and to a man who wastes his youth and his middle life in sin, and goes down into the vale of years a rebel against God, there is a dreadful probability that he will die as he lived. It will be found to be true, probably, that by far more than half who are saved are converted before they reach the age of twenty. Besides, it is foolish as well as wicked to spend the *best* of our days in the service of Satan, and to give to God only the poor remnant of our lives that we can no longer use in the cause of wickedness. God should have our *first* and *best* days.

8th. Neither this parable nor any part of the Bible should be so abused as to lead us to put off the time of repentance to old age. It is *possible*, though not *probable*, that *we* shall live to be old. Few, few, of all the world, live to old age. Thousands die in childhood. The time, the accepted time to serve God, is in early life; and God will require it at the hands of parents and teachers if they do not train up the children committed to them to love and obey him.

9th. One reason why we do not understand the plain doctrines of the Bible is our prejudice, ver. 17–19. Our Saviour plainly told his disciples that he must die. He stated the manner of his death, and the principal circumstances. To us, all this is plain, but *they* did not understand it (Luke). They had filled their heads with notions about his earthly glory and honour, and they were not *willing* to see the truth as he stated it. Never was there a juster proverb than that "none are so blind as those who *will* not see." So to us the Bible might be plain enough. The doctrines of truth are revealed as clear as a sunbeam, but we are filled with previous notions—we are determined to think differently; and the easiest way to gratify this is to say we do not *see* it so. The only correct principle of interpretation is, that the Bible is to be taken *just as it is.* The meaning that the sacred writers intended to teach is to be sought honestly; and when found, that, and that only, is religious truth.

10th. Mothers should be cautious about seeking places of honour for their sons, ver. 20–22. Doing this, they seldom know what they ask. They may be seeking the ruin of their children. It is not in posts of honour that happiness or salvation are certainly secured. Contentment and peace are found oftenest in the humble vale of honest and sober industry—in attempting to fill up our days with usefulness in the situation where God has placed us. As the purest and loveliest streams often flow in the retired grove, far from the thundering cataract or the stormy ocean, so is the sweet peace of the soul; it dwells oftenest far from the bustle of public life, and the storms and tempests of ambition.

11th. Ambition in the church is exceedingly improper, ver. 22–28. It is not the nature of religion to produce it. It is opposed to all the modest, retiring, and pure virtues that Christianity produces. An ambitious man will be destitute of religion just in proportion to his ambition, and piety may always be measured by humility. He that has the most lowly views of himself, and the highest of God—that is willing to stoop the lowest to aid his fellow-creatures and to honour God—has the most genuine piety. Such was the example of our Saviour, and it can never be any dishonour to imitate the Son of God.

12th. The case of the blind men is an expressive representation of the condition of the sinner, ver. 30–34. 1st. Men

CHAPTER XXI.

AND[a] when they drew nigh unto Jerusalem, and were come to Bethphage, unto the mount of Olives, then sent Jesus two disciples,

a Mar.11.1; Lu.19.29.

are blinded by sin. They do not by nature see the truth of religion. 2d. It is proper in this state of *blindness* to call upon Jesus to open our eyes. If we ever *see*, it will be by the grace of God. God is the fountain of light, and those in darkness should seek him. 3d. Present opportunities should be improved. This was the first time that Jesus had been in Jericho. It was the last time he would be there. He was passing *through it* on his way to Jerusalem. So he passes among us by his ordinances. So it may be the *last time* that we shall have an opportunity to call upon him. While he is near we should seek him. 4th. When people rebuke us and laugh at us, it should not deter us from calling on the Saviour. There is danger that they will *laugh* us out of our purpose to seek him, and we should cry the more earnestly to him. We should feel that our eternal all depends on our being heard. 5th. The persevering cry of those who seek the Saviour aright will not be in vain. They who cry to him, sensible of their blindness, and sensible that he only can open their eyes, will be heard. He turns none away who thus call upon him. 6th. Sinners must "rise" and come to Jesus. They must cast away everything that hinders their coming. As the blind Bartimeus threw off his "garments," so sinners should throw away everything that hinders their going to him—everything that obstructs their progress—and cast themselves at his feet. No man will be saved while *sitting still*. The command is, "Strive to enter in;" and the promise is made to those only who "ask," and "seek," and "knock." 7th. *Faith* is the only channel through which we shall receive mercy. According to our *faith*—that is, our *confidence* in Jesus, our trust and reliance on him—so will it be to us. Without that, we shall perish. 8th. They who apply to Jesus thus will receive sight. Their eyes will be opened and they will see clearly. 9th. They who are thus restored to sight should follow Jesus. They should follow him wherever he leads; they should follow him always; they should follow none else but him. He that can give sight to the blind cannot lead us astray. He that can shed light in the *beginning* of our faith, can enlighten our goings through all our pilgrimage, and even down through the dark valley of the shadow of death.

CHAPTER XXI.

1-16. See also Mar. xi. 1-11; Lu. xix. 29-44.

1. *And when they drew nigh unto Jerusalem.* They were going up now from Jericho, ch. xx. 29. The distance was about nineteen miles. The most of the way was a desert, or filled with caves, and rocks, and woods—a fit place for robbers. See Lu. x. 30. The Mount of Olives, or *Olivet*, is on the east of Jerusalem. Between this and Jerusalem there runs a small stream called the brook Kidron, or Cedron. It is dry in the hot seasons of the year, but swells to a considerable size in time of heavy rains. See Notes on Jn. xviii. 1. The Mount of Olives was so called from its producing in abundance the olive. It was from Jerusalem about a Sabbath-day's journey. See Notes on Ac. i. 12. On the *west* side of the mountain was the garden of Gethsemane, Lu. xxii. 39; Mar. xiv. 32. On the eastern declivity of the mountain were the villages of Bethphage and Bethany. Mark and Luke say that he came near to both those places. He appears to have come first to Bethany, where he passed the night (Jn. xii. 1, 9-11), and in the morning sent over to the adjacent village Bethphage. Bethany was the place where Lazarus dwelt, whom he raised from the dead (Jn. xi.); where Martha and Mary dwelt; and where Mary anointed him with ointment against the day of his burying, Jn. xii. 1-7. The Mount of Olives is about a mile in length and about 700 feet in height, and overlooks Jerusalem, so that from its summit almost every part of the city can be seen. The mountain is composed of three peaks or summits. The *olive* is a fruit well known among us as an article of commerce. The tree blooms in June, and bears white flowers. The fruit is small. It is first green, then whitish, and, when fully ripe, black. It incloses a hard stone in which are the seeds. The *wild olive* was common, and

2 Saying unto them, Go into the village over against you, and straightway ye shall find an ass tied, and a colt with her: loose *them*, and bring *them* unto me.

3 And if any *man* say aught unto you, ye shall say, The Lord hath need of them; and straightway he will send them.

4 All this was done, that it might be fulfilled which was spoken by the [b]prophet, saying,

5 Tell[c] ye the daughter of Sion, Behold, thy King cometh unto thee, meek, and sitting upon an ass, and a colt the foal of an ass.

6 And the disciples went, and did as Jesus commanded them,

7 And brought the ass, and the colt, and put on them their clothes, and they set *him* thereon.

8 And a very great multitude spread their garments in the way: others cut down branches from

b Zec.9.9.

c Is.62.11; Mar.11.4,&c.; Jn.12.15.

---

differed from the other only in being of a smaller size. There are two roads from Jerusalem to Bethany; one around the southern end of the Mount of Olives, and the other across the summit. The latter is considerably shorter, but more difficult, and it was probably along this road that the Saviour went.

2. *Go into the village over against you.* That is, to Bethphage. See Notes on ver. 1. ¶ *Ye shall find an ass tied*, &c. In Judea there were few horses, and those were chiefly used in war. Men seldom employed them in common life and in ordinary journeys. The ass, the mule, and the camel are still most used in Eastern countries. To ride on a horse was sometimes an emblem of war; on a mule and an ass, the emblem of peace. Kings and princes commonly rode on them in times of peace, and it is mentioned as a mark of rank and dignity to ride in that manner, Ju. x. 4; xii. 14; 1 Sa. xxv. 20. So Solomon, when he was inaugurated as king, rode on a *mule*, 1 Ki. i. 33. Riding in this manner, then, denoted neither poverty nor degradation, but was the appropriate way in which a king should ride, and in which, therefore, the King of Zion should enter into his capital, the city of Jerusalem.

Mark and Luke say that he told them they should find "a colt tied." This they were directed to bring. They mention only the *colt*, because it was this on which he rode.

3. *The Lord hath need of them.* This means no more than the *master* has need of them. The word *Lord* often means no more than *master* as opposed to *servant*, Mat. x. 24; Ep. vi. 5; 1 Pe. iii. 5, 6. The word is sometimes used in the Bible as applied to God, or as a translation of the name JEHOVAH. Its common use is a mere title of respect given by an inferior to a superior, by a servant to a master, by a disciple to a teacher. As a title of *high respect* it was given to Christ, or the Messiah. The persons to whom these disciples were sent were probably acquainted with the miracles of Jesus and favourably disposed toward him. He had attracted great notice in that region, particularly by raising Lazarus from the dead, and most of the people regarded him as the Messiah.

4, 5. *All this was done*, &c. The prophecy here quoted is found in Zec. ix. 9. It was always, by the Jews, applied to the Messiah. ¶ *Daughter of Zion.* That is, *Jerusalem. Zion* was one of the hills on which the city of Jerusalem was built. On this stood the city of David and some strong fortresses. The names *daughter* and *virgin* were given to it often, in accordance with the Oriental figurative manner of expression. See Notes on Is. i. 8. Comp. Am. v. 2; Ps. xlv. 13; cxxxvii. 8; Is. xlvii. 1. It was given to them as an expression of their beauty or comeliness. ¶ *Meek.* See Notes on Mat. v. 5. The expression here rather denotes *peaceful*, not *warlike;* not with pomp, and state, and the ensigns of ambition. He came in the manner in which kings were accustomed to ride, but with none of their pride and ambitious feeling. ¶ *Sitting upon an ass*, &c. He rode on the colt (Mark and Luke). This expression in Matthew is one which is common with all writers. See Ge. xix. 29; Ju. xii. 7.

7. *And put on them their clothes.* This was done as a token of respect, 2 Ki. ix. 13.

8. *And a very great multitude*, &c. Others showed the same respect by throwing their garments before him;

the trees, and strewed *them* in the way.

9 And the multitudes that went before, and that followed, cried, saying, Hosanna to the son of David! Blessed[d] is he that cometh

d Ps.118.26; ch.23.39.

others by cutting down branches of trees and casting them in the way. This was the way in which conquerors and princes were often honoured. To cast flowers, or garlands, or evergreens before a warrior returning from victory, or a king entering into his kingdom, was a common way of testifying joyful and triumphant feeling. Thus Josephus says that Alexander and Agrippa were received at Jerusalem. So in our own land some of the most acceptable tokens of rejoicing ever bestowed upon Washington were garlands of roses scattered in his path by children. So the path of Lafayette was often strewed with flowers, as a mark of respect and of a nation's gratitude. John says (xii. 13) that these branches were branches of the *palm-tree.* The *palm* was an emblem of *joy* and *victory.* It was used by the Roman soldiers, as well as the Jews, as a symbol of peace. See 1 Mac. xiii. 51; 2 Mac. x. 6, 7; Re. vii. 9.

The *palm-tree* is common in warm climates, and was abundant in Palestine. The finest grew about Jericho and Engedi. Hence Jericho was called the city of *palm-trees.* The palm has a long and straight body, a spreading top, and an appearance of very great beauty. It produces an agreeable fruit, a pleasant shade, a kind of *honey* little inferior to the honey of bees, and from it was drawn a pleasant *wine* much used in the East. On ancient coins the palm-tree is often a symbol of Judea. On coins made after Jerusalem was taken, Judea is represented by a female sitting and weeping under a palm-tree. A reference to the palm-tree occurs often in the Bible, and its general form and uses are familiar to most readers.

Strictly speaking, the palm has no branches, but at the summit from forty to eighty twigs or leaf-stalks spring forth. These are referred to in Ne. viii. 15. The leaves are set around the trunk in circles of about six. The lower row is of great length, and the vast leaves bend themselves in a curve toward the earth: as the circles ascend, the leaves are shorter. In the month of February, there sprout from between the junctures of the lower stalks and the trunk little scales, which develop a kind of bud, the germ of the coming fruit. These germs are contained in a thick and tough skin, not unlike leather. According to the account of a modern traveller, a single tree in Barbary and Egypt bears from fifteen to twenty large clusters of dates, weighing from 15 to 20 lbs. each. The palm-tree lives more than 200 years, and is most productive from the thirtieth until the eightieth year. The Arabs speak of 260 uses to which the different parts of the palm-tree are applied.

The inhabitants of Egypt, Arabia, and Persia depend much on the fruit of the palm-tree for their subsistence. Camels feed on the seed, and the leaves, branches, fibres, and sap are all very valuable.

The "branches" referred to by John (xii. 13) are the long *leaves* which shoot out from the top of the tree, and which were often carried about as the symbol of victory. Comp. Notes on Is. iii. 26.

9. *Hosanna to the son of David,* &c. The word *hosanna* means "save now," or "save, I beseech thee." It is a Syriac word, and was a form of acclamation used among the Jews. It was probably used in the celebration of their great festivals. During those festivals they sang the 115th, 116th, 117th, and 118th Psalms. In the chanting or singing of those psalms, the Jewish writers inform us that the people responded frequently *hallelujah,* or *hosanna.* Their use of it on this occasion was a joyful acclamation, and an invocation of a divine blessing by the *Messiah.* ¶ *Son of David.* The Messiah. ¶ *Blessed be he,* &c. That is, blessed be the *Messiah.* This passage is taken from Ps. cxviii. 25, 26. To come *in the name of the Lord* here means to come *by the authority* of the Lord, or to come *commissioned* by him to reveal his will. The Jews had commonly applied this to the Messiah. ¶ *Hosanna in the highest.* This may mean either "Hosanna in the highest, loftiest strains," or it may be for a prayer to God—"Save now, O thou that dwellest in the highest heaven, or among the highest angels." Perhaps the whole song of hosanna may be a prayer to the Supreme God, as well as a note of

in the name of the Lord; [e]Hosanna in the highest!

10 And when he was come into Jerusalem, all the city was moved, saying, Who is this?

11 And the multitude said, This is Jesus, the prophet of Nazareth of Galilee.

12 And[f] Jesus went into the temple of God, and cast out all

e Lu.2.14.

f Mar.11.11; Lu.19.45,&c.; Jn.2.15,&c.

---

triumphant acclamation: "Save now, O thou supremely great and glorious God; save by the Messiah that comes in thy name."

Mark adds that they shouted, "Blessed be the kingdom of our father David, that cometh in the name of the Lord." That is, the kingdom *promised* to David, 1 Ki. ii. 4; viii. 25. *Coming in the name of the Lord* here evidently means coming according to the *promise* of the Lord. The sense may be thus expressed: "Prosperity to the reign of our father David, advancing now according to the promise made to him, and about to be established by the long predicted Messiah, his descendant."

Luke adds (xix. 38) that they said, "Peace in heaven and glory in the highest." The word *peace* is used here as significant of joy, triumph, exultation at this event. There will be increased peace and rejoicing in heaven from the accession of the redeemed: there will be augmented glory—new songs of praise *among the highest angels*.

There is no contradiction here among the evangelists. Among such a multitude, the shouts of exultation and triumph would by no means be confined to the same words. Some would say one thing and some another; and one evangelist recorded what was said by a part of the multitude, and another what was said by another part.

10. *And when he was come into Jerusalem, all the city was moved.* There was great excitement. The sight of such a multitude, the shouts of the people, and the triumphant procession through the city, excited much attention and inquiry.

12–22. This paragraph contains the account of the barren fig-tree, and of the cleansing of the temple. See also Mar. xi. 12–19; Lu. xix. 45–48.

12. *And Jesus went into the temple of God*, &c. From Mar. xi. 11–15, it is probable that this cleansing of the temple did not take place on the day that he entered Jerusalem in triumph, but on the day following. He came and looked round upon all things, Mark says, and went out to Bethany with the twelve. On the day following, returning from Bethany, he saw the fig-tree. Entering into the temple, he purified it *on that day;* or perhaps he *finished* the work of purifying it on that day, which he commenced the day before. Matthew has mentioned the purifying of the temple, which was performed, probably, on two successive days, or has stated the *fact*, without being particular as to the order of events. Mark has stated the order more particularly, and has *divided* what Matthew mentions together.

The "temple of God," that is, the temple dedicated and devoted to the service of God, was built on Mount Moriah. The first temple was built by Solomon, about 1005 years before Christ, 1 Ki. vi. He was seven years in building it, 1 Ki. vi. 38. David, his father, had contemplated the design of building it, and had prepared many materials for it, but was prevented because he had been a man of war, 1 Ch. xxii. 1–9, 1 Ki. v. 5. This temple, erected with great magnificence, remained till it was destroyed by the Babylonians under Nebuchadnezzar, 584 years before Christ, 2 Ch. xxxvi. 6, 7, 19.

After the Babylonish captivity the temple was rebuilt by Zerubbabel, but with vastly inferior and diminished splendour. The aged men wept when they compared it with the glory of the former temple, Ezr. iii. 8, 12. This was called the *second* temple. This temple was often defiled in the wars before the time of Christ. It had become much decayed and impaired. Herod the Great, being exceedingly unpopular among the Jews on account of his cruelties (see Notes on Mat. ii.), was desirous of doing something to obtain the favour of the people, and accordingly, about sixteen years before Christ, and in the eighteenth year of his reign, he commenced the work of repairing it. This he did, not by taking it down entirely at once, but by removing one part after another, till it had become, in fact, a new temple, greatly surpassing the for-

them that sold and bought in the temple, and overthrew the tables of the money-changers, and the seats of them that sold doves;

mer in magnificence. It was still called by the Jews the *second* temple; and by Christ's coming to this temple thus repaired, was fulfilled the prophecy in Hag. ii. 9. On this building Herod employed eighteen thousand men, and completed it so as to be fit for use in nine years, or about eight years before Christ. But additions continued to be made to it, and it continued increasing in splendour and magnificence till A.D. 64. John says (ii. 20), forty and six years was this temple in building. Christ was then thirty years of age, which, added to the sixteen years occupied in repairing it before his birth, makes forty-six years.

The word *temple* was given not merely to the sacred edifice or house itself, but to all the numerous chambers, courts, and rooms connected with it on the top of Mount Moriah. The temple itself was a small edifice, and was surrounded by courts and chambers half a mile in circumference. Into the sacred edifice itself our Saviour never went. The high-priest only went into the holy of holies, and that but once a year, and none but priests were permitted to enter the holy place. Our Saviour was neither. He was of the tribe of *Judah*, and he consequently was allowed to enter no farther than the other Israelites into the temple. The works that he is said to have performed in the temple, therefore, are to be understood as having been performed in the *courts* surrounding the sacred edifice. These courts will now be described.

The temple was erected on Mount Moriah. The space on the summit of the mount was not, however, large enough for the buildings necessary to be erected. It was therefore enlarged by building high walls from the valley below and filling up the space within. One of these walls was 600 feet in height. The ascent to the temple was by high flights of steps. The entrance to the temple, or to the *courts* on the top of the mount, was by nine gates, all of them extremely splendid. On every side they were thickly coated with gold and silver. But there was one gate of peculiar magnificence: this was called *the Beautiful* gate, Ac. iii. 2. It was on the east side, and was made of Corinthian brass, one of the most precious metals in ancient times. See the Introduction to 1 Corinthians, § 1. This gate was 50 cubits, or 75 feet, in height.

The whole temple, with all its courts, was surrounded by a wall about 25 feet in height. This was built on the wall raised from the base to the top of the mountain, so that from the top of it to the bottom, in a perpendicular descent, was in some places not far from 600 feet. This was particularly the case on the south-east corner; and it was here, probably, that Satan wished our Saviour to cast himself down. See Notes on Mat. iv. 6.

On the inside of this wall, between the gates, were piazzas or covered porches. On the eastern, northern, and western sides there were two rows of these porches; on the south, three. These porches were covered walks, about 20 feet in width, paved with marble of different colours, with a flat roof of costly cedar, which was supported by pillars of solid marble, so large that three men could scarcely stretch their arms so as to meet around them. These walks or porches afforded a grateful shade and protection to the people in hot or stormy weather. The one on the east side was distinguished for its beauty, and was called Solomon's porch, Jn. x. 23; Ac. iii. 11. It stood over the vast terrace or wall which he had raised from the valley beneath, and which was the only thing of his work that remained in the second temple.

When a person entered any of the gates into this space within the wall he saw the temple rising before him with great magnificence; but the space was not clear all the way up to it. Going forward, he came to another wall, inclosing considerable ground, considered more holy than the rest of the hill. The space between this first and second wall was called *the court of the Gentiles*. It was so called because Gentiles might come into it, but they could proceed no farther. On the second wall and on the gates were inscriptions in Hebrew, Greek, and Latin, forbidding any Gentile or unclean person from proceeding farther on pain of death. This *court* was not of equal dimensions all the way round the temple. On the east, north, and west it was quite narrow. On the south it was wide, occupying nearly half of the whole surface of the hill. In this court the Gentiles might come. Here was the place where much secular business was transacted. This was the place occupied by the buyers and sellers, and by the money-changers, and which Jesus purified by casting them out.

The inclosure within the second wall was nearly twice as long from east to west as from north to south. This inclosure was also divided. The eastern part of it was called *the court of the women;* so called because women might advance thus far, but no farther. This court was square. It was entered by three gates; one on the north, one on the east directly opposite to the Beautiful gate, and one on the south. In passing from the court of the Gentiles to that of the women, it was necessary to ascend about 9 feet by steps. This court of the women was inclosed with a double wall, with a space between the walls about 15 feet in width, paved with marble. The inner of these two walls was much higher than the one outside. The court of the women was paved with marble. In the corners of that court were different structures for the various uses of the temple. It was in *this* court that the Jews commonly worshipped. Here, probably, Peter and John, with others, went up to pray, Ac. iii. 1. Here, too, the Pharisee and publican prayed—the Pharisee near the gate that led forward to the temple; the publican standing far off, on the other side of the court, Lu. xviii. 9-14. Paul also was seized here, and charged with defiling the temple by bringing the Gentiles into that holy place, Ac. xxi. 26-30.

A high wall on the west side of the court of the women divided it from the court of the Israelites, so called because all the *males* of the Jews might advance there. To this court there was an ascent of fifteen steps. These steps were in the form of a half circle. The great gate to which these steps led was called the gate *Nicanor*. Besides this, there were three gates on each side, leading from the court of the women to the court of the Israelites.

Within the court of the *Israelites* was the court of the *priests*, separated by a wall about 1½ foot in height. Within that court was the altar of burnt-offering and the laver standing in front of it. Here the priests performed the daily service of the temple. In this place, also, were accommodations for the *priests* when not engaged in conducting the service of the temple, and for the Levites who conducted the *music* of the sanctuary.

The temple, properly so called, stood within this court. It surpassed in splendour all the other buildings of the holy city; perhaps in magnificence it was unequalled in the world. It fronted the east, looking down through the gates Nicanor and the Beautiful gate, and onward to the Mount of Olives. From the Mount of Olives on the east there was a beautiful and commanding view of the whole sacred edifice. It was there that our Saviour sat when the disciples directed his attention to the goodly stones with which the temple was built, Mar. xiii. 1. The entrance into the temple itself was from the *court of the priests*, by an ascent of twelve steps. The *porch* in front of the temple was 150 feet high and as many broad. The open space in this porch through which the temple was entered was 115 feet high and 37 broad, without doors of any sort. The appearance of this, built, as it was, with white marble, and decorated with plates of silver, from the Mount of Olives was exceedingly dazzling and splendid. Josephus says that in the rising of the sun it reflected so strong and dazzling an effulgence that the eye of the spectator was obliged to turn away. To strangers at a distance, it appeared like a mountain covered with snow, for where it was not decorated with plates of gold it was extremely white and glistening.

The temple itself was divided into two parts. The first, called the *sanctuary* or holy place, was 60 feet in length 60 feet in height, and 30 feet in width. In this was the golden candlestick, the table of shew-bread, and the altar of incense. The *holy of holies* or the *most holy place*, was 30 feet each way. In the first temple this contained the ark of the covenant, the tables of the law, and over the ark was the mercy-seat and the cherubim. Into this place no person entered but the high-priest, and he but once in the year. These two apartments were separated only by a vail, very costly and curiously wrought. It was this vail which was rent from the top to the bottom when the Saviour died, Mat. xxvii. 51. Around the walls of the *temple*, properly so called, was a structure three stories high, containing chambers for the use of the officers of the temple. The temple was wholly razed to the ground by the Romans under Titus and Vespasian, and was effectually destroyed, according to the predictions of the Saviour. See Notes on ch. xxiv. 2. The site of it was made like a ploughed field. Julian the apostate attempted to rebuild it, but the workmen, according to his own historian, Ammianus Marcellinus, were prevented by balls of fire breaking out from the ground. See Warburton's *Divine Legation of Moses.* Its site is now occupied by the Mosque of Omar, one of the most splendid specimens of Saracenic architecture in the world.

The following is a view of the temple and its courts, as just described :—

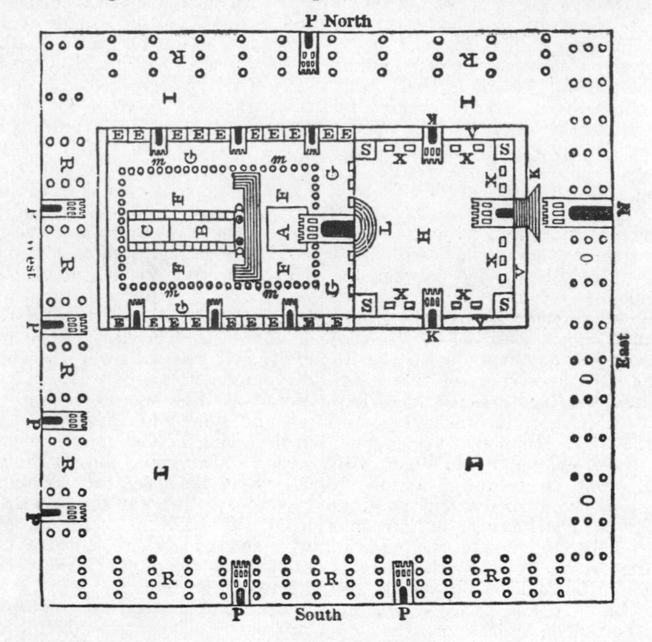

Explanation.

A Altar of burnt offerings. B Holy place.
C Holy of holies. D D Pillars of Jachin and Boaz.
E E E, &c. Rooms for the use of the Levites: for wood, instruments, beds, &c.
F F F F Court of the priests. G G G G Court of the Israelites.
H Court of the women. I I I I Court of the Gentiles.
K K K Gates from the court of the Gentiles to the court of the women.
L Ascent from the court of the women to the court of the Israelites.
M M M, &c. Inclosure between the court of the Israelites and that of the priests.
N The Beautiful gate of the temple. O O O Solomon's porch. P P P, &c. Gates of the temple.
R R R, &c. Porches or covered walks, supported by marble pillars.
X X X X X Boxes to receive money: the treasury, Mar. xi. 41.
S S S S Small rooms for various uses in the temple.
V V V V Space 15 feet wide between the court of the women and the Gentiles.

12. *And cast out all them that sold and bought in the temple.* The place where this was done was not the temple itself, but the outer court, or *the court of the Gentiles.* This was esteemed the least sacred part of the temple; and the Jews, it seems, did not consider it profanation to appropriate this to any business in any way connected with the temple service. The things which they bought and sold were at first those pertaining to the sacrifices. It is not improbable, however, that the traffic afterward extended to all kinds of merchandise. It gave rise to much confusion, noise, contention, and fraud, and was exceedingly improper in the temple of the Lord. ¶ *The tables of the money-changers.* Judea was subject to the Romans. The money in current use was Roman coin; yet the Jewish law required that every man should pay a tribute to the ser-

13 And said unto them, It is written, [g]My house shall be called the house of prayer; but ye have made it [h]a den of thieves.

14 And the blind and the lame came to him in the temple; and he[i] healed them.

15 And when the chief priests and scribes saw the wonderful things that he did, and the children crying in the temple, and saying, [k]Hosanna to the son of David! they were sore displeased,

16 And said unto him, Hearest thou what these say? And Jesus saith unto them, Yea: have ye

g Is.56.7. h Je.7.11. i Is.35.6. k ver.9.

---

vice of the sanctuary of *half a shekel*, Ex. xxx. 11–16. This was a Jewish coin, and the tribute was required to be paid in that coin. It became, therefore, a matter of convenience to have a place where the *Roman* coin might be exchanged for the Jewish half shekel. This was the *professed* business of these men. Of course, they would demand a small sum for the exchange; and, among so many thousands as came up to the great feasts, it would be a very profitable employment, and one easily giving rise to much fraud and oppression. ¶ *The seats of them that sold doves.* Doves were required to be offered in sacrifice—Le. xiv. 22; Lu. ii. 24—yet it was difficult to bring them from the distant parts of Judea. It was found much easier to purchase them in Jerusalem. Hence it became a business to keep them to sell to those who were required to offer them.

Mark adds (xi. 16) that he "would not suffer that any man should carry any vessel through the temple." That is, probably, any of the vessels or implements connected with the traffic in oil, incense, wine, &c., that were kept for sale in the temple.

13. *And said—It is written*, &c. This is written in Is. lvi. 7. The first part of this verse only is quoted from Isaiah. The rest—"but ye have made it a den of thieves"—was added by Jesus, denoting their abuse of the temple. Thieves and robbers live in dens and caves. Judea was then much infested with them. In their dens thieves devise and practise iniquity. These buyers and sellers imitated them. They made the temple a place of gain; they cheated and defrauded; they took advantage of the poor, and, by their being under a necessity of purchasing these articles for sacrifice, they *robbed* them by selling what they had at an enormous price.

The following reasons may be given why this company of buyers and sellers obeyed Christ: 1st. They were overawed by his authority, and struck with the consciousness that he had a right to command. 2d. Their own consciences reproved them; they knew they were guilty, and they dared make no resistance. 3d. The people generally were then on the side of Jesus, believing him to be the Messiah. 4th. It had always been the belief of the Jews that a *prophet* had a right to change, regulate, and order the various affairs relating to external worship. They supposed Jesus to be such, and they did not dare to resist him.

Mark and Luke add, that in consequence of this, the scribes and chief priests attempted to put him to death, Mar. xi. 18, 19; Lu. xix. 47, 48. This they did from *envy*, Mat. xxvii. 18. He drew off the people from them, and they envied and hated him. They were *restrained*, then, for the fear of the people; and this was the reason why they plotted *secretly* to put him to death, and why they afterward so gladly heard the proposals of the traitor, Mat. xxvi. 14, 15.

15, 16. *When the chief priests*, &c. The chief men of the nation were envious of his popularity. They could not prevent it; but, being determined to find fault, they took occasion to do so from the shouts of the children. Men often are offended that *children* have anything to do with religion, and deem it very improper that *they* should rejoice that the Saviour has come. Our Lord Jesus viewed this subject differently. He saw that it was proper that they should rejoice. *They* are interested in the concerns of religion, and before evil principles get fast hold of their minds is a proper time for them to love and obey him. The Lord Jesus silenced those who made the objection by appealing to a text of their own Scriptures. This text is found in Ps. viii. 2. The quotation is not made directly from the Hebrew, but from the Greek translation. This, however, should create no

never read, [l]Out of the mouth of babes and sucklings thou hast perfected praise?

17 And he left them, and went out of the city into Bethany; and he lodged there.

18 Now in the morning, as he returned into the city, he hungered.

19 And[m] when he saw [1]a fig-tree in the way, he came to it, and found nothing thereon but leaves only, and said unto it, Let no fruit

l Ps.8.2.

m Mar.11.13. 1 *one fig-tree.*

---

difficulty. The *point* of the quotation was to prove that *children* might offer praise to God. This is expressed in both the Hebrew and the Greek.

17. *Bethany.* See Notes on Mat. xxi. 1.

19. *And when he saw a fig-tree in the way*, &c. This tree was standing in the public road. It was therefore common property and anyone might lawfully use its fruit. Mark says (xi. 13), "Seeing a fig-tree afar off, having leaves, he came," &c. Not far off *from the road*, but at a considerable distance from the place where he was. Having leaves, and appearing healthy and luxuriant, they presumed that there would be fruit on it. Mark says (xi. 13), "he came, if haply he might find anything thereon." That is, judging from the *appearance* of the tree, it was *probable* that there would be fruit on it. We are not to suppose that our Lord was ignorant of the true condition of the tree, but he acted according to the appearance of things; being a man as well as divine, he acted, of course, as men *do act* in such circumstances. ¶ *And found nothing thereon but leaves only.* Mark (xi. 13) gives as a reason for this that "the time of figs was not yet." That is, the time *of gathering* the figs was not yet, or had not passed. It was a time when figs were ripe or fit to eat, or he would not have gone to it, expecting to find them; but the time *of gathering* them had not passed, and it was to be presumed that they were still on the tree. This took place on the week of the Passover, or in the beginning of April. Figs, in Palestine, are commonly ripe at the Passover. The summer in Palestine begins in March, and it is no uncommon thing that figs should be eatable in April. It is said that they sometimes produce fruit the year round.

Mark (xi. 12, 13) says that this took place on the morning of the day on which he purified the temple. Matthew would lead us to suppose that it was on the day following. Matthew records *briefly* what Mark records more *fully*. Matthew states the fact that the fig-tree was barren and withered away, without regarding minutely the order or the circumstances in which the event took place. There is no contradiction, for Matthew does not *affirm* that this took place on the morning *after* the temple was cleansed, though he places it in that order; nor does he say that a day did *not* elapse after the fig-tree was cursed before the disciples discovered that it was withered, though he does not affirm that it *was* so. Such circumstantial variations, where there is no *positive* contradiction, go greatly to confirm the truth of a narrative. They show that the writers were honest men, and did not *conspire* to deceive the world. ¶ *And said unto it, Let no fruit grow on thee*, &c. Mark calls this *cursing* the tree (ch. xi. 21). The word *curse*, as used by him, does not imply *anger*, or disappointment, or malice. It means only *devoting it to destruction*, or causing it to wither away. All the *curse* that was pronounced was in the words *that no fruit should grow on it.* The Jews used the word *curse* not as always implying *wrath* or *anger*, but to devote to *death*, or to any kind of destruction, He. vi. 8. It has been commonly thought that the Saviour wrought this miracle to denote the sudden *withering away* or destruction of the Jewish people. They, like the fig-tree, promised fair. That was full of leaves, and they full of professions. Yet both were equally barren; and as that was destroyed, so they were soon to be. It was certain that this would be a good *illustration* of the destruction of the Jewish people, but there is no evidence that Jesus *intended* it as such, and without such evidence we have no right to say that was its meaning. ¶ *And presently the fig-tree withered away.* That is, *before* another day. See Mark. It is probable that they were passing directly onward, and did not stop then to consider it. Matthew does not affirm that it withered away *in their presence*,

grow on thee henceforward for ever. And presently the fig-tree withered[n] away.

20 And when the disciples saw *it*, they marvelled, saying, How soon is the fig-tree withered away!

21 Jesus answered and said unto them, Verily I say unto you, [o]If ye have faith, and doubt not, ye shall not only do this *which is done* to the fig-tree, but also if ye shall say unto this mountain, [p]Be thou removed, and be thou cast into the sea, it shall be done.

22 And [q]all things whatsoever ye shall ask in prayer, believing, ye shall receive.

23 And[r] when he was come into the temple, the chief priests and the elders of the people came unto him as he was teaching, and said, [s]By what authority doest thou these things? and who gave thee this authority?

24 And Jesus answered and said unto them, I also will ask you one thing, which if ye tell me, I in like wise will tell you by what authority I do these things.

25 The baptism of John, whence

n Jude 12. *o* ch.17.20; Lu.17.6; Ja.1.6. *p* 1 Co.13.2. *q* ch.7.7; Mar.11.24; Ja.5.16; 1 Jn.3.22; 5.14.

r Mar.11.27; Lu.20.1. *s* Ex.2.14.

---

and Mark affirms that they made the discovery on the morning after it was "cursed."

20. *And when the disciples saw it.* That is, on the morning following that on which it was cursed, Mar. xi. 20. ¶ *They marvelled, saying,* &c. Peter said this, Mar. xi. 21. Matthew means only to say that this was said to him; Mark tells us which one of them said it.

21. *Jesus answered and said,* &c. Jesus took occasion from this to establish their faith in God, Mar. xi. 22. He told them that any difficulty could be overcome by faith. To remove a mountain denotes the power of surmounting or removing any difficulty. The phrase was so used by the Jews. There is no doubt that this was *literally* true—that if *they* had *the faith of miracles*, they could remove the mountain before them—the Mount of Olives—for this was as easy for God to do by them as to heal the sick or raise the dead. But the Saviour rather referred, probably, to the difficulties and trials which they would be called to endure in preaching the gospel.

22. *And all things,* &c. He adds an encouragement for them to pray, assuring them that they should have *all* things which they asked. This promise was evidently a *special* one, given to them in regard to working miracles. To them it was true, but it is manifest that we have no right to apply *this* promise to ourselves. It was designed specially for the apostles; nor have we a right to turn it from its original meaning. There are other promises in abundance on which we *may* rely in prayer, with confident assurance that our prayers will be heard. Comp. Notes on Mat. vii. 7-11.

23-27. See also Mar. xi. 27-33; Lu. xx. 1-9.

23. *When he was come into the temple.* That is, probably, into the inner court—the court of the Israelites. They took this opportunity of questioning him on this subject when he was not surrounded by the multitude. ¶ *By what authority,* &c. There was a *show* of propriety in this question. He was making great changes in the affairs of the temple, and they claimed the right to know why this was done, contrary to their permission. He was not a *priest;* he had no civil or ecclesiastical authority as a Jew. It was *sufficient* authority, indeed, that he came as a prophet and worked miracles. But they professed not to be satisfied with that. ¶ *These things.* The things which he had just done, in overturning the seats of those that were engaged in traffic, ver. 12.

24, 25. *And Jesus answered,* &c. Jesus was under no obligation to give them an answer. They well knew by what authority he did this. He had not concealed his power in working miracles, and had not kept back the knowledge that he was the Messiah. He therefore referred them to a similar case—that of John the Baptist. He knew the estimation in which John was held by the people, and he took the wise in their own craftiness. Whatever answer they gave, he knew they would convict themselves, and so they saw when they looked

was it? from heaven or of men? And they reasoned with themselves, saying, If we shall say, From heaven; he will say unto us, Why did ye not then believe him?

26 But if we shall say, Of men; we fear the people; for [t]all hold John as a prophet.

27 And they answered Jesus, and said, We cannot tell. And he said unto them, Neither tell I you by what authority I do these things.

28 But what think ye? A [u]*certain* man had two sons: and he came to the first, and said, Son, go work to-day in my vineyard.

29 He answered and said, I will not; but [v]afterward he repented, and went.

30 And he came to the second, and said likewise. And he answered and said, I *go*, sir; and went not.

31 Whether of them twain did the will of his father? They say unto him, The first. Jesus saith unto them, Verily I say unto you, that

t ch.14.5. *u* Lu.15.11,&c.

v 2 Ch.33.12,13; 1 Co.6.11; Ep.2.1-13.

---

at the question. They reasoned correctly. If they should say that John received authority to baptize from God or from heaven, he would directly ask why they did not believe him. They professed to hear all the prophets. If they said, "*Of men*," they would be in danger, for all the people believed that John was a prophet. ¶ *The baptism of John*. For an account of this, see Mat. iii. The word *baptism* here probably includes all his work. This was his principal employment; and hence he was called the Baptist, or the *Baptizer*. But our Saviour's question refers *to his whole ministry*. "The *ministry of John*—his baptism, preaching, prophecies—was it from God, or not?" If it *was*, then the inference was clear that Jesus was the Messiah, and then they might easily know by what authority he did those things. ¶ *From heaven*. By divine authority, or by the command of God. ¶ *From men*. By human authority.

26. *We fear the people*. They feared that the people would stone them (Luke). Such an unpopular sentiment as to profess that all that *John* did was *imposture*, would have probably ended in tumult, perhaps in their death.

27. *We cannot tell*. This was a direct falsehood. They *could* have told; and the answer should have been, "We *will* not tell." There was no reason but that why they did not tell. The reason, probably, why they would not acknowledge that John was a prophet, was that, if they did, they saw he could easily show them by *what authority* he did those things; that is, by his authority as Messiah. John came as his forerunner, pointed him out to the people, baptized him, and bore his public and solemn testimony to the fact that he was the Messiah, Mat. iii. 13-15; Jn. i. 29-34. If they acknowledged one, they must the other. In this way our Saviour was about to lead these crafty men to answer their own question, to their own confusion, about his authority. They saw this; and, having given them a *sufficient* answer, there was no need of stating anything farther.

28-32. *But what think ye?* A way of speaking designed to direct them particularly to what he was saying, that they might be self-convicted. ¶ *Two sons*. By those two sons our Lord intends to represent the conduct of the Jews, and that of the publicans and sinners. ¶ *In my vineyard*. See Notes on ver. 33. To work in the vineyard here represents the work which God requires man to do. ¶ *I will not*. This *had* been the language of the publicans and wicked men. They refused at first, and did not *profess* to be willing to go. ¶ *Repented*. Changed his mind. Afterward, at the preaching of John and Christ, the publicans—the wicked—repented and obeyed. ¶ *The second—said, I go sir; and went not*. This represented the conduct of the scribes and Pharisees—*professing* to obey God, observing the external rites of religion, but opposed *really* to the kingdom of God, and about to put his Son to death. ¶ *Whether of them twain*, &c. Which of the two. ¶ *They say unto him, The first*. This answer was correct; but it is strange that they did not perceive that it condemned themselves. ¶ *Go into the kingdom of God*. Become Christians, or more readily follow the Saviour. See Notes on Mat. iii. 2. ¶ *Before you*. Rather than you. They are more *likely* to do it than you. You are self-righteous, self-willed and obstinate. ¶ *John*

the publicans and the harlots go into the kingdom of God before you.

32 For John came unto you in the way of righteousness, and ye believed him not; but the [w]publicans and the [x]harlots believed him: and ye, when ye had seen *it*, [y]repented not afterward, that ye might believe him.

33 Hear another parable: There was a certain householder, which [z]planted a vineyard, and hedged it round about, and digged a winepress in it, and built a tower, and

w Lu.3.12. x Lu.7.37,&c.

y Re.2.21. z Ps.80.8-16; Ca.8.11,12; Is.5.1-7; Je.2.21; Mar.12.1; Lu.20.9,&c.

---

came in the way of righteousness. Many of them have believed, but you have not. That is, in the right way, or *teaching* the way to be righteous; to wit, by repentance. Publicans and harlots heard him and *became* righteous, but *they* did not. They *saw* it, but, as in a thousand other cases, it did not produce the proper effect on them, and they would not repent.

33–46. *The parable of the vineyard.* This is also recorded in Mar. xii. 1–12; Lu. xx. 9–19.

33. *Hear another parable.* See Notes on Mat. xiii. 3. ¶ *A certain householder.* See Notes on Mat. xx. 1. ¶ *Planted a vineyard.* A place for the cultivation of grapes. It is often used to represent the church of God, as a place *cultivated* and *valuable.* Judea was favourable to vines, and the figure is frequently used, therefore, in the sacred writers. See Mat. xx. 1. It is used here to represent the *Jewish people*—the people chosen of the Lord, cultivated with care, and signally favoured; or perhaps more definitely, *the city of Jerusalem.* ¶ *Hedged it round about.* This means he *inclosed it*, either with a fence of wood or stone, or more probably with *thorns*, thick set and growing—a common way of inclosing fields in Judea, as it is in England. ¶ *And digged a wine-press in it.* Mark says, *digged a place for the wine-fat.* This should have been so rendered in Matthew. The original word does not mean the *press* in which the grapes were trodden, but the *vat* or *large cistern* into which the wine ran. This was commonly made by digging into the side of a hill. The *wine press* was made of two receptacles. The upper one, in Persia at present, is about 8 feet square and 4 feet high. In this the grapes are thrown and *trodden* by men, and the juice runs into the large receptacle or cistern below. See Notes on Is. lxiii. 2, 3. ¶ *And built a tower.* See also Notes on Is. v. 2. In Eastern countries at present, these towers are often 80 feet high and 30 feet square. They were for the keepers, who defended the vineyards from thieves and animals, especially from foxes, Ca. i. 6; ii. 15. Professor Hackett (*Illustrations of Scripture*, p. 171, 172) says of such towers: "They caught my attention first as I was approaching Bethlehem from the south-east. They appeared in almost every field within sight from that direction. They were circular in shape, 15 or 20 feet high, and, being built of stones, looked, at a distance, like a little forest of obelisks. I was perplexed for some time to decide what they were; my travelling companions were equally at fault. Suddenly, in a lucky moment, the words crossed my mind, 'A certain man planted a vineyard, and set a hedge about it, and built a tower, and let it out to husbandmen, and went into a far country,' Mar. xii. 1. This recollection cleared up the mystery. There, before my eyes, stood the towers of which I had so often read and thought; such as stood there when David led forth his flocks to the neighbouring pastures; such as furnished to the sacred writers and the Saviour himself so many illustrations for enforcing what they taught.

"These towers are said to be sometimes square in form as well as round, and as high as 40 or 50 feet. Those which I examined had a small door near the ground, and a level space on the top, where a man could sit and command a view of the plantation. I afterwards saw a great many of these structures near Hebron, where the vine still flourishes in its ancient home; for there, probably, was Eshcol, whence the Hebrew spies returned to Joshua with the clusters of grapes which they had gathered as evidence of the fertility of the land. Some of the towers here are so built as to serve as houses; and during the vintage, it is said that the inhabitants of Hebron take up their abode in them in such numbers as to leave the

let it out to husbandmen, and went into a far country:

34 And when the time of the fruit drew near, he [a]sent his servants to the husbandmen, that they might receive the fruits of it.

35 And[b] the husbandmen took his servants, and beat one, and killed another, and stoned another.

36 Again, he sent other servants more than the first: and they did unto them likewise.

37 But, last of all, he sent unto them his son, saying, They will reverence my son.

38 But when the husbandmen saw the son, they said among themselves, [c]This is the heir; come, let

a 2 Ki.17.13,&c.
b 2 Ch.36.16; Ne.9.26; Je.25.3-7; ch.5.12; 23.34-37; Ac.7.52; 1 Th.2.15; He.11.36,37; Re.6.9.
c He.1.1,2.

town almost deserted." ¶ *And let it out*, &c. This was not an uncommon thing. Vineyards were often planted to be let out for profit. ¶ *Into a far country.* This means, in the original, only that he departed from them. It does not mean that he went out of the *land.* Luke adds, "for a long time." That is, as appears, till the time of the fruit; perhaps for a year. This vineyard denotes, doubtless, the Jewish people, or Jerusalem. But these circumstances are not to be particularly explained. They serve to *keep up* the story. They denote *in general* that God had taken proper care of his vineyard—that is, of his people; but beyond that we cannot affirm that these *circumstances* of building the tower, &c., mean any particular thing, for he has not told us that they do, and where he has not explained them we have no right to attempt it.

34. *And when the time of the fruit drew near*, &c. The time of gathering the fruit. The vineyard was let out, probably, for a part of the fruit, and the owner sent to receive the part that was his. ¶ *Sent his servants.* These, doubtless, represent the prophets sent to the Jewish people.

35. *And beat one.* The word here translated *beat* properly means to *flay* or to take off the skin; hence to beat or to whip so that the skin in many places is taken off. ¶ *And killed another.* Isaiah is said to have been put to death by sawing him asunder. Many other of the prophets were also put to death. See Lu. xiii. 34; He. xi. 37; 1 Sa. xxii. 18; 1 Ki. xix. 10. ¶ *And stoned another.* This was among the Jews a common mode of punishment, De. xiii. 10; xvii. 7; Jos. vii. 25. Especially was this the case in times of popular tumult, and of sudden indignation among the people, Ac. vii. 58; xiv. 19; Jn. viii. 59; x. 31. This does not imply, of necessity, that those who were stoned *died*, but they might be only severely wounded. Mark says, "At him they cast stones and wounded him in the head, and sent him away," &c.

There is a little variation in the circumstances as mentioned by Matthew, and by Mark and Luke, but the substance is the same. Mark and Luke are more particular, and state the *order* in which the servants were sent one after another. They all denote the dealing of the people of Israel towards the prophets. All these things had been done to them. See He. xi. 37; Je. xliv. 4-6; 2 Ch. xxxvi. 16; Ne. ix. 26; 2 Ch. xxiv. 20, 21.

37. *Last of all*, &c. Mark adds that this was an only son, greatly beloved. This beautifully and most tenderly exhibits the love of God in sending his only Son, Jesus Christ, into the world to die for men. Long had he sent the prophets, and they had been persecuted and slain. There was no use in sending any more prophets to the people. They had done all that they could do. God had one only-begotten and well-beloved Son, whom he might send, and whom the world *ought* to reverence even as they should the Father, Jn. v. 23. God is often represented in the Bible as giving his Son, his only-begotten and well-beloved Son, for a lost world, Jn. iii. 16, 17; 1 Jn. iv. 9, 14; Ro. viii. 3, 32; Ga. iv. 4. ¶ *Saying, They will reverence my son.* To *reverence* means to honour, to esteem, to show deference to. It is that feeling which we have in the presence of one who is greatly our superior. It means to give to such a person, in our feelings and our deportment, the honour which is due to his rank and character.

38. *But when the husbandmen*, &c. They determined to kill him, and as he was the only son, they supposed they could easily seize on the property. It

us kill him, and let us seize on his inheritance.

39 And [d]they caught him, and cast *him* out of the vineyard, and slew *him*.

40 When the lord, therefore, of the vineyard cometh, what will he do unto those husbandmen?

41 They say unto him, [e]He will miserably destroy those wicked men, and [f]let out *his* vineyard unto other husbandmen, which shall render him the fruits in their seasons.

42 Jesus saith unto them, Did ye never read in the scriptures, [g]The stone which the builders rejected, the same is become the head of the corner: this is the Lord's doing, and it is marvellous in our eyes?

43 Therefore I say unto you,

d Ac.2.23; 4.25-27. *e* Ps.2.4,5,9; Zec.12.2. *f* Lu.21.24; Ro.9.26; 11.11.

g Ps.118.22; Is.28 16; 1 Pe.2.6,7.

---

was rented to them; was in their possession; and they resolved to keep it. This circumstance has probably no reference to any particular conduct of the Jews, but is thrown in to keep up the story and fill up the narrative. An *heir* is one who succeeds to an estate, commonly a son; an *inheritance* is what an heir receives.

39. *And they caught him*, &c. This refers to the conduct of the Jews in putting the Saviour to death. So they understood it, ver. 45. The Jews put him to death after they had persecuted and slain the prophets. This was done by giving him into the hands of the Romans and seeking his crucifixion, Mat. xxvii. 20-25; Ac. ii. 23; vii. 51, 52. ¶ *And cast him out of the vineyard.* The vineyard in this parable may represent Jerusalem. Jesus was crucified *out* of Jerusalem, on Mount Calvary, Lu. xxiii. 23. See Notes on He. xiii. 12.

40. *When the lord, therefore*, &c. Jesus then asked them a question about the proper way of dealing with those men. The *design* of asking them this question was that they might condemn themselves, and admit the justice of the punishment that was soon to come upon them.

41. *They say*, &c. They answered according as they knew men would act, and would act justly in doing it. He would take away their privileges and confer them on others. This was the answer which Jesus wished. The case was so clear that they could not answer otherwise. He wished to show them the justice of taking away their national privileges, and punishing them in the destruction of their city and nation. Had he stated this at first they would not have heard him. He, however, by a parable, led them along to *state themselves* the very truth which he wished to communicate, and they had then nothing to answer. They did not, however, yet see the bearing of what they had admitted.

42, 43. *Jesus saith*, &c. Jesus, having led them to admit the justice of the great *principle* on which God was about to act towards *them* proceeds to apply it by a text of Scripture, declaring that this very thing which they admitted to be proper in the case of the *husbandmen* had been predicted respecting *themselves*. This passage is found in Ps. cxviii. 22, 23. It was first applicable to David, but no less to Jesus. ¶ *The stone.* The figure is taken from building a house. The principal stone for size and beauty is that commonly laid as the corner stone. ¶ *Which the builders rejected.* On account of its want of beauty or size it was laid aside, or deemed unfit to be a corner-stone. This represents the Lord Jesus, proposed to the Jews as the foundation or corner-stone on which to build the church, but rejected by them—the builders—on account of his want of comeliness or beauty; that is, of what *they* esteemed to be comely or desirable, Is. liii. 2, 3. ¶ *The same is become*, &c. Though rejected by *them*, yet God chose him, and made him the foundation of the church. Christ is often compared to a stone, a corner-stone, a *tried*, that is, a *sure*, firm foundation—all in allusion to the custom of building, Ac. iv. 11; Ro. ix. 33; Ep. ii. 20; 1 Pe. ii. 7. ¶ *Lord's doing.* The appointment of Jesus of Nazareth to be the foundation of the church is *proved* by miracle and prophecy to be the work of God. ¶ *Marvellous in our eyes.* Wonderful in the sight of his people. That he should select his only Son—that he should stoop so low, be despised, rejected, and put to death—

The[h] kingdom of God shall be taken from you, and given to [i]a nation bringing forth the fruits thereof.

44 And whosoever [k]shall fall on this stone shall be broken; but on whomsoever it shall fall, [l]it will grind him to powder.

45 And when the chief priests and Pharisees had heard his parables, they perceived that he spake of them.

46 But when they sought to lay hands on him, they feared the multitude, because [m]they took him for a prophet.

h ch.8.12. *i* Is.26.2. *k* Is.8.14,15. *l* He.2.2,3. *m* Lu.7.16; Jn.7.40.

that God should raise him up, and build a church on this foundation, embracing the Gentile as well as the Jew, and spreading through all the world, is a subject of wonder and praise to all the redeemed.

43. *The kingdom of God*, &c. Jesus applies the parable to *them*—the Jews. They *had* been the children of the kingdom, or under the *reign* of God; having his law and acknowledging him as King. They *had* been his chosen and peculiar people, but he says that now this privilege would be taken away; that they would cease to be the peculiar people of God, and that the blessing would be given to a nation who would bring forth the fruits thereof, or *be righteous*—that is, to the Gentiles, Ac. xxviii. 28.

44. *Whosoever shall fall*, &c. There is a reference here, doubtless, to Is. viii. 14, 15. Having made an allusion to himself *as a stone*, or a rock (ver. 42), he proceeds to state the consequences of coming in contact with it. He that falls upon it shall be broken; he that *runs against it*—a corner-stone, standing *out* from the other parts of the foundation—shall be injured, or broken in his limbs or body. He that is offended with *my* being the foundation, or that opposes me, shall by the act injure himself, or make himself miserable *by so doing*, even were there nothing farther. But there *is* something farther. ¶ *On whomsoever it shall fall, it will grind him to powder*. That is, in the original, will reduce him to dust, so that it may be scattered by the winds. There is an allusion here, doubtless, to the custom of stoning as a punishment among the Jews. A scaffold was erected twice the height of the man to be stoned. Standing on its edge, he was violently struck off by one of the witnesses: if he died by the blow and the fall, nothing farther was done; if not, a heavy stone was thrown down on him, which at once killed him. So the Saviour speaks of the *falling* of the stone on his enemies. They who oppose him, who reject him, and who continue impenitent, shall be *crushed* by him in the day of judgment, and perish for ever.

45, 46. They *at last* perceived that he spoke of them, and would have gratified their malice at once, but they feared the people.

REMARKS.

1st. Jesus is omniscient, and sees and knows all things, ver. 2.

2d. It is our duty to obey the Lord Jesus, and to do it at once, ver. 3. When *he* commands there should be no delay. What he orders is right, and we should not hesitate or deliberate about it.

3d. Especially is this the case where *he* is to be honoured, as he was on this occasion, ver. 3, 8. If it was for *our* interest or honour only that we obeyed him, it would be of less consequence; but *our* obedience will honour *him*, and we should seek that honour by any sacrifice or self-denial.

4th. We should be willing to give up our property to honour the Lord Jesus, ver. 3. He has a right to it. If given to spread the gospel, it goes, as this did, to increase "the triumphs of our King." We should be willing to give our wealth that he might "gird on his sword," and "ride prosperously among the heathen." Every one that is saved among the heathen by sending the gospel to them will be for the honour of Jesus. They will go to swell his train when he shall enter triumphantly into his kingdom at the day of judgment.

5th. It is our duty to *honour* him, ver. 7-9. He is King of Zion. He is Lord of all. He reigns, and shall always reign.

"Sinners! whose love can ne'er forget
The wormwood and the gall,
Go spread your trophies at his feet,
And crown him Lord of all.

"Ye chosen seed of Israel's race;
Ye ransomed from the fall;

Hail him who saves you by his grace,
And crown him Lord of all.

"Let every kindred, every tribe,
On this terrestrial ball,
To him all majesty ascribe,
And crown him Lord of all."

6th. *Children* should also honour him and shout *hosanna* to him, ver. 15. The chief priests and scribes, in the time of our Saviour, were displeased that they did it; and many of the great, and many formal professors since, have been displeased that *children* should profess to love and honour Jesus. They have opposed Sunday-schools, and opposed the praying of children, and opposed their singing to his praise, and opposed their *giving* their money to spread his gospel; but Jesus loves such praise and such service. The mouths of babes and sucklings should be taught to speak his name; and whatever the world may say, whatever the proud, the rich, or the formal may say, children should seek him early and give their first years to him. He loves their praises. Perhaps few of all the songs of thanksgiving are so pleasant to his ears as the *hosannas* of a Sabbath-school.

7th. We have here a view of the glory of Jesus, ver. 9-11. Though humble, yet he was King. Though most of his life *unhonoured*, yet once he had the honours of his station rendered to him, and entered the city of his father David as a triumphant King of Zion. He will be yet *more* honoured. He will come with all his saints, with the glory of his Father, and with the holy angels. There *we* shall be; and we should be prepared to join with the vast host in shouting hosanna to the returning King of Zion.

8th. Yet, amid all these honours, he was meek and lowly, ver. 5. Others would have been proud and lifted up, but he was always meek; his heart was not proud. He is the only one of kings that could bear triumph and honours without being lifted up by it and made proud.

9th. Yet amid all his triumphs he wept over Jerusalem (Luke). No king, no conqueror, ever before showed compassion like this. Men weep when *they* are afflicted, or are poor and needy; but what prince has ever, in the moment of his triumph, *wept* over the miseries and dangers of his subjects? Not an instance can be found in all history where an earthly conqueror ever showed compassion like this. So Jesus has still compassion over blind, ruined, wretched man. Amid all the triumphs of the gospel, he does not forget those who are yet in their sins, but stretches out his arms to welcome them to his embrace.

10th. Prophecy will be certainly and exactly fulfilled (Luke). That respecting Jerusalem was literally accomplished; and in like manner will *all* that is predicted of *all* sinners assuredly come to pass. If Jerusalem had repented it would have been saved; so if sinners repent they will be saved. If not, like Jerusalem, in due time they will perish.

11th. Jesus purified the temple, ver. 12. It was the house of God. So *our hearts* should be the dwelling-place of the Holy Spirit; so, also, they should be pure. All worldly cares, and traffic, and business, that would interfere with the dwelling of the Spirit there, and all wickedness, oppression, extortion, cheating, and pollution should be banished. God dwells not in such polluted temples; and unless we *are pure in heart*, he will not be with us, and we shall not see his face in peace. Comp. Notes on 1 Co. iii. 16, 17.

12th. Jesus only can purify our hearts. He does it by his blood and Spirit. Over all our sins he holds the same *power* as he did over the traffickers in the temple. At his command they will flee, and we shall be pure. If our hearts are ever purified, therefore, it will be by the power of Jesus. Nor should we wait in sin for him to do it. We should come to him, and beseech him to have mercy, and to save us from our pollutions.

13th. Envy and hatred will take hold of very small matters, to show itself against the good and even the prudent, ver. 15. When the enemies of Jesus could find nothing else to blame, they chose to find fault with the shouting of children. So always in a revival of religion, or any great work of the Lord, it is some small matter that is seized upon—something not exactly to the view of wicked objectors—that is made the occasion of reproach and opposition.

14th. We must produce *fruit* in our lives as well as *flowers*, ver. 19. A profession of religion is like the flowers of spring. A *revival* is like fragrant blossoms. They are beautiful, and promise much fruit; but how many wither, and droop, and fall useless to the ground! How few of all the blossoms of the spring produce ripe and mellow fruit in

CHAPTER XXII.

AND Jesus answered and spake unto them again in parables, and said,

2 The[a] kingdom of heaven is like unto a certain king, which made [b]a marriage for his son,

3 And [c]sent forth his servants

a Lu.14.16. b Re.19.7,9. c Ps.68.11; Je.25.4; 35.15; Re.22.17.

---

autumn! So, alas! it is often with those who appear well in revivals of religion.

15th. If we make a profession and do not produce fruit, Jesus will curse us, and we shall soon wither away, ver. 19, 20. He will suffer none to enter into his kingdom on the ground of profession only. If we bear fruit and live lives of piety, we are Christians; if not, all our professions are like the blossoms of spring or the leaves of the tree. They will not save us from the withering frown of Jesus.

16th. Men will do almost anything—right or wrong, and as often wrong as right—to court popularity, ver. 24. It is generally not asked by such men what is *right* or what is *true*, but what will secure popularity. If they have that, they are satisfied.

17th. Men often tell a direct falsehood rather than acknowledge the truth, ver. 27. Especially is this the case when the truth makes against them.

18th. Double-dealing and an attempt to evade the truth commonly lead into difficulty. If these men had been honest, they would have had far less trouble, ver. 27.

19th. A state of gross and open sin is often more *hopeful* than one of hypocrisy, pride, and self-conceit, together with external conformity to religion, ver. 28. Multitudes of profane and licentious people may be saved, while the proud and self-righteous will be cut off. The reasons are, 1st. That the wicked, the gross, have no righteousness on which they can pretend to rely. 2d. Nothing so effectually prevents religion as pride and self-confidence. 3d. There is often really more ingenuousness and candour, and less of malignity against the gospel, among the openly wicked, than among those who are outwardly righteous, but who are inwardly like whited sepulchres, full of dead men's bones and all uncleanness.

20th. Multitudes of people profess to go, and go not, ver. 30. They profess to love God, and love themselves better. They profess to obey him, and yet obey their lusts. They are hypocrites, and destruction must come upon them.

21st. Sinners, when they see the effect of truth on others, should repent, ver. 32. It is proof of the truth of religion, and they, as much as others, need it.

22d. We see the goodness of God in sending his messengers to a lost world, ver. 33–38. His prophets he sent one after another, and they were put to death. His well-beloved Son he sent, and *he* also was put to death. Nor is his mercy yet stayed. He still sends his message to sinners. Thousands have died, as his Son did, in attempting to spread the gospel, but still he sends it. We have often, often rejected it, yet still he sends it. What earthly monarch would be treated in this manner? What earthly parent would be so patient and so kind?

23d. If we improve not our privileges they will be taken away from us, ver. 43. The gospel will be sent to many of the heathen, and they will be saved, but woe to those who have had it all their lives and are not saved.

24th. All who reject the Saviour must perish, ver. 44.

CHAPTER XXII.

1. *And Jesus answered and spake unto them again in parables.* See Notes on Mat. xiii. 3. That is, he answered or made reply to the Pharisees, who had been enraged at him for what he had already spoken to them, ch. xxi. 45, 46. He made a still farther statement, to show how the gospel would be received and treated by them. The real *answer* here, as is frequently the case in the New Testament, refers to what was passing in the mind, or to the conduct of those who were addressed, not to what they *said.*

2. *The kingdom of heaven.* See Notes on Mat. iii. 2. The idea here is, "God deals with man in his kingdom, or in regard to the dispensation of the gospel, as a certain king did," &c. This parable refers, undoubtedly, to the rejection of the Jews and to the calling of the Gentiles. The gospel, with all its privileges, was offered to the Jewish people; but through their wickedness and pride

to call them that were bidden to the wedding: and they would not come.

4 Again, he sent forth other servants, saying, Tell them which are bidden, Behold, I have prepared my dinner; my oxen and *my* fatlings *are* killed, and all things *are* ready: come unto the marriage.

5 But they [d]made light of *it*, and went their ways, one to his farm, and another to his merchandise:

6 And the remnant took his servants, and [e]entreated *them* spitefully, and slew *them*.

7 But when the king heard *thereof*, he was wroth: and he sent forth his armies, and [f]destroyed those murderers, and burnt up their city.

8 Then saith he to his servants, The wedding is ready, but they which were bidden were not [g]worthy.

9 Go ye therefore into the high-

d Ps.106.24,25; Pr.1.24,25; Ac.24.25; Ro.2.4.

e 1 Th.2.15. f Da.9.26; Lu.19.27. g ch.10.11,13; Ac.13.46; Re.3.4; 22.14.

they rejected it, and all its blessings were offered to the Gentiles and accepted. This is the *general* truth. Many circumstances are thrown in to fill out the narrative which cannot be particularly explained. ¶ *A marriage for his son.* Rather a *marriage-feast*, or a feast on the occasion of the marriage of his son. The king here doubtless represents *God* providing for the salvation of the world.

3. *And sent forth his servants.* These represent the messengers that God has sent to invite men to his kingdom. ¶ *To call them that were bidden.* That is, to give notice to those who had before been invited that the feast was ready. It appears that there were two invitations—one considerably previous to the time of the feast, that they might have opportunity to prepare for it, and the other to give notice of the precise time when they were expected. ¶ *The wedding.* The marriage-feast. The same word in the original as in ver. 2. ¶ *They would not come.* They *might* have come if they had chosen, but they would not. So all the difficulty that sinners ever labour under in regard to salvation is in the *will.* It is a fixed determination *not* to come and be saved. See Notes on Jn. v. 45.

4. *Other servants.* Who might *press* it on their attention. So God repeats his message to sinners when they reject it. ¶ *My dinner.* This word literally denotes the meal taken about noon. It is also taken for a meal in general. As marriages were, among Eastern nations, in the evening, it refers here to a meal taken at that time. ¶ *Fatlings.* This word does not refer to any particular species of animals. It denotes any fat animals. As *oxen* are also mentioned, however, it refers here, probably, to lambs or calves, 2 Sa. vi. 13; 1 Ch. xv. 26.

5. *But they made light of* it. Treated it with contempt, as a thing of no consequence—an exact representation of the conduct of sinners in regard to the gospel. ¶ *One to his farm.* So men are engaged so much in their worldly employment that they pretend they have no time to attend to religion. The world is, in their view, of more value than God. ¶ *Merchandise.* Traffic; trading.

6. *And the remnant,* &c. That is, *a part* made light of it; treated it with silent contempt, and coolly went about their business. The others were not satisfied with that, but showed positive malignity. Some sinners seem to be well satisfied by merely neglecting religion; others proceed against it with open violence and bitter malice. ¶ *Entreated* them *spitefully.* Used harsh and opprobrious words. Reviled and abused them. This was done because they hated and despised the king. So sinners often abuse and calumniate ministers of religion because they themselves hate God, and can in no way else show their hatred so well.

7. *But when the king heard,* &c. This doubtless refers to the Jews and to Jerusalem. They were murderers, having slain the prophets; and God was about to send forth the armies of the Romans under his providential direction, and to burn up their city. See Notes on Mat. xxiv. ¶ *Wroth.* Angry; displeased.

9. *The highways.* Literally, the *exit* or *going out* of the *paths* or *roads.* It means the square or principal street, into which a number of smaller streets

ways; and as many as ye shall find, bid to the marriage.

10 So those servants went out into the highways, and [h]gathered together all, as many as they found, both bad and good: and the wedding was furnished with guests.

11 And when the king came in to[i] see the guests, he saw there a man which had not on a [k]wedding garment:

12 And he saith unto him, Friend, how camest thou in hither, not having a wedding garment? And he [l]was speechless.

13 Then said the king to the servants, Bind him hand and foot, and [m]take him away, and [n]cast *him* into outer darkness: there shall be weeping and gnashing of teeth.

14 For[o] many are called, but few *are* chosen.

h ch.13.47. *i* Zep.1.12. *k* Ps.45.14; Is.61.10; 2 Co.5.3; Ep.4.24; Re.16.15; 19.8.

l Je.2.26. *m* Is.52.1; Re.21.27. *n* ch.8.12. *o* ch.7.14; 20.16; Lu.13.23,24.

---

enter; a place, therefore, of confluence, where many persons would be seen, and persons of all descriptions. By this is represented the offering of the gospel to the Gentiles. They were commonly regarded among the Jews as living in highways and hedges—cast out and despised.

10. *Bad and good.* All descriptions of people. None are good by nature; if they were they would not need the gospel; but some are worse than others, and they have special need of it. None can be saved without it.

11. *A man which had not on a wedding garment.* Anciently kings and princes were accustomed to make presents of changes of raiment to their friends and favourites, to refuse to receive which was an expression of highest contempt, Ge. xlv. 22; 2 Ki. x. 22; Es. vi. 8; viii. 15. It was, of course, expected that such garments would be worn when they came into the presence of the benefactor. The garments worn on festival occasions were chiefly long white robes, and it was the custom of the person who made the feast to prepare such robes to be worn by the guests. This renders the conduct of this man more inexcusable. He came in his common and ordinary dress, as he was taken from the highway; and though he had not a garment of his own suitable for the occasion, yet one had been provided for him, if he had applied for it. His not doing it was expressive of the highest disrespect for the king. This beautifully represents the conduct of the hypocrite in the church. A garment of salvation might be his, wrought by the hands of the Saviour, and dyed in his blood; but the hypocrite chooses the filthy rags of his own righteousness, and thus offers the highest contempt for that provided in the gospel. He is to blame, not for being invited—not for coming, if he would come, for he is freely invited—but for offering the highest contempt to the King of Zion in presenting himself with all his filth and rags, and in refusing to be saved in the way provided in the gospel.

12. *Friend.* Rather, *companion.* The word does not imply friendship. ¶ *He was speechless.* He had no excuse. So it will be with all hypocrites.

13. *Cast* him *into outer darkness.* See Notes on Mat. viii. 12. This, without doubt, refers to the future punishment of the hypocrite, Mat. xxiii. 23–33; xxiv. 51.

14. *Many are called, but few* are *chosen.* Our Saviour often uses this expression. It was probably proverbial. The Jews had been called, but few of them had been chosen to life. The great mass of the nation was wicked, and they showed by their lives that they were not chosen to salvation. The Gentiles also were invited to be saved, Is. xlv. 22. Nation after nation has been called; but few, few have yet showed that they were real Christians, the elect of God. It is also true that many who are in the church may prove to be without the wedding garment, and show at last that they were not the chosen of God. This remark in the 14th verse is the inference from the *whole parable*, and not of the part about the man without the wedding garment. It does not mean, therefore, that the great mass in the church are simply called and not chosen, or are hypocrites; but the great mass in *the human family*, in the time of Christ, who had been *called*, had rejected the mercy of God.

15 Then[p] went the Pharisees and took counsel how they might entangle him in *his* talk.

16 And they sent out unto him their disciples, with the Herodians, saying, Master, we know that thou art true, and teachest the way of God in truth, neither carest thou for any *man:* for thou regardest not the person of men.

17 Tell us therefore, What thinkest thou? Is it lawful to give tribute unto Cæsar, or not?

18 But Jesus perceived their

p Mar.12.13,&c.; Lu.20.20,&c.

15–22. *The Pharisees and Herodians endeavour to entangle Jesus.* This narrative is also found in Mar. xii. 12–17; Lu. xx. 20–26.

15. *Then went the Pharisees.* See Notes on Mat. iii. 7. ¶ *How they might entangle him.* To *entangle* means to *ensnare*, as birds are taken by a net. This is done secretly, by leading them within the compass of the net and then suddenly springing it over them. So to entangle is artfully to lay a plan for enticing; to beguile by proposing a question, and by leading, if possible, to an incautious answer. This was what the Pharisees and Herodians endeavoured to do in regard to Jesus. ¶ *In* his *talk.* The word *his* is supplied by the translators, perhaps improperly. It means *in conversation*, or by *talking* with him; not alluding to anything that he had before said.

16. *The Herodians.* It is not certainly known who these were. It is probable that they took their name from Herod the Great. Perhaps they were first a political party, and were then distinguished for holding some of the peculiar opinions of Herod. Dr. Prideaux thinks that those opinions referred to two things. The first respected subjection to a foreign power. The law of Moses was, that a *stranger should not be set over the Jews as a king*, De. xvii. 15. Herod, who had received the kingdom of Judea by appointment of the Romans, maintained that the law of Moses referred only to a voluntary choice of a king, and did not refer to a necessary submission where they had been overpowered by force. His followers supposed, therefore, that it was lawful in such cases to pay tribute to a foreign prince. This opinion was, however, extensively unpopular among the Jews, and particularly the Pharisees, who looked upon it as a violation of their law, and regarded all the acts growing out of it as oppressive. Hence the difficulty of the question proposed by them. Whatever way he decided, they supposed he would be involved in difficulty. If he should say it was not lawful, the Herodians were ready to accuse him as being an enemy of Cæsar; if he said it was lawful, the Pharisees were ready to accuse him to the people of holding an opinion extremely unpopular among them, and as being an enemy of their rights. The other opinion of Herod, which they seem to have followed, was, that when a people were subjugated by a foreign force, it was right to adopt the rites and customs of their religion. This was what was meant by the *leaven of Herod*, Mar. viii. 15. The Herodians and Sadducees seem on most questions to have been united. Comp. Mat. xvi. 6; Mar. viii. 15. ¶ *We know that thou art true.* A hypocritical compliment, not believed by them, but artfully said, as compliments often are, to conceal their true design. ¶ *Neither carest thou for any* man. That is, thou art an independent teacher, delivering your sentiments without regard to the fear or favour of man. This was true, and probably they believed this. Whatever else they might believe about him, they had no reason to doubt that he delivered his sentiments openly and freely. ¶ *For thou regardest not the person of men.* Thou art not *partial.* Thou wilt decide according to truth, and not from any bias toward either party. To regard the person, or to respect the person, is in the Bible uniformly used to denote *partiality*, or being influenced in a decision, not by truth, but by previous attachment to a *person*, or to one of the parties—by friendship, or bias, or prejudice, Le. xix. 15; Jude 16; De. xvi. 19; 2 Sa. xiv. 14; Ac. x. 34; Ja. ii. 1, 3, 9; 1 Pe. i. 17.

17. *Is it lawful to give tribute unto Cæsar?* Tribute was the tax paid to the Roman government. ¶ *Cæsar.* The Roman emperor. The name *Cæsar*, after the time of Julius Cæsar, became common to all the emperors, as *Pharaoh* was the common name of all the kings of Egypt. *The Cæsar* that reigned at this time was *Tiberius*—a man distin-

wickedness, and said, Why tempt ye me, *ye* hypocrites?

19 Show me the tribute-money. And they brought unto him [1]a penny.

20 And he saith unto them, Whose *is* this image and [2]superscription?

21 They say unto him, Cæsar's. Then saith he unto them, [q]Render therefore unto Cæsar the things which are Cæsar's, and [r]unto God the things that are God's.

22 When they had heard *these words*, they marvelled, and left him, and went their way.

23 The[s] same day came to him the Sadducees,[t] which say that there is no resurrection, and asked him,

24 Saying, Master, Moses said, [u]If a man die, having no children, his brother shall marry his wife, and raise up seed unto his brother.

25 Now there were with us seven brethren: and the first, when he

1 in value 7 pence halfpenny. 2 or, *inscription.* q ch.17.25,27; Ro.13.7. r Mal.1.6-8; 3.8-10.

s Mar.12.18,&c.; Lu.20.27,&c. t Ac.23.8. u De.25.5; Ru.1.11.

---

guished for the grossest vices and most disgusting and debasing sensuality.

18. *Jesus perceived their wickedness.* This must have been done by his power of searching the heart, and proves that he was omniscient. No mere man has the power of discerning the motives of others. ¶ *Tempt ye me.* Try me, or endeavour to lead me into difficulty by an insidious question. ¶ *Hypocrites.* Dissemblers. Professing to be candid inquirers, when their only object was to lead into difficulty. See Notes on Mat. vi. 2.

19. *The tribute-money.* The money in which the tribute was paid. This was a Roman coin. The tribute for the temple service was paid in the Jewish shekel; that for the Roman government in foreign coin. Their having that coin about them, and using it, was proof that they themselves held it lawful to pay the tribute; and their pretensions, therefore, were mere hypocrisy. ¶ *A penny.* A Roman denarius, worth about fourteen cents = 7*d*.

20. *This image.* The likeness of the reigning prince was usually struck on the coins. ¶ *Superscription.* The name and titles of the emperor.

21. *Render, therefore, to Cæsar,* &c. Cæsar's image and name on the coin proved that it was his. It was proper, therefore, to give it back to him when he called for it. But while this was done, Jesus took occasion to charge them, also, to give to God what he claimed. This may mean either, 1st. The annual tribute due to the temple service, implying that paying tribute to Cæsar did not free them from the obligation to do that; or, 2d. That they should give their hearts, lives, property, and influence all to God, as his due.

22. *They marvelled.* They had been foiled in their attempt. Though he had apparently decided in favour of the Herodians, yet his answer confounded both parties, and wholly prevented the use which they intended to make of it. It was so wise; it so clearly detected their wickedness and foiled their aim, that they were confounded, and retired covered with shame.

23–33. *Conversation of Jesus with the Sadducees respecting the resurrection.* See also Mar. xii. 18–27; Lu. xx. 27–38.

23. *The same day came the Sadducees.* For an account of the Sadducees, see Notes on Mat. iii. 7. ¶ *No resurrection.* The word *resurrection* usually means the raising up the *body* to life after it is dead, Jn. xi. 24; v. 29; 1 Co. xv. 22. But the Sadducees not only denied this, but also a future state, and the separate existence of the soul after death altogether, as well as the existence of angels and spirits, Ac. xxiii. 8. Both these doctrines have commonly stood or fallen together, and the answer of our Saviour respects both, though it more distinctly refers *to the separate existence of the soul, and to a future state of rewards and punishments*, than to the resurrection of the body.

24. *Saying, Master, Moses said,* &c., De. xxv. 5, 6. This law was given by Moses in order to keep the families and tribes of the Israelites distinct, and to perpetuate them. ¶ *Raise up seed unto his brother.* That is, the children shall be reckoned in the genealogy of the deceased brother; or, to all civil purposes, shall be considered as his.

25–28. *There were with us seven brethren.* It is probable that they stated a case as difficult as possible; and though no such case might have occurred, yet it was

had married a wife, deceased, and, having no issue, left his wife unto his brother:

26 Likewise the second also, and the third, unto the [3]seventh.

27 And last of all the woman died also.

28 Therefore, in the resurrection, whose wife shall she be of the seven? for they all had her.

29 Jesus answered and said unto them, Ye do err, [v]not knowing the scriptures, nor the power of God.

30 For in the resurrection they neither marry, nor are given in marriage, but are as [w]the angels of God in heaven.

31 But as touching the resurrection of the dead, have ye not read that which was spoken unto you by God, saying,

32 I[x] am the God of Abraham,

3 *seven*.

v Jn.20.9. *w* ch.18.10; 1 Jn.3.2. *x* Ex.3.6,15,16; He.11.16.

---

supposable, and in their view it presented a real difficulty. The difficulty arose from the fact, that they supposed that, substantially, the same state of things must take place in the other world as here; that if there is such a world, husbands and wives must be there reunited; and they professed not to be able to see how *one* woman could be the wife of seven men.

29. *Ye do err, not knowing*, &c. They had taken a wrong view of the doctrine of the resurrection. It was not taught that men would marry there. The *Scriptures*, here, mean the books of the Old Testament. By appealing to them, Jesus showed that the doctrine of the future state was there, and that the Sadducees should have believed it as it was, and not have added the absurd doctrine to it that men must live there as they do here. The way in which the enemies of the truth often attempt to make a doctrine of the Bible ridiculous is by adding to it, and then calling it absurd. The reason why the Saviour produced a passage from the books of Moses (ver. 32) was that they had also appealed to his writings, ver. 24. Other places of the Old Testament, in fact, asserted the doctrine more clearly (Da. xii. 2; Is. xxvi. 19), but he wished to meet them on their own ground. None of those scriptures asserted that men would live there as they do here, and therefore their reasoning was false. ¶ *Nor the power of God*. They probably denied, as many have done since, that God could gather the scattered dust of the dead and remould it into a body. On this ground they affirmed that the doctrine could not be true—opposing reason to revelation, and supposing that infinite power could not reorganize a body that it had at first organized, and raise a body from its own dust which it had at first raised from nothing.

30. *Neither marry*, &c. This was a full answer to the objections of the Sadducees. ¶ *But are as the angels of God*. That is, in the manner of their intercourse; in regard to marriage and the mode of their existence. Luke adds that they shall be *equal with the angels*. That is, they shall be elevated above the circumstances of mortality, and live in a manner and in a kind of intercourse similar to that of the angels. It does not imply that they shall be equal in intellect, but only *in the circumstances of their existence*, as that is distinguished from the way in which mortals live. He also adds, "Neither do they die any more, but are the children of God, being the children of the resurrection," or being accounted worthy to be raised up to life, and therefore *sons of God raised up to him*.

31, 32. *As touching*, &c. That is, in proof that the dead are raised. The passage which he quotes is recorded in Ex. iii. 6, 15. This was at the burning bush (Mark and Luke). Abraham, Isaac, and Jacob had been long dead when Moses spoke this—Abraham 329 years, Isaac 224, and Jacob 198—yet God spake then as being still *their God*. They must, therefore, be still somewhere living, for God is not the God of the dead; that is, it is absurd to say that God rules over those who are *extinct* or *annihilated*, but he is the God only of those who have an existence. Luke adds, *all live unto him*. That is, all the righteous dead, all of whom he can be properly called their God, live unto his glory. This passage does not prove *directly* that the dead *body* would be raised, but only by consequence. It proves that Abraham, Isaac, and Jacob had an existence then, or that their

and the God of Isaac, and the God of Jacob? God is not the God of the dead, but of the living.

33 And when the multitude heard *this*, they were [y]astonished at his doctrine.

34 But when the Pharisees had heard that he had put the Sadducees to silence, they were gathered together.

35 Then [z] one of them, *which was* a lawyer, asked *him a question*, tempting him, and saying,

36 Master, which *is* the great commandment in the law?

37 Jesus said unto him, [a]Thou

y ch.7.28; Mar.12.17. z Lu.10.25,&c. a De.6.5; 10.12.

souls were alive. This the Sadducees denied (Ac. xxiii. 8), and this was the main point in dispute. If this was admitted—if there was a state of rewards and punishments—then it would easily follow that the bodies of the dead would be raised.

34–40. *Jesus converses with a Pharisee respecting the law.* See also Mar. xii. 28–34.

34. *The Pharisees—were gathered together.* That is, either to rejoice that their great rivals, the Sadducees, had been so completely silenced, or to lay a new plan for ensnaring him, or perhaps both. They would rejoice that the Sadducees had been confounded, but they would not be the less desirous to involve Jesus in difficulty. They therefore endeavoured, probably, to find the most difficult question in dispute among themselves, and proposed it to him to perplex him.

35. *A lawyer.* This does not mean one that *practised* law, as among us, but one learned or skilled in the law of Moses. Mark calls him *one of the scribes.* This means the same thing. The scribes were men of learning—particularly men skilled in the law of Moses. This lawyer had heard Jesus reasoning with the Sadducees, and perceived that he had put them to silence. He was evidently supposed by the Pharisees to be better qualified to hold a debate with him than the Sadducees were, and they had therefore put him forward for that purpose. This man was probably of a candid turn of mind; perhaps willing to know the truth, and not entering very fully into their malicious intentions, but acting as their agent, Mar. xii. 34. ¶ *Tempting him.* Trying him. Proposing a question to test his knowledge of the law.

36. *Which is the great commandment?* That is, the *greatest* commandment, or the one most important. The Jews are said to have divided the law into *greater* and *smaller* commandments. Which was of the greatest importance they had not determined. Some held that it was the law respecting sacrifice; others, that respecting circumcision; others, that pertaining to washings and purifying, &c. ¶ *The law.* The word *law* has a great variety of significations; it means, commonly, in the Bible, as it does here, *the law given by Moses*, recorded in the first five books of the Bible.

37. *Jesus said unto him*, &c. Mark says that he introduced this by referring to the doctrine of the unity of God —"Hear, O Israel! the Lord thy God is one Lord"—taken from De. vi. 4. This was said, probably, because all true obedience depends on the correct knowledge of God. None can keep his commandments who are not acquainted with his nature, his perfections, and his right to command. ¶ *Thou shalt love the Lord thy God with all thy heart.* The meaning of this is, thou shalt love him with all thy faculties or powers. Thou shalt love him supremely, more than all other beings and things, and with all the ardour possible. To love him with all the heart is to fix the affections supremely on him, more strongly than on anything else, and to be willing to give up all that we hold dear at his command. ¶ *With all thy soul.* Or, with all thy *life.* This means, to be willing to give up the life to him, and to devote it all to his service; to live to him, and to be willing to die at his command. ¶ *With all thy mind.* To submit the *intellect* to his will. To love his law and gospel more than we do the decisions of our own minds. To be willing to submit all our faculties to his teaching and guidance, and to devote to him all our intellectual attainments and all the results of our intellectual efforts. ¶ *With all thy strength* (Mark). With all the faculties of soul and body. To labour and toil for his glory, and to make that the great object of all our efforts.

shalt love the Lord thy God with all thy heart, and with all thy soul, and with all thy mind.

38 This is the first and great commandment.

39 And the second *is* like unto it, [b]Thou shalt love thy neighbour as thyself.

40 On [c]these two commandments hang all the law and the prophets.

41 While the Pharisees were gathered together, Jesus asked them,

42 Saying, [d]What think ye of Christ? whose son is he? They say unto him, *The son* of David.

43 He saith unto them, How

b Le.19.18. c Ro.13.9; Ja.2.8. d Mar.12.35,&c.; Lu.20.41,&c.

38. *This the first and great commandment.* This commandment is found in De. vi. 5. It is the first and greatest of all; *first*, not in *order of time*, but of *importance; greatest* in dignity, in excellence, in extent, and duration. It is the fountain of all others. All beings are to be loved according to their excellence. As God is the most excellent and glorious of all beings, he is to be loved supremely. If he is loved aright, then our affections will be directed toward all created objects in a right manner.

39. *The second* is *like unto it.* Le. xix. 18. That is, it resembles it in importance, dignity, purity, and usefulness. This had not been asked by the lawyer, but Jesus took occasion to acquaint him with the substance of the whole law. For its meaning, see Notes on Mat. xix. 19. Comp. Ro. xiii. 9. Mark adds, *there is none other commandment greater than these.* None respecting circumcision or sacrifice is greater. They are the fountain of all.

40. *On these two commandments hang*, &c. That is, these comprehend the substance of what Moses in the law and what the prophets have spoken. What they have said has been to endeavour to win men to love God and to love each other. Love to God and man comprehends the whole of religion, and to produce this has been the design of Moses, the prophets, the Saviour, and the apostles.

Mark (xii. 32–34) adds that the scribe said, "Well, Master, thou hast said the truth;" and that he assented to what Jesus had said, and admitted that to love God and man in this manner was more than all burnt-offerings and sacrifices; that is, was of more value or importance. Jesus, in reply, told him that he was "not far from the kingdom of heaven;" in other words, by his reply he had shown that he was almost prepared to receive the doctrines of the gospel. He had evinced such an acquaintance with the law as to prove that he was nearly prepared to receive the teachings of Jesus. See Notes on Mat. iii. 2.

Mark and Luke say that this had such an effect that no man after that durst ask him any question, Lu. xx. 40; Mar. xii. 34. This does not mean that none of his disciples durst ask him any question, but none of the Jews. He had confounded all their sects—the Herodians (Mat. xxii. 15–22); the Sadducees (23–33); and, last, the Pharisees (34–40). All, finding themselves unable to confound him, at last gave up the attempt.

41–46. *Jesus proposes a question concerning the Messiah.* See also Mar. xii. 35–37; Lu. xx. 41–44.

41. *While the Pharisees*, &c. Jesus, having confounded the great sects of the Jews, proceeds, in his turn, to propose to them a question for their solution. This was done, not for the purpose of vain parade and triumph, but, 1st. To show them how ignorant they were of their prophecies. 2d. To humble them in view of their ignorance. 3d. To bring to their attention the true doctrine respecting the Messiah—his being possessed of a character superior to that of David, the most mighty king of Israel—being his Lord, at the same time that he was his descendant.

42. *What think ye of Christ?* What are your views respecting THE MESSIAH, or *the Christ*, especially respecting his *genealogy?* He did not ask them their views respecting him in general, but only respecting his ancestry. The article should have been retained in the translation—*the* Christ or *the* Messiah. He did not ask them their opinion respecting himself, his person, and work, as would seem in our translation, but their views respecting the Messiah whom they expected. ¶ *Whose son is he?* Whose *descendant?* See the Notes on

then doth David in spirit [e] call him Lord? saying,

44 The LORD said unto my Lord, Sit thou on my right hand, till I make thine enemies thy footstool.

e Ps.110.1; Ac.2.34,35; He.1.13; 10.12,13.

45 If David then call him Lord, how is he his son?

46 And [f] no man was able to answer him a word; [g] neither durst any *man*, from that day forth, ask him any more *questions*.

f Lu.14.6. g Mar.12.34; Lu.20.40.

Mat. i. 1. ¶ The son *of David*. The descendant of David, according to the promise.

43. *How then*, &c. How is this doctrine that he is *descended* from David consistent with what David says when he calls him *lord?* How can your opinion be reconciled with that? That declaration of David is recorded in Ps. cx. 1. A *lord* or master is a superior. The word here does not necessarily imply divinity, but only superiority. David calls him his superior, his lord, his master, his lawgiver, and expresses his willingness to obey him. If the Messiah was to be merely a descendant of David, as other men descended from parents—if he was to have a human nature only—if he did not exist when David wrote—with what propriety could he, then, call him his lord? ¶ *In spirit.* By the inspiration of the Holy Spirit. As a prophet, Ac. ii. 30; i. 16; 2 Sa. xxiii. 2.

44. *The* LORD *said*, &c. This is the language of David. "Jehovah said to *my* lord—*the Messiah*—sit thou," &c. This was a prediction respecting the exaltation of Christ. To be raised to the right hand of a king was significant of favour, trust, and power. See Notes on Mat. xx. 21. This was done respecting Christ, Mar. xvi. 19; Ac. vii. 55; Ro. viii. 34; Ep. i. 20; He. i. 3; viii. 1; x. 12. *Thine enemies thy footstool.* A footstool is that which is under the feet when we are sitting—implying that we have it under subjection, or at our control. So Christ shall put all enemies under his feet—all his spiritual foes—all that rise up against him, Ps. ii. 9, 12; He. x. 13; 1 Co. xv. 25.

45. *If David*, &c. If he was then David's lord—if he was his superior—if he had an existence at that time—how could he be descended from him? They could not answer him. Nor is there any way of answering the question but by the admission that the Messiah was divine as well as human; that he had an existence at the time of David, and was his lord and master, his God and king, and that as man he was descended from him.

REMARKS.

1st. Multitudes of men, who are invited to be saved, reject the gospel and perish in their sins, ver. 3.

2d. If they perish, they only will be to blame. The offer was freely made, the salvation was provided, and the only reason why they were not saved was that they would not come, ver. 3.

3d. Attention to the affairs of this life, the love of the world, will shut many out of the kingdom of heaven, ver. 5. Some attention to those things is necessary; but such a devotion to these things as to lead to the loss of the soul never can be right.

4th. It is treating God ungratefully to reject his gospel, ver. 3–5. He has sent his Son to die for us; he has entreated us to be saved; he has followed us with mercies; and to reject all these, and refuse to be saved, is to treat him with contempt, as well as to overwhelm ourselves in condemnation. *Man has no right to be damned.* He is under the most solemn obligations to be *saved;* and after what God has done for us, deep and dreadful woe will await us if we are so foolish and wicked as to be lost.

5th. Many of the poor and needy will be saved, while the haughty and rich will perish for ever, ver. 9, 10.

6th. Let those who make a profession of religion look often to the great day when Christ will search them, ver. 11. There is a day coming that will try us. His eye will be upon us. He will read our hearts, and see whether we are clothed in his righteousness, or only the filthy rags of our own.

7th. A profession of religion will not save us, ver. 11–13. It is foolish to deceive ourselves. Nothing but genuine piety, true faith in Jesus, and a holy life, will save us. God asks not profession merely, but the heart. He asks not mockery, but sincerity; not pretension, but reality.

8th. The hypocrite must perish, ver. 13. It is right that he should perish. He knew his Master's will and would not do it. He must perish with an awful condemnation. No man sins amid so much light, none with so high a hand. No sin is so awful as to attempt to deceive God, and to palm pretensions on him for reality.

9th. Pretended friends are sometimes more dangerous than avowed enemies, ver. 16. Pretended friendship is often for the purpose of decoying us into evil. It throws us off our guard, and we are more easily taken.

10th. The truth is often admitted by wicked men from mere hypocrisy, ver. 16. It is only for the purpose of deceiving others and leading them into sin.

11th. Wicked men can decide correctly on the character of a public preacher, ver. 16. They often admit his claim in words, but for an evil purpose.

12th. It may be right for us sometimes to attend to artful and captious questions, ver. 18. It may afford opportunity to do good; to confound the wicked and to inculcate truth.

13th. No cunning can overreach God, ver. 18. He knows the heart, and he perceives the wickedness of all who attempt to deceive him.

14th. It is right, and it is our duty to obey the law of the land, when it does not contravene the law of God, ver. 21. *Conscientious Christians make the best citizens.* Comp. Notes on Ro. xiii. 1–7.

15th. We should give honour to civil rulers, ver. 21. We should pay respect to the *office*, whatever may be the character of the ruler. We should speak well of it, not abuse it; yield proper obedience to its requirements, and not rebel against it. Men may be wicked who hold an office, but the office is ordained by God (Ro. xiii. 1, 2); and for the sake of the office we must be patient, meek, submissive, and obedient, Mat. xxiii. 3.

16th. Yet we are to obey civil rulers no farther than their commands are consistent with the law of God, ver. 21. God is to be obeyed rather than man; and when a civil ruler commands a thing contrary to the laws of the Bible and the dictates of our consciences, we may, we must resist it, Ac. v. 29.

17th. The objections of men to the doctrines of the Bible are often founded on ignorance of what those doctrines are, and distrust of the power of God, ver. 29. Men often set up a notion which they call a doctrine of the Bible, and then fight a shadow, and think they have confuted the truth of God, while that truth was, in fact, untouched. It is a totally different thing from what they supposed.

18th. When men attack a doctrine they should be certain that they understand it, ver. 29. The Sadducees did not understand the true doctrine of the resurrection. The inquiry which they should have made was whether they had correct views of it. This is the inquiry which men ought always first to make when they approach a doctrine of the Bible.

19th. We learn the glory and happiness of the state after the resurrection, ver. 30 (Luke). We shall be in some respects equal to the angels. Like them we shall be free from sin, suffering, and death. Like them we shall be complete in knowledge and felicity. Like them we shall be secure of eternal joy. Happy are those—the good of all the earth—who shall have part in that resurrection of the just!

20th. The dead shall be raised, ver. 31, 32. There is a state of happiness hereafter. This the gospel has revealed; and it is the most consoling and cheering truth that has ever beamed upon the heart of man.

21st. Our pious friends that have died are now happy, ver. 31, 32. They are with God. God is still their God. A father, or mother, or sister, or friend that may have left us is there—there in perfect felicity. We should rejoice at that, nor should we wish them back to the poor comforts and the many sufferings of this world.

22d. It is our duty to love God with all the heart, ver. 37. No half, formal, cold, and selfish affection comes up to the requirement. It must be full, entire, absolute. It must be pleasure in *all* his attributes—his justice, his power, his purposes, as well as his mercy and his goodness. God is to be loved just as he is. If man is not pleased with his whole character he is not pleased with him at all.

23d. God is worthy of love. He is perfect. He should be *early* loved. Children should love him more than they do father, or mother, or friends. Their first affections should be fixed on God, and fixed on him supremely, till they die.

24th. We must love our neighbour, ver. 39. We must do to all as we would have them do to us. This is the law and

CHAPTER XXIII.

THEN spake Jesus to the multitude, and to his disciples,

2 Saying, [a]The scribes and the Pharisees sit in Moses' seat:

3 All, therefore, whatsoever they bid you observe, *that* observe and do; but do not ye after their works; for [b]they say, and do not.

4 For they bind [c]heavy burdens, and grievous to be borne, and lay *them* on men's shoulders; but they *themselves* will not move them with one of their fingers.

a Mal.2.7. b Ro.2.21-23. c Ac.15.10.

---

the prophets: this is the way of justice, of peace, of kindness, of charity, of benevolence. If all men obeyed these laws, the earth would be a paradise, and man would taste the bliss of heaven here below.

25th. We may ask here of each one, What think you of Christ? ver. 42. What think you of the necessity of a Saviour? What think you of his nature? Is he God as well as man, or do you regard him only as a man? What think you of his character? Do you see him to be lovely and pure, and is he such as to draw forth the warm affections of your heart? What think you of salvation by him? Do you depend on him, and trust in him, and expect heaven only on the ground of his merits? or do you reject and despise him, and would you have joined in putting him to death? Nothing more certainly tests the character, and shows what the feelings are, than the views which we entertain of Christ. Error here is fatal error; but he who has just views of the Redeemer, and right feelings toward him, is SURE OF SALVATION.

26th. We have in this chapter an illustrious specimen of the wisdom of Jesus. He successfully met the snares of his mighty and crafty foes, and with infinite ease confounded them. No art of man could confound him. Never was wisdom more clear, never more triumphant.

CHAPTER XXIII.

2. *Scribes and Pharisees.* See Notes on Mat. iii. 7. ¶ *Moses' seat.* Moses was the great legislator of the Jews. By him the law was given. The office of explaining that law among the Jews devolved on the scribes and Pharisees. In the synagogues they sat while expounding the law, and rose when they read it. By *sitting in the seat of Moses* we are to understand authority to teach the law; or, as he taught the nation by giving the law, so they taught it by explaining it.

3. *All, therefore, whatsoever,* &c. That is, all that they teach that is consistent with the law of Moses—all the commands of Moses which they read to you and properly explain. The word *all* could not be taken without such a restriction, for Christ himself accuses them of teaching many things contrary to that law, and of making it void by their traditions, Mat. xv. 1-6. ¶ *They say, and do not.* The interpretation which they give to the law is in the main correct, but their lives do not correspond with their teaching. It is not the duty of men to imitate their teachers unless their lives are pure; they are to obey the law of God, and not to frame their lives by the example of evil men.

4. *They bind heavy burdens,* &c. This phrase is derived from the custom of loading animals. The load or burden is bound up and then laid on the beast. So the Pharisees appointed weighty burdens, or grievous and heavy precepts, and insisted that the people should obey them, though they lent no assistance. The *heavy burdens* refer not here to the traditions and foolish customs of the Pharisees, for Jesus would not command the people to observe them; but they clearly mean the ceremonies and rights appointed by Moses, which Peter says neither *they nor their fathers were able to bear,* Ac. xv. 10. Those rites were numerous, expensive, requiring much time, much property, and laborious. The Pharisees were rigid in requiring that all the people should pay the taxes, give of their property, comply with every part of the law with the utmost rigour, yet they indulged themselves, and bore as little of the expense and trouble as possible; so that, where they could avoid it, they would not lend the least aid to the people in the toils and expense of their religious rites. ¶ *With one of their fingers.* In the least degree. They will not render the least aid.

5. *Their phylacteries.* The word *phy-*

5 But [d]all their works they do for to be seen of men: they make broad their [e]phylacteries, and enlarge the borders of their garments,

6 And [f]love the uppermost rooms at feasts, and the chief seats in the synagogues,

7 And greetings in the markets,

d ch.6.1-16. e Nu.15.38. f Mar.12.38,&c.; Lu.11.43,&c.

lactery comes from a word signifying to keep, preserve, or guard. The name was given because phylacteries were worn as amulets or charms, and were supposed to defend or preserve those who wore them from evil. They were small slips of parchment or vellum, on which were written certain portions of the Old Testament. The practice of using phylacteries was founded on a literal interpretation of that passage where God commands the Hebrews to have the law as a sign on their foreheads, and as frontlets between their eyes, Ex. xiii. 16; comp. Pr. iii. 1, 3; vi. 21. One kind of phylactery was called a *frontlet*, and was composed of four pieces of parchment, on the first of which was written Ex. xii. 2-10; on the second, Ex. xiii. 11-21; on the third, De. vi. 4-9; and on the fourth, De. xi. 18-21. These pieces of parchment, thus inscribed, they inclosed in a piece of tough skin, making a square, on one side of which is placed the Hebrew letter *shin*, ש, and bound them round their foreheads with a thong or ribbon when they went to the synagogue. Some wore them evening and morning; others only at the morning prayer.

As the token upon the hand was required, as well as the frontlets between the eyes (Ex. xiii. 16), the Jews made two rolls of parchment, written in square letters, with an ink made on purpose, and with much care. They were rolled up to a point, and inclosed in a sort of case of black calf-skin. They were put upon a square bit of the same leather, whence hung a thong of the same, of about a finger in breadth, and about 2 feet long. These rolls were placed at the bending of the left arm, and after one end of the thong had been made into a little knot in the form of the Hebrew letter *yod*, י, it was wound about the arm in a spiral line, which ended at the top of the middle finger. The Pharisees enlarged them, or made them wider than other people, either that they might make the letters larger or write more on them, to show, as they supposed, that they had peculiar reverence for the law. ¶ *Enlarge the borders of their garments.* This refers to the loose threads which were attached to the borders of the outer garment as a fringe. This fringe was commanded in order to distinguish them from other nations, and that they might remember to keep the commandments of God, Nu. xv. 38-40; De. xxii. 12. The Pharisees made them broader than other people wore them, to show that they had peculiar respect for the law.

6. *The uppermost rooms at feasts.* The word *rooms*, here, by no means expresses the meaning of the original. It would be correctly rendered the uppermost *places* or *couches* at feasts. To understand this, it is necessary to remark that the custom among the Jews was not to eat sitting, as we do, but reclining on couches. The table was made by *three* tables, raised like ours and placed so as to form a square, with a clear space in the midst, and one end quite open. Around these tables were placed cushions capable of containing three or more persons. On these the guests reclined, leaning on their left side, with their feet extended from the table, and so lying that the head of one naturally reclined on the bosom of another. To recline near to one in this manner denoted intimacy, and was what was meant by lying *in the bosom* of another, Jn. xiii. 23; Lu. xvi. 22, 23. As the feet were extended *from* the table, and as they reclined instead of sitting, it was easy to approach the feet behind, and even unperceived. Thus, in Lu. vii. 37, 38, while Jesus reclined in this manner, a woman that had been a sinner came to his feet *behind him*, and washed them with her tears, and wiped them with the hairs of her head. She stood on the outside of the couches. So our Saviour washed the feet of his disciples as they reclined on a couch in this manner, Jn. xiii. 4-12. Whenever we read in the New Testament of *sitting* at meals, it always means reclining in this manner, and never sitting as we do. The chief seat, or the *uppermost* one, was the middle couch at the upper end of the table. This the Pharisees loved, as a post of honour or distinction.

Chief seats in the synagogues. The

and to be called of men, Rabbi, Rabbi.

8 But[g] be not ye called Rabbi: for one is your Master, *even* Christ; and all ye are brethren.

9 And call no *man* your Father upon the earth: for one is your [h]Father, which is in heaven.

10 Neither be ye called masters: for one is your Master, *even* Christ.

g Ja.3.1. h ch.6.9.

---

seats usually occupied by the elders of the synagogue, near the pulpit. The meaning is, they love a place of distinction. See Notes on Mat. iv. 23.

7. *Greetings in the markets.* Markets were places where multitudes of people were assembled together. They were pleased with special attention in public places, and desired that all should show them particular respect. ¶ *Greetings.* Salutations. See Notes on Lu. x. 4. ¶ *To be called Rabbi, Rabbi.* This word literally signifies *great.* It was a title given to eminent teachers of the law among the Jews; a title of honour and dignity, denoting authority and ability to teach. They were gratified with such titles, and wished it given to themselves as denoting superiority. Every time it was given to them it implied their superiority to the persons who used it, and they were fond, therefore, of hearing it often applied to them. There were three titles in use among the Jews—Rab, Rabbi, and Rabban—denoting different degrees of learning and ability, as literary degrees do among us.

8. *Be not ye,* &c. Jesus forbade his disciples to seek such titles of distinction. The reason which he gave was that he was himself their Master and Teacher. They were on a level; they were to be equal in authority; they were brethren; and they should neither covet nor receive a title which implied either an elevation of one above another, or which appeared to infringe on the absolute right of the Saviour to be their only Teacher and Master. The direction here is an express command to his disciples not to *receive* such a title of distinction. They were not to covet it; they were not to seek it; they were not to do anything that implied a wish or a willingness that it should be appended to their names. Everything which would tend to make a distinction among them or destroy their parity—everything which would lead the world to suppose that there were ranks and grades among them as ministers, they were to avoid. It is to be observed that the command is that they were not to *receive* the title—"*Be not ye called Rabbi.*" The Saviour did not forbid them giving the title to others when it was customary or not regarded as improper (comp. Ac. xxvi. 25), but *they* were not to receive it. It was to be unknown among them. This title corresponds with the title "*Doctor of Divinity*" as applied to ministers of the gospel; and, so far as I can see, the spirit of the Saviour's command is violated by the reception of such a title, as really as it would have been by their being called Rabbi. It makes a distinction among ministers. It tends to engender pride and a sense of superiority in those who obtain it, and envy and a sense of inferiority in those who do not; and the whole spirit and tendency of it is contrary to the "simplicity that is in Christ."

9. *And call no* man *your Father,* &c. This does not, of course, forbid us to apply the term to our real father. Religion requires all proper honour to be shown to him, Ex. xx. 12; Mat. xv. 4; Ep. vi. 1–3. But the word *father* also denotes *authority, eminence, superiority, a right to command,* and *a claim to particular respect.* In this sense it is used here. In this sense it belongs eminently to God, and it is not right to give it to men. Christian brethren are equal. God only has supreme authority. He only has a right to give laws; to declare doctrines that shall bind the conscience; to punish disobedience. The Jewish teachers affected that title because they seem to have supposed that a teacher formed the man, or gave him real life, and sought, therefore, to be called father. Christ taught them that the source of all life and truth was God, and they ought not to seek or receive a title which properly belongs to him.

10. *Neither be ye called masters.* That is, *leaders, guides,* for this is the literal meaning of the word. It refers to those who go before others; who claim, therefore, the right to direct and control others. This was also a title conferred on Jewish teachers.

Neither of these commands forbids

11 But[i] he that is greatest among you shall be your servant.

12 And[k] whosoever shall exalt himself shall be abased; and he that shall humble himself shall be exalted.

13 But woe unto you, scribes and Pharisees, hypocrites! for ye shut up the kingdom of heaven against men: for ye neither go in *yourselves,* neither suffer ye them that are entering to go in.

14 Woe unto you, scribes and Pharisees, hypocrites! [l]for ye devour widows' houses, and for a pretence make long prayer: there-

i ch.20.26,27. k Pr.15.33; Ja.4.6. l 2 Ti.3.6; Tit.1.11.

us to give proper titles of civil office to men, or to render them the honour belonging to their station, Mat. xxii. 21; Ro. xiii. 7; 1 Pe. ii. 17. They prohibit the disciples of Jesus from seeking or receiving mere empty titles, producing distinctions among themselves, implying authority to control the opinions and conduct of others, and claiming that others should acknowledge them to be superior to them.

11, 12. See Notes on Mat. xx. 26. *He that shall humble himself,* &c. God will exalt or honour him that is humble, and that seeks a lowly place among men. That is true religion, and God will reward it.

13. *Woe unto you.* You are guilty, and punishment will come upon you. Jesus proceeds to state wherein they were guilty. This most eloquent, most appalling, and most terrible of all discourses ever delivered to mortals was pronounced in the temple, in the presence of multitudes. Never was there more faithful dealing, more terrible reproof, more profound knowledge of the workings of hypocrisy, or more skill in detecting the concealments of sin. This was the last of the Saviour's public discourses; and it is a most impressive summary of all that he had ever said, or that he had to say, of a wicked and hypocritical generation. ¶ *Scribes and Pharisees.* See Notes on Mat. iii. 7. ¶ *Hypocrites.* Note, Mat. vi. 2. ¶ *Ye shut up the kingdom of heaven.* Note, Mat. iii. 2. They shut it up by teaching false doctrines respecting the Messiah; by binding the people to an observance of their traditions; by opposing Jesus, and attempting to convince the people that he was an impostor, thus preventing many from becoming his followers. Many were ready to embrace him as the Messiah, and were about entering into the kingdom of heaven—that is, the church—but they prevented it. Luke says (xi. 52) they had taken away the key of knowledge, and thus prevented their entering in—that is, they had taken away the right interpretation of the ancient prophecies respecting the Messiah, and thus had done all that they could to prevent the people from receiving Jesus as their Redeemer.

14. *Devour widows' houses.* The word *houses* is here used to denote *property* or possessions of any kind. You take away or get possession of the property of widows by improper arts and pretences. This was done in two ways: 1st. They claimed a very exact knowledge of the law and a perfect observance of it. They pretended to extraordinary justice toward the poor, friendship for the distressed, and willingness to aid those who were in embarrassed circumstances. They thus induced *widows* and poor people to commit the management of their property to them as guardians and executors, and then took advantage of them and defrauded them. 2d. They put on the appearance of great sanctity, and induced many conscientious but credulous women to give them much, under pretence of devoting it to religious purposes. ¶ *Long prayer.* Their prayers are said to have been often three hours in length. One rule among them, says Lightfoot, was to meditate an hour, then pray an hour, and then meditate another hour—all of which was included in their *long prayers* or *devotions.* ¶ *Damnation.* Condemnation. The word here probably refers to future punishment. It does not always, however. It means, frequently, no more than *condemnation,* or the divine disapprobation of a certain course of conduct, as in 1 Co. xi. 29: "He that eateth and drinketh unworthily, eateth and drinketh *damnation* to himself;" that is, he that eateth and drinketh in an unworthy manner disorderly, not with reverence—is guilty, and his conduct will be disapproved or condemned by God—referring solely to the impropriety of the manner of partaking of the Lord's supper, and not at

fore ye shall receive the greater damnation.

15 Woe unto you, scribes and Pharisees, hypocrites! for ye compass sea and land to make one proselyte; and when he is made, ye make him twofold more [m]the child of hell than yourselves.

16 Woe unto you, *ye* [n]blind guides, which say, Whosoever shall swear by the temple, it is nothing; but whosoever shall swear by the gold of the temple, he is a debtor.

17 *Ye*[o] fools, and blind! for whether is greater, the gold, or the temple that sanctifieth the gold?

18 And, Whosoever shall swear by the altar, it is nothing; but whosoever sweareth by the gift that is upon it, he is [1]guilty.

19 *Ye* fools, and blind! for whe-

m Jn.8.44; Ac.13.10; Ep.2.3. *n* ch.15.14.

o Ps.94.8. 1 or, *debtor*, or, *bound*.

---

all to the worthiness or unworthiness of the person. See Notes on that place. Comp. Ro. xiv. 23. ¶ *For a pretence.* For appearance or show; in order that they might the better defraud poor people. They would not be condemned for *making* long prayers, but because they did it with an evil design. Public prayers should, however, be short, and always to the point. A man praying in a Sunday-school should pray for the school, and, usually, not for everything else.

15. *Ye compass sea and land.* You take every means, spare no pains, to gain proselytes. ¶ *Proselyte.* One that comes over from a foreign nation, religion, or sect to us—a convert. Among the Jews there were two kinds of proselytes: 1st. *Proselytes of righteousness,* or those who wholly and fully embraced the Jewish religion, who were baptized, who were circumcised, and who conformed to all the rites of the Mosaic institutions. 2d. *Proselytes of the gate,* or those who approved of the Jewish religion, renounced the Pagan superstitions, and conformed to some of the rites of the Jews, but were not circumcised or baptized. ¶ *Twofold more the child of hell.* That is, twice as bad. To be a child of hell was a Hebrew phrase, signifying to be deserving of hell, to be awfully wicked. Comp. Notes on Mat. i. 1. The Jewish writers themselves say that the proselytes were "scabs of Israel," and "hindered the coming of the Messiah" by their great wickedness. The Pharisees gained them either to swell their own numbers, or to make gain by extorting their money under various pretences; and when they had accomplished that, they took no pains to instruct them or to restrain them. They had renounced their superstition which had before somewhat restrained them, but the Pharisees had given them no religion in its place to restrain them, and they were consequently left to the full indulgence of their vices.

16. *Whosoever shall swear,* &c. See Notes on Mat. v. 33–37. ¶ *The temple.* See Notes on Mat. xxi. 12. ¶ *It is nothing.* It amounts to nothing—it is not binding. ¶ *The gold of the temple.* Either the golden vessels in the temple—the candlestick, &c.; or the gold with which the doors and other parts of the temple were covered; or the gold in the treasury. This, it seems, they considered far more sacred than any other part of the temple, but it is not known why. ¶ *He is a debtor.* He is bound to keep his oath. He is guilty if he violates it.

17. *The temple that sanctifieth the gold.* To sanctify is to make holy. The gold had no holiness but what it derived from the temple. If in any other place, it would be no more holy than any other gold. It was foolish, then, to suppose that that was more holy than the temple, from which it received all the sanctity which it possessed.

18. *The altar.* The altar of burnt-offerings, in the court of the priests. See Notes on Mat. xxi. 12. It was made of brass, about 30 feet in length and breadth, and 15 feet in height, 2 Ch. iv. 1. On this altar were offered all the beasts and bloody oblations of the temple. ¶ *The gift that is upon it.* The gift or offering made to God, so called because it was devoted or *given* to him. The gift upon this altar was always beasts and birds.

19. *The altar that sanctifieth the gift.* The altar, dedicated to God, gave all the value or holiness to the offering, and must therefore be the greatest or of the most importance. If, therefore, either bound to the fulfilment of an oath, it must be the altar.

ther *is* greater, the gift, or [p]the altar that sanctifieth the gift?

20 Whoso therefore shall swear by the altar, sweareth by it, and by all things thereon.

21 And whoso shall swear by the temple, sweareth by it, and by [q]him that dwelleth therein.

22 And he that shall swear by heaven, sweareth by [r]the throne of God, and by him that sitteth thereon.

23 Woe unto you, scribes and Pharisees, hypocrites! [s]for ye pay tithe of mint, and [2]anise, and cummin, and [t]have omitted the weightier *matters* of the law, judgment, mercy, and faith: these ought ye to have done, and not to leave the other undone.

p Ex.29.37; 30.29. q 2 Ch.6.2; Ps.26.8. r Ps.11.4; Is.66.1; ch.5.34.

s Lu.11.42. 2 *dill.* t 1 Sa.15.22; Je.22.15,16; Ho.6.6; Mi.6.8; ch.9.13.

---

21. *Him that dwelleth therein.* That is, God. The temple was his house, his dwelling. In the first, or Solomon's temple, he dwelt between the cherubims in the most holy place. He manifested himself there by a visible symbol, in the form of a cloud resting on the mercy-seat, 1 Ki. viii. 10, 13; Ps. lxxx. 1.

22. *The throne of God.* Heaven is his throne, Mat. v. 34. It is so called as being the place where he sits in glory. Jesus says, here, that all who swear at all do, in fact, swear by God, or the oath is good for nothing. To swear by an altar, a gift, or a temple is of no force unless it be meant to appeal to God himself. The essential thing in an oath is calling God to witness our sincerity. If a real oath is taken, therefore, God is appealed to. If not it is foolish and wicked to swear by anything else.

23. *Ye pay tithe.* A tenth part. The law required the Jews to devote a tenth part of all their property to the support of the Levites, Nu. xviii. 20-24. Another tenth part they paid for the service of the sanctuary, commonly in cattle or grain, but where they lived far from the place of worship they changed it to money, De. xiv. 22-24. Besides these, there was to be every third year a tenth part given to the poor, to be eaten at their own dwellings (De. xiv. 28, 29); so that nearly one-third of the property of the Jews was devoted to religious services by law. This was besides the voluntary offerings which they made. How much more mild and gentle are the laws of Christianity under which we live! ¶ *Mint.* A garden herb, in the original so called from its agreeable flavour. It was used to sprinkle the floors of their houses and synagogues to produce a pleasant fragrance. ¶ *Anise.* Known commonly among us as *dill.* It has a fine aromatic smell, and is used by confectioners and perfumers. ¶ *Cummin.* A plant of the same genus, like *fennel,* and used for similar purposes. These were all herbs of little value. The law of Moses said that they should pay tithes of the *fruits of the earth,* De. xiv. 22. It said nothing, however, about herbs. It was a question whether these should be tithed. The Pharisees maintained, in their extraordinary strictness, that they ought. Our Saviour says that they were precise in doing small matters which the law had not expressly commanded, while they omitted the greater things which it had enjoined. ¶ *Judgment.* Justice to others, as magistrates, neighbours, citizens. Giving to all their just dues. ¶ *Mercy.* Compassion and kindness to the poor and miserable. ¶ *Faith.* Piety toward God; confidence in him. Faith in God here means that we are to give to him what is his due; as mercy and justice mean to do to MEN, in all circumstances, what is right toward them. ¶ *These ought ye to have done.* Attention to even the smallest points of the law of God is proper, but it should not interfere with the *higher* and more important parts of that law.

24. *Which strain at a gnat,* &c. This is a proverb. There is, however, a mistranslation or misprint here, which makes the verse unmeaning. *To strain* AT *a gnat* conveys no sense. It should have been to strain OUT a gnat; and so it is printed in some of the earlier versions, and so it was undoubtedly rendered by the translators. The common reading is a *misprint,* and should be corrected. The Greek means to *strain out* by a cloth or sieve. ¶ *A gnat.* The gnat has its origin in the water; not in great rivers, but in pools and marshes. In the stagnant waters they appear in the form of small *grubs* or

24 *Ye* blind guides! which strain at a gnat, and swallow a camel.

25 Woe unto you, scribes and Pharisees, hypocrites! [u]for ye make clean the outside of the cup and of the platter, but within they are full of extortion and excess.

26 *Thou* blind Pharisee! cleanse first that *which is* within the cup and platter, that the outside of them may be clean also.

27 Woe unto you, scribes and Pharisees, hypocrites! [v]for ye are like unto whited sepulchres, which indeed appear beautiful outward, but are within full of dead *men's* bones, and of all uncleanness.

28 Even so ye also outwardly appear righteous unto men, but within ye are full of hypocrisy and iniquity.

29 Woe unto you, scribes and

u Mar.7.4,&c.

v Lu.11.44; Ac.23.3.

larvæ. These larvæ retain their form about three weeks, after which they turn to chrysalids, and after three or four days they pass to the form of gnats. They are then distinguished by their well-known sharp sting. It is probable that the Saviour here refers to the insect as it exists in its *grub* or *larva* form, before it appears in the form of a gnat. Water is then its element, and those who were nice in their drink would take pains to strain it out. Hence the proverb. See Calmet's *Dict.*, art. "Gnat." It is here used to denote a very small matter, as a camel is to denote a large object. "You Jews take great pains to avoid offence in very small matters, superstitiously observing the smallest points of the law, like a man carefully straining out the animalculæ from what he drinks, while you are at no pains to avoid great sins—hypocrisy, deceit, oppression, and lust—like a man who should swallow a camel." The Arabians have a similar proverb: "He eats an elephant, and is suffocated with a gnat." He is troubled with little things, but pays no attention to great matters.

25. *The cup and the platter.* The drinking-cup and the dish containing food. The Pharisees were diligent in observing all the washings and obligations required by their traditions. See Notes on Mar. vii. 4. ¶ *Full of extortion and excess.* The outside appeared well; the inside was filled with the fruit of extortion, oppression, and wickedness. The meaning is, that though they took much pains to appear well, yet they obtained a living by extortion and crime. Their cups, neat as they appeared outward, were filled, not with the fruits of honest industry, but with that which had been extorted from the poor by wicked arts. Instead of *excess*, many manuscripts and editions of the Greek Testament read *wickedness.*

26. *Cleanse first that* which is *within the cup and the platter.* Let them be filled with the fruits of honest industry, and then the outside and the inside will be really *clean.* By this allusion to the cup and platter he taught them that it was necessary to cleanse the heart first, that the external conduct might be really pure and holy.

27. *Like unto whited sepulchres.* For the construction of sepulchres, see Notes on Mat. viii. 28. Those tombs were annually whitewashed to prevent the people from accidentally coming in contact with them as they went up to Jerusalem. This custom is still continued. Dr. Thomson (*The Land and the Book*, vol. i. p. 148) says, "I have been in places where this is repeated very often. The graves are kept clean and white as snow, a very striking emblem of those painted hypocrites, the Pharisees, beautiful without, but full of dead men's bones and of all uncleanness within." The law considered those persons unclean who had touched anything belonging to the dead, Nu. xix. 16. Sepulchres were therefore often whitewashed, that they might be distinctly seen. Thus "whited," they appeared beautiful; but within they contained the bones and corrupting bodies of the dead. So the Pharisees. Their outward conduct appeared well, but their hearts were full of hypocrisy, envy, pride, lust, and malice—fitly represented by the corruption within a whited tomb.

29. *Ye build the tombs of the prophets.* That is, you build sepulchres or tombs over the prophets that have been slain. This they did professedly from veneration and respect for their character. This is often done at the East at the

Pharisees, hypocrites! because ye build the tombs of the prophets, and garnish the sepulchres of the righteous,

30 And say, If we had been in the days of our fathers, we would not have been partakers with them in the blood of the prophets.

31 Wherefore ye be witnesses unto yourselves that ye are the children of them which [w]killed the prophets.

32 Fill[x] ye up, then, the measure of your fathers.

33 *Ye* serpents, *ye* [y]generation of vipers! how can ye escape the damnation of hell?

34 Wherefore, behold, I send

w Ac.7.52; 1 Th.2.15.
x Ge.15.16; 1 Th.2.16.
y ch.3.7.

present day, and indeed elsewhere. Among the Mohammedans it is a common way of showing respect for any distinguished man to build a tomb for him. By doing this, they profess respect for his character and veneration for his memory. So the Pharisees, by building tombs in this manner, professedly approved of the character and conduct of the prophets, and disapproved of the conduct of their fathers in killing them. ¶ *And garnish*, &c. That is, adorn or ornament. This was done by rebuilding them with more taste, decorating them, and keeping them neat and clean. The original word means, also, to show any proper honour to the memory of the dead, as by speaking well of them, praying near them, or rearing synagogues near them in honour of their memory.

30. *And say*, &c. This they professed to say by rebuilding their tombs. They also, probably, publicly expressed their disapprobation of the conduct of their fathers. All this, in building and ornamenting tombs, was a profession of extraordinary piety. Our Lord showed them it was mere pretence.

31. *Ye be witnesses unto yourselves.* The emphasis, here, lies in the words "*to yourselves*." It is an appeal to their conscience. It was not by their building the tombs that they were witnesses that they were the children of those who slew the prophets; but that, in spite of all this pretence of piety, under all this cloak of profession, they knew in their consciences, and were witnesses to themselves, that it was mere hypocrisy, and that they really approved the conduct of those who slew the prophets. ¶ *Children of them*, &c. Resembling them; approving their conduct; inheriting their feelings. See Notes on Mat. i. 1. They not only showed that they were descended from them, but that they possessed their spirit, and that, in similar circumstances, they would have done as they did.

32. *Fill ye up, then*, &c. This is a prediction of what they were about to do. He would have them act out their true spirit, and show what they were, and evince to all that they had the spirit of their fathers. Comp. Notes on Jn. xiii. 27. This was done be putting him to death, and persecuting the apostles. ¶ *The measure.* The full amount, so as to make it complete. By your slaying me, fill up what is lacking of the iniquity of your fathers till the measure is full; till the national iniquity is complete; till as much has been committed as God can possibly bear, and then shall come upon you all this blood, and you shall be destroyed, ver. 34, 35.

33. Ye *serpents.* This name is given to them on account of their pretending to be pious, and very much devoted to God, but being secretly evil. At the heart, with all their pretensions, they were filled with evil designs, as the serpent was, Ge. iii. 1–5. ¶ *Generation of vipers.* See Notes on Mat. xii. 34. ¶ *Damnation of hell.* This refers, beyond all question, to future punishment. So great was their wickedness and hypocrisy, that, if they persevered in this course, it was impossible to escape the damnation that should come on the guilty. This is the sternest language that Jesus ever used to wicked men. But it by no means authorizes ministers to use such language to sinners now. Christ knew that this was true of them. He had an authority which none now have. It is not the province of ministers to denounce judgment, or to use severe names, least of all to do it on pretence of imitating Christ. He knew the hearts of men. We know them not. He had authority to declare certainly that those whom he addressed would be lost. We have no such authority. He addressed persons; we address characters.

unto you prophets, and wise men, and scribes: and [z]*some* of them ye shall kill and crucify; and [a]*some* of them shall ye scourge in your synagogues, and [b]persecute *them* from city to city:

35 That[c] upon you may come all the righteous blood shed upon the earth, [d]from the blood of righteous Abel unto [e]the blood of Zacharias, son of Barachias, whom ye slew between the temple and the altar.

36 Verily I say unto you, All these things shall come upon this generation.

37 O[f] Jerusalem, Jerusalem, *thou*

z Ac.7.59. a Ac.5.40; 2 Co.11.24,25. b He.11.37. c Re.18.24. d Ge.4.8. e 2 Ch.24.20,21. f Lu.13.34.

34. *I send unto you prophets*, &c. Jesus doubtless refers here to the apostles, and other teachers of religion. Prophets, wise men, and scribes were the names by which the teachers of religion were known among the Jews, and he therefore used the same terms when speaking of the messengers which he would send. *I send* has the force of the future, I *will* send. ¶ Some *of them ye shall kill.* As in the case of Stephen (Ac. vii. 59) and James (Ac. xii. 1, 2). ¶ *Crucify.* Punish with death on the cross. There are no cases of this mentioned; but few historical records of this age have come down to us. The Jews had not the power of crucifying, but they had power to deliver those whom they condemned to death into the hands of the Romans to do it. ¶ *Shall scourge.* See Notes on Mat. x. 17. This was done, Ac. xxii. 19-24; 2 Co. xi. 24, 25. *Persecute*, &c. See Notes on Mat. v. 10. This was fulfilled in the case of nearly all the apostles.

35. *That upon you may come*, &c. That is, the nation is guilty. Your fathers were guilty. You have shown yourselves to be like them. You are about, by slaying the Messiah and his messengers, to fill up the iniquity of the land. The patience of God is nearly exhausted, and the nation is about to be visited with signal vengeance. These national crimes deserve national judgments; and the proper judgment for all these crimes are about to come upon you in the destruction of your temple and city. ¶ *All the righteous blood.* That is, all the judgments due for shedding that blood. God did not hold them guilty for what their fathers had done; but temporal judgments descend on children in consequence of the wickedness of parents, as in the case of drunken and profligate parents. A drunken father wastes the property that his children might have possessed. A gambler reduces his children to poverty and want. An imprudent and foolish parent is the occasion of leading his sons into places of poverty, ignorance, and crime, materially affecting their character and destiny. See Notes on Ro. v. 12-19. So of the Jews. The appropriate effects of their fathers' crimes were coming on the nation, and they would suffer. ¶ *Upon the earth.* Upon the land of *Judea.* The word is often used with this limitation. See Mat. iv. 8. ¶ *Righteous Abel.* Slain by Cain, his brother, Ge. iv. 8. ¶ *Zacharias, son of Barachias.* It is not certainly known who this was. Some have thought that it was the Zecharias whose death is recorded in 2 Ch. xxiv. 20, 21. He is there called the son of Jehoiada; but it is known that it was common among the Jews to have two names, as Matthew is called Levi; Lebbeus, Thaddeus; and Simon, Cephas. Others have thought that Jesus referred to Zecharias the prophet, who might have been massacred by the Jews, though no account of his death is recorded. It might have been known by tradition. ¶ *Whom ye slew.* Whom you, Jews, slew. Whom your nation killed. ¶ *Between the temple and the altar.* Between the temple, properly so called, and the altar of burnt-offering in the court of the priests. See the plan of the temple, Mat. xxi. 12.

36. *Upon this generation.* The destruction of Jerusalem took place about forty years after this was spoken. See the next chapter.

37. *O Jerusalem*, &c. See Notes on Lu. xix. 41, 42. ¶ *Would I have gathered.* Would have protected and saved. ¶ *Thy children.* Thy people.

38. *Your house.* The temple. The house of worship of the Jews. The chief ornament of Jerusalem. ¶ *Desolate.* About to be desolate or destroyed. To be forsaken as a place of worship, and delivered into the hands of the Ro-

that killest the prophets, and stonest them which are sent unto thee, how often would [g]I have gathered thy children together, even as a hen gathereth her chickens under *her* wings, and ye would not!

38 Behold,[h] your house is left unto you desolate.

39 For I say unto you, Ye shall not see me henceforth till ye shall say, [i]Blessed *is* he that cometh in the name of the Lord.

g De.32.11,12; Ps.91.4. *h* Zec.11.6. *i* Ps.118.26; ch.21.9.

mans, and destroyed. See Notes on ch. xxiv.

39. *Ye shall not see me*, &c. The day of your mercy is gone by. I have offered you protection and salvation, and you have rejected it. You are about to crucify me, and your temple to be destroyed, and you, as a nation, to be given up to long and dreadful suffering. You will not see me as a merciful Saviour, offering you redemption any more, till you have borne these heavy judgments. They must come upon you, and be borne, until you would be glad to hail a deliverer, and say, Blessed is he that cometh in the name of the Lord. Blessed be he that comes as the Messiah, to bring deliverance. This has not been yet accomplished, but the days will come when the Jews, long cast out and rejected, will hail Jesus as the Messiah, and receive him whom their fathers slew as the merciful Saviour, Ro. xi. 25-32.

REMARKS.

1st. Proper respect should always be shown to teachers and rulers, ver. 3.

2d. We are not to copy the *example* of wicked men, though they *are* our teachers or rulers, ver. 3. We are to frame our conduct by the law of God, and not by the example of *men*.

3d. Men are often very rigid in exacting of others what they fail altogether of performing themselves, ver. 4.

4th. We are not to seek human honours (ver. 8), nor to *give* flattering titles to others, nor to allow others to give them to us (ver. 9). Our highest honour is in humility, and he is most exalted who is most lowly, ver. 11, 12.

5th. In the descriptions of the scribes and Pharisees in this chapter, we have a full-length portrait of a hypocrite. 1st. They shut up the kingdom of heaven against others, ver. 13. They made great pretensions to knowledge, but they neither entered in themselves, nor suffered others. 2d. They committed the grossest iniquity under a cloak of religion, ver. 14. They cheated widows out of their property, and made long prayers to hide their villainy. 3d. They showed great zeal in making proselytes, yet did it only for gain, and made them more wicked, ver. 15. 4th. They taught false doctrine, and they resorted to artful contrivances to destroy the force of oaths, and to shut out the Creator from their view, ver. 16-22. 5th. They were superstitious, ver. 23. Small matters they were exact in; matters of real importance they cared little about. 6th. They took great pains to *appear* well, while they themselves knew that it was all deceit and falsehood, ver. 25-28. 7th. They professed great veneration for the memory of the pious dead, while at the same time they were conscious that they really approved the conduct of those that killed them, ver. 29-31. Never, perhaps, was there a combination of more wicked feelings and hypocritical actions than among them; and never was there more profound knowledge of the human heart, and more faithfulness, than in him who tore off the mask, and showed them what they were.

6th. It is amazing with what power and authority our blessed Lord reproves this wicked people. It is wonderful that they ever waited for a mock trial, and did not kill him at once. But his time was not come, and they were restrained, and not suffered to act out the fury of their mad passions.

7th. Jesus pities dying sinners, ver. 37. He seeks their salvation. He pleads with them to be saved. He would gather them to him, if they would come. The most hardened, even like the sinners of Jerusalem, he would save if they would come to him. But they will not. They turn from him, and tread the road to death.

8th. The reason why the wicked are not saved is their own obstinacy. They choose not to be saved, and they die. If they will not come to Christ, it is right that they should die. If they do not come, they must die.

9th. The sinner will be destroyed, ver.

CHAPTER XXIV.

AND[a] Jesus went out, and departed from the temple; and his disciples came to *him* for to show him the buildings of the temple.

2 And Jesus said unto them, See ye not all these things? Verily I say unto you, [b]There shall not be left here one stone upon another, that shall not be thrown down.

3 And as he sat upon the Mount

a Mar.13.1; Lu.21.5.

b 1 Ki.9.7; Je.26.18; Lu.19.44.

38. The day will come when the mercy of God will be clean gone for ever, and the forbearance of God exhausted, and then the sinner must perish. When once God has given him over, he must die. No man, no parent, no minister, no friend, no angel, no archangel, can then save. Salvation is lost, for ever lost. Oh how amazing is the folly of the wicked, that they weary out the forbearance of God, and perish in their sins!

CHAPTER XXIV.

Jesus foretells the destruction of the temple as he takes his final leave of it, and teaches what were the signs of his coming. These predictions are also recorded in Mar. xiii.; Lu. xxi. 5–38.

1. *And Jesus went out.* He was going over to the Mount of Olives, ver. 3. ¶ *The buildings of the temple.* The temple itself, with the surrounding courts, porches, and other edifices. See Notes on Mat. xxi. 12. Mark says that they particularly pointed out the *stones* of the temple, as well as the buildings. "In that temple," says Josephus, the Jewish historian, "were several stones which were 45 cubits in length, 5 in height, and 6 in breadth;" that is, more than 70 feet long, 10 wide, and 8 high. These stones, of such enormous size, were principally used in building the high wall on the east side, from the base to the top of the mountain. They were also, it is said, beautifully painted with variegated colours.

2. *There shall not be left here one stone upon another.* At the time this was spoken, no event was more improbable than this. The temple was vast, rich, splendid. It was the pride of the nation, and the nation was at peace. Yet in the short space of forty years all this was exactly accomplished. Jerusalem was taken by the Roman armies, under the command of Titus, A.D. 70. The account of the siege and destruction of the city is left us by Josephus, a historian of undoubted veracity and singular fidelity. He was a Jewish priest. In the wars of which he gives an account, he fell into the hands of the Romans, and remained with them during the siege and destruction of the city. Being a Jew, he would of course say nothing designed to confirm the prophecies of Jesus Christ; yet his whole history appears almost like a running commentary on these predictions respecting the destruction of the temple. The following particulars are given on his authority:—

After the city was taken, Josephus says that Titus "gave orders that they should now *demolish the whole city and temple,* except three towers, which he reserved standing. But for the rest of the wall, it was laid so completely even with the ground by those who *dug it up from the foundation,* that there was nothing left to make those believe who came hither that it had ever been inhabited." Maimonides, a Jewish writer, has also recorded that "Terentius Rufus, an officer in the army of Titus, with a ploughshare tore up the foundations of the temple, that the prophecy might be fulfilled, 'Zion shall be plowed as a field,'" Mi. iii. 12. This was all done by the direction of divine Providence. Titus was desirous of preserving the temple, and frequently sent Josephus to the Jews to induce them to surrender and save the temple and city. But the prediction of the Saviour had gone forth, and, notwithstanding the wish of the Roman general, the temple was to be destroyed. The Jews themselves first set fire to the porticoes of the temple. One of the Roman soldiers, without any command, threw a burning firebrand into the golden window, and soon the temple was in flames. Titus gave orders to extinguish the fire; but, amid the tumult, none of his orders were obeyed. The soldiers pressed to the temple, and neither fear nor entreaties, nor stripes could restrain them. Their hatred of the Jews urged them on to the work of destruction, and thus, says Josephus, the temple was burned against the will of Cæsar.—*Jewish Wars,* b. vi. ch. 4, § 5-7.

of Olives, the disciples came unto him privately, saying, Tell us, when shall these things be? and [c]what *shall be* the sign of thy coming, and of the end of the world?

4 And Jesus answered and said unto them, [d]Take heed that no man deceive you.

5 For[e] many shall come in my name, saying, I am Christ; and shall deceive many.

6 And ye [f]shall hear of wars,

c 1 Th.5.1,&c. d Col.2.8; 2 Th.2.3. e Je.14.14. f Da.11.1,&c.

3. *He sat upon the Mount of Olives.* See Notes on Mat. xxi. 1. From that mount there was a magnificent view of the whole city. ¶ *The disciples came unto him privately.* Not all of them, but Peter, James, John, and Andrew, Mar. xiii. 3. The prediction that the temple would be destroyed (ver. 2) had been made in the presence of all the apostles. *A part* now came privately to know more particularly when this would be. ¶ *When shall these things be?* There are three questions here. 1st. When those things should take place. 2d. What should be the signs of his own coming. 3d. What should be the signs that the end of the world was near. To these questions he replies in this and the following chapters. This he does, not by noticing them distinctly, but by intermingling the descriptions of the destruction of Jerusalem and of the end of the world, so that it is sometimes difficult to tell to what particular subject his remarks apply. The *principle* on which this combined description of two events was spoken appears to be, that *they could be described in the same words*, and therefore the accounts are intermingled. A similar use of language is found in some parts of Isaiah, where the same language will describe the return from the Babylonish captivity, and deliverance by the Messiah. See Introduction to Isaiah, § 7. ¶ *Sign of thy coming.* Evidence that thou art coming. By what token shall we know that thou art coming?

4, 5. *Take heed*, &c. Jesus, in reply to their question, first gives them a caution to beware of deception. They were to be constantly on their guard, because many would arise to deceive the people. ¶ *Many shall come in my name.* Not in the name or by the authority of Jesus, or claiming to be *his* followers, and to be sent by *him*, but in the name of the *Messiah*, or claiming to be the Messiah. ¶ *I am Christ.* I am the Messiah. See Notes on Mat. i. 1. The Messiah was expected at that time, Mat. ii. 1, 2. Many would lay claims to being the Messiah, and, as he was universally expected, multitudes would easily be led to believe in them. There is abundant evidence that this was fully accomplished. Josephus informs us that there were many who pretended to divine inspiration; who deceived the people, leading out numbers of them into the desert. "The land," says he "was overrun with magicians, seducers, and impostors, who drew the people after them in multitudes into solitudes and deserts, to see the signs and miracles which they promised to show by the power of God." Among these are mentioned particularly Dositheus, the Samaritan, who affirmed that he was Christ; Simon Magus, who said he appeared among the Jews as the Son of God; and Theudas, who persuaded many to go with him to the river Jordan, to see the waters divided. The names of *twenty-four* false Messiahs are recorded as having appeared between the time of the Emperor Adrian and the year 1682.

6. *And ye shall hear of wars*, &c. It is recorded in the history of Rome that violent agitations prevailed in the Roman empire previous to the destruction of Jerusalem. Four emperors, Nero, Galba, Otho, and Vitellius, suffered violent deaths in the short space of eighteen months. In consequence of these changes in the government, there were commotions throughout the empire. Parties were formed, and bloody and violent wars were the consequence of attachment to particular emperors. This is the more remarkable, as at the time that the prophecy was made, the empire was in a state of peace. ¶ *Rumours of wars.* Wars declared or threatened, but not carried into execution. Josephus says that Bardanes, and after him Vologeses, declared war against the Jews, but it was not carried into execution, *Antiq.* xx. 34. He also says that Vitellius, governor of Syria, declared war against Aretas, king of Arabia, and wished to lead his army through Palestine, but the death of

and rumours of wars: see that ye be not troubled: for all *these things* must come to pass, but the end is not yet.

7 For[g] nation shall rise against nation, and kingdom against kingdom: and there shall be famines, and pestilences, and earthquakes, in divers places.

8 All these *are* the beginning of sorrows.

9 Then[h] shall they deliver you

g Hag.2.21,22.

h Lu.21.12.

Tiberius prevented the war, *Antiq*. xviii. 5. 3. ¶ *The end is not yet.* The end of the Jewish economy; the destruction of Jerusalem will not *immediately* follow. Be not, therefore, alarmed when you hear of those commotions. Other signs will warn you when to be alarmed and seek security.

7. *Nation shall rise against nation, and kingdom against kingdom.* At Cæsarea the Jews and Syrians contended about the right to the city, and twenty thousand of the Jews were slain. At this blow the whole nation of the Jews was exasperated, and carried war and desolation through the Syrian cities and villages. Sedition and civil war spread throughout Judea; Italy was also thrown into civil war by the contests between Otho and Vitellius for the crown. ¶ *And there shall be famines.* There was a famine foretold by Agabus (Ac. xi. 28), which is mentioned by Tacitus, Suetonius, and Eusebius, and which was so severe in Jerusalem, Josephus says, that many people perished for want of food, *Antiq*. xx. 2. Four times in the reign of Claudius (A.D. 41–54) famine prevailed in Rome, Palestine, and Greece. ¶ *Pestilences.* Raging epidemic diseases; the plague, sweeping off multitudes of people at once. It is commonly the attendant of famine, and often produced by it. A pestilence is recorded as raging in Babylonia, A.D. 40 (Joseph. *Antiq*. xviii. 9. 8); in Italy, A.D. 66 (Tacit. 16. 13). Both of these took place before the destruction of Jerusalem. ¶ *Earthquakes.* In prophetic language, earthquakes sometimes mean political commotions. Literally they are tremors or shakings of the earth, often shaking cities and towns to ruin. The earth opens, and houses and people sink indiscriminately to destruction. Many of these are mentioned as preceding the destruction of Jerusalem. Tacitus mentions one in the reign of Claudius, at Rome, and says that in the reign of Nero the cities of Laodicea, Hierapolis, and Colosse were overthrown, and the celebrated Pompeii was overwhelmed and almost destroyed by an earthquake, *Annales*, 15. 22. Others are mentioned as occurring at Smyrna, Miletus, Chios, and Samos. Luke adds, "*And fearful sights and great signs shall there be from heaven*," xxi. 11. Josephus, who had probably never heard of this prophecy, and who certainly would have done nothing designedly to show its fulfilment, records the prodigies and signs which he says preceded the destruction of the city. A star, says he, resembling a sword, stood over the city, and a comet that continued a whole year. At the feast of unleavened bread, during the night, a bright light shone round the altar and the temple, so that it seemed to be bright day, for half an hour. The eastern gate of the temple, of solid brass, fastened with strong bolts and bars, and which had been shut with difficulty by twenty men, opened in the night of its own accord. A few days after that feast, he says, "Before sunsetting, chariots and troops of soldiers in their armour were seen running about among the clouds, and surrounding of cities." A great noise, as of the sound of a multitude, was heard in the temple, saying, "LET US REMOVE HENCE." Four years before the war began, Jesus, the son of Ananus, a plebeian and a husbandman, came to the feast of the tabernacles when the city was in peace and prosperity, and began to cry aloud, "A voice from the east, a voice from the west, a voice from the four winds, a voice against Jerusalem and the holy house, a voice against the bridegroom and the brides, and a voice against this whole people!" He was scourged, and at every stroke of the whip he cried, "Woe, woe to Jerusalem!" This cry, Josephus says, was continued every day for more than seven years, till he was killed in the siege of the city, exclaiming, "Woe, woe to myself also!"—*Jewish Wars*, b. vi. ch. 9, § 3.

8. *The beginning of sorrows.* Far heavier calamities are yet to come before the end.

up to be afflicted, and [i]shall kill you: and ye shall be hated of all nations for my name's sake.

10 And then shall many be [k]offended, and shall betray one another, and shall hate one another.

11 And[l] many false prophets shall rise, and shall [m]deceive many.

i Jn.16.2; Ac.7.59. *k* ch.13.21. *l* 2 Pe.2.1; 1 Jn.4.3. *m* 1 Ti.4.1.

9. *To be afflicted.* By persecution, imprisonment, scourging, &c. ¶ *They shall deliver you up to councils* (Mark). To the great council, or Sanhedrim—for this is the word in the original. See Notes on Mat. v. 22. This was fulfilled when Peter and John were brought before the council, Ac. iv. 5-7. Mark farther adds (xiii. 9) that they should be delivered to synagogues and to prisons to be beaten, and should be brought before rulers and kings for his name's sake. All this was remarkably fulfilled. Peter and John were imprisoned (Ac. iv. 3); Paul and Silas were imprisoned (Ac. xvi. 24), and also beaten (Ac. xvi. 23); Paul was brought before Gallio (Ac. xviii. 12), before Felix (Ac. xxiv. 24), and before Agrippa (Ac. xxv. 23). ¶ *And shall kill you.* That is, shall kill some of you. Stephen was stoned (Ac. vii. 59); James was killed by Herod (Ac. xii. 2); and, in addition to all that the sacred writers have told us, the persecution under Nero took place before the destruction of Jerusalem, in which were put to death, with many others, Peter and Paul. Most of the apostles, it is believed, died by persecution.

When they were delivered up, Jesus told them not to premeditate what they should say, for he would give them a mouth and wisdom which all their adversaries would not be able to gainsay or resist, Lu. xxi. 14, 15. The fulfilment of this is recorded in the case of Stephen (Ac. vi. 10), and of Paul, who made Felix *tremble*, Ac. xxiv. 25. ¶ *Ye shall be hated of all nations.* This was fulfilled then, and has been in all ages. It was judged to be a crime to be a Christian. Multitudes for this, and for nothing else, were put to death. ¶ *For my name's sake.* On account of attachment to me, or because you bear my *name* as *Christians.*

10. *Many shall be offended.* See Notes on Mat. v. 29. Many shall stumble, fall, apostatize from a profession of religion. Many who *professed* to love me will then show that they had no *real* attachment to me; and in those trying times it will be seen that they knew nothing of genuine Christian love. See 1 Jn. ii. 19. ¶ *Shall betray one another.* Those who thus apostatize from professed attachment to me will betray others who really love me. This they would do to secure their own safety, by revealing the names, habitations, or places of concealment of others. ¶ *Shall hate one another.* Not that real Christians would do this, but those who had *professed* to be such would then show that they were not his true followers, and would hate one another. Luke adds that they should be betrayed *by parents, and brethren, and kinsfolks, and friends*, Lu. xxi. 16. They would break over the most tender ties to surrender Christians to punishment. So great would be their hatred of Christianity, that it would overcome all the natural endearments of kindred and home. This, in the persecutions of Christians, has often occurred, and nothing shows more fully the deep and deadly hatred of the human heart to the gospel. Comp. Notes on ch. x. 21.

11. *And many false prophets.* Many men pretending to be prophets or foretellers of future events. This refers not to the false *Messiahs* of which he had spoken (ver. 5), but to prophets who should appear during the *siege* of the city. Of them Josephus says: "The tyrannical zealots who ruled the city suborned *many false prophets* to declare that aid would be given to the people from heaven. This was done to prevent them from attempting to desert, and to inspire confidence in God."—*Jewish Wars*, b. vi. ch. 5, § 2, 3.

12. *And because iniquity,* &c. The word *iniquity* here seems to include the cruelty of the Jews and Romans in their persecutions; the betraying of Christians by those who professed to be such; and the pernicious errors of false prophets and others. The effect of all this would be, that the ardour of feeling of many Christians would be lessened. The word *wax* means to *become.* It is an old Saxon word, not used now in this sense except in the Bible. The fear of death, and the deluding influence of false teachers, would lessen the

12 And because iniquity shall abound, [n]the love of many shall wax cold.

13 But[o] he that shall endure unto the end, the same shall be saved.

14 And[p] this gospel of the kingdom shall be preached in all the world for a witness unto all nations; and then shall the end come.

15 When ye, therefore, shall see the abomination of desolation spoken of by [q]Daniel the prophet,

n Re.3.15,16. *o* Re.2.10. *p* ch.28.19; Ro.10.18; Re.14.6. *q* Da.9.27; 12.11.

zeal of many timid and weak professors; perhaps, also, of many real but feeble Christians.

13. *He that shall endure unto the end, the same shall be saved.* The word "end," here, has by some been thought to mean the destruction of Jerusalem, or the *end* of the Jewish economy, and the meaning has been supposed to be "he that perseveres in bearing these persecutions to the end of the wars shall be safe. God will protect his people from harm, so that not a hair of the head shall perish." Others, with more probability, have referred this to final salvation, and refer the "end" to the close of life. "He that bears afflictions and persecutions faithfully—that constantly adheres to his religion, and does not shrink till death—shall be saved, or shall enter heaven." So Luke (xxi. 18) says, *there shall not an hair of your head perish*—that is, they would be saved. *An hair of the head*, or the smallest part or portion, is a proverbial expression, denoting the *certainty* and *completeness* of their salvation. Luke (xxi. 19) farther adds, *In your patience possess ye your souls*—that is, keep your souls *patient;* keep proper possession of patience as your own. It is a part of religion to teach it, and in these trying times let it not depart from you.

14. *And this gospel of the kingdom shall be preached in all the world.* The evidence that this was done is to be chiefly derived from the New Testament, and there it is clear. Thus Paul declares that it was preached to every creature under heaven (Col. i. 6, 23); that the faith of the Romans was spoken of throughout the whole world (Ro. i. 8); that he preached in Arabia (Ga. i. 17), and at Jerusalem, and round about unto Illyricum (Ro. xv. 19). We know also that he travelled through Asia Minor, Greece, and Crete; that he was in Italy, and probably in Spain and Gaul, Ro. xv. 24–28. At the same time, the other apostles were not idle; and there is full proof that within thirty years after this prophecy was spoken, churches were established in all these regions. ¶ *For a witness unto all nations.* This preaching the gospel indiscriminately to *all* the Gentiles shall be a *proof* to them, or a witness, that the division between the Jews and Gentiles was about to be broken down. Hitherto the blessings of revelation had been confined to the Jews. They were the peculiar people of God. His messages had been sent to them only When, therefore, God sent the gospel to *all* other people, it was proof, or *a witness unto them*, that the peculiar Jewish economy was at an end. ¶ *Then shall the end come.* The end of the Jewish economy; the destruction of the temple and city.

15. *The abomination of desolation.* This is a Hebrew expression, meaning an abominable or hateful destroyer. The Gentiles were all held in abomination by the Jews, Ac. x. 28. The abomination of desolation means the Roman army, and is so explained by Lu. xxi. 20. The Roman army is farther called the *abomination* on account of the images of the emperor, and the eagles, carried in front of the legions, and regarded by the Romans with divine honours. ¶ *Spoken of by Daniel the prophet.* Da. ix. 26, 27; xi. 31; xii. 11. See Notes on those passages. ¶ *Standing in the holy place.* Mark says, *standing where it ought not*, meaning the same thing. All Jerusalem was esteemed *holy*, Mat. iv. 5. The meaning of this is, when you see the Roman armies standing in the holy city or encamped around the temple, or the Roman ensigns or standards in the temple. Josephus relates that when the city was taken, the Romans brought their idols into the temple, and placed them over the eastern gate, and sacrificed to them there, *Jewish Wars*, b. vi. ch. 6, § 1. *Whoso readeth*, &c. This seems to be a remark made by the evangelist to direct the attention of the reader particularly to the meaning of the prophecy by Daniel.

16. *Then let them*, &c. Then Chris-

stand in the holy place, (whoso readeth, let him understand:)

16 Then let them which be in Judea flee into the mountains:

17 Let him which is on the house-top not come down to take any thing out of his house:

18 Neither let him which is in the field return back to take his clothes.

19 And[r] woe unto them that are with child, and to them that give suck in those days.

20 But pray ye that your flight be not in the winter, neither on the sabbath-day;

r Lu.23.29.

---

tians may know that the end is come, and should seek a place of safety. Destruction would not only visit the *city*, but would extend to the surrounding part of Judea. ¶ *The mountains.* The mountains of Palestine abound in caves, a safe retreat for those who are pursued. In all ages these caves have been the favourite places of robbers, and they were also resorted to by those in danger, 1 Sa. xiii. 6; xxii. 1; 2 Sa. xxiii. 13; Jos. x. 16. In those mountains they would be safe.

17. *Him which is on the house-top.* The roofs of the houses in Eastern countries were made flat, so that they were favourable places for walking and retirement. See Notes on Mat. ix. 1–8. The meaning here is, that he who should be on the house-top when this calamity came upon the city *should flee without delay;* he should not even take time to secure any article of apparel from his house. So sudden would be the calamity, that by attempting to do this he would endanger his life.

18. *Return back to take his clothes.* His clothes which, in *working*, he had laid aside, or which, in fleeing, he should throw off as an encumbrance. *Clothes* here means the *outer* garment, commonly laid aside when men worked or ran. See Notes on Mat. v. 40.

These directions were followed. It is said that the Christians, warned by these predictions, fled from Jerusalem to Pella, and other places beyond the Jordan; so that there is not evidence that a single *Christian* perished in Jerusalem.—Euseb. *Hist. Eccl.*, lib. iii. ch. 6.

20. *But pray ye*, &c. The destruction was certainly coming. It could not be prevented; yet it was right to pray for a mitigation of the circumstances, that it might be as mild as possible. So we know that calamity is before us; sickness, pain, bereavement, and death are in our path; yet, though we know that these things *must* come upon us, it is right to pray that they may come in as mild a manner as may be consistent with the will of God. We *must die*, but it is right to pray that the pains of our dying may be neither long nor severe. ¶ *In the winter.* On account of the cold, storms, &c. To be turned then from home, and compelled to take up an abode in caverns, would be a double calamity. ¶ *Neither on the sabbath-day.* Long journeys were prohibited by the law on the Sabbath, Ex. xvi. 29. The law of Moses did not mention the distance to which persons *might* go on the Sabbath, but most of the Jews maintained that it should not be more than 2000 cubits. Some supposed that it was 7 furlongs, or nearly a mile. This distance was allowed in order that they might go to their places of worship. Most of them held that it was not lawful to go farther, under any circumstances of war or affliction. Jesus teaches his disciples to pray that their flight might not be on the Sabbath, because, if they should *not* go farther than a Sabbath-day's journey, they would not be beyond the reach of danger, and if they did, they would be exposed to the charge of violating the law. It should be added that it was almost impracticable to travel in Judea on that day, as the gates of the cities were usually closed, Ne. xiii. 19–22.

21. *There shall be great tribulation.* The word tribulation means *calamity* or *suffering*. Luke (xxi. 24) has specified in what this tribulation would consist: "They shall fall by the edge of the sword, and shall be led away captive into all nations, and Jerusalem shall be trodden down of the Gentiles, until the times of the Gentiles shall be fulfilled." That is, until the time allotted for the Gentiles *to do it* shall be fully accomplished, or as long as God is pleased to suffer them to do it.

The first thing mentioned by Luke is, that they should fall *by the edge of the sword*—that is, would be slain in war, as the sword was then principally used

21 For[s] then shall be great tribulation, such as was not since the beginning of the world to this time, no, nor ever shall be.

s Da.12.1.

22 And except those days should be shortened, there should no flesh be saved: [t] but for the elect's sake those days shall be shortened.

t Is.65.8,9.

in war. This was most strikingly fulfilled. Josephus, in describing it, uses almost the very words of our Saviour. *All the calamities*, says he, *which had befallen any nation from the beginning of the world* were but small in comparison with those of the Jews.—*Jewish Wars*, b. i. preface, § 4.

He has given the following account of one part of the massacre when the city was taken: "And now, rushing into the city, they slew whomsoever they found, without distinction, and burned the houses and all the people who had fled into them; and when they entered for the sake of plunder, they found whole families of dead persons, and houses full of carcasses destroyed by famine, then they came out with their hands empty. And though they thus pitied the dead, they had not the same emotion for the living, but killed all they met, whereby they filled the lanes with dead bodies. *The whole city ran with blood*, insomuch that many things which were burning were extinguished by the blood."—*Jewish Wars*, b. vi. ch. 8, § 5; ch. 9, § 2, 3. He adds that in the siege of Jerusalem not fewer than *eleven hundred thousand* perished (*Jewish Wars*, b. vi. ch. 9, § 3)—a number almost half as great as are in the whole city of London. In the adjacent provinces no fewer than *two hundred and fifty thousand* are reckoned to have been slain; making in all whose deaths were ascertained the almost incredible number of *one million three hundred and fifty thousand* who were put to death. These were not, indeed, all slain with the sword. Many were crucified. "Many hundreds," says Josephus (*Jewish Wars*, b. v. ch. 11, § 1), "were first whipped, then tormented with various kinds of tortures, and finally crucified; the Roman soldiers nailing them (out of the wrath and hatred they bore to the Jews), one after one way and another after another, to crosses, *by way of jest*, until at length the multitude became so great that room was wanting for crosses, and crosses for the bodies." So terribly was their imprecation fulfilled—*his blood be on us and on our children*, Mat. xxvii. 25. If it be asked how it was possible for so many people to be slain in a single city, it is to be remembered that the siege of Jerusalem commenced during the time of the Passover, when all the males of the Jews were required to be there, and when it is estimated that more than *three millions* were usually assembled. See Josephus, *Jewish Wars*, b. vi. ch. 9, § 3, 4.

A horrible instance of the distress of Jerusalem is related by Josephus. The famine during the siege became so great that they ate what the most sordid animals refused to touch. A woman of distinguished rank, having been plundered by the soldiers, in hunger, rage, and despair, killed and roasted her own babe, and had eaten one half of it before the deed was discovered.—*Jewish Wars*, b. vi. ch. 3, § 3, 4. This cruel and dreadful act was also in fulfilment of prophecy, De. xxviii. 53, 56, 57.

Another thing added by Luke (ch. xxi. 24), was, that *they should be led away captive into all nations*. Josephus informs us that the captives taken during the whole war amounted to *ninety-seven thousand*. The tall and handsome young men Titus reserved for triumph; of the rest, many were distributed through the Roman provinces to be destroyed by wild beasts in theatres; many were sent to the works in Egypt; many, especially those under seventeen years of age, were sold for slaves.—*Jewish Wars*, b. vi. ch. 9, § 2, 3.

22. *Except those days should be shortened.* If the calamities of the siege should be lengthened out. If famine and war should be suffered to rage. ¶ *No flesh be saved.* None of the nation would be preserved alive. All the inhabitants of Judea would perish. The war, famine, and pestilence would entirely destroy them. ¶ *But for the elect's sake.* The *elect* here doubtless means *Christians*. See 1 Pe. i. 2; Ro. i. 7; Ep. i. 4; 1 Th. i. 4. The word *elect* means *to choose*. It is given to Christians because they are *chosen to salvation through sanctification of the Spirit and belief of the truth*, 1 Pe. i. 2. It is probable that in Jerusalem and the adjacent parts of

23 Then[u] if any man shall say unto you, Lo, here *is* Christ, or there; believe *it* not.

24 For[v] there shall arise false Christs, and false prophets, [w]and shall show great signs and wonders; insomuch that, [x]if *it were* possible, they shall deceive the very elect.

25 Behold, I have told you before.

26 Wherefore if they shall say

u De.13.1-3. *v* ver.5,11. *w* 2 Th.2.9-11; Re.13.13. *x* Jn.10.28,29.

Judea there were many who were true followers of Christ. On *their* account—to preserve them alive, and to make them the instruments of spreading the gospel — Jesus said that those days should not be lengthened out so as to produce their destruction. It is related by Josephus (*Jewish Wars*, b. i. ch. 12, § 1) that Titus at first resolved to reduce the city by famine. He therefore built a wall around it to keep any provisions from being carried in, and any of the people from going out. The Jews, however, drew up their army near the walls, engaged in battle, and the Romans pursued them, provoked by their attempts, and broke into the city. The affairs of Rome, also, at that time demanded the presence of Titus there; and, contrary to his original intention, he pressed the siege and took the city by storm, thus *shortening* the time that *would* have been occupied in reducing it by famine. This was for the benefit of the "elect." So the designs of wicked men, intended *by them* for the destruction of the people of God, are intended by God for the good of his chosen people. See Notes on Is. x. 7.

23. *Lo, here* is *Christ.* The Messiah. The Jews expected the Messiah to deliver them from Roman oppression. In the time of these great calamities they would anxiously look for him. Many would claim *to be* the Messiah. Many would follow those who set up that claim. Many would rejoice to believe that he was come, and would call on others, Christians with the rest, to follow them. ¶ *Believe* it *not.* You have evidence that the Messiah *has* come, and you are not to be deceived by the plausible pretensions of others.

24. *False Christs.* Persons claiming to be the Messiah. ¶ *False prophets.* Persons claiming to be *the prophet* spoken of by Moses (De. xviii. 15); or persons pretending to declare the way of deliverance from the Romans, and calling the people to follow them. See ver. 5. ¶ *Shall show great signs and wonders.* That is, shall pretend to work miracles. They will so *nearly* resemble prophets in their miraculous power as to render it difficult to detect the imposture. Josephus represents the false Christs and prophets that appeared as *magicians* and *sorcerers.* He says they led the people out into the deserts, and promised to work miracles to deliver them, *Antiq*. b. xx. ch. 8, § 6. ¶ *If* it were *possible, they shall deceive the very elect.* So nearly would their pretended miracles resemble true miracles as to render it difficult to detect the imposture; so much so, that if it were possible they would persuade even true Christians that they were the Messiah. But that was not possible. His real friends would be too firmly established in the belief that he was the Christ to be wholly led away by others. Christians may be sometimes led far astray; they may be in doubt about some great doctrines of religion; they may be perplexed by the cavils and cunning craftiness of those who do not love the truth, but they cannot be *wholly* deceived and seduced from the Saviour. Our Saviour says that if this *were possible*, it would be done then; but it was not possible. Comp. Notes on Jn. x. 28, 29.

25. *Behold, I have told you before.* Mark adds (ch. xiii. 23), *take ye heed.* The reason why he told them before was that they might be on their guard, and be prepared for those calamities.

26. *Behold, he is in the desert.* The Jews had formed the expectation that the Messiah would appear suddenly from some unexpected quarter; hence many would be looking to desert places, expecting that he would come from them. Accordingly, most of the impostors and pretended prophets led their people into the deserts. ¶ *Go not forth.* Do not follow them; they will only deceive you. ¶ *In secret chambers.* Concealed in some house, or some retired part of the city. Many would, doubtless, pretend that the Messiah was *concealed* there, and, either for the purpose of encouraging or deceiving the

unto you, Behold, he is in the desert; go not forth: Behold, *he is* in the secret chambers; believe *it* not.

27 For as [y]the lightning cometh out of the east, and shineth even unto the west, so shall also the coming of the Son of man be.

28 For[z] wheresoever the carcase is, there will the eagles be gathered together.

29 Immediately after the tribu-

y Zec.9.14; Lu.17.24,&c.

z Job 39.30.

---

people, would pretend that they had discovered him.

27. *For as the lightning cometh out of the east*, &c. This is not designed to denote the *quarter* from which he would come, but the *manner*. He does not mean to affirm that the *Son of man* will come from the *east*, but that he will come in a rapid and unexpected manner, like the lightning. Many would be looking for him in the desert, many in secret places; but he said it would be useless to be looking in that manner; it was useless to look to any particular part of the heavens to know where the lightning would next flash. In a moment it would blaze in an unexpected part of the heavens, and shine at once to the other part. So rapidly, so unexpectedly, in so unlooked-for a quarter, would be his coming. See Lu. x. 18; Zec. ix. 14. ¶ *The coming of the Son of man.* It has been doubted whether this refers to the destruction of Jerusalem, or to the coming at the day of judgment. For the solution of this doubt let it be remarked—1st. That those two events are the principal scenes in which our Lord said he would come, either in person or in judgment. 2d. That the destruction of Jerusalem is described as *his* coming, *his* act. 3d. That these events—the judgment of Jerusalem and the final judgment—in many respects greatly resemble each other. 4th. That they *will bear*, therefore, to be described in the same language; and, 5th, therefore, that the same words often include *both* events, as properly described by them. The words had, doubtless, a primary reference to the destruction of Jerusalem, but they had, at the same time, such an amplitude of meaning as also to express his coming to judgment. See Introduction to Isaiah, § 7, (3).

28. *Wheresoever*, &c. The words in this verse are proverbial. Vultures and eagles easily ascertain where dead bodies are, and hasten to devour them. So with the Roman army. Jerusalem is like a dead and putrid corpse. Its life is gone, and it is ready to be devoured. The Roman armies will find it out, as the vultures do a dead carcass, and will come around it to devour it. This proverb also teaches a universal truth. Wherever wicked men are, there will be assembled the instruments of their chastisement. The providence of God will direct them there, as the eagles are directed to a dead carcass.

This verse is connected with the preceding by the word "for," implying that this is a reason for what is said there—that the Son of man would *certainly* come to destroy the city, and that he would come *suddenly*. The meaning is that he would come, by means of the Roman armies, as certainly, as suddenly, and as unexpectedly as whole flocks of vultures and eagles, though unseen before, see their prey at a great distance and suddenly gather in multitudes around it. Travellers in the deserts of Arabia tell us that they sometimes witness a speck in the distant sky which for a long time is scarcely visible. At length it grows larger, it comes nearer, and they at last find that it is a vulture that has from an immense distance seen a carcass lying on the sand. So keen is their vision as aptly to represent the Roman armies, though at an immense distance, spying, as it were, Jerusalem, a putrid carcass, and hastening in multitudes to destroy it.

29. *Immediately after the tribulation of those days.* That is, immediately after these tribulations, events will occur that *may be properly represented* by the darkening of the sun and moon, and by the stars falling from heaven. The word rendered *immediately*—εὐθέως—means, properly, *straightway*, *forthwith*, Mat. viii. 3; xiii. 5; Mar. i. 31; Ac. xii. 10; then *shortly*, 3 Jn. 14. This is the meaning here. Such events would *shortly* or *soon* occur. In the fulfilment of the predictions they would be *the next in order*, and would occur *before long*. The term here requires us to admit that, in order to the fulfilment

lation of those days [a]shall the sun be darkened, and the moon shall not give her light, and the stars shall fall from heaven, and the [b]powers of the heavens shall be shaken.

30 And then shall appear the sign of [c]the Son of man in heaven:

a Is.13.10; Eze.32.7; Am.5.20; Ac.2.20; Re.6.12. b 2 Pe.3.10. c Da.7.13; Re.1.7.

of the prophecy, it can be shown, or it actually happened, that things *did* soon occur "after the tribulation of those days" which would be *properly represented* or *described* by the images which the Saviour employs. It is not necessary to show that there could not have been *a more remote* reference to events lying far in the future, in which there would be a more complete fulfilment or *filling up* of the meaning of the words (comp. Notes on Mat. i. 22, 23); but it *is* necessary that there should have been events which would be *properly expressed* by the language which the Saviour uses, or which would have been in some proper sense *fulfilled*, even if there had not been reference to more remote events. It will be seen in the exposition that this was actually the case, and that therefore there was a propriety in saying that these events would occur *immediately*—that is, *soon*, or *the next in order*. Comp. Notes on Re. i. 1. ¶ *Shall the sun be darkened*, &c. The images here used are not to be taken literally. They are often employed by the sacred writers to denote *any great calamities*. As the darkening of the sun and moon, and the falling of the stars, would be an inexpressible calamity, so any great catastrophe—any overturning of kingdoms or cities, or dethroning of kings and princes—is represented by the darkening of the sun and moon, and by some terrible convulsion in the elements. Thus the destruction of Babylon is foretold in similar terms (Is. xiii. 10), and of Tyre (Is. xxiv. 23). The slaughter in Bozrah and Idumea is predicted in the same language, Is. xxxiv. 4. See also Is. l. 3; lx. 19, 20; Eze. xxxii. 7; Joel iii. 15. To the description in Matthew, Luke has added (ch. xxi. 25, 26), "And upon the earth distress of nations, with perplexity; the sea and the waves roaring; men's hearts failing them for fear, and for looking after those things which are coming on the earth." All these are figures of great and terrible calamities. The roaring of the waves of the sea denotes great tumult and affliction among the people. *Perplexity* means doubt, anxiety; not knowing what to do to escape. *Men's hearts should fail them for fear*, or by reason of *fear*. Their fears would be so great as to take away their courage and strength.

30. *The sign of the Son of man.* The *evidence* that he is coming to destroy the city of Jerusalem. It is not to be denied, however, that this description is applicable also to his coming at the day of judgment. The disciples had asked him (ver. 3) what should be the sign of his coming, and *of the end of the world.* In his answer he has reference to both events, and his language may be regarded as descriptive of both. At the destruction of Jerusalem, the *sign* or *evidence* of his coming was found in the fulfilment of these predictions. At the end of the world, the sign of his coming will be his personal approach with the glory of his Father and the holy angels, 1 Th. iv. 16; Lu. xxi. 27; Mat. xxvi. 64; Ac. i. 11. ¶ *All the tribes of the earth mourn.* That is, either all the *tribes* or *people* of the land of Judea shall mourn at the great calamities coming upon them, or all the nations of the world shall wail when he comes to judgment. All the wicked shall mourn at the prospect of their doom, Re. i. 7. The *cause* of their wailing at the day of judgment will be chiefly that they have pierced, killed, rejected the Saviour, and that they *deserve* the condemnation that is coming upon them, Jn. xix. 37; Zec. xii. 12. ¶ *And they shall see the Son of man.* The Lord Jesus coming to judgment. Probably this refers more directly to his coming at the last day, though it may also mean that the *evidence* of his coming to destroy Jerusalem will then be seen. ¶ *In the clouds of heaven.* He ascended in a cloud, Ac. i. 9. He shall return in like manner, Ac. i. 11. *The clouds of heaven* denote not the clouds *in* heaven, but the clouds that *appear* to shut heaven, or the sky, from our view. ¶ *With power.* Power, manifest in the destruction of Jerusalem, by the wonders that preceded it, and by the overturning of the temple and city. In the day of judgment, power manifest by consuming the material world (2 Pe. iii. 7, 10, 12); by raising the dead (Jn.

and then shall all the tribes of the earth mourn, and [d]they shall see the Son of man coming in the clouds of heaven, with power and great glory.

d ch.16.27; Mar.13.26; Lu.22.69.

31 And he shall send his angels [1]with a [e]great sound of a trumpet; and they shall [f]gather together his elect from the four winds, from one end of heaven to the other.

1 or, *with a trumpet and a great voice.*
e 1 Th.4.16. f Zec.14.5.

v. 29, 30; 1 Co. xv. 52); by changing those who may be alive when he shall come—that is, making their bodies like those who have died, and who have been raised up (1 Th. iv. 17; 1 Co. xv. 52); by bringing the affairs of the world to a close, receiving the righteous to heaven (Mat. xxv. 34; 1 Co. xv. 57), and sending the wicked, however numerous or however strong, down to hell, Mat. xxv. 41, 46; Jn. v. 29. ¶ *Great glory.* The word *glory* here means the visible display of honour and majesty. This glory will be manifested by the manner of his coming (Mat. xxvi. 64), by the presence of the angels (Mat. xxv. 31), and by the wonders that shall attend him down the sky.

31. *And he shall send his angels. Angels* signify, literally, *messengers*, Lu. vii. 24; ix. 52. The word is often applied to *inanimate* objects, or to anything that God employs to rescue his people from danger (Ps. civ. 4); but it most commonly refers to the race of intelligent beings more exalted than man, who are employed often in the work of man's rescue from ruin, and aiding his salvation, He. i. 14. In either of these senses it *might* here refer to deliverance granted to his people in the calamities of Jerusalem. It is said that there is reason to believe that not *one* Christian perished in the destruction of that city, God having in various ways secured their escape, so that they fled to Pella, where they dwelt when the city was destroyed. But the language seems to refer rather to the end of the world, and, no doubt, its *principal* application was intended to be to the gathering of his elect at the day of judgment. ¶ *With a great sound of a trumpet.* The Jewish assemblies used to be called together by the sound of a trumpet, as ours are by bells, Le. xxv. 9; Nu. x. 2; Ju. iii. 27. Hence, when they spoke of convening an assembly, they spoke also of doing it by sounding a trumpet. Our Saviour, speaking to Jews, used language to which they were accustomed, and described the *assembling* of the people at the last day in language which they were accustomed to use in calling assemblies together. It is not certain, however, that he meant that this would be *literally* so, but it may be designed only to denote the certainty that the *world would be assembled together.* Similar language is often used when speaking of the judgment, 1 Th. iv. 16; 1 Co. xv. 52. A *trump*, or *trumpet*, was a wind instrument, made at first of the horns of oxen, and afterward of rams' horns, cut off at the smaller extremity. In some instances it was made of brass, in the form of a horn. The common trumpet was straight, made of brass or silver, a cubit in length, the larger extremity shaped so as to resemble a small bell. In times of peace, in assembling the people, this was sounded softly. In times of calamity, or war, or any great commotion, it was sounded *loud.* Perhaps this was referred to when our Saviour said, with a *great* sound of a trumpet. ¶ *They shall gather together his elect.* Elect. See Notes on ver. 22. The word means *Christians*—the chosen of God. If this refers to the destruction of Jerusalem, it means, "God shall send forth his messengers—whatever he may choose to employ for that purpose: signs, wonders, human messengers, or the angels themselves—and gather Christians into a place of safety, so that they shall not be destroyed with the Jews." If it refers to the last judgment, as it doubtless in a primary or secondary sense does, then it means that he will send his angels to gather his chosen, his elect, together from all places, Mat. xiii. 39, 41–43. This shall be done before the living shall be changed, 1 Co. xv. 51, 52; 1 Th. iv. 16, 17. ¶ *From the four winds.* That is, from the four quarters of the globe—east, west, north, and south. The Jews expressed those quarters by the *winds* blowing from them. See Eze. xxxvii. 9. See also Is. xliii. 5, 6. ¶ *From one end of heaven*, &c. Mark says (xiii. 27), from the uttermost part of the earth to the uttermost part of heaven. The expression denotes that they shall be gathered from all parts of the earth where they

32 Now[g] learn a parable of the fig-tree: When his branch is yet tender, and putteth forth leaves, ye know that summer *is* nigh:

33 So likewise ye, when ye shall see all these things, know that [2]it is near, [h]*even* at the doors.

34 Verily I say unto you, This generation shall not pass till all these things be fulfilled.

35 Heaven[i] and earth shall pass away, but my words shall not pass away.

36 But[k] of that day and hour knoweth no *man*, no, not the angels of heaven, but my Father only.

37 But as the days of Noe *were*, so shall also the coming of the Son of man be.

38 For as in the days that were before the flood they were eating and drinking, marrying and giv-

g Lu.21.29. 2 or, *He*. *h* Ja.5.9. *i* Ps.102.26; Is.51.6. *k* Zec.14.7; 1 Th.5.2.

are scattered. The word *heaven* is here used to denote the *visible* heavens or the sky, meaning that through *the whole world* he would gather them. See Ps. xix. 1-7; De. iv. 32.

32. *Now learn a parable.* See Notes on Mat. xiii. 3. The word here means, rather, *an illustration*—make a *comparison*, or judge of this as you do respecting a fig-tree. ¶ *Fig-tree.* This was spoken on the Mount of Olives, which produced not only olives, but figs. Possibly one was near when he spoke this. ¶ *When his branch*, &c. When the juices return from the roots into the branches, and the buds swell and burst, *as if tender*, and too feeble to contain the pressing and expanding leaves—when you see that, you judge that spring and summer are near.

33. *So likewise ye*, &c. In the same manner, when you see what I have predicted—the *signs* around Jerusalem—then know that its destruction is at hand. ¶ *Is near.* Luke says (xxi. 28), *your redemption draweth nigh*, and (xxi. 31) *the kingdom of God is nigh at hand.* Your deliverance from the dangers that threaten the city approaches, and the kingdom of God will be set up in the earth; or your everlasting redemption from sin and death will come at the day of judgment, and his eternal kingdom will be established in the heavens.

34. *This generation*, &c. This age; this race of men. A generation is about thirty or forty years. The destruction of Jerusalem took place about forty years after this was spoken. See Notes on Mat. xvi. 28. ¶ *Till all these things*, &c. Till these things shall be accomplished. Till events shall take place which shall be a fulfilment of these words, if there were nothing farther intended. He does not mean to *exclude* the reference to the judgment, but to say that the destruction of Jerusalem would be such as to make *appropriate* the words of the prediction, were there nothing beyond. Comp. Notes on Mat. i. 22, 23. So when *death* was threatened to Adam, the propriety of the threatening would have been seen, and the threatening would have been fulfilled, had men suffered only *temporal death*. At the same time the threatening had *a fulness of meaning* that would cover also, and justify, eternal death. Thus the words of Christ describing the destruction of Jerusalem had a fulness of signification that would meet also the events of the judgment, and whose meaning would not be *entirely filled up* till the world was closed.

35. *Heaven and earth shall pass away*, &c. You may sooner expect to see the heaven and earth pass away and return to nothing, than my words to fail.

36. *But of that day and hour.* Of the precise time of the fulfilment. The *general signs* of its approach have been given, as the budding of the fig-tree is a *certain* indication that summer is near; but *the precise time* is not indicated by these things. One part of their inquiry was (ver. 3) *when* those things should be. He now replies to them by saying that the *precise* time would not be foretold. Comp. Notes on Ac. i. 7. ¶ *Knoweth no man, no, not the angels.* See Notes on Mar. xiii. 32.

37. *Noe.* The Greek way of writing *Noah*. See Ge. vi., vii., viii., ix. The coming of the Son of man would be as it was in the days of Noah—1st. In its being sudden and unexpected, the *precise time* not being made known, though the *general* indications had been given. 2d. The world would be found as it was then.

38. *For as in the days*, &c. The things mentioned here denote attention to the

ing in marriage, [l]until the day that Noe entered into the ark,

39 And knew not, until the flood came and took them all away; so shall also the coming of the Son of man be.

40 Then shall two be in the field; the one shall be taken, and the other left.

41 Two *women shall be* grinding at the mill; the one shall be taken, and the other left.

42 Watch,[m] therefore; for ye know not what hour your Lord doth come.

43 But know this, that if the goodman of the house had known in what watch the thief would come, he would have watched, and would not have suffered his house to be broken up.

44 Therefore be ye also ready; for in such an hour as ye think not, the Son of man cometh.

45 Who, then, is a faithful and wise servant, whom his lord hath

l Ge.6.2. m Lu.12.39,40; Re.3.3; 16.15.

---

affairs of this life rather than to what was coming on them. It does not mean that these things were wrong, but only that such was their actual employment, and that they were regardless of what was coming upon them.

39. *They knew not.* That is, they knew not the exact time until it came upon them. *So*, says he, it shall be when the Son of man shall come. They shall not know *the precise time* until he comes, and then they will be found engaged in the ordinary business of life unconcerned.

40. *Then shall two be in the field*, &c. The calamity will come suddenly. There will be no escape for those whom it overtakes. ¶ *One shall be taken.* The word *taken* may mean either to be taken away from the danger—that is, rescued, as Lot was (Lu. xvii. 28, 29), or to be taken away *by death*. Probably the latter is the meaning.

41. *Two* women, &c. Grinding in the East was performed, as it is now, chiefly by hand. The millstones were about 2 feet in diameter and ½ foot in thickness. The lower one was fixed, and the upper one was turned by a handle or crank. This was done by two persons, who sat opposite to each other. One took hold of the mill-handle and turned it half-way round; the other then seized it and completed the revolution. This was done by women—by servants of the lowest order—and was a very laborious employment. See Ex. xi. 5; Job xxxi. 10; Is. xlvii. 2; Ju. xvi. 21. The meaning of this verse is similar to the former. Of two persons sitting *near* to each other, one shall be taken and the other left. The calamity would be sudden, and would come upon them before they were aware.

42. *Watch.* Be looking for his coming. Be expecting it as near; as a great event; as coming in an unexpected manner. Watch the signs of his coming, and be ready.

43. *But know this*, &c. If a man knew the hour, or *about the hour*, when a robber would come, he would be ready for him. So you know not the exact hour, but you know it is near, when the Son of man will come. He will come suddenly, as a thief comes, without giving previous warning, 1 Th. v. 2; 2 Pe. iii. 10; Re. iii. 3; xvi. 15. ¶ *Goodman.* See Notes on Mat. xx. 11. ¶ *Thief.* A robber. A thief, with us, means one who takes goods without doing violence--secretly, silently. The original word means one who does it by housebreaking, or by highway violence, Lu. x. 30. ¶ *Broken up.* Broken into—either by the doors or windows. See Notes on ch. vi. 19. ¶ *In what watch.* In which of the four quarters of the night. See Notes on Mat. xiv. 25.

44. *Be ye also ready.* Luke (xxi. 36) says that he charged them to pray always, that they might be accounted worthy to escape those things—the judgments coming upon the wicked—and to stand before the Son of man—that is, to stand there *approved* by him, or to be admitted to his favour. He also charged them (Lu. xxi. 34) to take heed and not to suffer their hearts to be overcharged with surfeiting, or too much eating, or drunkenness, or the cares of this life, lest that day should come upon them unawares; things improper if there were no judgment—peculiarly mad and wicked when the judgment is near.

45-51. This passage is, in fact, a *parable*, though it is not expressly so called. The design is to show that his disciples should act *as if* they were each mo-

made [n]ruler over his household, [o]to give them meat in due season?

46 Blessed *is* that servant, whom his lord, when he cometh, shall find so doing.

47 Verily I say unto you, that he shall [p]make him ruler over all his goods.

48 But and if that evil servant shall say in his heart, My lord delayeth his coming;

49 And shall begin to smite *his* fellow-servants, and to eat and drink with the drunken;

50 The lord of that servant [q]shall come in a day when he looketh not for *him*, and in an hour that he is not aware of,

51 And shall [3]cut him asunder, and appoint *him* his portion with the hypocrites: [r]there shall be weeping and gnashing of teeth.

n Je.3.15. *o* ch.13.52. *p* ch.25.21.

q 1 Th.5.3; Re.3.3. 3 or, *cut him off.* *r* ch.25.30.

ment expecting his return. This he illustrates by the conduct of a servant who did not expect his master soon to return, who acted with great impropriety, and who was accordingly punished.

45. *Who, then, is a faithful and wise servant*, &c. By the conduct of a faithful and wise servant Jesus intends to denote a faithful Christian, a servant of God, or a teacher of religion. ¶ *Whom his lord.* His master. The word here has no reference to God. It means the *lord* or master of the servant. Applied to Christian teachers, in the spiritual meaning of the parable, it refers to *Christ*, who has appointed them as teachers, and who is their Lord and Master, Jn. xiii. 13, 14. ¶ *Over his household.* His family. Christian ministers are the servants of God appointed over the church, the family of Christ, 1 Th. v. 12, 13; 1 Co. iii. 5; iv. 1, 2; xii. 28. ¶ *Meat in due season.* The word *meat* here means food of all kinds. When the Bible was translated into English, the word included, as the original does, all kinds of provisions requisite to support and nourish life. ¶ *In due season.* As they need it, or in the accustomed times. This was the office of a steward. Among the ancients this office was often filled by *a slave*—one who had shown himself trusty and faithful. The duty was to have a general superintendence over the affairs of the family. Applied to Christian ministers, it means that they are to feed the flock of God, to *minister* to their wants, and to do it as they need it, Jn. xxi. 15–17; Ac. xx. 28; 1 Co. iv. 1, 2.

47. *Shall make him ruler*, &c. Shall confirm his appointment over his household, and, as a reward, shall place him over *all* his property. This does not mean that ministers will have a higher rank or office, but is a circumstance *of the parable* or story, designed to show the effect of faithfulness. Faithful servants of Christ shall be rewarded. This will be done by *his* approbation, and by the rewards of the heavenly world.

48. *That evil servant.* If that servant, so appointed, having this office, should be evil or wicked. ¶ *Say in his heart.* Secretly suppose. ¶ *Delayeth his coming.* Will not return in a long time; or does not return as soon as was expected, and perhaps may not at all.

49. *Smite* his *fellow-servants*, &c. This is the conduct of a wicked servant, who, supposing he would not be called to account, and abusing his authority, gave himself up to oppression, carousing, and debauchery. It is designed to represent the conduct of ministers who are unfaithful and overbearing, and who abuse their trust in the church.

51. *Shall cut him asunder.* This kind of punishment was anciently practised. Sometimes it was done by the sword, sometimes by saws. It was practised among the Chaldeans (Da. ii. 5; iii. 29), and among the Hebrews, 2 Sa. xii. 31; 1 Sa. xv. 33; 1 Ki. iii. 25; He. xi. 37. It was also practised by the Egyptians and Romans. It is not, perhaps, here to be taken *literally*, but signifies that the wicked servant should be severely punished. ¶ *Hypocrites.* See Notes on Mat. vi. 2. They are spoken of here as the worst of men. ¶ *Weeping and gnashing of teeth.* See Notes on Mat. viii. 12, 13. The unfaithful and wicked minister of God, who lives without expectation or fear of judgment, shall suffer the severest punishment inflicted on sinners in the world of woe.

CHAPTER XXV.

1. *Then shall the kingdom of heaven.* See Notes on Mat. iii. 2. The phrase

CHAPTER XXV.

THEN shall the kingdom of heaven be likened unto ten virgins,[a] which took their lamps, and went forth to meet [b]the bridegroom.

2 And [c]five of them were wise, and five *were* foolish.

a Ps.45.14; Ca.6.8,9; 2 Co.11.2. b Jn.3 29. c Je.24.2-9; ch.22.10.

---

here refers to his coming in the day of judgment. ¶ *Shall be likened.* Or shall resemble. The meaning is, "When the Son of man returns to judgment, it will be as it was in the case of ten virgins in a marriage ceremony." The coming of Christ to receive his people to himself is often represented under the similitude of a marriage, the church being represented as his spouse or bride. The marriage relation is the most tender, firm, and endearing of any known on earth, and on this account it fitly represents the union of believers to Christ. See Mat. ix. 15; Jn. iii. 29; Re. xix. 7; xxi. 9; Ep. v. 25-32. ¶ *Ten virgins.* These virgins, doubtless, represent the church—a name given to it because it is pure and holy. See 2 Co. xi. 2; La. i. 15; ii. 13. ¶ *Which took their lamps, and went forth to meet the bridegroom.* The *lamps* used on such occasions were rather *torches* or *flambeaux.* They were made by winding rags around pieces of iron or earthenware, sometimes hollowed so as to contain oil, and fastened to handles of wood. These torches were dipped in oil, and gave a large light. Marriage ceremonies in the East were conducted with great pomp and solemnity. The *ceremony* of marriage was performed commonly in the open air, on the banks of a stream. Both the bridegroom and bride were attended by friends. They were escorted in a *palanquin,* carried by four or more persons. After the ceremony of marriage succeeded a feast of seven days if the bride was a virgin, or three days if she was a widow. This feast was celebrated in her father's house. At the end of that time the bridegroom conducted the bride with great pomp and splendour to his own home. This was done in the evening, or at night, Je. vii. 34; xxv. 10; xxxiii. 11. Many friends and relations attended them; and besides those who went with them from the house of the bride, there was another company that came out from the house of the bridegroom to meet them and welcome them. These were probably female friends and relatives of the bridegroom, who went out to welcome him and his new companion to their home. These are the virgins mentioned in this parable. Not knowing *precisely* the time when the procession would come, they probably went out early, and waited till they should see indications of its approach. In the celebration of marriage in the East at the present day, many of the peculiar customs of ancient times are observed. "At a Hindoo marriage," says a modern missionary, "the procession of which I saw some years ago, the bridegroom came from a distance, and the bride lived at Serampore, to which place the bridegroom was to come by water. After waiting two or three hours, at length, near midnight, it was announced, in the very words of Scripture, '*Behold the bridegroom cometh; go ye out to meet him.*' All the persons employed now lighted their lamps, and ran with them in their hands to fill up their stations in the procession. Some of them had lost their lights and were unprepared, but it was then too late to seek them, and the cavalcade moved forward to the house of the bride, at which place the company entered a large and splendidly illuminated area before the house, covered with an awning, where a great multitude of friends, dressed in their best apparel, were seated upon mats. The bridegroom was carried in the arms of a friend, and placed in a superb seat in the midst of the company, where he sat a short time, and then went into the house, the door of which was immediately shut and guarded by sepoys. I and others expostulated with the doorkeepers, but in vain. Never was I so struck with our Lord's beautiful parable as at this moment—*And the door was shut.*"

The journal of one of the American missionaries in Greece contains an account of an Armenian wedding which she attended; and, after describing the dresses and previous ceremonies, she says that at twelve o'clock at night precisely the cry was made by some of the attendants, *Behold, the bridegroom cometh;* and immediately five or six men set off to meet him. ¶ *Bridegroom.* A man newly married.

2, 3, 4. *And five of them were wise.*

3 They that *were* foolish took their lamps, and took [d]no oil with them:

4 But the wise [e]took oil in their vessels with their lamps.

5 While the bridegroom tarried, they all [f]slumbered and slept.

6 And at [g]midnight there was a cry[h] made, Behold, the bridegroom cometh; [i]go ye out to meet him.

7 Then all those virgins arose, and trimmed their lamps.

8 And the foolish said unto the wise, Give us of your oil; [k]for our lamps are [1]gone out.

9 But the wise answered, saying, *Not so;* lest there be not enough for us and you: but [l]go ye rather to them that sell, and buy for yourselves.

d Is.48.1. *e* 1 Jn.2.20. *f* 1 Th.5.6. *g* Re.16.15. *h* 1 Th.4.16. *i* Am.4.12.

k Lu.12.35. 1 or, *going out.* *l* Is.55.1,6.

The words *wise* and *foolish,* here, refer only to their conduct in regard to the oil. The one part was *wise* in taking oil, the other *foolish* in neglecting it. The conduct of those who were *wise* refers to those who are *prepared* for the coming of Christ—prepared by possessing *real* piety, and not being merely his professed followers. The conduct of those *without* oil expresses the conduct of those who *profess* to love him, but are destitute of true grace, and are therefore unprepared to meet him. Nothing can be argued from the *number* here in regard to the proportion of sincere Christians among professors. *Circumstances* in parables are not to be pressed literally. They are necessary to keep up the story, and we must look chiefly or entirely to the *scope* or *design* of the parable to understand its meaning. In this parable the scope is to teach us to *watch* or be ready, ver. 13. It is *not* to teach us the relative *number* of those who shall be saved and who shall not. In teaching us to *watch* and *to be ready,* our Lord gives great additional interest by the circumstances of this narrative; but there is no authority for saying that he meant to teach that *just half* of professing Christians would be deceived. The moral certainty is that *nothing like* that number will be found to have been hypocrites. ¶ *Oil in their vessels.* The five foolish virgins probably expected that the bridegroom would come immediately; they therefore made no provision for any delay. The wise virgins knew that the time of his coming was uncertain, and they therefore furnished themselves with oil. This was carried in vessels, so that it could be poured on the torches when it was necessary. ¶ *Vessels.* Cups, cans, or anything to hold oil.

5. *The bridegroom tarried.* That is, while they waited for him. It was uncertain at what time he would come. He delayed longer than they expected. ¶ *All slumbered and slept.* Waiting till near midnight, they fell into repose. This circumstance is not to be pressed to prove that all *Christians* will be asleep, or cold and careless, when the Lord Jesus shall come. *Many* may be so, but many, also, will be looking for his coming. This circumstance is designed simply to show more clearly the *duty of being ready,* ver. 13. It does not mean to affirm it as *a fact* that none will be ready.

6. *At midnight.* Later than was the usual custom, and hence they had fallen asleep. ¶ *A cry made.* Of those who were coming with the bridegroom.

7. *Trimmed their lamps.* Burning till midnight, the oil was exhausted: they gave a dim and obscure light. They trimmed them by removing the burnt parts of the *linen* or the torch, so that they would burn clear. It was needful, also, to dip them again in oil, or to pour oil upon them. This strikingly represents the conduct of most men at the approach of death. They *then* begin to make ready. They are alarmed, anxious, and trembling, and then they ask the aid of others, but often when it is for ever too late.

10. *Went in with him to the marriage.* The *marriage-feast.* The marriage *ceremony* took place before the bride left her father's house, but a feast was given at the house of her husband, which was also called the *marriage,* or a part of the marriage solemnities. This part of the parable doubtless represents the entrance of those who *are ready,* or prepared, into the kingdom of God, when the Son of man shall come. They will be *ready* who have repented of their sins; who truly believe on the Lord Jesus; who live a holy life; and who wait for his coming. See Mar. xvi. 16; Jn. v. 24; Ac. iii. 19; Re. xxiii.

10 And [m]while they went to buy, the bridegroom came; and they that were ready went in with him to the marriage: [n]and the door was shut.

11 Afterward came also the other virgins, saying, [o]Lord, Lord, open to us.

12 But he answered and said, Verily I say unto you, [p]I know you not.

13 Watch,[q] therefore, for ye know neither the day nor the hour wherein the Son of man cometh.

14 For[r] *the kingdom of heaven is* as a man travelling into a far

m Am.8.12,13. n He.3.18,19; Re.22.11. o ch.7.21-23; He.12.17.

p Hab.1.13. q ch.24.42,44; Mar.13.33,35; Lu.21.36. r Lu.19.12,&c.

11; 2 Pe. iii. 11, 12; 1 Ti. vi. 17–19; 2 Ti. iv. 6–8. ¶ *The door was shut.* No more could be admitted to the marriage-feast. So, when the truly righteous shall all be received into heaven, the door will be closed against all others. There will be no room for preparation afterward, Re. xxii. 11; Ec. xi. 3; ix. 10; Mat. xxv. 46.

11. *Open unto us.* This is not to be understood as implying that any will come after the righteous shall be admitted into the kingdom, and claim admission then. It is a part of the *parable* to illustrate the general truth inculcated, or to prepare the way for what is afterwards said, and to keep up the narrative and make it consistent.

12. *I know you not.* You were not in the company of those who attended me to the marriage-feast, and are unknown to me. Applied to professing Christians, having *only* a profession of religion, but no real piety, it means, I do not know or *acknowledge* you as Christians. I do not approve of you, or delight in you, or admit that you are my friends. The word *know* is often used in the sense of approving, loving, acknowledging as real friends and followers. See Mat. vii. 23; Ps. i. 6; 2 Ti. ii. 19; 1 Th. v. 12.

13. *Watch, therefore,* &c. This is the scope or design of the whole parable. This is the great truth that Christ wished to inculcate, and all parts of the parable are to be interpreted in reference to this admonition. Like the virgins, many are professedly going to meet the Bridegroom—the Lord Jesus Christ. Like the coming of the bridegroom, his advent will be sudden. It will be to many at an unexpected time. Many, even professing Christians, will be engaged in the business of the world; thoughtless about eternity; not expecting his approach, and not prepared. They will only *profess* to know him, but in *works* they will deny him. So death will come. All approaches of the Son of God to judge men are *sudden*, and to many unexpected. So many, when they shall see him coming, at death or the judgment, will begin, like the foolish virgins, to be active, and to prepare to die; but it will be too late. They that are ready will enter in, and heaven will be closed for ever against all others. The *coming* of the Saviour is certain. The precise time *when* he will come is not certain. As the virgins should all have watched and been ready, so should we. They who are Christians should be ever watchful; and they who are not should lose no time to be ready, for in such an hour as they think not the Son of man shall come. ¶ *The Son of man cometh.* This refers, doubtless, to his coming in the day of judgment. The circumstances of the parable do not seem at all to apply to his coming to destroy Jerusalem, but are aptly expressive of his advent to judge the world.

14. *For* the kingdom of heaven, &c. The *parable of the talents* was spoken still farther to illustrate the manner in which he would deal with men at his return to judgment. The words *the kingdom of heaven* are not in the original, but are very properly inserted by the translators. The design of the parable is to teach that those who improve their talents or faculties in the cause of religion—who improve them to their own salvation and in doing good to others—shall be proportionally rewarded; but they who neglect their talents, and who neither secure their own salvation nor do good to others, will be punished. The kingdom of heaven is like such a man—that is, *God deals with men in his government as such a man did.* ¶ *His own servants.* That is, such of them as he judged to be worthy of such a trust. These represent the apostles, Christian ministers, professing Christians, and perhaps all men. The going into a far country

country, *who* called his own servants, and delivered unto them his goods.

15 And unto one he gave five talents,[2] to another two, and to another one; [s]to every man according to his several ability; and straightway took his journey.

16 Then he that had received the five talents went and traded with the same, and made *them* other five talents.

17 And likewise he that *had received* two, he also gained other two.

18 But he that had received one went and digged in the earth, and hid his lord's money.

19 After a [t]long time, the lord of those servants cometh, and [u]reckoneth with them.

20 And so he that had received five talents came, and brought other five talents, saying, Lord, thou deliveredst unto me five talents; behold, I have gained beside them five talents more.

21 His lord said unto him, Well done, *thou* good and faithful servant: thou hast been faithful over a

2 A talent is £187, 10s., ch.18.24.
s Ro.12.6; 1 Co.12.4,&c.; Ep.4.11.
t ch.24.48. u ch.18.23,24.

may represent the Lord Jesus going into heaven. He has given to all talents to improve, Ep. iv. 8; ii. 12. ¶ *His goods.* His property—representing the offices, abilities, and opportunities for doing good, which he has given to his professed followers.

15. *Five talents.* See Notes on Mat. xviii. 24. The word *talents* here is used to denote indefinitely *a large sum*, and is designed to refer to the endowments conferred on men. We have retained in our language the word *talent* as referring to the abilities or gifts of men. ¶ *According to his several ability.* According to the ability of each one. According as he saw each one was adapted to improve it. So in the church and the world. God gives men stations which he judges them adapted to fill, and requires them to fill them. He makes *distinctions* among men in regard to abilities, and in the powers and opportunities of usefulness, requiring them only to occupy those stations, and to discharge their duties there, 1 Co. iv. 7.

16, 17. The two who had received most employed their money in trade, and by honest industry doubled it before their master returned, representing the conduct of those who make a good improvement of their abilities, and employ them in doing good.

18. *Digged in the earth,* &c. This represents the conduct of those who neglect the abilities that God has given, and fail to do what he has required. This is done often: 1st. On the plea that they do not occupy a high station. 2d. That they have slender abilities, and can do little good. 3d. As it was in this case, that God had not given them as much as he did others, and they will therefore do nothing. These pleas are without foundation; for, First. God does not require us to do as much as those who have greater abilities; but this is not a reason why we should do nothing, 2 Co. viii. 12. Second. Any situation is honourable, and may be useful, where God has placed us; and though humble, yet in that we may do much good, 1 Co. xii. 11-31. Third. Men of slender abilities may often do more good in the world than men of much greater talents. It is rather a *warm heart* than a *strong head* which is required to do good. A humble Christian, by his life, example, and conversation, may often do much more good than *is* done by those in more elevated stations and with far greater gifts.

We are not to suppose by this, however, that our Saviour meant to teach that only those of *feeble* talents neglected their duty. The parable does not require us to do this; and the *fact* is, perhaps, that those most highly endowed are the farthest from properly improving their talents.

19. *After a long time,* &c. By the return of the lord of those servants to reckon with them is denoted the return of Christ to call men to an account for the manner in which they have improved their talents. See Ro. xiv. 12; 2 Co. v. 10; 1 Th. iv. 16; Ac. i. 11; xvii. 31. ¶ *Reckon with them.* To reckon is to settle accounts. Here it means to inquire into their faithfulness, and to reward or punish them accordingly.

few things, I will make thee [v]ruler over many things: enter thou into the joy of thy lord.

22 He also that had received two talents came, and said, Lord, thou deliveredst unto me two talents: behold, I have gained two other talents beside them.

23 His lord said unto him, Well done, good and faithful servant: thou hast been faithful over a few things, I will make thee ruler over many things: enter thou into the joy of thy lord.

24 Then he which had received the one talent came, and said, Lord, I knew thee that thou art [w]an hard man, [x]reaping where thou hast not sown, and gathering where thou hast not strawed:

25 And I was [y]afraid, and went and hid thy talent in the earth: lo, *there* thou hast *that is* thine.

26 His lord answered and said unto him, [z]*Thou* wicked and slothful servant, thou knewest that I reap where I sowed not, and gather where I have not strawed:

v Lu.12.44; 22.29; Re.3.21.

w Job 21.15. x Je.2.31. y Pr.26.13; Re.21.8. z Job 15.5,6; ch.18.32; Lu.19.22; Jude 15.

---

20. *I have gained.* Gained by trading or by honest industry, ver. 16.

21. *Ruler over many things.* I will promote thee to greater honours and to more important trusts. ¶ *Joy of thy lord.* In the meantime share the pleasures and enjoyments of his palace; be his companion, and receive the rewards which he has promised thee. *The joy of his lord* may mean either the festivals and rejoicings at his return, or the rewards which his lord had prepared for his faithful servants. Applied to Christians, it means that they who rightly improve their talents will, at the return of Christ, be promoted to great honours in heaven, and be partakers of the joys of their Lord in the world of glory. See ver. 34; also 1 Jn. ii. 28.

24. *The one talent.* The design of this part of the parable is to show that no one is excused for neglecting his duty because he has few talents. God will require of him only according to his ability, 1 Co. iv. 2; Lu. xii. 48; 2 Co. viii. 12. ¶ *A hard man.* Of a sordid, griping disposition; taking advantage of the poor, and oppressing them. ¶ *Reaping,* &c. This is indicative of an avaricious and overbearing disposition; compelling the poor to sow for him, and reaping all the benefit himself. ¶ *Hast not strawed.* The word *straw* means to *scatter*—as men scatter seed in sowing it. It may mean, also, to *ventilate,* or to *fan* by *ventilating* or winnowing. As *sowing* the seed is mentioned just before, it may be that this refers to gathering grain fanned or winnowed by others, while he did nothing—indicating, also, a hard or sordid disposition.

25. *I was afraid.* I feared lest, by some accident, thy talent would be lost if I put it out to trade, and that I should be severely punished by a hard master. I therefore kept it laid up safely, and hid it where it could not be lost. ¶ That is *thine.* There is what properly belongs to thee. There is the original talent that thou gavest me, and that is all that can be reasonably required. Observe here—1st. That this expresses exactly the feelings of all sinners. God, in their view, is hard, cruel, unjust. 2d. All the excuses of sinners are excuses for indolence and sin, and the effect is to cheat themselves out of heaven. The effect of this excuse was that the reward was lost, and such will always be the result of the excuses of sinners for not doing their duty. 3d. Sinners grudge everything to God. They are never willing to be liberal toward him, but are stinted and close; and if they give, they do it with hard feelings, and say that *that* is all that he can claim.

26. *Slothful.* Indolent, lazy, who had done nothing. God will judge men not merely for doing wrong, but for *not doing* right. See ver. 45. That servant was *wicked,* because he had such an opinion of his master; he had shown that he was slothful by not making good use of the talent, ver. 27. ¶ *Thou knewest,* &c. This should be understood, and might have been translated, as a question. If you knew that I was such a man you ought to have acted accordingly, so as to have escaped punishment. Didst thou know that I reap, &c.? Then thou shouldst have given my money to the exchangers, &c. This is not in-

27 Thou oughtest therefore to have put my money to the exchangers, and *then* at my coming I should have received mine own with usury.

28 Take, therefore, the talent from him, and give *it* unto him which hath ten talents.

29 For[a] unto every one that hath shall be given, and he shall have abundance; but from him that hath not shall be [b]taken away even that which he hath.

30 And cast ye the unprofitable servant into [c]outer darkness: there shall be weeping and gnashing of teeth.

31 When[d] the Son of man shall

a ch.13.12; Mar.4.25; Lu.8.18; 19.26.

b Lu.10.42. *c* ch.8.12.
d Da.7.13; Zec.14.5; ch.16.27; 19.28; Mar.8.38; Ac. 1.11; 1 Th.4.16; 2 Th.1.7; Jude 14; Re.1.7.

tended to *admit* that he was such a man, but to convict the slothful servant of guilt and folly in not having been prepared to meet him.

27. *The exchangers.* The *exchangers* were persons who were in the habit of borrowing money, or receiving it on deposit at a low rate of interest, to be loaned to others at higher interest. They commonly sat by *tables* in the temple, with money ready to exchange or loan. See Mat. xxi. 12. This money was left with the servant, not to exchange, nor to increase it by any such idle means, but by honest industry and merchandise; but since he was too indolent for that, he ought at least to have loaned it to the exchangers, that his master might have received some benefit from it. ¶ *With usury.* With interest, increase, or gain. The word *usury*, in our language, has a bad signification, meaning unlawful or exorbitant interest. This was contrary to the law, Ex. xxii. 25; Le. xxv. 36. The original means *gain*, increase, or lawful interest.

29. *For unto every one that hath shall be given.* See Notes on Mat. xiii. 12. This seems to be a proverbial expression. It means, whosoever rightly improves what is committed to him shall receive more, or shall be rewarded; but he that misimproves what is committed to him shall *not* be rewarded. In pecuniary matters—in the *literal* sense of this parable—they who improve their money by industry or merchandise increase it. They who do not—who are indolent or vicious—lose what they did possess, and it goes into the hands of the faithful and industrious. In the spiritual sense of the parable it means that they who are faithful shall be rewarded—not, however, that anything shall be taken from the unfaithful and given to them; and it means also that the unfaithful and indolent shall be taken away from their privileges and punished.

30. *And cast*, &c. See Notes on Mat. viii. 12. The spiritual meaning of the parable may be thus summed up: 1st. The servants of God are not all endowed with equal gifts and talents. 2d. All, whatever may be their ability, are bound to employ their talents in promoting his honour, and in a proper improvement of them. 3d. By employing their talents in a proper manner, they improve and strengthen them. 4th. They will be judged according to the improvements which they have made. 5th. All sinners look on God as a hard master, and as unreasonable and tyrannical. 6th. Men will be judged not merely for *doing wrong*, but for *neglecting to do right.* 7th. If the servant who kept the talent entire without injuring it, and who returned it to his master as he received it, was nevertheless judged, condemned, and cast away, what must they expect who abuse their talents, destroy by drunkenness and lust the noble faculties conferred on them, and squander the property that might be employed in advancing the interests of morals and religion!

31. *When the Son of man*, &c. This is in answer to the question which the disciples proposed to Jesus respecting the end of the world, ch. xxiv. 3. That this refers to the last judgment, and not, as some have supposed, to the destruction of Jerusalem, appears—1st. From the fact that it was in answer to an express inquiry respecting *the end* of the world. 2d. *All nations* were to be assembled, which did not take place at the destruction of Jerusalem. 3d. A separation was to take place between the righteous and the wicked, which was not done at Jerusalem. 4th. The rewards and punishments are declared to be *eternal.* None of these things took place at the destruction of Jerusalem. ¶ *In his glory.* In his own

come in his glory, and all the holy angels with him, then shall he sit upon the throne of his glory:

32 And[e] before him shall be gathered all nations; and he[f] shall separate them one from another, as a [g]shepherd divideth *his* sheep from the goats:

33 And he shall set the sheep on his [h]right hand, but the goats on the left.

34 Then shall the King say unto them on his right hand, Come, [i]ye blessed of my Father, [k]inherit the [l]kingdom [m]prepared for you from the foundation of the world:

e Ro.14.10; 2 Co 5.10; Re.20.12. *f* Eze.20.38; ch.13.49. *g* Ps.78.52; Jn.10.14,27.

h He.1.3. *i* Ps.115.15. *k* Ro.8.17; 1 Pe.1.4. *l* 1 Th.2.12; Re.5.10. *m* 1 Co.2.9; He.11.16.

proper honour. With his glorified body, and as the head and king of the universe, Ac. i. 11; Ep. i. 20–22; 1 Th. iv. 16; 1 Co. xv. 24, 25, 52. ¶ *The throne of his glory.* This means, in the language of the Hebrews, his glorious or splendid throne. It is not to be taken literally, as if there would be a material throne or seat for the King of Zion. It expresses the idea that he will come *as a king and judge* to assemble his subjects before him, and to appoint them their rewards.

32. *And before him,* &c. At his coming to judgment the world will be burned up, 2 Pe. iii. 10, 12; Re. xx. 11. The dead in Christ—that is, all true Christians—will be raised up from their graves, 1 Th. iv. 16. The living will be changed—*i.e.* will be made like the glorified bodies of those that are raised from the dead, 1 Co. xv. 52–54; 1 Th. iv. 17. All the wicked will rise and come forth to judgment, Jn. v. 28, 29; Da. xii. 2; Mat. xiii. 41, 42; Re. xx. 13. Then shall the world be judged, the righteous saved, and the wicked punished. ¶ *And he shall separate,* &c. Shall determine respecting their character, and shall appoint them their doom accordingly.

33. *Shall set the sheep,* &c. By *the sheep* are denoted, here, the righteous. The name is given to them because the sheep is an emblem of innocence and harmlessness. See Jn. x. 7, 14, 15, 16, 27; Ps. c. 3; lxxiv. 1; xxiii. ¶ *On the right hand.* The right hand is the place of honour, and denotes the situation of those who *are* honoured, or those who are virtuous. See Ec. x. 2; Ep. i. 20; Ps. cx. 1; Ac. ii. 25, 33. ¶ *The goats.* The wicked. See Eze. xxxiv. 17. ¶ *The left.* That is, the left hand. This was the place of dishonour, denoting condemnation. See Ec. x. 2.

34. *The King.* That is, the Lord Jesus, the King of Zion and of the universe, now acting as Judge, Lu. xix. 38; Jn. xviii. 37; Re. xvii. 14; xix. 16. ¶ *Blessed of my Father.* Made happy or raised to felicity by my Father. See Notes on Mat. v. 3. ¶ *Inherit the kingdom.* Receive *as heirs* the kingdom, or be received there as the sons of God. Christians are often called heirs of God, Ro. viii. 17; Ga. iv. 6, 7; He. i. 14; 1 Jn. iii. 2. ¶ *Prepared for you,* &c. That is, *designed* for you, or appointed for you. The phrase *from the foundation of the world* is used to denote that this was appointed for them in the beginning; that God has no new plan; that the rewards which he will now confer on them he always *intended* to confer. Christ says to the righteous that the kingdom was prepared for *them.* Of course, God meant to confer it on *them.* They were individuals, and it follows that he intended to bestow his salvation on them *as* individuals. Accordingly, the salvation of his people is universally represented as the result of the free gift of God, according to his own pleasure, bestowed on individuals, and by a plan which is eternal, Ro. viii. 29, 30; Ep. i. 4, 5, 11, 12; 2 Th. ii. 13; 1 Pe. i. 2; Jn. vi. 37. This is right and consistent with justice; for, 1st. All men are by nature equally undeserving. 2d. Bestowing favours on one does not do injustice to another, where neither deserves favour. Pardoning one criminal is not injuring another. Bestowing great talents on Locke, Newton, or Paul did not injure me. 3d. If it is right for God to *give* eternal life to his people, or to *admit* them to heaven, it was right to *determine* to do it, which is but another way of saying that God resolved from all eternity to *do right.* 4th. Those who perish *choose* the paths which lead to death, and *will* not be saved by the merits of Jesus. No blame can be charged on God if he does not save them against their will, Jn. v. 40; Mar. xvi. 15, 16.

35 For[n] I was an hungered, and ye gave me meat: I was thirsty, and ye gave me drink: I was [o]a stranger, and ye took me in:

36 Naked,[p] and ye clothed me: I was sick, and [q]ye visited me: I was in[r] prison, and ye came unto me.

37 Then shall the righteous answer him, saying, Lord, when saw we thee an hungered, and fed *thee?* or thirsty, and gave *thee* drink?

38 When saw we thee a stranger, and took *thee* in? or naked, and clothed *thee?*

39 Or when saw we thee sick, or in prison, and came unto thee?

40 And the King shall answer and say unto them, Verily I say unto you, [s]Inasmuch as ye have done *it* unto one of the least of these my brethren, ye have done *it* unto me.

41 Then shall he say also unto

n Is.58.7; Eze.18.7. o 1 Pe.4.9; 3 Jn.5. p Ja.2.15,16. q Ja.1.27. r 2 Ti.1.16; He.13.2.

s Pr.19.17; Mar.9.41; He.6.10.

35, 36. *I was an hungered.* The union between Christ and his people is the most tender and endearing of all connections. It is represented by the closest unions of which we have knowledge, Jn. xv. 4-6; Ep. v. 23-32; 1 Co. vi. 15. This is a union—not physical, but moral; a union of feelings, interests, plans, destiny; or, in other words, he and his people have similar feelings, love the same objects, share the same trials, and inherit the same blessedness, Jn. xiv. 19; Re. iii. 5, 21; Ro. viii. 17. Hence he considers favours shown to his people as shown to himself, and will reward them accordingly, Mat. x. 40, 42. They show attachment to him, and love to his cause. By showing kindness to the poor, the needy, and the sick, they show that they possess *his* spirit, for he did it when on earth; they evince attachment to him, for *he* was poor and needy; and they show that they have the proper spirit to fit them for heaven, 1 Jn. iii. 14, 17; Ja. ii. 1-5; Mar. ix. 41. ¶ *Was a stranger.* The word *stranger* means a *foreigner* or traveller; in our language, one unknown to us. To receive such to the rites of hospitality was, in Eastern countries, where there were few or no public houses, a great virtue. See Ge. xviii. 1-8; He. xiii. 2. ¶ *Took me in.* Into your house. Received me kindly. ¶ *Naked.* Poorly clothed. Among the Jews they were called *naked* who were clad in poor raiment, or who had on only the *tunic* or inner garment, without any outer garment. See Notes on Mat. v. 40; also Ac. xix. 16; Mar. xiv. 51, 52; Job xxii. 6; Is. lviii. 7.

37-39. *Then shall the righteous,* &c. This answer is indicative of humility—a deep sense of their being unworthy such commendation. They will feel that their poor acts of kindness have come so far short of what they *should* have been, that they have no claim to praise or reward. It is not, however, to be supposed that in the day of judgment this will be actually *said* by the righteous, but that this would be a proper expression of their feelings.

40. *One of the least of these.* One of the obscurest, the least known, the poorest, the most despised and afflicted. ¶ *My brethren.* Either those who are Christians, whom he condescends to call brethren, or those who are afflicted, poor, and persecuted, who are his brethren and companions in suffering, and who suffer as he did on earth. See He. ii. 11; Mat. xii. 50. How great is the condescension and kindness of the Judge of the world, thus to reward our actions, and to consider what *we* have done to the poor as done to him!

41. *On the left hand.* The wicked. ¶ *Ye cursed.* That is, you who are devoted to destruction, whose characters deserve everlasting punishment, and who are about to enter into it. *To curse* is the opposite of *to bless.* It implies a negation of all the blessings of heaven, and a positive infliction of eternal sufferings. ¶ *Everlasting fire. Fire,* here, is used to denote punishment. The image is employed to express extreme suffering, as a death by burning is one of the most horrible that can be conceived. The image was taken, probably, from the *fires* burning in the Valley of Hinnom. See Notes on Mat. v. 22. It has been asked whether the wicked will be burned in literal fire, and the common impression has been that they will be. Respecting that, however, it is to be observed—1st. That the *main truth* intended to be taught refers not to the

them on the left hand, [t]Depart from me, ye cursed, into [u]everlasting fire, [v]prepared for the devil and his angels:

42 For I was an hungered, and ye gave me no meat: I was thirsty, and ye gave me no drink:

43 I was a stranger, and ye took me not in: naked, and ye clothed me not: sick, and in prison, and ye visited me not.

44 Then shall they also answer him, saying, Lord, when saw we thee an hungered, or athirst, or a stranger, or naked, or sick, or in prison, and did not minister unto thee?

45 Then shall he answer them, saying, Verily I say unto you, [w]Inasmuch as ye did *it* not to one of the least of these, ye did *it* not to me.

t Lu.13.27. u ch.13.40,42; Re.14.11. v Jude 6; Re.20.10.

w Zec.2.8; Ac.9.5.

manner of suffering, but to the *certainty* and *intensity* of it. 2d. That the design, therefore, was to present an image of terrific and appalling suffering—an image well represented by fire. 3d. That this image was well known to the Jews (Is. lxvi. 24), and therefore expressed the idea in a very strong manner. 4th. That all the *truth* that Christ intended to convey appears to be expressed in the certainty, intensity, and eternity of future torment. 5th. That there is no distinct affirmation respecting the *mode* of that punishment, where the *mode* was the subject of discourse. 6th. That to us it is a subject of comparatively little consequence what will be the *mode* of punishment. The fact that the wicked will be eternally punished, cursed of God, should awe every spirit, and lead every man to strive most earnestly to secure his salvation. As, however, the *body* will be raised, it is not unreasonable to suppose that a mode of punishment will be adopted suited to the body—perhaps bearing some analogy to suffering here, in its various forms of flames, and racks, and cold, and heat, and disease, and ungratified desire, and remorse—perhaps the concentration of all earthly woes, all that makes man miserable here, poured upon the naked body and spirit of the wicked in hell for ever and ever. ¶ *Prepared for the devil.* The devil is the prince of evil spirits. This place of punishment was fitted up for *him* when he rebelled against God, Jude 6; Re. xii. 8, 9. ¶ *His angels.* His messengers, his servants, or those angels that he drew off from heaven by his rebellion, and whom he has employed as his *messengers* to do evil. The word *may* extend also to *all* his followers—fallen angels or men. There is a remarkable difference between the manner in which the righteous will be addressed, and the wicked. Christ will say to the one that the kingdom was prepared for *them;* to the other, that the fire was not prepared for *them*, but for another race of beings. *They* will inherit it because they have the same character *as the devil*, and are therefore fitted to the same place—not because it was originally *prepared for them.*

45. *Inasmuch as ye did it not*, &c. By not doing good to the *followers* of Christ, they showed that they had no real love to *him*. By not doing good to the poor and needy, to the stranger and the prisoner, they showed that they had not his spirit, and were not like him, and were unfit for his kingdom. Let it be observed here that the public ground of their condemnation is the *neglect* of duty, or because *they did it not.* We are not to suppose that they will not also be condemned for their open and positive sins. See Ro. ii. 9; Ep. v. 5; Col. iii. 5, 6; 1 Co. vi. 9, 10; Re. xxi. 8; Ps. ix. 17. But their neglect of doing good to him and his people may be the *public* reason of condemning them: 1st. Because he wished to give *pre-eminence* to those virtues, to excite his followers to do them. 2d. Men should be punished for *neglect* as well as for positive sin. Sin is a violation of the law, or *refusing* to do what God commands. 3d. Nothing better shows the true state of the *heart* than the proper performance of those duties, and the true character can be as well tested by neglecting them as by open crimes.

If it be asked how the heathen who never heard of the name of Christ can be justly condemned in this manner, it may be answered—1st. That Christ acknowledges all the poor, and needy, and strangers of every land, as his brethren. See ver. 40. 2d. That by ne-

46 And[x] these shall go away into everlasting punishment; but the righteous into life eternal.

x Da.12.2; Jn.5.29.

glecting the duties of charity they show that they have not his spirit—are not like him. 3d. That these duties are clearly made known by conscience and by the light of nature, as well as by revelation, and men may therefore be condemned for the neglect of them. 4th. That they are not condemned for not believing in Christ, of whom they have not heard, but for a wrong spirit, neglect of duty, open crime; for being *unlike Christ*, and therefore *unfit* for heaven. ¶ *One of the least of these.* These on my right hand. My brethren. Those who are saved.

46. *And these shall go away.* These *persons.* Many, holding the doctrine of universal salvation have contended that God would punish *sin* only. Christ says that *those on his left hand*, shall go away—not *sins*, but *sinners.* Besides, *sin*, as an abstract thing, cannot be punished. Sin is nothing but an *act*—the act of a transgressor, and, to be reached at all, it must be reached by punishing the offender himself. ¶ *Into everlasting punishment.* The original word here translated *punishment* means torment, or suffering inflicted for crime. The noun is used but in one other place in the New Testament—1 Jn. iv. 18: "Fear hath *torment.*" The verb from which the noun is derived is twice used—Ac. iv. 21; 2 Pe. ii. 9. In all these places it denotes anguish, suffering, punishment. It does not mean simply a *state* or *condition*, but absolute, positive suffering; and if this word does not teach it, no word *could* express the idea that the wicked would suffer. It has been contended that the sufferings of the wicked will not be *eternal* or *without end.* It is not the purpose of these *Notes* to enter into debates of that kind farther than to ascertain the meaning of the language used by the sacred writers. In regard to the meaning of the word *everlasting* in this place, it is to be observed—1st. That the *literal* meaning of the word expresses absolute eternity—*always being*, Mat. xviii. 8; xix. 16; Mar. iii. 29; Ro. ii. 7; He. v. 9. 2d. That the obvious and plain interpretation of the word demands this signification in this place. The original word—*aionion*—is employed in the New Testament sixty-six times. Of these, in fifty-one instances it is used of the happiness of the righteous; in two, of God's existence; in six, of the church and the Messiah's kingdom; and in the remaining seven, of the future punishment of the wicked. If in these seven instances we attach to the word the idea of limited duration, consistency requires that the same idea of limited duration should be given it in the fifty-one cases of its application to the future glory of the righteous, and the two instances of its application to God's existence, and the six cases of its appropriation to the future reign of the Messiah and the glory and perpetuity of the church. But no one will presume to deny that in these instances it denotes unlimited duration, and therefore, in accordance with the sound laws of interpretation and of language itself, the same sense of unlimited duration must be given it when used of future punishment.—Owen, *in loc.* 3d. That, admitting that it was the Saviour's design *ever* to teach this doctrine, this would be *the very word* to express it; and if this does not teach it, it *could not* be taught. 4th. That it is not taught in any plainer manner in any confession of faith on the globe; and if this may be explained away, all those may be. 5th. That our Saviour knew that this would be so understood by nine-tenths of the world; and if he did *not* mean to teach it, he has knowingly led them into error, and his honesty cannot be vindicated. 6th. That he knew that the doctrine was calculated to produce *fear* and *terror;* and if he was benevolent, and actually used language calculated to produce this fear and terror, his conduct cannot be vindicated in exciting unnecessary alarms. 7th. *That the word used here is the same in the original as that used to express the eternal life of the righteous;* if one can be proved to be limited in duration, the other can by the *same arguments.* *The proof that the righteous will be happy for ever is precisely the same, and no other, than that the wicked will be miserable for ever.* 8th. That it is confirmed by many other passages of Scripture, 2 Th. i. 7-9; Lu. xvi. 26; Re. xiv. 11; Ps. ix. 17; Is. xxxiii. 14; Mar. xvi. 16; Jn. iii. 36. ¶ *Life eternal.* Man by sin has plunged himself into death, temporal, spiritual, eternal. Christ, by coming and dying, has abolished death,

CHAPTER XXVI.

AND it came to pass, when Jesus had finished all these sayings, he said unto his disciples,

2 Ye[a] know that after two days is *the feast of the* passover, and the Son of man is betrayed to be crucified.

a Mar.14.1,&c.; Lu.22.1,&c.; Jn.13.1,&c.

---

and brought life and immortality to light, 2 Ti. i. 10. *Life* is the opposite of death. It denotes, here, freedom from death, and positive holiness and happiness for ever.

CHAPTER XXVI.

1-16. See also Mar. xiv. 1-11; Lu. xxii. 1-6; Jn. xii. 1-7.

2. *After two days is* the feast of the *passover*. See Notes on Mat. xii. 1-8. The festival of the Passover was designed to preserve among the Jews the memory of their liberation from Egyptian servitude, and of the safety of their first-born in that night when the first-born of the Egyptians perished, Ex. xii. The name *Passover* was given to the feast because the Lord *passed over* the houses of the Israelites without slaying their first-born, while the Egyptians were cut off, Ex. xii. 13. It was celebrated seven days, viz. from the 15th to the 21st of the month ABIB or NISAN (April), Ex. xii. 15-20; xxiii. 15. During all this period the people ate unleavened bread, and hence the festival was sometimes called *the feast of unleavened bread*, Ex. xii. 18; Le. xxiii. 6. On the evening of the fourteenth day, all the leaven or yeast in the family was removed with great care, as it is to the present time—a circumstance to which the apostle alludes in 1 Co. v. 7. On the tenth day of the month the master of a family separated a lamb or a goat of a year old from the flock (Ex. xii. 1-6), which he slew on the fourteenth day before the altar, De. xvi. 2, 5, 6. The lamb was commonly slain at about 3 o'clock P.M. The blood of the paschal lamb was, in Egypt, sprinkled on the door-posts of the houses; afterward it was poured by the priests at the foot of the altar, Ex. xii. 7. The lamb thus slain was roasted whole, with two spits thrust through it—one lengthwise and one transversely—crossing each other near the forelegs, so that the animal was in a manner, crucified. Not a bone of it might be broken—a circumstance strongly representing the sufferings of our Lord Jesus, the Passover slain for us, Jn. xix. 36; 1 Co. v. 7. Thus roasted, the lamb was served up with wild and bitter herbs. Not fewer than ten, nor more than twenty persons, were admitted to these sacred feasts. At first it was observed with their loins girt about, with sandals on their feet, and with all the preparations for an immediate journey. This, in Egypt, was significant of the haste with which they were about to depart from the land of bondage. The custom was afterward retained.

The order of the celebration of this feast was as follows:—The ceremony commenced with drinking a cup of wine mingled with water, after having given thanks to God for it. This was the *first cup*. Then followed the *washing of hands*, with another short form of thanksgiving to God. The table was then supplied with the provisions, viz. the bitter salad, the unleavened bread, the lamb, and a thick sauce composed of dates, figs, raisins, vinegar, &c. They then took a small quantity of salad, with another thanksgiving, and ate it; after which, all the dishes were removed from the table, and a second cup of wine was set before each guest, as at first. The dishes were removed, it is said, to excite the curiosity of children, and to lead them to make inquiry into the cause of this observance. See Ex. xii. 26, 27. The leading person at the feast then began and rehearsed the history of the servitude of the Jews in Egypt, the manner of their deliverance, and the reason of instituting the Passover. The dishes were then returned to the table, and he said, "*This is the Passover which we eat, because that the Lord passed over the houses of our fathers in Egypt;*" and then, holding up the salad and the unleavened bread, he stated the *design*, viz. that the one represented the *bitterness* of the Egyptian bondage, and the other the *suddenness* of their deliverance. This done, he repeated the 113th and 114th Psalms, offered a short prayer, and all the company drank the wine that had been standing some time before them. This was the *second cup*. The hands were then again washed, and the meal then eaten with the usual forms and solemnities; after which they washed the hands again, and then drank another cup of

3 Then assembled together the chief priests, and the scribes, and the elders of the people, unto the palace of the high-priest, who was called Caiaphas,

4 And[b] consulted that they might take Jesus by subtilty and kill *him.*

5 But they said, Not on the feast-*day*, lest there be an uproar among the people.

b Ps.2.2.

wine, called *the cup of blessing*, because the leader was accustomed in a particular manner, over that cup, to offer thanks to God for his goodness. This is the cup which our Saviour is supposed to have taken when he instituted the Lord's Supper, called by Paul *the cup of blessing*, 1 Co. x. 16. There was still another cup, which was drunk when they were about to separate, called the Hallel, because in connection with it they were accustomed to repeat the lesser *Hallel*, or the 115th, 116th, 117th, 118th Psalms. In accordance with this, our Saviour and his disciples sang a hymn as they were about to go to the Mount of Olives, ver. 30. It is probable that our Saviour complied with these rites according to the custom of the Jews. While doing it, he signified that the *typical* reference of the Passover was about to be accomplished, and he instituted in place of it *the supper*—the communion—and, of course, the obligation to keep the Passover then ceased. ¶ *The Son of man is betrayed.* Will be betrayed. He did not mean to say that they then knew that he would be betrayed, for it does not appear that they had been informed of the precise time; but they knew that the Passover was at hand, and *he then* informed them that he would be betrayed. ¶ *To be crucified.* To be put to death on the cross. See Notes on Mat. xxvii. 35.

3. *Then assembled*, &c. This was a meeting of the great council or Sanhedrim. See Notes on Mat. v. 22. ¶ *The palace.* The original word properly denotes the *hall* or large area in the centre of the dwelling, called the court. See Notes on Mat. ix. 1–8. It may be understood, however, as referring to the palace itself. ¶ *The high-priest.* Holding the office that was first conferred on Aaron, Ex. xxviii. The office was at first hereditary, descending on the oldest son, Nu. iii. 10. Antiochus Epiphanes (B.C. 160), when he had possession of Judea, sold the office to the highest bidder. In the year 152 B.C., Alexander, King of Syria, conferred the office on JONATHAN (1 Mac. x. 18–20), whose brother Simon was afterward created by the Jews both prince and high-priest, 1 Mac. xiv. 35–47. His posterity, who at the same time sustained the office of kings, occupied the station of high-priest till the time of Herod, who changed the incumbents of the office at pleasure—a liberty which the Romans ever afterward exercised without any restraint. The office was never more fluctuating than in the time of our Saviour. Hence it is said that *Caiaphas* was high-priest *for that year*, Jn. xi. 51. Persons who *had been* high-priests, and had been removed from office, still retained the name. Hence more than one high-priest is sometimes mentioned, though strictly there was but one who held the office.

4. *By subtilty.* By guile, deceit, or in some secret manner, so that the people would not know it. Jesus was regarded by the people as a distinguished prophet, and by most of them, probably, as the Messiah; and the Sanhedrim did not dare to take him away openly, lest the people should rise and rescue him. They were probably aware that he had gone out to Bethany, or to some place adjacent to the city; and as he passed his nights there and not in the city, there was need of guile to ascertain the place to which he had retired, and to take him.

5. *Not on the feast*-day. Not during the *feast*. The feast lasted seven days. A vast multitude attended from all parts of Judea. Jerusalem is said to have contained at such times *three millions of people*. Amid such a multitude there were frequent tumults and seditions, and the Sanhedrim was justly apprehensive there *would* be now, if, in open day and in the temple, they took away a teacher so popular as Jesus, and put him to death. They therefore sought how they might do it secretly and by guile.

6. *In Bethany.* See Notes on ch. xxi. 1. ¶ *Simon the leper.* Simon, who *had been* a leper. ¶ *Leper.* See Notes on Mat. viii. 1. It was *unlawful* to eat with persons that *had* the leprosy, and it is more than probable, therefore,

6 Now when Jesus was in Bethany, in the house of Simon the leper,

7 There[c] came unto him a woman having an alabaster box of very precious ointment, and poured it on his head as he sat *at meat.*

c Jn.11.1,2; 12.3.

that this Simon had been healed—perhaps by our Lord himself. John (xii. 1) says that this was the house where Lazarus was, who had been raised from the dead. Probably Lazarus was a relative of Simon's, and was living with him. He farther says that they made Jesus a supper, and that Martha served. He says that this was six days before the Passover. From the order in which Matthew and Mark mention it, it would have been supposed that it was but *two days* before the Passover, and *after* the cleansing of the temple; but it is to be observed, 1st. That Matthew and Mark often neglect the exact order of the events that they record. 2d. That they do not *affirm* at what time this was. They leave it indefinite, saying that *while* Jesus was in Bethany he was anointed by Mary. 3d. That Matthew introduced it here for the purpose of giving a *connected* account of the conduct of *Judas. Judas* murmured at the waste of the ointment (Jn. xii. 4), and one of the *effects* of his indignation, it seems, was to betray his Lord.

7. *There came to him a woman.* This woman was *Mary*, the sister of Lazarus and Martha, Jn. xii. 3. ¶ *Having an alabaster box.* The *alabaster* is a species of marble, distinguished for being light, and of a beautiful white colour, almost transparent. It was much used by the ancients for the purpose of preserving various kinds of ointment in. ¶ *Of very precious ointment.* That is, of ointment *of great value;* that was rare and difficult to be obtained. Mark (xiv. 3) and John (xii. 3) say that it was ointment of spikenard. In the original it is *nard.* It was procured from an herb growing in the Indies, chiefly obtained from the root, though sometimes also from the bark. It was liquid, so as easily to flow when the box or vial was open, and was distinguished particularly for an agreeable smell. See Ca. i. 12. The ancients were much in the habit of *anointing* or *perfuming* their bodies, and the *nard* was esteemed one of the most precious perfumes. John says there was a *pound* of this, ch. xii. 3. The *pound* in use among the Jews was the Roman, of twelve ounces, answering to our troy weight. That there was a large quantity is farther evident from the fact that Judas says it might have been sold for three hundred pence (about £9), and that the *house* was filled with the odour of the ointment (John). ¶ *And poured it on his head.* They were accustomed chiefly to anoint the head or hair. John says (xii. 3) that she poured it on the *feet* of Jesus, and wiped them with her hair. There is, however, no contradiction. She probably poured it *both* on his head and his feet. Matthew and Mark having recorded the former, John, who wrote his gospel in part to record events omitted by them, completes the account by saying that the ointment was also poured on the feet of the Saviour. To pour ointment on the *head* was common. To pour it on the *feet* was an act of distinguished *humility* and of attachment to the Saviour, and therefore deserved to be particularly recorded. ¶ *As he sat* at meat. That is, at supper. In the original, as he *reclined* at supper. The ancients did not *sit* at their meals, but *reclined* at length on couches. See Notes on Mat. xxiii. 6. She came up, therefore, *behind him* as he lay reclined at the table, and, bending down over the couch, poured the ointment on his head and his feet, and, probably kneeling at his feet, wiped them with her hair.

8. *They had indignation.* John says that *Judas expressed* indignation. Probably some of the others *felt* indignation, but Judas only gave vent to his feelings. The reason why Judas was indignant was, that he had the *bag* (Jn. xii. 6)—that is, the *purse*, or repository of articles *given* to the disciples and to the Saviour. He was a thief, and was in the habit, it seems, of taking out and appropriating to his own use what was put in for them in common. The leading trait of Judas's character was *avarice*, and no opportunity was suffered to pass without attempting by base and wicked means to make money. In his example an avaricious man may learn the true nature and the effect of that grovelling and wicked passion. It led him to commit the enormous crime of betraying his Lord to death, and it will always lead its possessor to guilt. No small part of the sins of the world can be traced to avarice, and many and many

8 But when his disciples saw *it*, they had indignation, saying, To what purpose *is* this waste?

9 For this ointment might have been sold for much, and given to the poor.

10 When Jesus understood *it*, he said unto them, Why trouble ye the woman? for she hath wrought a good work upon me.

11 For[d] ye have the poor always with you; [e]but me ye have not always.

12 For in that she hath poured this ointment on my body, she did *it* for my burial.

13 Verily I say unto you, Wheresoever this gospel shall be preached in the whole world, *there* shall also this, that this woman hath done, be told for a memorial of her.

14 Then [f]one of the twelve, called

d De.15.11. e Jn.14.19; 17.11. f Ch.10.4.

a time since the days of Judas has the Lord Jesus been betrayed among his professed friends by the same base propensity. ¶ Is *this waste.* This *loss* or *destruction* of property. They could see no use in it, and they therefore supposed it was lost.

9. *Sold for much.* Mark and John say for three hundred pence—that is, for about £9. This, to them, was a large sum. Mark says they murmured against her. There was also an *implied* murmuring against the Saviour for suffering it to be done. The murmuring was, however, without cause. It was the *property* of Mary. She had a right to dispose of it as she pleased, answerable not to *them*, but *to God.* *They* had no right over it, and no cause of complaint if it *had* been wasted. So Christians now are at liberty to dispose of their property as they please, either in distributing the Bible, in supporting the gospel, in sending it to heathen nations, or in aiding the poor. The men of the world, like Judas, regard it as *wasted.* Like Judas, they are indignant. They say it might be disposed of in a better way. Yet, like Judas, they are interfering in that which concerns them not. Like other men, Christians have a right to dispose of their property as they please, answerable only to God. And though an avaricious world esteems it to be *wasted*, yet, if their Lord commands it, it will be found to be the *only way* in which it was *right* for them to dispose of that property, and will be found not to have been in vain.

10. *Trouble ye the woman.* That is, disturb her mind by insinuations, as if she had done wrong. ¶ *A good work on me.* She has done it with a mind grateful, and full of love to me. The work was *good*, also, as it was preparative for his death, ver. 12.

11. *For ye have the poor*, &c. Mark adds, "Whensoever ye will, ye may do them good." It was right that they should regard the poor. It was a plain precept of religion (see Ps. xli. 1; Pr. xiv. 21; xxix. 7; Ga. ii. 10), and our Saviour would not prohibit it, but do all that was possible to excite his followers to the duty. But every duty should be done in its place, and the duty *then* incumbent was that which Mary had performed. They would afterward have abundant occasion to show their regard for the poor. ¶ *Me ye have not always.* He alludes here to his dying, and his going away to heaven. He would still be their friend and their Saviour, but would not be *bodily* present with them always, so that they could show kindness *in this way* to him.

12. *She did* it *for my burial.* It is not to be supposed that Mary understood clearly that he was *then* about to die—for the apostles, it seems, did not fully comprehend it, or that she *intended* it for his burial; but she had done it as an act of kindness and love, to show her regard for her Lord. *He* said that it was a *proper preparation* for his burial. Anciently, bodies were anointed and embalmed for the purpose of the sepulchre. Jesus said that this was *really* a preparation for that burial; a fitting him in a proper manner for the tomb.

13. *A memorial.* Anything to produce *remembrance.* This would be told to her honour and credit, as a memorial of her piety and self-denial; and it is right that the good deeds of the pious should be recorded and had in recollection.

14. *Then one of the twelve*, &c. Luke says that Satan entered into Judas. That is, Satan *tempted* or instigated him to do it. Probably he tempted Judas by appealing to his avarice, his ruling passion, and by suggesting that now

Judas Iscariot, went unto the chief priests,

15 And said *unto them*, What will ye give me, and I will deliver him unto you? And they [g]covenanted with him for thirty pieces of silver.

16 And from that time he sought opportunity to betray him.

17 Now[h] the first *day* of the *feast of* unleavened bread, the disciples came to Jesus, saying unto him, Where wilt thou that we prepare for thee to eat the passover?

g Zec.11.12,13; ch.27.3.

h Ex.12.6,18.

was a favourable opportunity to make money rapidly by selling his Lord. ¶ *Judas Iscariot.* See Notes on Mat. x. 4. ¶ *Unto the chief priests.* The high-priest, and those who *had* been high-priests. The ruling men of the Sanhedrim. Luke adds that he went also to *the captains* (xxii. 4). It was necessary, on account of the great wealth deposited there, and its great sacredness, to *guard* the temple by night. Accordingly, men were stationed around it, whose leaders or commanders were called *captains*, Ac. iv. 1. These men were commonly of the tribe of Levi, were closely connected with the priests, were men of influence, and Judas went to them, therefore, as well as to the priests, to offer his services in accomplishing what they so much desired to secure. Probably his object was to get as much money as possible, and he might therefore have attempted to make a bargain with several of them apart from each other.

15. *And they covenanted with him.* Made a bargain with him. Agreed to give him. Mark says they *promised* to give him money. They did not pay it to him *then*, lest he should deceive them. When the deed was done, and before he was made sensible of its guilt, they paid him. See Mat. xxvii. 3; Ac. i. 18. ¶ *Thirty pieces of silver.* Mark and Luke do not mention the sum. They say that they promised him *money*—in the original, *silver*. In Matthew, in the original, it is thirty *silvers*, or *silverlings*. This was the price *of a slave* (see Ex. xxi. 32), and it is not unlikely that this sum was fixed on by them to show their *contempt* of Jesus, and that they regarded him as of little value. There is no doubt, also, that they understood that such was the anxiety of Judas to obtain money, that he would betray his Lord for *any* sum. The money usually denoted by *pieces* of silver, when the precise sum is not mentioned, is a *shekel*—a silver Jewish coin amounting to about 50 cents, or 2*s.* 3*d.* The whole sum, therefore, for which Judas committed this crime was $15, or £3, 7*s.* 6*d.*

16. *Sought opportunity to betray him.* Luke adds, "in the absence of the multitude." This was the chief difficulty—to deliver him into the hands of the priests so as not to have it known by the people, or so as not to excite tumult. The *opportunity* which he sought, therefore, was one in which the multitude *would* not see him, or *could* not rescue the Saviour. ¶ *To betray him.* The word *betray* commonly means to deliver into the hands of an enemy by treachery or breach of trust; to do it while friendship or faithfulness is *professed*. All this took place in the case of Judas. But the word in the original does not necessarily imply this. It means simply to *deliver up*, or to give into their hands. He sought opportunity *how he might deliver him up to them*, agreeably to the contract.

17–19. See also Mar. xiv. 12–16; Lu. xxii. 7–13.

17. *The first* day, &c. The feast continued *eight* days, including the day on which the paschal lamb was killed and eaten, Ex. xii. 15. That was the fourteenth day of the month Abib, answering to parts of our March and April. ¶ Of *unleavened bread.* Called so because during those eight days no bread made with yeast or leaven was allowed to be eaten. Luke says, "in which the passover must be killed"—that is, in which the *paschal lamb*, or the lamb eaten on the occasion, was killed. The word in the original, translated *Passover*, commonly means, not the *feast* itself, but the *lamb* that was killed on the occasion, Ex. xii. 43; Nu. ix. 11; Jn. xviii. 28. See also 1 Co. v. 7, where Christ, *our Passover*, is said to be slain for us; that is, our paschal lamb, so called on account of his innocence, and his being offered as a victim or *sacrifice* for our sins.

18. *Go into the city to such a man.* That is, Jerusalem, called *the* city by way of eminence. Luke says that the

18 And he said, Go into the city to such a man, and say unto him, The Master saith, My time is at hand: I will keep the passover at thy house with my disciples.

19 And the disciples did as Jesus

---

disciples whom he sent were Peter and John. The man to whom they were to go he did not mention by name, but he told them that when they came into the city, a man would meet them bearing a pitcher of water. See Mark and Luke. Him they were to follow, and in the house which he entered they would find a room prepared. The *name* of the man was not mentioned. The *house* in which they were to keep the Passover was not mentioned. The reason of this probably was, that Christ was desirous of concealing from *Judas* the place where they would keep the Passover. He was acquainted with the design of Judas to betray him. He knew that if Judas was acquainted with the place *beforehand*, he could easily give information to the chief priests, and it would give them a favourable opportunity to surprise them, and apprehend *him* without making a tumult. Though it was certain that he would not be delivered up before the time appointed by the Father, yet it was proper *to use the means* to prevent it. There can be little doubt that Jesus was acquainted with this man, and that he was a disciple. The direction which he gave his disciples most clearly proves that he was omniscient. Amid so great a multitude going at that time into the city, it was impossible to know that *a particular man would be met*—a man bearing a pitcher of water—unless Jesus had all knowledge, and was therefore divine. ¶ *The Master saith.* This was the name by which Jesus was probably known among the disciples, and one which he directed them to give him. See Mat. xxiii. 8, 10. It means, literally, *the teacher*, as opposed to *the disciple*, or learner; not the *master*, as opposed to the *servant* or *slave*. The fact that they used this name *as if* the man would know whom they meant, and the fact that the man understood them and made no further inquiries, shows that he was acquainted with Jesus, and was probably himself a disciple. ¶ *My time is at hand.* That is, *is near.* By *his time*, here, may be meant either his time to eat the Passover, or the time of his death. It has been supposed by many that Jesus, in accordance with a part of the Jews who rejected traditions, anticipated the usual observance of the Passover, or kept it one day sooner. The Pharisees had devised many forms of ascertaining when the month commenced. They placed witnesses around the heights of the temple to observe the first appearance of the new moon; they examined the witnesses with much formality, and endeavoured also to obtain the exact time by astronomical calculations. Others held that the month properly commenced when the moon was *visible.* Thus it is said a difference arose between them about the time of the Passover, and that Jesus kept it one day sooner than most of the people. The foundation of the opinion that he anticipated the usual time of keeping the Passover is the following: 1st. In Jn. xviii. 28, it is said that on the day on which our Lord was crucified, and of course the *day after* he had eaten the Passover, the chief priests would not go into the judgment-hall lest they should be defiled, *but that they might eat the passover*, evidently meaning that it was to be eaten that day. 2d. In Jn. xix. 14, the day on which he was crucified is called *the preparation of the passover*—that is, the day on which it was prepared to be eaten in the evening. 3d. In Jn. xix. 31, the day in which our Lord lay in the grave was called the great day of the Sabbath—"a high day;" that is, the day after the Passover was killed, the Sabbath occurring on the first day of the feast properly, and therefore a day of peculiar solemnity; yet our Saviour had partaken of it *two* days before, and therefore the *day before* the body of the people. If this opinion be true, then the phrase "my time is at hand" means *my* time for keeping the Passover is near. Whether this opinion be true or not, there may be a reference also *to his death.* The man with whom they were to go was probably a disciple of his, though perhaps a secret one. Jesus might purpose to keep the Passover at his house, that he might inform him more particularly respecting his death, and prepare him for it. He sent, therefore, to him and said, "I will keep the passover *at thy house.*"

Mark and Luke add that he would

had appointed them; and they made ready the passover.

20 Now when the even was come, he sat down with the twelve.

21 And as they did eat, he said, Verily I say unto you, that one of you shall betray me.

22 And they were exceeding

---

show them "a large upper room, furnished and prepared." Ancient writers remark that, at the time of the great feasts, the houses in Jerusalem were all open to receive guests—that they were in a manner common to the people of Judea; and there is no doubt, therefore, that the master of a house would have it ready on such occasions for company. It is possible, also, that there might have been an agreement between this man and our Lord that he would prepare his house for him, though this was unknown to the disciples. The word rendered *furnished* means, literally, *spread;* that is, *spread* with carpets, and with *couches* on which to recline at the table, after the manner of the East. See Notes on Mat. xxiii. 6.

19. *They made ready the passover.* That is, they procured a *lamb*, multitudes of which were kept for sale in the temple; they had it killed and flayed by the priests, and the blood poured by the altar; they roasted the lamb, and prepared the bitter herbs, the sauce, and the unleavened bread. This was done, it seems, while our Lord was absent, by the two disciples.

20. *When the even was come.* The lamb was killed *between the evenings*, Ex. xii. 6 (Hebrew)—that is between three o'clock, P.M., and nine in the evening. The Jews reckoned two evenings—one from three o'clock P.M. to sunset, the other from sunset to the close of the first watch in the night, or nine o'clock. The paschal supper was commonly eaten *after* the setting of the sun, and often in the night, Ex. xii. 8. ¶ *He sat down.* At first the supper was eaten standing, with their loins girded and their staff in their hand, denoting the haste with which they were about to flee from Egypt. Afterward, however, they introduced the practice, it seems, of partaking of this as they did of their ordinary meals. The original word is, *he reclined*—that is, he placed himself on the couch in a reclining posture, in the usual manner in which they partook of their meals. See Notes on Mat. xxiii. 6. While reclining there at the supper, the disciples had a dispute which should be the greatest. See Notes on Lu. xxii. 24-30. At this time, also, before the institution of the Lord's supper, Jesus washed the feet of his disciples, to teach them humility. See Notes on Jn. xiii. 1-20.

21-24. *As they did eat*, &c. The account contained in these verses is also recorded in Mar. xiv. 18-21; Lu. xxii. 21-23; Jn. xiii. 21, 22. John says that before Jesus declared that one of them should betray him, *he was troubled in spirit, and testified;* that is, he *felt deeply* in view of the greatness of the crime that Judas was about to commit, and the sufferings that he was to endure, and *testified*, or gave utterance to his inward feelings of sorrow.

22. *They were exceeding sorrowful.* John says (ch. xiii. 22) "they looked one on another, doubting of whom he spake"—that is, they anxiously looked one at another, conscious each one, except Judas, of no such intention, and each one beginning to examine himself to find whether he was the person intended. This showed their innocence, and their attachment to Jesus. It showed how *sensitive* they were to the least suspicion of the kind. It showed that they were willing to know themselves, thus evincing the spirit of the true Christian. Judas only was silent, and was the last to make the inquiry, and that after he had been plainly pointed out (ver. 25), thus showing, 1st, that guilt is slow to suspect itself; 2d, that it shrinks from the light; 3d, that it was his purpose to conceal his intention; and, 4th, that nothing but the consciousness that his Lord *knew his design* could induce him to make inquiry. The guilty would, if possible, always conceal their crimes. The innocent are ready to suspect that they *may* have done wrong. Their feelings are tender, and they inquire with solicitude whether there may not be something in their bosoms, unknown to themselves, that may be a departure from right feeling.

23. *He that dippeth* his *hand with me in the dish.* The Jews, at the observance of this ordinance, used a bitter *sauce*, made of bunches of raisins, mixed with vinegar and other seasoning of the like kind, which they said represented the *clay* which their fathers were com-

sorrowful, and began every one of them to say unto him, Lord, is it I?

23 And he answered and said, He[i] that dippeth *his* hand with me in the dish, the same shall betray me.

24 The Son of man goeth [k]as *it* is written of him: but woe unto that man by whom the Son of

i Ps.41.9; 55.12-15.

k Ps.22.; Is.53.

pelled to use in Egypt in making brick, thus reminding them of their bitter bondage there. This was probably the *dish* to which reference is made here. It is not improbable that Judas reclined near to our Saviour at the feast, and by his saying it was one that dipped *with him* in the dish, he meant one that was near to him, designating him more particularly than he had done before. John adds (xiii. 23-30; see Notes on that place), that "there was leaning on Jesus' bosom one of his disciples whom Jesus loved"—referring to himself; that Simon Peter beckoned to him to ask Jesus more particularly who it was; that Jesus signified who it was by giving *Judas a sop*—that is, a piece of *bread* or *meat* dipped in the thick sauce; and that Judas, having received it, went out to accomplish his wicked design of betraying him. Judas was not, therefore, present at the institution of the Lord's supper.

24. *The Son of man goeth.* That is, the Messiah—the Christ. See Notes on Mat. viii. 20. ¶ *Goeth.* Dies, or will die. The Hebrews often spoke in this manner of death, Ps. xxxix. 13; Ge. xv. 2. ¶ *As it is written of him.* That is, as it is *written* or prophesied of him in the Old Testament. Comp. Ps. xli. 9 with Jn. xiii. 18. See also Da. ix. 26, 27; Is. liii. 4-9. Luke (xxii. 22) says, *as it was determined.* In the Greek, as it was *marked out by a boundary*—that is, in the divine purpose. It was the previous *intention* of God to give him up to die for sin, or it could not have been certainly predicted. It is also declared to have been by his *determinate counsel and foreknowledge.* See Notes on Ac. ii. 23. ¶ *Woe unto that man,* &c. The crime is great and awful, and he will be punished accordingly. He states the greatness of his misery or "*woe*" in the phrase following. ¶ *It had been good,* &c. That is, it would have been better for him if he had not been born; or it would be better *now* for him if he was to be as *if* he had not been born, or if he was annihilated. This was a proverbial mode of speaking among the Jews in frequent use. In relation to *Judas,* it *proves* the following things: 1st, that the crime which he was about to commit was exceedingly great; 2d, that the misery or punishment *due to it* would *certainly* come upon him; 3d, that he would certainly *deserve* that misery, or it would not have been threatened or inflicted; and, 4th, that his punishment would be *eternal.* If there should be any *period* when the sufferings of Judas should *end,* and he be restored and raised to heaven, the blessings of that *happiness without end* would infinitely overbalance all the sufferings he could endure in a limited time, and consequently it would *not* be true that it would have been better for him not to have been born. Existence, to him, would, on the whole, be an infinite blessing. This passage proves farther that, in relation to *one* wicked man, the sufferings of hell will be eternal. If of *one,* then it is equally certain and proper that *all* the wicked will perish for ever.

If it be asked how this crime of Judas could be so great, or could be a crime at all, when it was determined beforehand that the Saviour should be betrayed and die in this manner, it may be answered—1st. That the crime was what it was *in itself,* apart from any determination of God. It was a violation of all the duties he owed to God and to the Lord Jesus—awful ingratitude, detestable covetousness, and most base treachery. As such it *deserved* to be punished. 2d. The previous purpose of God did not *force* Judas to do this. In it he acted freely. He did just what his wicked heart prompted him to do. 3d. A previous *knowledge* of a thing, or a previous *purpose* to permit a thing, does not alter *its nature,* or cause it to be a different thing from what it is. 4th. God, who is the best judge of the nature of crime, holds all that was done in crucifying the Saviour, though it was by his determinate counsel and foreknowledge, *to be by wicked hands,* Ac. ii. 23. This punishment of Judas proves, also, that sinners cannot take shelter for their sins in the decrees of God, or

man is betrayed! it had been good for that man if he had not been born.

25 Then Judas, which betrayed him, answered and said, Master, is it I? He said unto him, Thou hast said.

26 And *l* as they were eating, Jesus took bread, and [1]blessed *it*, and brake *it*, and gave *it* to the

l 1 Co.11.23,&c.
[1] Many Greek copies have, *gave thanks*.

plead them as an excuse. God will punish crimes for what they *are in themselves*. His own deep and inscrutable purposes in regard to human actions will not change *the nature* of those actions, or screen the sinner from the punishment which he deserves.

25. *Thou hast said*. That is, thou hast said the truth. It is so. Thou art the man. Comp. ver. 64 of this chapter with Mar. xiv. 62.

26–30. See also Mar. xiv. 22–26; Lu. xxii. 15–20; 1 Co. xi. 23–25.

26. *As they were eating*. As they were eating the paschal supper, near the close of the meal. Luke adds that he said, just before instituting the sacramental supper, "With desire have I desired to eat this passover with you before I suffer." This is a Hebrew manner of expression, signifying *I have greatly desired*. He had desired it, doubtless, (1), that he might institute the Supper, to be a perpetual memorial of him; (2), that he might strengthen them for their approaching trials; (3), that he might explain to them the true nature of the Passover; and, (4), that he might spend another season with them in the duties of religion. Every *Christian* about to die will also seek opportunities of drawing specially near to God, and of holding communion with him and with his people. ¶ *Jesus took bread*. That is, the unleavened bread which they used at the celebration of the Passover, made into thin cakes, easily broken and distributed. ¶ *And blessed* it. Or sought a blessing on it; or *gave thanks* to God for it. The word rendered *blessed* not unfrequently means *to give thanks*. Comp. Lu. ix. 16 and Jn. vi. 11. It is also to be remarked that some manuscripts have the word rendered *gave thanks*, instead of the one translated *blessed*. It appears from the writings of Philo and the Rabbins that the Jews were never accustomed to eat without giving thanks to God and seeking his blessing. This was especially the case in both the bread and the wine used at the Passover. ¶ *And brake* it. This *breaking* of the bread represented the sufferings of Jesus about to take place—his body *broken* or wounded for sin. Hence Paul (1 Co. xi. 24) adds, "This is my body which is *broken* for you;" that is, which is *about to be* broken for you by death, or wounded, pierced, bruised, to make atonement for your sins. ¶ *This is my body*. This *represents* my body. This broken bread shows the manner in which my body will be broken; or this will serve to recall my dying sufferings to your remembrance. It is not meant that his body would be literally *broken* as the bread was, but that the bread would be a significant emblem or symbol to recall to their recollection his sufferings. It is not improbable that our Lord pointed to the broken bread, or laid his hands on it, as if he had said, "Lo, my body!" or, "Behold my body!—that which *represents* my broken body to you." This *could not* be intended to mean that that bread was literally his body. It was not. His body was then before them *living*. And there is no greater absurdity than to imagine his *living body* there changed at once to *a dead body*, and then the *bread* to be changed *into* that dead body, and that all the while the *living* body of Jesus was before them. Yet this is the absurd and impossible doctrine of the Roman Catholics, holding that the *bread* and *wine* were literally changed into the *body* and *blood* of our Lord. The language employed by the Saviour was in accordance with a common mode of speaking among the Jews, and exactly similar to that used by Moses at the institution of the Passover (Ex. xii. 11): "It"—that is, the lamb—"*is* the Lord's passover." That is, the lamb and the feast *represent* the Lord's *passing over* the houses of the Israelites. It serves to *remind* you of it. It surely cannot be meant that that lamb was the literal *passing over* their houses—a palpable absurdity—but that it *represented* it. So Paul and Luke say of the bread, "This is my body broken for you: *this do* IN REMEMBRANCE *of me*." This expresses the whole design of the sacramental bread. It is to call *to remembrance*, in a vivid manner, the dying

disciples, and said, Take, eat; this is my body.

27 And he took the cup, and gave thanks, and gave *it* to them, saying, Drink ye all of it;

28 For this is my blood of the [m]new testament, which is shed for many for the remission of sins.

29 But I say unto you, I will not drink henceforth of this fruit

m Je.31.31.

---

sufferings of our Lord. The sacred writers, moreover, often denote that one thing is *represented* by another by using the word *is*. See Mat. xiii. 37: "He that soweth the good seed IS the Son of man"—that is, represents the Son of man. Ge. xli. 26: "The seven good kine ARE seven years"—that is, *represent* or signify seven years. See also Jn. xv. 1, 5; Ge. xvii. 10. The meaning of this important passage may be thus expressed: "As I give this broken bread to you to eat, *so* will I deliver my body to be afflicted and slain for your sins."

27. *And he took the cup.* That is, the cup of wine which was used at the feast of the Passover, called the cup of *Hallel*, or praise, because they commenced then repeating the *Psalms* with which they closed the Passover. See ver. 30. This cup, Luke says, he took *after supper*—that is, after they had finished the ordinary celebration of *eating* the Passover. The *bread* was taken *while* they were eating, the cup after they had done eating. ¶ *And gave thanks.* See Notes on ver. 26. ¶ *Drink ye all of it.* That is, "all of you, disciples, drink of it;" not, "drink *all* the wine."

28. *For this is my blood.* This *represents* my blood, as the bread does my body. Luke and Paul vary the expression, adding what Matthew and Mark have omitted. "This cup is the new testament in my blood." By this *cup* he meant the wine *in* the cup, and not the cup itself. Pointing to it, probably, he said, "This—*wine*—represents my blood about to be shed." The phrase "new testament" should have been rendered *new covenant*, referring to the *covenant* or *compact* that God was about to make with men through a Redeemer. The *old* covenant was that which was made with the Jews by the sprinkling of the blood of sacrifices. See Ex. xxiv. 8: "And Moses took the blood and sprinkled it on the people, and said, Behold the blood of the covenant which the Lord hath made with you," &c. In allusion to that, Jesus says, this cup is the NEW *covenant* in my blood; that is, which is *ratified, sealed,* or *sanctioned by my blood.* Anciently, covenants or contracts were ratified by slaying an animal; by the shedding of its blood, imprecating similar vengeance if either party failed in the compact. See Notes on He. ix. 16. So Jesus says the covenant which God is about to form with men—the new covenant, or the gospel economy—is sealed or ratified with *my* blood. ¶ *Which is shed for many for the remission of sins.* In order that sins may be remitted, or forgiven. That is, this is the appointed way by which God will pardon transgressions. That blood is efficacious for the pardon of sin—1st. Because it is *the life* of Jesus, the *blood* being used by the sacred writers as representing *life itself*, or as containing the elements of life, Ge. ix. 4; Le. xvii. 14. It was forbidden, therefore, to eat blood, because it contained the life, or was the life, of the animal. When, therefore, Jesus says that his blood was shed for many, it is the same as saying that *his life* was given for many. See Notes on Ro. iii. 25. 2d. His life was given for sinners, or he died in the place of sinners as their substitute. By his death on the cross, the death or punishment due to them in hell may be removed and their souls be saved. He endured *so much* suffering, bore *so much* agony, that God was pleased to accept it in the place of the eternal torments of all the redeemed. The interests of justice, the honour and stability of his government, would be as secure in saving them in this manner as if the suffering were inflicted on them personally in hell. God, by giving his Son to die for sinners, has shown his infinite abhorrence of sin; since, according to his view, and therefore according to *truth*, nothing else would show its evil nature but the awful sufferings of his own Son. That he died *in the stead* or *place* of sinners is abundantly clear from the following passages of Scripture: Jn. i. 29; Ep. v. 2; He. vii. 27; 1 Jn. ii. 2; iv. 10; Is. liii. 10; Ro. viii. 32; 2 Co. v. 15.

of the vine, until [n]that day when I drink it new with you in my Father's kingdom.

30 And when they had sung an hymn,[2] they went out into the mount of Olives.

31 Then saith Jesus unto them, All ye shall be offended because of me this night: for it is written, [o]I will smite the Shepherd, and the sheep of the flock shall be scattered abroad.

32 But after I am risen again, [p]I will go before you into Galilee.

n Is.25.6. 2 or, *psalm*. o Zec.13.7. p ch.28.7,10,16.

29. *But I say unto you*, &c. That is, the observance of the Passover, and of the rites shadowing forth future things, here end. I am about to die. The design of all these types and shadows is about to be accomplished. This is the last time that I shall partake of them with you. Hereafter, when my Father's kingdom is established in heaven, we will partake together of the thing represented by these *types* and *ceremonial observances*—the blessings and triumphs of redemption. ¶ *Fruit of the vine.* *Wine*, the *fruit* or *produce* of the vine—made of the grapes of the vine. ¶ *Until that day.* Probably the time when they should be received to heaven. It does not mean here on earth, farther than that they would partake with him in the happiness of spreading the gospel and the triumphs of his kingdom. ¶ *When I drink it new with you.* Not that he would partake with them of *literal* wine there, but in the thing represented by it. Wine was an important part of the feast of the Passover, and of all feasts. The kingdom of heaven is often represented under the image of a feast. It means that he will partake of joy with them in heaven; that they will share together the honours and happiness of the heavenly world. ¶ *New.* In a new manner, or perhaps *afresh.* ¶ *In my Father's kingdom.* In heaven. The place where God shall reign in a kingdom fully established and pure.

30. *And when they had sung a hymn.* The Passover was observed by the Jews by singing or *chanting* the 113th, 114th, 115th, 116th, 117th, and 118th Psalms. These they divided into two parts. The 113th and 114th Psalms they sung during the observance of the Passover, and the others at the close. There can be no doubt that our Saviour, and the apostles also, used the same psalms in their observance of the Passover. The word rendered *sung a hymn* is a participle, literally meaning *hymning*—not confined to a single hymn, but admitting many. ¶ *Mount of Olives.* See Notes on Mat. xx. 1.

31-35. *Jesus foretells the fall of Peter.* This is also recorded in Mar. xiv. 27-31; Lu. xxii. 31-34; Jn. xiii. 34-38.

31. *Then saith Jesus unto them.* The *occasion* of his saying this was Peter's bold affirmation that he was ready to *die* with him, Jn. xiii. 36. Jesus had told them that he was going away—that is, was about to die. Peter asked him whither he was going. Jesus replied that he could not follow him then, but should afterward. Peter, not satisfied with that, said that he was ready to lay down his life for him. Jesus then distinctly informed them that all of them would forsake him that very night. ¶ *All ye shall be offended because of me.* See Notes on Mat. v. 29. This language means, here, you will all *stumble* at my being taken, abused, and set at naught; you will be *ashamed* to own me as a teacher, and to acknowledge yourselves as my disciples; or, my being betrayed will prove a snare to you all, so that you will be guilty of the sin of forsaking me, and, by your conduct, of denying me. ¶ *For it is written*, &c. See Zec. xiii. 7. This is affirmed here to have reference to the Saviour, and to be fulfilled in him. ¶ *I will smite.* This is the language of God the Father. *I* will smite means either that I will give him up to be smitten (comp. Ex. iv. 21 with viii. 15, &c.), or that *I* will do it myself. Both of these things were done. God gave him up to the Jews and Romans, to be smitten for the sins of the world (Ro. viii. 32); and he himself *left* him to deep and awful sorrows—to bear "the burden of the world's atonement" alone. See Mar. xv. 34. ¶ *The Shepherd.* The Lord Jesus—the Shepherd of his people, Jn. x. 11, 14. Comp. Notes on Is. xl. 11. ¶ *The sheep.* This means *here* particularly *the apostles*. It also refers sometimes to all the followers of Jesus, the friends of God, Jn. x. 16; Ps. c. 3. ¶ *Shall be scattered abroad.* This refers

33 Peter answered and said unto him, Though all *men* shall be offended because of thee, *yet* will I never be offended.

34 Jesus said unto him, Verily I say unto thee, That this night, before the cock crow, thou shalt deny me thrice.

35 Peter said unto him, Though I should die with thee, yet will I

---

to their *fleeing*, and was fulfilled in that. See ver. 56 of this chapter.

32. *But after I am risen*, &c. This promise was given them to encourage and support them, and also to give them an indication where he might be found. He did not deny that he would first appear to a part of them before he met them all together (comp. Lu. xxiv. 13-31, 34; 1 Co. xv. 5), but that he would meet them *all* in Galilee. This was done. See Mar. xvi. 7; Mat. xxviii. 16. ¶ *Galilee.* See Notes on Mat. ii. 22.

33. *Peter answered—Though all* men, &c. The word *men* is improperly inserted here by the translators. Peter meant only to affirm this of *the disciples.* This confidence of Peter was entirely characteristic. He was ardent, sincere, and really attached to his Master. Yet this declaration was made evidently, 1st. From true love to Jesus. 2d. From too much reliance on his own strength. 3d. From ignorance of himself, and of the trials which he was soon to pass through. And it most impressively teaches us, 1st. That no strength of attachment to Jesus can justify such confident promises of fidelity, made without dependence on him. 2d. That all promises to adhere to him should be made relying on him for aid. 3d. That we little know how feeble we are till we are tried. 4th. That Christians *may be left* to great and disgraceful sins to show them their weakness.

Luke adds that Jesus said to Peter that Satan had desired to have him, that he might sift him as wheat—that is, that he might thoroughly *try* him. But Jesus says that he had prayed for him that his faith should not fail, and charged him when he was *converted*—that is, when he was *turned* from this sin—to strengthen his brethren; to wit, by teaching them to take warning by his example. See Notes on Lu. xxii. 31-33.

34. *This night.* This was in the *evening* when this was spoken, after the observance of the Passover, and, we may suppose, near nine o'clock. ¶ *Before the cock crow.* Mark and Luke add, before the cock crow *twice.* The cock is accustomed to crow twice—once at midnight, and once in the morning at break of day. The latter was commonly called cock-crowing. See Mar. xiii. 35. This was the time familiarly known as the cock-crowing, and of this Matthew and John speak, without referring to the other. Mark and Luke speak of the *second* crowing, and mean the same time, so that there is no contradiction between them. ¶ *Deny me thrice.* That is, as Luke adds, deny that *thou knowest* me. See ver. 74.

35. *Will I not deny thee.* Will not deny my connection with thee, or that I knew thee. *All* the disciples said the same thing, and all fled at the approach of danger, *forsaking* their Master and Friend, and practically denying that they knew him, ver. 56.

36-45. *Jesus's agony in Gethsemane.* This account is also recorded in Mar. xiv. 32-42; Lu. xxii. 39-46; Jn. xviii. 1.

36. *Then cometh*, &c. After the institution of the Supper, in the early part of the night, he went out to the Mount of Olives. In his journey he passed over the brook Cedron (Jn. xviii. 1), which bounded Jerusalem on the east. ¶ *Unto a place.* John calls this *a garden.* This garden was on the western side of the Mount of Olives, and a short distance from Jerusalem. The word used by John means not properly a garden for the cultivation of *vegetables*, but a place planted with the olive and other trees, perhaps with a fountain of water, and with walks and groves; a proper place of refreshment in a hot climate, and of retirement from the noise of the adjacent city. Such places were doubtless common in the vicinity of Jerusalem. Messrs. Fisk and King, American missionaries, were at the place which is commonly supposed to have been the garden of Gethsemane in 1823. They tell us that the garden is about a stone's cast from the brook of Cedron; that it now contains eight large and venerable-looking olives, whose trunks show their great antiquity. The spot is sandy and barren, and appears like a forsaken place. A low broken wall surrounds it. Mr.

not deny thee. Likewise also said all the disciples.

36 Then[q] cometh Jesus with them unto a place called Gethsemane, and saith unto the disciples, Sit ye here, while I go and pray yonder.

37 And he took with him Peter and the two sons of Zebedee, and began to be sorrowful and very heavy.

38 Then saith he unto them, [r]My soul is exceeding sorrowful, even unto death: tarry ye here, and watch with me.

39 And he went a little farther,

q Mar.14.32,&c.; Lu.22.39,&c.; Jn.18.1,&c.

r Ps.116.3; Is.53.3,10; Jn.12.27.

King sat down beneath one of the trees and read Is. liii., and also the gospel history of our Redeemer's sorrow during that memorable night in which he was there betrayed; and the interest of the association was heightened by the passing through the place of a party of Bedouins, armed with spears and swords. A recent traveller says of this place that it "is a field or garden about fifty paces square, with a few shrubs growing in it, and eight olive-trees of great antiquity, the whole inclosed with a stone wall." The place was probably fixed upon, as Dr. Robinson supposes, during the visit of Helena to Jerusalem, A.D. 326, when the places of the crucifixion and resurrection were believed to be identified. There is, however, no absolute certainty respecting the places. Dr. Thomson (*The Land and the Book*, vol. ii. p. 484) supposes it most probable that the real "Garden of Gethsemane" was several hundred yards to the northwest of the present Gethsemane, in a place much more secluded than the one usually regarded as that where the agony of the Saviour occurred, and therefore more likely to have been the place of his retirement. Nothing, however, that is of importance depends on ascertaining the exact spot.

Luke says that Jesus "went as he was wont"—that is, accustomed—"to the Mount of Olives." Probably he had been in the habit of retiring from Jerusalem to that place for meditation and prayer, thus enforcing by his example what he had so often done by his precepts—the duty of retiring from the noise and bustle of the world to hold communion with God. ¶ *Gethsemane.* This word is made up either of two Hebrew words, signifying *valley of fatness*—that is, a fertile valley; or of two words, signifying *an olive-press*, given to it, probably, because the place was filled with olives. ¶ *Sit ye here.* That is, in one part of the garden to which they first came. ¶ *While I go and pray yonder.* That is, at the distance of a stone's cast, Lu. xxii. 41. Luke adds that when he came to the garden he charged them to pray that they might not enter into temptation—that is, into deep *trials* and *afflictions*, or, more probably, into scenes and dangers that would tempt them to deny him.

37. *And he took with him Peter and the two sons of Zebedee.* That is, James and John, Mat. x. 2. On two other occasions he had favoured these disciples in a particular manner, suffering them to go with him to witness his power and glory, viz. at the healing of the ruler's daughter (Lu. viii. 51), and at his transfiguration on the mount, Mat. xvii. 1. ¶ *Sorrowful.* Affected with grief. ¶ *Very heavy.* The word in the original is much stronger than the one translated *sorrowful.* It means, to be pressed down or overwhelmed with great anguish. This was produced, doubtless, by a foresight of his great sufferings on the cross in making an atonement for the sins of men.

38. *My soul is exceeding sorrowful.* His human nature—his soul—was much and deeply affected and pressed down. ¶ *Even unto death.* This denotes extreme sorrow and agony. The sufferings of death are the greatest of which we have any knowledge; they are the most feared and dreaded by man; and those sufferings are therefore put for extreme and indescribable anguish. The meaning may be thus expressed: My sorrows are so great that under their burden I am ready to die; such is the anxiety of mind, that I seem to bear the pains of death! ¶ *Tarry ye here and watch with me.* The word rendered *watch* means, literally, to abstain from sleep; then to be vigilant, or to guard against danger. Here it seems to mean to sympathize with him, to unite with him in seeking divine support, and to prepare themselves for approaching dangers.

and fell on his face, and [s]prayed, saying, O my Father, if it be possible, let [t]this cup pass from me! nevertheless, [u]not as I will, but as thou *wilt*.

s He.5.7. t ch.20.22. u Jn.5.30; 6.38; Ro.15.3; Phi.2.8.

40 And he cometh unto the disciples, and findeth them asleep, and saith unto Peter, What! could ye not watch with me one hour?

41 Watch,[v] and pray, that [w]ye

v Mar.13.33; 14.38; Lu.22.40; Ep.6.18; Re.16.15. w Pr.4.14,15.

39. *And he went a little farther.* That is, at the distance that a man could conveniently cast a stone (Luke). ¶ *Fell on his face.* Luke says "he kneeled down." He did both. He *first* kneeled, and then, in the fervency of his prayer and the depth of his sorrow, he fell with his face on the ground, denoting the deepest anguish and the most earnest entreaty. This was the usual posture of prayer in times of great earnestness. See Nu. xvi. 22; 2 Ch. xx. 18; Ne. viii. 6. ¶ *If it be possible.* That is, if the world can be redeemed—if it be consistent with justice, and with maintaining the government of the universe, that men should be saved *without* this extremity of sorrow, let it be done. There is no doubt that if it had been possible it would have been done; and the fact that these sufferings were *not* removed, and that the Saviour went forward and bore them without mitigation, shows that it was *not* consistent with the justice of God and with the welfare of the universe that men should be saved without the awful sufferings of *such an atonement.* ¶ *Let this cup.* These bitter sufferings. These approaching trials. The word *cup* is often used in this sense, denoting sufferings. See Notes on Mat. xx. 22. ¶ *Not as I will, but as thou* wilt. As Jesus was man as well as God, there is nothing inconsistent in supposing that, *as* man, he was deeply affected in view of these sorrows. When he speaks of *his* will, he expresses what *human nature*, in view of such great sufferings, would desire. It naturally shrunk from them and sought deliverance. Yet he sought to do the will of God. He chose rather that the high purpose of God should be done, than that *that* purpose should be abandoned from regard to the fears of his human nature. In this he has left a model of prayer in all times of affliction. It is *right*, in times of calamity, to seek deliverance. Like the Saviour, also, in such seasons we *should*, we *must* submit cheerfully to the will of God, confident that in all these trials he is wise, and merciful, and good.

40. *And findeth them asleep.* It may seem remarkable that in such circumstances, with a suffering, pleading Redeemer near, surrounded by danger, and having received a special charge to *watch*—that is, not to sleep—they should so soon have fallen asleep. It is frequently supposed that this was proof of wonderful stupidity, and indifference to their Lord's sufferings. The truth is, however, that it was just the reverse; *it was proof of their great attachment, and their deep sympathy in his sorrows.* Luke has added that *he found them sleeping* FOR SORROW—that is, *on account* of their sorrow; or their grief was so great that they naturally fell asleep. Multitudes of facts might be brought to show that this is in accordance with the regular effects of grief. Dr. Rush says: "There is another symptom of grief, which is not often noticed, and that is *profound sleep.* I have often witnessed it even in mothers, immediately after the death of a child. Criminals, we are told by Mr. Akerman, the keeper of Newgate, in London, often sleep soundly the night before their execution. The son of General Custine slept nine hours the night before he was led to the guillotine in Paris."—*Diseases of the Mind*, p. 319. ¶ *Saith unto Peter,* &c. This earnest appeal was addressed to Peter particularly on account of his warm professions, his rash zeal, and his self-confidence. If he could not keep awake and watch with the Saviour for one hour, how little probability was there that he would adhere to him in the trials through which he was soon to pass!

41. *Watch.* See ver. 38. Greater trials are coming on. It is necessary, therefore, still to be on your guard. ¶ *And pray.* Seek aid from God by supplication, in view of the thickening calamities. ¶ *That ye enter not into temptation.* That ye be not *overcome* and *oppressed* with these trials of your faith so as to deny me. The word *temptation* here properly means what would *try* their faith in the approaching calamities—in his rejection and death. It

enter not into [x]temptation: [y]the spirit indeed *is* willing, but the flesh *is* weak.

42 He went away again the second time, and prayed, saying, O my Father, if this cup may not pass away from me, except I drink it, thy will be done.

x Re.3.10. y Is.26.8,9; Ro.7.18-25; Ga.5.17.

would *try* their faith, because, though they believed that he was the Messiah, they were not very clearly aware of the necessity of his death, and they did not fully understand that he was to rise again. They had cherished the belief that he was to establish a kingdom *while he lived.* When they should see him, therefore, rejected, tried, crucified, dead—when they should see him submit to all this *as if* he had not power to deliver himself—*then* would be the trial of their faith; and, in view of that, he exhorted them to pray that they might not *so* enter temptation as to be overcome by it and fall. ¶ *The spirit indeed* is *willing,* &c. The mind, the heart is ready and disposed to bear these trials, but the *flesh,* the natural feelings, through the fear of danger, is weak, and will be likely to lead you astray when the trial comes. Though you may have strong faith, and believe now that you will not deny me, yet human nature is weak, and shrinks at trials, and you should therefore seek strength from on high. This was intended to excite them, notwithstanding he knew that they loved him, to be on their guard, lest the weakness of human nature should be insufficient to sustain them in the hour of their temptation.

42-44. It is probable that our Lord spent considerable time in prayer, and that the evangelists have recorded rather *the substance* of his petitions than the very *words.* He returned repeatedly to his disciples, doubtless to caution them against danger, to show the deep interest which he had in their welfare, and to show them the extent of his sufferings on their behalf. Each time that he returned these sorrows deepened. Again he sought the place of prayer, and as his approaching sufferings overwhelmed him, this was the burden of his prayer, and he prayed the same words. Luke adds that amid his agonies an angel appeared from heaven strengthening him. His human nature began to sink, as unequal to his sufferings, and a messenger from heaven appeared, to support him in these heavy trials. It may seem strange that, since Jesus was divine (Jn. i. 1), the *divine nature* did not minister strength to the human, and that he that was *God* should receive strength from an *angel.* But it should be remembered that Jesus came in his human nature not only to make an atonement, but to be a perfect example of a holy man; that, as such, it was necessary to submit to the *common conditions* of humanity—that he should live as other men, be sustained as other men, suffer as other men, and be strengthened as other men; that he should, so to speak, take no advantage in favour of his piety, from his divinity, but submit in all things to the common lot of pious men. Hence he supplied his wants, not by his being divine, but in the ordinary way of human life; he preserved himself from danger, not *as God,* but by seeking the usual ways of human prudence and precaution; he met trials as a man; he received comfort as a man; and there is no absurdity in supposing that, in accordance with the condition of his people, his human nature should be strengthened, *as they are,* by those who are sent forth to be ministering spirits to the heirs of salvation, He. i. 14.

Luke farther adds (xxii. 44) that, being in an agony, he prayed more earnestly, and his sweat was as it were great drops of blood falling down to the ground. The word *agony* is taken from the anxiety, effort, and strong emotion of the *wrestlers* in the Greek games about to engage in a mighty struggle. Here it denotes the extreme anguish of mind, the strong conflict produced in sinking human nature from the prospect of deep and overwhelming calamities. ¶ *Great drops of blood,* Lu. xxii. 44. The word here rendered *great drops* does not mean drops gently falling on the ground, but rather thick and clammy masses of gore, pressed by inward agony through the skin, and, mixing with the sweat, falling thus to the ground. It has been doubted by some whether the sacred writer meant to say that there was actually *blood* in this sweat, or only that the sweat was *in the form* of great drops. The natural meaning is, doubtless, that the blood was mingled with his sweat; that it fell profusely—falling masses of gore; that it was pressed out by his inward anguish; and that this was caused

43 And he came and found them asleep again; for their eyes were heavy.

44 And he left them, and went away again, and prayed the [z]third time, saying the same words.

45 Then cometh he to his disciples, and saith unto them, Sleep on now and take *your* rest; behold, the hour is at hand, and the Son of man is betrayed into the hands of sinners.

z 2 Co.12.8.

in some way in view of his approaching death. This effect of extreme sufferings, of mental anguish, has been known in several other instances. Bloody sweats have been mentioned by many writers as caused by extreme suffering. Dr. Doddridge says (Note on Lu. xxii. 44) that "Aristotle and Diodorus Siculus both mention bloody sweats as attending some extraordinary agony of mind; and I find Loti, in his *Life of Pope Sextus V.*, and Sir John Chardin, in his *History of Persia*, mentioning a like phenomenon, to which Dr. Jackson adds another from Thuanus." It has been objected to this account that it is improbable, and that such an event could not occur. The instances, however, which are referred to by Doddridge and others show sufficiently that the objection is unfounded. In addition to these, I may observe that Voltaire has himself narrated a fact which ought for ever to stop the mouths of infidels. Speaking of Charles IX. of France, in his *Universal History*, he says: "He died in his thirty-fifth year. His disorder was of a very remarkable kind; the blood oozed out of all his pores. This malady, of which there have been other instances, was owing to either excessive fear, or violent agitation, or to a feverish and melancholy temperament."

Various opinions have been given of the probable causes of these sorrows of the Saviour. Some have thought it was a strong shrinking from the manner of dying on the cross, or from an apprehension of being *forsaken* there by the Father; others, that Satan was permitted in a peculiar manner to try him, and to fill his mind with horrors, having departed from him at the beginning of his ministry for a season (Lu. iv. 13), only to renew his temptations in a more dreadful manner now; and others that these sufferings were sent upon him as the wrath of God manifested against sin—that God *inflicted* them directly upon him by his own hand, to show his abhorrence of the sins of men for which he was about to die. Where the Scriptures are silent about *the cause*, it does not become us confidently to express an opinion. We may suppose, perhaps, without presumption, that a part or all these things were *combined* to produce this awful suffering. There is no need of supposing that there was a *single* thing that produced it; but it is rather probable that this was a *rush* of feeling from every quarter—his situation, his approaching death, the temptations of the enemy, the awful suffering on account of men's sins, and God's hatred of it about to be manifested in his own death—all coming upon his soul at once—sorrow flowing in from every quarter—the *concentration* of the sufferings of the atonement pouring together upon him and filling him with unspeakable anguish.

45. *Sleep on now and take* your *rest.* Most interpreters have supposed that this should be translated as a *question* rather than a command. "Do you sleep *now* and take your rest? Is this a time, amid so much danger and so many enemies, to give yourselves to sleep?" This construction is strongly countenanced by Lu. xxii. 46, where the expression, Why sleep ye? evidently refers to the same point of time. There is no doubt that the Greek will bear this construction, and in this way the apparent inconsistency will be removed between this command *to sleep*, and that in the next verse, *to rise* and be going. Others suppose that, his agony being over, and the necessity of watching *with him* being now past, he kindly *permitted* them to seek repose till they should be roused by the coming of the traitor; that while they slept Jesus continued still awake; that some considerable time elapsed between what was spoken here and in the next verse; and that Jesus suffered them to sleep until he saw Judas coming, and then aroused them. This is the most probable opinion. Others have supposed that he spoke this in irony: "Sleep on now, if you can; take rest, if possible, in such dangers and at such a time." But this supposition is un-

46 Rise, let us be going: behold, he is at hand that doth betray me.

47 And while he yet spake, lo, [a] Judas, one of the twelve, came, and with him a great multitude, with swords and staves, from the chief priests and elders of the people.

48 Now he that betrayed him gave them [b] a sign, saying, Whomsoever I shall kiss, that same is he: hold him fast.

a Ac.1.16. *b* Ps.38.12.

---

worthy the Saviour and the occasion. Mark adds, "It is enough." That is, sufficient time has been given to sleep. It is time to arise and be going. ¶ *The hour is at hand.* The *time* when the Son of man is to be betrayed is near. ¶ *Sinners.* Judas, the Roman soldiers, and the Jews.

46. *Rise, let us be going.* That is, probably, *with them.* Let us go wheresoever they shall lead us. The time when *I must die* is come. It is no longer proper to attempt an escape, and no more time can be given to repose.

47-57. The account of Jesus's being betrayed by Judas is recorded by all the evangelists. See Mar. xiv. 43-52; Lu. xxii. 47-53; Jn. xviii. 2-12.

47. *Judas, one of the twelve, came.* This was done while Jesus was addressing his disciples. John informs us that Judas knew the place, because Jesus was in the habit of going there with his disciples. Judas had passed the time, after he left Jesus and the other disciples at the Passover, in arranging matters with the Jews, collecting the band, and preparing to go. Perhaps, also, on this occasion they *gave* him the money which they had promised. ¶ *A great multitude with swords and staves.* John says that he had *received a band of men and officers from the chief priests and Pharisees.* Josephus says (*Antiq.* b. xx. ch. iv.) that at the festival of the Passover, when a great multitude of people came to observe the feast, lest there should be any disorder, a band of men was commanded to keep watch at the porches of the temple, to repress a tumult if any should be excited. This *band*, or guard, was at the disposal of the chief priests, Mat. xxvii. 65. It was composed of Roman soldiers, and was stationed chiefly at the tower of Antonia, at the north-west side of the temple. In addition to this, they had *constant* guards stationed around the temple, composed of Levites. The Roman soldiers were armed with *swords.* The other persons that went out carried, probably, whatever was accessible as a weapon. These were the persons *sent* by the priests to apprehend Jesus. Perhaps other desperate men might have joined them. ¶ *Staves.* In the original, "*wood;*" used here in the plural number. It means rather *clubs* or *sticks* than spears. It does not mean *staves.* Probably it means any weapon at hand, such as a mob could conveniently collect. John says that they had *lanterns* and *torches.* The Passover was celebrated at the *full moon;* but this night might have been cloudy. The place to which they were going was also shaded with trees, and lights, therefore, might be necessary.

48. *Gave them a sign.* That is, told them of a way by which they might know whom to apprehend—to wit, by his kissing him. It was night. Jesus was, besides, probably personally unknown to the *Romans*—perhaps to the others also. Judas, therefore, being well acquainted with him, to prevent the possibility of mistake, agreed to designate him by one of the tokens of friendship.

John tells us that Jesus, knowing all things, that should come upon him, when they approached him, asked them whom they sought, and that they replied, Jesus of Nazareth. He then informed them that he was the person they sought. They, when they heard it, overawed by his presence and smitten with the consciousness of guilt, went backward and fell to the ground. He again asked them whom they sought. They made the same declaration—Jesus of Nazareth. Jesus then, since they *professed* to seek only *him*, claimed the right that his disciples should be suffered to escape, "that the saying might be fulfilled which he spake (Jn. xviii. 9): Of them which thou gavest me have I lost none."

49. *Hail, Master.* The word translated *hail*, here, means to *rejoice*, to have joy, and also to have *cause* of joy. It thus expresses the *joy* which one friend has when he meets another,

49 And forthwith he came to Jesus, and said, Hail, Master; and [c]kissed him.

50 And Jesus said unto him, Friend,[d] wherefore art thou come? Then came they and laid hands on Jesus, and took him.

51 And, behold, one of them which were with Jesus stretched out *his* hand and drew his sword, and struck a servant of the high-priest, and smote off his ear.

52 Then said Jesus unto him, Put up again thy sword into his place; [e]for all they that take the sword shall perish with the sword.

53 Thinkest thou that I cannot now pray to my Father, and he

c 2 Sa.3.27; 20.9; Ps.28.3. d Ps.41.9; 55.13. e Ge.9.6; Eze.35.5,6; Re.13.10.

especially after an absence. It was used by the Jews and Greeks as a mode of salutation among friends. It would here seem to express the *joy* of Judas at finding his Master and again being *with him.* ¶ *Master.* In the original, *Rabbi.* See Notes on Mat. xxiii. 7. ¶ *Kissed him.* Gave him the common salutation of friends when meeting after absence. This mode of salutation was more common among Eastern nations than with us.

50. *And Jesus said unto him, Friend.* It seems strange to us that Jesus should give the endeared name *friend* to a man that he knew was his enemy, and that was about to betray him. It should be remarked, however, that this is the fault of *our language,* not of the original. In the Greek there are two words which our translators have rendered *friend*—one implying *affection* and *regard,* the other not. One is properly rendered *friend;* the other expresses more nearly what we mean by *companion.* It is this *latter* word which is given to the disaffected labourer in the vineyard: "*Friend,* I do thee no wrong" (Mat. xx. 13); to the guest which had not on the wedding-garment, in the parable of the marriage feast (Mat. xxii. 12); and to *Judas* in this place. ¶ *Wherefore art thou come?* This was said, not because he was ignorant why he had come, but probably to fill the mind of Judas with the consciousness of his crime, and by a striking question to *compel* him *to think* of what he was doing.

51. *One of them which were with Jesus.* John informs us that this was *Peter.* The other evangelists concealed the name, probably because they wrote while Peter was living, and it might have endangered Peter to have it known. ¶ *And drew his sword.* The apostles were not commonly armed. On this occasion they had provided *two swords,* Lu. xxii. 38. In seasons of danger, when travelling, they were under a necessity of providing means of defending themselves against the robbers that infested the country. This will account for their having *any* swords in their possession. See Notes on Lu. x. 30. Josephus informs us that the people were accustomed to carry swords under their garments as they went up to Jerusalem. ¶ *A servant of the high-priest.* His name, John informs us, was *Malchus.* Luke adds that Jesus touched the ear and healed it, thus showing his benevolence to his foes when they sought his life, and giving them proof that they were attacking him that was sent from heaven.

52. *Thy sword into his place.* Into the sheath. ¶ *For all they that take the sword,* &c. This passage is capable of different significations. 1st. They who resist by the sword the civil magistrate shall be punished; and it is dangerous, therefore, to oppose those who come with the authority of the civil ruler. 2d. These men, Jews and Romans, who have taken the sword against the innocent, shall perish by the sword. God will take vengeance on them. But, 3d. The most satisfactory interpretation is that which regards it as a *caution* to Peter. Peter was rash. Alone he had attacked the whole band. Jesus told him that his unseasonable and imprudent defence might be the occasion of his own destruction. In doing it he would endanger his life, for they who took the sword perished by it. This was probably a proverb, denoting that they who engaged in wars commonly perished there.

53. *Thinkest thou,* &c. Jesus says that not only would Peter endanger himself, but his resistance implied a distrust of the protection of God, and was an improper resistance of his will. If it had been proper that they should be rescued, God could easily have furnished far more efficient aid than that of Peter—a mighty host of angels. ¶ *Twelve*

shall presently give me [f] more than twelve legions of angels?

54 But how then shall the scriptures be fulfilled, that [g] thus it must be?

55 In that same hour said Jesus to the multitudes, Are ye come out, as against a thief, with swords and staves for to take me? I sat daily with you teaching in the temple, and ye laid no hold on me.

56 But all this was done that the [h] scriptures of the prophets might be fulfilled. Then all the disciples forsook him, and fled.

57 And [i] they that had laid hold on Jesus led *him* away to Caiaphas

f 2 Ki.6.17; Da.7.10; ch.4.11. *g* Lu.24.26,46.

h Ge.3.15; Ps.22.; 69.; Is.53.; La.4.20; Da.9.24,26; Zec.13.7; Ac.1.16.
i Mar.14.53,&c.; Lu.22.54,&c.; Jn.18.12,&c.

legions. A legion was a division of the Roman army amounting to more than six thousand men. See Notes on Mat. viii. 29. The number *twelve* was mentioned, perhaps, in reference to the number of his apostles and himself. Judas being away, but eleven disciples remained. God could guard *him*, and each disciple, with a legion of angels: that is, God could easily protect him, if he should pray to him, and if it was his will.

54. *But how then shall the scriptures be fulfilled*, &c. That is, the Scriptures which foretold of his dying for the world. In *some way* that must be accomplished, and the time had come when, having finished the work which the Father gave him to do, it was proper that he should submit to death. This was said, doubtless, to comfort his disciples; to show them that his death was not a matter of surprise or disappointment to him; and that *they*, therefore, should not be offended and forsake him.

55. *Against a thief.* Rather a *robber.* This was the *manner* in which they would have sought to take a highwayman of desperate character, and armed to defend his life. It adds not a little to the depth of his humiliation that he consented to be *hunted down* thus by wicked men, and to be treated as if he had been the worst of mankind. ¶ *Daily with you teaching in the temple.* For many days before the Passover, as recorded in the previous chapter.

56. *Scriptures of the prophets.* The *writings* of the prophets, for that is the meaning of the word *scriptures.* He alludes to those parts of the prophetic writings which foretold his sufferings and death. ¶ *Then all the disciples*, &c. Overcome with fear when they saw their Master actually taken; alarmed with the terrific appearance of armed men and torches in a dark night, and forgetting their promises *not* to forsake him, they all left their Saviour to go *alone* to trial and to death! Alas! how many, when attachment to Christ would lead them to danger, leave him and flee! Mark adds that after the disciples had fled, a young man, having a linen cloth cast about his naked body, attempted to follow him. It is not known who he was, but not improbably he may have been the *owner* of the garden and a friend of Jesus. Aroused by the noise from his repose, he came to defend, or at least to follow the Saviour. He cast, in his hurry, such a covering as was at hand around his body, and came to him. The young men among the Romans and Jews attempted to seize him also, and he only secured his safety by leaving in their hands the covering that he had hastily thrown around him. It is not known *why* this circumstance was recorded by Mark, but it would seem to be probable that it was to mention him with honour, as showing his interest in the Saviour, and his willingness to aid him. See Notes on Mar. xiv. 50, 51. This circumstance *may* have been recorded for the purpose of honouring him by placing his conduct in strong contrast with that of the apostles, who had all forsaken the Saviour and fled.

57–75. The trial of our Lord before the council, and the denial of Peter happening at the same time, might be related one before the other, according to the evangelists' pleasure. Accordingly, Matthew and Mark relate the *trial* first, and Peter's denial afterward; Luke mentions the denial first, and John has probably observed the natural order. The parallel places are recorded in Mar. xiv. 53–72; Lu. xxii. 54–71; and Jn. xviii. 13–27.

57. *To Caiaphas.* John says that they led him first to Annas, the father-in-law of Caiaphas. This was done, probably as a mark of respect, he having

the high-priest, where the scribes and the elders were assembled.

58 But Peter followed him afar off, unto the high-priest's palace, and went in, and sat with the servants, to see the end.

59 Now the chief priests and elders, and all the council, sought

---

been high-priest, and perhaps distinguished for prudence, and capable of *advising* his son-in-law in a difficult case. The Saviour was *detained* there, probably, until the chief priests and elders were assembled. ¶ *The high-priest.* Note, Mat. xxvi. 3. John says he was high-priest for that year. Annas had been high-priest some years before. In the time of our Saviour the office was frequently changed by the civil ruler. This Caiaphas had prophesied that it was expedient that one should die for the people. See Notes on Jn. xi. 49, 50. ¶ *The scribes and elders.* The men composing the great council of the nation, or Sanhedrim, Mat. v. 22. It is not probable that they could be immediately assembled, and some part of the transaction respecting the denial of Peter probably took place while they were collecting.

58. *Peter followed afar off.* By this he evinced two things: 1st. Real attachment to his Master; a desire to be near him and to witness his trial. 2d. Fear respecting his personal safety. He therefore kept so far off as to be out of danger, and yet so near as that he might witness the transactions respecting his Master. Perhaps he expected to be lost and unobserved in the crowd. Many, in this, imitate Peter. They are afraid to follow the Saviour closely. They fear danger, ridicule, or persecution. They *follow him*, but it is at a great distance—*so far* that it is difficult to discern that they are in the train, and are his friends at all. Religion requires us to be near to Christ. We may measure our piety by our desire to be with him, to be like him, and by our willingness to follow him always—through trials, contempt, persecution, and death. Comp. Notes on Phi. iii. 10. John says that another disciple went with Peter. By that other disciple it is commonly supposed, as he did not mention his name, that he meant himself. He was acquainted with the high-priest, and went immediately into the hall. ¶ *Unto the high-priest's palace.* The word rendered *palace* means, rather, the *hall*, or middle court, or *area* of his house. It was situated in the centre of the palace, and was commonly uncovered. See Notes and plan of a house in Mat. ix. 1–8. ¶ *And went in.* John informs us that he did not go immediately in; but the other disciple, being known to the high-priest, went in first, while Peter remained at the *gate* or entrance. The other disciple then went out and brought in Peter. Matthew, Mark, and Luke have omitted this circumstance. John recorded it, probably, *because* they had omitted it, and because *he* was the "other disciple" concerned in it. ¶ *Sat with the servants to see the end.* That is, the end of the trial, or to see how it would go with his Master. The other evangelists say that he stood with the servants warming himself. John says, it being cold, they had made a fire of coals and warmed themselves. It was then, probably, not far from midnight. The place where they were was uncovered; and travellers say that, though the *days* are warm in Judea at that season of the year, yet that the nights are often uncomfortably cold. This fire was made *in the hall* (Luke). The fire was not in *a fireplace*, as we commonly suppose, but was probably made of *coals* laid on the pavement. At this place and time was Peter's first *denial* of his Lord, as is recorded afterward. See ver. 69.

59. *False witness.* That is, they sought for witnesses who would accuse him of crime—of violation of the laws of the land or of God. We are not to suppose that *they wished* them to be *false* witnesses. They were indifferent, probably, whether they were true or false, if they could succeed in condemning him. *The evangelist* calls it false testimony. Before these witnesses were sought, we learn from John (xviii. 19–23) that the high-priest asked Jesus of his disciples and his doctrine. Jesus replied that he had taught openly in the temple, and in secret had said nothing; that is, he had no *secret doctrines* which he had not been willing openly to teach, and he referred the high-priest to those who had heard him. In a firm, dignified manner he put himself on trial, and insisted on his rights. "If I have spoken evil, bear witness of the evil; but if well, why smitest thou me?" Jn. xviii. 23.

false witness against Jesus, to put him to death;

60 But found none; yea, though many false witnesses came, *yet* found they none. At the last came [k]two false witnesses,

61 And said, This *fellow* said, I[l] am able to destroy the temple of God, and to build it in three days.

62 And the high-priest arose, and said unto him, Answerest thou nothing? What *is it which* these witness against thee?

63 But [m]Jesus held his peace. And the high-priest answered and said unto him, I [n]adjure thee by the living God that thou tell us whether thou be [o]the Christ, the Son of God.

k Ps.27.12; 35.11. l Jn.2.19,21.

m Is.53.7; ch.27.12,14. n 1 Sa.14.26,28; 1 Ki.22.16. o ch.16.16; Jn.1.34.

This conversation took place, probably, before the council was assembled, and during this time the denials by Peter occurred. Luke informs us (xxii. 66) that the council came together as soon as it was day; that is, probably, near the morning, or not far from the break of day—after Peter had denied him and gone out.

60. *Found none.* That is, they found none on whose testimony they could with any show of reason convict him. The reason was, as Mark says (xiv. 56), that "their witnesses agreed not together." They differed about facts, times, and circumstances, as all false witnesses do. Two witnesses were required by their law, and they did not *dare* to condemn him without conforming, *in appearance* at least, to the requirements of the law.

61. *And said, This* fellow *said*, &c. Mark has recorded this testimony differently. According to him, they said, "We heard him say, I will destroy this temple that is made with hands, and within three days I will build another made without hands." Probably both forms of giving in the testimony were used on the trial, and Matthew has recorded it as it was given at one time and Mark at another, so that there is no contradiction. Mark adds, "But neither so did their witnesses agree together." That which they *attempted* to accuse him of is what he had said respecting his body and their destroying it, Jn. ii. 19: "Destroy this temple, and in three days I will raise it up." This he spoke of his body; they perverted it, endeavouring to show that he meant the temple at Jerusalem. They neither stated it as it was, nor did they state correctly its meaning, nor did they agree about the *words* used. It was therefore very little to their purpose.

62, 63. *Jesus held his peace.* Was silent. He knew that the evidence did not even *appear* to amount to anything worth a reply. He knew that they were aware of that, and that feeling that, the high-priest attempted to draw something from him on which they could condemn him. ¶ *I adjure thee by the living God.* I put thee upon thy oath before God. This was the usual form of putting an oath among the Jews. It implies calling God to witness the truth of what was said. The law respecting witnesses also made it a violation of an oath to *conceal* any part of the truth; and though our Saviour might have felt that such a question, put in such a manner, was very improper or was unlawful, yet he also knew that to be silent would be construed into a denial of his being the Christ. The question was probably put in anger. They had utterly failed in their proof. They had no way left to accomplish their purpose of condemning him but to draw it from his own lips. This cunning question was therefore proposed. The difficulty of the question consisted in this: If he *confessed* that he was the Son of God, they stood ready to condemn him for *blasphemy;* if he *denied it*, they were prepared to condemn him for being an *impostor*, and for deluding the people under the pretence of being the Messiah. ¶ *The living God.* Jehovah is called the *living* God in opposition to *idols*, which were without life. ¶ *The Christ.* The Messiah, the Anointed. See Notes on Mat. i. 1. ¶ *The Son of God.* The Jews uniformly expected that the Messiah would be the Son of God. In their view it denoted, also, that he would be *divine*, or equal to the Father, Jn. x. 31–36. To claim that title was therefore, in their view, *blasphemy;* and as they had determined beforehand in their own minds that he was *not* the Messiah, they were ready at once to accuse him of blasphemy.

64 Jesus saith unto him, Thou hast said: nevertheless I say unto you, [p]Hereafter shall ye see the Son of man sitting on the [q]right hand of power, and coming in the clouds of heaven.

65 Then the high-priest rent his clothes, saying, He hath spoken blasphemy; what further need have we of witnesses? behold, now ye have heard his blasphemy.

66 What think ye? They answered and said, [r]He is guilty of death.

67 Then[s] did they spit in his face, and buffeted him; and others

p Da.7.13; Jn.1.51; 1 Th.4.16; Re.1.7.
q Ps.110.1; Ac.7.55.
r Le.24.16; Jn.19.7.
s Is.50.6.

---

64. *Thou hast said.* This is a form of *assenting* or affirming. Thou hast said the *truth;* or, as Luke (xxii. 70) has it, "Ye say that I am." This was not, however, said *immediately*. Before Jesus acknowledged himself to be the Messiah, he said to them (Lu. xxii. 67, 68), "*If I tell you ye will not believe, and if I also ask you*"—that is, propose the proofs of my mission, and require you to give your opinion of them—"*ye will not answer me, nor let me go.*" ¶ *Nevertheless.* This word should have been translated *moreover* or *furthermore*. What follows is designed to explain and give confirmation to what he had said. ¶ *Sitting on the right hand of power.* That is, of God, called here *the Power*—equivalent to *the Mighty*, or *the Almighty*. It denotes dignity and majesty; for to sit at the right hand of a prince was the chief place of honour. See Notes on Mat. xx. 21. ¶ *Coming in the clouds of heaven.* See Notes on Mat. xxiv., xxv. The meaning of this is, You shall see *the sign from heaven* which you have so often demanded; even the Messiah returning himself *as the sign*, with great glory, to destroy your city and to judge the world.

65. *Then the high-priest rent his clothes.* The Jews were accustomed to rend their clothes as a token of grief. This was done often as a matter of form, and consisted in tearing a particular part of the garment reserved for this purpose. It was not lawful for the high-priest to rend his clothes, Le. x. 6; xxi. 10. By that was probably intended the robes of his priestly office. The garment which he *now* rent was probably his ordinary garment, or the garments which he wore as president of the Sanhedrim—not those in which he officiated as high-priest in the things of religion. This was done on this occasion to denote the *great grief* of the high-priest that so great a sin as blasphemy had been committed in his presence. ¶ *He hath spoken blasphemy.* That is, he has, under oath, arrogated to himself what belongs to God. In asserting that he is the Son of God, and therefore equal in dignity with the Father, and that he would yet sit at his right hand, he has claimed what belongs to no *man*, and what is therefore an invasion of the divine prerogative. If he had not been the *Messiah*, the charge would have been true; but the question was whether he had not given evidence that he *was* the Messiah, and that therefore his claims were just. This point—the only *proper* point of inquiry—they never examined. They *assumed* that he was an *impostor*, and that point being assumed, everything like a pretension to being the Messiah was, in their view, proof that he deserved to die.

66. *What think ye?* What is your *opinion?* What *sentence* do you pronounce? As president of the Sanhedrim he demanded their judgment. ¶ *He is guilty of death.* This was the form which was used when a criminal was condemned to die. The meaning is, he is guilty of a crime to which the law annexes death. This sentence was used before the Jews became subject to the Romans, when they had the power of inflicting death. After they were subject to the Romans, though the power of *inflicting* capital punishment was taken away, yet they retained the *form* when they expressed their opinion of the guilt of an offender. The law under which they condemned him was that recorded in Le. xxiv. 10–16, which sentenced him that was guilty of blasphemy to death by *stoning*. The chief priests, however, were unwilling to excite a popular tumult by stoning him, and they therefore consulted to deliver him to the Romans to be crucified, *under the authority of the Roman name*, and thus to prevent any excitement among the people.

67. *Then did they spit in his face.* This, among the Jews, as among us,

smote *him* with [3]the palms of their hands,

68 Saying, Prophesy unto us, thou Christ, who is he that smote thee?

69 Now[t] Peter sat without in the palace: and a damsel came unto him, saying, Thou also wast with Jesus of Galilee.

70 But he denied before *them* all, saying, I know not what thou sayest.

71 And when he was gone out into the porch, another *maid* saw

3 or, *rods.*
t Mar.14.66,&c.; Lu.22.55,&c.; Jn.18.16,&c.

was significant of the highest contempt and insult, Nu. xii. 14; Isa. l. 6; Job xxx. 10. ¶ *And buffeted him.* That is, they struck him with their hands closed, or with the *fist.* ¶ *Others smote* him *with the palms of their hands.* The word used in the original here means literally to strike with *rods.* It also means to strike *the mouth* with the open hand, as if to prevent a person's speaking, or to evince abhorrence of what he had spoken.

68. *Saying, Prophesy unto us,* &c. Mark informs us that before they said this they had blindfolded him. Having prevented his seeing, they ridiculed his pretensions of being the Messiah. If he was the Christ, they supposed he could tell who smote him. As he bore it patiently and did not answer, they doubtless supposed that they had discovered another reason to think he was an impostor. The word *prophesy* does not mean only to foretell future events, although that is the proper meaning of the word, but also to declare anything that is unknown, or anything which cannot be known by natural knowledge or without revelation. Luke adds, "And many other things blasphemously spake they against him." There is something very remarkable in this expression. They had charged *him* with *blasphemy* in claiming to be the Son of God. This charge they were not able to prove; but the evangelist *fixes* the charge of *blasphemy* on them, because he really *was* the Son of God, and they denied it.

69. *Now Peter sat without in the palace.* Mark says the first denial took place while Peter was "beneath in the palace." This *palace* was the large *hall* or court belonging to the residence of the high-priest. The part of it where Jesus and the council were was *elevated,* probably above the rest for a tribunal. Peter was *beneath,* or in the *lower part* of the hall, with the servants at the fire. Yet, as Matthew says, he sat *without* in the palace—that is, *out of* the palace where they were trying Jesus—to wit, in the lower part of the hall with the servants; both narratives are therefore consistent. ¶ *And a damsel came unto him.* John (xviii. 17) says that this damsel was one that kept the door. ¶ *Thou also wast with Jesus of Galilee.* Probably she suspected him from his being in company with John. This was in the early part of the trial of Jesus.

70. *But he denied before* them *all,* &c. He denied that he was a disciple; he denied that he knew Jesus; he denied (Mark) that he *understood* what was meant—that is, he did not see any reason why this question was asked. All this was palpable falsehood, and Peter must have known that it was such. This is remarkable, because Peter had just before been so confident. It is more remarkable, because the edge of the charge was taken off by the insinuation that *John* was known to be a disciple—thou *also* wast with Jesus of Galilee.

71. *When he was gone out into the porch.* The *entrance,* or the small apartment between the outer door and the large hall in the centre of the building. See plan of a house, Notes, Mat. ix. 1–8. Peter was embarrassed and confused by the question, and to save his confusion from attracting notice, he went away from the fire into the porch, where he expected to be unobserved—yet in vain. By the very movement to avoid detection, he came into contact with another who knew him and repeated the charge. How clearly does it prove that our Lord was omniscient, that all these things were foreseen! ¶ *Another* maid *saw him.* Mark simply says that *a maid* saw him. From Luke it would appear that *a man* spoke to him, Lu. xxii. 58. The truth probably is that both were done. When he first went out, *a maid* charged him with being a follower of Jesus. He was probably there a considerable time. To this charge he might have been silent, thinking, perhaps, that he was con-

him, and said unto them that were there, This *fellow* was also with Jesus of Nazareth.

72 And again he denied with an oath, I do not know the man.

73 And after a while came unto *him* they that stood by, and said to Peter, Surely thou also art *one* of them, for thy speech bewrayeth thee.

74 Then began he to curse and to swear, *saying*, I know not the man. And immediately the cock crew.

75 And Peter remembered [u]the word of Jesus, which said unto

u ver.34; Lu.22.31-34.

cealed, and there was no need of denying Jesus then. Yet it is very likely that the charge would be repeated. A *man*, also, might have repeated it; and Peter, irritated, provoked, perhaps thinking that he was in danger, *then* denied his Master the second time. This denial was in a stronger manner and with an oath. While in the porch, Mark says, the cock crew—that is, the first crowing, or not far from midnight.

73. *And after a while.* That is, about an hour after (Luke). Peter by this time had returned into the palace or hall, and stood warming himself by the fire, Jn. xviii. 25. ¶ *Thy speech bewrayeth thee.* Your language makes it manifest that you are of his company. That is, as Mark adds, he was *a Galilean*, and in this way his speech betrayed him. It is probable that the Galileans were distinguished for some peculiarity of pronunciation, perhaps some peculiar rusticity or coarseness in their manner of speaking, that distinguished them from the refinement of the capital, Jerusalem. This charge, John says (xviii. 26), was supported by the express affirmation of a kinsman of Malchus, the servant of the high-priest, that he had seen him in the garden.

74. *Then began he to curse*, &c. Peter was now irritated beyond endurance. He could no longer resist the evidence that he was known. It had been repeatedly charged on him. His language had betrayed him, and there was a positive witness who had seen him. He felt it necessary, therefore, to be still more decided, and he accordingly added to the sin of denying his Lord the deep aggravation of profane cursing and swearing, affirming what he must have known was false, that he knew not the man. Immediately then the cock crew — that is, the second crowing, or not far from three in the morning.

75. *And Peter remembered the word of Jesus*, &c. Luke has mentioned a beautiful and touching circumstance omitted by the other evangelists, that when the cock crew, *Jesus turned and looked upon Peter*, and that then he remembered his words. They were in the same room—Jesus at the upper end of the hall, elevated for a tribunal and Peter below with the servants, so that Jesus could look down upon Peter standing near the fire. By a tender and compassionate look—a single glance of his eye—the injured Saviour brought to remembrance all Peter's promises, his own predictions, and the great guilt of the disciple; he overwhelmed him with the remembrance of his sin, and pierced his heart through with many sorrows. The consciousness of deep and awful guilt rushed over Peter's soul; he flew from the palace, he went where he might be alone in the darkness of the night, and *wept bitterly*.

The fall of Peter is one of the most melancholy instances of depravity ever committed in our world. But a little while before so confident; seated at the table of the Lord; distinguished throughout the ministry of Christ with peculiar favours; cautioned against this very thing; yet so soon denying him, forgetting his promises, and profanely calling on God to witness what he knew to be false—that he did not *know* him! Had it been but *once*, it would have been awful guilt—guilt deeply piercing the Redeemer's soul in the day of trial; but it was three times repeated, and at last with profane cursing and swearing. Yet, while we weep over Peter's fall, and seek not to palliate his crime, we should draw from it important practical uses: 1st. The danger of self-confidence. He that thinketh he standeth should take heed lest he fall. True Christian confidence is that which relies on God for strength, and feels safety only in the belief that *He* is able and willing to keep from temptation. 2d. The highest favours, the most exalted privileges, do not secure us from the danger of falling

him, Before the cock crow, thou shalt deny me thrice. And he went out and wept bitterly.

CHAPTER XXVII.

WHEN the morning was come, all the chief priests and

into sin. Few men were ever so highly favoured as Peter; few ever so dreadfully departed from the Saviour, and brought so deep a scandal on religion. 3d. When a man *begins* to sin, his fall from one act to another is easy—perhaps almost certain. At first Peter's sin was only simple denial; then it increased to more violent affirmation, and ended with open profaneness. So the downward road of crime is easy. When sin is *once* indulged, the way is open for a whole deluge of crime, nor is the course easily stayed till the soul is overwhelmed in awful guilt. 4th. True repentance is deep, thorough, bitter. Peter wept bitterly. It was sincere sorrow — sorrow proportioned to the nature of the offence he had committed. 5th. A look from Jesus—a look of mingled affection, pity, and reproof—produces bitter sorrow for sin. *Him* we injure by our crimes; and *his* tender look, when we err, pierces the soul through with many sorrows, opens fountains of tears in the bosom, and leads us to weep with bitterness over our transgressions. 6th. When we sin —when we fall into temptation—let us retire from the world, seek the place of solitude, and pour out our sorrows before God. He will mark our groans; he will hear our sighs; he will behold our tears; and he will receive us to his arms again. 7th. Real Christians may be suffered to go far astray. To show them their weakness, to check self-confidence, and to produce dependence on Jesus Christ, they may be permitted to show how weak, and feeble, and rash they are. Peter was a real believer. Jesus had prayed for him *that his faith should fail not*, Lu. xxii. 32. Jesus was *always* heard in his prayer, Jn. xi. 42. He was heard, therefore, then. Peter's *faith* did not fail—that is, his *belief* in Jesus, his real piety, his *true* attachment to the Saviour. He *knew* during the whole transaction that Jesus was the Messiah, and that *he himself* was well acquainted with him; but he was suffered to declare that which he knew was not true, and in *this* consisted his sin. Yet, 8th. Though a Christian *may* be suffered to go astray—*may* fall into sin—yet he who should, from this example of Peter, think that he might lawfully do it, or who should *resolve* to do it, thinking that he might, like Peter, weep and repent, would give evidence that he knew nothing of the grace of God. He that *resolves* to sin under the expectation of repenting hereafter *cannot be a Christian.*

It is worthy of further remark, that the fact that the fall of Peter is recorded by *all* the evangelists is high proof of their *honesty.* They were willing to tell the truth as it was; to conceal no fact, even if it made much against themselves, and to make mention of their *own* faults without attempting to *appear* to be better than they were. And it is worthy of special observation that *Mark* has recorded this with *all* the circumstances of aggravation, perhaps even more so than the others. Yet, by the universal belief of antiquity, the Gospel of *Mark* was written under *Peter's* direction, and every part of it submitted to him for examination. Higher proof of the *honesty* and *candour* of the evangelists could not be demanded.

CHAPTER XXVII.

1, 2. *Jesus is brought before Pilate.* See also Mar. xvi. 1; Lu. xxiii. 1; Jn. xviii. 28.

1. *When the morning was come.* This was not long after Jesus had been condemned by the Sanhedrim. Peter's last denial was probably not far from three o'clock, or near the break of day. As soon as it was light, the Jews consulted together for the purpose of taking his life. The sun rose at that season of the year in Judea not far from five o'clock, and the time when they assembled, therefore, was not long after Peter's denial. ¶ *The chief priests and elders of the people took counsel.* They had on his trial (ch. xxvi. 65, 66) agreed that he deserved to die, *on a charge of blasphemy;* yet they did not *dare* to put him to death by stoning, as they did afterward Stephen (Ac. vii.), and as the law commanded in case of blasphemy; for they feared the people. They therefore *consulted*, or took counsel together, to determine on what pretence they could deliver him to the Roman emperor, or to fix some charge of a civil nature by which Pilate might be in-

elders of the people [a]took counsel against Jesus to put him to death.

2 And when they had bound him, they led *him* away, and [b]delivered him to Pontius Pilate the governor.

3 Then Judas, which had betrayed him, when he saw that he was condemned, repented himself, and brought again the thirty pieces of silver to the chief priests and elders,

4 Saying, I have sinned, in that I have betrayed the [c]innocent

a Ps.2.2. b ch.20.19. c 2 Ki.24.4.

duced to condemn him. The charge which they fixed on was not that on which *they* had tried him, and on which they had determined he ought to die, but *that of perverting the nation, and of forbidding to give tribute to Cæsar*, Lu. xxiii. 2. On *this* accusation, if made out, they supposed Pilate could be induced to condemn Jesus. On a charge of *blasphemy* they knew he could not, as that was not an offence against the Roman laws, and over which, therefore, Pilate claimed no jurisdiction. ¶ *To put him to death.* To devise some way by which he might be put to death under the authority of the Roman governor.

2. *And when they had bound him.* He was *bound* when they took him in the garden, Jn. xviii. 12. Probably when he was tried before the Sanhedrim in the palace of Caiaphas, he had been loosed from his bonds, being there surrounded by multitudes, and supposed to be safe. As they were about to lead him to another part of the city now, they again bound him. The binding consisted, probably, in nothing more than tying his hands. ¶ *Pontius Pilate, the governor.* The governor appointed by the Romans over Judea. The governor commonly resided at *Cesarea;* but he came up to Jerusalem usually at the great feasts, when great numbers of the Jews were assembled, to administer justice, and to suppress tumults if any should arise. The *title* which Pilate received was that of *governor* or *procurator.* The duties of the office were, chiefly, to collect the revenues due to the Roman emperor, and in certain cases to administer justice. Pilate was appointed governor of Judea by Tiberius, then Emperor of Rome. John says (xviii. 28) that they led Jesus from Caiaphas to the hall of judgment—that is, to the part of the *prætorium*, or governor's palace, where justice was administered. The Jews did not, however, enter in themselves, lest they should be defiled, but that they might eat the Passover. In Nu. xix. 22 it is said that whosoever touched an unclean thing should be unclean. For this reason they would not enter into the house of a *heathen*, lest they should contract some defilement that would render them unfit to keep the Passover.

3. *Then Judas, when he saw that he was condemned, repented himself.* This shows that Judas did not suppose that the affair would have resulted in this calamitous manner. He probably expected that Jesus would work a miracle to deliver himself, and not suffer this condemnation to come upon him. When he saw him taken, bound, tried, and condemned—when he saw that all probability that he would deliver himself was taken away—he was overwhelmed with disappointment, sorrow, and remorse. The word rendered *repented himself*, it has been observed, does not of necessity denote a change *for the better*, but *any* change of views and feelings. Here it evidently means no other change than that produced by the horrors of a guilty conscience, and by deep remorse for crime at its unexpected results. It was not saving repentance. That leads to a holy life—this led to an increase of crime in his own death. True repentence leads the sinner to the Saviour. This led *away* from the Saviour to the gallows. Judas, if he had been a true penitent, would have come *then* to Jesus; would have confessed his crime at his feet, and sought for pardon there. But, overwhelmed with remorse and the conviction of vast guilt, he was not willing to come into his presence, and added to the crime of *treason* that of *self-murder*. Assuredly such a man could not be a true penitent.

4. *I have sinned.* I have been guilty. I have done wrong. ¶ *In that I have betrayed the innocent blood.* That is, in betraying an innocent being to death. *Blood* is put here for *life*, or for the *man.* The meaning is, that he knew and felt that Jesus was innocent. This

blood. And they said, What *is that* to us? See thou *to that.*

5 And he cast down the pieces of silver in the temple, and departed, and went and [d]hanged himself.

6 And the chief priests took the

d Ps.55.23; 2 Sa.17.23; Ac.1.18.

confession is a remarkable proof that Jesus *was* innocent. Judas had been with him three years. He had seen him in public and private; he had heard his public teaching and his private views; he had seen him in all circumstances; and if he *had* done anything evil, or advanced anything against the Roman emperor, Judas was competent to testify it. Had he *known* any such thing he would have stated it. *His* testimony, being a disciple of Jesus, would have been to the chief priests far more valuable than that of any other man; and he might not only have escaped the horrors of a troubled conscience and an awful death, but have looked for an ample reward. That he did *not* make such a charge—that he fully and frankly confessed that Jesus *was* innocent—and that he gave up the ill-gotten price of *treason*, is full proof that, in the belief of Judas, the Saviour was free from crime, and even the *suspicion of crime.* ¶ *What* is that *to us?* This form of speaking denoted that they had nothing to do with his remorse of conscience, and his belief that Jesus was innocent. *They* had secured what they wanted—the person of Jesus—and they cared little now for the feelings of the traitor. So all wicked men who make use of the agency of others for the accomplishment of crime or the gratification of passion care little for the effect on the instrument. They will soon cast him off and despise him, and in thousands of instances the instruments of villainy and the panders to the pleasures of others are abandoned to remorse, wretchedness, crime, and death.

5. *And he cast down*, &c. This was an evidence of his remorse of conscience for his crime. His ill-gotten gain now did him no good. It would not produce relief to his agonized mind. He *attempted*, therefore, to obtain relief by throwing back the price of treason; but he attempted it in vain. The consciousness of guilt was fastened to his soul; and Judas found, as all will find, that to cast away or abandon ill-gotten wealth will not alleviate a guilty conscience. ¶ *In the temple.* It is not quite certain what part of the temple is here meant. Some have thought that it was the place where the Sanhedrim were accustomed to sit; others, the treasury; others, the part where the priests offered sacrifice. It is probable that Judas cared little or thought little to what particular part of the temple he went. In his deep remorse he hurried to the temple, and probably cast the money down in the most convenient spot, and fled to some place where he might take his life. ¶ *And went and hanged himself.* The word used in the original, here, has given rise to much discussion, whether it means that he was suffocated or strangled by his great grief, or whether he took his life by suspending himself. It is acknowledged on all hands, however, that the latter is its most usual meaning, and it is certainly the most obvious meaning. Peter says, in giving an account of the death of Jesus (Ac. i. 18), that Judas, "falling headlong, burst asunder in the midst, and all his bowels gushed out." There has been supposed to be some difficulty in reconciling these two accounts, but there is really no necessary difference. Both accounts are true. Matthew records the *mode* in which Judas *attempted* his death by hanging. Peter speaks of *the result.* Judas probably passed out of the temple in great haste and perturbation of mind. He sought a place where he might perpetrate this crime. He would not, probably, be very careful about the fitness of the means he used. In his anguish, his haste, his desire to die, he seized upon a rope and suspended himself; and it is not at all remarkable, or indeed unusual, that the rope might prove too weak and break. Falling headlong—that is, on his face—he burst asunder, and in awful horrors died—a double death, with double pains and double horrors—the reward of his aggravated guilt. The explanation here suggested will be rendered more probable if it be supposed that he hung himself near some precipitous valley. "Interpreters have suggested," says Professor Hackett (*Illustrations of Scripture*, p. 275, 276), "that Judas may have hung himself on a tree near a precipice over the valley of Hinnom, and that, the limb or rope breaking, he fell to the bottom, and was

silver pieces, and said, It is not lawful for to put them into the treasury, because it is the price of blood.

7 And they took counsel, and bought with them the potter's field, to bury strangers in.

8 Wherefore that field was called, The field of blood, unto this day.

---

dashed to pieces by the fall. For myself, I felt, as I stood in this valley and looked up to the rocky terraces which hang over it, that the proposed explanation was a perfectly natural one. I was more than ever satisfied with it. I measured the precipitous, almost perpendicular walls in different places, and found the height to be, variously, 40, 36, 33, 30, and 25 feet. Trees still grow quite near the edge of these rocks, and, no doubt, in former times were still more numerous in the same place. A rocky pavement exists, also, at the bottom of the ledges, and hence on that account, too, a person who should fall from above would be liable to be crushed and mangled as well as killed. The traitor may have struck, in his fall, upon some pointed rock, which entered the body and caused 'his bowels to gush out.'"

6. *It is not lawful*, &c. It was forbidden (De. xxiii. 18) to take what was esteemed as an abomination and to offer it to God. The price of blood—that is, of the life of a man—they justly considered as an improper and unlawful offering. ¶ *The treasury.* The *treasury* was kept in the court of the women. See plan of the temple, Mat. xxi. 12. It was composed of a number of small *chests* placed in different parts of the *courts* to receive the voluntary offerings of the people, as well as the half shekel required of every Jew. The original word here rendered *treasury* contains the notion of an *offering to God.* What was given there was considered as an offering made to him. ¶ *The price of blood.* The life is in the blood. See Notes on Ro. iii. 25. The word *blood* here means the same as *life.* The price of blood means the price by which the life of a man has been purchased. This was an acknowledgment that in their view Jesus was innocent. They had *bought* him, not condemned him justly. It is remarkable that they were so scrupulous now about so small a matter, comparatively, as putting this money in the treasury, when they had no remorse about *murdering an innocent man*, and crucifying him who had given full evidence that he was the Messiah. Men are often very scrupulous in *small* matters, who stick not at great crimes.

7. *And they took counsel*, &c. They consulted among themselves about the proper way to dispose of this money. ¶ *And bought with them.* In Ac. i. 18 it is said of Judas that "*he* purchased a field with the reward of his iniquity." By the passage in the Acts is meant no more than that he *furnished the means* or *was the occasion* of purchasing the field. It is not of necessity implied that *Judas* actually made the contract and paid down the money to buy a field to bury strangers in—a thing which would be in itself very improbable, but that it was *by his means* that the field was purchased. It is very frequent in the Scriptures, as well as in other writings, to represent a man as doing that which he is only the cause or occasion of another's doing. See Ac. ii. 23; Jn. xix. 1; Mat. xxviii. 59, 60. ¶ *The potter's field.* Probably this was some field well known by that name, which was used for the purpose of making earthen vessels. The price paid for a field so near Jerusalem may appear to be very small; but it is not improbable that it had been worked till the clay was exhausted, and was neither fit for that business nor for tillage, and was therefore considered as of little value. ¶ *To bury strangers in. Jews*, who came up from other parts of the world to attend the great feasts at Jerusalem. The high-priests, who regarded the *Gentiles* as abominable, would not be inclined to provide a burial-place for *them.*

8. *The field of blood.* The field purchased by the price of blood. The name by which this field was called was *Aceldama*, Ac. i. 19. It was just without the walls of Jerusalem, on the south of Mount Zion. It is now used as a burying-place by the Armenian Christians in Jerusalem, who have a magnificent convent on Mount Zion.—*Missionary Herald*, 1824, p. 66. See Plan of Jerusalem. ¶ *To this day.* That is, to the day when Matthew wrote this gospel, about thirty years after the field was purchased.

9. *Spoken by Jeremy the prophet.* The

9 (Then was fulfilled that which was spoken by Jeremy the prophet, saying, [e]And they took the thirty pieces of silver, the price of him that was valued, [1]whom they of the children of Israel did value;

10 And gave them for the potter's field, as the Lord appointed me.)

e Zec.11.12,13.

1 or, *whom they bought of the children of Israel.*

words quoted here are not to be found in the prophecy of Jeremiah. Words similar to these are recorded in Zec. xi. 12, 13, and from that place this quotation has been doubtless made. Much difficulty has been experienced in explaining this quotation. Anciently, according to the Jewish writers, *Jeremiah* was reckoned the first of the prophets, and was placed first in the Book of the Prophets, thus: Jeremiah, Ezekiel, Isaiah, and the twelve minor prophets. Some have thought that Matthew, quoting this place, quoted the *Book of the Prophets* under the name of that which had the *first* place in the book, that is, Jeremiah; and though the words are those of Zechariah, yet they are quoted correctly as the words of the Book of the Prophets, the first of which was Jeremiah. Others have thought that there was a mistake made by ancient transcribers, writing the name Jeremiah instead of Zechariah; and it is observed that this might be done by the change of only a single letter. It was often the custom to *abridge* words in writing them. Thus, instead of writing the name of Jeremiah in full, it would be written in Greek, *Iriou.* So Zechariah would be written *Zriou.* By the mere change of *Z* into *I*, therefore, the mistake might easily be made. Probably this is the correct explanation. Others have supposed that the words were *spoken* by *Jeremiah*, and that *Zechariah* recorded them, and that Matthew quoted them as they *were*—the words of Jeremiah. The passage is not quoted literally; and by its being *fulfilled* is meant, probably, that the language used by Zechariah on a similar occasion would *express* also this event. See Notes on Mat. i. 22, 23. It was language appropriate to this occasion. ¶ *The price of him that was valued.* That is, the price of him on whom a value was set. The word rendered "valued," here, does not, as often in our language, mean to *esteem*, but to *estimate;* not to love, approve, or regard, but to fix a *price on*, to *estimate the value of.* This they considered to be thirty pieces of silver, *the common price of a slave.* ¶ *They of the children of Israel did value.* Some of the Jews, the leaders or priests, acting in the name of the nation. ¶ *Did value.* Did estimate, or fix a price on.

10. *And gave them.* In Zechariah it is, *I* gave them. Here it is represented as being given by the priests. The meaning is not, however, different. It is, that this price *was given* for the potter's field. ¶ *As the Lord appointed me.* That is, *commanded* me. The meaning of the place in Zechariah is this: He was directed to go to the Jews as a prophet—a pastor of the people. They treated him, as they had done others, with great contempt. He asks them to give him *his price*—that is, the price which they thought he and his pastoral labours were worth, or to show *their* estimate of his office. If they thought it of value, they were to pay him accordingly; if not, they were to "forbear"—that is, to give nothing. To show their *great contempt* of him and his office, and of God who had sent him, they gave him thirty pieces of silver—*the price of a slave.* This God commanded or *appointed him* to give to the potter, or to throw into the pottery—to throw away. So in the time of Jesus the same thing was substantially repeated. Jesus came as the Messiah. They hated and rejected him. To show their contempt of him and his cause, they *valued* him *at the price of a slave.* This was thrown down in the temple, taken by the priests, and appropriated to the purchase of a field owned by a *potter*—worn-out land of little or no value; *all* showing at how low a price, through the whole transaction, the Son of God was estimated. Though the *words* quoted here are not *precisely* like those in Zechariah, yet the *sense* and *general structure* are the same.

11. *And Jesus stood before the governor.* Many things are omitted by Matthew, in the account of this trial, which are recorded by the other evangelists. A much more full account is found in Jn. xviii. 28–40. ¶ *And the governor asked him*, &c. This question was asked on account of the *charge* which the Jews brought against Jesus, *of perverting the nation, and forbidding to give tribute to Cæsar*, Lu. xxiii. 2. It was on *this*

11 And Jesus stood before the governor: and the governor asked him, saying, Art thou the King of the Jews? And Jesus said unto him, Thou sayest.

12 And when he was accused of the chief priests and elders, he [f]answered nothing.

13 Then saith Pilate unto him, Hearest thou not how many things they witness against thee?

14 And he answered him to never

[f] ch. 26. 63.

charge that, after consultation, they had agreed to arraign him before Pilate. See Notes on ver. 1. *They* had condemned him for *blasphemy*, but they well knew that Pilate would altogether disregard an accusation of that kind. They therefore attempted to substitute a totally different accusation from that on which they had professed to find him guilty, to excite the jealousy of the Roman governor, and to procure his death on a charge of treason against the Roman emperor. ¶ *Thou sayest.* That is, thou sayest right, or thou sayest the truth. We may wonder why the Jews, if they heard this confession, did not press it upon the attention of Pilate as a full confession of his guilt. It was what they had accused him of. But it might be doubtful whether, in the confusion, they heard the confession; or, if they did, Jesus took away all occasion of triumph by explaining to Pilate the *nature* of his kingdom, Jn. xviii. 36. Though he acknowledged that he was a king, yet he stated fully that *his kingdom was not of this world*, and that therefore it could not be alleged against him as treason against the Roman emperor. This was done *in the palace*, apart from the Jews, and fully satisfied Pilate of his innocence, Jn. xviii. 23.

12. *When he was accused*, &c. To wit, of perverting the nation, and of forbidding to give tribute to Cæsar, Lu. xxiii. 2, 5. Probably this was done in a tumultuous manner and in every variety of form. ¶ *He answered nothing.* He was conscious of his innocence. He knew that they could not *prove* these charges. They offered no testimony to prove them, and, in conscious innocence, he was silent.

13. *They witness against thee.* This means, rather, that they *accused* him. They were not *witnesses*, but accusers. These accusations were repeated and pressed. They charged him with exciting the people, teaching throughout all Judea from Galilee to Jerusalem, and exciting the nation to sedition, Lu. xxiii. 5.

14. *To never a word.* That is, not at all. He said nothing. This is, an *emphatic* way of saying that he answered nothing. There was no *need* of his replying. He was innocent, and they offered no proof of guilt. Besides, his *appearance* was full evidence in his favour. He was poor, unarmed, without powerful friends, and alone. His life had been public, and his sentiments were well known, and the charge had on the face of it the aspect of absurdity. It deserved, therefore, no answer. ¶ *Marvelled greatly.* Wondered exceedingly, or was much surprised. He was probably more surprised that he bore this *so meekly*, and did not return railing for railing, than that he did not set up a defence. The latter was unnecessary—the former was unusual. The governor was not accustomed to see it, and was therefore greatly amazed.

It was at this time that Pilate, having heard them speak of Galilee (Lu. xxiii. 5), asked if he was a Galilean. Having ascertained that he was, and being probably desirous of freeing himself from any farther trouble in the affair, under pretence that he belonged to Herod's jurisdiction, he sent Jesus to Herod, who was then at Jerusalem attending the feast of the Passover, Lu. xxiii. 6–12. Herod, having examined him, and finding no cause of death in him, sent him back to Pilate. Pleased with the respect which had been shown him, Herod laid aside his enmity against Pilate, and they became friends. The cause of their friendship does not appear to be at all that they were united in opposing the claims of Jesus to be the Messiah, but the respect which Pilate had shown in sending Jesus to him.

15–23. See also the parallel places in Mar. xv. 6–14; Lu. xxiii. 17–23; Jn. xviii. 39, 40.

15. *At* that *feast.* The feast of the Passover. ¶ *The governor was wont to release*, &c. Was *accustomed* to release. From what this custom arose, or by whom it was introduced, is not known.

a word; insomuch that the governor marvelled greatly.

15 Now[g] at *that* feast the governor was wont to release unto the people a prisoner, whom they would.

16 And they had then a notable prisoner, called Barabbas.

17 Therefore, when they were gathered together, Pilate said unto them, Whom will ye that I release unto you? Barabbas, or Jesus, which is called Christ?

18 For he knew that [h]for envy they had delivered him.

g Mar.15.6,&c.; Lu.23.17,&c.; Jn.18.39,&c.

h Pr.27.4; Ec.4.4.

It was probably adopted to secure popularity among the Jews, and to render the government of the Romans less odious. Any little indulgence granted to the Jews during the heavy oppression of the Romans would serve to conciliate their favour, and to keep the nation from sedition. It might happen often that when persons were arraigned before the Romans on charge of sedition, some peculiar favourite of the people, or some leader, might be among the number. It is evident that if they had the privilege of recovering such a person, it would serve much to allay their feelings, and make tolerable the yoke under which they groaned.

16. *A notable prisoner.* The word *notable* means one that is *distinguished* in any way either for great virtues or great crimes. In this place it evidently means the latter. He was perhaps the leader of a band who had been guilty of sedition, and had committed murder in an insurrection, Lu. xxiii. 19.

17. *Whom will ye that I release,* &c. Pilate was satisfied of the innocence of Jesus, Lu. xxiii. 13-16. He was therefore desirous of releasing him. He expected to release one to the people. He knew that Jesus, though condemned by the chief priests, was yet popular among the *people.* He therefore attempted in this manner to rescue him from the hands of the priests, and expected that the *people* would prefer *him* to an odious and infamous robber and murderer. Had the people been left to themselves it would probably have been done. ¶ *Jesus, which is called Christ.* That is, Jesus, who claims to be the Messiah. Pilate probably did not believe it, or care much for it. He used the name which Jesus had acquired among the people. Perhaps, also, he thought that they would be more likely to ask him to be released if he was presented to them as the Messiah. Mark (xv. 9) adds that he asked them whether they would that he should release *the King of the Jews?* It is probable that he asked the question in both ways. Perhaps it was several times repeated, and Matthew has recorded one way in which it was asked, and Mark another. He asked them whether they would demand him who *was called the Christ,* expecting that they would be moved by the claims of the Messiah—claims which, when he entered Jerusalem in triumph, and in the temple, they had acknowledged. He asked them whether they would have the *King of the Jews*—probably to ridicule the priests who had delivered him on that charge. He did it to show the *people* how absurd the accusation was. There Jesus stood, apparently a poor, inoffensive, unarmed, and despised man. Herod had set him at naught and scourged him, and sent him back. The charge, therefore, of the priests, that he was a *king* opposed to the Roman emperor, was *supremely ridiculous;* and Pilate, expecting that the people would see it so, hoped also that they would ask that he might be released.

18. *For he knew that for envy,* &c. This was envy at his popularity. He drew away the people from them. This Pilate understood, probably, from his knowledge of the pride and ambition of the rulers, and from the fact that no danger *could* arise from a person that appeared like Jesus. If Pilate *knew* this, he was bound to release him himself. As a governor and judge, he was under obligation to protect the innocent, and should, in spite of all the opposition of the Jews, at once have set him at liberty. But the Scriptures could not then have been fulfilled. It was necessary, in order that an atonement should be made, that Jesus should be condemned to die. At the same time, it shows the wisdom of the overruling providence of God, that he was condemned by a man who was satisfied of his innocence, and who proclaimed before his accusers his *full belief* that there was no fault in him.

19. *When he was set down on the judgment-seat.* Literally, *While he was sit-*

19 When he was set down on the judgment-seat, his wife sent unto him, saying, Have thou nothing to do with [i]that just man; for I have suffered many things this day in a dream because of him.

20 But the chief priests and elders persuaded the multitude that they should [k]ask Barabbas, and destroy Jesus.

21 The governor answered and said unto them, Whether of the twain will ye that I release unto you? They said, Barabbas.

22 Pilate saith unto them, What shall I do, then, with Jesus, which is called Christ? *They* all say unto him, Let him be crucified.

23 And the governor said, Why, what evil hath he done? But they cried out the more, saying, [l]Let him be crucified.

24 When Pilate saw that he could prevail nothing, but *that* rather a

i Is.53.11; Zec.9.9; Lu.23.47; 1 Pe.2.22; 1 Jn.2.1.
k Ac.3.14.
l ch.21.38,39.

---

ting. This message was probably received when he had resumed his place on the judgment-seat, after Jesus had been sent to Herod. See Notes on ver. 14. ¶ *His wife sent unto him.* The reason why she sent to him is immediately stated—that she had a *dream* respecting him. We know nothing more of her. We do not know whether she had ever seen the Saviour herself, but it would seem that she was apprised of what was taking place, and probably anticipated that the affair would involve her husband in trouble. ¶ *Have thou nothing to do,* &c. That is, do not condemn him. Perhaps she was afraid that the vengeance of heaven would follow her husband and family if he condemned the innocent. ¶ *That just man.* The word *just,* here, has the sense of *innocent,* or not guilty. She might have been satisfied of his innocence from other sources as well as from the dream. ¶ *I have suffered many things,* &c. Dreams were considered as indications of the divine will, and among the Romans and Greeks, as well as the Jews, great reliance was placed on them. Her mind was probably agitated with the subject. She was satisfied of the innocence of Jesus; and, knowing that the Jews would make every effort to secure his condemnation, it was not unnatural that her mind should be excited during her sleep, perhaps with a frightful prospect of the judgments that would descend on the family of Pilate if Jesus was condemned. She therefore sent to him to secure, if possible, his release. ¶ *This day.* It was now early in the morning. The Jewish *day* began at sunset, and she employed the usual language of the Jews respecting time. The dream was, in fact, in the night.

20. *Persuaded the multitude.* The release of a prisoner was to be to the *people,* not to the *rulers.* The rulers, therefore, in order to secure the condemnation of Jesus, urged on the people to demand Barabbas. The people were greatly under the influence of the priests. Galileans among the citizens of Jerusalem were held in contempt. The priests turned the pretensions of Jesus into ridicule. Hence, in a popular tumult, among a flexible and changing multitude, they easily excited those who, but a little before, had cried Hosanna, to cry, Crucify him.

21. *Whether of the twain?* Which of the two, Jesus or Barabbas?

23. *And the governor said, Why?* Luke informs us that Pilate put this question to them *three times,* so anxious was he to release him. He affirmed that he had found no cause of death in him. He said, therefore, that he would chastise him and let him go. He expected, probably, by causing him to be publicly whipped, to excite their compassion, to satisfy *them,* and thus to evade the demands of the priests, and to set him at liberty with the consent of the people. So weak and irresolute was this Roman governor! Satisfied of his innocence, he should at once have preferred *justice* to *popularity,* and acted as became a magistrate in acquitting the innocent. ¶ *Let him be crucified.* See Notes on ver. 39. Luke says they were *instant* with loud voices demanding this. They *urged* it. They demanded it with a popular clamour.

24. *He took water,* &c. The Jews were accustomed to wash their hands when they wished to show that they were innocent of a crime committed by others. See De. xxi. 6; Ps. xxvi. 6. Pilate, in doing this, meant to denote that they

tumult was made, he [m]took water, and washed *his* hands before the multitude, saying, I am innocent of the blood of this just person: see ye *to it.*

25 Then answered all the people, and said, [n]His blood *be* on us, and on our children.

26 Then released he Barabbas unto them: and when he had [o]scourged Jesus, he delivered *him* to be crucified.

27 Then the soldiers of the governor took Jesus into the [2]common hall, and gathered unto him the whole band *of soldiers.*

m De.21.6.
n De.19.10; Jos.2.19; ch.21.44; Ac.5.28.
o Is.53.5; Lu.18.33. 2 or, *governor's house.*

were guilty of his death, but that he was innocent. But the mere washing of his hands did not free him from guilt. He was *bound* as a magistrate to free an innocent man; and whatever might be the clamour of the Jews, *he* was guilty at the bar of God for suffering the holy Saviour to be led to execution, in order to gratify the malice of enraged priests and the clamours of a tumultuous populace. ¶ *See ye* to it. That is, take it upon yourselves. You are responsible for it, if you put him to death.

25. *His blood* be *on us,* &c. That is, let the guilt of putting him to death, if there be any, be on us and our children. We will be answerable for it, and will consent to bear the punishment for it. It is remarked by writers that, among the Athenians, if anyone accused another of a capital crime, he devoted himself and children to the same punishment if the accused was afterward found innocent. So in all countries the conduct of the parent involves the children in the consequences of his conduct. The Jews had no *right* to call down this vengeance on their children, but, in the righteous judgment of God, it has come upon them. In less than forty years their city and temple were overthrown and destroyed. More than a million of people perished in the siege. Thousands died by famine; thousands by disease; thousands by the sword; and their blood ran down the streets like water, so that, Josephus says, it extinguished things that were burning in the city. Thousands were *crucified*—suffering the same punishment that they had inflicted on the Messiah. So great was the number of those who were crucified, that, Josephus says, they were obliged to cease from it, "room being wanted for the crosses, and crosses for the men." See Notes on ch. xxiv. To this day, also, the curse has remained. They have been a nation scattered and peeled; persecuted almost everywhere, and a hissing and a byword among men. No single nation, probably, has suffered so much; and yet they have been preserved. All classes of men, all the governments of the earth, have conspired to overwhelm them with calamity, and yet they still live as monuments of the justice of God, and as proofs, going down from age to age, that the Christian religion is true—standing demonstrations of the crime of their fathers in putting the Messiah to death, and in calling down vengeance on their heads.

26. *And when he had scourged Jesus.* See Notes on Mat. x. 17. Among the Romans it was customary to scourge or whip *a slave* before he was crucified. This was done to inflict greater suffering than crucifixion would be alone, and to add to the horrors of the punishment. Our Lord, being about to be put to death after the manner of a *slave,* was also treated as a slave—as one of the lowest and most despised of mankind. ¶ *He delivered* him *to be crucified.* Not merely gave him up to *them* to crucify him, as if *they* only were answerable, but he gave him up *as a judge,* when he ought to have saved his life and might have done it. Crucifixion was a Roman punishment; it was performed by Roman soldiers; Pilate pronounced the sentence from a Roman tribunal, and Pilate affixed the title to the cross. Pilate, therefore, as well as the Jews, was answerable to God for the death of the Saviour of the world.

27-31. See also Mar. xv. 15-20; Jn. xix. 1-3.

27. *Into the common hall.* The original word here means, rather, the governor's palace or dwelling. The trial of Jesus had taken place outside of the palace. The Jews would not enter in (Jn. xviii. 28), and it is probable that courts were held often in a larger and more public place than would be a room in his dwelling. Jesus,

28 And they stripped him, and put on him a scarlet robe.

29 And when they had platted a crown of thorns, they put *it* upon his head, and a reed in his right hand: and they bowed the knee before him, and [p] mocked him, saying, Hail, King of the Jews!

p Ps.69.19,20.

being condemned, was led by the soldiers away from the Jews *within* the palace, and subjected there to their profane mockery and sport. ¶ *The whole band.* The *band* or cohort was a tenth part of a Roman legion, and consisted of from 400 to 600 men, according to the size of the legion. Comp. Notes on ch. viii. 29.

28. *And they stripped him.* That is, they either took off all his upper garments or removed all his clothing, probably the former. ¶ *A scarlet robe.* Mark says they clothed him in *purple.* The *scarlet* colour was obtained from a species of fruit; *purple* from shell-fish. See Notes on Is. i. 18. The ancients gave the name *purple* to any colour that had a mixture of *red* in it, and consequently these different colours might be sometimes called by the same name. The *robe* here used was the same kind worn by Roman generals and other distinguished officers of the Roman army, and also by the Roman governors. It was made so as to be placed on the shoulders, and was bound around the body so as to leave the right arm at liberty. As we cannot suppose that Pilate would array him in a new and splendid robe, we must suppose that this was one which had been worn and cast off as useless, and was now used to array the Son of God as an object of ridicule and scorn.

29. *Had platted.* The word *platted* here means *woven together.* They made a *wreath* of a thorn-bush. ¶ *A crown.* Or perhaps, rather, a *wreath.* A crown was worn by kings, commonly made of gold and precious stones. To ridicule the pretensions of Jesus that he was a king, they probably plucked up a thorn-bush growing near, made it into something resembling in shape a royal crown, so as to correspond with the old purple robe, and to complete the mockery. ¶ *Of thorns.* What was the precise species of shrub denoted here is not certainly known. It was, however, doubtless, one of that species that has sharp points of very hard wood. They could therefore be easily pressed into the skin and cause considerable pain. Probably they seized upon the first thing in their way that could be made into a crown, and this happened to be a *thorn,* thus increasing the sufferings of the Redeemer. Palestine abounds with thorny shrubs and plants. "The traveller finds them in his path, go where he may. Many of them are small, but some grow as high as a man's head. The Rabbinical writers say that there are no less than twenty-two words in the Hebrew Bible denoting thorny and prickly plants."—Professor's Hackett's *Illustrations of Scripture,* p. 135. Comp. Pr. xxiv. 30, 31; xv. 19; Je. iv. 3. ¶ *And a reed in his right hand.* A *reed* is a straight, slender herb, growing in marshy places, and abundant on the banks of the Jordan. It was often used for the purpose of making *staves* for walking, and it is not improbable that this was such a staff in the possession of some person present. The word is several times thus used. See 2 Ki. xviii. 21; Is. xxxvi. 6; Eze. xxix. 6. Kings commonly carried a *sceptre,* made of ivory or gold, as a sign of their office or rank, Es. iv. 11; viii. 4. This *reed* or *staff* they put in his hand, in imitation of a *sceptre,* to deride, also, his pretensions of being a king. ¶ *And they bowed the knee.* This was done for mockery. It was an act of pretended homage. It was to ridicule his saying that he was a king. The common mode of showing respect or homage for kings was by kneeling or prostration. It shows amazing forbearance on the part of Jesus that he thus consented to be ridiculed and set at naught. No mere *human* being would have borne it. None but he who loved us unto death, and who saw the grand results that would come from this scene of sufferings, could have endured such mockery. ¶ *Hail, King of the Jews!* The term *hail* was a common mode of salutation to a king, or even to a friend. It implies, commonly, the highest respect for office as well as the person, and is an invocation of blessings. Here it was used to carry on what they thought to be the *farce* of his being a king; to ridicule in every possible way the pretensions of a poor, unattended, unarmed man of Nazareth, as if he was a weak impostor or was deranged.

30. *And they spit upon him.* This was

30 And they [q]spit upon him, and took the reed, and smote him on the head.

31 And after that they had mocked him, they took the robe off from him, and put his own raiment on him, and [r]led him away to crucify *him.*

32 And as they came out, they found a man of Cyrene, Simon by name: him they compelled to bear his cross.

33 And when they were come unto a place called Golgotha, that is to say, A place of a skull,

q Is.49.7; 50.6; 53.3,7.
r Nu.15.35; 1 Ki.21.10,13; Ac.7.58; He.13.12.

a token of the deepest contempt and insult. See Notes on Mat. xxvi. 67. ¶ *And took the reed.* The cane, probably so large as to inflict a heavy blow. ¶ *And smote him on the head.* Not merely to injure him by the force of the blow, but to press the *thorns* into his head, and thus to add cruelty to insult.

31, 32. *As they came out.* That is, either out of the governor's palace where he had been treated with such cruelty and contempt, or out of the gates of the city, to crucify him. ¶ *A man of Cyrene.* Cyrene was a city of Libya, in Africa, lying west of Egypt. There were many Jews there, and they were in the habit, like others, of going frequently to Jerusalem. ¶ *Him they compelled to bear his cross.* John says (xix. 17) that Jesus went forth *bearing his cross.* Luke says (xxiii. 26) that they laid the cross on Simon, that he might bear it after Jesus. There is no contradiction in these accounts. It was a part of the usual punishment of those who were crucified that they should bear their own cross to the place of execution. It was accordingly laid at first on Jesus, and he went forth, as John says, bearing it. Weak, however, and exhausted by suffering and watchfulness, he probably sunk under the heavy burden, and they laid hold of Simon that he might bear *one end* of the cross, as Luke says, *after Jesus.* The cross was composed of two pieces of wood, one of which was placed upright in the earth, and the other crossed it after the form of the figure †. The upright part was commonly so high that the feet of the person crucified were 2 or 3 feet from the ground. On the middle of that upright part there was usually a projection or seat on which the person crucified sat, or, as it were, *rode.* This was necessary, as the hands were not alone strong enough to bear the weight of the body; as the body was left exposed often many days, and not unfrequently suffered to remain till the flesh had been devoured by vultures or putrefied in the sun. The feet were fastened to this upright piece either by nailing them with large spikes driven through the tender part, or by being lashed by cords. To the cross-piece at the top, the hands, being extended, were also fastened, either by spikes or by cords, or perhaps, in some cases, by both. The hands and feet of our Saviour were both fastened by spikes. Crosses were also sometimes made in the form of the letter X, the limbs of the person crucified being extended to the four parts, and he suffered to die a lingering death in this cruel manner. The cross used in the crucifixion of Christ appears to have been the former. The mention of the cross often occurs in the New Testament. It was the instrument on which the Saviour made atonement for the sins of the world. The whole of the Christian's hope of heaven, and all his peace and consolation in trial and in death, depend on the sacrifice there made for sin, and on just views and feelings in regard to the fact and the design of the Redeemer's death. See Notes on Jn. xxi. 18.

33. *Golgotha.* This is a Hebrew word, signifying the place of a skull. This is the word which in Luke is called *Calvary.* The original Greek, there, also means *a skull.* The word *calvary* is a *Latin* word meaning *skull,* or place of *skulls.* It is not known certainly why this name was given to this place. Some have supposed that it was because the mount resembled in shape a human skull. The most probable opinion, however, is that it was a place of execution; that malefactors were beheaded there or otherwise put to death, and that their bones remained unburied or unburned. Golgotha, or Calvary, was probably a small eminence on the north-west of Jerusalem, without the walls of the city, but at a short distance. Jesus was put to death *out* of the city, because capital punishments were not allowed within the walls. See Nu. xv. 35; 1 Ki.

34 They[s] gave him vinegar to drink, mingled with gall: and when he had tasted *thereof*, he would not drink.

s Ps.69.21.

35 And[t] they crucified him, and parted his garments, casting lots; that it might be fulfilled which was spoken by the prophet, [u]They

t Ps.22.16; Mar.15.24,&c.; Lu.23.34,&c.; Jn.19. 24,&c. u Ps.22.18.

xxi. 13. This was a law among the Romans as well as the Jews. He also died there, because the bodies of the beasts slain in sacrifice as typical of him were *burned without the camp*. He also, as the antitype, suffered *without the gate*, He. xiii. 11, 12. The place which is shown as Calvary now is within the city, and must also have been within the ancient walls, and there is no reason to suppose that it is the place where the Saviour was put to death.

34. *They gave him vinegar*, &c. Mark says that, "*they gave him to drink wine mingled with myrrh.*" The two evangelists mean the same thing. Vinegar was made of light wine rendered acid, and was the common drink of the Roman soldiers, and this might be called either vinegar or wine in common language. *Myrrh* is a bitter substance produced in Arabia, but is used often to denote anything bitter. The meaning of the name is *bitterness*. See Notes on Mat. ii. 11. *Gall* is properly a bitter secretion from the liver, but the word is also used to denote anything exceedingly *bitter*, as wormwood, &c. The drink, therefore, was vinegar or sour wine, rendered *bitter* by the infusion of wormwood or some other very bitter substance. The effect of this, it is said, was to stupefy the senses. It was often given to those who were crucified, to render them insensible to the pains of death. Our Lord, knowing this, when he had tasted it refused to drink. He was unwilling to blunt the pains of dying. The *cup* which his *Father* gave him he rather chose to drink. He came to suffer. His sorrows were necessary for the work of the atonement, and he gave himself up to the unmitigated sufferings of the cross. This was presented to him in the early part of his sufferings, or when he was about to be suspended on the cross. *Afterward*, when he was on the cross and just before his death, vinegar was offered to him *without the myrrh*—the vinegar which the soldiers usually drank—and of this he drank. See ver. 49, and Jn. xix. 28-30. When Matthew and Mark say that he "would not drink," they refer to a different thing and a different time from John, and there is no contradiction.

35. *And they crucified him.* To *crucify* means to put to death on a cross. The *cross* has been described at ver. 32. The usual *manner* of the crucifixion was as follows: After the criminal had carried the cross, attended with every possible gibe and insult, to the place of execution, a hole was dug in the earth to receive the foot of it. The cross was laid on the ground; the person condemned to suffer was stripped and was extended on it, and the soldiers fastened the hands and feet either by nails or thongs. After they had driven the nails deeply in the wood, they elevated the cross with the agonizing sufferer on it, and, in order to fix it more firmly in the earth, they let it fall violently into the hole which they had dug to receive it. This sudden fall gave to the person that was nailed to it a violent and convulsive shock, and greatly increased his sufferings. The crucified person was then suffered to hang, commonly, till pain, exhaustion, thirst, and hunger ended his life. Sometimes the sufferings continued for days; and when friendly death terminated the life, the body was often suffered to remain—a loathsome object, putrefying in the sun or devoured by birds.

This punishment was deemed the most disgraceful and ignominious that was practised among the Romans. It was the way in which slaves, robbers, and the most notorious and abandoned wretches were commonly put to death. It was this, among other things, that exposed those who preached the gospel to so much shame and contempt among the Greeks and Romans. They despised everything that was connected with the death of one who had been put to death as a slave and an outlaw.

As it was the most ignominious punishment known, so it was the most painful. The following circumstances made it a death of peculiar pain: 1st. The position of the arms and the body was unnatural, the arms being extended back and almost immovable. The least motion gave violent pain in the hands

parted my garments among them, and upon my vesture did they cast lots.

36 And sitting down, they watched him there;

37 And set up over his head his accusation written, THIS IS JESUS, THE KING OF THE JEWS.

38 Then were there two [v]thieves crucified with him; one on the right hand, and another on the left.

39 And they that passed by reviled him, [w]wagging their heads,

v Is.53.12. w Ps.22.7; 109.25.

---

and feet, and in the back, which was lacerated with stripes. 2d. The nails, being driven through the parts of the hands and feet which abound with *nerves*, created the most exquisite anguish. 3d. The exposure of so many wounds to the air brought on a violent inflammation, which greatly increased the poignancy of the suffering. 4th. The free circulation of the blood was prevented. More blood was carried out in the *arteries* than could be returned by the *veins*. The consequence was, that there was a great increase of blood in the veins of the head, producing an intense pressure and violent pain. The same was true of other parts of the body. This intense pressure in the blood-vessels was the source of inexpressible misery. 5th. The pain gradually increased. There was no relaxation and no rest. There was no prospect but death. The sufferer was commonly able to endure it till the third, and sometimes even to the seventh day. The intense sufferings of the Saviour, however, were sooner terminated. This was caused, perhaps, in some measure, by his previous fatigue and exhaustion, but still more by the intense sufferings of his soul in bearing *our* griefs and carrying *our* sorrows—in making an atonement for the sins of the world. See Notes on Mat. xv. 44. ¶ *And parted his garments.* It was customary to crucify a person naked. The clothes of the sufferer belonged to those who were executioners. John says (xix. 23) that they divided his garments into four parts, to each soldier a part, but for his coat they cast lots. See Notes on the place. When Matthew says, therefore, that they parted his garments, casting lots, it is to be understood that they *divided* one part of them, and for the other part of them they cast lots. ¶ *That it might be fulfilled*, &c. The words here quoted are found in Ps. xxii. 18. The whole psalm is usually referred to Christ, and is a most striking description of his sufferings and death.

36. *They watched him there.* That is, the four soldiers who had crucified him. They watched him lest his friends should come and release him.

37. *And set up over his head.* John says (xix. 19) that Pilate wrote the title and put it upon the cross. Probably Pilate wrote it or caused it to be written, and directed the soldiers to set it up. A man is often said to do what he directs others to do. It was customary to set up over the heads of persons crucified the crime for which they suffered, and the name of the sufferer. The accusation on which Jesus had been condemned by Pilate was his claiming to be the King of the Jews. ¶ *This is Jesus, the King of the Jews.* The evangelists differ in the account of this title. Mark (xv. 26) says it was, "The King of the Jews." Luke (xxiii. 38), "This is the King of the Jews." John (xix. 19), "Jesus of Nazareth, the King of the Jews." But the difficulty may be easily removed. John says that the title was written in Hebrew, Greek, and Latin. It is not at all improbable that the inscription *varied* in these languages. One evangelist may have translated it from the Hebrew, another from the Greek, a third from the Latin, and a fourth may have translated one of the inscriptions a little differently from another. Besides, the evangelists all agree in the main point of the inscription, viz. that he was the King of the Jews.

38. *Two thieves crucified*, &c. Rather two *robbers*. Pilate did not reside in Jerusalem. When he came there on the great feasts, or at other times, it was, in part, to hold courts for the trial of criminals. These robbers had been probably condemned at that time; and to show greater contempt for Jesus, he was crucified between men of that abandoned character, and on a cross that *should* have been occupied by their companion and leader, *Barabbas*.

39. *Wagging their heads.* In token of derision and insult. See Job xvi. 4; Ps. cix. 25.

40 And saying, Thou that destroyest the temple, and buildest *it* in three days, save thyself. If thou be the Son of God, come down from the cross.

41 Likewise, also, the chief priests, mocking[x] *him*, with the scribes and elders, said,

42 He saved others, himself he cannot save. If he be the King of Israel, let him now come down from the cross, and we will believe him.

43 He trusted in God; [y]let him deliver him now, if he will have him: for he said, [z]I am the Son of God.

44 The thieves also, which were crucified with him, cast the same in his teeth.

45 Now from the sixth hour

x Job 13.9; Ps.35.16; Is.28.22; Lu.18.32.

y Ps.3.2; 22.8; 42.10; 71.11. *z* Jn.5.17,18; 10.30,36.

40. *Thou that destroyest the temple*, &c. Meaning, Thou that didst boast that thou couldst do it. This was one of the things that had been falsely charged on him. It was intended for painful sarcasm and derision. If he could destroy the *temple*, they thought he might easily come down from the cross.

42, 43. *He saved others.* It does not seem probable that they meant to admit that he had actually saved others, but only that he *pretended* to save them from death by miracles, or that he claimed to be the Messiah, and thus affirmed that he *could* save them. This is, therefore, cutting irony. ¶ *If he be the King of Israel*, &c. It may seem strange to some that Jesus did not vindicate by a miracle his claims to be the Messiah, and come down from the cross. But the time had come for him to make an atonement. He *had* given full and sufficient proof that he was the Christ. Those who had rejected him, and who mocked and taunted him, would have been little likely to admit his claims if he *had* come down from the cross, since they had set at naught all his other miracles. They said this for the purpose of insult; and Jesus chose rather to suffer, though his character was assailed, than to work a new miracle for their gratification. He had foretold his death, and the time had come; and now, amid revilings, and gibes, and curses, and the severe sarcasms of an angry and apparently triumphant priesthood, he chose to die for the sins of the world. To this they added *insult* to God, profanely calling upon him to interpose by miracle and save him, if he was his friend; and all this when their prophets had foretold this very scene, and when they were fulfilling the predictions of their own Scriptures. See Notes on Is. liii., and Da. ix. 24-27. So wonderful is the way by which God causes his word to be fulfilled.

44. *The thieves also.* The robbers, or highwaymen. Luke says (xxiii. 39) that one of them did it, and that the other reproved him and was penitent. The account in Luke may, however, easily be reconciled with that in Matthew by supposing that *at first both* of them reviled the Saviour, and that it is of this fact that Matthew speaks. Afterward one of them relented and became penitent—perhaps from witnessing the patient sufferings of Christ. It is of this one particularly that Luke speaks. Or it may be that what is true of one of the malefactors is by Matthew attributed to both. The evangelists, when for the sake of brevity they avoid particularizing, often attribute to many what is said or done by single persons, meaning no more than that it was done by some one or more of them, without specifying the one. Comp. Mar. vii. 17 with Mat. xv. 15; Mar. v. 31 with Lu. viii. 45; Lu. ix. 13 with Jn. vi. 8, 9. ¶ *Cast the same in his teeth.* This is a most unhappy translation. It means in the original simply, they upbraided him or reproached him in the same manner.

45. *Now from the sixth hour.* That is, from our twelve o'clock. The Jews divided their day into twelve hours, beginning to count at sunrise. ¶ *There was darkness.* This could not have been an eclipse of the sun, for the Passover was celebrated at the time of the full moon, when the moon is opposite to the sun. Luke says (xxiii. 45) that *the sun was darkened*, but it was not by an eclipse. The only cause of this was the interposing power of God—furnishing testimony to the dignity of the sufferer, and causing the elements to sympathize with the pains of his dying Son. It was also peculiarly proper to furnish this testimony when the *Sun of righte-*

there was [a]darkness over all the land unto the ninth hour.

46 And about the ninth hour Jesus cried with a loud voice, saying, Eli, Eli, lama sabachthani? that is to say, [b]My God, my God, why hast thou forsaken me?

47 Some of them that stood

a Am.8.9.

b Ps.22.1; Is.53.10; La.1.12.

ousness was withdrawing his beams for a time, and the Redeemer of men was expiring. A thick darkness, shutting out the light of day, and clothing every object with the gloom of midnight, was the appropriate drapery with which the world should be clad when the Son of God expired. This darkness was noticed by one at least of the Pagan writers. *Phlegon*, a Roman astronomer, speaking of the fourteenth year of the reign of Tiberius, which is supposed to be that in which our Saviour died, says "that the greatest eclipse of the sun that was ever known happened then, for the day was so turned into night that the stars appeared." ¶ *Over all the land.* That is, probably, over the whole land of Judea, and perhaps some of the adjacent countries. The extent of the darkness is not known. ¶ *The ninth hour.* Till about three o'clock in the afternoon, at which time the Saviour is supposed to have died.

46. *Eli, Eli*, &c. This language is not pure Hebrew nor Syriac, but a mixture of both, called commonly *Syro-Chaldaic.* This was probably the language which the Saviour commonly spoke. The words are taken from Ps. xxii. 1. ¶ *My God, my God*, &c. This expression is one denoting intense suffering. It has been difficult to understand in what sense Jesus was *forsaken by God.* It is certain that God *approved* his work. It is certain that he was innocent. He had done nothing to forfeit the favour of God. As his own Son—holy, harmless, undefiled, and obedient—God still loved him. In either of these senses God could not have forsaken him. But the expression was probably used in reference to the following circumstances, viz.: 1st. His great bodily sufferings on the cross, greatly aggravated by his previous scourging, and by the want of sympathy, and by the revilings of his enemies on the cross. A person suffering thus might address God as if he was forsaken, or given up to extreme anguish. 2d. He himself said that this was "the power of darkness," Lu. xxii. 53. It was the time when his enemies, including the Jews and Satan, were suffered to do *their utmost.* It was said of the serpent that he should bruise the heel of the seed of the woman, Ge. iii. 15. By that has been commonly understood to be meant that, though the Messiah would finally crush and destroy the power of Satan, yet he should himself suffer *through the power of the devil.* When he was tempted (Lu. iv.), it was said that the tempter *departed from him for a season.* There is no improbability in supposing that he might be permitted to return at the time of his death, and exercise his power in increasing the sufferings of the Lord Jesus. In what way this might be done can be only conjectured. It might be by horrid thoughts; by temptation to despair, or to distrust God, who thus permitted his innocent Son to suffer; or by an increased horror of the pains of dying. 3d. There might have been *withheld* from the Saviour those strong religious consolations, those clear views of the justice and goodness of God, which would have blunted his pains and soothed his agonies. Martyrs, under the influence of strong religious feeling, have gone triumphantly to the stake, but it is possible that those views might have been withheld from the Redeemer when he came to die. His sufferings were accumulated sufferings, and the design of the atonement seemed to require that he should suffer all that human nature *could be made to endure* in so short a time. Yet, 4th. We have reason to think that there was still something more than all this that produced this exclamation. Had there been no deeper and more awful sufferings, it would be difficult to see why Jesus should have shrunk from these sorrows and used such a remarkable expression. Isaiah tells us (liii. 4, 5) that *he bore our griefs and carried our sorrows; that he was wounded for our transgressions, and bruised for our iniquities; that the chastisement of our peace was laid upon him; that by his stripes we are healed.* He hath redeemed us from the curse of the law, being made a curse for us (Ga. iii. 13); he was made a sin-offering (2 Co. v. 21); he died *in our place*, on *our* account, that he might

there, when they heard *that*, said, This *man* calleth for Elias.

48 And straightway one of them ran, and took a sponge, and [c]filled *it* with vinegar, and put *it* on a reed, and gave him to drink.

49 The rest said, Let be; let us see whether Elias will come to save him.

50 Jesus, when he had cried again with a loud voice, yielded up the ghost.

51 And, behold, [d]the vail of the temple was [e]rent in twain, from

c Ps.69.21.

d Ex.26.31; Le.16.2,15; 21.23; 2 Ch.3.14. e Is.25.7.

---

bring us near to God. It was this, doubtless, which caused his intense sufferings. It was the manifestation of God's hatred of sin, in some way which he has not explained, that he experienced in that dread hour. It was suffering endured by *him* that was due to *us*, and suffering by which, and by which alone, we can be saved from eternal death.

47. *This* man *calleth for Elias.* This was done purposely to deride him and his pretensions to be the Messiah. The words Eli, Eli, they might easily pretend that they understood to mean Elias, or so pervert them. The taunt would be more cutting, because it was the universal belief of the Jews, as well as the doctrine of Christ, that *Elias* would come before the Messiah. They derided him now, as calling upon *Elias* when *God* would not help him; still keeping up the pretensions to being the Messiah, and invoking *Elijah* to come from the dead to aid him. Or it is possible that this might have been said by some by-standers who did not understand the language in which he spoke, or who might not have been near enough to hear him distinctly.

48. *One of them ran.* John (xix. 28) says that this was in consequence of Jesus' saying "I thirst." One of the effects of crucifixion was excessive thirst. ¶ *Took a sponge.* A sponge is a well-known porous substance that easily absorbs water. It was used in this case because, Jesus being elevated, it was difficult to convey a cup to his lips. ¶ *Filled* it *with vinegar.* This was the common drink of Roman soldiers. It was a light wine, turned sour and mixed with water. John says (xix. 29) there was a vessel set full of vinegar, probably for the use of the soldiers who watched his crucifixion. ¶ *And put* it *on a reed.* John says it was put upon *hyssop.* The *hyssop* was a *shrub*, growing so large sometimes as to be called a *tree*, 1 Ki. iv. 33. The *stalk* of this was what Matthew calls a *reed.* The sponge fastened to this could easily be *extended* to reach the mouth of *Jesus.* This vinegar Jesus drank, for it was not intended to *stupefy* him or blunt his sense of pain, like the *wine and myrrh.*

49. *The rest said*, &c. Still deriding his sufferings, and refusing to allow even the poor consolation of a drink, to assuage the thirst of the Saviour of the world in his dying agonies.

50. *Cried again with a loud voice.* He cried, "It is finished," Jn. xix. 30. It was in the height of his agony, probably attended with deep groaning, and uttered amid sorrows which were never else experienced in our world. It finished the work of atonement, made the way of salvation possible, rolled away the curse from guilty men, and opened the kingdom of heaven to all true believers. ¶ *Yielded up the ghost.* This, though a literal translation, is unhappy. It means resigned his spirit, or *expired.* The same phrase is used by the LXX. in describing the death of Rachel, Ge. xxxv. 18.

51. *The vail of the temple.* This was doubtless the vail, curiously wrought, which separated the holy from the most holy place, dividing the temple into two apartments, Ex. xxvi. 31–33. ¶ *In twain.* In two pieces or parts. This was the time of day when the priest was burning incense in the holy place, and it is probable that he witnessed it. The most holy place has been usually considered as a type of heaven, and the rending of the vail to signify that the way to heaven was now open to all —the great High-priest, the Lord Jesus, being about to enter in as the forerunner of his people. However, about the *design* of the rending of the vail, the Scriptures are silent, and conjecture is useless. ¶ *And the earth did quake.* Or shook. Earthquakes are violent convulsions of the ground, caused commonly by confined and rarefied air. This was probably, however, a miraculous convulsion of the earth, in attes-

the top to the bottom; and the earth did quake, and the rocks rent;

52 And[f] the graves were opened, and [g]many bodies of the saints which slept arose,

53 And [h]came out of the graves after his resurrection, and went into the holy city, and appeared unto many.

54 Now[i] when the centurion, and they that were with him watching Jesus, saw the earthquake, and those things that were done, they feared greatly, saying, Truly this was the Son of God.

55 And many women were there beholding afar off, [k]which followed Jesus from Galilee, ministering unto him;

f Is.25.8; 26.19; Ho.13.14; Jn.5.25,28. g Da.12.2; 1 Th.4.14. h 1 Co.15.20.

i Mar.15.39; Lu.23.47,&c. k Lu.8.2,3.

tation of the truth that the sufferer was the Messiah, the Son of God, and as an exhibition of *wrath* at the crimes of those who put him to death. It was not confined to Judea, but was felt in other countries. It is mentioned by Roman writers. ¶ *The rocks rent.* That is, were torn asunder. Rocks are still seen at Mount Calvary thus rent asunder, which are *said* to be the ones that were convulsed when the Saviour died.

52. *And the graves were opened. Graves* or sepulchres were most commonly made, among the Jews, in solid rocks or in caves of rocks. The rending of the rocks, therefore, would lay them open. The graves were *opened* by this earthquake, but the dead in them did not rise till after his resurrection. ¶ *And many bodies of the saints arose.* Of course, it is not known who these were, nor what became of them. It is probable that they were persons who had recently died, and they appear to have been known in Jerusalem; at least, had the ancient saints risen, they would not have been known, and would not so soon have been credited as those who had recently died. ¶ *Which slept.* Which had died. The death of saints is often called *sleep*, Da. xii. 2; 1 Co. xv. 18; 1 Th. iv. 15.

53. *And came out of the graves after his resurrection.* The narrative of Matthew does not determine whether they came to life *before* Jesus rose, and remained in the tombs, or came to life *after* he died. The latter is probably the correct opinion. There is nothing said of the *reason* why they were raised. It is not improbable to suppose that it was, amid the other wonders attending the death of Jesus, to convince the Jews that he was the Messiah. Perhaps some who had been his open friends were raised up now as an attestation that he in whom they had believed was the Christ. What became of them after they had entered into the city—whether they again died or ascended to heaven, is not revealed, and conjecture is vain. ¶ *The holy city.* Jerusalem, called holy because the temple was there, because it was devoted to God, and because it was the place of religious solemnities.

54. *Now when the centurion*, &c. Centurion, a captain of a hundred soldiers. He was here placed over the band that attended the crucifixion. ¶ *They feared greatly.* They regarded these things as proof that God was angry, and they were terrified at the prospect that vengeance was coming on them. ¶ *Truly this was the Son of God.* They had heard, probably, that Jesus professed to be the Son of God. Seeing these wonders, they believed that God was now attesting the truth of his professions. The centurion was a heathen, and had probably no very distinct notions of the phrase *the Son of God*—perhaps understanding by it only that he was like the heathen heroes who had been deified; but he certainly regarded these wonders as proof that he was *what he professed to be.* In the original it is "a son of a god;" an expression perfectly suitable to a polytheist, who believed in the existence of many gods. Mark (xv. 39) says that they affirmed that "this man was the Son of God." Luke (xxiii. 47), that they said, "Certainly this was a righteous man." These things were said by *different persons*, or at different periods of his sufferings—one evangelist having recorded one saying, and another another.

55. *Beholding afar off.* These women were probably not suffered to come near the cross because it was surrounded by soldiers. They witnessed with intense feelings his sufferings from some con-

56 Among which was Mary Magdalene, and Mary the mother of James and Joses, and the mother of Zebedee's children.

57 When[l] the even was come, there came a rich man of Arimathea, named Joseph, who also himself was Jesus' disciple:

58 He went to Pilate, and begged the body of Jesus. Then Pilate commanded the body to be delivered.

59 And when Joseph had taken the body, he wrapped it in a clean linen cloth,

60 And[m] laid it in his own new tomb, which he had hewn out in

l Mar.15.42; Lu.23.50; Jn.19.38.

m Is.53.9.

venient place as near as they could approach. ¶ *Ministering unto him.* Attending him and providing for his wants. While multitudes of *men* joined in the cry Crucify him! and forsook him in his trying moments, it does not appear that any of his *female* followers were thus unfaithful. In the midst of all his trials, and all the contempt poured upon him, they adhered to their Redeemer. Never did female constancy shine more brightly, and never was a happier example set for all who should afterward believe on him.

56. *Mary Magdalene.* Mary of Magdala. She had peculiar cause of attachment to the Saviour, having been relieved by him of a most dreadful calamity and restored to her right mind, after being possessed by seven devils. See Notes on Lu. viii. 2. ¶ *And the mother of Zebedee's children.* That is, of James and John, Mat. x. 2. Her name was Salome, Mar. xv. 40.

57 *When the even was come.* That is, some time after three o'clock in the afternoon. Before this, the Jews had besought Pilate that the legs of those who were crucified might be broken and the bodies be taken down, that they might not remain on the cross during the Sabbath. The soldiers, coming to Jesus for that purpose, found that he was already dead, contrary to their expectation. A soldier, however, thrust a spear into his side, and there was furnished the fullest proof that he had expired. See Notes on Jn. xix. 31-37. ¶ *A rich man of Arimathea.* It is uncertain where Arimathea was. There were several cities of that name in Judea. It is commonly supposed to be the same as Rama. See Notes on ch. ii. 17. Luke says that this was a *city of the Jews,* and it is probable, therefore, that it was in the tribe of Benjamin, and but a short distance from Jerusalem. This man sustained a high character. He was an "honourable counsellor, who also waited for the kingdom of God" (Mar. xv. 43); he was "a good man and a just" (Lu. xxiii. 50); he had nobly set himself against the wicked purposes of the Sanhedrim (Lu. xxiii. 51); he was a disciple of Jesus, though he was not openly his follower, because he feared the Jews, Jn. xix. 38.

58. *He went to Pilate.* Because no one had a right to remove the body but by authority of the magistrate. Jesus was condemned to be crucified, usually a long and most bitter death, and in common cases it would have been unlawful to have removed the body so soon.

59. *He wrapped it in a clean linen cloth.* John adds that this was done *with spices* (xix. 40). The Jews were accustomed to use myrrh, aloes, and other aromatics in large quantities when they buried their dead. When they were not regularly embalmed, which was a long and tedious process, they inclosed the spices in the folds of the linen, or wrapped the body in it. Spices were sometimes used in such quantities as to form a *heap* or *bed,* on which the dead body was laid. Thus it is said of Asa (2 Ch. xvi. 14), "they laid him in the bed which was filled with sweet odours and spices," &c. There not being time properly to embalm the body of Jesus, he was buried in this manner. The women who attended him, either not being aware of this, or desirous of showing a farther regard for him, returned from the sepulchre and prepared other spices with which to embalm him on the first day of the week, Lu. xxiii. 56; xxiv. 1.

60. *In his own new tomb.* John says (xix. 41) that this was in a garden that was *in* or *near* the place where he was crucified. This tomb Joseph had prepared for himself, as was not uncommon among the Jews. Comp. Notes on Isa. xxii. 16. In this tomb Luke and John inform us that no man had been laid. This was so ordered, in the pro-

the rock: and he rolled a great stone to the door of the sepulchre, and departed.

61 And there was Mary Magdalene, and the other Mary, sitting over against the sepulchre.

62 Now the next day, that followed the day of the preparation, the chief priests and Pharisees came together unto Pilate,

63 Saying, Sir, we remember that that [n]deceiver said, while he was yet alive, [o]After three days I will rise again.

64 Command, therefore, that the sepulchre be made sure until the third day, lest his disciples [p]come by night and steal him away, and say unto the people, He is risen from the dead: so the last error shall be worse than the first.

65 Pilate said unto them, Ye have a watch: go your way, make *it* as sure as you can.

n Jn.7.12,47; 2 Co.6.8.

o ch.16.21; 17.23; 20.19; Lu.24.6,7; Jn.2.19.
p ch.28.13.

vidence of God, doubtless, that there might be no suspicion about his identity when he rose; that it might not be alleged that another person had risen, or that he was raised by touching the bones of some prophet, as happened to the corpse that touched the bones of Elisha, 2 Ki. xiii. 21. Farther, by being buried here an important prophecy was remarkably fulfilled (Is. liii. 9): *He made his grave—with the rich in his death.* The fulfilment of this is the more remarkable, because during his life he associated with the poor and was himself poor. See Notes on Is. liii. 9. ¶ *Which he had hewn out in the rock.* This was a common way of constructing tombs in Judea. See Notes on Mat. viii. 28. Being cut out of a rock, there was no way by which the disciples could have access to it but by the entrance, at which the guard was placed, and consequently it was impossible for them to steal him away. The sepulchre, thus secure, was rendered more so by rolling a great stone at its entrance; all possible precautions thus being used, in the providence of God, against imposition and deceit.

62. *Now the next day, that followed the day of the preparation.* The first day of the feast of the Passover was called the day of *preparation,* because all things were on that day got in readiness for the observances of the paschal week. The Jewish day closed at sunset, and the Sabbath at that time commenced. The *next day* mentioned here does not mean the following day in *our* acceptation of the word, or the following *morning,* but the next day in the Jewish way of speaking—that is, after the next day had commenced, or after sundown. To suppose them to have waited till the next morning would be absurd, as the disciples would be as likely to steal him away the first night as the second.

63. *We remember.* They had either heard him say this, or, more probably, had understood that this was one of his doctrines. ¶ *That deceiver.* One of the charges against him was that he deceived the people, Jn. vii. 12. By this title they still chose to designate him, thinking that his death had fully confirmed the truth of the charges against him.

64. *Until the third day.* That is, during two nights and the intervening day. This proves that when the Jews spoke of *three days,* they did not of necessity mean three *whole days,* but *parts* of three days, as was the case in our Saviour's lying in the grave. See Notes on ch. xii. 40. ¶ *The last error shall be worse than the first.* That is, the last *deception,* or the taking him from the tomb, pretending that he rose, will have a wider influence among the people than the *first,* or his pretending to be the Messiah.

65. *Ye have a watch.* The Jews had a guard of Roman soldiers, who kept watch in the tower of Antonia, on the north-west of the temple. Pilate either referred to these, or to the *watch* that attended the crucifixion—the whole *band* that had been appointed for that. As the torments of crucifixion sometimes lasted many days, the band had been probably granted to them during that time, and they were therefore still at the direction of the chief priests.

66. *Sealing the stone.* The sepulchre was made sure by affixing the large stone to the entrance in such a way that it could not be removed without detection. It was sealed. In what way this

66 So they went, and made the sepulchre sure, [q]sealing the stone, and setting a watch.

q Da.6.17.

CHAPTER XXVIII.

IN[a] the end of the sabbath, as it began to dawn toward the first

a Mar.16.1; Lu.24.1,&c.; Jn.20.1,&c.

---

was done cannot now be certainly told. The cave in which Daniel was cast was fastened in the same manner, and sealed with the king's signet (Da. vi. 17), perhaps by fastening the stone in its place with cords, and bringing them together and uniting them with wax, and impressing on that the seal of the king. In this way letters and books were anciently sealed. Possibly on the sepulchre of Jesus was impressed in this manner the seal of Pilate—the seal of office—making it doubly sure; or it may be that the stone was fitted into the tomb with clay or cement, and on that was impressed the seal of Pilate. ¶ *Setting a watch.* That is, as large a number of soldiers as they judged necessary to secure the tomb.

We cannot but be struck with the wisdom of God in ordering the circumstances of the Saviour's burial in such a manner as to avoid the possibility of deception. Had all this been done by his *friends*, it might have been said that they only pretended to secure the tomb, and only pretended that he was dead. But he was adjudged to be dead *by the Jews themselves;* Pilate was satisfied that that was the fact; they had their own way about his burial; he was buried alone; the place of his sepulchre was made sure, *expressly to prevent his being removed;* and they placed around him a guard in their own judgment large enough to prevent his being taken away by force or strength. His very enemies, therefore, took every possible precaution to place his resurrection beyond the possibility of suspicion of fraud and imposture, and those precautions were the very means of furnishing the most striking proof that his death, burial, and resurrection were not impositions, but most affecting, awful, and yet cheering realities.

CHAPTER XXVIII.

1. *In the end of the sabbath.* The word *end* here means the same as *after* the Sabbath—that is, after the Sabbath was fully completed or finished, and may be expressed in this manner: "In the night following the Sabbath, for the Sabbath closed at sunset, as it began to dawn," &c. ¶ *As it began to dawn toward the first* day *of the week.* The word *dawn* is not of necessity in the original. The word there properly means as the first day *approached*, or drew on, without specifying the precise time. Mark says (xvi. 1, 2) that it was after "the sabbath was past, and very early in the morning, at the rising of the sun"—that is, not that the sun *was risen*, but that it was *about to rise*, or at the early break of day. Luke says (xxiv. 1) that it was "very early in the morning;" in the Greek, *deep twilight*, or when there was scarcely any light. John (xx. 1) says it was "very early, while it was yet dark"—that is, it was not yet full daylight, or the sun had not yet risen. The time when they came, therefore, was at the break of day, when the sun was about to rise, but while it was yet so dark as to render objects obscure, or not distinctly visible. ¶ *The first* day *of the week.* The day which is observed by Christians as the Sabbath. The Jews observed the seventh day of the week, or our Saturday. During that day our Saviour was in the grave. As he rose on the morning of the first day, that day has always been observed in commemoration of so glorious an event. ¶ *Came Mary Magdalene and the other Mary.* From Mary Magdalene Christ had cast out seven devils. Grateful for his great mercy, she was one of his firmest and most faithful followers, and was first at the sepulchre, and was first permitted to see her risen Lord. The *other Mary* was not the mother of Jesus, but the mother of James and Joses (Mark). Mark says that *Salome* attended them. Salome was the wife of Zebedee, and the mother of James and John. From Luke (xxiv. 10) it appears that Joanna, wife of Chusa, Herod's steward (see Lu. viii. 3), was with them. These four women, Mark says (ch. xvi. 1), having bought sweet spices, came to anoint him. They had prepared a part of them on the evening before the Sabbath, Lu. xxiii. 56. They now, according to Mark, *completed* the preparation and bought more; or the meaning in Mark may be merely that, *having bought* sweet spices, without specifying the time *when*, they came now to embalm him. John men-

day of the week, came [b]Mary Magdalene, and the other Mary, to see the sepulchre.

2 And, behold, there [1]was a great earthquake; for the angel of the Lord descended from heaven, and came and rolled back the stone from the door, and sat upon it.

3 His[c] countenance was like lightning, and his raiment white as snow:

4 And for fear of him the keepers did shake, and became as dead *men*.

5 And[d] the angel answered and said unto the women, Fear not ye; for[e] I know that ye seek Jesus, which was crucified.

b ch.27.56. 1 or, *had been*.

c Ps.104.4; Eze.1.4-14; Da.10.6; Re.1.14-16. d He.1.14. e Ps.105.3,4.

tions only Mary Magdalene. He does this, probably, because his object was to give a particular account of her interview with the risen Saviour. There is no contradiction among the evangelists; for while one mentions only the names of a part of those who were there, he does not deny that *others* were present also. It is an old maxim, that "he who mentions a few does not deny that there are more." ¶ *To see the sepulchre.* To see whether it was as it had been left on the evening when he was laid there. To see if the stone was still there, by which they would know that he had not been removed. Mark and Luke say that the design of their coming was to anoint him with the sweet spices which they had prepared. Matthew does not mention that, but he does not *deny* that that was the ultimate design of their coming. It is not improbable that they might have known the manner in which he was buried, with a large quantity of myrrh and aloes; but that was done in in haste—it was done by depositing the myrrh and aloes, without mixture or preparation, in the grave-clothes. *They* came that they might embalm his body more deliberately, or at least that they might *anoint the bandages* and complete the work of embalming.

2. *There was a great earthquake.* Rather there *had been*. It does not mean that this was while they were there, or while they were going, but that there *had been* so violent a commotion as to remove the stone. The word here rendered *earthquake* does not of necessity mean that the convulsion extended to the earth, but only that there had been such a concussion as to remove the stone. ¶ *And sat upon it.* Sat upon it when the keepers saw him, ver. 4. It is not said that he was sitting when he appeared to the women. From Luke it would rather appear that he was standing.

3. *His countenance.* In our language the word *countenance* refers to the *face only;* in the original it refers to his *whole person*. His *general aspect*, or *the appearance of the angel himself*, was, &c. ¶ *Like lightning.* Peculiarly bright and shining. ¶ *His raiment white as snow.* Celestial beings are usually represented as clothed in white, Ac. i. 10; Da. vii. 9; Re. iii. 4, 5; iv. 4; vii. 13, 14. *White*, among the Jews, was the symbol of *purity* or *innocence*.

4. *The keepers did shake.* It was night. The appearance was sudden and unexpected, and to them terrific. The stone was probably suddenly removed. At the noise, the light, the suddenness of the appearance, they were affrighted. ¶ *And became as dead* men. Probably by terror they fainted, or were thrown into a swoon. At this time it is probable that the Lord Jesus arose, and hence he was not seen by them when he came forth. At what *precise time* of the night this was we are not certainly informed. The narrative, however, leads us to suppose that it was not long before the women came to the sepulchre, or near the break of day.

5. *And the angel answered and said,* &c. This was not on the *outside* of the tomb, for Matthew does not say that the angel appeared to the *women* there, but only to the keepers. Mark says, "entering into the sepulchre, they saw a young man sitting on the right side, clothed in a long white garment" (xvi. 5). Luke says (xxiv. 3), "they entered in, and found not the body of the Lord Jesus; and as they were much perplexed thereabout, behold, two men stood by them in shining garments." Seeing the stone rolled away and the sepulchre open, they of course anxiously entered into it, to see if the body was there. They did not find it, and *there* they saw the vision of the angels, who gave them information respecting his resurrection. Infidels have objected that there are three inconsistencies in the accounts by Mark and Luke: 1st.

6 He is not here; for he is risen, as[f] he said. Come, see the place where the Lord lay.

7 And go quickly, and tell his disciples that [g]he is risen from the dead; and, behold, he goeth before you into Galilee; [h]there shall ye see him: lo, I have told you.

8 And they departed quickly from the sepulchre, with fear and great joy, and did run to bring his disciples word.

9 And as they went to tell his disciples, behold, Jesus met them, saying, [i]All hail. And they came and held him by the feet, and worshipped him.

10 Then said Jesus unto them,

f ch.27.63. g Lu.24.34; 1 Co.15.4. h ver.16,17. i Jn.20.19.

That Mark says the angel was sitting, and Luke says they were standing. *Answer*. The word in Luke does not of necessity mean that they *stood*, but only that they were *present*. Or it may be that the one that *Mark* mentions was sitting when they entered, and then arose. 2d. It is objected that Luke mentions *two*, but Mark and Matthew *one*. *Answer*. Mark mentions the one who spoke; for it cannot be supposed they both spake the same thing. He does not *deny* that another was present with him. Luke affirms that there was. This way of speaking is not unfrequent. Thus Mark and Luke mention only one demoniac who was cured at Gadara. Matthew mentions two. In like manner Mark and Luke speak of only one blind man who was cured at Jericho, while from Matthew it is certain that two were. The fact that but one is mentioned, where it is not *denied* that there were others, does not prove that there could not be others. 3d. Matthew calls this an *angel*. Mark and Luke *a man*. *Answer*. Angels, in the Scriptures, from *appearing* in the form of men, are often called as they *appear*, and are mentioned as men. See Ge. xviii. 2, 16, 22; xix. 1, 5. ¶ *Fear not ye*. That is, "Be not agitated, or troubled, that you do not find the body of the Saviour. I know that ye seek him, and are troubled that he is removed; but you need not *fear* that he has been stolen. You will see him again in Galilee."

6. *He has risen, as he said*. Jesus had often predicted that he would rise, but the disciples did not understand it, and consequently did not expect it, Mat. xvi. 21; xx. 19. ¶ *The place where the Lord lay*. The place where a body was deposited in a sepulchre was commonly a *niche* cut in the wall of the sepulchre. The sepulchre was usually large; that of David was more than 100 feet in length, cut out of solid rock under ground, and separated into various apartments. All round the sides of those apartments were *niches* for the dead; or they were ranged around the sides, in places cut in the solid rock just large enough to contain the body. In such a place, probably, our Lord lay.

7. *Tell his disciples*. Mark adds particularly, "tell Peter." This was a kind message to Peter, who had so recently denied his Lord. It would serve to cheer him in his despondency, and to assure him that his sin had been forgiven; and it shows the tender love and remembrance of Jesus, even for his unfaithful friends.

8. *And they departed quickly*. Joyful at the *news*, and wishing to impart it to all, they fled to find the disciples, and to tell them that the Lord was risen. ¶ *With fear and great joy*. Fear, 1st, at the wonderful scenes which they had witnessed—the stone rolled away, and the presence of an angel; 2d, a confused state of mind, apprehensive, perhaps, that it might not, after all, be true. The news was too good to be credited at once, yet they had sufficient faith in it to fill them with great and unexpected joy. Perhaps no language could better express the state of their minds—the mingled awe and rejoicing—than that which is here used. ¶ *And did run*, &c. They ran to announce what they had seen to the disciples. The city, where the disciples were, was half a mile or more from the place.

9. *And as they went—Jesus met them*. This was when they left the sepulchre the *second* time. Jesus *first* appeared to Mary Magdalene when alone, Jn. xx. 14. *Afterward* he appeared to the other women, as related by Matthew. See the accounts of the resurrection harmonized at the end of this chapter. ¶ *All hail*. This is a term of salutation. The word "all" has been supplied by the translators. It is not in the original. The meaning of the word "hail," here,

Be not afraid: go tell [k]my brethren that they go into Galilee, and there shall they see me.

11 Now when they were going, behold, some of the watch came into the city, and showed unto the chief priests all the things that were done.

12 And when they were assembled with the elders, and had taken counsel, they gave large money unto the soldiers,

13 Saying, Say ye, [l]His disciples came by night, and stole him *away* while we slept.

14 And if this come to the gov-

k He.2.11.

l ch.27.64.

is *rejoice;* a term of salutation connected with the idea of joy—joy at his resurrection, and at meeting them again. ¶ *Held him by the feet.* Or threw themselves prostrate before him. This was the usual posture of supplication. See 2 Ki. iv. 37. It does not mean that they took hold of his feet, but only that they cast themselves down before him. ¶ *And worshipped him.* See Notes on Mat. viii. 2. In this place the word *worship* seems to denote the homage due to the Messiah risen from the dead; regarded by *them* now in a proper light, and entitled to the honour which was due to God, agreeably to Jn. v. 23.

10. *Be not afraid.* The ancients, when in the presence of a heavenly being—an angel, or one who was supposed to be possessed of divine power—were commonly struck with great *fear*, as well as a great sense of their unworthiness. See Lu. v. 8; Ju. vi. 22, 23; xiii. 21, 22. These women were in like manner alarmed when they saw Jesus, believing him now peculiarly to be a divine being; seeing him returning from the regions of the dead, and doubtless impressed with a new consciousness that they were unworthy of being in his presence. Jesus comforted them. He was the *same Jesus* with whom they had been before his death, and they had no reason now to fear him. ¶ *Go tell my brethren.* There is something exceedingly tender in the appellation here used—"my brethren." Though he was risen from the dead, though about to be exalted to heaven, yet he did not disdain to call his disciples his brethren. This was calculated still farther to silence the fears of the women and to inspire them with confidence. ¶ *Into Galilee.* Galilee was the northern part of the land. There the Saviour commenced his ministry; and there, away from the noise and confusion of the city, he purposed again to meet them, in retirement and quietness, to satisfy them of his resurrection, and to commission them to go forth and preach the everlasting gospel.

11. *When they were going.* Or when they had gone from the tomb. ¶ *Some of the watch.* Some of the guard that had been set around the tomb to keep it safe. Probably the leaders or officers came to give a true account of what had happened. ¶ *Showed unto the chief priests.* To Annas and Caiaphas.

12. *And when they were assembled,* &c. They deemed the matter of so much importance as to justify the calling together of the great council of the nation. Notwithstanding all their caution, it was plain that the body of Jesus was gone. It was farther plain that the disciples would affirm that he was restored to life again. It was not improbable that Jesus would himself appear, and convince multitudes that he was the Messiah, and that the guilt of putting him to death would, after all their caution and cunning, be charged on them. They had been at great pains to procure his death. They had convinced Pilate that he was dead. They had placed a guard for the express purpose of preventing his being taken away. It would be in vain, after this, to *pretend* that he was not dead; that he was in a swoon; that he died in appearance only. They had shut themselves out from this, which would have been the most plausible plea, and, whatever course they might now adopt, they were *obliged* to proceed on the admission that he had been *really dead*, and that all proper measures had been taken to prevent his being stolen. They concluded, after consultation, that but one way was left—to bribe the soldiers—to induce them to tell a falsehood—and to attempt to convince the world that Jesus, in spite of themselves, and in the face of all probability, had been really stolen. ¶ *Large money.* Much money. This was given to bribe them; to induce them to conceal the truth, and to affirm what they knew was false.

ernor's ears, we will persuade him, and secure you.

15 So they took the money, and did as they were taught: and

14. *The governor's ears.* To Pilate. If it is reported to him that Jesus was stolen while you slept. ¶ *We will persuade him.* We will convince or satisfy him, so that he shall not punish you. This they might promise with safety; for, 1st. They knew from the character of Pilate that he could be easily bribed. 2d. Pilate, after the feast of the Passover, was accustomed to return to Cesarea. 3d. He had not been inclined at all to interfere in anything concerning the Saviour until it was urged upon him by the Jews. He would not be disposed, *of himself*, to take any farther trouble about the matter. He would feel that all that could be demanded of him had been done, and would not be disposed farther to interfere, unless the Sanhedrim should demand it. This, of course, they would not do.

15. *This saying is commonly reported.* This account of the disappearance of the body of Jesus from the sepulchre is commonly given. ¶ *Until this day.* The time when Matthew wrote this gospel—that is, about thirty years after the resurrection.

The *resurrection* of the Lord Jesus, of which an account is given in this chapter, is one of the most important doctrines of the Christian religion, and is attested by the strongest evidence that can be adduced in favour of any ancient fact. Let it be considered—1st. That he had often foretold his own death and resurrection. See Mat. xii. 40; xvi. 21; xx. 19. 2d. There was no doubt that he was really dead. Of this the Jews, the Romans, and the disciples were all equally well satisfied. 3d. Every proper precaution was taken to prevent his removal by stealth. A guard, usually consisting of sixty men, was placed there for the express purpose of keeping him, and the sepulchre was secured by a large stone and by a seal. 4th. On the third day the body was missing. In this all were agreed. The high-priests did not dare to call that in question. They laboured, therefore, to account for it. The disciples affirmed that he was alive. The Jews hired the Roman soldiers to affirm that he was stolen while they slept, and succeeded in making many of the people believe it. This account of the Jews is attended with the following difficulties and absurdities: 1st. The Roman guard was composed usually of sixty men, and they were stationed there for the express purpose of guarding the body of Jesus. 2d. The punishment of *sleeping* while on guard in the Roman army was *death*, and it is perfectly incredible that those soldiers should expose themselves in this manner to death. 3d. The disciples were few in number, unarmed, weak, and timid. They had just fled before those who took Jesus in the garden, and how can it be believed that in so short a time they would dare to *attempt* to take away from a Roman guard of armed men what they were expressly set to defend? 4th. How could the disciples *presume* that they would find the Roman soldiers asleep? or, if they should, how was it possible to remove the stone and the body without awaking even *one* of their number? 5th. The *regularity* and *order* of the grave-clothes (Jn. xx. 6, 7) show that the body had not been stolen. When men rob graves of the bodies of the dead, they do not wait coolly to fold up the grave-clothes and lay them carefully by themselves. 6th. If the soldiers were *asleep*, how did they, or how could they know that the disciples stole the body away? If they were *awake*, why did they suffer it? The whole account, therefore, was intrinsically absurd. On the other hand, the account given by the disciples is perfectly natural and credible. 1st. They account for the reason why the soldiers did not see the Saviour when he rose. Terrified at the vision of an angel, they became as dead men. 2d. They affirmed that they saw him. All the apostles affirmed this, and many others. 3d. They affirmed it in Jerusalem, in the presence of the Jews, before the high-priests and the people. See the Acts of the Apostles. If the Jews really *believed* the account which they themselves had given, why did they not apprehend the apostles, and *prove* them guilty of the theft and of falsehood?—things which they never attempted, and which show, therefore, that they did not credit their own report. 4th. In regard to the Saviour they could not be deceived. They had been with him three years. They knew him as a friend. They again ate and drank with him; they put their fingers

this saying is commonly reported among the Jews until this day.

16 Then[m] the eleven disciples went away into Galilee, into a mountain where Jesus had appointed them.

17 And when they [n]saw him, they worshipped him: but some doubted.

18 And Jesus came and spake unto them, saying, [o]All power is given unto me in heaven and in earth.

m ch.26.32. n ch.16.28.

o Ps.2.6; 89.19; 110.1-3; Is.9.6,7; Da.7.14; ch.11.27; Lu.1.32; Jn.17.2; Ro.14.9; Ep.1.20,21; He.2.8; 1 Pe. 3.22; Re.11.15.

---

into his hands and side; they conversed with him; they were with him forty days. There were *enough* of them to bear witness. Law commonly requires not more than one or two competent witnesses, but here were *eleven* plain, honest men, who affirmed in all places and at all times that they had seen him. Can it be possible that they could be deceived? Then all faith in testimony must be given up. 5th. They gave every possible evidence of their sincerity. They were persecuted, ridiculed, scourged, and put to death for affirming this. Yet not one of them ever expressed the least doubt of its truth. They bore everything rather than to deny that they had seen him. They had no motive in doing this but the love of truth. They obtained no wealth by it, no honour, no pleasure. They gave themselves up to great and unparalleled sufferings—going from land to land; crossing almost every sea; enduring the dangers, toils, and privations of almost every clime—for the simple object of affirming everywhere that a Saviour died and rose. If they knew this was an imposition—and if it *had been* they would have known it—in what way is this remarkable conduct to be accounted for? Do men conduct in this way for nought? and especially in a *plain case*, where all that can be required is the testimony of the senses? 6th. The world believed them. Three thousand of the Jews themselves believed in the risen Saviour on the day of Pentecost, but fifty days after his resurrection, Ac. ii. 41. Multitudes of other Jews believed during the lives of the apostles. Thousands of Gentiles believed also, and in three hundred years the belief that Jesus rose had spread over and changed the whole Roman empire. *Had* the apostles been deceivers, that was the age in which they could most easily have been detected. Yet *that* was the age when converts were most rapidly multiplied, and God affixed his seal to their testimony that it was true.

16. *Then the eleven disciples.* Judas was dead, leaving but eleven of the original number of the apostles. ¶ *Into a mountain where Jesus had appointed them.* This *appointment* is recorded in Mat. xxvi. 32. On what particular mountain this was is not known. It is probable that Jesus, when he made the appointment, specified the place, which has been omitted by the evangelists. Matthew has omitted many appearances which Jesus made to his disciples which have been recorded by Luke, John, and Paul. See the harmony of the resurrection at the end of the chapter.

17. *They worshipped him.* Paid him honour as the Messiah. ¶ *But some doubted.* As, for example, Thomas, Jn. xx. 25. The disciples had not expected his resurrection; they were therefore slow to believe. The mention of their doubting shows that they were honest men—that they were not easily imposed on—that they had not previously *agreed* to affirm that he had risen—that they were convinced only by the strength of the evidence. Their caution in examining the evidence; their slowness to believe; their firm conviction after all their doubts; and their willingness to show their conviction even by their *death*, is most conclusive proof that they were *not* deceived in regard to the fact of his resurrection.

18. *All power is given unto me in heaven and in earth.* The *Son of God*, as *Creator*, had an original right to all things, to control them and dispose of them. See Jn. i. 3; Col. i. 16, 17; He. i. 8. But the universe is put under him more particularly as Mediator, that he might redeem his people; that he might gather a church; that he might defend his chosen; that he might subdue all their enemies, and bring them off conquerors and more than conquerors, Ep. i. 20-23; 1 Co. xv. 25-27; Jn. v. 22, 23; Phi. ii. 6-11. It is in reference to *this*, doubtless, that he speaks here—power or *authority* committed to him over all things, that he might redeem, defend,

19 Go[p] ye, therefore, [q]and [2]teach all nations, baptizing them in the name of the Father, and of the Son, and of the Holy Ghost;

p Mar.16.15. q Is.52.10; Ro.10.18.
2 or, *make disciples*, or, *Christians*, *of all nations.*

and save the church purchased with his own blood. His mediatorial government extends, therefore, over the material world, over angels, over devils, over wicked men, and over his own people.

19. *Go ye therefore.* *Because* all power is mine, go. I can defend you. The world is placed under my control. It is redeemed. It is given me in promise by my Father, as the purchase of my death. Though you are weak, yet I am strong. Though you will encounter many troubles and dangers, yet I can defend you. Though *you* die, yet *I* live, and the work shall be accomplished. ¶ *Teach all nations.* The word rendered *teach*, here, is not the one that is usually so translated in the New Testament. This word properly means *disciple*, or *make disciples of.* This was to be done, however, by teaching, and by administering the rite of baptism. ¶ *All nations.* This gracious commission was the foundation of their authority to go to the Gentiles. The Jews had expected that the offers of life under the Messiah would be confined to their own nation. Jesus broke down the partition wall, and commissioned his disciples to go everywhere, and bring the *world* to the knowledge of himself. ¶ *Baptizing them.* Applying to them water, as an emblem of the purifying influences of the Christian religion through the Holy Spirit, and solemnly devoting them to God. ¶ *In the name*, &c. This phrase does not mean, here, *by the authority* of the Father, &c. To be baptized *in* the name of the Father, &c., is the same as to be baptized *unto* the Father; as to believe on the *name* of Christ is the same as to believe *on Christ*, Jn. i. 12; ii. 23; iii. 18; 1 Co. i. 13. To be baptized *unto* anyone is publicly to receive and adopt him as a religious teacher or lawgiver; to receive his system of religion. Thus the Jews were baptized *unto Moses*, 1 Co. x. 2. That is, they received the system that he taught; they acknowledged him as their lawgiver and teacher. So Paul asks (1 Co. i. 13), "Were ye baptized in the name of Paul?"—that is, Were you devoted to Paul by this rite? Did you bind yourselves to *him*, and give yourselves away to *him*, or to God? So to be baptized in the name of the Father, or unto the Father, means publicly, by a significant rite, to receive his system of religion; to bind the soul to obey his laws; to be devoted to him; to receive, as the guide and comforter of the life, his instructions, and to trust to his promises. To be baptized unto the Son, in like manner, is to receive him as the Messiah—our Prophet, Priest, and King—to submit to his laws, and to receive him as a Saviour. To be baptized unto the Holy Ghost is to receive him publicly as the Sanctifier, Comforter, and Guide of the soul. The meaning, then, may be thus expressed: Baptizing them unto the Father, Son, and Holy Ghost by a solemn profession of the only true religion, and by a solemn consecration to the service of the sacred Trinity.

The union of these three names in the form of baptism proves that the Son and Holy Ghost are *equal* with the Father. Nothing would be more absurd or blasphemous than to unite the name of a creature—a man or an angel—with the name of the ever-living God in this solemn rite. If Jesus was a mere man or an angel, as is held by many who deny his divinity, and if the Holy Ghost was a mere *attribute* of God, then it would have been the height of absurdity to use a form like this, or to direct the apostles to baptize men under them. How absurd would be the direction—nay, how blasphemous—to have said, "Baptize them unto God, and unto Paul, and unto the *wisdom* or *power* of God!" Can we believe that our Saviour would have given a direction so absurd as this? Yet, unless he himself is divine, and the Holy Spirit is divine, Jesus gave a direction substantially the same as this. The form of baptism, therefore, has been always regarded as an irrefragable argument for the doctrine of the Trinity, or that the Son and Holy Spirit are equal with the Father.

20. *Lo, I am with you.* That is, by my Spirit, my providence, my attending counsel and guidance. I will strengthen, assist, and direct you. This also proves that Christ is divine. If he is a mere man, or a creature, though of the highest order, how could he promise to be *with* his disciples *always*, or

20 Teaching[r] them to observe all things whatsoever I have commanded you: and, lo, [s]I am with you alway, *even* unto the end of the world. Amen.

r Ac.2.42; 1 Co.11.2.

s ch.18.20; Re.1.18.

at all? They would be scattered far and wide. His disciples would greatly increase. If he was *with them* always, he was God; for no finite creature could thus be present with many men scattered in different parts of the world. ¶ *Unto the end of the world.* The word rendered *world*, here, sometimes means *age* or *state;* and by some it has been supposed to mean, I will be with you until the end of this *age*, or during the continuance of the Jewish state, to the destruction of Jerusalem. But as the presence of Christ was no less necessary *after* that than before, there seems to be no propriety in limiting the promise to his own age. It may therefore be considered as a gracious assurance that he would aid, strengthen, guide, and defend all his disciples, but more especially his ministers, to the end of time.

HARMONY OF THE ACCOUNTS

OF THE

RESURRECTION, APPEARANCES, AND ASCENSION OF CHRIST.

I. THE RESURRECTION.

As much difficulty has been felt in reconciling the accounts of the different evangelists respecting the resurrection of Christ, and as infidels have maintained that they are utterly irreconcilable, it may be proper, in closing the Notes on Matthew, to give these accounts at *one view.* One thing should always be borne in mind by all who read the Gospels, viz. *that the sacred narrative of an event is what it is declared to be by* ALL *the evangelists.* That a thing is omitted by *one* does not prove that another is false because he has recorded it, for the very object of the different Gospels was to give the testimony of independent witnesses to the great facts of the life and death of Jesus. Nor does it prove that there is a contradiction because one relates facts in a different *order* from another, for neither of them professes to relate facts in the *precise order* in which they occurred. The object was to relate the *facts themselves.* With these principles in view, which are conceded to *profane* historians always, let us look at the accounts which are presented in the *sacred narrative* respecting the resurrection, appearance, and ascension of Christ.

1. Jesus was laid in the tomb on Friday evening, having been wrapped in linen with myrrh and aloes in a hurried manner, Jn. xix. 39, 40. The *women,* not apprised of that, or desiring also to testify their regard for him, prepared spices on the same evening to embalm him, Lu. xxiii. 56. As it was too late that night to complete the preparation, they deferred it till the first day of the week, resting on the Sabbath, Lu. xxiii. 56.

2. On the first day of the week, early, the women completed their preparation, purchased more spices, and properly mixed them to make an *unguent* to anoint the bandages in which the body was rolled, Mar. xvi. 1. Or this *may* refer to the purchase which is mentioned by Luke, meaning that they *had* bought them—that is, on Friday evening.

3. They came to the sepulchre just as the day began to dawn, or just as the light appeared in the east, yet so *dark* as to render objects indistinct. It was "in the end of the Sabbath, as it began to dawn toward the first day of the week," Mat. xxviii. 1. "Very early in the morning, at the rising of the sun," or as the sun was *about* to rise, Mar. xvi. 2. "Very early in the morning," Lu. xxiv. 1. "Early, while it was yet dark," Jn. xx. 1.

4. Those who came were Mary Magdalene, Mat. xxviii. 1, Jn. xx. 1; Mary the mother of James and Joses, Mat. xxviii. 1, Lu. xxiv. 10, Mar. xv. 40; Salome, the wife of Zebedee, and mother of James and John, comp. Mat. xxvii. 56, Mar. xv. 40; Joanna, the wife of Chuza, Herod's steward, comp. Lu. xxiv. 10, viii. 3; and certain others not specified, Lu. xxiv. 1, 10.

5. The objects of their coming were, 1st. To see the sepulchre, Mat. xxviii. 1. 2d. To embalm him, or to *finish* embalming him, Mar. xvi. 1, Lu. xxiv. 1.

6. While on the way they inquired who should roll away the stone for them, that they might have access to the body of Jesus, Mar. xvi. 3.

7. When they arrived they found that there *had been* an earthquake or shaking of the tomb, so that the stone was rolled away, Mat. xxviii. 2; Mar. xvi. 4.

8. The angel who rolled the stone away *had* sat down on it, and had appeared to the *keepers* and frightened them; though he did not appear in this place to the *women*, but only to the *keepers*, Mat. xxviii. 2–4. At that time probably our Saviour had risen—how long before the women came is not known and cannot be ascertained.

9. When they came there, *Mary Magdalene*, greatly agitated with the appearance of things, and probably supposing that the body had been stolen, left the other women, and ran to the city, at the distance of half a mile, to inform the disciples, Jn. xx. 2.

10. While Mary was gone the others probably looked round the garden in search of the body, and then came and examined the sepulchre to see if it was not there. The tomb was large, and they entered *into* it. *There* "the angel spake unto them," Mat. xxviii. 5. "They saw a young man"—that is, an angel in the appearance of a young man—"sitting on the right side," Mar. xvi. 5. When they entered he was *sitting;* as they entered he *rose* and stood, Lu. xxiv. 4. Luke adds that there was another with him, xxiv. 4; this *other one* was not seen when they entered into the sepulchre at the time mentioned by *Mark*, but was seen when they had fully entered in, as mentioned by Luke.

11. The angel charged them to go and tell the disciples and Peter, Mat. xxviii. 7, Mar. xvi. 7; and to assure them that he would see them in Galilee. He also reminded them of what Jesus had said when they were in Galilee, Lu. xxiv. 6, 7.

12. They went immediately toward the city, yet taking a different way from the one that Mary had taken, or going in such a way that they did not meet her when she was returning from the city with Peter and John, Mat. xxviii. 8, Mar. xvi. 8. "They said nothing to any man," Lu. xxiv. 9, 10. In Lu. xxiv. 10 it is said that it was Mary Magdalene, and Joanna, and Mary the mother of James, that told these things to the disciples. Not that Luke affirms that they were *together* when they told them, but that the information was given *by them*, though perhaps at different times.

13. While they were gone Mary Magdalene returned to the sepulchre, following Peter and John, who came running, Jn. xx. 2–9. They examined the sepulchre, and found that the body was really gone, but as yet they did not know the reason, not having seen the other women to whom the angel had told the cause, and Mary Magdalene having left the women before the angel had spoken to them. As yet, therefore, *she* was ignorant of the reason of his removal.

14. Peter and John then left the sepulchre, returned to the city, and left Mary alone, Jn. xx. 10.

15. While Mary was there alone she looked into the sepulchre, and saw two angels, probably the same that had appeared to the other women, Jn. xx. 11–13.

16. Jesus appeared to Mary while she sat alone at the sepulchre, Jn. xx. 14–18. Thus, according to Mark (xvi. 9), he appeared to Mary Magdalene "*first*."

17. Mary then went to tell the disciples that she had seen him, but they did not fully believe her, Jn. xx. 18; Mar. xvi. 10, 11.

18. *Afterward* Jesus appeared to the other women, Mat. xxviii. 9: "As they went to tell his disciples, behold, Jesus met them, saying, All hail." This would *seem*, in Matthew, to be immediately after they left the sepulchre the first time; but many critics observe that the words "to tell his disciples" are wanting in many manuscripts, and of doubtful authority. It may be far-

ther said that the words "as they were going" might have been rendered "*after* they were gone." They do not imply of necessity that the appearance took place *immediately*, but only *after* they were gone, without specifying the time. Probably it was not long after he had appeared to Mary Magdalene. They would naturally return to the garden after they had informed the disciples, and linger around there, that they might ascertain what had become of him, or learn whether he had been seen by anyone. It was, then, probably *after* they had been away and returned, and *after* he had been seen by Mary, that they saw him.

II. APPEARANCES OF JESUS AFTER THE RESURRECTION.

1. To Mary Magdalene, Jn. xx. 14; Mar. xvi. 9.
2. To the other women, Mat. xxviii. 9.
3. To Peter, 1 Co. xv. 5; Lu. xxiv. 34.
4. To two disciples as they were going to Emmaus, Mar. xvi. 12, 13; Lu. xxiv. 13–32.
5. The same day, at evening, to the apostles, in the absence of Thomas, 1 Co. xv. 5; Mar. xvi. 14; Lu. xxiv. 36; Jn. xx. 19, 24.
6. To the apostles when Thomas was present, Jn. xx. 24–29.
7. In Galilee, at the Sea of Tiberias, to Peter, Thomas, Nathaniel, James and John, and two others, Jn. xxi. 1–14. This is said to be *the third time* that he showed himself to the disciples—that is, *to the apostles when they were assembled together*, Jn. xxi. 14.
8. To the disciples on a mountain in Galilee, Mat. xxviii. 16.
9. To more than five hundred brethren at once, 1 Co. xv. 6.
10. To James, one of the apostles, 1 Co. xv. 7.
11. To all the apostles assembled together, 1 Co. xv. 7. He was seen by them forty days after he rose—probably conversing with them familiarly.
12. To the apostles at his ascension, Lu. xxiv. 50, 51; Ac. i. 9, 10.
13. To Paul, 1 Co. xv. 8; Ac. ix. 3–5; xxii. 6–10.

III. THE ASCENSION.

1. It was forty days after his resurrection, Ac. i 3
2. He ascended from the Mount of Olives, near Bethany, Lu. xxiv. 50; Ac. i. 12.
3. It was in the presence of all the apostles, Lu. xxiv. 50; Ac. i. 9, 10.
4. He was received into a cloud, and ascended to heaven, Ac. i. 9, 11; Lu. xxiv. 51; Ep. i. 20–22.

PREFACE

TO THE GOSPEL ACCORDING TO MARK.

Of Mark, the writer of this Gospel, little is certainly known. He is commonly supposed to be the same that is several times mentioned in the New Testament. He was not an apostle, or companion of the Lord Jesus, during his ministry, though some of the fathers affirm that he was one of the seventy disciples. This is improbable, as he is mentioned by Peter (1 Pe. v. 13) as *his son;* from which it is supposed that he was converted by the instrumentality of Peter.

From the New Testament we learn that he was sister's son to Barnabas (Col. iv. 10); and that his mother's name was Mary, a pious woman in Jerusalem, at whose house the apostles and primitive Christians often assembled, Ac. xii. 12.

His Hebrew name was John (Ac. xii. 12), and it is probable that he adopted a name better known or more familiar when he visited the Gentiles, a practice not uncommon in that age. He was at first the companion of Paul and Barnabas in their journeys to propagate Christianity, Ac. xii. 25; xiii. 5; xv. 37. He chose not to attend them through their whole journey, but left them in Pamphylia, and probably returned to Jerusalem, Ac. xv. 38. Probably at this time he was the companion of Peter, and travelled with him to Babylon, 1 Pe. vi. 13. Afterward he went with Barnabas to Cyprus, Ac. xv. 39. Subsequently he went to Rome, at the express desire of Paul, in company with Timothy, 2 Ti. iv. 11. He remained at Rome while Paul was a captive there, but how long is uncertain, Col. iv. 10; Phile. 24. From Eusebius, Epiphanius, and Jerome we hear that Mark went from Rome to Alexandria, in Egypt, where he planted a church, and died in the eighth year of the reign of Nero, A.D. 64.

The time when this Gospel was written is not certainly known. It is supposed to have been between the years 56 and 63. It is allowed by all that it was written at Rome; of course it was during the latter years of his life, after the apostles had left Judea, Mar. xvi. 20. Mark was for a considerable time the companion of Peter. Though he had not himself been with the Saviour in his ministry, yet, from his long acquaintance with *Peter*, he was familiar with the events of his life, and with his instructions. The uniform testimony of the fathers is that he was the *interpreter* of Peter, and that he wrote this Gospel under the eye of Peter and with his approbation. It has come down to us, therefore, with the sanction of Peter's authority. Its right to a place among the inspired books has never been questioned. That it was written by Mark, that it was with Peter's approbation, that it was a record of the *facts* which Peter stated in his ministry, and that it was therefore an inspired book, has never been questioned.

THE GOSPEL ACCORDING TO MARK.

CHAPTER I.

THE beginning of the gospel of Jesus Christ, the [a]Son of God;

2 As it is written in the prophets, [b]Behold, I send my messenger before thy face, which shall prepare thy way before thee.

3 The[c] voice of one crying in the wilderness, Prepare ye the way of the Lord, make his paths straight.

4 John[d] did baptize in the wilderness, and preach the baptism of repentance, [1]for the [e]remission of sins.

5 And there went out unto him all the land of Judea, and they of Jerusalem, and were all baptized of him in the river of Jordan, [f]confessing their sins.

6 And John was clothed with camel's hair, and with a girdle of a skin about his loins; and he did eat [g]locusts and wild honey;

7 And preached, saying, [h]There cometh one mightier than I after me, the latchet of whose shoes I am not worthy to stoop down and unloose.

8 I indeed have baptized you with water; but [i]he shall baptize you with the Holy Ghost.

9 And it came to pass in those days that Jesus came from Nazareth of Galilee, and [k]was baptized of John in Jordan.

10 And straightway coming up out of the water, he saw the heavens [2]opened, and [l]the Spirit, like a dove, descending upon him:

11 And there came a voice from heaven, *saying*, [m]Thou art my beloved Son, in whom I am well pleased.

12 And immediately the Spirit driveth him into the wilderness.

13 And[n] he was there in the wilderness forty days, tempted of

a He.1.1,2. *b* Mal.3.1. *c* Is.40.3.
d Mat.3.1; Lu.3.3; Jn.3.23. [1] or, *unto*. *e* Ac.22.16.
f Le.26.40-42; Ps.32.5; Pr.28.13; 1 Jn.1.8-10.
g Le.11.22.

h Mat.3.11; Jn.1.27; Ac.13.25.
i Joel 2.28; Ac.1.5; 2.4; 10.45; 11.15,16; 1 Co.12.13.
k Mat.3.13; Lu.3.21. [2] or, *cloven*, or, *rent*.
l Is.42.1; Jn.1.32. *m* Ps.2.7.
n Mat.4.1,&c.; Lu.4.1,&c.

---

1. *The beginning of the gospel.* The word *gospel* literally signifies good tidings, and particularly the good tidings respecting the way of salvation by the Lord Jesus Christ. Some have understood the word *gospel* here to mean *history* or *life—the beginning of the history*, &c.; but Mark says nothing of the early life of the Saviour. The word *gospel* here has reference rather to the preaching of John, an account of which immediately follows, and means the beginning of the good news, or annunciation respecting the Messiah. It was very customary thus to prefix a title to a book. ¶ *The Son of God.* This title was used here to attract attention, and secure the respect of those who should read the gospel. It is no common history. It does not recount the deeds of man—of a hero or a philosopher—but the doctrines and doings of THE SON OF GOD. The history, therefore, *commands* respect.

2, 3. *As it is written in the prophets.* Mark mentions *prophets* here without specifying which. The places are found in Mal. iii. 1, and in Is. xli. 3. See Notes on Mat. iii. 3.

4–8. See Notes on Mat. iii. 3, 5, 6, 11.

9–11. See Notes on Mat. iii. 13–17.

12, 13. Mark here relates concisely what Matthew has recorded more at length in ch. iv. ¶ *The Spirit driveth.* The word *driveth* does not mean that he was compelled forcibly against his will to go there, but that he was inclined to go there by the Spirit, or was led there. The Spirit of God, for important purposes, *caused* him to go. Comp. Mat. ix. 25, where the same word is

Satan; and was with the wild beasts; and the angels ministered unto him.

14 Now after that John was put in prison, [o]Jesus came into Galilee, preaching the [p]gospel of the kingdom of God,

15 And saying, [q]The time is fulfilled, and the kingdom of God is at hand: [r]repent ye, and [s]believe the gospel.

16 Now[t] as he walked by the sea of Galilee, he saw Simon, and Andrew his brother, casting a net into the sea: (for they were fishers.)

17 And Jesus said unto them, Come ye after me, and I will make you to become fishers of men.

18 And straightway they forsook their nets and followed him.

19 And when he had gone a little further thence, he saw James the *son* of Zebedee, and John his brother, who also were in the ship mending their nets.

20 And straightway he called them: and they left their father Zebedee in the ship with the hired servants, and went after him.

21 And they went into Capernaum: and straightway on the sabbath-day he entered into the synagogue and taught.

22 And[u] they were astonished at his doctrine: for he taught them as one that had authority, and not as the scribes.

23 And[v] there was in their synagogue a man with an unclean spirit; and he cried out,

24 Saying, Let *us* alone; what

o Mat.4.23. p Lu.8.1. q Da.2.44; 9.25; Ga.4.4; Ep.1.10. r Ac.2.38. s Ro.16.26. t Mat.4.18,&c.; Lu.5.4,&c. u Mat.7.28. v Lu.4.33,&c.

used in the original: "And when they were all *put forth*"—in Greek, *all driven out*. ¶ *And was with the wild beasts.* This is added to show the desolation and danger of his dwelling there. In this place, surrounded by such dangers, the temptations offered by Satan were the stronger. Amid want and perils, Satan might suppose that he would be more easily seduced from God. But he trusted in his Father, and was alike delivered from dangers, from the wild beasts, and from the power of temptation, thus teaching *us* what to do in the day of danger and trial. ¶ *And the angels ministered unto him.* From Lu. iv. 2 we learn that in those days he did eat nothing. When Mark says, therefore, that the angels ministered to him, it means *after* the days of temptation had expired, as is said by Mat. iv. 11.

14. *Now after that John was put in prison.* John was imprisoned by Herod, Mat. xiv. 3. ¶ *Jesus came into Galilee.* He left Judea and went into the more retired country of Galilee. He supposed that if he remained in Judea, Herod would also persecute him and attempt to take his life. His time of death had not come, and he therefore prudently sought safety in retirement. Hence we may learn that when we have great duties to perform for the church of God we are not wantonly to endanger our lives. When we can secure them without a sacrifice of *principle*, we are to do it. See Mat. xxiv. 16.

15. *The time is fulfilled.* That is, the time for the appearance of the Messiah, the time so long foretold, has come. ¶ *The kingdom of God is at hand.* See Notes on Mat. iii. 2. ¶ *Repent ye.* Exercise sorrow for sins, and turn from them. ¶ *And believe the gospel.* Literally, trust in the gospel, or believe the good tidings—to wit, respecting salvation. See Notes on Mat. iv. 17.

16–20. See Notes on Mat. iv. 18–22.

21–27. See also Lu. iv. 31–37.

21. *And they went into Capernaum.* For the situation of Capernaum see Notes on Mat. iv. 13. ¶ *Straightway.* Immediately. On the following Sabbath. ¶ *The synagogue.* See Notes on Mat. iv. 23. ¶ *And taught.* In the synagogue, the presiding elder, after reading the Scriptures, invited any who chose to address the people, Ac. xiii. 15. Though our Saviour was not a *priest* of the Levitical order or an *officer* of the synagogue, yet we find him often availing himself of this privilege, and delivering his doctrines to the Jews.

22. *He taught them as one that had authority,* &c. See Notes on Mat. vii. 29.

23. *A man with an unclean spirit.*

have we to do with thee, thou Jesus of Nazareth? art thou come to destroy us? I know thee who thou art, the Holy One of God.

25 And Jesus rebuked him, saying, Hold thy peace, and come out of him.

26 And when the unclean spirit had torn him, and cried with a loud voice, he came out of him.

27 And they were all amazed, insomuch that they questioned among themselves, saying, What thing is this? what new doctrine *is* this? for with authority commandeth he even the unclean spirits, and they do obey him.

28 And immediately his fame spread abroad throughout all the region round about Galilee.

See Mat. iv. 24. It is probable that this man had lucid intervals, or he would not have been admitted into the synagogue. When there, one of his fits came on, and he suddenly cried out.

24. *Let us alone.* Though but *one* impure spirit is mentioned as possessing this man, yet that spirit speaks also in the name of others. They were leagued together in the work of evil, and this one knew that if *he* was punished, others would also share the same fate. ¶ *What have we to do with thee?* See Notes on Mat. viii. 29. By this the spirit meant to say that if Jesus cast him out he would use an improper interference. But this was untrue. The possession of the man was a direct assault on God and his works. Jesus came to destroy the works of the devil, and he had a right, therefore, to liberate the captive, and to punish him who had possessed him. So Satan still considers it an infringement of his rights when God frees a *sinner* from bondage and destroys his influence over the soul. So he still asks to be let alone, and to be suffered to lead men captive at his will. ¶ *Art thou come to destroy us?* Implying that this could not be the intention of the *benevolent* Messiah; that to be cast out of that man would, in fact, be his destruction, and that therefore he might be suffered still to remain. Or it may imply, as in Mat. viii. 29, that the time of their destruction had not come, and that he ought not to destroy them before that. ¶ *I know thee who thou art.* Evil spirits seem to have been acquainted at once with the Messiah. Besides, they had learned from his miracles that he was the Messiah, and had power over them. ¶ *The Holy One of God.* The Messiah. See Da. ix. 24. He is called the Holy One of God because—1st. He was eminently pure. 2d. Because he was the only begotten Son of God—equal with the Father. And, 3d. Because he was anointed or set apart to the work of the Messiah, the mediator between God and man.

25. *And Jesus rebuked him.* Chid him, or commanded him, with a threatening. This was not the *man* that he rebuked, but the *spirit*, for he instantly commanded the same being to come out of the man. In all this Jesus did not once *address the man.* His conversation was with the *evil spirit*, proving conclusively that it was not a mere disease or mental derangement—for how could the Son of God hold converse with *disease* or *insanity?*—but that he conversed with a *being* who also conversed, reasoned, cavilled, felt, resisted, and knew him. There *are*, therefore, evil spirits, and those spirits *have* taken possession of men. ¶ *Hold thy peace.* Greek, *Be muzzled.* Restrain thyself. Cease from complaints, and come out of the man. This was a very signal proof of the power of Jesus, to be able by a word to silence an evil angel, and, against his will, to compel him to leave a man whom he delighted to torment.

26. *And when the unclean spirit,* &c. Still malignant, though doomed to obey—submitting because he was obliged to, not because he chose—he exerted his last power, inflicted all the pain he could, and then bowed to the Son of God and came out. This is the nature of an evil disposition. Though compelled to obey, though prevented by the command and providence of God from doing what it *would*, yet, in seeming to obey, it does all the ill it can, and makes even the appearance of obedience the occasion for increased crime and mischief.

27, 28. *And they were all amazed,* &c. The power of casting out devils was to them new. It was done by a word. Jesus did it in his own name and by his own authority. This proved that he was *superior* to all the unclean spirits. In consequence, his fame spread throughout all the country, and the

29 And[w] forthwith, when they were come out of the synagogue, they entered into the house of Simon and Andrew, with James and John.

30 But Simon's wife's mother lay sick of a fever; and anon they tell him of her.

31 And he came, and took her by the hand, and lifted her up; and immediately the fever left her, and she ministered unto them.

32 And at even, when the sun did set, they brought unto him all that were diseased, and them that were possessed with devils.

33 And all the city was gathered together at the door.

34 And he healed many that were sick of divers diseases, and cast out many devils; and suffered not the devils [3]to speak, because they knew him.

35 And in the morning, rising up a great while before day, he went out, and departed into a solitary place, and there prayed.

36 And Simon, and they that were with him, followed after him.

37 And when they had found him, they said unto him, All *men* seek for thee.

w Mat.8.14; Lu.4.38.

3 or, *to say that they knew him.*

---

impression became prevalent that he was the Messiah.

29–31. See Notes on Mat. viii. 14, 15.

32–34. See Notes on Mat. viii. 16, 17. ¶ *And at even, when the sun did set.* See Notes on Mat. viii. 16.

33. *All the city.* A great part of the city. A great multitude from the city.

34. *And suffered not the devils to speak, because they knew him.* They knew that he was the Messiah. If they had spoken, they would have made that known to the people. Jesus was not desirous at that time that that should be publicly known, or that his name should be blazoned abroad. The time had not come when he wished it to be promulgated that he was the Messiah, and he therefore imposed silence on the evil spirits.

35–37. *And in the morning, rising up a great while before day.* Luke says (iv. 42), *when it was day.* The passage in Mark means, in the original, not literally *a great while before day*, but very early, or while there was yet *much appearance of night.* The place in Luke means *at daybreak*, at the beginning of day. Then, also, there is much appearance of night; and Luke and Mark therefore refer to the same time—before it was fully light, or just at daybreak. ¶ *And departed into a solitary place, and there prayed.* Here observe, 1st. That the Saviour, though perfectly holy, regarded the duty of secret prayer as of great importance. 2d. That he sought a solitary place for it—far away from the world and even from his disciples. 3d. That it was early in the morning—always the *best* time, and a time when it should not be omitted. 4th. If Jesus prayed, how much more important is it for us! If *he* did it in the morning, how much more important is it for *us*, before the world gets possession of our thoughts; before Satan fills us with unholy feelings; when we rise fresh from beds of repose, and while the world around us is still! David also thus prayed, Ps. v. 3; cxix. 147. He that wishes to enjoy religion will seek a place of secret prayer in the morning. If that is omitted, all will go wrong, our piety will wither. The world will fill our thoughts. Temptations will be strong. Through the day we shall find it impossible to raise our feelings to a state of proper devotion. It will be found to be true universally, *that the religious enjoyment through the day will be according to the state of the heart in the morning, and can therefore be measured by our faithfulness in early secret prayer.* How different, too, was the conduct of the Saviour from those who spend the precious hours of the morning in sleep! He knew the value of the morning hours; he rose while the world was still; he saw the light as it spread abroad in the east with fresh tokens of his Father's presence, and joined with the universal creation in offering praise to the everywhere present God.

36. *And Simon.* Simon Peter. ¶ *They that were with him.* The other apostles.

37. *All* men *seek for thee.* That is, many men, or multitudes. The inquiry after him was general. They told him this, evidently, with a view to induce

38 And he said unto them, Let us go into the next towns, that I may preach there also; for [x]therefore came I forth.

39 And he preached in their synagogues throughout all Galilee, and cast out devils.

40 And[y] there came a leper to him, beseeching him, and kneeling down to him, and saying unto him, If thou wilt, thou canst make me clean.

41 And Jesus, moved with compassion, put forth *his* hand, and touched him, and saith unto him, I will; be thou clean.

42 And as soon as he had spoken, [z]immediately the leprosy departed from him, and he was cleansed.

43 And he straitly charged him, and forthwith sent him away;

44 And saith unto him, See thou say nothing to any man; but go thy way, show thyself to the priest,

x Is.61.1,2; Jn.17.8. *y* Mat.8.2; Lu.5.12. *z* Ps.33.9; Jn.15.3.

---

him to leave his place of retirement, and to prevail upon him to appear publicly to instruct the multitudes.

38. *And he said unto them*, &c. This was said in answer to their *implied* request that he would go and meet the multitudes. "Since the anxiety to hear the truth is so great, since such multitudes are waiting to hear the word, let us go into the next towns," &c. ¶ *Next towns.* Towns in the neighbourhood or vicinity of Capernaum. He proposed to carry the gospel to them, rather than that multitudes should leave their homes and attend him in his ministry. The word here rendered *towns* denotes places in size between *cities* and *villages*, or large places, but without walls. ¶ *For therefore came I forth.* That is, came forth from God, or was sent by God. Luke says (iv. 43), "for therefore am I sent." Comp. Jn. xvi. 28: "I came forth from the Father, and am come into the world." The meaning of this verse therefore is, "Since multitudes press to hear the word, let us not remain here, but go into the neighbouring towns also; for I was sent by God not to preach at Capernaum only, but *throughout Judea*, and it is therefore improper to confine my labours to this place."

39. *And he preached in their synagogues.* See Mat. iv. 23. ¶ *All Galilee.* See Mat. i. 22. ¶ *And cast out devils.* See Mat. iv. 24.

40–45. *And there came a leper*, &c. See Notes on Mat. viii. 1–4. ¶ *Kneeling down to him.* He kneeled and inclined his face to the ground, in token of deep humiliation and earnest entreaty. Comp. Lu. v. 12. ¶ *If thou wilt.* This was an acknowledgment of the almighty power of Jesus, and an appeal to his benevolence. ¶ *Make me clean.* Canst heal me of this loathsome and offensive disease, in the eye of the law justly regarded as *unclean*, and render me *legally* clean, and restore me to the privileges of the congregation. ¶ *And Jesus—touched him.* It was by the law considered as unclean to touch a leprous man. See Nu. v. 2. The fact that Jesus *touched* him was evidence that the requisite power had been already put forth to heal him; that Jesus regarded him as already clean. ¶ *I will.* Here was a most manifest proof of his divine power. None but God can work a miracle; yet Jesus does it by his *own will*—by an exertion of his own power. He is therefore divine. ¶ *See thou say nothing to any man.* The law of Moses required that a man who was healed of the leprosy should be pronounced clean by the priest before he could be admitted again to the privileges of the congregation, Le. xiv. Christ, though *he* had cleansed him, yet required him to be obedient to the law of the land—to go at once to the priest, and not to make delay by stopping to converse about his being healed. It was also possible that, if he did not go at once, evil-minded men would go before him and prejudice the priest, and prevent his declaring the healing to be thorough because it was done by Jesus. It was farther of importance that *the priest* should pronounce it to be a genuine cure, that there might be no cavils among the Jews against its being a real miracle. ¶ *Offer for thy cleansing those things*, &c. Two birds, and cedar-wood, and scarlet, and hyssop; and after eight days, two he-lambs, without blemish, and one ewe-lamb, and fine flour, and oil, Le. xiv. 4, 10. ¶ *For a testimony unto them.* Not to the *priest*, but to the *people*, that they may have evidence

and offer for thy cleansing [a]those things which Moses commanded, for a [b]testimony unto them.

45 But he went out, and began to [c]publish *it* much, and to blaze abroad the matter, insomuch that Jesus could no more openly enter into the city, but was without in desert places: and [d]they came to him from every quarter.

CHAPTER II.

AND again he entered into Capernaum after *some* days; and it was noised that he was in the house.

2 And straightway many were gathered together, insomuch that there was no room to receive *them*, no, not so much as about the door: and he [a]preached the word unto them.

3 And[b] they come unto him, bringing one sick of the palsy, which was borne of four.

4 And when they could not come nigh unto him for the press, they uncovered the roof where he was: and when they had broken *it* up, they let down the bed wherein the sick of the palsy lay.

5 When Jesus [c]saw their faith, he said unto the sick of the palsy, Son, thy sins be forgiven thee.

a Le.14.2-32. *b* Ro.15.4; 1 Co.10.11. *c* Ps.77.11,12; Tit.1.10. *d* ch.2.13.

a Ps.40.9. *b* Mat.9.1,&c.; Lu.5.18,&c. *c* Ac.14.9; Ep.2.8.

---

that it is a real cure. The testimony of the priest on the subject would be decisive.

45. *Began to publish* it *much.* That is, he made known his own cure. He was so deeply affected with it, and so much rejoiced, that he followed the natural dictates of his own feelings rather than the command of the Saviour. ¶ *Jesus could no more enter openly into the city.* The word *could*, here, does not refer to any natural inability, or to any physical obstacle in his way, but only denotes that there was difficulty, inconvenience, or impropriety in his doing it then; that he judged it best *not* then to enter into the city. The difficulty was, probably, that his being in the city drew such crowds of people as rendered it difficult to accommodate them, or so as to excite the opposition of civil rulers. ¶ *The city.* The city or large town where the leper was cured. The same reason for not entering that city applied also to others, so that he remained in the deserts, where the multitudes could come to him without any difficulty or opposition.

CHAPTER II.

1. *Into Capernaum.* See Notes on Mat. iv. 13. ¶ *After* some *days.* The number of days is not known. Probably he remained long enough in the desert to heal the sick that were brought to him, and to give instructions to the multitudes that attended his preaching. Capernaum was not *the city* mentioned in ch. i. 45, and it is probable that there was no difficulty in his remaining there and preaching. ¶ *And it was noised,* &c. He entered the city, doubtless, privately; but his being there was soon known, and so great had his popularity become that multitudes pressed to hear him.

2. *So much as about the door.* In the *court* or *yard* before the door. They could not get near enough to hear him. ¶ *Preached the word unto them.* The word of God; the revelation or doctrine which he came to deliver, called *the Word*, and *the Word of God*, because it was spoken or revealed by God. Comp. Ac. vi. 2–7.

3–12. See this miracle explained in Mat. ix. 2–8. ¶ *Palsy.* See Notes on Mat. iv. 24. ¶ *Borne of four.* Borne on a couch (Mat. ix. 2) by four men.

4. *The press.* The crowd, the multitude of people. Jesus was probably in the large open area or hall in the centre of the house. See Notes on Mat. ix. 2. The people pressed into the area, and blocked up the door so that they could not have access to him. ¶ *They uncovered the roof where he was.* See Notes on Mat. ix. 2. ¶ *When they had broken it up.* When they had removed the awning or covering, so that they could let the man down. See Notes on Mat. ix. 2.

5. *Their faith.* Their confidence or belief that he could heal them. ¶ *Son.* Literally *child.* The Hebrews used the

6 But there were certain of the scribes sitting there, and reasoning in their hearts,

7 Why doth this *man* thus speak blasphemies? Who can [d]forgive sins but God only?

8 And immediately, when Jesus perceived in his spirit that they so reasoned within themselves, he said unto them, Why reason ye these things in your hearts?

9 Whether is it easier to say to the sick of the palsy, *Thy* sins be forgiven thee; or to say, Arise, and take up thy bed, and walk?

10 But that ye may know that the Son of man hath [e]power on earth to forgive sins, (he saith to the sick of the palsy,)

11 I say unto thee, Arise, and take up thy bed, and go thy way into thine house.

12 And immediately he arose, took up the bed, and went forth before them all; insomuch that they were all amazed, and glorified God, saying, [f]We never saw it on this fashion.

13 And he went forth again by the sea-side; and all the multitude resorted unto him, and he taught them.

14 And[g] as he passed by, he saw Levi, the son of Alpheus, sitting [1]at the receipt of custom, and said unto him, Follow me. And he arose and followed him.

15 And[h] it came to pass, that, as Jesus sat at meat in his house, many [i]publicans and sinners sat also together with Jesus and his disciples: for there were many, and they followed him.

16 And when the scribes and Pharisees saw him eat with publicans and sinners, they said unto his disciples, How is it that he eateth and drinketh with publicans and sinners?

17 When Jesus heard *it*, he saith

d Is.43.25; Da.9.9. *e* Ac.5.31.

f Jn.7.31; 9.32. *g* Mat.9.9; Lu.5.27.
[1] or, *at the place where the custom was received.*
h Mat.9.10,&c. *i* Lu.15.1-5.

---

words *son* and *child* with a great latitude of signification. They were applied to children, to grandchildren, to adopted children, to any descendants, to disciples, followers, young people, and to dependants. See Notes on Mat. i. 1. In this place it denotes affection or kindness. It was a word of consolation—an endearing appellation, applied by the Saviour to the sick man to show his *compassion*, to inspire confidence, and to assure him that he would heal him.

12. *We never saw it on this fashion.* Literally, "We never saw it so." We never saw anything like this.

13. *By the sea-side.* That is, by the Sea of Tiberias, on the shore of which Capernaum was situated. See Notes on Mat. iv. 13.

14. *Levi, the son of Alpheus.* The same, undoubtedly, as *Matthew*, the writer of the gospel which bears his name. It was not uncommon among the Jews to have two names. ¶ *The receipt of custom.* See Notes on Mat. ix. 9.

15. *Sat at meat in the house.* The words "at meat" are not in the original. The phrase means "as he reclined at his meal," or "as he was eating." This feast was made by Matthew in honour of the Saviour. See Lu. v. 29. ¶ *Publicans.* See Notes on Mat. v. 47. ¶ *Sinners.* Sinners of abandoned character—of the same character that publicans commonly sustained—fit companions of publicans—great sinners. ¶ *There were many.* That is, many *disciples.* Their following him, leaving their homes, and going with him from place to place, was proof of their attachment to him. There is no doubt that our Saviour, in the early part of his ministry, was extremely popular. Multitudes of the common people attended him, and gave conclusive evidence that they were his real disciples, and it was only after much opposition from the rich and the great that he ever became unpopular among the people. Perhaps no preacher has ever attracted so universal attention, and produced so decisive effects on mankind, as our Lord did in his personal ministry.

16, 17. See Notes on Mat. ix. 12, 13.

unto them, [k]They that are whole have no need of the physician, but they that are sick: I came not to call the righteous, [l]but sinners to repentance.

18 And the disciples of John and of the Pharisees used to fast: and they come and say unto him, Why do the disciples of John and of the Pharisees fast, but thy disciples fast not?

19 And Jesus said unto them, Can the children of the bride-chamber fast while the [m]bridegroom is with them? As long as they have the bridegroom with them, they cannot fast.

20 But the days will come when the bridegroom shall be taken away from them, and [n]then shall they fast in those days.

21 No man also seweth a piece of [2]new cloth on an old garment; else the new piece that filled it up taketh away from the old, and the rent is made worse.

22 And no man putteth new wine into old bottles; else the new wine doth burst the bottles, and the wine is spilled, and [o]the bottles will be marred: but new wine must be put into new bottles.

23 And[p] it came to pass, that he went through the corn-fields on the sabbath-day; and his disciples began, as they went, to [q]pluck the ears of corn.

24 And the Pharisees said unto him, Behold, why do they on the sabbath-day that which is not lawful?

25 And he said unto them, Have ye never read [r]what David did, when he had need, and was an hungered, he, and they that were with him?

26 How he went into the house of God in the days of Abiathar the

k Mat.9.12,13; Lu.5.31,32.
l Is.1.18; 55.7; Mat.18.11; Lu.19.10; 1 Co.6.9-11; 1 Ti.1.15. *m* Mat.25.1. *n* Ac.13.2.
2 or, *raw*, or, *unwrought*.

o Job 32.19; Ps.119.80,83.
p Mat.12.1,&c.; Lu.6.1,&c. *q* De.23.25. *r* 1 Sa.21.6.

18. *And the disciples of John and of the Pharisees used to fast.* Were accustomed often to fast. Comp. Lu. v. 33; xviii. 12. ¶ *And they come and say.* The disciples of John come, Mat. ix. 4.

19–22. See Notes on Mat. ix. 15–17.

23–28. See Mat. xii. 1–8. ¶ *The corn-fields.* The fields sown with wheat or barley. The word *corn*, in the Bible, refers only to grain of that kind, and never to *maize* or *Indian corn.* ¶ *To pluck the ears of corn.* They were hungry, Mat. xii. 1. They therefore gathered the wheat or barley as they walked, and rubbed it in their hands to shell it, and thus to satisfy their appetite. Though our Lord was with them, and though he had all things at his control, yet he suffered them to resort to this method of supplying their wants. When Jesus, thus *with* his disciples, suffered them to be *poor*, we may learn that poverty is not disgraceful; that God often suffers it for the good of his people; and that he will take care, in some way, that their wants shall be supplied. It was *lawful* for them thus to supply their wants. Though the property belonged to another, yet the law of Moses allowed the poor to satisfy their wants when hungry. See De. xxiii. 25.

24. *That which is not lawful.* That is, that which they esteemed to be unlawful on the *Sabbath-day.* It was made lawful by Moses, without any distinction of days, but *they* had denied its lawfulness on the Sabbath. Christ shows them from their own law that it was *not* unlawful.

25. *Have ye never read,* &c. See Notes on Mat. xii. 3.

26. *Abiathar the priest.* From 1 Sa. xxi. 1, it appears that *Ahimelech* was high-priest at the time here referred to. And from 1 Sa. xxiii. 6, it appears that *Abiathar* was the son of *Ahimelech.* Some difficulty has been felt in reconciling these accounts. The probable reason why Mark says it was in the days of *Abiathar* is that Abiathar was better known than Ahimelech. The son of the high-priest was regarded as his successor, and was often associated with him in the duties of his office. It was not improper, therefore, to designate him as high-priest even during the life of his father, especially as that was the name by which he was afterward known.

high-priest, and did eat the [s]shew-bread, which is not lawful to eat but for the priests, and gave also to them which were with him?

27 And he said unto them, [t]The sabbath was made for man, and not[u] man for the sabbath:

28 Therefore [v]the Son of man is Lord also of the sabbath.

CHAPTER III.

AND[a] he entered again into the synagogue; and there was a man there which had a withered hand.

s Ex.29.32,33; Le.24.9.
t Ne.9.14; Is.58.13; Eze.20.12,20. u Col.2.16.
v Jn.9.14; Ep.1.22; Re.1.10.
a Mat.12.9,&c.; Lu.6.6,&c.

Abiathar, moreover, in the calamitous times when David came to the throne, left the interest of Saul and fled to David, bringing with him the ephod, one of the peculiar garments of the high-priest. For a long time, during David's reign, he was high-priest, and it became natural, therefore, to associate *his* name with that of David; to speak of David as king, and Abiathar the high-priest of his time. This will account for the fact that he was spoken of rather than his father. At the same time this was strictly true, that this was done in the days of *Abiathar*, who was afterward high-priest, and was familiarly spoken of as such; as we say that *General* Washington was present at the defeat of Braddock and saved his army, though the title of *General* did not belong to him till many years afterward. Comp. Notes on Lu. ii. 2. ¶ *Shew-bread.* See Notes on Mat. xii. 4.

27. *The sabbath was made for man.* For his rest from toil, his rest from the cares and anxieties of the world, to give him an opportunity to call off his attention from earthly concerns and to direct it to the affairs of eternity. It was a kind provision for man that he might refresh his body by relaxing his labours; that he might have undisturbed time to seek the consolations of religion to cheer him in the anxieties and sorrows of a troubled world; and that he might render to God that homage which is most justly due to him as the Creator, Preserver, Benefactor, and Redeemer of the world. And it is easily capable of proof that no institution has been more signally blessed to man's welfare than the Sabbath. To that we owe, more than to anything else, the peace and order of a civilized community. Where there is no Sabbath there is ignorance, vice, disorder, and crime. On that holy day the poor and the ignorant, as well as the learned, have undisturbed time to learn the requirements of religion, the nature of morals, the law of God, and the way of salvation. On that day man may offer his praises to the Great Giver of all good, and in the sanctuary seek the blessing of him whose favour is life. Where that day is observed in any manner as it should be, order prevails, morals are promoted, the poor are elevated in their condition, vice flies away, and the cmomunity puts on the appearance of neatness, industry, morality, and religion. The Sabbath was therefore pre-eminently intended for man's welfare, and the best interests of mankind demand that it should be sacredly regarded as an appointment of merciful heaven intended for our best good, and, where improved aright, infallibly resulting in our temporal and eternal peace. ¶ *Not man for the sabbath.* Man was made *first*, and then the Sabbath was appointed for his welfare, Ge. ii. 1–3. The Sabbath was not *first* made or contemplated, and then the man made with reference to that. Since, therefore, the Sabbath was intended for man's *good*, the law respecting it must not be interpreted so as to oppose his real welfare. It must be explained in consistency with a proper attention to the duties of mercy to the poor and the sick, and to those in peril. It must be, however, in accordance with man's *real good on the whole*, and with the law of God. The law of God contemplates man's *real good on the whole;* and we have no right, under the plea that the Sabbath was made for man, to do anything contrary to what the law of God admits. It would not be for our *real good*, but for our real and eternal injury, to devote the Sabbath to vice, to labour, or to amusement.

28. *Therefore the Son of man*, &c. See Notes on Mat. xii. 8.

CHAPTER III.

1–5. See this explained in Mat. xii. 9–13.

4. *Or to do evil? to save life, or to kill?*

2 And they [b]watched him whether he would heal him on the sabbath-day, that they might accuse him.

3 And he saith unto the man which had the withered hand, Stand[1] forth.

4 And he saith unto them, Is it lawful to do good on the sabbath-days, or to do evil? [c]to save life, or to kill? But they held their peace.

5 And when he had looked round about on them with anger, being grieved for the [2]hardness of their hearts, he saith unto the man, Stretch forth thine hand. And he stretched *it* out; and his hand was restored whole as the other.

6 And the Pharisees went forth, and straightway took counsel with the [d]Herodians against him, how they might destroy him.

b Lu.14.1. 1 *Arise in the midst.* c Ho.6.6. 2 or, *blindness.* d Mat.22.16.

It seems to have been a maxim with the Jews that *not* to do good when we have an opportunity is to do evil; *not* to save life is to kill or to be guilty of murder. If a man has an opportunity of saving a man's life when he is in danger, and does not do it, he is evidently guilty of his death. On this principle our Saviour puts this question to the Jews—whether it was better for him, having the *power* to heal this man, to do it, or to suffer him to remain in this suffering condition; and he illustrates it by an example, showing that in a manner of much less importance—that respecting their cattle—they would do on the Sabbath just as *he* would if he should heal this man. The same remark may apply to all opportunities of doing good. "The ability to do good imposes an *obligation* to do it" (Cotton Mather). He that has the means of feeding the hungry, and clothing the naked, and instructing the ignorant, and sending the gospel to the destitute, and that does it not, is guilty, for he is practically doing evil; he is suffering evils to exist which he might remove. So the wicked will be condemned in the day of judgment because *they did it not*, Mat. xxv. 45. If this be true, what an obligation rests on the rich to do good!

5. *With anger.* With a severe and stern countenance; with indignation at their hypocrisy and hardness of heart. This was not, however, a spiteful or revengeful passion; it was caused by excessive *grief* at their state: "being *grieved* for the hardness of their hearts." It was not hatred of the *men* whose hearts were so hard; it was hatred of the *sin* which they exhibited, joined with the extreme grief that neither his teaching nor the law of God, nor any means which could be used, overcame their confirmed wickedness. Such anger is not unlawful, Ep. iv. 26. But in this instance our Lord has taught us that anger is never lawful except when it is tempered with grief or compassion for those who have offended. ¶ *Hardness of their hearts.* The heart, figuratively the seat of feeling or affection, is said to be tender when it is easily affected by the sufferings of others—by our own sin and danger—by the love and commands of God; when we are easily made to *feel* on the great subjects pertaining to our interest, Eze. xi. 19, 20. It is hard when nothing moves it; when a man is alike insensible to the sufferings of others, to the dangers of his own condition, and to the commands, the love, and the threatenings of God. It is most tender in youth, or when we have committed fewest crimes. It is *made* hard by indulgence in sin, by long resisting the offers of salvation, or by opposing any great and affecting appeals which God may make to us by his Spirit or providence, by affliction, or by a revival of religion. Hence it is that the most favourable period for securing an interest in Christ, or for becoming a Christian, is in youth—the first, the tenderest, and the best days of life. Nay, in the days of childhood, in the Sabbath-school, God may be found, and the soul prepared to die.

6. *Straightway.* Immediately, or as soon as possible. ¶ *Took counsel.* Laid a plan. Consulted with them. Literally, "made a consultation." ¶ *The Herodians.* See Notes on Mat. xxii. 16. ¶ *How they might destroy him.* They hated him, he was so holy; because he reproved them; because he laid open their hypocrisy; and because he won the hearts of the people and lessened their influence. They therefore determined to remove him, if possible, and thus avoid his reproofs.

7 But Jesus withdrew himself with his disciples to the sea: and a great[e] multitude from Galilee followed him, and from Judea,

8 And from Jerusalem, and from Idumea, and *from* beyond Jordan; and they about Tyre and Sidon, a great multitude, when they had heard what great things he did, came unto him.

9 And he spake to his disciples, that a small ship should wait on him because of the multitude, lest they should throng him.

10 For he had [f]healed many; insomuch that they [3]pressed upon him for to touch him, as many as had plagues.

11 And[g] unclean spirits, when they saw him, fell down before him, and cried, saying, Thou art the Son of God.

e Lu.6.17.

f Mat.12.15; 14.14. 3 or, *rushed.*
g ch.1.24; Mat.14.33; Lu.4.41; Ja.2.19.

Sinners would often rather put to death the man that reproves them than forsake their sins. The Pharisees had rather commit any crime, even to the murder of the Messiah, than forsake the sins for which he rebuked them.

7, 8. *To the sea.* The Sea of Galilee, or to the lonely regions which surrounded the sea, where he might be in obscurity, and avoid their designs against his life. His time had not yet come, and he prudently took care of his life, thus showing that we are not needlessly to throw ourselves into danger. ¶ *Galilee.* See Notes on Mat. ii. 22. ¶ *Judea.* The southern division of the land of Palestine. ¶ *Jerusalem.* Jerusalem was *in* Judea. It is mentioned particularly to show that not only the people of the surrounding *country* came, but also many from the capital, the place of wealth, and honour, and power. ¶ *Idumea.* The country formerly inhabited by the *Edomites.* In the time of the Saviour it was embraced in the country belonging to the Jews. It was south of Judea proper. The word *Idumea* is a Greek word made from the Hebrew *Edom.* It signifies the land of Edom, a name given to Esau, one of the sons of Isaac, Ge. xxv. 30. The word signifies *red,* and the name was given to him because he sought of Jacob red pottage as the price of his birthright. He settled in Mount Seir (De. ii. 5), on the south of the land of Canaan, and the country of Idumea was bounded by Palestine on the north. During the Babylonish captivity the Edomites spread themselves into the country of Judea, and occupied a considerable part of the south of Palestine. They had, however, submitted to the rite of circumcision, and were incorporated with the Jews. From them sprang Herod the Great. ¶ From *beyond Jordan.* From the region lying *east* of the river Jordan. The sacred writers lived on the *west* side of Jordan, and by the country *beyond Jordan* they meant that on the *east* side. ¶ *Tyre and Sidon.* See Notes on Mat. xi. 21.

9. *A small ship.* Rather a *boat.* There were properly speaking, no *ships* on the Sea of Tiberias. This was probably a small boat that belonged to the disciples, in which he could draw off from the shore, and teach the people without being pressed by them. ¶ *Lest they should throng him.* They pressed upon him in great numbers. He had healed many, and those who were still diseased pressed or crowded on him, so that his labours were interrupted and embarrassed. He therefore withdrew from the multitude, and sought a situation where he might address them to greater advantage. ¶ *As many as had plagues.* As many as had diseases or maladies of body or mind. The word *plague,* now confined to the pestilence, does not express the meaning of the original, and tends to mislead.

11, 12. *Unclean spirits.* Persons who were possessed of evil spirits. ¶ *Thou art the Son of God.* The Son of God, by way of eminence. In this place it is equivalent to the Messiah, who was, among the Jews, called the Son of God. Hence they were charged not to make him known, because he was not desirous that it should be blazoned abroad that he claimed to be the Messiah. He had not yet done what he wished in order to establish his claims to the Messiahship. He was poor and unhonoured, and the claim would be treated as that of an impostor. *For the present,* therefore, he did not wish that it should be proclaimed abroad that he was the Messiah.

The circumstance here referred to

12 And[h] he straitly charged them that they should not make him known.

13 And[i] he goeth up into a mountain, and calleth *unto him* whom[k] he would; and they came unto him.

14 And he ordained twelve, that they should be with him, and that he might send them forth to preach,

15 And to have power to heal sicknesses, and to cast out devils:

16 And [l]Simon he surnamed Peter;

17 And James the *son* of Zebedee, and John the brother of James, and he surnamed them Boanerges, which is, [m]The sons of thunder;

18 And Andrew, and Philip, and Bartholomew, and Matthew, and Thomas, and James the *son* of Alpheus, and Thaddeus, and Simon the Canaanite,

19 And Judas Iscariot, which also betrayed him: and they went [4]into an house.

20 And the multitude cometh together again, [n]so that they could not so much as eat bread.

21 And when his [5]friends heard *of it*, they went out to lay hold on

h ch.1.25,34. *i* Mat.10.1. *k* Jn.15.16. *l* Jn.1.42.
m Is.58.1; Je.23.29. *n* ch.6.31.
4 or, *home.* 5 or, *kinsmen.*

demonstrates the existence of evil spirits. If these were merely diseased or deranged persons, then it is strange that they should be endowed with knowledge so much superior to those in health. If they were under the influence of an order of spirits superior to man — whose appropriate habitation was in another world—then it is not strange that they should know him, even in the midst of his poverty, to be the Messiah, the Son of God.

13–19. For an account of the appointment of the apostles, see Notes on Mat. x. 1–4. ¶ *And calleth* unto him *whom he would.* Those whom he chose; whom he was about to appoint to the apostleship. See Notes on Jn. xv. 16.

14. *He ordained twelve.* The word rendered *ordained* here does not express our notion of ordination to the ministry. It means, literally, "he made" —that is, he *appointed* twelve to be with him. ¶ *Twelve.* The reason why *twelve* were chosen was, probably, that such a number would be deemed competent witnesses of what they saw; that they could not be easily charged with being excited by sympathy, or being deluded, as a multitude might; and that, being destined to go into all the world, a considerable number seemed indispensable. Perhaps, also, there was some reference to the fact that *twelve* was the number of the twelve tribes of Israel.

17. *Boanerges.* This word is made up of two Hebrew words signifying *sons of thunder*, meaning that they, on some accounts, *resembled* thunder. See Notes on Mat. i. 1. It is not known why this name was given to James and John. They are nowhere else called by it. Some suppose it was because they wished to call down fire from heaven and consume a certain village of the Samaritans, Lu. ix. 54. It is, however, more probable that it was on account of something fervid, and glowing, and powerful in their genius and eloquence.

20. *They could not so much as eat bread.* Their time and attention were so occupied that they were obliged to forego their regular meals. The affairs of religion *may* so occupy the attention of ministers and others as to prevent their engaging in their customary pursuits. Religion is all-important—far more important than the ordinary business of this life; and there is nothing unreasonable if our *temporal* affairs sometimes give way to the higher interests of our own souls and the souls of others. At the same time, it is true that religion is ordinarily consistent with a close attention to worldly business. It promotes industry, economy, order, neatness, and punctuality—all indispensable to worldly prosperity. Of these there has been no more illustrious example than that of our Saviour himself.

21. *When his friends.* Greek, "they who were of him." Not the apostles, but his relatives, his friends, who were in the place of his nativity. ¶ *Heard* of it. Heard of his conduct; his preaching; his appointing the apostles; his drawing such a multitude to his preaching. This shows that by "his friends" were not meant the apostles, but his

him: for they said, [o]He is beside himself.

22 And the scribes which came down from Jerusalem said, [p]He hath Beelzebub, and by the prince of the devils casteth he out devils.

23 And he called them *unto him*, and said unto them in parables, How can Satan cast out Satan?

24 And if a kingdom be divided against itself, that kingdom cannot stand.

25 And if a house be divided against itself, that house cannot stand.

26 And if Satan rise up against himself, and be divided, he cannot stand, but hath an end.

27 No[q] man can enter into a strong man's house, and spoil his goods, except he will first bind the strong man; and then he will spoil his house.

28 Verily I say unto you, [r]All sins shall be forgiven unto the sons of men, and blasphemies wherewith soever they shall blaspheme:

29 But he that shall [s]blaspheme against the Holy Ghost hath never forgiveness, but is in danger of eternal damnation:

30 Because they said, He hath an unclean spirit.

31 There[t] came then his brethren and his mother, and, standing without, sent unto him, calling him.

32 And the multitude sat about him; and they said unto him, Behold, thy mother and thy brethren without seek for thee.

33 And he answered them, saying, Who is my mother, or my brethren?

34 And he looked round about on them which sat about him, and said, Behold my mother and my brethren!

35 For whosoever shall [u]do the

o Ho.9.7; Jn.10.20.
p Mat.9.34; 10.25; 12.24; Lu.11.15; Jn.7.20; 8.48,52.
q Is.49.24,26; 61.1; Mat.12.29.
r Mat.12.31; Lu.12.10.
s He.10.29. t Mat.12.46-48; Lu.8.19-21.
u Ja.1.25; 1 Jn.2.17.

neighbours and others who *heard* of his conduct. ¶ *They went out to lay hold on him.* To take him away from the multitude, and to remove him to his home, that he might be treated as a maniac, so that, by absence from the *causes* of excitement, he might be restored to his right mind. ¶ *They said.* That is, common report said; or his friends and relatives said, for they did not believe on him, Jn. vii. 5. Probably the enemies of Jesus raised the report, and his relatives were persuaded to believe it to be true. ¶ *He is beside himself.* He is delirious or deranged. The reason why this report gained any belief was, probably, that he had lived among them as a carpenter; that he was poor and unknown; and that now, at thirty years of age, he broke off from his occupations, abandoned his common employment, spent much time in the deserts, denied himself the common comforts of life, and set up his claims to be the Messiah who was expected by all the people to come with great pomp and splendour. The charge of *derangement* on account of attention to religion has not been confined to the Saviour. Let a man be made deeply sensible of his sins, and spend much of his time in prayer, and have no relish for the ordinary amusements or business of life; or let a Christian be much impressed with his obligation to devote himself to God, and *act* as if he believed there was an *eternity*, and warn his neighbours of their danger; or let a minister show uncommon zeal and spend his strength in the service of his Master, and the world is not slow to call it derangement. And none will be more ready to originate or believe the charge than an ungodly and infidel parent or brother, a self-righteous Pharisee or professor in the church. At the same time, men may endanger themselves on the bosom of the deep or in the bowels of the earth for wealth; or may plunge into the vortex of fashion, folly, and vice, and break in upon the hours of repose, and neglect their duties to their family and the demands of business, and in the view of the world it is wisdom and proof of a sane mind! Such is the consistency of boasted reason; such the wisdom and prudence of worldly men!

22-30. *And the scribes*, &c. See Notes

will of God, the same is my brother, and my sister, and my mother.

CHAPTER IV.

AND[a] he began again to teach by the sea-side: and there was gathered unto him a great multitude, so that he entered into a ship, and sat in the sea; and the whole multitude was by the sea on the land.

2 And he taught them many things by [b]parables, and said unto them in his doctrine,

3 Hearken:[c] Behold, there went out a sower to sow:

4 And it came to pass, as he sowed, some fell by the way-side, and [d]the fowls of the air came and devoured it up.

5 And some fell on [e]stony ground, where it had not much earth; and immediately it sprang up, because it had no depth of earth:

6 But when the sun was up, it was scorched; and [f]because it had no root, it withered away.

7 And some fell [g]among thorns; and the thorns grew up, and choked it, and it yielded no fruit.

8 And other fell on [h]good ground, and did [i]yield fruit that sprang up and increased, and brought forth, some thirty, and some sixty, and some an hundred.

9 And he said unto them, He that hath ears to hear, let him hear.

10 And[k] when he was alone, they that were about him with the twelve asked of him the parable.

11 And he said unto them, [l]Unto you it is given to know the mystery of the kingdom of God; but unto [m]them that are without, all *these* things are done in parables:

12 That[n] seeing they may see, and not perceive; and hearing they may hear, and not understand; lest at any time they should be converted, and *their* sins should be forgiven them.

13 And he said unto them, Know ye not this parable? and how then will ye know all parables?

14 The sower [o]soweth the word.

15 And these are they by the way-side, where the word is sown; but when they have heard, [p]Satan cometh immediately, and [q]taketh away the word that was sown in their hearts.

16 And these are they likewise which are sown on stony ground; who, when they have heard the word, immediately receive it with gladness;

17 And have [r]no root in themselves, and so endure [s]but for a

a Mat.13.1,&c.; Lu.8.4,&c. b Ps.78.2; ver.34. c ver.9,23; ch.7.16. d Ge.15.11. e Eze.11.19; 36.26. f Ps.1.4; Ja.1.11. g Je.4.3. h He.6.7,8. i Col.1.6.

k Mat.13.10,&c. l Ep.1.9. m Col.4.5; 1 Th.4.12; 1 Ti.3.7. n Is.6.9,10; Jn.12.40; Ac.28.26,27; Ro.11.8. o Is.32.20; 1 Pe.1.25. p 1 Pe.5.8; Re.12.9. q He.2.1. r Job 19.28. s Job 27.10.

---

on Mat. xii. 24–32. The occasion of their saying this was, that he had healed a man possessed with a devil. The scribes, who came from Jerusalem to watch his conduct, charged him with having made a compact or agreement with the prince of the devils.

31–35. See Notes on Mat. xii. 46–50.

CHAPTER IV.

1–9. See the parable of the sower explained in the Notes on Mat. xiii. 1–9.

10–13. See Notes on Mat. xiii. 10–17. On ver. 12, see Notes on Jn. xii. 39, 40. ¶ *When he was alone.* That is, separate from the multitude. When he withdrew from the multitude a few followed him for the purpose of farther instruction.

13. *Know ye not this parable?* This which is so plain and obvious. ¶ *How then will ye know all parables?* Those which are more difficult and obscure. As they were themselves to be *teachers*, it was important that they should be acquainted with the whole system of religion—of much more importance for them at that time than for the mass of the people.

time: afterward, when affliction or persecution ariseth for the word's sake, [t]immediately they are offended.

18 And these are they which are sown among thorns; such as hear the word,

19 And the [u]cares of this world, and the [v]deceitfulness of riches, and the [w]lusts of other things entering in, choke the word, and [x]it becometh unfruitful.

20 And these are they which are sown on good ground; such as hear the word, and receive *it*, and bring[y] forth fruit, some thirty-fold, some sixty, and some an hundred.

21 And he said unto them, Is a candle brought to be put under a [1]bushel, or under a bed, and not to be set on a candlestick?

22 For[z] there is nothing hid which shall not be manifested, neither was any thing kept secret but that it should come abroad.

23 If any man have ears to hear, let him hear.

24 And he saith unto them, Take heed [a]what ye hear: [b]with what measure ye mete, it shall be measured to you; and unto you that hear shall more be given.

25 For he that hath, to him shall be given; and he that hath not, [c]from him shall be taken even that which he hath.

t 2 Ti.1.15. *u* Lu.14.18-20; 1 Ti.6.9,17; 2 Ti.4.10. *v* Pr.23.5. *w* 1 Jn.2.16,17. *x* Is.5.2,4. *y* Ro.7.4; Col.1.10; 2 Pe.1.8.

1 See on Mat.5.15. *z* Ec.12.14; Mat.10.26; Lu.12.2; 1 Co.4.5. *a* 1 Pe.2.2. *b* Mat.7.2. *c* Lu.8.18.

14–20. See Notes on Mat. xiii. 18–23.

21. *Is a candle brought*, &c. A candle is not lit up to be put immediately under a measure or a bed, where it can give no light. Its design is to give light. So my preaching by parables is not designed to obscure the truth, but to throw light on it. You should understand those parables, and, understanding them, should impart the truth to others also, as a candle throws its beams upon a dark world. ¶ *Bushel.* The word here used in the original means a measure for grain containing about 12 quarts. ¶ *Bed.* A couch, either to sleep on at night or to recline on at their meals. Probably the latter is here meant, and is equivalent to our saying a candle is not brought to be put *under* the table, but *on* it. See Notes on Mat. xxiii. 6.

22. *There is nothing hid*, &c. See Notes on Mat. x. 26.

24. *Take heed what ye hear.* Or, consider well what you hear. Make a good improvement of it. ¶ *With what measure ye mete*, &c. You shall be treated according to the use you make of your opportunities of learning. If you consider it well, and make a good improvement of what you hear, you shall be well rewarded. If not, your reward shall be small. This is a proverbial expression. See it explained in the Notes on Mat. vii. 1, 2. ¶ *Mete.* Measure. With what measure ye measure. ¶ *Unto you that hear.* To you who are *attentive*, and who improve what you hear.

25. *For he that hath*, &c. See Notes on Mat. xiii. 12. The meaning here seems to be, he that diligently attends to my words shall increase more and more in the knowledge of the truth; but he that neglects them and is inattentive shall become more ignorant; the few things which he had learned he will forget, and his trifling knowledge will be diminished. ¶ *Hath not.* Does not improve what he possessed, or does not make proper use of his means of learning. ¶ *That which he hath.* That which he had already learned. By this we are taught the indispensable necessity of giving attention to the means of instruction. The attention must be *continued.* It is not sufficient that we have learned some things, or appear to have learned much. All will be in vain unless we go forward, and improve every opportunity of learning the will of God and the way of salvation. So what children are taught will be of little use unless they follow it up and endeavour to improve themselves.

26. *So is the kingdom of God.* The gospel, or religion in the soul, may be compared to this. See Notes on Mat. iii. 2. This parable is recorded only by Mark.

27. *And should sleep, and rise night and day.* Should sleep in the night and rise by day, for so the expression is to

26 And he said, [d]So is the kingdom of God, as if a man should cast seed into the ground;

27 And should sleep, and rise night and day, and the seed should spring and grow up, he knoweth not how.

28 For[e] the earth bringeth forth fruit of herself; [f]first the blade, then the ear; after that, the full corn in the ear.

29 But when the fruit is [2]brought forth, immediately [g]he putteth in the sickle, because the harvest is come.

30 And he said, Whereunto shall

d Mat.13.24. e Ge.1.11,12. f Ec.3.1,11. 2 or, *ripe*, Job 5.26. g Re.14.15.

be understood. That is, should live in his usual way, without exerting any influence over the growing grain. By this we are not to infer that men are to use no diligence in the obtaining and in the growth of piety; but the illustration shows only that as we cannot tell *how* grain grows, so we cannot tell the *mode* in which piety increases in the heart. ¶ *He knoweth not how.* This is still true. After all the researches of philosophers, no one has been able to tell the way in which grain grows. They can observe one fact after another; they can see the changes; they can see the necessity of rains and suns, of care and shelter, but beyond this they cannot go. So in religion. We can mark the change; we can see the need of prayer, and self-examination, and searching the Scriptures, and the ordinances of religion, but we cannot tell *in what way* the religious principle is developed and strengthened. As God unseen, yet by the use of proper means, makes the grass to flourish, so God unseen, but by proper means, nourishes the soul, and the plants of piety spring up, and bloom, and bear fruit. Comp. Notes on Jn. iii. 8.

28. *For the earth bringeth forth fruit of herself.* That is, it is done without the power of man. It is done while man is engaged in other things. The scope of this passage does not require us to suppose that our Saviour meant to say that the earth had any productive power *of itself*, but only that it produced its fruits not by the *power of man.* God gives it its power. It has no power of its own. So religion in the heart is not by the *power* of man. It grows he cannot tell how, and of course he cannot, without divine aid, control it. It is by the power of God. At the same time, as without industry man would have no harvest, so without active effort he would have no religion. Both are connected with his effort; both are to be measured commonly by his effort (Phi. ii. 12); both grow he cannot tell how; both increase when the proper means are used, and both depend on God for increase. ¶ *First the blade.* The green, tender shoot, that first starts out of the earth before the stalk is formed. ¶ *Then the ear.* The original means the *stalk* or *spire* of wheat or barley, as well as the ear. ¶ *The full corn.* The ripe wheat. The grain swollen to its proper size. By this is denoted, undoubtedly, that grace or religion in the heart is of gradual growth. It is at first tender, feeble, perhaps almost imperceptible, like the first shootings of the grain in the earth. Perhaps also, like grain, it often lies long in the earth before there are signs of life. Like the tender grain, also, it needs care, kindness, and culture. A frost, a cold storm, or a burning sun alike injure it. So tender piety in the heart needs care, kindness, culture. It needs shelter from the frosts and storms of a cold, unfeeling world. It needs the genial dews and mild suns of heaven; in other words, it needs instruction, prayer, and friendly counsel from parents, teachers, ministers, and experienced Christians, that it may grow, and bring forth the full fruits of holiness. Like the grain, also, in due time it will grow strong; it will produce its appropriate fruit—a full and rich harvest—to the praise of God.

29. *Immediately he putteth in the sickle.* This is the way with the husbandman. As soon as the grain is ripe it is cut down. So it is often with the Christian. As soon as he is prepared for heaven he is taken there. But we are not to press this part of the parable, as if it meant that *all* are removed as soon as they are fit for heaven. Every parable contains circumstances thrown in to fill up the story, which cannot be literally interpreted. In this, the circumstance of *sleeping* and *rising* cannot be applied to Christ; and in like manner, the harvest, I suppose, is not to be literally in-

we liken the kingdom of God? or with what comparison shall we compare it?

31 It[h] *is* like a grain of mustard-seed, which, when it is sown in the earth, is less than all the seeds that be in the earth:

32 But when it is sown, it groweth up, and becometh [i]greater than all herbs, and shooteth out great branches; so that the fowls of the air may lodge under the shadow of it.

33 And with many such parables spake he the word unto them, [k]as they were able to hear *it*.

34 But without a parable spake he not unto them: and when they were alone he expounded all things to his disciples.

35 And the same day, when the even was come, he saith unto them, Let us pass over unto the other side.

36 And when they had sent away the multitude, they took him even

h Mat.13.31,32; Lu.13.18,19.
i Pr.4.18; Is.11.9; Da.2.44; Mal.1.11.
k Jn.16.12.

terpreted. Perhaps the whole parable may be differently interpreted. The seed sown may mean the gospel which he was preaching. In Judea its beginnings were small; yet he would leave it, commit it to his disciples, and return to his Father. The gospel, in the mean-time, left by him, would take root, spring up, and produce an abundant harvest. In due time he would return, send forth the angels, and gather in the harvest, and save his people for ever. Comp. Notes on Mat. xiii. 31–33.

30. *Whereunto shall we liken*, &c. This shows the great solicitude which Jesus had to adapt his instructions to the capacity of his disciples. He sought out the most plain and striking illustrations—an example which should be followed by all the ministers of the gospel. At the same time that the instructions of the pulpit should be dignified—as our Saviour's always were—they should be adapted to the capacity of the audience and easily understood. To do this the following things are necessary in a minister: 1st. *Humility*. A freedom from a desire to shine, and to astonish the world by the splendour of his talents, and by his learning and eloquence. 2d. *Good sense*. A satisfaction in being understood. 3d. Acquaintance with the habits of thought and manner of speaking among the people. To do this, frequent intercourse with them is necessary. 4th. *A good sound education*. It is the men of ignorance, with some smattering of learning, and with a desire to confound and astonish men by the use of unintelligible words, and by the introduction of matter that is wholly unconnected with the subject, that most often shoot over the heads of the people. Preachers of humility, good sense, and education are content with being understood, and free from the affectation of saying things to amaze and confound their auditors. ¶ *The kingdom of God*. See Notes on Mat. iii. 2.

31, 32. See Notes on Mat. xiii. 31, 32.

33. *Spake he the word*. The word of God. The doctrines of his gospel. ¶ *As they were able to hear* it. As they could comprehend it. They were like children; and he was obliged to lead them along cautiously and by degrees to a full understanding of the plan of salvation.

34. *Without a parable spake he not unto them*. That is, the things pertaining to his kingdom. On other subjects he spake without parables. On these, such was their prejudice, so many notions had they contrary to the nature of his kingdom, and so liable would plain instructions have been to give offence, that he employed this method to *insinuate* truth gradually into their minds, and to prepare them fully to understand the nature of his kingdom. ¶ *They were alone*. His disciples. ¶ *He expounded*. Explained. Showed them more at length the spiritual meaning of the parables.

35–41. See Notes on Mat. viii. 18–27.

36. *Even as he was in the ship*. They took him without making any preparation for the voyage; without providing any food or raiment. He was sitting in a ship, or boat, instructing the people. In the same boat, probably ill fitted to encounter a storm on the lake, they sailed. This would render their danger more imminent and the miracle more striking. ¶ *There were with him other little ships*. Belonging probably to the people, who, seeing him sail, resolved to follow him.

as he was in the ship: and there were also with him other little ships.

37 And[l] there arose a great storm of wind, and the waves beat into the ship, so that it was now full.

38 And he was in the hinder part of the ship, asleep on a pillow: and they awake him, and say unto him, Master,[m] carest thou not that we perish?

39 And he arose, and rebuked the wind, and said unto the sea, Peace, be still. And[n] the wind ceased, and there was a great calm.

40 And he said unto them, [o]Why are ye so fearful? how is it that ye have no faith?

41 And they [p]feared exceedingly, and said one to another, What manner of man is this, that even the wind and the [q]sea obey him?

CHAPTER V.

AND[a] they came over unto the other side of the sea, into the country of the Gadarenes,

l Mat.8.24; Lu.8.23. *m* Ps.10.1; Is.40.27; La.3.8. *n* Ps.89.9; La.3.31,32. *o* Ps.46.1,2; Is.43.2. *p* Jonah 1.10,16. *q* Job 38.11. *a* Mat.8.28,&c.; Lu.8.26,&c.

39. *Peace, be still.* There is something exceedingly authoritative and majestic in this command of our Lord. Standing amid the howling tempest, on the heaving sea, and in the darkness of night, by his own power he stills the waves and bids the storm subside. None but the *God* of the storms and the billows could awe by a word the troubled elements, and send a universal peace and stillness among the winds and waves. He *must*, therefore, be divine. The following remarks by Dr. Thomson, long a resident in Syria, and familiar with the scenes which occur there, will farther illustrate this passage, and the parallel account in Mat. viii. 18–27, and also the passage in Mat. xiv. 23–32. The extract which follows is taken from *The Land and the Book*, vol. ii. p. 32, 33:—"To understand the causes of these sudden and violent tempests, we must remember that the lake lies low—600 feet lower than the ocean; that the vast and naked plateaus of the Jaulan rise to a great height, spreading backward to the wilds of the Hauran and upward to snowy Hermon; that the water-courses have cut out profound ravines and wild gorges, converging to the head of this lake, and that these act like gigantic *funnels* to draw down the cold winds from the mountains. On the occasion referred to we subsequently pitched our tents at the shore, and remained for three days and nights exposed to this tremendous wind. We had to double-pin all the tent-ropes, and frequently were obliged to hang with our whole weight upon them to keep the quivering tabernacle from being carried up bodily into the air. No wonder the disciples toiled and rowed hard all that night; and how natural their amazement and terror at the sight of Jesus walking on the waves! The faith of Peter in desiring and *daring* to set foot on such a sea is most striking and impressive; more so, indeed, than its failure after he made the attempt. The whole lake, as we had it, was lashed into fury; the waves repeatedly rolled up to our tent door, tumbling over the ropes with such violence as to carry away the tent-pins. And moreover, those winds are not only violent, but they come done suddenly, and often when the sky is perfectly clear. I once went in to swim near the hot baths, and, before I was aware, a wind came rushing over the cliffs with such force that it was with great difficulty I could regain the shore. Some such sudden wind it was, I suppose, that filled the ship with waves 'so that it was now full,' while Jesus was asleep on a pillow in the hinder part of the ship; nor is it strange that the disciples aroused him with the cry of Master! Master! carest thou not that we perish!"

CHAPTER V.

1–20. See this account of the demoniacs fully explained in the Notes on Mat. viii. 28–34.

4. *He had been often bound with fetters and chains.* Efforts had been made to confine him, but his great strength—his strength increased by his malady—had prevented it. There often appears to be a great increase of strength produced by insanity, and what is here stated in regard to this maniac often

2 And when he was come out of the ship, immediately there met him out of the tombs a man with an unclean spirit,

3 Who[b] had *his* dwelling among the tombs; and no man could bind him, no, not with chains:

4 Because that he had been often bound with fetters and chains, and the chains had been plucked asunder by him, and the fetters broken in pieces: neither could any *man* tame him.

5 And always, night and day, he was in the mountains, and in the tombs, crying, and cutting himself with stones.

6 But when he saw Jesus afar off, he ran and [c]worshipped him,

7 And cried with a loud voice, and said, What have I to do with thee, Jesus, *thou* Son of the most high God? I adjure thee by God that thou torment me not.

8 (For he said unto him, [d]Come out of the man, *thou* unclean spirit.)

9 And he asked him, What *is* thy name? And he answered, saying, My name *is* Legion; [e]for we are many.

10 And he besought him much that he would not send them away out of the country.

11 Now there was there, nigh unto the mountains, a great herd of [f]swine feeding.

12 And all the devils [g]besought him, saying, Send us into the swine, that we may enter into them.

13 And forthwith [h]Jesus gave them leave. And the unclean spirits went out, and entered into the swine; and the herd ran violently down a steep place into the sea, (they were about two thousand,) and were choked in the sea.

14 And they that fed the swine fled, and told *it* in the city, and in the country. And they went out to see what it was that was done.

15 And they came to Jesus, and see him that was possessed with the devil, and [i]had the legion, sit-

b Is.65.4. c Ps.72.9. d Ac.16.18; He.2.14; 1 Jn.3.8.
e Mat.12.45. f Le.11.7,8; De.14.8.
g Job 1.10,12; 2.3,6. h Re.13.7; 1 Pe.3.22.
i Is.49.25; Col.1.13.

---

occurs in Palestine and elsewhere now. Dr. Thomson (*The Land and the Book*, vol. i. p. 213) says respecting this case: "There are some very similar at the present day—furious and dangerous maniacs, who wander about the mountains, and sleep in tombs and caves. In their worst paroxysms they are quite unmanageable and prodigiously strong." Luke (ch. viii. 27) says of him that "he wore no clothes," or that he was naked, which is also implied in the account in Mark, who tells us that after he was healed he was found "*clothed* and in his right mind," ver. 15. This is often a striking characteristic of insanity. Dr. Pritchard (on *Insanity*, p. 26) quotes from an Italian physician's description of raving madness or mania: "A striking and characteristic circumstance is the propensity to go quite naked. The patient tears his clothes to tatters." So Dr. Thomson (*The Land and the Book*, vol. i. p. 213) says: "It is one of the most common traits in this madness that the victims refuse to wear clothes. I have often seen them absolutely naked in the crowded streets of Beirut and Sidon. There are also cases in which they run wildly about the country and frighten the whole neighbourhood. These poor wretches are held in the greatest reverence by Moslems, who, through some monstrous perversion of ideas, believe them to be inspired and peculiarly holy."

5. *Cutting himself with stones.* These are all marks of a *madman*—a man bereft of reason, a wretched outcast, strong and dangerous. The inspired penman says that this madness was caused by an unclean spirit, or by his being under the influence of a devil. That this account is not irrational, see Notes on Mat. iv. 24.

6. *Worshipped him.* Bowed down before him; rendered him homage. This was an acknowledgment of his power, and of his control over fallen spirits.

9. *My name* is *Legion.* See Notes on Mat. viii. 29.

ting, and clothed, and in his right mind: and [k]they were afraid.

16 And they that saw *it* told them how it befell to him that was possessed with the devil, and *also* concerning the swine.

17 And they began to pray him to [l]depart out of their coasts.

18 And when he was come into the ship, he that had been possessed with the devil prayed him that he might be with him.

19 Howbeit, Jesus suffered him not, but saith unto him, Go home to thy friends, and [m]tell them how great things the Lord hath done for thee, and hath had compassion on thee.

20 And he departed, and began to publish in Decapolis how great things Jesus had done for him: and all *men* did marvel.

21 And when Jesus was passed over again by ship unto the other side, much people gathered unto him; and he was nigh unto the sea.

22 And,[n] behold, there cometh one of the rulers of the synagogue, Jairus by name; and when he saw him, he fell at his feet,

23 And besought him greatly, saying, My little daughter lieth at the [o]point of death: *I pray thee* come and lay thy hands on her, that she may be healed; and she shall live.

24 And *Jesus* went with him; and much people followed him, and thronged him.

25 And a certain woman, which had an [p]issue of blood twelve years,

26 And had suffered many things of many physicians, and had spent all that she had, and was [q]nothing bettered, but rather grew worse,

27 When she had heard of Jesus, came in the press behind and [r]touched his garment:

k Job 13.11; Ps.14.5; 2 Ti.1.7.
l Job 21.14; Lu.5.8; Ac.16.39.
m Ps.66.16; Is.38.19.
n Mat.9.18,&c.; Lu.8.41,&c.
o Ps.107.18.
p Le.15.19,&c.
q Job 13.4; Ps.108.12; Je.30.12,13.
r 2 Ki.13.21; Mat.14.36; Ac.5.15; 19.12.

---

15. *Sitting, and clothed, and in his right mind.* There could be no doubt of the reality of this miracle. The man had been well known. He had long dwelt among the tombs, an object of terror and alarm. To see him all at once peaceful, calm, and rational, was proof that it was the power of God only that had done it. ¶ *They were afraid.* They were *awed*, as in the presence of God. The word does not mean here that they feared that any *evil* would happen to them, but that they were affected with *awe;* they felt that God was there; they were struck with astonishment at what Jesus had done.

19. *Jesus suffered him not.* Various reasons have been conjectured why Jesus did not suffer this man to go with him. It might have been that he wished to leave him among the people as a conclusive evidence of his power to work miracles. Or it might have been that the man feared that if Jesus left him the devils would return, and that Jesus told him to remain to show to him that the cure was complete, and that he had power over the devils when absent as well as when present. But the probable reason is, that he desired to restore him to his family and friends. Jesus was unwilling to delay the joy of his friends, and to prolong their anxiety by suffering him to remain away from them.

20. *In Decapolis.* See Notes on Mat. iv. 25. ¶ *How great things*, &c. This was the natural expression of right feeling at being cured of such a calamity. So the desire of sinners freed from sin is to honour Jesus, and to invite the world to participate in the same salvation, and to join them in doing honour to the Son of God. Comp. Ps. lxvi. 16.

22–43. See the account of the raising of Jairus's daughter, and the healing of the woman with an issue of blood, fully explained in the Notes on Mat. ix. 18–26.

23. *Lieth at the point of death.* Is dying; in the last agonies.

26. *Had suffered many things.* Had resorted to many things painful, by the direction of the physicians, in order to be healed.

28 For she said, If I may touch but his clothes, I shall be whole.

29 And straightway the fountain of her blood was dried up, and she felt in *her* body that she was healed of that plague.

30 And Jesus, immediately knowing in himself that [s]virtue had gone out of him, turned him about in the press, and said, Who touched my clothes?

31 And his disciples said unto him, Thou seest the multitude thronging thee, and sayest thou, Who touched me?

32 And he looked round about to see her that had done this thing.

33 But the woman, fearing and trembling, knowing what was done in her, came and fell down before him, and [t]told him all the truth.

34 And he said unto her, Daughter, [u]thy faith hath made thee whole: [v]go in peace, and be whole of thy plague.

35 While he yet spake, there came from the ruler of the synagogue's *house certain* which said, [w]Thy daughter is dead: why troublest thou the Master any further?

36 As soon as Jesus heard the word that was spoken, he saith unto the ruler of the synagogue, Be not afraid, [x]only believe.

37 And he suffered no man to follow him, [y]save Peter, and James, and John the brother of James.

38 And he cometh to the house of the ruler of the synagogue, and seeth the tumult, and them that wept and wailed greatly.

39 And when he was come in, he saith unto them, Why make ye this ado and weep? the damsel is not dead, but [z]sleepeth.

40 And they laughed him to scorn. But when he had put them all out, he taketh the father and the mother of the damsel, and them that were with him, and entereth in where the damsel was lying.

41 And he took the damsel by the

s Lu.6.19. t Ps.30.2. u ch.10.52; Ac.14.9. v 1 Sa.1.17; 20.42; 2 Ki.5.19.
w Jn.5.25; 11.25. x 2 Ch.20.20; Jn.11.40. y ch.9.2; 14.33. z Jn.11.11-16.

---

27. *Came in the press behind.* In the crowd that pressed upon him. This was done to avoid being noticed. It was an act of faith. She was full of confidence that Jesus was *able* to heal, but she trembled on account of her conscious unworthiness, thus illustrating the humility and confidence of a sinner coming to God for pardon and life.

30. *Virtue had gone out of him.* Power to heal. The word in the original means *power.* ¶ *Who touched my clothes?* This he said, not to obtain information, for he had healed her, and must have known on whom the blessing was conferred; but he did it that the woman might herself make a confession of the whole matter, so that the power of her faith and the greatness of the miracle might be manifested to the praise of God.

34. *Daughter.* A word of kindness, tending to inspire confidence and to dissipate her fears. ¶ *Be whole.* That is, *continue* to be whole, for she was already cured. ¶ *Of thy plague.* Thy disease; literally, thy *scourge.* So a word from Jesus heals the moral malady of the sinner.

35, 36. *Why troublest thou,* &c. It seems that the people had not yet confidence that Jesus could raise the dead. He had not yet done it; and as the child was now dead, and as they supposed that his power over her was at an end, they wished no farther to trouble him. Jesus kindly set the fears of the ruler at rest, and assured him that he had equal power over the dead and the living, and could as easily raise those who had expired as those who were expiring.

38. *The tumult.* The confusion and weeping of the assembled people. ¶ *Wailed.* Making inarticulate, mournful sounds; howling for the dead.

39. *This ado.* This tumult, this bustle or confusion. ¶ *And weep.* Weep in this inordinate and improper manner. See Notes on Mat. ix. 23. ¶ *But sleepeth.* See Notes on Mat. ix. 24

hand, and said unto her, Talitha cumi; which is, being interpreted, Damsel, (I say unto thee,) [y]arise.

42 And straightway the damsel arose and walked; for she was *of the age* of twelve years. And they were astonished with a great astonishment.

43 And he [z]charged them straitly that no man should know it; and commanded that something should be given her to eat.

CHAPTER VI.

AND he went out from thence, and came into his own country; and his disciples follow him.

2 And[a] when the sabbath-day was come, he began to teach in the synagogue: and many, hearing *him*, were astonished, saying, From[b] whence hath this man these things? and what wisdom *is* this which is given unto him, that even such mighty works are wrought by his hands?

3 Is not this the carpenter, the son of Mary, the brother of [c]James, and Joses, and of Juda, and Simon? and are not his sisters here with us? And they were [d]offended at him.

4 But Jesus said unto them, [e]A prophet is not without honour, but in his own country, and among his own kin, and in his own house.

5 And he [f]could there do no mighty work, save that he laid his hand upon a few sick folk and healed *them*.

6 And he [g]marvelled because of their unbelief. And [h]he went round about the villages, teaching.

7 And[i] he called *unto him* the twelve, and began to send them forth by two and two, and gave them power over unclean spirits;

8 And commanded them that they should take nothing for *their* journey save a staff only; no scrip, no bread, no [1]money in *their* purse;

9 But *be* [k]shod with [l]sandals; and not put on two coats.

10 And he said unto them, In what place soever ye enter into an house, there abide till ye depart from that place.

11 And whosoever shall not re-

y Ac.9.40. z Mat.8.4; 12.16-18; ch.3.12; Lu.5.14. a Mat.13.54,&c.; Lu.4.16,&c. b Jn.6.42. c Ga.1.19.

d Mat.11.6. e Mat.13.57; Jn.4.44. f Ge.19.22; ch.9.23. g Is.59.16; Je.2.12. h Mat.9.35; Lu.13.22; Ac.10.38. i Mat.10.1,&c.; ch.3.13,&c.; Lu.9.1,&c.; 10.3,&c.

1 The word signifies a piece of brass money, in value somewhat less than a farthing, Mat.10.9, but here it is taken in general for money: Lu.9.3.

k Ep.6.15. l Ac.12.8.

41. *Talitha cumi.* This is the language which our Saviour commonly spoke. It is a mixture of Syriac and Chaldee, called Syro-Chaldaic. The proper translation is given by the evangelist—"Damsel, arise."

43. *Something should be given her to eat.* "He had raised her by *extraordinary* power, but he willed that she should be sustained by *ordinary* means." He also in this gave full evidence that she was really restored to life and health. The changes were great, sudden, and certain. There could be no illusion. So, when the Saviour had risen, he gave evidence of his own resurrection by eating with his disciples, Jn. xxi. 1-13.

CHAPTER VI.

1-6. See this passage explained in the Notes on Mat. xiii. 54-58.

7. *And he called* unto him *the twelve.* See Notes on Mat. x. 1. ¶ *And began to send them forth by two and two.* In order that they might *support* and *encourage* each other in their work. Amid the trials and opposition with which they would meet, mutual counsel and aid would greatly lighten their burdens and alleviate their calamities. Mutual counsel might also contribute to their success, and lead to *united* plans to advance the kingdom of the Redeemer. Jesus here, as in all the work of religion, consulted at the same time the *happiness* and the *usefulness* of his disciples; nor are they ever separated. Whatever contributes to the *usefulness* of his people produces also their happiness; or, in other words, the secret of being happy is to be *useful*.

8-11. See these verses fully explained in the Notes on Mat. x. 9-15. In Mat.

ceive you, nor hear you, when ye depart thence, [m]shake off the dust under your feet for a testimony against them. Verily I say unto you, It shall be more tolerable for Sodom [2]and Gomorrah in the day of judgment than for that city.

12 And they went out, and preached[n] that men should repent.

13 And they [o]cast out many devils, and [p]anointed with oil many that were sick, and healed *them*.

14 And[q] king Herod heard *of him;* (for his name was spread abroad;) and he said, That John the Baptist was risen from the dead, and therefore mighty works do show forth themselves in him.

15 Others[r] said, That it is Elias. And others said, That it is a prophet, or as one of the prophets.

16 But when Herod heard *thereof*, he said, It is John, whom I beheaded: he is risen from the dead.

17 For Herod himself had sent forth, and laid hold upon John, and bound him in prison, for Herodias' sake, his brother Philip's wife: for he had married her.

18 For John had said unto Herod, [s]It is not lawful for thee to have thy brother's wife.

19 Therefore Herodias had [3]a quarrel against him, and would have killed him; but she could not.

20 For [t]Herod feared John, knowing that he was a just man and an holy, and [4]observed him; and when he heard him, he did many things, and heard him gladly.

m Ne.5.13; Ac.13.51. [2] *or.*
n Lu.24.47; Ac.2.38; 3.19. *o* Lu.10.17. *p* Ja.5.14.
q Mat.14.1,&c.; Lu.9.7,&c. *r* Mat.16.14; ch.8.28.
s Le.18.16. [3] or, *an inward grudge.*
t Ex.11.3; Eze.2.5-7. [4] or, *kept him*, or, *saved him.*

x. 5 they were commanded not to go among the Gentiles or Samaritans. Mark omits that direction, perhaps, because he was writing for the *Gentiles*, and the direction might create unnecessary difficulty or offence. Perhaps he omits it also because the command was given for a temporary purpose, and was not in force at the time of his writing.

12. *Preached that men should repent.* See the nature of repentance explained in Notes on Mat. iii. 2. They were now called upon to repent and reform their lives because sin was evil, because the Messiah had come to preach forgiveness to the penitent, and because at *his* presence it was fit that the nation should turn from its sins and prepare to receive him.

13. *Cast out many devils.* See Notes on Mat. iv. 24. ¶ *And anointed with oil*, &c. Anointing with oil was in common use among the Jews in cases of sickness. It was supposed to have a mild, soothing, and alleviating effect on the body. In Ja. v. 14, the elders of the church, in connection with prayer, were directed also to anoint the sick with oil. See Notes on that passage. It was also used in wounds. See Notes on Is. i. 6. The good Samaritan poured *oil* and wine into the wounds of the waylaid Jew, Lu. x. 34. Josephus says that in the last sickness of Herod his physicians commanded him to be anointed with oil. It need not be supposed, however, that the apostles used oil for mere *medical* purposes. It was used, probably, like the imposition of hands, or like our Saviour's anointing the eyes of the blind with clay; also as a sign, in expectation of imparting that aid and comfort from God which was sought, and which was *represented* by the soothing and gentle effect of oil.

14-20. See this account of the death of John the Baptist fully explained in the Notes on Mat. xiv. 1-12.

20. *For Herod feared John.* That is, he stood in awe of him on account of his sanctity, and his boldness and fearlessness in reproving sin. ¶ *Knowing that he was a just man and an holy.* A holy, pious, upright, *honest* man—a man who would not be afraid of him, or afraid to speak his real sentiments. ¶ *And observed him*—marg. "*kept him*, or *saved him.*" This does not mean that he "observed" or obeyed his teachings, but that he kept him in safe custody in order to preserve him from the machinations of Herodias. He was willing to show his respect for John, and to secure him from danger, and even to do "many things" which might indicate respect for him—at least, to do

21 And when a convenient day was come, that Herod on [u]his birthday made a supper to his lords, high captains, and chief *estates* of Galilee;

22 And when the daughter of the said Herodias came in, and danced,[v] and pleased Herod and them that sat with him, the king said unto the damsel, Ask of me whatsoever thou wilt, and I will give *it* thee.

23 And he sware unto her, Whatsoever[w] thou shalt ask of me, I will give *it* thee, unto the half of my kingdom.

24 And she went forth, and said unto her mother, What shall I ask? And she said, The head of John the Baptist.

25 And she came in straightway with haste unto the king, and asked, saying, I will that thou give me by and by, in a charger, [x]the head of John the Baptist.

26 And the king was exceeding sorry; *yet* for his oath's sake, and for their sakes which sat with him, he would not reject her.

27 And immediately the king sent [5]an executioner, and commanded his head to be brought; and he went and beheaded him in the prison,

28 And brought his head in a charger, and gave it to the damsel: and the damsel gave it to her mother.

29 And when his disciples heard *of it*, [y]they came and took up his corpse, and laid it in a tomb.

30 And[z] the apostles gathered themselves together unto Jesus, and told him all things, both what they had done, and what they had taught.

31 And he said unto them, Come ye yourselves apart into a desert place and rest a while: for there were many coming and going, and they had no leisure so much as to eat.

32 And they departed into a desert place by ship privately.

u Ge.40.20. *v* Is.3.16. *w* Es.5.3,6; 7.2. *x* Ps.37.12,14.

5 or, *one of his guard.* *y* Ac.8.2. *z* Lu.9.10.

so much as to guard him from his enemies. ¶ *And did many things.* But he did not do the thing which was demanded of him—to break off from his sins. He attempted to make a compromise with his conscience. He still loved his sins, and did *other* things which he supposed might be accepted in the place of putting away, as he ought, the wife of his brother—the polluted and adulterous woman with whom he lived. Perhaps he treated John kindly, or spoke well of him, or aided him in his wants, and attempted in this way to silence his rebukes and destroy his faithfulness. This was probably before John was imprisoned. So sinners often treat ministers kindly, and do much to make them comfortable, and hear them gladly, while they are still unwilling to do *the thing* which is demanded of them—to repent and believe the gospel. They expect that their kind attentions will be accepted in the place of what God demands—repentance and the forsaking of their sins.

30. *And the apostles gathered themselves together.* That is, those whom he had sent out two and two, ver. 7. Having travelled around the country, they returned and met the Saviour at Capernaum.

31. *A desert place.* A retired place, across the sea from Capernaum, where they would be free from interruption. ¶ *There were many coming and going.* Coming to be healed and retiring, or coming to hear him preach. It means that they were *thronged*, or that there was a vast multitude attending his preaching.

32–44. See this narrative explained in the Notes on Mat. xiv. 13–21.

32. *By ship.* By a boat or a small vessel. ¶ *Privately.* Without making their plan known. They *intended* to go privately. It appears, however, that their intention became known, and multitudes followed them.

33. *Afoot thither.* On foot to the place where they saw them going. ¶ *Out of all cities.* All cities or large towns in the neighbourhood.

33 And the people saw them departing, and many knew him, and ran afoot thither out of all cities, and outwent them, and came together unto him.

34 And Jesus, when he came out, saw much people, and was moved with compassion toward them, because [a]they were as sheep not having a shepherd: and he began to teach them many things.

35 And[b] when the day was now far spent, his disciples came unto him and said, This is a desert place, and now the time *is* far passed:

36 Send them away, that they may go into the country round about, and into the villages, and buy themselves bread; for they have nothing to eat.

37 He answered and said unto them, Give ye them to eat. And they say unto him, [c]Shall we go and buy two hundred [6]pennyworth of bread, and give them to eat?

38 He saith unto them, How many loaves have ye? go and see. And when they knew, they say, Five, and two fishes.

39 And[d] he commanded them to make all sit down by companies upon the green grass.

40 And they sat down in ranks, by hundreds and by fifties.

41 And when he had taken the five loaves and the two fishes, he looked up to heaven, and [e]blessed and brake the loaves, and gave *them* to his disciples to set before them; and the two fishes divided he among them all.

42 And[f] they did all eat, and were filled.

43 And they took up twelve baskets full of the fragments, and of the fishes.

44 And they that did eat of the loaves were about five thousand men.

45 And[g] straightway he constrained his disciples to get into the ship, and to go to the other side before [7]unto Bethsaida, while he sent away the people.

46 And when he had sent them

a 1 Ki.22.17. b Mat.14.15,&c.; Lu.9.12,&c.; Jn.6.5,&c. c Nu.11.13,22; 2 Ki.4.43. 6 See on Mat.18.28.

d Mat.15.35; ch.8.6. e 1 Sa.9.13; Mat.26.26; Lu.24.30. f De.8.3. g Mat.14.22,&c.; Jn.6.17,&c. 7 or, *over against Bethsaida.*

---

34. *Much people—as sheep*, &c. They had no one to teach them and guide them. The priests and scribes were proud and corrupt; they despised the common people and neglected them.

35. *The time* is *far passed.* The day is almost gone. It is drawing near night.

37. *Two hundred pennyworth of bread.* About twenty-eight dollars, or £6. See Notes on Mat. xiv. 16. As the disciples had a common purse in which they carried their little property, consisting of the donations of their friends and money to be given to the poor (comp. Jn. xii. 6; Mat. xxvi. 8, 9; Lu. viii. 3), it is not improbable that they had at this time about this sum in their possession. Philip—for it was he who asked the question (Jn. vi. 7)—asked, with a mixture of wonder and agitation, whether they should take *all* their little property and spend it on a single meal? And even if we should, said he, it would not be sufficient to satisfy such a multitude. It was implied in this that, in *his* view, they could not provide for them if they wished to, and that it would be better to send them away than to attempt it.

40. *In ranks.* Literally, in the form of square beds in a garden. By regularly formed companies. ¶ *By hundreds and by fifties.* Some companies had a hundred in, and some fifty. We need not suppose that these were *exactly* formed or arranged, but that this was *about* the number. The expression indicates a *multitude.* There were so many that they sat down, by *hundreds* and by *fifties*, in separate companies, on the green grass.

43. *Twelve baskets.* Baskets belonging to the disciples, in which they carried their provisions, or, perhaps, belonging to some of the multitude. ¶ *Fragments.* Broken pieces of the bread that remained.

45–56. See this passage explained in the Notes on Mat. xiv. 22–36.

away, [h]he departed into a mountain to pray.

47 And when even was come, the ship was in the midst of the sea, and he alone on the land.

48 And he saw them [i]toiling in rowing; for the wind was contrary unto them: and about the fourth watch of the night he cometh unto them, walking upon the sea, and [k]would have passed by them.

49 But when they saw him walking[l] upon the sea, [m]they supposed it had been a spirit, and cried out:

50 (For they all saw him, and were troubled:) and immediately he talked with them, and saith unto them, [n]Be of good cheer: it is I; be not afraid.

51 And he went up unto them into the ship; and [o]the wind ceased; and they were sore amazed in themselves beyond measure, and wondered.

52 For they considered not *the miracle* of the loaves; for [p]their heart was hardened.

53 And[q] when they had passed over, they came into the land of Gennesaret, and drew to the shore.

54 And when they were come out of the ship, straightway they knew him,

55 And[r] ran through that whole region round about, and began to carry about in beds those that were sick, where they heard he was.

56 And whithersoever he entered, into villages, or cities, or country, they laid the sick in the streets, and besought him that they might [s]touch if it were but the [t]border of his garment: and as many as touched [8]him were made whole.

CHAPTER VII.

THEN[a] came together unto him the Pharisees, and certain of the scribes, which came from Jerusalem.

2 And when they saw some of his disciples eat bread with [1]defiled (that is to say, with unwashen) hands, they found fault.

3 For the Pharisees, and all the

h Mat.6.6; ch.1.35; Lu.6.12. *i* Jonah 1.13. *k* Lu.24.28. *l* Job 9.8. *m* Lu.24.37. *n* Is.43.2. *o* Ps.93.3,4. *p* Is.63.17.

q Mat.14.34. *r* Mat.4.24; ch.2.1-3. *s* Mat.9.20; ch.5.27,28; Ac.19.12. *t* Nu.15.38,39. [8] or, *it*. *a* Mat.15.1,&c. [1] or, *common*.

52. *They considered not* the miracle *of the loaves.* They did not remember or call to mind the *power* which Jesus had shown in feeding the five thousand by a miracle, and that, having done that, he had power also to save them from the storm. ¶ *Their heart was hardened.* Their *mind* was dull to perceive it. This does not mean that they were *opposed* to Jesus, or that they had what we denominate *hardness of heart*, but simply that they were slow to perceive his power. They did not quickly learn, as they ought to have done, that he had *all* power, and could therefore allay the storm. The word *heart* is frequently used in this sense. See Ep. i. 18, in Greek; Ro. i. 21; ii. 15; 2 Co. iv. 6.

54. *They knew him.* They *recollected* him, for he had been there before and worked miracles.

56. *The border of his garment.* Comp. Notes on Mat. ix. 20.

CHAPTER VII.

1-23. See this passage explained in the Notes on Mat. xv. 1-20.

1. *Came from Jerusalem.* Probably to observe his conduct, and to find matter of accusation against him.

2. *Defiled hands.* The hands were considered defiled or polluted unless they were washed previous to every meal.

3. *Except they wash their hands oft.* Our word *oft* means frequently, often. The Greek word translated *oft* has been rendered various ways. Some have said that it means "*up to the wrist*"—unless they wash their hands up to the wrist. Others have said "up to the elbow." There is evidence that the Pharisees had some such foolish rule as this about washing, and it is likely that they practised it faithfully. But the Greek word πυγμῇ—*pugmē*—means properly the *fist*, and the meaning here

Jews, except they wash *their* hands oft,[2] eat not, holding the [b]tradition of the elders.

4 And *when they come* from the market, except they [c]wash, they eat not. And many other things there be which they have received to hold, *as* the washing of cups, and [3]pots, brazen vessels, and of tables.[4]

5 Then the Pharisees and scribes asked him, Why walk not thy disciples according to the tradition of the elders, but eat bread with unwashen hands?

6 He answered and said unto them, Well hath [d]Esaias prophesied of you hypocrites, as it is written, This people honoureth me with *their* lips, but their heart is far from me.

7 Howbeit, in vain do they worship me, teaching *for* doctrines the commandments of men.

8 For [e]laying aside the commandment of God, ye hold the tradition of men, *as* the washing of pots and cups: and many other such like things ye do.

9 And he said unto them, Full

2 or, *diligently:* Gr. *with the fist:* Theophylact, *up to the elbow.*
b Ga.1.14; Col.2.8,22,23. c Job 9.30,31.
3 Sextarius is about a pint and a half. 4 or, *beds.*
d Is.29.13. e Is.1.12.

is, "Unless they wash their hands (rubbing them) *with the fist*"—that is, not merely dipping the finger or hands in water as a sign of ablution, but rubbing the hands together as a ball or fist, in the usual Oriental manner when water is poured over them. Hence the phrase comes to mean *diligently, carefully, sedulously.*—Robinson, *Lex.* The idea is, unless they pay the utmost attention to it, and do it carefully and according to rule. ¶ *The tradition.* What had been handed down; not what was delivered *by writing* in the law of Moses, but what had been communicated from father to son as being proper and binding. ¶ *The elders.* The ancients; not the old men *then living*, but those who had lived formerly.

4. *Market.* This word means either the place where provisions were sold, or the place where men were convened for any purpose. Here it probably means the former. ¶ *Except they wash.* In the original, "Except they *baptize.*" In this place it does not mean to immerse the whole body, but the hands only. There is no evidence that the Jews washed their *whole bodies* every time they came from market. It is probable that they often washed with the use of a very small quantity of water. ¶ *The washing of cups.* In the Greek, the *baptism of cups.* ¶ *Cups.* Drinking vessels. Those used at their meals. ¶ *Pots.* Measures of *liquids.* Vessels made of wood, used to hold wine, vinegar, &c. ¶ *Brazen vessels.* Vessels made of brass, used in cooking or otherwise. These, if much polluted, were commonly passed through the fire; if slightly polluted they were washed. Earthen vessels, if defiled, were usually broken. ¶ *Tables.* This word means, in the original, *beds or couches.* It refers not to the *tables* on which they ate, but to the *couches* on which they reclined at their meals. See Notes on Mat. xxiii. 6. These were supposed to be defiled when any unclean or polluted person had reclined on them, and they deemed it necessary to purify them with water. The word *baptism* is here used—in the original, *the baptism of tables;* but as it cannot be supposed that *couches* were entirely *immersed* in water, the word *baptism* here must denote some other application of water, by sprinkling or otherwise, and shows that the term is used in the sense of washing in any way. If the word is used *here*, as is clear it is, to denote anything except entire immersion, it may be elsewhere, and baptism is lawfully performed, therefore, without immersing the whole body in water.

7. For *doctrines.* For commands of God binding on the conscience. Imposing *your* traditions as equal in authority to the laws of God.

8. *Laying aside.* Rejecting, or making it give place to traditions; considering the traditions as superior in authority to the divine law. This was the uniform doctrine of the Pharisees. See Notes on Mat. xv. 1–9. ¶ *The tradition of men.* What has been handed down by men, or what rests solely on their authority.

9. *Full well.* These words are capable of different interpretations. Some read them as a question: "Do ye do *well* in

well ye [5]reject the commandment of God, that ye may keep your own tradition.

10 For Moses said, [f]Honour thy father and thy mother; and, Whoso[g] curseth father or mother, let him die the death.

11 But ye say, If a man shall say to his father or mother, *It is* Corban,[h] that is to say, a gift, by whatsoever thou mightest be profited by me, *he shall be free.*

12 And ye suffer him no more to do aught for his father or his mother;

13 Making the word of God of none effect through your tradition, which ye have delivered: and many such like things do ye.

14 And when he had called all the people *unto him,* he said unto them, [i]Hearken unto me every one *of you,* and understand:

15 There is nothing from without a man that, entering into him, can defile him; but the things which come out of him, those are they that defile the man.

16 If[k] any man have ears to hear, let him hear.

17 And[l] when he was entered into the house from the people, his disciples asked him concerning the parable.

18 And he saith unto them, Are ye so without understanding also? Do ye not perceive, that whatsoever thing from without entereth into the man, *it* cannot defile him;

19 Because it entereth not into

[5] or, *frustrate,* ver.13. *f* Ex.20.12; De.5.16. *g* Ex.21.17; Le.20.9; Pr.20.20. *h* Mat.15.5; 23.18.

i Pr.8.5; Is.6.9; Ac.8.30. *k* Mat.11.15. *l* Mat.15.15,&c.

rejecting?" &c. Others suppose they mean *skilfully, cunningly.* "You show great cunning, or art, in laying aside God's commands and substituting in their place those of men." Others suppose them to be ironical. "How nobly you act! From conscientious attachment to your traditions you have made void the law of God;" meaning to intimate by it that they had acted wickedly and basely.

17. *The parable.* The *obscure* and difficult remarks which he had made in ver. 15. The word *parable,* here, means *obscure* and *difficult saying.* They could not understand it. They had probably imbibed many of the popular notions of the Pharisees, and they could not understand why a man was not defiled by external things. It was, moreover, a doctrine of the law that men were ceremonially polluted by contact with dead bodies, &c., and they could not understand how it could be otherwise.

18. *Cannot defile him.* Cannot render his *soul* polluted; cannot make him a *sinner* so as to need this purifying as a *religious* observance.

19. *Entereth not into his heart.* Does not reach or affect the *mind,* the *soul,* and consequently cannot pollute it. Even if it should affect the *body,* yet it cannot the *soul,* and consequently cannot need to be cleansed by a religious ordinance. The notions of the Pharisees, therefore, are not founded in *reason,* but are mere *superstition.* ¶ *The draught.* The sink, the vault. ¶ *Purging all meats.* The word *purging,* here, means to purify, to cleanse. What is thrown out of the body is the innutritious part of the food taken into the stomach, and leaving only that which is proper for the support of life; and it cannot, therefore, defile the soul. ¶ *All meats.* All food; all that is taken into the body to support life. The meaning is, that the economy or process by which life is supported *purifies* or *renders nutritious* all kinds of food. The unwholesome or innutritious parts are separated, and the wholesome only are taken into the system. This agrees with all that has since been discovered of the process of digestion and of the support of life. The food taken into the stomach is by the gastric juice converted into a thick pulp called chyme. The nutritious part of this is conveyed into small vessels, and changed into a milky substance called *chyle.* This is poured by the thoracic duct into the left subclavian vein, and mingles with the blood, and conveys nutriment and support to all parts of the system. The useless parts of the food are thrown off.

20. *That which cometh out of the man.* His words; the expression of his thoughts and feelings; his conduct, as the development of inward malice, anger,

his heart, but [m]into the belly, and goeth out into the draught, purging all meats?

20 And he said, That which cometh out of the man, that defileth the man.

21 For[n] from within, out of the heart of men, proceed evil thoughts, adulteries, fornications, murders,

22 Thefts, [6]covetousness, wickedness, deceit, lasciviousness, an evil eye, blasphemy, pride, foolishness:

23 All these evil things come from within, and defile the man.

24 And[o] from thence he arose, and went into the borders of Tyre and Sidon, and entered into an house, and would have no man know *it:* but [p]he could not be hid.

25 For a *certain* woman, whose young daughter had an unclean spirit, heard of him, and came and fell at his feet:

26 The woman was a [7]Greek, a Syrophenician by nation: and she besought him that he would cast forth the devil out of her daughter.

27 But Jesus said unto her, Let the children first be filled: for [q]it is not meet to take the children's bread, and to cast *it* unto the dogs.

28 And she answered and said unto him, Yes, Lord; yet [r]the dogs under the table eat of the children's crumbs.

29 And he said unto her, [s]For this saying go thy way; the devil is gone out of thy daughter.

30 And when she was come to her house, she found [t]the devil gone out, and her daughter laid upon the bed.

31 And[u] again, departing from the coasts of Tyre and Sidon, he came unto the sea of Galilee, through the midst of the coasts of Decapolis.

32 And they bring unto him one that was deaf, and had an impediment in his speech; and they beseech him to put his hand upon him.

33 And he took him aside from the multitude, and put his fingers

m 1 Co.6.13. n Ge.6.5; Ps.14.1,3; 53.1,3; Je.17.9. 6 *covetousnesses, wickednesses.* o Mat.15.21,&c. p ch.2.1. 7 or, *Gentile,* Is.49.12.

q Mat.7.6; 10.5,6. r Ro.15.8,9; Ep.2.12-14. s Is.66.2. t 1 Jn.3.8. u Mat.15.29,&c.

---

covetousness, lust, &c. ¶ *Defileth the man.* Makes him *really* polluted or offensive in the sight of God. This renders the soul corrupt and abominable in his sight. See Mat. xv. 18–20.

24–30. See this miracle explained in the Notes on Mat. xv. 21–28.

24. *Would have no man know* it. To avoid the designs of the Pharisees he wished to be retired.

26. *A Greek.* The Jews called all persons *Greeks* who were not of their nation. Comp. Ro. i. 14. The whole world was considered as divided into Jews and Greeks. Though she might not have been strictly a *Greek,* yet she came under this general appellation as a foreigner.

31. *Departing from the coasts.* The country or regions of Tyre. ¶ *Came unto the sea of Galilee.* The Sea of Tiberias. See Notes on Mat. iv. 18. ¶ *Decapolis.* See Notes on Mat. iv. 25. He did not go immediately into Capernaum, or any city where he was known, but into the retired regions around the Sea of Galilee. This was done to avoid the designs of the Pharisees, who sought his life.

32. *They bring.* That is, his friends brought, or the people brought. ¶ *One that was deaf, and had an impediment in his speech.* Not entirely dumb, but who spoke indistinctly or with difficulty. His deafness might not have been of long standing, and his speech, therefore, not entirely ruined. ¶ *To put his hand upon him.* That is, to cure him. Blessings were commonly imparted by laying on the hands.

33. *And he took him aside from the multitude.* Why this was done we have no means of information. It might have been to conceal from the multitude everything respecting the *manner* of cure, in order that none might attempt to cure in a similar way. ¶ *And he put his fingers into his ears,* &c. Why this was done it has been found exceedingly difficult to explain. Jesus had power at once to open his ears and loose his tongue, but for some cause he

into his ears, and [u]he spit, and touched his tongue;

34 And [v]looking up to heaven, he [w]sighed, and saith unto him, Ephphatha, that is, Be opened.

35 And[x] straightway his ears were opened, and the string of his tongue was loosed, and he spake plain.

36 And he charged them that they should tell no man: but the more he charged them, so much the more a great deal they published *it;*

37 And were beyond measure astonished, saying, [y]He hath done all things well: [z]he maketh both the deaf to hear and the dumb to speak.

CHAPTER VIII.

IN[a] those days, the multitude being very great, and having nothing to eat, Jesus called his disciples *unto him*, and saith unto them,

2 I have [b]compassion on the multitude, because they have now been with me three days, and have nothing to eat:

3 And if I send them away fasting to their own houses, they will faint by the way: for divers of them came from far.

4 And his disciples answered him, [c]From whence can a man satisfy these *men* with bread here in the wilderness?

5 And he asked them, How many loaves have ye? And they said, Seven.

6 And he commanded the people to sit down on the ground: and he took the seven loaves, and gave thanks, and brake, and gave to his disciples to set before *them;* and they did set *them* before the people.

7 And they had a few small fishes: and [d]he blessed, and commanded to set them also before *them*.

8 So they did eat, and [e]were filled: and [f]they took up of the broken *meat* that was left seven baskets.

9 And they that had eaten were

u ch.8.23; Jn.9.6. v ch.6.41; Jn.11.41; 17.1. w Jn.11.33,38. x Is.35.5,6; Mat.11.5. y Ps.139.14; Ac.14.11. z Ex.4.10,11. a Mat.15.32,&c. b Ps.145.8,15; He.5.2.

c ch.6.36,37,&c. d Mat.14.19. e Ps.107.5,6; 145.16. f 1 Ki.17.14-16; 2 Ki.4.2-7,42-44.

chose to accompany it with a sign. This was intended, probably, simply to denote that the power of healing came from him; to satisfy the man by the touch that he had this power, and that it could come from no other quarter. Our Saviour often used signs in this way to denote his power to heal. See Mar. viii. 23; Jn. ix. 6.

34. *Looked up to heaven.* To lift up the eyes to heaven is an act imploring aid from God, and is an attitude of prayer, Ps. cxxi. 1, 2; Mar. vi. 41; Jn. xi. 41. ¶ *He sighed.* Pitying the sufferings of the man who stood before him. ¶ *Ephphatha.* This word is *Syriac*, the language which our Lord used in addressing the man, and means "Be opened."

35. *The string of his tongue was loosed.* The difficulty in his speaking was removed.

36. *Tell no man.* Do not noise it abroad. He was not ambitious of being known, and he knew that if much was said of his cures, it would excite the jealousy of the Pharisees and endanger his life.

37. *Beyond measure.* Exceedingly; very much. In the Greek, "Very abundantly." ¶ *He hath done all things well.* All things in a remarkable manner; or, he has perfectly effected the cure of the deaf and the dumb.

CHAPTER VIII.

1-9. See this passage explained in the Notes on Mat. xv. 32-39.

1. *In those days.* While in the wilderness, where he had cured the deaf and dumb man. ¶ *Having nothing to eat.* Having come unprovided, or having consumed what they had brought.

2. *I have compassion.* I pity their condition. I am disposed to relieve them.

9. *Four thousand.* Four thousand *men*, besides women and children. See Mat. xv. 38.

about four thousand; and he sent them away.

10 And[g] straightway he entered into a ship with his disciples, and came into the parts of Dalmanutha.

11 And[h] the Pharisees came forth, and began to question with him, seeking of him a sign from heaven, tempting him.

12 And he sighed deeply in his spirit, and saith, Why doth this generation seek after a sign? Verily I say unto you, There shall no sign be given unto this generation.

13 And he left them, and, entering into the ship again, departed to the other side.

14 Now *the disciples* had forgotten to take bread, neither had they in the ship with them more than one loaf.

15 And he charged them, saying, Take heed, [i]beware of the leaven[k] of the Pharisees, and *of* the leaven of Herod.

16 And they reasoned among themselves, saying, *It is* because we have no bread.

17 And when Jesus knew *it*, he saith unto them, Why reason ye, because ye have no bread? [l]perceive ye not yet, neither understand? have ye your [m]heart yet hardened?

18 Having[n] eyes, see ye not? and having ears, hear ye not? and [o]do ye not remember?

19 When I brake the [p]five loaves among five thousand, how many baskets full of fragments took ye up? They say unto him, Twelve.

20 And when the [q]seven among four thousand, how many baskets full of fragments took ye up? And they said, Seven.

21 And he said unto them, How is it that ye do not understand?

22 And he cometh to Bethsaida; and they bring a blind man unto him, and besought him to [r]touch him.

23 And he took the blind man by the hand, and led him out of

g Mat.15.39. h Mat.12.38; 16.1,&c.; Jn.6.30. i Pr.19.27; Lu.12.1. k Ex.12.20; Le.2.11; 1 Co.5.6-8.

l ch.6.52. m ch.3.5; 16.14. n Is.44.18. o 2 Pe.1.12. p ch.6.38,44; Mat.14.17-21; Lu.9.12-17; Jn.6.5-13. q ver.1-9; Mat.15.34-38. r Mat.8.3,15.

10. *Dalmanutha.* In Mat. xv. 39 it is said that he came into the coasts of *Magdala.* See Note on the place.

11-21. See this passage explained in Mat. xvi. 1-12.

12. *Sighed deeply in his spirit.* His heart was deeply affected at their wickedness and hypocrisy. The word *spirit* here is taken as the seat of the emotions, passions, affections. He drew groans deeply from his breast. ¶ *No sign be given.* That is, no such sign as they asked, to wit, a sign *from heaven.* He said a sign should be given, the same as was furnished by Jonas, Mat. xvi. 4. But this was not what they *asked*, nor would it be given *because* they asked it.

15. *Beware of the leaven of the Pharisees.* See Mat. xvi. 6. ¶ *Of Herod.* Of the Herodians—of Herod and his followers. Matthew, instead of "Herod," has "the Sadducees." It is not improbable that he cautioned them against them all. The Pharisees sought his life, and were exceedingly corrupt in their doctrine and practice; the Sadducees denied some of the essential doctrines of religion, and the Herodians probably were distinguished for irreligion, sensuality, and corrupt living. They were united, therefore, with the Pharisees and Sadducees in opposing the claims of Jesus. Matthew has recorded his caution to avoid the Pharisees and Sadducees, and Mark has added, what Matthew had omitted, the caution likewise to beware of the Herodians. Thus the evangelists speak the same thing.

22. *To Bethsaida.* See Notes on Mat. xi. 21. ¶ *And they bring a blind man unto him.* The healing of the blind man of Bethsaida is recorded only by Mark. ¶ *Besought him to touch him.* That is, to *heal* him, for they believed that his touch would restore his sight.

23. *Led him out of the town.* Why this was done the sacred writers have not told us. It *might* have been to avoid the collecting of a multitude, and thus to have escaped the designs

the town; and when he had [s]spit on his eyes, and put his hands upon him, he asked him if he saw aught.

24 And he looked up, and said, I[t] see men, as trees, walking.

25 After that, he put *his* hands again upon his eyes, and made him look up: and he was restored, [u]and saw every man clearly.

26 And he sent him away to his house, saying, Neither go into the town, nor tell *it* to any in the town.

27 And[v] Jesus went out, and his disciples, into the towns of Cesarea Philippi: and by the way he asked his disciples, saying unto them, Whom do men say that I am?

28 And they answered, [w]John the Baptist: but some *say* Elias; and others, One of the prophets.

29 And he saith unto them, But whom say ye that I am? And Peter answereth and saith unto him, [x]Thou art the Christ.

30 And he charged them that they should tell no man.

31 And he began to teach them,

s ch.7.33. t Ju.9.36; Is.29.18; 1 Co.13.11,12. u Pr.4.18; Is.32.3; 1 Pe.2.9. v Mat.16.13,&c.; Lu.9.18,&c.

w Mat.14.2. x Jn.1.41-49; 6.69; 11.27; Ac.8.37; 1 Jn.5.1.

---

of the Pharisees who were attempting to take his life, and chiefly on a charge of sedition and of exciting the people. On this account Jesus chose to perform the miracle alone, thus showing that while he did good, he desired to do it in such a way as to avoid the *appearance* of evil, and to prevent, at the same time, ostentation and the malice of his enemies. ¶ *Spit on his eyes.* Why this was done is not known. It was evidently not intended to perform the cure by any natural effect of the spittle. It was to the man a *sign*, an evidence that it was the power of Jesus. The eyes were probably closed. They were perhaps "gummed" or united together by a secretion that had become hard. To apply spittle to them—to wet them—would be a *sign*, a natural expression of removing the obstruction and opening them. The power was not in the spittle, but it attended the application of it. ¶ *Saw aught.* Saw anything.

24. *I see men, as trees, walking.* I see men walking, but see them so indistinctly that, but for their *motion*, I could not distinguish them from trees. I cannot distinctly see their shapes and features. Probably our Lord did not *at once* restore him fully to sight, that he might strengthen his faith. Seeing that Jesus had *partially* restored him, it was evidence that he could *wholly*, and it led him to exercise faith anew in him, and to feel more strikingly his dependence on him.

25. *Every man clearly.* Could see their form and features. His sight was completely restored. Though our Lord did not by this, probably, *intend* to teach any lesson in regard to the way in which the mind of a sinner is enlightened, yet it affords a striking illustration of it. Sinners are by nature blind, 2 Co. iv. 4; 1 Jn. ii. 11; Jn. ix. 39. The effect of religion, or of the influence of the Holy Spirit, is to open the eyes, to show the sinner his condition and his danger, and to lead him to *look* on him as a Saviour. Yet at first he sees indistinctly. He does not soon learn to distinguish objects. When converted he is in a new world. Light is shed on every object, and he sees the Scriptures, the Saviour, and the works of creation, the sun, the stars, the hills, the vales, in a new light. He sees the beauty of the plan of salvation, and wonders that he has not seen it before. Yet he sees at first indistinctly. It is only by repeated applications to the Source of light that he sees all things clearly. At first religion appears full of mysteries. Doctrines and facts are brought before his mind that he cannot fully comprehend. He is still perplexed, and he may doubt whether he has ever seen anything aright, or has been ever renewed. Yet let him not despair. Light, in due time, will be shed on these obscure and mysterious truths. Faithful and repeated application to the Father of lights in prayer, and in searching the Scriptures, and in the ordinances of religion, will dissipate these doubts, and he will see all things clearly, and the universe will appear to be filled with one broad flood of light.

26. *The town.* The town of Bethsaida. ¶ *Nor tell* it, &c. Lest it excite the

that the Son of man must suffer many things; and be rejected of the elders, and *of* the chief priests and scribes, and be killed; and after three days rise again.

32 And he spake that saying openly. And Peter took him, and began to rebuke him.

33 But when he had turned about, and looked on his disciples, he [y]rebuked Peter, saying, Get thee behind me, [z]Satan; for thou savourest not the things that be of God, but the things that be of men.

34 And when he had called the people *unto him*, with his disciples also, he said unto them, [a]Whosoever will come after me, let him deny himself, and take up his cross, and follow me.

35 For [b]whosoever will save his life shall lose it; but whosoever shall lose his life for my sake or the gospel's, the same shall save it.

36 For what shall it profit a man if he shall gain the whole world and lose his own soul?

37 Or what shall a man give in exchange for his soul?

38 Whosoever,[a] therefore, shall be ashamed of me, and of my words, in this adulterous and sinful generation, of him also shall the Son of man be ashamed, when he cometh in the glory of his Father, with the holy angels.

CHAPTER IX.

AND he said unto them, [b]Verily I say unto you, that there be some of them that stand here which shall not [c]taste of death till they have seen the kingdom of God come with power.

2 And[d] after six days Jesus taketh *with him* Peter, and James, and John, and leadeth them up into an high mountain apart by themselves: and he was transfigured before them.

3 And his raiment became shining, exceeding [e]white as snow; so as no fuller on earth can white them.

4 And there appeared unto them

y Re.3.19. z 1 Co.5.5.
a Mat.10.38; 16.24; Lu.9.23; 14.27; Tit.2.12.
b Es.4.14; Mat.10.39; 16.25; Lu.9.24; 17.33; Jn.12.25; 2 Ti.2.11; 4.6,8; Re.2.10; 7.14-17.

a Lu.12.9; 2 Ti.1.8.
b Mat.16.28; Lu.9.27. c Jn.8.52; He.2.9.
d Mat.17.1,&c.; Lu.9.28,&c. e Da.7.9; Mat.28.3.

---

jealousy of the Pharisees, and produce commotion and danger.

27-38. See this passage illustrated in the Notes on Mat. xvi. 13-28.

32. *He spake that saying openly.* With boldness or confidence, or without parables or figures, so that there could be no possibility of misunderstanding him.

38. *Ashamed of me.* Ashamed to own attachment to me on account of my lowly appearance and my poverty. ¶ *And of my words.* My doctrines, my instructions. ¶ *This adulterous and sinful generation.* This age given to wickedness, particularly to adultery. ¶ *In the glory of his Father.* In the day of judgment. See Notes on Mat. xxvi. 64. The meaning of this verse is, Whosoever shall refuse, through pride or wickedness, to acknowledge and serve Christ here, shall be excluded from his kingdom hereafter. He was lowly, meek, and despised; yet there was an inimitable beauty in his character even then. But he will come again in awful grandeur; not as the babe of Bethlehem, not as the man of Nazareth, but as the Son of God, in majesty and glory. They that would not acknowledge him *here* must be rejected by him *there;* they that would not serve him on earth will not enjoy his favour in heaven; they that would cast *him* out and despise him must be cast out *by* him, and consigned to eternal, hopeless sorrow.

CHAPTER IX.

1. *Verily I say,* &c. See Notes on Mat. xvi. 28. This verse properly belongs to the preceding chapter and the preceding discourse.

2-10. *And after six days,* &c. See this passage explained in the Notes on Mat. xvii. 1-9.

3. *No fuller.* Rather, no *scourer.* The office of the person here mentioned was to *scour* or *whiten* cloth; not to *full* it, or to render it thicker.

Elias, with Moses; and they were talking with Jesus.

5 And Peter answered and said to Jesus, Master, it is [e]good for us to be here: and let us make three tabernacles; one for thee, and one for Moses, and one for Elias.

6 For he [f]wist not what to say; for they were sore afraid.

7 And there was a cloud that overshadowed them; and a voice came out of the cloud, saying, This[g] is my beloved Son; [h]hear him.

8 And suddenly, when they had looked round about, they saw no man any more, save Jesus only with themselves.

9 And as they came down from the mountain, he charged them that they should tell no man what things they had seen till the Son of man were risen from the dead.

10 And they kept that saying with themselves, questioning one with another [i]what the rising from the dead should mean.

11 And they asked him, saying, Why say the scribes that [k]Elias must first come?

12 And he answered and told them, Elias verily cometh first, and restoreth all things; and how it is [l]written of the Son of man that he must suffer many things, and [m]be set at nought.

13 But I say unto you, [n]That Elias is indeed come, and they have done unto him whatsoever they listed, as it is written of him.

14 And when he came to *his* disciples, he saw a great multitude about them, and the scribes questioning with them.

15 And straightway all the people, when they beheld him, were greatly amazed; and running to *him*, saluted him.

16 And he asked the scribes, What question ye [1]with them?

17 And one of the multitude answered and said, Master, I have brought unto thee my son, which hath a [o]dumb spirit:

18 And wheresoever he taketh him, he [2]teareth him; and he [p]foameth, and gnasheth with his teeth, and pineth away: and I spake to thy disciples, that they should cast him out; and they could not.

19 He answereth him, and saith,

e Ps.63.2; 84.10. f Da.10.15; Re.1.17. g Ps.2.7; Mat.3.17; 2 Pe.1.17. h De.18.15. i Ac.17.18. k Mal.4.5.

l Ps.22.; Is.53.; Da.9.26; Zec.13.7. m Ps.74.22; Lu.23.11; Phi.2.7. n Mat.11.14; Lu.1.17. 1 or, *among yourselves*. o Mat.12.22; Lu.11.14. 2 or, *dasheth him*. p Jude 13.

---

6. *He wist not.* He *knew* not. He was desirous of saying something, and he knew not what would be proper.

11-13. *Why say the scribes*, &c. See Notes on Mat. xvii. 10-13.

14-29. See this passage explained in the Notes on Mat. xvii. 14-21.

14. *Questioning with them.* Debating with the disciples, and attempting to confound them. This he saw as he came down from the mount. In his absence they had taken occasion to attempt to perplex and confound his followers.

15. *Were greatly amazed.* Were astonished and surprised at his sudden appearance among them. ¶ *Saluted him.* Received him with the customary marks of affection and respect. It is probable that this was not by any *formal* manner of salutation, but by the *rush* of the multitude, and by hailing him as the Messiah.

16. *What question ye?* What is the subject of your inquiry or debate with the disciples?

17. *A dumb spirit.* A spirit which deprived his son of the power of speaking.

18. *And wheresoever.* In whatever place —at home or abroad, alone or in public. ¶ *He teareth him.* He rends, distracts, or throws him into convulsions. ¶ *He foameth.* At the mouth, like a mad animal. Among us these would all be considered as marks of violent derangement or madness. ¶ *And pineth away.* Becomes thin, haggard, and emaciated. This was the effect of the violence of his struggles, and perhaps of the want of food.

O [q]faithless generation! how long shall I be with you? how long shall I suffer you? Bring him unto me.

20 And they brought him unto him: and when he saw him, straightway the spirit tare him; and he fell on the ground, and wallowed foaming.

21 And he asked his father, How long is it ago since this came unto him? And he said, [r]Of a child:

22 And ofttimes it hath cast him into the fire, and into the waters, to destroy him; but if thou canst do any thing, have compassion on us and help us.

23 Jesus said unto him, [s]If thou canst believe, all things *are* possible to him that believeth.

24 And straightway the father of the child cried out, and said [t]with tears, Lord, I believe; [u]help thou mine unbelief.

25 When Jesus saw that the people came running together, he rebuked the foul spirit, saying unto him, *Thou* dumb and deaf spirit, I charge thee, come out of him, and enter no more into him.

26 And *the spirit* cried, and [v]rent him sore, and came out of him; and he was as one dead, insomuch that many said, He is dead.

27 But Jesus [w]took him by the hand, and lifted him up, and he arose.

28 And when he was come into the house, his disciples asked him privately, Why could not we cast him out?

29 And he said unto them, This

q De.32.20; Ps.78.8; He.3.10. r Job 5.7; Ps.51.5. s 2 Ch.20.20; Mat.17.20; ch.11.23; Lu.17.6; Jn.11.40; He.11.6.

t Ps.126.5. u He.12.2. v Re.12.12. w Is.41.13.

22. *If thou canst do any thing.* I have brought him to the disciples, and they could not help him. If THOU canst do anything, have compassion.

23. *If thou canst believe.* This was an answer to the request, and there was a reference in the answer to the *doubt* in the man's mind about the power of Jesus. *I* can help him. If THOU *canst believe*, it shall be done. Jesus here demanded *faith* or confidence in his power of healing. His design here is to show the man that the difficulty in the case was not in the want of *power* on his part, but in the want of *faith* in the man; in other words, to rebuke him for having *doubted* at all whether he *could* heal him. So he demands faith of every sinner that comes to him, and none that come without *confidence* in him can obtain the blessing. ¶ *All things are possible to him that believeth.* All things can be effected or accomplished—to wit, by God—in favour of him that believes, and if thou canst believe, this will be done. God will do nothing in our favour without faith. It is right that we should have confidence in him; and if we *have* confidence, it is easy for him to help us, and he willingly does it. In our weakness, then, we should go to God our Saviour; and though we have no strength, yet *he* can aid us, and he will make all things easy for us.

24. *Said with tears.* The man felt the implied rebuke in the Saviour's language; and feeling grieved that he should be thought to be destitute of faith, and feeling deeply for the welfare of his afflicted son, he wept. Nothing can be more touching or natural than this. An anxious father, distressed at the condition of his son, having applied to the disciples in vain, now coming to the Saviour, and not having full confidence that he had the proper qualification to be aided, he wept. Any man would have wept in his condition, nor would the Saviour turn the weeping suppliant away. ¶ *I believe.* I have faith. I do put confidence in thee, though I know that my faith is not as strong as it should be. ¶ *Lord.* This word here signifies merely *master*, or *sir*, as it does often in the New Testament. We have no evidence that he had any knowledge of the divine nature of the Saviour, and he applied the word, probably, as he would have done to any other teacher or worker of miracles. ¶ *Help thou mine unbelief.* Supply thou the defects of my faith. Give me strength and grace to put *entire* confidence in thee. Everyone who comes to the Saviour for help has need of offering this prayer. In our unbelief

kind can come forth by nothing but by [x]prayer and [y]fasting.

30 And they departed thence, and passed through Galilee; and he would not that any man should know *it*.

31 For he taught his disciples, and said unto them, The Son of man is delivered into the hands of men, and they shall kill him; and after that he is killed, he shall rise the third day.

32 But they understood not that saying, and were afraid to [z]ask him.

33 And[a] he came to Capernaum: and being in the house, he asked them, What was it that ye disputed among yourselves by the way?

34 But they held their peace: for by the way they had disputed among themselves who *should be* the greatest.

35 And he sat down, and called the twelve, and saith unto them, [b]If any man desire to be first, *the same* shall be last of all, and servant of all.

36 And he took a child, and set him in the midst of them: and when he had taken him in his arms, he said unto them,

37 Whosoever[c] shall receive one of such children in my name, receiveth me; and whosoever shall receive me, receiveth not me, but him that sent me.

38 And John answered him, saying, [d]Master, we saw one casting out devils in thy name, and he followeth not us; and we forbad him, because he followeth not us.

39 But Jesus said, Forbid him not; [e]for there is no man which shall do a miracle in my name that can lightly speak evil of me.

40 For[f] he that is not against us is on our part.

x Ep.6.18. *y* 1 Co.9.27. *z* Jn.16.19. *a* Mat.18.1,&c.; Lu.9.46,&c.; 22.24,&c. *b* Mat.20.26,27; ch.10.43. *c* Lu.9.48. *d* Nu.11.26-28. *e* 1 Co.12.3. *f* Mat.12.30.

and our doubts we need his aid, nor shall we ever put sufficient reliance on him without his gracious help.

30–33. See Notes on Mat. xvii. 22, 23.

31. *Is delivered.* Is given to men to make an atonement by his sufferings and death, and will in due time be taken and killed.

33–37. See Notes on Mat. xviii. 1–5.

38. *We saw one,* &c. There is no improbability in supposing that this might have been one of the disciples of John, or one of the seventy whom Jesus had sent out, and who, though he did not *personally* attend on Jesus, yet had the power of working miracles. There is no evidence that he was merely an *exorcist*, or that he used the name of Jesus merely as a pretence.

39. *Forbid him not.* Do not prevent his doing good. If he can work a miracle in my name, it is sufficient proof of attachment to me, and he should not be prevented. ¶ *Can lightly speak evil of me.* The word here rendered *lightly* means *quickly* or *immediately*. The meaning of the passage is, that he to whom God gave the power of working a miracle, by that gave evidence that he could not be found among the enemies of Jesus. He ought not, therefore, to be prevented from doing it. There is no reason to think here that John had any improper designs in opposing the man. He thought that it was evidence that he could not be right, because he did not join them and follow the Saviour. Our Lord taught him differently. He opposed no one who gave evidence that he loved him. Wherever he might be or whatever his work, yet, if he did it in the name of Jesus and with the approbation of God, it was evidence sufficient that he was right. Christians should rejoice in good done by their brethren of any denomination. There are men calling themselves Christians who seem to look with doubt and suspicion on all that is done by those who do not walk with them. They undervalue their labours, and attempt to lessen the evidences of their success and to diminish their influence. True likeness to the Saviour would lead us to rejoice in *all* the good accomplished, by whomsoever it may be done—to rejoice that the kingdom of Christ is advanced, whether by a Presbyterian, an Episcopalian, a Baptist, or a Methodist. Comp. Phi. i. 18.

41 For[g] whosoever shall give you a cup of water to drink in my name, because ye belong to Christ, verily I say unto you, he shall not lose his reward.

42 And whosoever shall [h]offend one of *these* little ones that believe in me, it is better for him that a millstone were hanged about his neck, and he were cast into the sea.

43 And[i] if thy hand [3]offend thee, cut it off: it is better for thee to enter into life maimed, than, having two hands, to go into hell, into the fire that never shall be quenched;

44 Where[k] their worm dieth not, and the fire is not quenched.

45 And if thy foot [4]offend thee, cut it off: it is better for thee to enter halt into life, than, having two feet, to be cast into hell, into the fire that never shall be quenched;

46 Where their worm dieth not, and the fire is not quenched.

47 And if thine eye [5]offend thee, pluck it out: it is better for thee to enter into the kingdom of God with one eye, than, having two eyes, to be cast into hell-fire;

48 Where their worm dieth not, and the [l]fire is not quenched.

49 For every one shall be salted

g Mat.10.42; 25.40.
h Mat.18.6; Lu.17.1,2. i De.13.6; Mat.5.29.
3 or, *cause thee to offend;* and so ver. 45 and 47.
k Is.66.24; Re.14.11. 4 See ver.43.
5 See ver.43. l ver.44,46; Lu.16.24.

---

41. *Whosoever shall give you a cup,* &c. How easy it is to be a Christian! What is easier than to give a cup of cold water to a thirsty disciple of Jesus! But it must be in his name—that is, because he *is* a Christian, and therefore from love *to the Saviour.* This is very different from giving it from a mere motive of common kindness. If done from love to Christ, it *will* be rewarded; and hence we learn that the humblest acts of Christians—the lowest service that is rendered—will be graciously noticed by Jesus and rewarded. None are so humble in his kingdom as not to be able to do good, and none so poor that he may not show attachment to him. The feeblest service will be accepted, and acts of love that may be forgotten by *man,* will be remembered by *him,* and rewarded in heaven.

42–50. See Notes on Mat. xviii. 7–9. *Millstone.* See Mat. xviii. 6.

44–46. *Their worm.* This figure is taken from Is. lxvi. 24. See Notes on that passage. In describing the great prosperity of the kingdom of the Messiah, Isaiah says that the people of God "shall go forth, and look upon the carcases of the men who have transgressed against God." Their enemies would be overcome. They would be slain. The people of God would triumph. The figure is taken from heaps of the dead slain in battle; and the prophet says that the number would be so great that their worm—the worm feeding on the dead—would not die, would live long—as long as there were carcasses to be devoured; and that the fire which was used to burn the bodies of the dead would continue long to burn, and would not be extinguished till they were consumed. The figure, therefore, denotes great misery, and certain and terrible destruction. In these verses it is applied to the state beyond the grave, and is intended to denote that the destruction of the wicked will be awful, wide-spread, and eternal. It is not to be supposed that there will be any *real* worm in hell—perhaps no *material* fire; nor can it be told what was particularly intended by the undying worm. There is no authority for applying it, as is often done, to remorse of conscience, any more than to any other of the pains and reflections of hell. It is a mere image of loathsome, dreadful, and *eternal* suffering. In what that suffering will consist it is probably beyond the power of any living mortal to imagine. The word "their," in the phrase "their worm," is used merely to keep up the *image* or *figure.* Dead bodies putrefying in that valley would be overrun with worms, while the *fire* would not be confined to them, but would spread to other objects kindled by combustibles through all the valley. It is *not* meant, therefore, that every particular sufferer has a peculiar worm, or has particular sins that cause remorse of conscience. That is a truth, but it does not appear that it is intended to be taught here.

49. *Every one shall be salted with fire.*

with fire, and [m]every sacrifice shall be salted with salt.

50 Salt *is* good; [n]but if the salt have lost his saltness, wherewith will ye season it? Have [o]salt in yourselves, and [p]have peace one with another.

CHAPTER X.

AND[a] he arose from thence, and cometh into the coasts of Judea, by the farther side of Jordan: and the people resort unto him again; and, as he was wont, he taught them again.

2 And the Pharisees came to him, and asked him, Is it lawful for a man to put away *his* wife? tempting him.

3 And he answered and said unto them, What did Moses command you?

4 And they said, [b]Moses suffered to write a bill of divorcement, and to put *her* away.

5 And Jesus answered and said

m Le.2.13; Eze.43.24. *n* Mat.5.13; Lu.14.34. *o* Col.4.6. *p* Ps.34.14; 2 Co.13.11; He.12.14. *a* Mat.19.1,&c.; Jn.10.40.

b De.24.1; Mat.5.31.

Perhaps no passage in the New Testament has given more perplexity to commentators than this, and it may be impossible now to fix its precise meaning. The common idea affixed to it has been, that as salt preserves from putrefaction, so fire, applied to the wicked in hell, will have the property of preserving them in existence, or they will *be* preserved amid the sprinkling of fire, to be continually in their sufferings a sacrifice to the justice of God; but this meaning is not quite satisfactory. Another opinion has been, that as salt was sprinkled on the victim preparatory to its being devoted to God (see Le. ii. 13), so would *the apostles*, by trials, calamities, &c., represented here by *fire*, be prepared as a sacrifice and offering to God. Probably the passage has not reference at all to future punishment; and the difficulty of interpreting it has arisen from supposing it to be connected with the 48th verse, or given as a *reason* for what is said in *that* verse, rather than considering it as designed to illustrate the *general design* of the passage. The main scope of the passage was not to discourse of future punishment; that is brought in incidentally. The chief object of the passage was—1st. To teach the apostles that *other men*, not *with them*, might be true Christians, ver. 38, 39. 2d. That they ought to be disposed to look favourably upon the slightest evidence that they *might be true believers*, ver. 41. 3d. That they ought to avoid giving *offence* to such feeble and obscure Christians, ver. 42. 4th. That *everything* calculated to give offence, or to dishonour religion, should be removed, ver. 43. And 5th. That everything which would endanger their salvation should be sacrificed; that they should *deny* themselves in every way in order to obtain eternal life. In this way they would be *preserved* to eternal life. The word "fire," here, therefore denotes self-denials, sacrifices, trials, in keeping ourselves from the gratification of the flesh. As if he had said, "Look at the sacrifice on the altar. It is an offering to God, about to be presented to him. It is sprinkled with *salt*, *emblematic of* PURITY, *of* PRESERVATION, *and of fitting it, therefore, for a sacrifice.* So *you* are devoted to God. You are sacrifices, victims, offerings to him in his service. To make you *acceptable* offerings, everything must be done to *preserve* you from sin and to *purify* you. Self-denials, subduing the lusts, enduring trials, removing offences, are the proper *preservatives* in the service of God. Doing this, you will be acceptable offerings and be saved; without this, you will be *unfit* for his eternal service and will be lost."

50. *Lost its saltness*, &c. See Notes on Mat. v. 13. ¶ *Have salt in yourselves.* Have the preserving, purifying principle always; the principles of denying yourselves, of suppressing pride, ambition, contention, &c., and thus you will be an acceptable offering to God. ¶ *Have peace.* Avoid contention and quarrelling, struggling for places, honours, and office, and seek each other's welfare, and religion will be honoured and preserved in the world.

CHAPTER X.

1–12. See this question about divorce explained in the Notes on Mat. xix. 1–12.

12. *And if a woman shall put away her husband.* It would seem, from this, that

unto them, For the hardness of your heart he wrote you this precept:

6 But from the beginning of the creation [c]God made them male and female.

7 For[d] this cause shall a man leave his father and mother, and cleave to his wife;

8 And they twain shall be [e]one flesh: so then they are no more twain, but one flesh.

9 What therefore God hath joined together, let not man put asunder.

10 And in the house his disciples asked him again of the same *matter*.

11 And he saith unto them, Whosoever[f] shall put away his wife, and marry another, committeth adultery against her.

12 And if a woman shall put away her husband, and be married to another, she committeth adultery.

13 And[g] they brought young children to him, that he should touch them; and *his* disciples rebuked those that brought *them*.

14 But when Jesus saw *it* he was [h]much displeased, and said unto them, Suffer the little children to come unto me, and forbid them not; [i]for of such is the kingdom of God.

15 Verily I say unto you, Whosoever shall not receive the kingdom of God as a little child, he shall not enter therein.

c Ge.1.27; 5.2; Mal.2.15. d Ge.2.24. e 1 Co.6.16; Ep.5.31. f Mat.5.32; 19.9; Lu.16.18; Ro.7.3; 1 Co.7.10,11. g Mat.19.13; Lu.18.15. h Ep.4.26. i Mat.18.10; 1 Co.14.20; 1 Pe.2.2; Re.14.5.

---

a woman, among the Jews, had the power of separating herself from her husband, yet this right is not given her by the law of Moses. There is not, however, any positive evidence that females often claimed or exercised this right. Cases had occurred, indeed, in which it had been done. The wife of Herod had rejected her former husband and married Herod. And though instances of this kind *might* have been attempted to be defended by the example of Pagans, yet our Saviour was desirous of showing them that it did not free them from the charge of adultery. The apostles were going forth to teach Pagan nations, and it was proper for Christ to teach them how to act in such cases, and to show them that they were cases of real adultery.

13-16. See Notes on Mat. xix. 13-15.

13. *Should touch them.* That is, should lay his hands on them, and pray for them, and bless them. Comp. Mat. xix. 13. It was common to lay the hands on the head of a person for whom a blessing was asked. See the case of Jacob, Ge. xlviii. 14.

14. *Saw* it. Saw the conduct of his disciples. ¶ *Was much displeased.* Because, first, it was a pleasure *to him* to receive and bless little children; and, secondly, they were doing what they were not commanded to do—interfering in a case where it was evidently improper.

15. *Whosoever shall not receive.* Whosoever shall not manifest the spirit of a little child. ¶ *The kingdom of God.* The gospel. The new dispensation by the Messiah, *or the reign of God through a Mediator.* See Notes on Mat. iii. 2. ¶ *As a little child.* With the temper and spirit of a child—teachable, mild, humble, and free from prejudice and obstinacy. ¶ *Shall not enter therein.* Shall not be a Christian; shall not be a *real* member of the family of Christ on earth, though he may be a *professor*, and shall never enter heaven.

16. *Took them up in his arms.* These were small children. ¶ *Blessed them.* Prayed for them, sought a blessing on them, or gave them the assurance of his favour as the Messiah.

How happy would it be if *all* parents thus felt it to be their privilege to present their children to Christ! The question with a parent should be, not whether he *ought* to present them by prayer, but whether he *may* do it. And so, too, the question respecting infant baptism is not so much whether a parent OUGHT to devote his children to God in this ordinance, as whether he MAY do it. It is an inestimable privilege to do it; it is not a matter of mere stern and iron-handed duty; and a parent with right feelings will come to God with his

16 And he took them up in his arms, put *his* hands upon them, and blessed them.

17 And[k] when he was gone forth into the way, there came one running, and kneeled to him, and asked him, Good Master, what shall I do that I may inherit eternal life?

18 And Jesus said unto him, Why callest thou me good? *There is* none good [l]but one, *that is* God.

19 Thou knowest [m]the commandments, Do not commit adultery, Do not kill, Do not steal, Do not bear false witness, Defraud not, Honour thy father and mother.

20 And he answered and said unto him, Master, [n]all these have I observed from my youth.

21 Then Jesus beholding him, loved him, and said unto him, [o]One thing thou lackest: go thy way, sell whatsoever thou hast, and give

k Mat.19.16,&c.; Lu.18.18,&c. *l* Ps.86.5; 119.68.
m Ex.20.; Ro.13.9.
n Is.58.2; Eze.33.31,32; Mal.3.8; Ro.7.9; Phi.3.6.
o Ja.2.10.

---

children *in every way*, and seek his blessing on them in the beginning of their journey of life. Our children are given to us but for a little time. They are in a world of danger, sin, and woe. They are exposed to temptation on every hand. If God be not their friend, they *have* no friend that can aid them in the day of adversity, or keep them from the snares of the destroyer. If *he* is their friend they have nothing to fear. The *proper expression, then, of parental feeling*, is to come and offer them early to God. A parent should ask only the *privilege* of doing it. He should seek *God's* favour as the best inheritance of his children; and if a parent *may* devote his offspring to God—if he *may* daily seek his blessing on them by prayer—it is all that he should ask. With proper feelings he will rush to the throne of grace, and daily seek the protection and guidance of God for his children amid the temptations and snares of an ungodly world, and implore *him* to be their guide when the parent shall be laid in the silent grave.

So children who have been devoted to God—who have been the daily objects of a father's prayers and a mother's tears—who have been again and again presented to Jesus in infancy and childhood—are under the most sacred obligations to live to God. They should never forget that a parent sought the favour of God as the chief blessing; and, having been offered to *Jesus* by prayer and baptism in their first days on earth, they should make it their great aim to be prepared to meet *him* when he shall come in the clouds of heaven.

17–31. See this passage illustrated in the Notes on Mat. xix. 16–30.

17. *Gone forth.* From the place where he had been teaching. ¶ *Into the way.* Into the road or path on his journey. ¶ *Running.* Thus showing the intensity with which he desired to know the way of life. Zeal to know the way to be saved is proper, nor is it possible that it should be too intense if well directed. Nothing else is so important, and nothing demands, therefore, so much effort and haste.

19. *Defraud not.* Do not take away your neighbour's property by fraud or dishonesty. To *cheat* or *defraud*, supposes a covetous desire of a neighbour's property, and is usually attended with *falsehood* or *false witness* against a neighbour in obtaining it. It is thus a violation of the ninth and tenth commandments; and our Saviour very properly, therefore, *condensed* the two, and expressed their substance in this—not to defraud. It is, besides, expressly forbidden in Le. xix. 13: "Thou shalt not defraud thy neighbour."

21. *Jesus beholding him, loved him.* What occurred afterward showed that the young man did not love the Saviour, or was not a true disciple; so that this expression denotes simply natural affection, or means that Jesus was pleased with his amiableness, his morality, and his *external* regard for the law of God. At the same time, this was entirely consistent with deep sorrow that he would not give his heart to God, and with deep abhorrence of such a love of the world as to blind the mind to the beauty of true religion, and to lead to the rejection of the Messiah and the destruction of the soul. ¶ *One thing thou lackest.* When the young man came to Jesus he asked him, "What lack I yet?" Mat. xix. 20. This *question*

to the poor, and thou shalt have treasure[p] in heaven; and come, take up the cross and follow me.

22 And he was sad at that saying, and went away grieved; for he had great possessions.

23 And Jesus looked round about, and saith unto his disciples, How hardly shall they that have riches enter into the kingdom of God!

24 And the disciples were astonished at his words. But Jesus answereth again, and saith unto them, Children, how hard is it for them that [q]trust in riches to enter into the kingdom of God!

25 It is easier for a camel to go through the eye of a needle, than for a rich man to enter into the kingdom of God.

26 And they were astonished out of measure, saying among themselves, Who then can be saved?

27 And Jesus looking upon them, saith, With men *it is* impossible, but not with God; for [r]with God all things are possible.

28 Then Peter began to say unto him, Lo, we have left all, and have followed thee.

29 And Jesus answered and said, Verily I say unto you, there is no man that hath left house, or brethren, or sisters, or father, or mother, or wife, or children, or lands, for my sake, and the gospel's,

30 But he shall receive an hun-

p Mat.6.19,20, Lu.12.33, 16.9.
q Job 31.24; Ps.52.7; 62.10; Hab.2.9; 1 Ti.6.17; Re.3.17.

r Ge.18.14, Job 42.2, Je.32.17; Lu.1.37.

Mark has omitted, but he has retained the *answer*. The answer means, there is *one thing* yet wanting. Though all that you have said should be *true*, yet, to make the system complete, or to show that you *really* are disposed to keep the commands of God, go and sell your property. See whether you love *God* more than you do your *wealth*. By doing that you will show that your love of God is supreme; that your obedience is not merely *external* and *formal*, but *sincere* and *real;* the thing now *lacking* will be made up.

24. *Children.* An expression of affection, perhaps also implying a reproof that their slowness of understanding was like that of children. When they should have seen at once the truth of what he said, they were slow to learn it. It became necessary, therefore, to *repeat* what he had said. ¶ *How hard.* With how much difficulty.

26. *Out of measure.* Very much, or exceedingly. The Greek means no more than this.

30. *An hundred-fold.* A hundred times as much. ¶ *In this time.* In this life. In the *time* that he forsakes all. ¶ *Houses,* &c. This cannot be taken literally, as promising a hundred times as many *mothers, sisters,* &c. It means, evidently, that the loss shall be a hundred times *compensated* or made up; or that, in the possession of religion, we have a hundred times the *value* of all we forsake. This consists in the pardon of sin, in the favour of God, in peace of conscience, in support in trials and in death, and in raising up *friends* in the place of those who are left—*spiritual brethren, and sisters, and mothers,* &c. And this corresponds to the experience of all who ever became Christians. At the same time, it is true that godliness is profitable *for all things,* having the promise of the life that is, as well as of that which is to come. See Notes on 1 Ti. iv. 8. *The favour of God* is the security for every blessing. Obedience to his law secures industry, temperance, chastity, economy, prudence, health, and the confidence of the world—all indispensable to success in life, and all connected, commonly, with success. Though the wicked *sometimes* prosper, yet the *surest* way of prosperity is to fear God and keep his commandments. Thus will all *needed* blessings descend on us *here*, and *eternal* blessings *hereafter.* ¶ *With persecutions.* Persecutions, or the contempt of the world, and bodily sufferings on account of their religion, they *must* meet. Jesus did not conceal this; but he consoled them. He assured them that *amid* these, or perhaps it should be rendered "*after*" these, they should find friends and comfort. It is well to bear trial if *God* be our Friend. With the promises of the Bible in our hand, we may hail

dred-fold now in this time, houses, and brethren, and sisters, and mothers, and children, and lands, with persecutions; and in the world to come eternal life.

31 But[s] many *that are* first shall be last, and the last first.

32 And[t] they were in the way going up to Jerusalem; and Jesus went before them: and they were amazed; and as they followed, they were afraid. And he took again the twelve, and began to tell them what things should happen unto him,

33 *Saying*, Behold, [u]we go up to Jerusalem; and the Son of man shall be delivered unto the chief priests, and unto the scribes; and they shall condemn him to death, and shall deliver him to the Gentiles;

34 And[v] they shall mock him, and shall scourge him, and shall spit upon him, and shall kill him; and the third day he shall rise again.

35 And James and John, the sons of Zebedee, come unto him, saying, Master, we would that thou shouldest do for us whatsoever we shall desire.

36 And he said unto them, What would ye that I should do for you?

37 They said unto him, Grant unto us that we may sit, one on thy right hand, and the other on thy left hand, in thy glory.

38 But Jesus said unto them, [w]Ye know not what ye ask. Can ye drink of the cup that I drink of? and be baptized with [x]the baptism that I am baptized with?

39 And they say unto him, We can. And Jesus said unto them, [y]Ye shall indeed drink of the [z]cup that I drink of, and with the baptism that I am baptized withal shall ye be baptized:

40 But to sit on my right hand and on my left hand is not mine to give; but *it shall be given to them* [a]for whom it is prepared.

41 And when the ten heard *it*, they began to be much displeased with James and John.

42 But Jesus called them *to him*, and saith unto them, [b]Ye know that they which [1]are accounted to rule over the Gentiles exercise lordship over them; and their great ones exercise authority upon them.

43 But so shall it not be among you; [c]but whosoever will be great among you shall be your minister,

44 And whosoever of you will be the chiefest, shall be servant of all.

45 For even the Son of man came not to be ministered unto, but [d]to minister, and [e]to give his life a ransom for many.

46 And[f] they came to Jericho,

s Mat.20.16; Lu.13.30. *t* Mat.20.17,&c.; Lu.18.31,&c. *u* Ac.20.22. *v* Ps.22.6,7,13.

w Ja.4.3. *x* Lu.12.50. *y* Mat.10.25; Jn.17.14. *z* ch.14.36. *a* Mat.25.34; He.11.16. *b* Lu.22.25. [1] or, *think good*. *c* Mat.20.26,28; ch.9.35; Lu.9.48. *d* Jn.13.14; Phi.2.7. *e* Is.53.11,12; Da.9.26; 2 Co.5.21; Ga.3.13; 1 Ti.2.6; Tit.2.14. *f* Mat.20.29,&c.; Lu.18.35,&c.

---

persecutions, and thank God that, amid so many sorrows, he has furnished such abundant consolations.

32–34. See Notes on Mat. xx. 17–19.

32. *Jesus went before him.* In the manner of an intrepid, fearless leader and guide, exposing *himself* to danger and death rather than his followers. ¶ *And they were amazed*, &c. They were afraid that evil would befall him in the city; that the scribes and Pharisees, who had so often sought to kill him, would then do it. Their fear and amazement were increased when he told them what would befall him there. They were *amazed* that, when he knew so well what would happen, he should still persevere in going up to the city.

35–45. See Notes on Mat. xx. 20–28.

35. *And James and John—came unto him.* They did this through the instrumentality of their mother. They did not come in *person*, but they got their mother to make the request for them. Comp. Notes on Mat. xx. 20.

46–52. See this passage explained in the Notes on Mat. xx. 29–34.

46. *Blind Bartimeus.* Matthew says

and as he went out of Jericho, with his disciples and a great number of people, blind Bartimeus, the son of Timeus, sat by the highway side begging.

47 And when he heard that it was Jesus of Nazareth, he began to cry out, and say, Jesus, *thou* son of David, have mercy on me.

48 And many charged him that he should hold his peace; but he cried[g] the more a great deal, *Thou* son of David, [h]have mercy on me.

49 And Jesus stood still and commanded him to be called. And they called the blind man, saying unto him, Be of good comfort, rise; he[i] calleth thee.

50 And he, [k]casting away his garment, rose and came to Jesus.

51 And Jesus answered and said unto him, What wilt thou that I should do unto thee? The blind man said unto him, Lord, that I might receive my sight.

52 And Jesus said unto him, Go thy way: [l]thy faith hath [2]made thee whole. And immediately he received his sight, and followed Jesus in the way.

CHAPTER XI.

AND[a] when they came nigh to Jerusalem, unto Bethphage, and Bethany, at the mount of Olives, he sendeth forth two of his disciples,

2 And saith unto them, Go your way into the village over against you; and as soon as ye be entered into it ye shall find a colt tied, whereon never man sat; loose him and bring *him*.

3 And if any man say unto you, Why do ye this? say ye that the [b]Lord hath need of him; and straightway he will send him hither.

4 And they went their way, and found the colt tied by the door without, in a place where two ways met, and they loose him.

5 And certain of them that stood there said unto them, What do ye loosing the colt?

6 And they said unto them even as Jesus had commanded; and they let them go.

7 And they brought the colt to Jesus, and cast their garments on him, and [c]he sat upon him.

8 And many spread their garments in the way; and others cut down branches off the trees and strawed *them* in the way.

9 And they that went before, and they that followed, cried, saying, [d]Hosanna, Blessed *is* he that cometh in the name of the Lord:

10 Blessed *be* the [e]kingdom of

g Je.29.13. h Ps.62.12. i Jn.11.28. k Phi.3.7-9. l Mat.9.22; ch.5.34. 2 or, *saved thee.* a Mat.21.1,&c.; Lu.19.29,&c.; Jn.12.14,&c.

b Ac.17.25. c Zec.9.9. d Ps.118.26. e Is.9.7; Je.33.15.

---

there were two. Mark mentions but one, though he does not deny that there was another. He mentio s this man because he was well known—Bartimeus, THE *blind man*

50. *Casting away his garment.* That is, his *outer* garment—the one that was thrown loosely over him. See Notes on Mat. v. 40. He threw it off, full of joy at the prospect of being healed, and that he might run without impediment to Jesus. This may be used to illustrate —though it had no such original reference—the manner in which a sinner should come to Jesus. He should throw away the garments of his own righteousness—he should rise speedily —should run with joy—should have full faith in the power of Jesus, and cast himself entirely upon his mercy.

CHAPTER XI.

1-11. See this passage illustrated in the Notes on Mat. xxi. 1-16.

4. *Two ways met.* Cross-roads. A public place, probably near the centre of the village.

5. *What do ye, loosing the colt?* Or, why do ye do this? What authority have you for doing it?

11-26. See this passage explained in the Notes on Mat. xxi. 18-22.

11. *Into the temple.* Not into the

our father David, that cometh in the name of the Lord: Hosanna in[f] the highest.

11 And Jesus entered into Jerusalem, and into the temple: and when[g] he had looked round about upon all things, and now the eventide was come, he went out unto Bethany with the twelve.

12 And[h] on the morrow, when they were come from Bethany, he was hungry:

13 And seeing a fig-tree afar off, having leaves, he came, if haply he might find anything thereon: and when he came to it [i]he found nothing but leaves; for the time of figs was not *yet.*

14 And Jesus answered and said unto it, No man eat fruit of thee hereafter for ever. And his disciples heard *it.*

15 And[k] they come to Jerusalem: and Jesus went into the temple, and began to cast out them that sold and bought in the temple, and overthrew the tables of the money-changers,[l] and the seats of them that sold doves;

16 And would not suffer that any man should carry *any* vessel through the temple.

17 And he taught, saying unto them, Is it not written, [m]My house shall be called [1]of all nations the house of prayer? but ye have made it a [n]den of thieves.

18 And the scribes and chief priests heard *it,* and sought how they might destroy him; for they feared him, because all the people was [o]astonished at his doctrine.

19 And when even was come, he went out of the city.

20 And in the morning, as they passed by, they saw the fig-tree dried up from the roots.

21 And Peter, calling to remembrance, saith unto him, Master, behold, the fig-tree which thou cursedst is withered away!

22 And Jesus, answering, saith unto them, [2]Have faith in God.

23 For verily I say unto you, That [p]whosoever shall say unto this mountain, Be thou removed, and be thou cast into the sea, and shall not doubt in his heart, but

f Ps.148.1. *g* Zep.1.12; Eze.8.9. *h* Mat.21.18,&c. *i* Is.5.7. *k* Mat.21.12,&c.; Lu.19.45,&c.; Jn.2.14,&c. *l* De.14.25,26.

m Is.56.7. 1 or, *an house of prayer for all nations.* *n* Je.7.11. *o* Mat.7.28; ch.1.22; Lu.4.32. 2 or, *Have the faith of God.* *p* Mat.17.20; Lu.17.6.

edifice properly called *the temple,* but into the *courts* which surrounded the principal edifice. Our Saviour, not being of the tribe of Levi, was not permitted to enter into the holy or most holy place; and when, therefore, it is said that he went into the *temple,* it is always to be understood of the *courts* surrounding the temple. See Notes on Mat. xxi. 12. ¶ *And when he had looked round about upon all things.* Having seen or examined everything. He saw the abominations and abuses which he afterward corrected. It may be a matter of wonder that he did not *at once* correct them, instead of waiting to another day; but it may be observed that God is slow to anger; that he does not *at once* smite the guilty, but waits patiently before he rebukes and chastises. ¶ *The eventide.* The evening; the time after three o'clock P.M. It is very probable that this was before sunset. The religious services of the temple closed at the offering of the evening sacrifice, at three o'clock, and Jesus probably soon left the city.

13, 14. *Afar off.* See Notes on Mat. xxi. 19.

15–24. See Notes on Mat. xxi. 12–22.

16. Any *vessel.* Any vessel used in cooking, or connected with the sale of their articles of merchandise.

18. *All the people were astonished.* He became popular among them. The Pharisees saw that their authority was lessened or destroyed. They were therefore envious of him, and sought his life. ¶ *His doctrine.* His teaching. He taught with power and authority so great that the multitudes were awed, and were constrained to obey.

21. *Thou cursedst.* To curse means to devote to destruction. This is its meaning here. It does not in this place imply blame, but simply that it should be destroyed.

22. *Have faith in God.* Literally,

shall believe that those things which he saith shall come to pass, he shall have whatsoever he saith.

24 Therefore I say unto you, What[q] things soever ye desire when ye pray, believe that ye receive *them*, and ye shall have *them*.

25 And when ye stand praying, forgive,[r] if ye have aught against any; that your Father also which is in heaven may forgive you your trespasses.

26 But [s]if ye do not forgive, neither will your father which is in heaven forgive your trespasses.

27 And they come again to Jerusalem: [t]and as he was walking in the temple, there come to him the chief priests, and the scribes, and the elders,

28 And say unto him, [u]By what authority doest thou these things? and who gave thee this authority to do these things?

29 And Jesus answered and said unto them, I will also ask of you one [3]question, and answer me, and I will tell you by what authority I do these things.

30 The baptism of John, was *it* from heaven or of men? Answer me.

31 And they reasoned with themselves, saying, If we shall say, From heaven, he will say, Why then did ye not believe him?

32 But if we shall say, Of men, they feared the people; [v]for all *men* counted John that he was a prophet indeed.

33 And they answered and said unto Jesus, [w]We cannot tell. And Jesus answering, saith unto them, Neither do [x]I tell you by what authority I do these things.

CHAPTER XII.

AND he began to speak unto them by parables. A[a] *certain* man planted a vineyard, and set an hedge about *it*, and digged *a place for* the wine-fat, and built a tower, and let it out to husbandmen, and went into a far country.

2 And at the season he sent to the husbandmen a servant, that he might receive from the husbandmen of the [b]fruit of the vineyard.

3 And they caught *him*, and beat him, and sent *him* away empty.

4 And again he sent unto them another servant; and at him they [c]cast stones, and wounded *him* in the head, and sent *him* away shamefully handled.

5 And again he sent another,

q Mat.7.7; Lu.11.9; 18.1; Jn.14.13; 15.7; 16.24; Ja. 1.5,6. r Mat.6.14; Col.3.13. s Mat.18.35. t Mat.21.23,&c.; Lu.20.1,&c. u Nu.16.3. 3 or, *thing*.

v Mat.3.5,6; 14.5; ch.6.20. w Is.1.3; 29.14; Je.8.7; Ho.4.6. x Lu.10.21,22. a Mat.21.33; Lu.20.9,&c. b Ca.8.11; Mi.7.1; Lu.12.48; Jn.15.1-8. c He.11.37.

"Have the faith of God." This may mean, have strong faith, or have confidence in God; a strong belief that he is able to accomplish things that appear most difficult with infinite ease, as the fig-tree was made to wither away by a word.

25. *And when ye stand praying.* When ye pray. It seems that the posture in prayer was sometimes standing and sometimes kneeling. God looks upon *the heart* rather than upon our position in worship; and if the heart be right, any posture may be proper. It cannot be doubted, however, that in private, in the family, and wherever it can be conveniently done, the kneeling posture is more proper, as expressing more humility and reverence, and more in accordance with Scripture examples. Comp. Ps. xcv. 6; 2 Ch. vi. 13; Da. vi. 10; Lu. xxii. 41; Ac. vii. 60; ix. 40. Yet a subject like this may be made of too much consequence, and we should be careful that anxiety about a mere *form* should not exclude anxiety about a far more important matter—the state of the soul. ¶ *Forgive*, &c. See Notes on Mat. vi. 12, 15.

27-33. See Notes on Mat. xx. 23-27.

CHAPTER XII.

1-12. See this parable explained in the Notes on Mat. xxi. 33-46.

13-17. See Notes on Mat. xxii. 15-22.

18-27. See this passage fully ex-

and him they killed; [d]and many others, beating some and [e]killing some.

6 Having yet, therefore, one son, his well-beloved, [f]he sent him also last unto them, saying, They will reverence my son.

7 But those husbandmen said among themselves, This is the heir; come, let us kill him, and the inheritance shall be ours.

8 And they took him, and killed *him*, and cast *him* [g]out of the vineyard.

9 What shall therefore the lord of the vineyard do? He will [h]come and destroy the husbandmen, and will [i]give the vineyard unto others.

10 And have ye not read this scripture? [k]The stone which the builders rejected is become the head of the corner:

11 This was the Lord's doing, and it is marvellous in our eyes.

12 And[l] they sought to lay hold on him, but feared the people; for they knew that he had spoken the parable against them: and they left him and went their way.

13 And [m]they sent unto him certain of the Pharisees, and of the Herodians, to catch him in *his* words.

14 And when they were come, they say unto him, Master, we know that thou art true, and carest for no man; for thou regardest not the person of men, but teachest the way of God in truth: Is it lawful to give tribute to Cæsar, or not?

15 Shall we give, or shall we not give? But he, knowing their hypocrisy, said unto them, Why tempt ye me? Bring me a [1]penny, that I may see *it*.

16 And they brought *it*. And he saith unto them, Whose *is* this image and superscription? And they said unto him, Cæsar's.

17 And Jesus, answering, said unto them, [n]Render to Cæsar the things that are Cæsar's, and [o]to God the things that are God's. And they marvelled at him.

18 Then[p] come unto him the Sadducees, [q]which say there is no resurrection; and they asked him, saying,

19 Master, [r]Moses wrote unto us, If a man's brother die, and leave *his* wife *behind him*, and leave no children, that [s]his brother should take his wife and raise up seed unto his brother.

20 Now there were seven brethren: and the first took a wife, and dying, left no seed.

21 And the second took her, and died, neither left he any seed; and the third likewise.

22 And the seven had her, and left no seed: last of all the woman died also.

23 In the resurrection, therefore, when they shall rise, whose wife shall she be of them? for the seven had her to wife.

24 And Jesus, answering, said unto them, Do ye not therefore err because ye know not the scriptures, neither the power of God?

25 For when they shall rise from the dead, they neither marry nor are given in marriage, [t]but are as the angels which are in heaven.

d Ne.9.30; Je.7.25,&c. *e* Mat.23.37. *f* He.1.1,2. *g* He.13.12. *h* Ps.1.24-31; Is.5.5-7; Da.9.26. *i* Je.17.3. *k* Ps.118.22. *l* ch.11.18; Jn.7.30. *m* Mat.22.15; Lu.20.20,&c.

1 Valuing of our money seven pence halfpenny, as Mat.22.19. *n* Mat.17.25-27; Ro.13.7; 1 Pe.2.17. *o* Ec.5.4,5; Mal.1.6. *p* Mat.22.23; Lu.20.27,&c. *q* Ac.23.8. *r* De.25.5. *s* Ru.1.11,13. *t* 1 Co.15.42-53.

plained in the Notes on Mat. xxii. 23–33.

25. *Are as the angels.* That is, as the angels in respect to connections and relations. What those connections and relations may be we know not, but this passage teaches that the peculiar relation of *marriage* will not exist. It does not affirm, however, that there will be no recollection of former marriages, or

26 And as touching the dead, that they rise; have ye not read in the book of Moses how in the bush God spake unto him, saying, I[u] *am* the God of Abraham, and the God of Isaac, and the God of Jacob?

27 He is not the God of the dead, but the God of the living: ye[v] therefore do greatly err.

28 And[w] one of the scribes came, and having heard them reasoning together, and perceiving that he had answered them well, asked him, Which is the first commandment of all?

29 And Jesus answered him, The first of all the commandments *is*, Hear,[x] O Israel; the Lord our God is one Lord:

30 And thou shalt love the Lord thy God with all thy heart, and with all thy soul, and with all thy mind, and with all thy strength. This *is* the first commandment.

31 And the second *is* like, *namely* this, [y]Thou shalt love thy neighbour as thyself. There is none other commandment greater than these.

32 And the scribe said unto him, Well, Master, thou hast said the truth; for there is one God, [z]and there is none other but he:

33 And to love him with all the heart, and with all the understanding, and with all the soul, and with all the strength, and to love *his* neighbour as himself, is [a]more than all whole burnt-offerings and sacrifices.

34 And when Jesus saw that he answered discreetly, he said unto him, Thou art not far from the kingdom of God. And no man after that durst [b]ask him *any question*.

u Ex.3.6. v ver.24. w Mat.22.35.
x De.6.4,5; Lu.10.27.

y Lc.19.18; Mat.22.39; Ro.13.9.
z De.4.39; Is.45.5,6,14; 46.9.
a 1 Sa.15.22; Ho.6.6; Mi.6.6-8. b Mat.22.46.

no recognition of each other as having existed in this tender relation.

26. *How in the bush.* At the burning bush. See Ex. iii. 16. The meaning is, "in that part of the *book* of Exodus which contains the account of the burning bush." When there were no chapters and verses, it was the easiest way of quoting a book of the Old Testament *by the subject*, and in this way it was often done by the Jews.

28-34. See Notes on Mat. xxii. 34-40.

28. *Perceiving that he answered them well.* That is, with wisdom, and with a proper understanding of the law. In this case the opinion of the Saviour corresponded with that of the Pharisees; and the question which this scribe put to him now seems to have been one of the very few candid inquiries of him by the Jews for the purpose of obtaining information. Jesus answered it in the spirit of kindness, and commended the conduct of the man.

29. *Hear, O Israel!* This was said to call the attention of the Jews to the great importance of the truth about to be proclaimed. See De. vi. 4, 5. ¶ *The Lord our God*, &c. Literally, "Jehovah, our God, is one Jehovah." The other nations worshipped many gods, but the God of the Jews was one, and one only. Jehovah was undivided; and this great truth it was the design of the separation of the Jewish people from other nations to keep in mind. This was the *peculiar* truth which was communicated to the Jews, and this they were required to keep and remember for ever.

30. *And thou shalt love*, &c. If Jehovah was the *only* God, then they ought not to love any other being supremely—then they might not bow down before any idol. They were required to love God above all other beings or things, and with all the faculties of their minds. See Notes on Mat. xxii. 37.

32-34. This answer of the scribe is not found in Matthew. ¶ *Is more than all.* Is of more importance and value. ¶ *Discreetly.* Wisely, according to truth. ¶ *Not far from the kingdom of God.* Thou who dost prefer the *internal* to the *external* worship of God—who hast so just a view of the requirements of the law—canst easily become a follower of me, and art almost fit to be numbered among my disciples. This shows that a proper understanding of the Old Testament, of its laws and requirements, would prepare the mind for

35 And[c] Jesus answered and said, while he taught in the temple, How say the scribes that Christ is the son of David?

36 For David himself said [d]by the Holy Ghost, [e]The Lord said to my Lord, Sit thou on my right hand, till I make thine enemies thy footstool.

37 David therefore himself calleth him Lord; and whence is he *then* his son? And the common people heard him gladly.

38 And he [f]said unto them in his doctrine, [g]Beware of the scribes, which love to go in long clothing, and *love* salutations in the marketplaces,

39 And [h]the chief seats in the synagogues, and the uppermost rooms at feasts;

40 Which [i]devour widows' houses, and for a pretence make long prayers: these shall receive greater damnation.

41 And[k] Jesus sat over against the treasury, and beheld how the people cast [2]money into the treasury; and many that were rich cast in much.

c Mat.22.41; Lu.20.41,&c. d 2 Sa.23.2; 2 Ti.3.16. e Ps.110.1. f ch.4.2. g Mat.23.1; Lu.20.46,&c.

h Lu.11.43. i 2 Ti.3.6. k Lu.21.1,&c. 2 *a piece of brass money;* see Mat.10.9.

Christianity, and fit a man at once to embrace it when presented. One system is grafted on the other, agreeably to Ga. iii. 24. ¶ *And no man after that durst ask him* any question. That is, no one of the scribes, the Pharisees, or the Sadducees durst ask him a question for the purpose of *tempting* him or entangling him. He had completely silenced them. It does not appear, however, but that his *disciples* dared to ask him questions for the purpose of information.

35-37. See Notes on Mat. xxii. 41-46.

37. *The common people heard him gladly.* The success of the Saviour in his preaching was chiefly among the common or the poorer class of people. The rich and the mighty were too proud to listen to his instructions. So it is still. The main success of the gospel is there, and there it pours down its chief blessings. This is not the fault of *the gospel.* It would bless the rich and the mighty as well as the poor, if they came with like humble hearts. God knows no distinctions of men in conferring his favours; and wherever there is a poor, contrite, and humble spirit—be it clothed in rags or in purple—be it on a throne or on a dunghill—there he confers the blessings of salvation.

38. *In his doctrine.* In his *teaching,* for so it should be rendered. ¶ *Beware of the scribes.* Be on your guard. Be cautious about hearing them or following them. ¶ *Scribes.* The learned men of the Jewish nation. ¶ *Which love to go in long clothing.* In long, flowing robes, as significant of their consequence, leisure, and learning. ¶ *Salutations,* &c. See Notes on Mat. xxiii. 6, 7.

40. *Which devour widows' houses.* Which devour the families of widows, or the means of supporting their families. This they did under pretence of counselling them in the knowledge of the law and in the management of their estates. They took advantage of their ignorance and their unprotected state, and either extorted large sums for their counsel, or perverted the property to their own use.

No wonder that our Saviour denounced them! If there is any sin of peculiar enormity, it is that of taking advantage of the circumstances of the poor, the needy, and the helpless, to wrong them out of the pittance on which they depend for the support of their families; and as God is the friend of the widow and the fatherless, it may be expected that such will be visited with heavy condemnation. ¶ *For a pretence.* For show, or *pretending* great devotion.

41. *Sat over against.* Opposite to, in full sight of. ¶ *The treasury.* This was in the court of the women. See Notes on Mat. xxi. 12. In that court there were fixed a number of places or coffers, made with a large open mouth in the shape of a trumpet, for the purpose of receiving the offerings of the people; and the money thus contributed was devoted to the service of the temple—to incense, sacrifices, &c.

42. *Two mites.* The word translated *mite* denotes a small coin made of brass—the smallest in use among the Jews. The precise value cannot now be easily estimated. It was much less than any

42 And there came a certain poor widow, and she threw in two mites,[3] which make a farthing.

43 And he called *unto him* his disciples, and saith unto them, Verily I say unto you, [l]That this poor widow hath cast more in than all they which have cast into the treasury:

44 For all *they* did cast in [m]of their abundance; but she of her want did cast in all that she had, *even* [n]all her living.

3 7th part of that piece of brass money.
l 2 Co.8.2,12. m 1 Ch.29.3,17; 2 Ch.24.10. n De.24.6.

CHAPTER XIII.

AND[a] as he went out of the temple, one of his disciples saith unto him, Master, see what manner of stones and what buildings *are here!*

2 And Jesus, answering, said unto him, Seest thou these great buildings? [b]there shall not be left one stone upon another that shall not be thrown down.

3 And as he sat upon the mount of Olives, over against the temple,

a Mat.24.1,&c.; Lu.21.5,&c. b Lu.19.44.

coin we have, as the *farthing* was less than an English farthing. It was in value about three mills and a half, or one-third of a cent.

43. *This poor widow hath cast more in*, &c. That is, more in proportion to her means, and therefore more that was acceptable to God. He does not mean that this was more in value than all which the others had put in, but it showed more love to the sacred cause, more self-denial, and, of course, more sincerity in what she did. This is the rule by which God will reward us. Comp. 2 Co. viii. 12.

44. *Of their abundance*. Of their superfluous store. They have given what they did not *need*. They could afford it as well as not, and in doing it they have shown no self-denial. ¶ *She of her want*. Of her poverty. ¶ *All her living*. All that she had to live on. She trusted in God to supply her wants, and devoted her little property entirely to him.

From this passage we may learn—1st. That God is pleased with offerings made to him and his cause. 2d. That it is our duty to devote our property to God. We received it from him, and we shall not employ it in a proper manner unless we feel that we are stewards, and ask of him what we shall do with it. Jesus approved the conduct of all who had given money to the treasury. 3d. That the highest evidence of love to the cause of religion is not the *amount* given, but the amount compared with our means. 4th. That it *may be* proper to give *all* our property to God, and to depend on his providence for the supply of our wants. 5th. That God does not despise the humblest offering, if made in sincerity. He loves a cheerful giver. 6th. That there are none who may not in this way show their love to the cause of religion. There are few, very few scholars in Sabbath-schools who may not give as much to the cause of religion as this poor widow; and Jesus would be as ready to approve their offerings as he was hers; and the time to *begin* to be benevolent and to do good is in early life, in childhood. 7th. That it is every man's duty to inquire, not how *much* he gives, but how much compared with what he *has;* how much self-denial he practises, and what is the *motive* with which it is done. 8th. We may remark that few practise self-denial for the purpose of charity. Most give of their abundance—that is, what they can spare without feeling it, and many feel that this is the same as throwing it away. Among all the thousands who give to these objects, how few deny themselves of *one* comfort, even the least, that they may advance the kingdom of Christ!

CHAPTER XIII.

The principal things in this chapter are fully explained in Mat. xxiv.

1. *What manner of stones*. The stones here referred to were those used in the building of the temple, and the walls on the sides of Mount Moriah, on which the temple stood. The temple was constructed of white marble, and the blocks were of a prodigious size. Josephus says that these stones were, some of them, 50 feet long, 24 broad, and 16 in thickness.

3. *On the mount of Olives, over against the temple*. The Mount of Olives was

Peter, and James, and John, and Andrew asked him privately,

4 Tell us, when shall these things be? and what *shall be* the sign when all these things shall be fulfilled?

5 And Jesus, answering them, began to say, [c]Take heed lest any *man* deceive you:

6 For many shall [d]come in my name, saying, I am *Christ*, and shall deceive many.

7 And when ye shall hear of wars and rumours of wars, [e]be ye not troubled; for *such things* must needs be; but the end *shall* not *be* yet.

8 For nation shall rise against nation, and kingdom against kingdom; and there shall be earthquakes in divers places, and there shall be famines and troubles: these *are* the beginnings of [1]sorrows.

9 But take heed to yourselves; for they [f]shall deliver you up to councils; and in the synagogues ye shall be beaten; and ye shall be brought before rulers and kings for my sake, for a testimony against them.

10 And[g] the gospel must first be published among all nations.

11 But when they shall lead *you*, and deliver you up, take no thought beforehand what ye shall speak, neither do ye premeditate; but whatsoever shall be given you in that hour, that speak ye; for it is not ye that speak, but [h]the Holy Ghost.

12 Now the [i]brother shall betray the brother to death, and the father the son; and children shall rise up against *their* parents, and shall cause them to be put to death.

13 And ye shall be [k]hated of all *men* for my name's sake; but [l]he that shall endure unto the end, the same shall be saved.

c Je.29.8; Ep.5.6; 2 Th.2.3; Re.20.7,8.
d Ac.5.36-39; 1 Jn.4.1.
e Ps.27.3; 46.1,2; Pr.3.25; Jn.14.1,27.
1 The word in the original importeth *the pains of a woman in travail.*

f Mat.10.17,&c.; Re.2.10. g Mat.28.19; Re.14.6.
h Ac.2.4; 4.8,31; 6.10. i Mi.7.6.
k Lu.6.22; Jn.17.14. l Da.12.12; Re.2.10.

---

directly east of Jerusalem, and from it there was a fine view of the temple.

9. *Take heed to yourselves.* Be cautious that no man deceive you; or, take care of your lives, not to run into unnecessary danger. ¶ *To councils.* The higher ecclesiastical courts of the Jews, including the Sanhedrim, or great council of the nation. ¶ *Rulers and kings.* Referring to Roman officers. ¶ *For a testimony against them.* Rather to bear testimony *to* them, or to be witnesses *before them* of the truth. This was *for the sake* of Jesus, or because they were attached to him; and God would overrule it so that at the same time they should bear witness *to* the rulers of the truth, as was the case with Peter and John, Ac. iv.; with Stephen, Ac. vi. vii.; and with Paul, Ac. xxiii.; xxiv. 24, 25.

11. *Neither do ye premeditate.* Do not think beforehand, or *prepare* an answer. You know not what the accusations will be, and God will furnish you with a reply that shall be adapted to the occasion. ¶ *Not ye that speak, but the Holy Ghost.* This is a full promise that they should be inspired, and consequently their defences recorded in the Acts of the Apostles are the words of the Holy Ghost. There could be no more explicit promise that they should be under an infallible guidance, and we are not left to doubt that they were taught of God. At the same time, this was a most desirable and gracious aid. They were illiterate, unknown, without power. They were unfit of themselves to make the important statements of religion which were requisite, but God gave them power, and they spake with a wisdom, fearlessness, pungency, and ability which no other men have ever manifested—full proof that these illiterate fishermen were under the influence of the Holy Ghost.

12. *The brother shall betray*, &c. The brother shall give up in a treacherous manner his brother to be put to death, on account of his attachment to Jesus. Through fear, or from the hope of reward and from the hatred of the gospel, he will overcome all the natural ties of brotherhood, and give up his own kindred to be burnt or crucified.

14 But when ye shall see the abomination of desolation, spoken of by [m]Daniel the prophet, standing where it ought not, (let him that readeth understand,) then let them that be in Judea flee to the mountains;

15 And let him that is on the house-top not go down into the house, neither enter *therein* to take any thing out of his house.

16 And let him that is in the field not turn back again for to take up his garment.

17 But woe to them that are with child, and to them that give suck in those days!

18 And pray ye that your flight be not in the winter.

19 For[n] *in* those days shall be affliction, such as was not from the beginning of the creation which God created unto this time, neither shall be.

20 And except that the Lord had shortened those days, no flesh should be saved: but for the elect's sake, whom he hath chosen, he hath shortened the days.

21 And then if any man shall say to you, [o]Lo, here *is* Christ, or, Lo, *he is* there, believe *him* not;

22 For false Christs and false prophets shall rise, and shall show signs and wonders, to seduce, if *it were* possible, even the elect.

23 But[p] take ye heed: behold, I have foretold you all things.

24 But in those days, after [q]that tribulation, the sun shall be darkened, and the moon shall not give her light;

25 And[r] the stars of heaven shall fall, and the powers that are in heaven shall be shaken.

26 And[s] then shall they see the Son of man coming in the clouds, with great power and glory.

27 And then shall he send his angels, and shall gather together his elect from the four winds, from the uttermost part of the earth to the uttermost part of heaven.

28 Now learn a parable of the fig-tree: When her branch is yet tender, and putteth forth leaves, ye know that summer is near:

29 So ye in like manner, when ye shall see these things come to pass, know that it is nigh, *even* at the doors.

30 Verily I say unto you, that this generation shall not pass till all these things be done.

31 Heaven and earth shall pass away, but [t]my words shall not pass away.

32 But of that day and *that* hour

m Da.9.27. *n* Da.12.1; Joel 2.2. *o* Lu.17.23.

p 2 Pe.3.17. *q* Da.12.1; Zep.1.15-17. *r* Is.13.10; 24.20,23; Je.4.28; 2 Pe.3.10,12; Re.6.12-14; 20.11. *s* Da.7.9-14; Mat.16.27; 24.30; ch.14.62; Ac.1.11; 1 Th.4.16; 2 Th.1.7,10; Re.1.7. *t* Is.40.8.

Perhaps nothing could more clearly show the dreadful evil of those times, as well as the natural opposition of the heart to the religion of Christ.

15. *On the house-top.* See Notes on Mat. ix. 1–8.

32. *Neither the Son.* This text has always presented serious difficulties. It has been asked, If Jesus had a divine nature, how could he say that he knew not the day and hour of a future event? In reply, it has been said that the passage was wanting, according to Ambrose, in some Greek manuscripts; but it is now found in all, and there can be little doubt that the passage is genuine. Others have said that the verb rendered "knoweth" means sometimes to *make* known or to reveal, and that the passage means, "that day and hour none makes known, neither the angels, nor the Son, but the Father." It is true that the word has sometimes that meaning, as in 1 Cor. ii. 2, but then it is natural to ask where has *the Father* made it known? In what place did he reveal it? After all, the passage has no more difficulty than that in Lu. ii. 52, where it is said that Jesus increased in wisdom and stature. He had a human nature. He grew as a man in knowledge. As a man his knowledge must be finite, for the faculties of the human soul are not infinite. As a man he often spoke, reasoned,

knoweth no man, no, not the angels which are in heaven, neither the Son, but the Father.

33 Take[u] ye heed, watch and pray; for ye know not when the time is.

34 *For the Son of man is* as a man taking a far journey, who left his house, and gave authority to his servants, and to every man his work, and commanded the porter to watch.

35 Watch ye, therefore; for ye know not when the master of the house cometh, at even, or at midnight, or at the cock-crowing, or in the morning;

36 Lest, coming suddenly, [v]he find you sleeping.

37 And what I say unto you, I say unto all, [w]Watch.

CHAPTER XIV.

AFTER two days was *the feast of* the passover, and of unleavened bread; and the chief priests and the scribes sought how they might take him by craft and put *him* to death.

2 But they said, Not on the feast-*day*, lest there be an uproar of the people.

3 And[a] being in Bethany, in the house of Simon the leper, as he sat

u Mat.24.42; 25.13; Lu.12.40; 21.34; Ro.13.11,12; 1 Th.5.6; Re.16.15.

v Mat.25.5. w ver.33,35.
a Mat.26.6,&c.; Lu.7.37; Jn.12.1,&c.

---

inquired, felt, feared, read, learned, ate, drank, and walked. Why are not all these, which imply that he was a *man*—that, *as a man*, he was not infinite—why are not these as difficult as the want of knowledge respecting the particular *time* of a future event, especially when that time must be made known by God, and when he chose that the man Christ Jesus should grow, and think, and speak *as a man?*

34. *Who left his house.* The word *house* often means family. Our Saviour here represents himself as going away, leaving his household the church, assigning to the apostles and all his servants their duty, and leaving it uncertain when he would return. As his return was a matter of vast consequence, and as the affairs of his kingdom were intrusted to them, just as the affairs of a house are to servants when the master is absent, so it was of vast importance that they should be faithful at their post, that they should defend the house from danger, and be ready for his return. ¶ *The porter.* The doorkeeper. To the janitor or doorkeeper was intrusted particularly the care of the house, whose duty it was to attend faithfully on those who came and those who left the house.

35. *Watch ye.* Be diligent, faithful, and waiting for the return of your Lord, who will come at an unexpected hour. ¶ *Master of the house.* Denoting here the Lord Jesus. ¶ *At even, or at midnight, or,* &c. This refers to the four divisions into which the Jews divided the night.

36. *Find you sleeping.* Inattentive to your post, neglecting your duty, and unprepared for his coming.

37. *I say unto all, Watch.* This command was proper, not only for those who were expecting the calamities that were soon to come upon the Jews, but for all who are soon to die and to go to the judgment. We know not the time of our death. We know not how soon we shall be called to the judgment. The Son of man may come at any moment, and we should therefore be ready. If we are his friends; if we have been renewed and pardoned; if we have repented of our sins, and have believed on him, and are leading a holy life, we *are* ready. If not, we are unprepared, and soon—probably while we are not expecting it—the cold hand of death will be laid on us, and we shall be hurried to the place where is weeping, and wailing, and gnashing of teeth. Oh how important it is to be ready, and to escape the awful sufferings of an ETERNAL HELL!

CHAPTER XIV.

1-11. See this passage explained in the Notes on Mat. xxvi. 1-16.

1. *And of unleavened bread.* So called because at that feast no other bread was used but that which had been made without leaven or yeast. ¶ *By craft.* By subtilty (Matthew); that is, by some secret plan that would secure possession

at meat, there came a woman having an alabaster-box of ointment of [1]spikenard, very precious; and she brake the box, and poured *it* on his head.

4 And there were some that had indignation within themselves, and said, Why was this waste of the ointment made?

5 For it might have been sold for more than three hundred pence,[2] and have been given to the poor. And they murmured against her.

6 And Jesus said, Let her alone; why trouble ye her? She hath wrought a good work on me.

7 For[b] ye have the poor with you always, and whensoever ye will ye may do them good; but me ye have not always.

8 She hath done what she could: she is come aforehand to anoint my body to the burying.

9 Verily I say unto you, Wheresoever this gospel shall be preached throughout the whole world, *this* also that she hath done shall be spoken of for a memorial of her.

10 And[c] Judas Iscariot, one of the twelve, went unto the chief priests, to [d]betray him unto them.

11 And when they heard *it* they were glad, and promised to [e]give him money. And he sought how he might conveniently betray him.

12 And the first day of [f]unleavened bread, when they [3]killed the passover, his disciples said unto him, Where wilt thou that we go and prepare, that thou mayest eat the passover?

13 And he sendeth forth two of his disciples, and saith unto them, [g]Go ye into the city, and there shall meet you a man bearing a pitcher of water: follow him,

14 And wheresoever he shall go

1 or, *pure nard*; or, *liquid nard*.
2 See Mat.18.28. *b* De.15.11.

c Mat.26.14,&c.; Lu.22.3,&c. *d* Jn.13.2.
e 1 Ki.21.20; Pr.1.10-16. *f* Ex.12.8,&c.
3 or, *sacrificed*. *g* ch.11.2,3; He.4.13.

---

of him without exciting the opposition of the people.

3. *Ointment*. This word does not convey quite the proper meaning. This was a perfume. It was used only to give a pleasant odour, and was liquid. ¶ *Of spikenard*. The *nard*, from which this perfume was made, is a plant of the East Indies, with a small, slender stalk, and a heavy, thick root. The best perfume is obtained from the root, though the stalk and fruit are used for that purpose. ¶ *And she brake the box*. This may mean no more than that she broke the *seal* of the box, so that it could be poured out. Boxes of perfumes are often sealed or made fast with wax, to prevent the perfume from escaping. It was not likely that she would break the box itself when it was unnecessary, and when the unguent, being liquid, would have been wasted; nor from a broken box or vial could she easily have *poured it* on his head.

5. *Three hundred pence*. About forty dollars (or £9). See Notes on Mat. xxvi. 7.

8. *She hath done what she could*. She has showed the highest attachment in her power; and it was, as it is now, a sufficient argument against there being any *real* waste, that it was done for the honour of Christ.

12–16. See Notes on Mat. xxvi. 17–19.

12. *They killed the passover*. The *paschal lamb*, which was slain in keeping the Passover. ¶ *Go and prepare*. Go and provide a lamb, have it roasted, and properly prepared with the usual things to eat with it.

13. *The city*. The city of Jerusalem. They were now in Bethany, about 2 miles from the city. ¶ *A man bearing a pitcher of water*. This could have been known only by the infinite knowledge of Christ. Such a thing could not have been conjectured, nor was there any concert between him and the man that *at that time* he should be in a particular place to meet them, for the disciples themselves proposed the inquiry. If Jesus knew a circumstance like that, then he in the same way must have known all things; then he sees *all* the actions of men—hears every word, and marks every thought; then the righteous are under his care, and the wicked, much as they may wish to be unseen, cannot escape the notice of his eye.

in, say ye to the goodman of the house, The [h]Master saith, Where is the guest-chamber, where I shall eat[i] the passover with my disciples?

15 And he will show you a large upper room furnished *and* prepared: there make ready for us.

16 And his disciples went forth, and came into the city, and [k]found as he had said unto them: and they made ready the passover.

17 And in the evening he cometh with the twelve.

18 And as they sat and did eat, Jesus said, Verily I say unto you, One[l] of you which eateth with me shall betray me.

19 And they began to be sorrowful, and to say unto him one by one, *Is* it I? and another *said*, *Is* it I?

20 And he answered and said unto them, *It is* one of the twelve, that dippeth with me in the dish.

21 The Son of man indeed goeth, as it is written of him; but woe to that man by whom the Son of man is betrayed! [m]good were it for that man if he had never been born.

22 And[n] as they did eat, Jesus took bread, and blessed, and brake *it*, and gave to them, and said, Take,[o] eat; this is my body.

23 And he took the cup; and when he had given thanks he gave *it* to them: and they all drank of it.

24 And he said unto them, [p]This is my blood of the new testament, which is shed for many.

25 Verily I say unto you, I will drink no more of the fruit of the vine, until that day that I [q]drink it new in the kingdom of God.

26 And when they had sung an [4]hymn, they went out into the mount of Olives.

27 And Jesus saith unto them, All ye shall be offended because of me this night; for it is written, [r]I will smite the shepherd, and the sheep shall be scattered.

28 But[s] after that I am risen, I will go before you into Galilee.

29 But[t] Peter said unto him, Although all shall be offended, yet *will* not I.

30 And Jesus saith unto him, Verily I say unto thee, That this day, *even* in this night, before the cock crow twice, thou shalt deny me thrice.

31 But he spake the more vehemently, If I should die with thee, I will not deny thee in any wise. Likewise also said they all.

32 And[u] they came to a place which was named Gethsemane; and he saith to his disciples, Sit ye here, while I shall pray.

33 And he taketh with him Peter, and James, and John, and began to be sore amazed, and to be very heavy;

34 And saith unto them, [v]My soul is exceeding sorrowful unto death: tarry ye here, and watch.

35 And he went forward a little,

h Jn.11.28; 13.13. *i* Re.3.20. *k* Jn.16.4. *l* Ps.41.9; 55.13,14. *m* Mat.18.6,7. *n* Mat.26.26,&c.; Lu.22.19; 1 Co.11.23,&c. *o* Jn.6.48-58. *p* 1 Co.10.16; Jn.6.53.

q Joel 3.18; Am.9.13,14. [4] or, *psalm*. *r* Zec.13.7. *s* ch.16.7. *t* Mat.26.33,34; Lu.22.33,34; Jn.13.37,38. *u* Mat.26.36,&c.; Lu.22.39,&c.; Jn.18.1,&c. *v* Jn.12.27.

14. *The goodman of the house.* This signifies simply the *master* of the house. The original word expresses nothing respecting his character, whether it was good or bad. ¶ *The guest-chamber.* A chamber for guests or friends—an unoccupied room.

15. *A large upper room.* The word used here denotes the upper room devoted to purposes of prayer, repose, and often of eating. See Notes on Mat. ix. 1–8. ¶ *Furnished* and *prepared.* Literally *spread* and *ready.* Spread with a carpet, or with *couches* such as were used in eating. See Notes on Mat. xxiii. 6.

17–31. See this passage explained in the Notes on Mat. xxvi. 20–35.

31. *More vehemently.* More earnestly, more confidently.

and fell on the ground, and [w]prayed that, if it were possible, the hour might pass from him.

36 And he said, [x]Abba, Father, all things *are* possible unto thee; take away this cup from me: nevertheless, [y]not what I will, but what thou wilt.

37 And he cometh, and findeth them sleeping, and saith unto Peter, Simon, sleepest thou? couldst not thou watch one hour?

38 Watch ye, and pray, lest ye enter into temptation. The [z]spirit truly *is* ready, but the flesh *is* weak.

39 And again he went away, and prayed, and spake the same words.

40 And when he returned, he found them asleep again, (for their eyes were heavy,) neither wist they what to answer him.

41 And he cometh the third time, and saith unto them, Sleep on now, and take *your* rest: it is enough, the [a]hour is come: behold, the Son of man is betrayed into the hands of sinners.

42 Rise up, let us go; lo, he that betrayeth me is at hand.

43 And[b] immediately, while he yet spake, cometh Judas, one of the twelve, and with him a [c]great multitude with swords and staves, from the [d]chief priests, and the scribes, and the elders.

44 And he that betrayed him had given them a token, saying, Whomsoever I shall [e]kiss, that same is he: take him and lead *him* away safely.

45 And as soon as he was come, he goeth straightway to him, and saith, [f]Master, master; and kissed him.

46 And they laid their hands on him, and took him.

47 And one of them that stood by drew a sword, and smote a servant of the high-priest, and cut off his ear.

48 And Jesus answered and said unto them, Are ye come out, as against a thief, with swords and *with* staves to take me?

49 I was daily with you in the temple, teaching, and ye took me not: but the [g]scriptures must be fulfilled.

50 And[h] they all forsook him and fled.

51 And there followed him a certain young man, having a linen cloth cast about *his* naked *body*,

w He.5.7. *x* Ro.8.15; Ga.4.6.
y Ps.40.8, Jn.4.34; 5.30; 6.38,39; 18.11; Phi.2.8.
z Ro.7.18-25; Ga.5.17. *a* Jn.7.30; 8.20; 13.1.
b Mat.26.47; Lu.22.47,&c.; Jn.18.3,&c.

c Ps.3.1,2. *d* Ps.2.2. *e* 2 Sa.20.9; Ps.55.21; Pr.27.6.
f Lu.6.46. *g* Ps.22.; Is.53.; Lu.24.44.
h Ps.88.8; Is.63.3, ver.27.

32-42. See Notes on Mat. xxvi. 36-46.

36. *Abba.* This word denotes *father.* It is a Syriac word, and is used by the Saviour as a word denoting filial affection and tenderness. Comp. Ro. viii. 15.

40. *Neither wist they,* &c. Neither *knew* they. They were so conscious of the impropriety of sleeping at that time, that they could not find any answer to give to the inquiry why they had done it.

41. *It is enough.* There has been much difficulty in determining the meaning of this phrase. Campbell translates it, "all is over"—that is, the time when you could have been of service to me is gone by. They *might* have aided him by watching for him when they were sleeping, but now the time was past, and he was already, as it were, in the hands of his enemies. It is not improbable, however, that *after* his agony some time elapsed before Judas came. He had required them to watch—that is, to keep awake during that season of agony. After that they might have been suffered to sleep, while Jesus watched alone. As he saw Judas approach he probably roused them, saying, It is sufficient—as much repose has been taken as is allowable—the enemy is near, and the Son of man is about to be betrayed.

43-52. See Notes on Mat. xxvi. 47-57.

45. *Master, master.* As if expressing great joy that he had found him again.

51. *A certain young man.* Who this was we have no means of determining,

and the young men laid hold on him;

52 And he [i]left the linen cloth, and fled from them naked.

53 And[k] they led Jesus away to the high-priest: and with him were assembled all the chief priests, and the elders, and the scribes.

54 And Peter followed him afar off, even into the palace of the high-priest: and he sat with the servants, and warmed himself at the fire.

55 And the chief priests and all the council sought for witness against Jesus to put him to death, and found none.

56 For[l] many bare false witness against him, but their witness agreed not together.

57 And there arose certain, and bare false witness against him, saying,

58 We heard him say, I will destroy[m] this temple that is made with hands, and within three days I will build another made without hands.

59 But neither so did their witness agree together.

60 And[n] the high-priest stood up in the midst, and asked Jesus, saying, Answerest thou nothing? What *is it which* these witness against thee?

61 But he [o]held his peace and answered nothing. Again the high-priest asked him, and said unto him, Art thou the Christ, the Son of the Blessed?

62 And Jesus said, I am; and [p]ye shall see the Son of man sitting on the right hand of power, and coming in the clouds of heaven.

63 Then the high-priest [q]rent his clothes, and saith, What need we any further witnesses?

64 Ye have heard the blasphemy; what think ye? And they all condemned him to be guilty of death.

65 And some began to [r]spit on him, and to cover his face, and to buffet him, and to say unto him, Prophesy: and the servants did strike him with the palms of their hands.

66 And[s] as Peter was beneath in the palace, there cometh one of the maids of the high-priest.

67 And when she saw Peter warming himself, she looked upon him and said, And thou also wast with Jesus of Nazareth.

68 But he [t]denied, saying, I know not, neither understand I what thou sayest. And he went out into the porch; and the cock crew.

69 And a maid saw him again, and began to say to them that stood by, This is *one* of them.

i ch.13.16.
k Mat.26.57,&c.; Lu.22.54,&c.; Jn.18.13,&c.
l Ps.35.11. *m* ch.15.29; Jn.2.19.
n Mat.26.62,&c. *o* Ps.39.9; Is.53.7; 1 Pe.2.23.
p Da.7.13; Mat.24.30; 26.64; Lu.22.69; Re.1.7.
q Is.37.1. *r* Is.50.6; ch.15.19.
s Mat.26.69,&c.; Lu.22.55,&c.; Jn.18.16,&c.
t 2 Ti.2.12,13.

but it seems not improbable that he may have been the owner of the garden, and that he may have had an understanding with Jesus that he should visit it for retirement when he withdrew from the city. That he was not one of the apostles is clear. It is probable that he was roused from sleep by the noise made by the rabble, and came to render any aid in his power in quelling the disturbance. It is not known why this circumstance is recorded by Mark. It is omitted by all the other evangelists. It may have been recorded to show that the conspirators had instructions to take the *apostles* as well as Jesus, and supposing *him* to be one of them, they laid hold of him to take him before the high-priest; or it *may* have been recorded in order to place his conduct in strong and honourable contrast with the timidity and fear of the disciples, who had all fled. Comp. Notes on Mat. xxvi. 56. ¶ *A linen cloth cast about* his *naked* body. He was roused from sleep, and probably threw around him, in his haste, what was most convenient. It was common to sleep in linen bed-

70 And he denied it again. And a little after, they that stood by said again to Peter, Surely thou art *one* of them; for thou art a Galilean,[u] and thy speech agreeth *thereto.*

71 But he began to curse and to swear, *saying*, I know not this man of whom ye speak.

72 And the second time the cock crew. And Peter called to mind the word that Jesus said unto him, Before the cock crow twice thou shalt deny me thrice. And [5]when he thought thereon, he [v]wept.

CHAPTER XV.

AND straightway in the morning the [a]chief priests held a consultation with the elders and scribes and the whole council, and bound Jesus, and carried *him* away, and delivered *him* to Pilate.

2 And Pilate asked him, Art thou the King of the Jews? And he, answering, said unto him, Thou sayest *it*.

3 And the chief priests accused him of many things, but he answered nothing.

4 And Pilate asked him again, saying, Answerest thou nothing? behold how many things they witness against thee.

5 But[b] Jesus yet answered nothing; so that Pilate marvelled.

6 Now[c] at *that* feast he released unto them one prisoner, whomsoever they desired.

7 And there was *one* named Barabbas, *which lay* bound with them that had made insurrection with him, who had committed murder in the insurrection.

8 And the multitude, crying aloud, began to desire *him to do* as he had ever done unto them.

9 But Pilate answered them, saying, Will ye that I release unto you the King of the Jews?

10 (For he knew that the chief priests had delivered him [d]for envy.)

11 But the chief priests moved the people that he should rather release [e]Barabbas unto them.

12 And Pilate answered, and said again unto them, What will ye, then, that I shall do *unto him* whom ye call the [f]King of the Jews?

13 And they cried out again, Crucify him.

14 Then Pilate said unto them, Why, [g]what evil hath he done? And they cried out the more exceedingly, Crucify him.

15 And *so* Pilate, willing to content the people, released Barabbas unto them, and delivered Jesus, when he had scourged *him*, to be crucified.

16 And[h] the soldiers led him away into the hall called Pretorium; and they call together the whole band.

17 And they clothed him with purple, and platted a crown of thorns, and put it about his *head;*

u Ac.2.7.
5 or, *he wept abundantly; or, he began to weep.*
v 2 Co.7.10.
a Ps.2.2; Mat.27.1,&c.; Lu.23.1,&c.; Jn.18.28,&c.; Ac.3.13; 4.26.
b Is.53.7; Jn.19.9. c Mat.27.15; Lu.23.17; Jn.18.39.
d Pr.27.4; Ec.4.4; Ac.13.45; Tit.3.3. e Ac.3.14.
f Ps.2.6; Je.23.5; Ac.5.31. g Is.53.9.
h Mat.27.27; Jn.18.28,33; 19.9.

---

clothes, and he seized a part of the clothes and hastily threw it round him. ¶ *The young men.* The Roman soldiers. They were called *young men* because they were made up chiefly of youth. This was a Jewish mode of speaking. See Ge. xiv. 24; 2 Sa. ii. 14; Is. xiii. 18. ¶ *Laid hold on him.* Supposing him to be one of the apostles.

53–72. See this fully explained in the Notes on Mat. xxvi. 57–75.

CHAPTER XV.

See the principal events in this chapter explained in the Notes on Mat. xxvii.

16. *Called Pretorium.* The hall of the *prætor*, or Roman governor, where he sat to administer justice. ¶ *Whole band.* See Notes on Mat. xxvii. 27.

18 And began to salute him, Hail, King of the Jews!

19 And they smote him on the head with a reed, and did [i]spit upon him, and, bowing *their* knees, worshipped him.

20 And when they had [k]mocked him, they took off the purple from him, and put his own clothes on him, and led him out to crucify him.

21 And they compel one Simon, a Cyrenian, who passed by, coming out of the country, the father of Alexander and Rufus, to bear his cross.

22 And[l] they bring him unto the place Golgotha, which is, being interpreted, The place of a skull.

23 And they gave him to drink wine mingled with myrrh; but he received *it* not.

24 And when they had crucified him, [m]they parted his garments, casting lots upon them, what every man should take.

25 And it was the third hour; and they crucified him.

i ch.14.65. *k* Job 13.9; Ps.35.16; Mat.20.19; ch.10.34; Lu.22.63; 23.11,36.

l Mat.27.33,&c.; Lu.23.33,&c.; Jn.19.17,&c. *m* Ps.22.18.

17. *With purple.* Matthew says *scarlet.* See Notes on Mat. xxvii. 28. ¶ *About his* head. In the form of a garland or diadem. The whole head was not covered, but it was placed in a circle round the temples.

19. *Worshipped him.* Mocked him with the *appearance* of homage. The word *worship* here denotes only the respect and honour shown to princes and kings. It does not refer to any *religious* homage. They regarded him as foolishly and madly claiming to be *a king* —not as claiming to be *divine.*

23. *Wine mingled,* &c. Matthew says *vinegar.* It was probably *wine soured,* so that it might be called either. This was the common drink of the Roman soldiers. ¶ *Myrrh.* See Notes on Mat. xxvii. 34.

25. *And it was the third hour,* &c. In Jn. xix. 14 it is said, "And it was the preparation of the passover, and about the sixth hour," &c. Much difficulty has been felt in reconciling these passages, and infidels have usually adduced them to prove that the evangelists have contradicted themselves. In reconciling them the following remarks may perhaps make the matter clear: (1.) The Jews divided both the night and the day into four equal parts of three hours each. See Notes on Mat. xiv. 25. The first division of the day commenced at six o'clock in the morning, and ended at nine; the second commenced at nine and ended at twelve, &c. The *third* hour mentioned by Mark would therefore correspond with our nine o'clock; the *sixth* hour mentioned by John would correspond with our twelve, or noon. (2.) Mark professes to give the time accurately; John does not. He says "it was *about* the sixth hour," without affirming that this was exactly the time. (3.) A mistake in *numbers* is easily made; and if it should be admitted that such an error had crept into the text here, it would be nothing more than has occurred in many ancient writings. It has been proved, moreover, that it was common not to write the *words* indicating numbers *at length,* but to use *letters.* The Greeks designated numbers by the letters of the alphabet, and this mode of computation is found in ancient manuscripts. For example, the Cambridge MS. of the New Testament has in this very place in Mark, not the word *third* written at length, but the letter γ, gamma, the usual notation for third. Now it is well known that it would be easy to mistake this for the mark denoting *six,* ϛ. An error of this kind in an early MS. might be extensively propagated, and might have led to the present reading of the text. Such an error is actually known to exist in the *Chronicon* of Paschal, where Otho is said to have reigned ϛ (six) months, whereas it is known that he reigned but three, and in this place, therefore, the γ, three, was mistaken for ϛ, six. (4.) There is some external authority for reading "third" in Jn. xix. 14. The Cambridge MS. has this reading. Nonnus, who lived in the fifth century, says that this was the true reading (Wetstein). Peter of Alexandria, in a fragment concerning the Passover, as quoted by Usher, says, "It was the preparation of the Passover, and about the *third* hour, as," he adds, "the most accurate copies of the Bible have it;

26 And the superscription of his accusation was written over, THE KING OF THE JEWS.

27 And with him they crucify two thieves; the one on his right hand, and the other on his left.

28 And the scripture was fulfilled which saith, [n]And he was numbered with the transgressors.

29 And[o] they that passed by railed on him, wagging their heads, and saying, Ah, thou that [p]de-

n Is.53.12. o Ps.22.7. p ch.14.58; Jn.2.19.

and this was the handwriting of the evangelist (John), which is kept, by the grace of God, in his most holy church at Ephesus" (Mill). It is to be admitted, however, that no great reliance is to be placed on this account. That a mistake *might* have occurred in the early MSS. is not improbable. No man can *prove* that it did *not* so occur, and so long as this cannot be proved, the passages should not be adduced as conclusive proof of contradiction.

After all, perhaps, without the supposition that there is any error in the text, the whole difficulty may be removed by the following statements: (1.) Calvary was *without* the walls of Jerusalem. It was a considerable distance from the place where Jesus was tried and condemned. Some time, more or less, would be occupied in going there, and in the preparatory measures for crucifying him. (2.) It is not necessary to understand *Mark* as saying that it was precisely nine o'clock, according to our expression. With the Jews it was six until seven; it was the third hour until the fourth commenced; it was the ninth until it was the tenth. They *included* in the *third* hour the whole time from the third to the fourth. The same mode they adopted in regard to their days. See Notes on Mat. xii. 40. (3.) It is not unduly pressing the matter to suppose that Mark spoke of the time when the process for crucifixion commenced—that is, when he was condemned—when they entered upon it—when they made the preparation. Between that and the time when he was taken *out* of Jerusalem to Mount Calvary, and when he was actually nailed to the tree, there is no improbability in supposing that there might have been an interval of more than an hour. Indeed, the presumption is that considerably more time than that would elapse. (4.) John does not profess, as has been remarked, to be strictly accurate. He says "it was *about* the sixth hour," &c. (5.) Now suppose that John meant to indicate the time when he was *actually* suspended on the cross—that he spoke of the *crucifixion* denoting the *act of suspension*, as it struck *him*—and there is no difficulty. Any other two men—any witnesses—might give just such an account now. One man would speak of the time when the process for an execution commenced; another, perhaps, of the very *act* of the execution, and would *both* speak of it in general terms, and say that a man was executed at such a time; and the circumstantial variation would *prove* that there was no collusion, no agreement to *impose* on a court—that they were honest witnesses. That is *proved* here. (6.) That this is the true account of the matter is clear from the evangelists themselves, and *especially* from *Mark*. The three first evangelists concur in stating that there was a remarkable *darkness* over the whole land from the *sixth* to the *ninth* hour, Mat. xxvii. 45; *Mar. xv. 33;* Lu. xxiii. 44. This fact—in which *Mark* concurs—would seem to indicate that *the actual crucifixion* continued only during that time—that he was, in fact, *suspended* at about the sixth hour, though the preparations for crucifying him had been going on (Mark) for two hours before. The fact that *Mark* (xv. 33) mentions this darkness as commencing at the *sixth* and not at the *third* hour, is one of the circumstances undesignedly occurring that seems to signify that the crucifixion then had *actually* taken place, though the various arrangements for it (ver. 25) had been going on from the *third* hour.

One thing is conclusively proved by this—that the evangelists did not *conspire together* to impose on the world. They are independent witnesses, and they were honest men; and the circumstance adverted to here is one that is allowed to be of great value in testimony in courts of justice—*circumstantial variation with essential agreement.*

26. *The superscription.* The writing over his head on the cross. ¶ *The King of the Jews.* See Notes on Mat. xxvii. 37.

28. *And the scripture was fulfilled,* &c.

stroyest the temple, and buildest *it* in three days,

30 Save thyself, and come down from the cross.

31 Likewise also the chief priests, mocking, said among themselves with the scribes, He saved others; himself he cannot save.

32 Let Christ the King of Israel descend now from the cross, that we may [q]see, and believe. And they that were crucified with him reviled him.

33 And[r] when the sixth hour was come, there was darkness over the whole land until the ninth hour.

34 And at the ninth hour Jesus cried with a loud voice, saying, Eloi,[s] Eloi, lama sabachthani? which is, being interpreted, My God, my God, why hast thou [t]forsaken me?

35 And some of them that stood by, when they heard *it*, said, Behold, he calleth Elias.

36 And one ran and filled a sponge full of vinegar, and put *it* on a reed, and [u]gave him to drink, saying, Let alone; Let us see whether Elias will come to take him down.

37 And[v] Jesus cried with a loud voice, and gave up the ghost.

38 And the vail of the temple was rent in twain, from the top to the bottom.

39 And when the centurion, which stood over against him, saw that he so cried out, and gave up the ghost, he said, Truly this man was the Son of God.

40 There were also women looking on [w]afar off; among whom was Mary Magdalene, and Mary the mother of James the less, and of Joses, and Salome;

41 (Who also, when he was in Galilee, followed him, and [x]ministered unto him;) and many other women which came up with him unto Jerusalem.

42 And now when the even was come, because it was the Preparation, that is, the day before the sabbath,

43 Joseph of Arimathea, an honourable counsellor, which also [y]waited for the kingdom of God,

q Ro.3.3; 2 Ti.2.13.
r Mat.27.45; Lu.23.44.
s Ps.22.1.
t Ps.42.9; 71.11; La.1.12.
u Ps.69.21.
v Mat.27.50; Lu.23.46; Jn.19.30.
w Ps.38.11.
x Lu.8.2,3.
y Lu.2.25,38.

This passage of Scripture is found in Is. liii. 12. This does not mean that he *was* a transgressor, but simply that in dying he *had a place with* transgressors. Nor does it mean that GOD regarded him as a sinner; but that at his death, in popular estimation, or by the sentence of the judge, he was *regarded as* a transgressor, and was treated in the same manner as the others who were put to death for their transgressions. Jesus died, the *just* for the *unjust*, and in his death, as well as in his life, he was *holy*, *harmless*, *undefiled*.

42. *The even.* The time after three o'clock in the afternoon. ¶ *The Preparation*, &c. The following day was to be a day of peculiar solemnity, called the *great day* of the feast. More than ordinary preparation was therefore made for *that* Sabbath on the day before. Hence the day was known as a day of preparation. This consisted in the preparation of food, &c., to be used on the Sabbath.

43. *Joseph, an honourable counsellor.* A distinguished man, who probably held a high office among the Jews, as one of their great council, or a Jewish senator. The word *honourable*, here, is not a mere title of *office*, but is given in reference to his personal character, as being a man of integrity and blameless life. ¶ *Waited for the kingdom of God.* Waited for, or expected, the coming of the Messiah. But this expression means more than an *indefinite* expectation that the Messiah *would* come, for all the Jews expected that. It implies that he believed *Jesus* to be the Messiah, and that he had *waited* for *him* to build up the kingdom of God; and this agrees with what John says (xix. 38), that he was a disciple of Jesus, but secretly, for fear of the Jews. He had retained his *secret* belief, in the hope that Jesus would be proclaimed and treated as the

came, and went in boldly unto Pilate, and craved the body of Jesus.

44 And Pilate marvelled if he were already dead: and calling *unto him* the centurion, he asked him whether he had been any while dead.

45 And when he knew *it* of the centurion, he gave the body to Joseph.

46 And he bought fine linen, and took him down, and wrapped him in the linen, and laid him in a sepulchre which was hewn out of a rock, and [z]rolled a stone unto the door of the sepulchre.

47 And Mary Magdalene and Mary *the mother* of Joses beheld where he was laid.

z ch.16.3,4.

Messiah, and then he probably proposed openly to acknowledge his attachment to him. But God called him to a public profession of attachment in a different manner, and gave this distinguished man grace to evince it. So men often delay a profession of attachment to Christ. They cherish a secret love, they indulge a hope in the mercy of God, but they conceal it for fear of man; whereas God requires that the attachment should be made known. "Whosoever is ashamed of me," said the Saviour, "and of my words, of him also shall the Son of man be ashamed when he cometh in the glory of his Father and with the holy angels," Mar. viii. 38. Those who love the Saviour have no right to hide their light under a bushel. As soon as they have evidence satisfactory to their own mind that they are Christians, or have a *prevalent* belief, after faithful examination, that they truly love God, and that they depend on the Lord Jesus for salvation, so soon are they bound to profess Christ before men. This is the command of God, and this is the way of peace. None have the prospect of *comfort* in religion who do not have respect to *all* of the commandments of God. ¶ *Went in boldly unto Pilate.* God had raised up this distinguished counsellor and secret disciple for a special and most important occasion. The disciples of Jesus had fled, and if they had not, they had no influence with Pilate. Unless there had been a special application to Pilate in behalf of Jesus, his body would have been buried *that night* in the same grave with the malefactors, for it was a law of the Jews that the body of an executed man should not remain on the cross on the Sabbath. At this critical juncture God called forward this secret disciple—this friend of Jesus, though unknown as such to the world—and gave him confidence. He dared to express sympathy for the Saviour; he went in boldly and begged the body of Jesus. It needed no small measure of courage to do this. Jesus had just been condemned, mocked, spit on, crucified—the death of a slave or of the most guilty wretch. To avow attachment for him *now* was proof of sincere affection; and the Holy Spirit has thought this worthy of special notice, and has set down this bold attachment of a senator for Jesus for our imitation. ¶ *Craved the body.* Begged, or asked.

44. *And Pilate marvelled if.* Wondered if he was dead, or wondered that he was so soon dead. It was not common for persons crucified to expire under two or three days, sometimes not until the sixth or seventh. Joseph had asked for the *body*, implying that he was dead. That he *was*, had been ascertained by the soldiers. See Jn. xix. 33.

45. *When he knew* it *of the centurion.* Being informed by the centurion of the fact that he was dead. The centurion had charge of the soldiers who watched him, and could therefore give correct information.

47. *Beheld where he was laid.* The affection of these pious females never forsook them, in all the trials and sufferings of their Lord. With true love they followed him to the cross; they came as near to him as they were permitted to come in his last moments; they followed him when taken down and laid in the tomb. The strong, the mighty, the youthful, had fled; but female love never forsook him, even in his deepest humiliation. This is the nature of true love; it is strongest in such scenes. While *professed* attachment will abound in prosperity and live most in sunshine, it is only genuine love that will go into the dark shades of adversity and flourish there. In

CHAPTER XVI.

AND[a] when the sabbath was past, Mary Magdalene, and Mary the *mother* of James, and Salome, had bought [b]sweet spices, that they might come and anoint him.

2 And very early in the morning, the first *day* of the week, they came unto the sepulchre at the rising of the sun.

3 And they said among themselves, Who shall roll us away the stone from the door of the sepulchre?

4 (And when they looked, they saw that the stone was rolled away:) for it was very great.

5 And entering into the sepulchre, they saw a young man sitting on the right side, clothed in a long white garment; and they were affrighted.

6 And he saith unto them, Be not affrighted: Ye seek Jesus of Nazareth, which was crucified: [c]he is risen; he is not here; behold the place where they laid him.

7 But go your way, tell his disciples and Peter that he goeth before you into Galilee; there shall ye see him, as he said unto you.

8 And they went out quickly, and fled from the sepulchre; for they trembled and were amazed: neither said they any thing to any *man;* for they were afraid.

9 Now when *Jesus* was risen early the first *day* of the week, he appeared first to Mary Magdalene, out of whom he had cast seven devils.

10 *And* she went and told them that had been with him, as they mourned and wept.

11 And they, when they had

a Mat.28.1,&c.; Lu.24.1,&c.; Jn.20.1,&c.
b Lu.23.56.
c Ps.71.20.

---

scenes of poverty, want, affliction, and death, it shows its genuineness. That which lives there is genuine. That which turns away from such scenes is spurious.

CHAPTER XVI.

1-8. See this passage explained in the Notes on Mat. xxviii. 1-8.

1. *Sweet spices. Aromatics.* Substances used in embalming. The idea of sweetness is not, however, implied in the original. Many of the substances used for embalming were *bitter* — as, *e.g.* myrrh — and none of them, perhaps, could properly be called *sweet.* The word *spices* expresses all that there is in the original. ¶ *Anoint him.* Embalm him, or apply these spices to his body to keep it from putrefaction. This is proof that they did not suppose he would rise again; and the fact that they did not *expect* he would rise, gives more strength to the evidence for his resurrection.

4. *It was very great.* These words belong to the third verse: "Who shall roll us away the stone from the door of the sepulchre?" for, the evangelist adds, it was very great.

5. *Sitting on the right side.* As they entered. The sepulchre was large enough to admit persons to go into it; not unlike, in that respect, our vaults.

7. *Tell his disciples and Peter.* It is remarkable that Peter is singled out for special notice. It was proof of the kindness and mercy of the Lord Jesus. Peter, just before the death of Jesus, had denied him. He had brought dishonour on his profession of attachment to him. It would have been right if the Lord Jesus had from that moment cast him off and noticed him no more. But he loved him still. Having loved him once, he loved unto the end, Jn. xiii. 1. As a proof that he forgave him and still loved him, he sent him this *special* message — the assurance that though he had denied him, and had done much to aggravate his sufferings, yet he had risen, and was still his Lord and Redeemer. We are not to infer, because the angel said, "Tell his disciples *and* Peter," that Peter was not still a disciple. The meaning is, "Tell his disciples, and especially Peter," sending to him a particular message. Peter was still a disciple. Before his fall, Jesus had prayed for him that his faith should not fail (Lu. xxii. 32); and as the prayer of Jesus was *always* heard (Jn. xi. 42), so it follows that

heard that he was alive, and had been seen of her, believed not.

12 After that he appeared in another form unto [d]two of them, as they walked, and went into the country.

13 And they went and told *it* unto the residue; neither believed they them.

14 Afterward[e] he appeared unto the eleven as they sat [1]at meat, and [f]upbraided them with their unbelief and hardness of heart, because they believed not them which had seen him after he was risen.

15 And he said unto them, [g]Go ye into all the world, and preach the gospel [h]to every creature.

16 He[i] that believeth, and is

d Lu.24.13. e Lu.24.36; 1 Co.15.5.

1 or, *together*. f Lu.24.25. g Mat.28.19; Jn.20.21. h Ro.10.18; Col.1.23. i Jn.3.18,36; Ac.16.31-33; Ro.10.9; 1 Pe.3.21.

Peter still retained faith sufficient to be a disciple, though he was suffered to fall into sin.

11. *Believed not.* This is proof that they did not *expect* his resurrection; proof that they were not easily deceived, and that nothing but the clearest evidence could undeceive them.

12. *He appeared in another form.* In a form unlike his ordinary appearance—so much so that they did not at first know him. See Notes on Lu. xxiv. 13–31. ¶ *As they walked and went into the country.* To Emmaus, Lu. xxiv. 13.

13. *The residue.* The remainder. Those who remained at Jerusalem.

14. *Afterward he appeared unto the eleven.* Judas was dead, and the apostles were then called "*the eleven.*" This was done even when one of them was absent, as Thomas was on this occasion. See the "Harmony of the Accounts of the Resurrection, Appearances, and Ascension of Christ," ii. 5, at the close of the Notes on Matthew. ¶ *As they sat at meat.* The word *meat* here means food, or meals. As they were reclining at their meals. ¶ *And upbraided them,* &c. Rebuked them, or reproached them. This was done because, after all the evidence they had had of his resurrection, still they did not believe. This is a most important circumstance in the history of our Lord's resurrection. Never were men more difficult to be convinced of anything than *they* were of that fact. And this shows conclusively that they had not conspired to impose on the world; that they had given up all for lost when he died; that they did not expect his resurrection; and all this is the strongest proof that he truly rose. *They* were not convinced until it was impossible for them longer to deny it. Had they expected it, they would have caught easily at the slightest evidence, and would have turned every circumstance in favour of such an event. It may be added that it was impossible that eleven men of good natural understanding should have been deceived in so plain a case. They had been with Jesus three years; they perfectly knew his features, voice, manner; and it is not credible that they should have been deceived by anyone who might have *pretended* to have been the Lord Jesus.

15. *Into all the world.* To the Gentiles as well as the Jews. It was contrary to the opinions of the Jews that the Gentiles should be admitted to the privileges of the Messiah's kingdom, or that the partition wall between them should be broken down. See Ac. xxii. 21, 22. It was long before the disciples could be trained to the belief that the gospel was to be preached to all men; and it was only by special revelation, even *after* this command, that Peter preached to the Gentile centurion, Ac. x. Jesus has graciously ordered that the preaching of the gospel shall be stopped by no barriers. Wherever there is man, there it is to be proclaimed. To every sinner he offers life, and all the world is included in the message of mercy, and every child of Adam is offered eternal salvation. ¶ *Preach.* Proclaim; make known; offer. To do this to every creature is to offer pardon and eternal life to him on the terms of the plan of mercy—through repentance, and faith in the Lord Jesus. ¶ *The gospel.* The good news. The tidings of salvation. The assurance that the Messiah has come, and that sin may be forgiven and the soul saved. ¶ *To every creature.* That is, to every human being. Man has no right to limit this offer to any class of men. God commands his servants to offer the salva-

baptized, shall be saved; but he[k] that believeth not, shall be damned.

17 And these signs shall follow them that believe: In [l]my name shall they cast out devils; they shall [m]speak with new tongues;

18 They shall [n]take up serpents;

k Jn.12.48; 2 Th.2.12.

l Lu.10.17; Ac.5.16; 8.7; 16.18; 19.12.
m Ac.2.4; 10.46; 1 Co.10.12,28. n Lu.10.19; Ac.28.5.

---

tion to *all men*. If *they* reject, it is at their peril. God is not to blame if they do not choose to be saved. His mercy is manifest; his grace is boundless in offering life to a creature so guilty as man.

16. *He that believeth*. That is, believeth the gospel. *He who credits it to be true, and acts as if it were true.* This is the whole of faith. Man is a sinner. He should act on the belief of this truth and repent. There is a God. Man should believe it, and fear and love him, and seek his favour. The Lord Jesus died to save him. To have faith in him is to believe that this is true, and to *act* accordingly; that is, to trust him, to rely on him, to love him, to feel that we have no merit, and to cast our all upon him. There is a heaven and a hell. To *believe* this is to credit the account and act as if it were true—to seek the one and avoid the other. We are to die. To believe this is to act as if this were so; to be in readiness for it, and to expect it daily and hourly. In one word, faith is feeling and acting as if there were a God, a Saviour, a heaven, a hell; as if we were sinners and must die; as if we deserved eternal death and were in danger of it; and, in view of all, casting our eternal interests on the mercy of God in Christ Jesus. To do this is to be a Christian: not to do it is to be an infidel. ¶ *Is baptized*. Is initiated into the church by the application of water, as significant that he is a sinner, and needs the purifying influences of the Holy Ghost. It is worthy of remark that Jesus has made *baptism* of so much importance. He did not say, indeed, that a man *could not* be saved without baptism, but he has strongly implied that where this is neglected *knowing it to be a command of the Saviour*, it endangers the salvation of the soul. *Faith* and *baptism* are the beginnings of a Christian life: the one the beginning of piety *in the soul*, the other of its manifestation *before men*, or of a *profession* of religion. Every man endangers his eternal interest by being ashamed of Christ before men. See Mar. viii. 38. ¶ *Shall be saved*. Saved from sin (Mat. i. 21) and from eternal death (Jn. v. 24; iii. 36), and raised to eternal life in heaven, Jn. v. 28; xvii. 2, 24. ¶ *Shall be damned*. That is, condemned by God and cast off from his presence, 2 Th. i. 6–9. It implies that they will be adjudged to be guilty by God in the day of judgment (Ro. ii. 12, 16; Mat. xxv. 41); that they will deserve to die for ever (Ro. ii. 6, 8), and that they will be cast out into a place of woe to all eternity, Mat. xxv. 46. It may be asked how it can be *just* in God to condemn men for ever for not believing the gospel? I answer—1st. God has a right to appoint his own terms of mercy. 2d. Man has no claim on him for heaven. 3d. The sinner rejects the terms of salvation, knowingly, deliberately, and perseveringly. 4th. He has a special disregard and contempt for the gospel. 5th. His unbelief is produced by the love of sin. 6th. He shows by this that he has no love for God, and his law, and for eternity. 7th. He slights the objects dearest to God and most like him; and, 8th. He *must* be miserable. A creature who has *no confidence* in God; who does not believe that he is *true* or worthy of his regard, and who never seeks his favour, *must* be wretched. He rejects God, and he must go into eternity without a Father and without a God. He has no source of comfort in himself, and *must* die for ever. There is no being in eternity *but* God that can make man happy, and without his favour the sinner *must* be wretched.

17. *And these signs*. These miracles. These evidences that they are sent from God. ¶ *Them that believe*. The apostles, and those in the primitive age who were endowed with like power. This promise was fulfilled if it can be shown that these signs followed in the case of *any* who believed, and it is not necessary to suppose that they would follow in the case of *all*. The meaning is, that they would be the result of *faith*, or of the belief of the gospel. It is true that they were. These signs were shown in the case of the apostles and early Chris-

and if they drink any deadly thing, it shall not hurt them; they shall lay[o] hands on the sick, and they shall recover.

o Ac.5.15,16; 28.8; Ja.5.14,15.

19 So then [p]after the Lord had spoken unto them, he was received up into heaven, and [q]sat on the right hand of God.

p Ac.1.2,3; Lu.24.51.
q Ps.110.1; 1 Pe.3.22; Re.3.21.

tians. The infidel cannot say that the promise has not been fulfilled unless he can show that this *never* occurred; the Christian should be satisfied that the promise was fulfilled if these miracles were *ever* actually wrought, though they do not occur now; and the believer now should not expect a miracle in his case. Miracles were necessary for the establishment of religion in the world; they are not necessary for its continuance now. ¶ *In my name.* By my authority, and using the power that I would in such cases, if bodily present. This was done; and in this they differed essentially from the manner in which Jesus himself wrought miracles. He did it in *his own name*, and as possessing original, underived authority. See the account of his stilling the sea (Mat. viii. 26, &c.); of his healing the sick (Mat. ix. 5, 6); of his raising Lazarus, Jn. xi. The prophets spoke *in the name of the Lord.* The apostles did likewise, Ac. iii. 6, &c. There was, therefore, an important difference between Jesus and all the other messengers that God has sent into the world. He acted in his own name; they in the name of another. He wielded *his own* power; they were the *instruments* by which God put forth the omnipotence of his arm to save. *He* was therefore God; *they* were men, of like passions as other men, Ac. xiv. 15. ¶ *Shall they cast out devils.* See Notes on Mat. iv. 24. Comp. Ac. xvi. 16–18. ¶ *Shall speak with new tongues.* Shall speak other languages than their native language. This was remarkably fulfilled on the day of Pentecost, Ac. ii. 4–11. It existed, also, in other places. See 1 Co. xii. 10.

18. *They shall take up serpents.* When it is necessary for the sake of establishing religion, they shall handle poisonous reptiles without injury, thus showing that *God* was with them to keep them from harm. This was literally fulfilled when Paul shook the viper from his hand. See Ac. xxviii. 5, 6. ¶ *Any deadly thing.* Any poison usually causing death. ¶ *Shall not hurt them.* There is a similar promise in Is. xliii. 2. ¶ *They shall lay hands on the sick*, &c. See instances of this in the Acts of the Apostles, ch. iii. 6, 7; v. 15, &c.

19. *He was received up into heaven.* In a cloud from the Mount of Olives. See Ac. i. 9. ¶ *The right hand of God.* We are not to suppose that God has *hands*, or that Jesus sits in any particular *direction* from God. This phrase is taken from the manner of speaking among men, and means that he was exalted to honour and power in the heavens. It was esteemed the place of the *highest* honour to be seated at the right hand of a prince. So, to be seated at the right hand of God, means that Jesus is exalted to the highest honour of the universe. Comp. Ep. i. 20–22.

20. *They went forth.* The apostles. ¶ *Every where.* In all parts of the world. See the account in the Acts and the Epistles. ¶ *The Lord working with them.* By miracles; by removing obstacles; by supporting them; and by giving the gospel success and making it effectual to saving men. ¶ *Confirming the word.* Showing it to be the word of God or a revelation from heaven. ¶ *By signs following.* By attending miracles. By raising the dead, healing the sick, &c., as *signs* that God was with them, and had sent them forth to preach. ¶ *Amen.* Truly, verily. So be it. This word here, however, is of no authority. There is no reason to think that it was added by Mark.

Mark is more concise than either of the other evangelists. In most instances he coincides with Matthew, though he has added some circumstances which Matthew had omitted. There is no evidence, however, that he copied from Matthew. The last chapter in Mark contains some things omitted in Matthew, and some things of fearful import. We learn from it that the gospel is to be preached to all mankind. Every man is to be offered eternal life, and he rejects it at his peril. The condition of the man who *will* not believe is fearfully awful. The Son of God has solemnly declared that he shall be damned. *He* will judge the world, and there is none that can deliver out of his hand. No excuse will be allowed for

20 And they went forth, and preached every where, [r] the Lord working with *them*, and confirming the word with signs following. Amen.

r Ac.5.12; 14.3; He.2.4.

---

not believing. Unless a man has faith he *must* be lost for ever. This is the solemn assurance of the Bible; and in view of this awful declaration of the *merciful* Redeemer, how sad is the condition of him who has no confidence in Jesus, and who has never looked to him for eternal life! And how important that without delay he should make his peace with God, and possess that faith which is connected with everlasting salvation!

SCRIPTURE WEIGHTS, MEASURES, AND MONEY.

I.—Scriptural Measures of Length, reduced to English Measure.

							Measure	Feet.	Inches.
							A Digit,	0	0·912
4							A Palm,	0	3·648
12	3						A Span,	0	10·944
24	6	3					A Cubit,	1	9·888
96	24	6	2				A Fathom,	7	3·552
144	36	12	6	1·5			Ezekiel's Reed,	10	11·328
192	48	16	8	2	1·3		An Arabian Pole,	14	7·104
1920	480	160	80	20	13·3	10	A *Schœnus*, or Measuring Line,	145	11·04

II.—The Long Scripture Measures.

					Measure	Miles.	Paces.	Feet.
					A Cubit,	0	0	1·824
400					A Stadium, or Furlong,	0	145	4·6
2000	5				A Sabbath Day's Journey,	0	729	3
4000	10	2			An Eastern Mile,	1	403	1
12000	30	6	3		A Parasang,	4	153	3
96000	240	48	24	8	A Day's Journey,	33	172	4

III.—Jewish Money reduced to our Standard.

				Money	£	s.	d.
				A Gerah,	0	0	1·2687
10				A Bekah,	0	1	1·6875
20	2			A Shekel,	0	2	3·375
1200	120	50		A Maneh, or Mina,	5	14	0·75
60000	6000	3000	60	A Talent of Silver,	342	3	9
				A gold Shekel was worth	1	16	6
				A Talent of gold was worth	5475	0	0

IV.—Roman Money, mentioned in the New Testament, reduced to our Standard.

A Mite, about three-eighths of a farthing.
A Farthing, about three-fourths of a farthing.
A Penny or Denarius, sevenpence three farthings.
A Pound or Mina, three pounds two shillings and sixpence.

INDEX

TO THE NOTES ON THE GOSPELS BY

MATTHEW AND MARK.